Handbook of Research on Building Inclusive Global Knowledge Societies for Sustainable Development

Cristina Raluca Gh. Popescu
University of Bucharest, Romania & The Bucharest University of Economic Studies, Romania

A volume in the Practice, Progress, and
Proficiency in Sustainability (PPPS) Book Series

Published in the United States of America by
IGI Global
Information Science Reference (an imprint of IGI Global)
701 E. Chocolate Avenue
Hershey PA, USA 17033
Tel: 717-533-8845
Fax: 717-533-8661
E-mail: cust@igi-global.com
Web site: http://www.igi-global.com

Copyright © 2022 by IGI Global. All rights reserved. No part of this publication may be reproduced, stored or distributed in any form or by any means, electronic or mechanical, including photocopying, without written permission from the publisher. Product or company names used in this set are for identification purposes only. Inclusion of the names of the products or companies does not indicate a claim of ownership by IGI Global of the trademark or registered trademark.
    Library of Congress Cataloging-in-Publication Data

Names: Popescu, Cristina Raluca Gh., 1983- editor.
Title: Handbook of research on building inclusive global knowledge
   societies for sustainable development / Cristina Raluca Gh. Popescu,
   editor.
Description: Hershey, PA : Engineering Science Reference, an imprint of IGI
   Global, [2022] | Includes bibliographical references and index. |
   Summary: "This book provides an updated view of the newest trends, novel
   practices and latest tendencies concerning building inclusive global
   knowledge societies for sustainable development in the Post-COVID-19
   Era, while focusing on the benefits and the opportunities derived from
   the new economy and the global knowledge societies"-- Provided by
   publisher.
Identifiers: LCCN 2022003081 (print) | LCCN 2022003082 (ebook) | ISBN
   9781668451090 (h/c) | ISBN 9781668451106 (ebook)
Subjects: LCSH: Information society. | Sustainable development.
Classification: LCC HM851 .H348184 2022 (print) | LCC HM851 (ebook) | DDC
   303.48/33--dc23/eng/20220404
LC record available at https://lccn.loc.gov/2022003081
LC ebook record available at https://lccn.loc.gov/2022003082

This book is published in the IGI Global book series Practice, Progress, and Proficiency in Sustainability (PPPS) (ISSN: 2330-3271; eISSN: 2330-328X)

British Cataloguing in Publication Data
A Cataloguing in Publication record for this book is available from the British Library.

All work contributed to this book is new, previously-unpublished material. The views expressed in this book are those of the authors, but not necessarily of the publisher.

For electronic access to this publication, please contact: eresources@igi-global.com.

Practice, Progress, and Proficiency in Sustainability (PPPS) Book Series

Ayman Batisha
International Sustainability Institute, Egypt

ISSN:2330-3271
EISSN:2330-328X

Mission

In a world where traditional business practices are reconsidered and economic activity is performed in a global context, new areas of economic developments are recognized as the key enablers of wealth and income production. This knowledge of information technologies provides infrastructures, systems, and services towards sustainable development.

The **Practices, Progress, and Proficiency in Sustainability (PPPS) Book Series** focuses on the local and global challenges, business opportunities, and societal needs surrounding international collaboration and sustainable development of technology. This series brings together academics, researchers, entrepreneurs, policy makers and government officers aiming to contribute to the progress and proficiency in sustainability.

Coverage

- Strategic Management of IT
- Global Business
- Environmental informatics
- ICT and knowledge for development
- Technological learning
- Innovation Networks
- Sustainable Development
- E-Development
- Outsourcing
- Knowledge clusters

IGI Global is currently accepting manuscripts for publication within this series. To submit a proposal for a volume in this series, please contact our Acquisition Editors at Acquisitions@igi-global.com or visit: http://www.igi-global.com/publish/.

The Practice, Progress, and Proficiency in Sustainability (PPPS) Book Series (ISSN 2330-3271) is published by IGI Global, 701 E. Chocolate Avenue, Hershey, PA 17033-1240, USA, www.igi-global.com. This series is composed of titles available for purchase individually; each title is edited to be contextually exclusive from any other title within the series. For pricing and ordering information please visit http://www.igi-global.com/book-series/practice-progress-proficiency-sustainability/73810. Postmaster: Send all address changes to above address. © © 2022 IGI Global. All rights, including translation in other languages reserved by the publisher. No part of this series may be reproduced or used in any form or by any means – graphics, electronic, or mechanical, including photocopying, recording, taping, or information and retrieval systems – without written permission from the publisher, except for non commercial, educational use, including classroom teaching purposes. The views expressed in this series are those of the authors, but not necessarily of IGI Global.

Titles in this Series

For a list of additional titles in this series, please visit: http://www.igi-global.com/book-series/practice-progress-proficiency-sustainability/73810

Innovative Economic, Social, and Environmental Practices for Progressing Future Sustainability
Chai Lee Goi (Curtin University, Malaysia)
Engineering Science Reference • © 2022 • 369pp • H/C (ISBN: 9781799895909) • US $195.00

Impact of Artificial Reefs on the Environment and Communities
Jorge H. P. Ramos (CinTurs, University of Algarve, Portugal)
Engineering Science Reference • © 2022 • 304pp • H/C (ISBN: 9781668423448) • US $215.00

Wetland Biodiversity, Ecosystem Services, and the Impact of Climate Change
Abdelkrim Ben Salem (Mohammed V University, Morocco) Laila Rhazi (Mohammed V University, Morocco) and Ahmed Karmaoui (University of Moulay Ismail, Morocco & Southern Center of Culture and Science, Morocco)
Engineering Science Reference • © 2022 • 310pp • H/C (ISBN: 9781799892892) • US $225.00

Handbook of Research on Organizational Sustainability in Turbulent Economies
Rafael Ignacio Perez-Uribe (Santo Tomas University, Bogota, Colombia) Carlos Salcedo-Perez (Politecnico GranColombiano University Institución, Colombia) and Andres Carvajal-Contreras (EAN University, Colombia)
Business Science Reference • © 2022 • 428pp • H/C (ISBN: 9781799893011) • US $295.00

Examining Algae as a Sustainable Solution for Food, Energy, and the Environment
Mostafa M. El-Sheekh (Tanta University, Egypt) Norhayati Abdullah (Universiti Teknologi Malaysia, Malaysia) and Imran Ahmad (Universiti Teknologi Malaysia, Malaysia)
Engineering Science Reference • © 2022 • 330pp • H/C (ISBN: 9781668424384) • US $195.00

Implications for Entrepreneurship and Enterprise Development in the Blue Economy
Lukman Raimi (Universiti Brunei Darussalam, Brunei) and Jainaba M. L. Kah (Office of the President, Gambia)
Business Science Reference • © 2022 • 302pp • H/C (ISBN: 9781668433935) • US $245.00

Technological Development and Impact on Economic and Environmental Sustainability
Yilmaz Bayar (Bandirma Onyedi Eylul University, Turkey) Mahmut Unsal Sasmaz (Usak University, Turkey) and Omer Faruk Ozturk (Usak University, Turkey)
Engineering Science Reference • © 2022 • 352pp • H/C (ISBN: 9781799896487) • US $215.00

701 East Chocolate Avenue, Hershey, PA 17033, USA
Tel: 717-533-8845 x100 • Fax: 717-533-8661
E-Mail: cust@igi-global.com • www.igi-global.com

Dedication

The editor would like to dedicate this book entitled *Handbook of Research on Building Inclusive Global Knowledge Societies for Sustainable Development*, published by IGI Global – International Academic Publisher, to all the outstanding professionals worldwide as well as to all the marvelous academics all around the world that are truly passionate about helping our society accomplish the targets required in order to ensure the Sustainable Development (SD) – in terms of the most powerful and the most rewarding paradigm of the United Nations (UN).

In like manner, the editor would like to dedicate this book to all the phenomenal and the magnificent leaders that are truly engaged in reaching the Sustainable Development Goals (SDGs) – in terms of the most expected and the most needed call for action by all regions and all countries, in a continuously globalizing society, that targets the desire of the present generations to accomplish their needs without compromising the desires and the future of the generations due to come.

The editor would like to encourage all individuals to be part of the amazing and the astonishing adventure of promoting all forms of protection for our Planet, in order to ensure that specialists and entrepreneurs will become more and more aware of the necessity to learn how to develop those action plans capable to support sustainability in the business practices, while addressing the new challenges and the great opportunities derived from the COVID-19 pandemic and the COVID-19 crisis, thus being able to better manage the overwhelming Global Goals that will become most likely a must in the Post-COVID-19 Era.

Also, the editor would like to take this opportunity to invite readers to reflect on a few brilliant questions, which when properly answered might offer the key for better lives, secure and sustainable living, well-being, happiness, and an intact Planet – where nature and climate are called to support decent and responsible human actions and human activities: (a) How can economic growth become sustainable economic growth, while targeting responsible development for all?; (b) How can individuals worldwide be motivated to be part of the complex and phenomenal Sustainable Development Goals (SDGs) actions, in the attempt of changing the world in seventeen major steps?; (c) Will the Sustainable Development Goals (SDGs) implicate a constraint upon the individuals' present level of consumption, or will these Sustainable Development Goals (SDGs) represent, in fact, the solution that the present generations have in order to create a paramount resource base due to be inherited by the future generations?; and (d) What can we all do in order to make sure that we have reached a global consensus in terms of the economic, the financial, the demographic, the political, and the cultural cohesion, for the Sustainable Development (SD) implementation, in a society that is rapidly evolving and constantly changing from one second to another?

In the spirit of all the aspects highlighted in the lines above, the editor would like to show her immeasurable gratitude to two reputed specialists in the fields of this book, namely to Dr. Esthela Galván-Vela (affiliated to the School of Administration and Business, CETYS University, Tijuana, México & National System of Researchers (SNI), National Council for Science and Technology (CONACYT), ORCID ID: https://orcid.org/0000-0002-8778-3989), to Associate Professor Dr. Jarmila Duháček Šebestová (affiliated to the Department of Business Economics and Management, Silesian University in Opava, School of Business Administration in Karviná, Czech Republic & Moravian Business College Olomouc, Czech Republic, ORCID ID: https://orcid.org/0000-0002-7493-0759), and to Associate Professor PhD. Renáta Pakšiová (affiliated to the University of Economics in Bratislava, Department of Accounting and Auditing, doc. Ing. Mgr. PhD., ORCID ID: https://orcid.org/0000-0002-3833-9339).

Dr. Esthela Galván-Vela, Associate Professor Dr. Jarmila Duháček Šebestová, and Associate Professor PhD. Renáta Pakšiová have displayed a great interest as well as an outstanding dedication to this current book, closely and consciously analyzing its content, remarking the eye-catching contribution of all the works, while showing an exceptional support in order to make a noteworthy contribution to the success of this fabulous scientific project.

Hence, it should be mentioned that Dr. Esthela Galván-Vela is a level 1 member of the National System of Researchers (SNI), of the National Council for Science and Technology (CONACYT) and works as a Full-Time Research Professor at CETYS University, Campus Tijuana, Mexico, since January 2020, where she has also been a liaison for the Center of Excellence in Competitiveness and Entrepreneurship. Her professional profile is oriented to the area of Economic-Administrative Sciences, because she is a Commercial Engineer, Master in Academic Communication, Master in Business Management with emphasis in Strategic Administration and Doctor in Administrative Sciences from the Autonomous University of Tamaulipas. As for her international training, she has spent time at the University of Santiago de Chile, at the University of San Diego (USD) in California, United States, and at the Western University of New Mexico (WUNM), in Arizona, United States. Her lines of research are: entrepreneurship, intrapreneurship, innovation, happiness management and other elements of organizational behavior. On these lines of research, in the last 5 years, Dr. Esthela Galván-Vela has published more than 20 articles in indexed journals of international recognition such as Frontiers in Psychology, Cogent Business and Management, Quality and Quantity, Journal of Risk and Financial Management, The Journal of Asian Finance, Economics and Business, Corporate Governance, Journal of Legal, Ethical and Regulatory Issues, Innovar, among others; of which she has more than 150 citations, her H index is 7 and her i10 index is 4. Likewise, Dr. Esthela Galván-Vela has been the author and co-author of books and book chapters. She has participated as a speaker in Colloquiums, Congresses and Research Symposiums, in which she also usually acts as an organizer and as a reviewer or commentator in the workshops. She is currently a member of some research networks such as the International University Network of Happiness, where she collaborates with the University of Cadiz and the Multidisciplinary Study network of the influence of creativity and corporate happiness on the sustainable economic, social and environmental development of territories (IGOMSOH) where she collaborates with the Salesian Polytechnic University of Ecuador.

In the same line, it ought to be highlighted that Associate Professor Dr. Jarmila Duháček Šebestová is an experienced researcher focusing on Small Businesses and alternative business concepts. She published several monographs and scientific papers focused on sustainable strategy and development in small business. She cooperates with several non-profit organisations to include SDG goals to their strategy. She has participated in several international projects, including COST project Cost Action 18115 TRIBES: Transnational Collaboration on Bullying, Migration and Integration at School Level (focused on minority enterprises to help integration), IPREG (Innovative Policy Research for Economic Growth) and the E-WORLD project (International Entrepreneurs Network). She is Vice President of the European Council of Small Businesses for the Czech Republic. She is a head of study programme of Management in Social Services. Associate Professor Dr. Jarmila Duháček Šebestová research interests are: small business performance, small business dynamics, minority entrepreneurship, social entrepreneurship, and SDG goals within business strategy.

Furthermore, it needs to be underlined that Associate Professor Ing. Mgr. Renáta Pakšiová, PhD. is currently in the appointment procedure for a professor and works in the position of professor at the Department of Accounting and Auditing of the Faculty of Business Informatics, the University of Economics in Bratislava. She has long focused on research into the nature and importance of accounting and reporting of financial and non-financial information and CSR. Due to its key importance in today's open economy and societal goals, it addresses the issue from a theoretical and practical point of view. Her research is oriented on the analysis of information provided by accounting, mostly in financial reports, and on the importance of critical analysis of profit creation and quantification for decision-making on its allocation. In the accounting theory, her most investigated topics include sustainability and maintenance of business property of companies for the support of their sustainable development. She focuses on research of reporting of business entities in terms of both, financial and non-financial information in the context of national and international laws area.

All in all, the editor would like to affectionately and to graciously thank to all the IGI Global team members for their time and for their dedication to this current project, which might be regarded as up-to-date, daring, and valorous due to the knowledge that it successfully manages to transmit to the readers. Thus, the editor would like to dedicate this marvelous book to all the IGI Global team members, as a token of heartfelt and profound appreciation and in remembrance of such a constructive and marvelous collaboration.

May you all have a formidable experience when reading and when analyzing the content of the chapters of this book and may you all feel part of the amazing world that the authors managed to paint in order to attract positive actions intended to lead to building inclusive Global Knowledge Societies (GKS) for Sustainable Development (SD) in the present as well as in the future!

Editorial Advisory Board

Elham Ataei, *Zanjan University, Iran*
Hikmet H. Gülçin Beken, *Gümüşhane University, Turkey*
María Delgado-Rodríguez, *Independent Researcher, Spain*
Ayşegül Ermeç, *Hacettepe Üniversitesi, Turkey*
Pınar Hayaloğlu, *Gumushane University, Turkey*
Hossein Khajehpour, *Technical University of Berlin, Germany*
Yutong Li, *University of Reading, UK*
Estela Núñez-Barriopedro, *University of Alcalá, Spain & Carlos III University, Spain*
Fahri Özsungur, *Mersin University, Turkey*
Hüseyin Erbil Özyörük, *Türk Hava Kurumu Üniversitesi, Turkey*
Veronica Adriana A. V. Popescu, *The Bucharest University of Economic Studies, Romania*
Gheorghe N. Popescu, *The Bucharest University of Economic Studies, Romania*
Luis Manuel Ruiz Gómez, *Independent Researcher, Spain*
Rahul Verma, *Meera Bai Institute of Technology, Delhi University, India*
Meg Warren, *Western Washington University, USA*

List of Reviewers

Esna Betul Buğday, *Hacettepe University, Turkey*
María Higuera-Cota, *Autonomous University of Baja California, Mexico*
Esra Karapınar Kocağ, *Gümüşhane University, Turkey*
Arturo Luque González, *Universidad Técnica de Manabí, Ecuador*
Nima Norouzi, *Bournemouth University, UK*
Sajedeh Rabipour, *Islamic Azad University, Dubai, UAE*
Niray Tuncel, *Hacettepe Univertesi Beytepe Kampusu, Turkey*
José Vargas-Hernández, *Tecnológico Mario Molina Unidad Zapopan, Mexico*

List of Contributors

Buğday, Esna Betül / *Hacettepe University, Turkey* 36
Dixit, Ramnath / *Symbiosis International University (Deemed), India* 185
Foncubierta-Rodríguez, María-José / *University of Cádiz, Spain* 1
González, Arturo Luque / *Universidad Técnica de Manabí, Ecuador & Observatorio
    Euromediterráneo de Espacio Público y Democraca, Ecuador* 166
Higuera Cota, María Fernanda F. / *Autonomous University of Baja California, Mexico* 280
Karapınar Kocağ, Esra / *Gümüşhane University, Turkey* 244
Marco-Lajara, Bartolomé / *University of Alicante, Spain* 111
Martínez Falcó, Javier / *University of Alicante, Spain* 111
Millan-Tudela, Luis A. / *University of Alicante, Spain* 111
Norouzi, Nima / *Bournemouth University, UK* 97, 130, 143, 204, 225, 263
Popescu, Cristina Raluca Gh. / *University of Bucharest, Romania & The Bucharest University of
    Economic Studies, Romania* 1, 60, 166
Rabipour, Sajedeh / *Islamic Azad University, UAE* 97
Ravina-Ripoll, Rafael / *University of Cádiz, Spain* 1
Sinha, Vinita / *Symbiosis Centre for Management and Human Resource Development, Symbiosis
    International University (Deemed), India* 185
Tuncel, Niray / *Hacettepe University, Turkey* 36
Vargas-Hernández, José G. / *Posgraduate and Research Department, Tecnológico Mario
    Molina Unidad Zapopan, Mexico* 280, 299, 317
Zaragoza-Saez, Patrocinio / *University of Alicante, Spain* 111

Table of Contents

Foreword xx

Preface xxiv

Acknowledgment xxxiii

Chapter 1
A New Leadership for a New Era: Effects of Association of Socio-Demographic Variables on the Leader's Competencies 1
    María-José Foncubierta-Rodríguez, University of Cádiz, Spain
    Rafael Ravina-Ripoll, University of Cádiz, Spain
    Cristina Raluca Gh. Popescu, University of Bucharest, Romania & The Bucharest University of Economic Studies, Romania

Chapter 2
A Literature Review on Sustainable Consumption in the COVID Era 36
    Niray Tuncel, Hacettepe University, Turkey
    Esna Betül Buğday, Hacettepe University, Turkey

Chapter 3
Impressive, Inspiring, and Profound Mindfulness Movement in Organizations: Boosting Productivity, Cultivating Joy, and Sharping Awareness 60
    Cristina Raluca Gh. Popescu, University of Bucharest, Romania & The Bucharest University of Economic Studies, Romania

Chapter 4
An Analysis of the Health Economic Impacts of COVID-19 and Government Financial Packages in Its Management 97
    Nima Norouzi, Bournemouth University, UK
    Sajedeh Rabipour, Islamic Azad University, UAE

Chapter 5
Analysing the Relationship Between Green Intellectual Capital and the Achievement of the
Sustainable Development Goals 111
    Bartolomé Marco-Lajara, University of Alicante, Spain
    Patrocinio Zaragoza-Saez, University of Alicante, Spain
    Javier Martínez Falcó, University of Alicante, Spain
    Luis A. Millan-Tudela, University of Alicante, Spain

Chapter 6
Green Economics and Urbanization in OIC Member Countries 130
    Nima Norouzi, Bournemouth University, UK

Chapter 7
Mathematics of the Circular Economics: A Case Study for the MENA Region 143
    Nima Norouzi, Bournemouth University, UK

Chapter 8
Legendary, Life-Changing, and Memorable Benefits of Digitalization to Restart the Economy:
Impact of COVID-19 on Global Economic Environment for Sustainable Development 166
    Cristina Raluca Gh. Popescu, University of Bucharest, Romania & The Bucharest University
        of Economic Studies, Romania
    Arturo Luque González, Universidad Técnica de Manabí, Ecuador & Observatorio
        Euromediterráneo de Espacio Público y Democraca, Ecuador

Chapter 9
Role of Training Transfer in the Aftermath of the COVID-19 Pandemic 185
    Ramnath Dixit, Symbiosis International University (Deemed), India
    Vinita Sinha, Symbiosis Centre for Management and Human Resource Development,
        Symbiosis International University (Deemed), India

Chapter 10
Water Utilization Rate: Impact on Iranian Economic Growth 204
    Nima Norouzi, Bournemouth University, UK

Chapter 11
Structure of Gas-Exporting Countries Forum: Heterogeneity of Members and Their Ranking
Criteria in Influencing the Global Gas Market 225
    Nima Norouzi, Bournemouth University, UK

Chapter 12
Would You Pay for the Environment? An Application of the Environmental Preferences 244
    Esra Karapınar Kocağ, Gümüşhane University, Turkey

Chapter 13
Strategies of Green Economics: Analyzing the Renewable Energy Impact in Making the Economy
Green 263
    Nima Norouzi, Bournemouth University, UK

Chapter 14
Strategic Organizational Resilience as a Response to the Crisis: Towards a Recovery of SMEs 280
    José G. Vargas-Hernández, Posgraduate and Research Department, Tecnológico Mario
        Molina Unidad Zapopan, Mexico
    María Fernanda F. Higuera Cota, Autonomous University of Baja California, Mexico

Chapter 15
Implications of the Environmental Planning and Policing Systems to Promote Organizational
Green Practices, Marketing Management, and Strategic Change 299
    José G. Vargas-Hernández, Posgraduate and Research Department, Tecnológico Mario
        Molina Unidad Zapopan, Mexico

Chapter 16
Strategic Analysis of Organizational Learning Approaches to Dynamic Resilient Capability 317
    José G. Vargas-Hernández, Posgraduate and Research Department, Tecnológico Mario
        Molina Unidad Zapopan, Mexico

Compilation of References 338

About the Contributors 397

Index 402

Detailed Table of Contents

Foreword xx

Preface xxiv

Acknowledgment xxxiii

Chapter 1
A New Leadership for a New Era: Effects of Association of Socio-Demographic Variables on the Leader's Competencies 1
    María-José Foncubierta-Rodríguez, University of Cádiz, Spain
    Rafael Ravina-Ripoll, University of Cádiz, Spain
    Cristina Raluca Gh. Popescu, University of Bucharest, Romania & The Bucharest University of Economic Studies, Romania

Organizations face their work in a rapidly changing environment, where globalization, technological advances, and the generation, management, and transfer of knowledge have become fundamental processes for competitiveness. This VUCA environment forces entities to readjust continuously. This implies attracting and retaining people with adequate and sufficient skills to work in this context and committing to management models based on leadership that contributes, as never before, to giving visibility, voice, participation, and well-being to its members. In the conviction, demonstrated by recent literature, the most satisfied collaborators are the most productive. This study is of an empirical, exploratory, and transversal nature, in which, firstly, the degree of conformity with individual capacities of the new leader is tested among personnel managers in organizations in the Bay of Algeciras Arch. Secondly, it is analyzed whether these opinions are related to specific socio-demographic characteristics of the respondents.

Chapter 2
A Literature Review on Sustainable Consumption in the COVID Era 36
    Niray Tuncel, Hacettepe University, Turkey
    Esna Betül Buğday, Hacettepe University, Turkey

The COVID-19 pandemic has made significant differences in consumers' sustainable consumption behaviors and their attitudes toward environmental issues. After the global spread of the virus, a growing number of people became more aware of the environmental impact of their consumption habits, and their purchasing decisions shifted to favoring products and brands that place a higher value on environmental issues. Therefore, this chapter aims to introduce what the existing knowledge has presented about the impact of the COVID-19 pandemic on consumers' sustainable consumption practices and presents an overview of the existing literature. For this purpose, the current study focused on the recent research that addressed the changes in the sustainable consumption behaviors of consumers from different aspects, such as consumer spending habits, adopting a voluntarily simple life, consumption of energy and natural resources, the purchase, consumption, and use of environmentally friendly products and participating in sustainable practices.

Chapter 3
Impressive, Inspiring, and Profound Mindfulness Movement in Organizations: Boosting Productivity, Cultivating Joy, and Sharping Awareness 60
Cristina Raluca Gh. Popescu, University of Bucharest, Romania & The Bucharest University of Economic Studies, Romania

These days, individuals are part of business environments far more overwhelming than ever before as a result of COVID-19 pandemic and COVID-19 crisis, thus having to deal with competitive, demographic, global, economic, legal, political, social, and technological adjustments, advances, and provocations. The post-COVID-19 era has to find the answers and the solutions derived from the key question: "How can people bring mindfulness into the business environment, in order to make individuals more aware of their inner power and their surroundings, and act towards achieving the Sustainable Development Goals (SDGs)?" This study centers, on the one hand, on analyzing the importance and the role of mindfulness for individuals, thus enhancing the tremendous benefits of the impressive, inspiring, and profound mindfulness movement in organizations, and focuses, on the other hand, on presenting those solutions that empower individuals to proceed to the next stages that represent embracing the mindfulness state of mind, by boosting productivity, cultivating joy, and sharping awareness.

Chapter 4
An Analysis of the Health Economic Impacts of COVID-19 and Government Financial Packages in Its Management.. 97
Nima Norouzi, Bournemouth University, UK
Sajedeh Rabipour, Islamic Azad University, UAE

This chapter focuses on the extent of government intervention against COVID-19 and compares and evaluates support packages in different countries based on available statistical evidence. Economic interventions were described by collecting statistical data from government reports and international organizations. The statistical sample includes 46 countries with the highest number of patients as of May 20, 2021. Comparing the success rate of the health system (net ratio of the number of recovered to the number of patients with COVID-19) and the share of government support in countries affected by the COVID-19 virus shows a positive correlation coefficient of 0.26. The high recovery rate of COVID-19 patients in Iran has been achieved while the Iranian economy is under inhumane US sanctions. The experience of COVID-19 crisis management in Iran shows that the general mobilization of facilities and capabilities can turn any threat into an opportunity for the country's progress, growth, and excellence.

Chapter 5
Analysing the Relationship Between Green Intellectual Capital and the Achievement of the
Sustainable Development Goals 111
    Bartolomé Marco-Lajara, University of Alicante, Spain
    Patrocinio Zaragoza-Saez, University of Alicante, Spain
    Javier Martínez Falcó, University of Alicante, Spain
    Luis A. Millan-Tudela, University of Alicante, Spain

The research aims to analyze the link between the green intellectual capital (GIC) and the Sustainable Development Goals (SDGs) in the wine industry, contributing to the academic literature in a remarkable way, since, to the authors' knowledge, there is no previous research that has addressed this relationship. To achieve the proposed objective, the research follows a qualitative approach, given that the case study method was used. The research results show the positive effect of the three dimensions of the GIC (green human capital, green structural capital, green relational capital) on the achievement of SDGs 5, 6, 7, 9, 11, 12, 13, 15, and 17.

Chapter 6
Green Economics and Urbanization in OIC Member Countries 130
    Nima Norouzi, Bournemouth University, UK

Although urbanization is often discussed in the context of economic modernization, it is nevertheless a population indicator that increases urban density and changes the structure of human behavior and, as a result, affects household energy consumption patterns. Accordingly, the purpose of this study is to investigate the effect of urbanization on carbon dioxide emissions in the member countries of the Organization of the Islamic Conference using the Paneldita approach and the application of the STIRPAT model. The method used in the present study is scientific-analytical and the purpose of the research is applied. Statistics and information about the variables used in the research are extracted from the WDI2014 CD. The econometric tools used in the research are EViews software and the econometric method used in the research is the Paneldita method. The research period is 2000 to 2020 and the research area is 43 countries selected from the member countries of the Islamic conference.

Chapter 7
Mathematics of the Circular Economics: A Case Study for the MENA Region 143
    Nima Norouzi, Bournemouth University, UK

Based on the findings of economic studies on the consequences of industrialization in emerging economies, this study aims to evaluate rotational economy processes in the Middle East and North Africa (MENA) using a Shannon entropy algorithm. An entropy-based analysis was performed for 19 MENA countries in the period 2000-2020. The modeling process involves constructing a hybrid index that consists of a weighted sum of all the indices developed by an algorithm based on Shannon's entropy. The weight assigned to each index in the analysis measures the importance of each index involved in developing the composite index. The results are similar to the international balancing, which combines and confirms the precision and reliability of this method.

Chapter 8
Legendary, Life-Changing, and Memorable Benefits of Digitalization to Restart the Economy:
Impact of COVID-19 on Global Economic Environment for Sustainable Development 166
    Cristina Raluca Gh. Popescu, University of Bucharest, Romania & The Bucharest University
        of Economic Studies, Romania
    Arturo Luque González, Universidad Técnica de Manabí, Ecuador & Observatorio
        Euromediterráneo de Espacio Público y Democraca, Ecuador

The COVID-19 pandemic and COVID-19 crisis suddenly, abruptly accentuated both individual and business needs to move at an accelerated rate to digital activities like never before in history of mankind, which led to increased importance of digitalization in terms of use of digital technologies. The post-COVID-19 era seeks to create novel communication patterns and business models capable to ensure new revenue and value-producing benefits and opportunities in accordance to the Sustainable Development Goals by launching tremendous provocations on global economic environment for sustainable development: How can people and entities adapt, implement digitalization in their daily lives, in order to restart the economy? What will the world's digital business transformation roadmap look like, in order to find a balance between individuals' expectations and planet's needs? Will the digital skills transformation enhance the role of human resources in society, or will these new acquired skills create an even larger gap between people than ever before? Is artificial intelligence the future?

Chapter 9
Role of Training Transfer in the Aftermath of the COVID-19 Pandemic 185
    Ramnath Dixit, Symbiosis International University (Deemed), India
    Vinita Sinha, Symbiosis Centre for Management and Human Resource Development,
        Symbiosis International University (Deemed), India

This chapter aims to highlight the significance of training transfer in organizations in the aftermath of the COVID-19 pandemic. Transfer of training has always been sidelined in companies for various reasons, and this problem aggravates during situations such as the pandemic or economic upheavals. It is imperative that workplace transfer is given its due credit in the learning and development framework to ensure successful implementation of trained skills and knowledge thereby justifying the training investments made. The chapter highlights the bottlenecks that need to be addressed towards training transfer in the context of a post-pandemic scenario and also suggests practical recommendations to overcome these challenges.

Chapter 10
Water Utilization Rate: Impact on Iranian Economic Growth.. 204
    Nima Norouzi, Bournemouth University, UK

In economic growth models, less attention is paid to natural resources and their importance on economic growth. The decline of the world's water resources, especially in countries with inherently limited water resources, such as Iran, has caused a water supply and demand crisis. This chapter deals with the effect of water utilization rate on economic growth. The hypothesis of this research is based on Barrow and Sala's Martin model developed by Barber. According to this model, the effect of the water utilization rate on economic growth can be nonlinear. The tool for measuring the amount of water in this study is the water utilization rate. Other explanatory variables used in the model include the share of water exports, the share of water activities, and the share of gross capital. This chapter uses a self-regression model with distributive interruption with the shore test approach for 1990-2020 for Iran. The estimation results indicate that the relationship between water utilization rate and economic growth for Iran is inversely U-shaped.

Chapter 11
Structure of Gas-Exporting Countries Forum: Heterogeneity of Members and Their Ranking Criteria in Influencing the Global Gas Market 225
   Nima Norouzi, Bournemouth University, UK

The main focus of the studies, which have been conducted mainly by experts from gas-consuming countries, is to evaluate and measure the impact of this forum on the price of natural gas in the main consumer markets. Unfortunately, the issue of homogeneity or heterogeneity of members and the role that this issue can play in the success of the policies and goals of this organization has received less attention. In this chapter, the authors first show the heterogeneity of members and then, with the help of appropriate indicators, rank member countries in influencing policies and achieving the goals of the assembly in the short, medium, and long term. Based on the presented indicators, it can be concluded that Russia, Qatar, and Algeria are the countries that play the most important role in influencing the policies of the assembly in the short and medium-term, while Russia, Qatar, and Iran, respectively, are three influential members in the long-term policies of the assembly.

Chapter 12
Would You Pay for the Environment? An Application of the Environmental Preferences 244
   Esra Karapınar Kocağ, Gümüşhane University, Turkey

Environmental degradation is a rising global concern. Many countries aim a sustainable development that could reduce the pressure on the environment. Macro-level actions are mostly investigated in the literature. However, micro-level components to ensure a sustainable future are very limited. This chapter argues that individuals as micro-level actors in the system are extremely important actors to stop the depletion of the nature and to help restoring it. Who is more supportive to protect the environment? What kind of factors influence this behaviour? This chapter aims to shed light on individual determinants of environmentally friendly preferences. To do so, the WVS was used, and findings indicate that gender and unemployment status have no significant effect. However, age, income level, and education level of individuals significantly influence preferences of individuals. Bearing in mind potential limitations, this chapter nevertheless acknowledges the importance of individual characteristics that can help protect the environment.

Chapter 13
Strategies of Green Economics: Analyzing the Renewable Energy Impact in Making the Economy Green.. 263
   Nima Norouzi, Bournemouth University, UK

The crises that threaten countries and human societies are the limited resources of non-renewable (fossil) energy sources and the increasing environmental pollution caused by the excessive consumption of fossil fuels, which are necessary for paying attention to energy resources. The close relationship between economic and environmental issues has led to the emergence of new approaches in international environmental law, one of the most important of which is the green economy. Since one of the most important goals of the green economy is to reduce greenhouse gas emissions, the use of renewable energy sources is a shortcut to the green economy. In this regard, the main purpose of this chapter is to compare the impact of renewable energy on the green economy in selected middle-income and high-income countries.

Chapter 14
Strategic Organizational Resilience as a Response to the Crisis: Towards a Recovery of SMEs 280
    José G. Vargas-Hernández, Posgraduate and Research Department, Tecnológico Mario
        Molina Unidad Zapopan, Mexico
    María Fernanda F. Higuera Cota, Autonomous University of Baja California, Mexico

SMEs, like other organizations, are subject to risk and change in an uncertain environment today more than ever with the economic effects of the COVID-19 pandemic. That is why this study aims to analyze resilience at a strategic level in organizations and the factors that make up organizational resilience. The analysis starts from the assumption that SMEs need to implement a cultural change to respond to crises and disruptions. From a strategic perspective, the chapter provides the concept of organizational resilience, the elements that make it up, and identifies the necessary actions to carry out more flexible and progressive strategies. The study concludes that SMEs require a cultural change, where the main objective is the creation of innovative and creative environments to face crises, through an adaptation and response system based on strategies that consider the resources and capacities of each productive unit.

Chapter 15
Implications of the Environmental Planning and Policing Systems to Promote Organizational
Green Practices, Marketing Management, and Strategic Change 299
    José G. Vargas-Hernández, Posgraduate and Research Department, Tecnológico Mario
        Molina Unidad Zapopan, Mexico

This study has the objective to analyze the implications of the environmental planning and policing systems to promote organizational green practices, marketing management, and strategic change. It is assumed that organizational environmental strategic change must be planned and policed based on the transformation of green practices and marketing management. The method employed is the analytical-descriptive and reflective steaming from the theoretical and empirical research on these environmental issues. It is concluded that organizational environmental planning and policing systems are relevant to promote the strategic change in organizations towards green activities and marketing management.

Chapter 16
Strategic Analysis of Organizational Learning Approaches to Dynamic Resilient Capability 317
    José G. Vargas-Hernández, Posgraduate and Research Department, Tecnológico Mario
        Molina Unidad Zapopan, Mexico

The purpose of this study is to analyze the strategic organizational learning approach to dynamic resilient capabilities. A scoping review of the theoretical and empirical literature on organizational dynamic resilience capability reveals gaps to be addressed to improve the conceptualization. Under the assumption of some attributes and properties, it is viable to study the organizational resilience learning process leading to the analysis of the organizational resilience strategies.

Compilation of References 338

About the Contributors 397

Index 402

Foreword

These days, the profound and the irreversible impact of the COVID-19 pandemic and of the COVID-19 crisis on our society have drawn considerable attention to the need to create inclusive knowledge societies for sustainable development, especially in the context in which knowledge is believed to be, according to prominent specialists, the most important resource that mankind holds as well as the most relevant resource in terms of adding value to the social, cultural, political and economic development of our societies as a whole.

In this particular context, the book suggestively entitled *Handbook of Research on Building Inclusive Global Knowledge Societies for Sustainable Development*, published by IGI Global, proves to be ideal for academics, leaders, scientists, researchers, students, Ph.D. scholars, and postdoctoral students, since it brings to light new visions as well as new solutions capable to add value to our knowledge-based societies, as follows:

- Chapter 1 is profoundly focused on the impressive and the up-to-date subject of creating a New Leadership for a New Era, while centering the attention on the analysis of the effects of the association of socio-demographic variables on the leader's competencies, while exploring the individual capacities of the New Leader.
- Chapter 2 is highly anchored in presenting a literature review on sustainable consumption in the COVID Era, while showing a great interest in the implications of the COVID-19 pandemic, which has made significant differences in consumers' sustainable consumption behaviors and their attitudes toward environmental issues.
- Chapter 3 is mainly targeting the impressive, inspiring, and profound mindfulness movement in organizations, while centering on identifying solutions capable of boosting productivity, cultivating joy, and sharping awareness as a result of the COVID-19 pandemic and of the COVID-19 crisis.
- Chapter 4 is taking into consideration an analysis of the health economic impacts of covid-19 and government financial packages in its management, while focusing on the extent of government intervention against the COVID-19 and compares and evaluates support packages in different countries based on available statistical evidence.
- Chapter 5 is centered on an analysis on the relationship between green intellectual capital and the achievement of the Sustainable Development Goals (SDGs), since the research aims to analyze the link between the Green Intellectual Capital (GIC) and the Sustainable Development Goals (SDGs) in the wine industry, contributing to the academic literature in a remarkable way, since, to our knowledge, there is no previous research that has addressed this relationship.

Foreword

- Chapter 6 addresses green economics and urbanization in OIC member countries, while focusing on sustainable economics, sustainable city, energy intensity, STIRPAT model, green economics, energy economics, and ecological economics.
- Chapter 7 centers on the mathematics of the circular economics, while presenting a case study for the MENA Region.
- Chapter 8 addresses the legendary, life-changing, and memorable benefits of digitalization to restart the economy, while centering on the impact of COVID-19 on global economic environment for sustainable development, by launching tremendous provocations on global economic environment for sustainable development: "How can people and entities adapt, implement digitalization in their daily lives, in order to restart the economy?", "How will the world's digital business transformation roadmap look like, in order to find a balance between individuals' expectations and planet's needs?", and "Is artificial intelligence the future?"
- Chapter 9 addresses the role of training transfer in the aftermath of COVID-19 pandemic, highlighting the significance of training transfer in organizations in the aftermath of the COVID-19 pandemic, since the transfer of training has always been sidelined in companies for various reasons.
- Chapter 10 stresses the importance of water utilization rate impact on the Iranian economic growth, while showing that the decline of the world's water resources, especially in countries with inherently limited water resources, such as Iran, has caused a water supply and demand crisis, thus being forced to deal with the effect of water utilization rate on economic growth.
- Chapter 11 deals with the structure of gas exporting countries forum, while addressing heterogeneity of members and their ranking criteria in influencing the global gas market.
- Chapter 12 attempts to answer the vital question: "Would you pay for the environment?" while centering on an application of the environmental preferences, centering on the fact that the environmental degradation is a rising global concern, thus many countries aim a sustainable development that could reduce the pressure on the environment.
- Chapter 13 centers on the strategies to the green economics, while analyzing the renewable energy impact in making economy green, while addressing the fact that the crises that threaten countries and human societies are the limited resources of non-renewable (fossil) energy sources and the increasing environmental pollution caused by the excessive consumption of fossil fuels, which are necessary for paying attention to energy resources.
- Chapter 14 presents the case of the strategic organizational resilience as a response to the crisis, towards a recovery of SMEs, based on the fact that SMEs, like other organizations, are subject to risk and change in an uncertain environment, today more than ever with the economic effects of the COVID-19 pandemic, thus aiming to analyze resilience at a strategic level in organizations, and the factors that make up organizational resilience.
- Chapter 15 highlights the implications of the environmental planning and policing systems to promote organizational green practices, marketing management and strategic change.
- Chapter 16 focuses on the strategic analysis of organizational learning approach to dynamic resilient capability.

It is both our great pleasure and our great honor to invite academics, leaders, scientists, researchers, students, Ph.D. scholars, and postdoctoral students to seriously consider this book entitled *Handbook of Research on Building Inclusive Global Knowledge Societies for Sustainable Development* for reading, since it represents a great value in terms of building, promoting, and developing knowledge as an essential prerequisite of the Post-COVID-19 Era.

We would like to take this chance to profoundly congratulate, on the one hand, the authors of the book chapters for their strenuous work, and, on the other hand, the Editorial Advisory Board members, and the Editorial Review Board members for the very difficult and the highly demanding work throughout the entire process.

Also, we would like to take this invaluable opportunity to intensely and enthusiastically congratulate the editor of the *Handbook of Research on Building Inclusive Global Knowledge Societies for Sustainable Development*, Professor Dr. Cristina Raluca Gh. Popescu, from the University of Bucharest, Bucharest, Romania, and The Bucharest University of Economic Studies, Bucharest, Romania, for having the initiative to collaborate with the IGI Global team members, and for having the patience and the dedication to finalize all the steps required by such a complex and laborious project, thus being able to ensure its timely success.

Since we have also collaborated in the past with the editor, Professor Dr. Cristina Raluca Gh. Popescu, it is our great pleasure to communicate in these lines the fact that we have received with-open-arms the new project and new contribution belonging to Professor Dr. Cristina Raluca Gh. Popescu, which led to our distinct desire to share with you now our delight and our good wishes of a pleasant and noteworthy reading. It is our strong hope that this current book will be able to make a significant contribution in terms of building and developing the necessary skills that scholars and specialists worldwide ought to possess in order to help build inclusive global knowledge societies for sustainable development as a desiderate of the Post-COVID-19 Era.

In the end, we would like to express our deepest appreciation and our warmest consideration to the publisher IGI Global for offering us this tremendous opportunity to express our thoughts concerning the content of the *Handbook of Research on Building Inclusive Global Knowledge Societies for Sustainable Development* as well as our admiration for this exceptional work that will most certainly draw the attention on the newest trends, novel practices, and most recent tendencies that surround a highly competitive business environment as part of the new economy and the global knowledge societies.

May you have a delightful and insightful reading!

Esthela Galván-Vela
School of Administration and Business, CETYS University, Tijuana, Mexico

Jarmila Duháček Šebestová
Department of Business Economics and Management, School of Business Administration in Karviná, Silesian University in Opava, Czech Republic & Moravian Business College, Olomouc, Czech Republic

Renáta Pakšiová
Department of Accounting and Auditing, University of Economics in Bratislava, Slovakia

Esthela Galván-Vela *is a level 1 member of the National System of Researchers (SNI), of the National Council for Science and Technology (CONACYT) and works as a Full-Time Research Professor at CETYS University, Campus Tijuana, Mexico, since January 2020, where she has also been a liaison for the Center of Excellence in Competitiveness and Entrepreneurship.*

Foreword

Her professional profile is oriented to the area of Economic-Administrative Sciences, because she is a Commercial Engineer, Master in Academic Communication, Master in Business Management with emphasis in Strategic Administration and Doctor in Administrative Sciences from the Autonomous University of Tamaulipas. As for her international training, she has spent time at the University of Santiago de Chile, at the University of San Diego (USD) in California, United States, and at the Western University of New Mexico (WUNM), in Arizona, United States. Her lines of research are entrepreneurship, intrapreneurship, innovation, happiness management and other elements of organizational behavior. On these lines of research, in the last 5 years, Dr. Esthela Galván-Vela has published more than 20 articles in indexed journals of international recognition such as Frontiers in Psychology, Cogent Business and Management, Quality and Quantity, Journal of Risk and Financial Management, The Journal of Asian Finance, Economics and Business, Corporate Governance, Journal of Legal, Ethical and Regulatory Issues, Innovar, among others; of which she has more than 150 citations, her H index is 7 and her i10 index is 4. Likewise, Dr. Esthela Galván-Vela has been the author and co-author of books and book chapters. She has participated as a speaker in Colloquiums, Congresses and Research Symposiums, in which she also usually acts as an organizer and as a reviewer or commentator in the workshops. She is currently a member of some research networks such as the International University Network of Happiness, where she collaborates with the University of Cadiz and the Multidisciplinary Study network of the influence of creativity and corporate happiness on the sustainable economic, social and environmental development of territories (IGOMSOH) where she collaborates with the Salesian Polytechnic University of Ecuador.

Jarmila Duháček Šebestová, *PhD, is an Associate Professor, is an experienced researcher focusing on Small Businesses and alternative business concepts. She published several monographs and scientific papers focused on sustainable strategy and development in small business. She cooperates with several non-profit organisations to include SDG goals to their strategy. She has participated in several international projects, including COST project Cost Action 18115 TRIBES: Transnational Collaboration on Bullying, Migration and Integration at School Level (focused on minority enterprises to help integration), IPREG (Innovative Policy Research for Economic Growth) and the E-WORLD project (International Entrepreneurs Network). She is Vice President of the European Council of Small Businesses for the Czech Republic. She is a head of study programme of Management in Social Services. Research interests: small business performance, small business dynamics, minority entrepreneurship, social entrepreneurship and SDG goals within business strategy.*

Renáta Pakšiová, *PhD, is currently in the appointment procedure for a professor and works in the position of professor at the Department of Accounting and Auditing of the Faculty of Business Informatics, the University of Economics in Bratislava. She has long focused on research into the nature and importance of accounting and reporting of financial and non-financial information and CSR. Due to its key importance in today's open economy and societal goals, it addresses the issue from a theoretical and practical point of view. Her research is oriented on the analysis of information provided by accounting, mostly in financial reports, and on the importance of critical analysis of profit creation and quantification for decision-making on its allocation. In the accounting theory, her most investigated topics include sustainability and maintenance of business property of companies for the support of their sustainable development. She focuses on research of reporting of business entities in terms of both, financial and non-financial information in the context of national and international laws area.*

Preface

The main objective of this reference book is to provide valuable insight of today's context concerning building inclusive global knowledge societies for sustainable development in the Post-COVID-19 Era. It is known that knowledge and information have a significant impact on individuals' daily lives and daily activities, especially when referring to the new economy and the global knowledge societies. What is more, the need to ensure inclusive global knowledge societies comes from the desire to support sustainable development and to empower communities to become more concerned with aspects related to well-being, health, preservation, quality of life, and commitment for people-centered and environmental-centered programs and policies. Furthermore, the COVID-19 pandemic and the COVID-19 crisis have managed to severely affect the balance existing in the daily lives, threatening the entire society and creating massive disruptions in the creation of the vital inclusive global information society. These days, while reflecting on the global knowledge societies, while targeting sustainable development in the Post-COVID-19 Era, there are several questions that have succeeded in becoming more and more persistent: (1.) Is global knowledge the key to a bright and well-balanced future for all? (2.) Is the individuals' commitment to building inclusive global knowledge societies the optimum solution for sustainable development in the Post-COVID-19 Era? (3.) Do information and communication technologies help create the basis of the knowledge society on truer and more realistic values capable to support healthier lifestyles? (4.) Does showing concern by building inclusive global knowledge societies for sustainable development in the Post-COVID-19 Era implicate strengthening regional and international cooperation and fostering alliances encouraging information dissemination and knowledge production?

This book aims at providing an updated view of the newest trends, novel practices and latest tendencies concerning building inclusive global knowledge societies for sustainable development in the Post-COVID-19 Era, while focusing on the benefits and the opportunities derived from the new economy and the global knowledge societies.

The target audience is represented by academics, scientists, researchers, students, PhD scholars and Post - doctoral students. Also, this reference book will present important features concerning sustainability, sustainable development, the Sustainable Development Goals (SDGs), the challenges specific to the process of building inclusive global knowledge societies for sustainable development in the Post-COVID-19 Era, which will prove to be extremely valuable for specialists, practitioners, governmental institutions, and policy makers' worldwide. Nevertheless, this scientific book will represent a well - documented and well - developed work for (potential) business leaders, entrepreneurs and managers, as well as highly prominent individuals involved in decision making processes.

The main objective of this reference book is to provide a platform for sharing researchers' and professionals' most recent ideas, findings and works concerning sustainability, sustainable development,

Preface

the Sustainable Development Goals (SDGs), while building inclusive global knowledge societies for sustainable development in the Post-COVID-19 Era. In this context, researchers and professionals are kindly invited to submit their contributions in form of original research papers, case studies or essays, in particular on the following topics (but not limited to the following topics) highlighted below. It should also be stated that interdisciplinary and cross section contributions are welcomed as long as they fall in the area specific to sustainability and challenges of Post-COVID-19 era, with a special focus on finding the best solutions able to support building inclusive global knowledge societies for sustainable development in the Post-COVID-19 Era.

- Agricultural innovation
- Artificial Intelligence and the power to influence the future
- Business Excellence and Innovation
- Climate chance
- Circular economies
- Cybernetics
- Competency-based education
- Constructing modern knowledge
- COVID-19 domains
- Ecosystems Management and water and land preservation
- Energy transitioning to sustainability
- Entrepreneurship and Greening Economy
- Entrepreneurship measuring indicators
- Entrepreneurial finance
- Environmental sustainability and justice
- Financial security and safety
- Food security
- Future energy scenarios, with focus on smart energy markets
- Health education and awareness
- Health disparities
- Health management and trust in health systems
- Intellectual capital, sustainability and resilience
- International entrepreneurship
- intragroup relations and immigrants
- Intelligence
- New and sustainable agribusiness management models
- Pandemic-Related Domains
- Resiliency
- Risk Assessments for Coronavirus Threats
- Smart cities
- Stability
- Sustainable agriculture and organic farming
- Sustainable Conservation Management
- Sustainable Development in Business Reporting
- Sustainable Entrepreneurship

- Sustainable Entrepreneurship skills and competences
- Sustainable Human Resource Development
- Sustainable Rural Community Development
- Global Entrepreneurship
- Social Entrepreneurship
- Women Entrepreneurship
- Corporate social responsibility
- Creativity
- Creating an inclusive and competitive entrepreneurship
- Information technology
- Innovation
- Innovative Business Models
- Innovation for sustainable agriculture and food chains
- Intellectual capital
- Leadership
- Knowledge management
- Migration
- Organizational performance
- Public policies and influences on entrepreneurship
- Responsible Innovation, Performance and Excellence for a sustainable future
- Responsible consumption and production
- Social responsibility
- Sustainable entrepreneurial ecosystems
- Sustainable energy, with responsible consumption and production
- Sustainability practices
- Sustainable society, with responsible consumption and production
- Technologies and policies for a sustainable society
- Technological and social innovation for sustainable business
- Travel resilience and sustainability challenges
- Tourism resilience and sustainability challenges

ORGANIZATION OF THE BOOK

The book is organized into 16 chapters. A brief description of each of the chapters may be found below, as it results based on the authors' own statements:

Chapter 1 focuses on the impressive and up-to-date subject of creating a New Leadership for a New Era, while centering their attention on the analysis of the effects of the association of socio-demographic variables on the leader's competencies. In this matter, the authors of this highly elaborate book chapter have focused on today's organizations which face their work in a rapidly changing environment, where globalization, technological advances, and the generation, management, and transfer of knowledge have become fundamental processes for competitiveness. Also, the authors have turned their attention in this book chapter on this VUCA environment which forces entity to readjust continuously, which implies attracting and retaining people with adequate and sufficient skills to work in this context and

Preface

committing to management models based on leadership that contributes, as never before, to giving visibility, voice, participation, and well-being to its members. In the conviction, demonstrated by recent literature, the most satisfied collaborators are the most productive. In essence, this current profound study is of an empirical, exploratory, and transversal nature, in which, firstly, the degree of conformity with individual capacities of the New Leader is tested among personnel managers in organizations in the Bay of Algeciras Arch, and in which, secondly, it is analyzed whether these opinions are related to specific socio-demographic characteristics of the respondents. In terms of keywords, the authors of this book chapter have successfully concentrated their attention on business, creativity, knowledge, human resource, innovation, intangible asset, intellectual capital, leadership, sustainable development goals, well-being, VUCA environment, and organizational culture.

Chapter 2 presents a literature review on sustainable consumption in the COVID Era. The authors have showed a great interest in the implications of the COVID-19 pandemic, which has made significant differences in consumers' sustainable consumption behaviors and their attitudes toward environmental issues. Also, the authors stressed the fact that after the global spread of the virus, a growing number of people became more aware of the environmental impact of their consumption habits, and their purchasing decisions shifted to favoring products and brands that place a higher value on environmental issues. Therefore, this chapter aims to introduce what the existing knowledge has presented about the impact of the COVID-19 pandemic on consumers' sustainable consumption practices and presents an overview of the existing literature. For this purpose, the current study focused on the recent research that addressed the changes in the sustainable consumption behaviors of consumers from different aspects, such as consumer spending habits, adopting a voluntarily simple life, consumption of energy and natural resources, the purchase, consumption, and use of environmentally friendly products and participating in sustainable practices. The keywords believed to be the most relevant ones for the authors of this book chapter are environmentally friendly consumption, natural sources, energy consumption, sustainable packaging, sustainable food consumption, voluntary simple life, recycling, reuse, and "do it yourself".

Chapter 3 draws on the impressive, inspiring, and profound mindfulness movement in organizations, while centering on identifying solutions capable of boosting productivity, cultivating joy, and sharping awareness as a result of the COVID-19 pandemic and of the COVID-19 crisis. According to the authors of this book chapter, these days' individuals are part of business environments far more overwhelming than ever before as a result of COVID-19 pandemic and COVID-19 crisis, thus having to deal with competitive, demographic, global, economic, legal, political, social, and technological adjustments, advances, and provocations. Also, the Post-COVID-19 Era has to find the answers and the solutions derived from the key question: "How can people bring mindfulness into the business environment, in order to make individuals more aware of their inner power and their surroundings, and act towards achieving the Sustainable Development Goals (SDGs)?" This study centers, on the one hand, on analyzing the importance and the role of mindfulness for individuals, thus enhancing the tremendous benefits of the impressive, inspiring, and profound mindfulness movement in organizations, and focuses, on the other hand, on presenting those solutions that empower individuals to proceed to the next stages that represent embracing the mindfulness state of mind, by boosting productivity, cultivating joy, and sharping awareness. In terms of keywords, it ought to be mentioned that the authors of this book chapter are particularly attracted to pivotal and powerful concepts such as business, knowledge, human resource, innovation, intangible asset, intellectual capital, leadership, sustainable development goals, well-being, mindfulness, environment, organizational culture, and create.

Chapter 4 presents an analysis of the health economic impacts of covid-19 and government financial packages in its management. This book chapter focuses on the extent of government intervention against the COVID-19 and compares and evaluates support packages in different countries based on available statistical evidence. According to the authors, economic interventions were described by collecting statistical data from government reports and international organizations. In like manner, the authors noted that the statistical sample includes 46 countries with the highest number of patients as of May 20, 2021. Comparing the success rate of the health system (net ratio of the number of recovered to the number of patients with COVID-19) and the share of government support in countries affected by the COVID-19 virus shows a positive correlation coefficient of 0.26. The high recovery rate of COVID-19 patients in Iran has been achieved while the Iranian economy is under inhumane US sanctions. Also, the authors mentioned that the experience of COVID-19 crisis management in Iran shows that the general mobilization of facilities and capabilities can turn any threat into an opportunity for the country's progress, growth, and excellence. In terms of keywords, the authors have centered their work on health financing, COVID-19, pandemic costs, healthcare economics, healthcare policy, healthcare management, healthcare financial management, COVID-19 and economy.

Chapter 5 analyzes the relationship between green intellectual capital and the achievement of the Sustainable Development Goals (SDGs), since the research aims to analyze the link between the Green Intellectual Capital (GIC) and the Sustainable Development Goals (SDGs) in the wine industry, contributing to the academic literature in a remarkable way, since, to our knowledge, there is no previous research that has addressed this relationship. Based on the authors' notes, to achieve the proposed objective, the research follows a qualitative approach, given that the case study method was used. In continuation, according to the authors, the research results show the positive effect of the three dimensions of the GIC (Green Human Capital, Green Structural Capital, Green Relational Capital) on the achievement of SDGs 5, 6, 7, 9, 11, 12, 13, 15 and 17. The keywords on which this book chapter centers are Green Intellectual Capital, Sustainable Development Goals, Green Human Capital, Green Structural Capital, Green Relational Capital, wine industry, case study, and wineries for climate protection.

Chapter 6 addresses green economics and urbanization in OIC member countries. The authors mentioned that although urbanization is often discussed in the context of economic modernization, it is nevertheless a population indicator that increases urban density and changes the structure of human behavior and, as a result, affects household energy consumption patterns. Accordingly, the authors stated that the purpose of this study is to investigate the effect of urbanization on carbon dioxide emissions in the member countries of the Organization of the Islamic Conference using the Paneldita approach and the application of the STIRPAT model. Also, according to the authors' notes, the method used in the present study is scientific-analytical and the purpose of the research is applied. Statistics and information about the variables used in the research are extracted from the WDI2014 CD. The econometric tools used in the research are EViews software and the econometric method used in the research is the Paneldita method. The research period highlighted by the authors is 2000 to 2020 and the research area is 43 countries selected from the member countries of the Islamic Conference. The keywords that have a profound impact on this work are, according to the authors, the following ones: sustainable economics, sustainable city, energy intensity, STIRPAT model, green economics, energy economics, and ecological economics.

Chapter 7 centers on the mathematics of the circular economics, while presenting a case study for the MENA Region. The authors have stated that based on the findings of economic studies on the consequences of industrialization in emerging economies, this study aims to evaluate rotational economy processes

Preface

in the Middle East and North Africa (MENA) using a Shannon entropy algorithm. An entropy-based analysis was performed by the authors for 19 MENA countries in the period 2000-2020. The modeling process involves, according to the authors, constructing a hybrid index that consists of a weighted sum of all the indices developed by an algorithm based on Shannon's entropy. Based on the authors' comments, the weight assigned to each index in our analysis measures the importance of each index involved in developing the composite index; and the results are similar to the international balancing, which combines and confirms the precision and reliability of this method. In terms of keywords, the following aspects should be emphasized: energy economics, green economics, circular economics, sustainable economics, sustainability, sustainable development, Middle East, and climate change economics.

Chapter 8 addresses the legendary, life-changing, and memorable benefits of digitalization to restart the economy, while centering on the impact of COVID-19 on global economic environment for sustainable development. According to the authors, the COVID-19 pandemic and the COVID-19 crisis suddenly, abruptly accentuated both individuals and businesses need to move at an accelerated rate to digital activities like never before in history of mankind, which led to increased importance of digitalization in terms of use of digital technologies. Also, based on the authors' elaborate work, the Post-COVID-19 Era seeks to create novel communication patterns and business models capable to ensure new revenue and value-producing benefits and opportunities in accordance to the Sustainable Development Goals (SDGs), by launching tremendous provocations on global economic environment for sustainable development: "How can people and entities adapt, implement digitalization in their daily lives, in order to restart the economy?", "How will the world's digital business transformation roadmap look like, in order to find a balance between individuals' expectations and planet's needs?", "Will the digital skills transformation enhance the role of human resources in society, or will these new acquired skills create an even larger gap between people than ever before?", and "Is artificial intelligence the future?". In continuation to the aspects highlighted in the lines above, it needs to be emphasized that there are several keywords that were considered essential according to the authors, namely: business, knowledge, Human Resources (HR), innovation, Intangible Assets (IA), Intellectual Capital (IC), Sustainable Development Goals (SDGs), digitalization, global economic environment, restart the economy, and COVID-19.

Chapter 9 addresses the role of training transfer in the aftermath of COVID-19 pandemic. This chapter aims, as the authors have stated, to highlight the significance of training transfer in organizations in the aftermath of the Covid-19 pandemic. In continuation, the authors have mentioned that transfer of training has always been sidelined in companies for various reasons, and this problem aggravates during situations such as the pandemic or economic upheavals. It is imperative, based on the authors' research, that workplace transfer is given is due credit in the learning and development framework to ensure successful implementation of trained skills and knowledge thereby justifying the training investments made. The chapter highlights, as the authors have prompted, the bottlenecks that need to be addressed towards training transfer in the context of a post-pandemic scenario and also suggests practical recommendations to overcome these challenges. The keywords believed to be essential according to the authors are COVID-19, employee training, learning and development, learning transfer, training barriers, training intervention, training investments, training strategy, and training transfer.

Chapter 10 stresses the importance of water utilization rate impact on the Iranian economic growth. The authors have mentioned in their work that in economic growth models, less attention is paid to natural resources and their importance on economic growth. Also, based on the authors' notes, the decline of the world's water resources, especially in countries with inherently limited water resources, such as Iran, has caused a water supply and demand crisis. This article deals with the effect of water utilization rate on economic growth. The hypothesis of this research is based on Barrow and Sala-'s-Martin-model developed by Barber. According to this model, the effect of the water utilization rate on economic growth can be nonlinear. The tool for measuring the amount of water in this study is the water utilization rate. Other explanatory variables used in the model include the share of water exports, the share of water activities, and the share of gross capital. This paper uses a self-regression model with distributive interruption with the shore test approach for 1990-2020 for Iran. The estimation results indicate that the relationship between water utilization rate and economic growth for Iran is inversely U-shaped. In terms of keywords, the authors have centered on sustainable development, water economy, sustainable economy, economic growth, development theory, green economy, and resource economy.

Chapter 11 deals with the structure of gas exporting countries forum, while addressing heterogeneity of members and their ranking criteria in influencing the global gas market. Based on the authors' comments, the main focus of the studies, which have been conducted mainly by experts from gas-consuming countries, is to evaluate and measure the impact of this forum on the price of natural gas in the main consumer markets. The authors have mentioned that unfortunately, the issue of homogeneity or heterogeneity of members and the role that this issue can play in the success of the policies and goals of this organization has received less attention. In this book chapter, the authors have noted that there intention is first to show the heterogeneity of members and then, with the help of appropriate indicators, rank member countries in influencing policies and achieving the goals of the assembly in the short, medium, and long term. Based on the presented indicators, it can be concluded according to the authors that Russia, Qatar, and Algeria are the countries that play the most important role in influencing the policies of the assembly in the short and medium-term, while Russia, Qatar, and Iran, respectively. Also, based on the authors' results, there are three influential members in the long-term policies of the assembly. The keywords are natural gas, assembly of gas exporting countries, ranking of assembly members, gas trade, and international gas market.

Chapter 12 attempts to answer the vital question: "Would you pay for the environment?" while centering on an application of the environmental preferences. The authors have mentioned that environmental degradation is a rising global concern, thus many countries aim a sustainable development that could reduce the pressure on the environment, while Macro level actions are mostly investigated in the literature. However, according to the authors, Micro level components to ensure a sustainable future are very limited. This chapter argues – according to the authors – that individuals' as micro level actors in the system are extremely important actors to stop the depletion of the nature and to help restoring it. The authors have also mentioned several pivotal questions that they targeted: Who is more supportive to protect the environment? What kinds of factors influence this behavior? This chapter aims – according to the authors – to shed light on individual determinants of environmentally friendly preferences. To do so, the authors have used the WVS used and the authors findings indicate that gender and unemployment status have no significant effect. However, based on the authors' results, age, income level, and education level of individuals significantly influence preferences of individuals. Bearing in mind potential limitations, the authors have showed that this chapter nevertheless acknowledges the importance of individual characteristics that can help protecting the environment. The keywords that the authors have considered as being vital for this current work are environment, degradation, climate change, decision-making, preferences, environmental-friendly behavior, World Values Survey, and Ordered Probit Model.

Preface

Chapter 13 centers on the strategies to the green economics, while analyzing the renewable energy impact in making economy green. The authors have drawn their attention to the fact that the crises that threaten countries and human societies are the limited resources of non-renewable (fossil) energy sources and the increasing environmental pollution caused by the excessive consumption of fossil fuels, which are necessary for paying attention to energy resources. Also, the authors have noted that the close relationship between economic and environmental issues has led to the emergence of new approaches in international environmental law, one of the most important of which is the green economy. Since one of the most important goals of the green economy is to reduce greenhouse gas emissions, the authors have mentioned in their work that the use of renewable energy sources is a shortcut to the green economy. In this regard, the main purpose of this chapter is to compare the impact of renewable energy on the green economy in selected middle-income and high-income countries. In terms of valuable keywords, the following ones ought to be presented, as follows: renewable energies, green economy, greenhouse gases, renewable energy market, climate change, sustainable economics, ecological economics, energy economics, and sustainability.

Chapter 14 presents the case of the strategic organizational resilience as a response to the crisis, towards a recovery of SMEs. The authors have stated in their work that SMEs, like other organizations, are subject to risk and change in an uncertain environment, today more than ever with the economic effects of the COVID-19 pandemic. That is why, based on the authors notes, this study aims to analyze resilience at a strategic level in organizations, and the factors that make up organizational resilience. According to the authors, the analysis starts from the assumption that SMEs need to implement a cultural change to respond to crises and disruptions. From a strategic perspective, the paper provides, according to the authors, the concept of organizational resilience, the elements that make it up, and identifies the necessary actions to carry out more flexible and progressive strategies. The study concludes, as the authors have mentioned, that SMEs require a cultural change, where the main objective is the creation of innovative and creative environments to face crises, through an adaptation and response system based on strategies that consider the resources and capacities of each productive unit. The keywords are, in this case, organizational resilience, strategies, SMEs, and crisis.

Chapter 15 presents the implications of the environmental planning and policing systems to promote organizational green practices, marketing management and strategic change. As mentioned by the authors, this study has the objective to analyze the implications of the environmental planning and policing systems to aim to promote organizational green practices, marketing management and strategic change. Also, according to the authors, it is assumed that organizational environmental strategic change must be planned and policed based on the transformation of green practices and marketing management. The method employed by the authors is the analytical-descriptive and reflective steaming from the theoretical and empirical research on these environmental issues. It is concluded by the authors that organizational environmental planning and policing systems are relevant to promote the strategic change in organizations towards green activities and marketing management. In terms of the keywords employed by the authors, the following concepts are perceived as being highly relevant for this current research: environmental planning, green practices, marketing management, policing, and strategic change.

Chapter 16 addresses a strategic analysis of organizational learning approach to dynamic resilient capability. According to the authors, the purpose of this study is to analyze the strategic organizational learning approach to dynamic resilient capabilities. Based on the authors' notes, a scoping review of the theoretical and empirical literature on organizational dynamic resilience capability reveals gaps to be addressed to improve the conceptualization. Under the assumption of some attributes and properties, according to the authors it is viable to study the organizational resilience learning process leading to the analysis of the organizational resilience strategies. The keywords considered vital by the authors are: dynamic resilient capability, organizational learning, and strategic analysis.

Cristina Raluca Gh. Popescu
University of Bucharest, Romania & The Bucharest University of Economic Studies, Romania

Acknowledgment

The editor would like to point out on this festive occasion the fact that this scientific book entitled *Handbook of Research on Building Inclusive Global Knowledge Societies for Sustainable Development*, published by IGI Global, is the result of the vigorous work and the sedulousness that characterized the activity and the actions belonging to the authors, to the members of the Editorial Advisory Board (EAB), and to the members of the Editorial Review Board (ERB).

On top of that, the editor would like to call attention to the devotion that was characteristic at all times to Dr. Esthela Galván-Vela (affiliated to the School of Administration and Business, CETYS University, Tijuana, México & National System of Researchers (SNI), National Council for Science and Technology (CONACYT), ORCID ID: https://orcid.org/0000-0002-8778-3989), to Associate Professor Dr. Jarmila Duháček Šebestová (affiliated to the Department of Business Economics and Management, Silesian University in Opava, School of Business Administration in Karviná, Czech Republic & Moravian Business College Olomouc, Czech Republic, ORCID ID: https://orcid.org/0000-0002-7493-0759), and to Associate Professor PhD. Renáta Pakšiová (affiliated to the University of Economics in Bratislava, Department of Accounting and Auditing, doc. Ing. Mgr. PhD., ORCID ID: https://orcid.org/0000-0002-3833-9339), since these three renown specialists and dedicated researchers in the fields of the book on *Handbook of Research on Building Inclusive Global Knowledge Societies for Sustainable Development* successfully managed to support this project, and display tenacity and persistence during the entire preparation and publication process.

Over and above that, the editor would like to prompt the attention to the commitment, the wholeheartedness, and the enthusiasm that accompanied at all times and in all circumstances the IGI Global team members, starting from the very first moment when the ideas surrounding this powerful project were born and ending with the moment when this wonderful quest came to an end with the publication of the *Handbook of Research on Building Inclusive Global Knowledge Societies for Sustainable Development*.

Nevertheless, the editor firmly and fully believes that this current project targeting the activities and the actions surrounding the temerarious process of building inclusive, resilient, and robust Global Knowledge Societies (GKS) for Sustainable Development (SD) might develop new ramifications in the near future, due to the belief that the *Handbook of Research on Building Inclusive Global Knowledge Societies for Sustainable Development* ought to offer novel and deeper ways of addressing the Sustainable Development Goals (SDGs), seeking brighter and firmer solutions capable to reconcile economic growth with the Planet's heath, the environment's balance, the individuals' well-being and mental health, and the social progress.

Acknowledgment

Under these given circumstances, the editor would like to offer the warmest appreciation to all the IGI Global team members that made a contribution to this project, while accentuating with great enthusiasm the positive collaboration and the solid contribution made to the field with the aid of this current research.

Cristina Raluca Gh. Popescu
University of Bucharest, Romania & The Bucharest University of Economic Studies, Romania

Chapter 1
A New Leadership for a New Era:
Effects of Association of Socio-Demographic Variables on the Leader's Competencies

María-José Foncubierta-Rodríguez
https://orcid.org/0000-0003-3231-5261
University of Cádiz, Spain

Rafael Ravina-Ripoll
University of Cádiz, Spain

Cristina Raluca Gh. Popescu
https://orcid.org/0000-0002-5876-0550
University of Bucharest, Romania & The Bucharest University of Economic Studies, Romania

ABSTRACT

Organizations face their work in a rapidly changing environment, where globalization, technological advances, and the generation, management, and transfer of knowledge have become fundamental processes for competitiveness. This VUCA environment forces entities to readjust continuously. This implies attracting and retaining people with adequate and sufficient skills to work in this context and committing to management models based on leadership that contributes, as never before, to giving visibility, voice, participation, and well-being to its members. In the conviction, demonstrated by recent literature, the most satisfied collaborators are the most productive. This study is of an empirical, exploratory, and transversal nature, in which, firstly, the degree of conformity with individual capacities of the new leader is tested among personnel managers in organizations in the Bay of Algeciras Arch. Secondly, it is analyzed whether these opinions are related to specific socio-demographic characteristics of the respondents.

DOI: 10.4018/978-1-6684-5109-0.ch001

INTRODUCTION

This book chapter entitled "A New Leadership for a New Era: Effects of Association of Socio-Demographic Variables on the Leader's Competencies" represents an integrating part of the "Handbook of Research on Building Inclusive Global Knowledge Societies for Sustainable Development", and is specially designed by the authors in order to present, to analyze, and to offer valuable solutions in terms of leadership, as an immediate and most natural result derived from the sudden and inevitable appearance of the COVID-19 pandemic and the COVID-19 crisis. In continuation, it should be mentioned that both the COVID-19 pandemic and the COVID-19 crisis have forced our society to regroup and to readjust to the new tendencies and the new requirements, thus implementing the need for more powerful, more empathetic and more capable leaders in order to create a New Leadership for a New Era. In addition, the authors ought to mention that the tendencies to create, to discover, and to implement a New Leadership for a New Era could have been foreseen long before the current situation that occurred due to the COVID-19 pandemic and the COVID-19 crisis, since humanity was striving for the creation of a more human environment, with higher concern for individuals and the environment, in particular, and for the Planet Earth, in general. In essence, the need for a more secure, more robust, more resilient, and a healthier future for all was the new resolution for all countries and all individuals alike, since for many, many years the general economic, social, political and demographical tendencies were towards ensuring the sustainable development (SD), the Sustainable Development Goals (SDGs), and building inclusive global knowledge societies for sustainable development (SD) (Núñez-Barriopedro *et al.* 2021).

The COVID-19 pandemic and the COVID-19 crisis have brought immeasurable challenges and sudden changes to individuals daily lives, transforming the society in a very abrupt and profound way. These days, specialists and leaders worldwide are highly focused on building inclusive global knowledge societies for sustainable development, thus promoting a safer and a better future for all. In like manner, nowadays researchers' immediate focus concerns discovering the best and the most important characteristics that belong to a New Leadership for a New Era, while addressing the most relevant effects of association of socio-demographic variables on the leader's competencies.

These days, according to specialists worldwide, the pressure that our society experiences due to the involvement of the COVID-19 pandemic and the COVID-19 crisis factors in our day-to-day activities is incapable of being estimated or assessed, while compared with the time periods before the COVID-19 pandemic and the COVID-19 crisis (Bostancı and Yıldırım, 2022; Özsungur, 2021a). Thus, the motivation of understanding better today's business environment needs and requirements is extremely high in terms of leaders and leadership at a general scale (Özsungur, 2021b; Popescu, 2022a).

Since the beginning of the 21-st century, there has been a great interest on the part of the social science researchers – especially the specialists in the area of human resources, in exploring what type of management or leadership organizations need to achieve advantages of a competitive and sustainable nature in the digital era (Adamik and Nowicki, 2020; Khan, 2022). This era is characterized by robust automation in production or manufacturing processes. This has brought with it, among other consequences, the fact that employees have an exhaustive knowledge of new technologies' performance and a more open mind towards innovation, disruptive thinking, or creativity. In this way, companies aim to face the intense competition demanded by the market to achieve high productivity (Bauer *et al.*, 2015). Traditionally, this objective has been pursued by an essential number of companies through human resources policies based on precarious employment and authoritarian or bureaucratic leadership. Far from these principles, other companies understand that their organizational culture must pivot in the generation of a climate that favors their workforce's commitment and the transfer of internal knowledge. As is well known, this source of added value helps to improve the quality of their products or services, and therefore, customer satisfaction (Geisler *et al.*, 2019).

In this sense, scientific literature shows us that workers' happiness or subjective well-being play a vital role in achieving business success. Happiness thus becomes a powerful predictor of positive employee behavior (Rego *et al.*, 2011). The most satisfied, happiest workers in their jobs are sources of commitment, entrepreneurship, and productivity (Salazar Estrada *et al.*, 2009). Therefore, it is necessary to explore or identify, on the one hand, the psychological and social factors which contribute significantly to the collective welfare of employees in the digital society (Sherman and Barokas, 2019); and, on the other hand, to analyze, from a theoretical and empirical point of view, what type of leadership is the most appropriate in order to promote organizational policies aimed at enriching the socio-emotional resources of its human talent (Ciulla, 2020).

Under this umbrella of Positive Psychology (Seligman, 1990), management approaches based on the well-being, motivation, and satisfaction of the collaborators emerge. One of them is *Happiness Management (HM)*, a management model that maximizes its financial results through leadership that holistically energizes its workers' collective happiness (López-Regalado *et al.*, 2020). Through this specific intangible resource, together with other multiple psycho-organizational specific vectors, employees will have a more proactive psycho-organizational work, personal involvement, internal effort, collaborative learning, emotional commitment, or work performance (Salas-Vallina *et al.*, 2018). Models, such as *Happiness Management (HM)*, teach us that the use of a stable human capital-leadership construct through happiness contributes by boosting workers' socio-emotional needs (Sánchez-Vázquez, 2018). As a result of the aspects mentioned in the lines above, companies will demand a type of leadership that is in line with the strategic value given to this type of management.

In this context, this book chapter entitled "A New Leadership for a New Era: effects of association of socio-demographic variables on the leader's competencies" aims to carry out an empirical study of a descriptive, quantitative, correlational, exploratory, and transversal nature, to inferentially examine the influence of the socio-demographic factors of the human resources managers of companies in the Campo de Gibraltar region – namely, in the province of Cádiz, Spain, which is in the southwestern part of the autonomous community of Andalusia, the southernmost part of mainland Europe, on the competencies and skills that the new leaders of companies in the digital era must possess, *stricto sensu*. In this way, it will be possible to understand better the socio-demographic factors' role in the management of human talent from the perspective of their managers' leadership (Bonesso *et al.*, 2020).

After this introduction, the next section provides the conceptual framework for this study. It then sets out the methodology used, the empirical study, and the results' evaluation. Finally, the most relevant conclusions of the work carried out are shown, and the limitations and future lines of research are derived from it. Hence, the section that successfully continues the ideas highlighted in the "Introduction" section, is represented by the "Background" section, which is dedicated to reflecting the most important concepts that are analyzed and displayed in this book chapter, thus focusing on a strong literature review analysis. In addition, the next section is represented by the "Main focus of the chapter", where the authors have successfully and synthetically underlined the purpose of this book chapter, thus closely presenting the reasoning behind choosing this theme as well as the motivation that comes to support the need for such a novel and comprehensive approach in terms of scientific research. Also, this section is immediately continued by the "Research design and methodology" and by the "Data collection analysis and presentation", which mainly centers on the following three subsections, namely: "Main descriptive study", "Analysis of the association relations with the profile variables", and "Exploratory Factor Analysis". Besides these sections, the next section is represented by the "Discussion and synthesis of results", where the authors focused also on the "Analysis of the association relations of the factors with the profile variables". It should also be underlined that the next sections are represented by the "Solutions and recommendations", the "Future research directions", the "Conclusion", and the "References", thus completing the current scientific work and providing the readers with a relevant and most recent image of the subject taken under close analysis.

Background

The background section of this book chapter focuses on presenting a literature review containing the most significant and up-to-date elements which are specific to the theme chosen for analysis.

Two processes drive business activity in our era: the first one is represented by the economic-financial globalization and the second one is represented by the rapid advance of technology. In this matter, it should be considered that there are numerous important processes that force new forms of action by organizations and transform the social paradigm of our planet. In this particular case, the reference made is about a VUCA environment, which is represented by an acronym that arose in the United States military field (Whiteman, 1998). Hence, it should be pointed out that in the daily lives of organizations and individuals, in general, are marked by volatility, uncertainty, complexity, and ambiguity (Bennett and Lemoine, 2014).

Today, entrepreneurship represents a vital component of today's environment, which also leads to the need to better analyze and to better understand the implications of leadership, while referring to companies' development, growth, and performance (Vargas-Hernández, 2021). Also, concentrating on the forms of leadership that are specific to the small and medium-sized enterprises (SMEs) represents a crucial step in today's business context (Duháček Šebestová, 2021).

Thus, given the current circumstances, organizations have either to provide an evolutionary response or one of continuous adaptation. This implies a renewal of the leadership exercised by all those in an organization responsible for the direction and the management functions. Leadership and performance management have a fundamental role in helping the organization maintain, or achieve, a competitive advantage that guarantees its survival (Hall and Rowland, 2016). Today's leadership needs appropriate mental models for this new world (Bolman and Deal, 2015), this "unstable and chaotic Terrae Incognitae" (Lagadec, 2009, p.5), this "phantom threat" (Bennett and Lemoine, 2014, p.7) that the environment has become. Table 1 which is entitled "Characteristics of leadership in a VUCA environment" reflects the main characteristics that different authors maintain leadership should have in an era like the present one (see Table 1. Characteristics of leadership in a VUCA environment).

In such a context, there is no doubt that information and knowledge become the leading resources. The progress of the Information and Communications Technology (ICTs) is contributing to this in an increasingly accelerated manner. Those organizations that will be able to adapt the best will be the ones that will be able to capture, create, disseminate, and manage knowledge more efficiently. The leader has an essential role in this function; he or she must manage it in favor of its objectives, starting with those of their team or group of collaborators. Moreover, in this process, the leader has to combat two phenomena linked to the wide dissemination through ICTs: on the one hand, that of "over information" and "intoxication" or "involution" (Cornellá, 2009; Manovich, 2006; Lyman and Varian, 2003; Moles and Costa, 1998); on the other hand, that of the deficit of reflection before decision making to which the ease of obtaining data can lead (Lash, 2005). Leaders and collaborators must be e-competent, i.e., they must have the right skills in the Information and Communications Technology (ICT) and, through them, in knowledge management (Cobo Roma, 2010, pp. 9-10).

Curiously, alongside this facet of "homo technologies", or "homo digitalis", the emotional facet of the team leaders is now back on the agenda, in a new version of the social man of the Human Relations Theories of the early and mid-20th century.

Table 1. Characteristics of leadership in a VUCA environment

Doh and Quigley (2014) and Sarkar (2016), "Responsible Leadership"	Caldwell *et al.* (2012)	Rodriguez and Rodriguez (2015)	Elkington *et al.* (2017)
Communicating: with the team members, with the company, with the *stakeholders* and with the society as a whole	Informing	Discovering the potential of employees: empowering them	Self-leadership
Encouraging teamwork	Listening actively		Passion
Encouraging the employees to achieve objectives			Understanding people
Encouraging innovative thinking and creativity			Value-based leadership
Promoting ethical integrity			Stimulus and influence
Promoting Corporate Social Responsibility (CSR)			Ethics and values
			Social Responsibility
			Understanding the human factor
			Communication
			Diversity Management
			Teamwork
			Conflict resolution
			Networking
			Empowering human resources
			Customer orientation
			Relations with *stakeholders*
			Boosting innovation
			Knowledge of technologies
			International networks

Source: Authors' own elaboration, based on the referenced works (see the "References" section of this book chapter).

In line with this, it should be noted that since the beginning of the 21-st century, the studies in the area of the business organization that have emerged, focus on demonstrating empirically that corporations should also become an essential source of socio-emotional resources for their workforce (e.g., Tomprou *et al.*, 2020; Vandekerkhof *et al.*, 2018; Shore *et al.*, 2009). This requires, on the one hand, the existence of technological and emotional leaders, who can cultivate a positive environment within the organizations (Ouakouak et al., 2020; Kováč *et al.*, 2010); and, on the other hand, management that designs human resources policies that focuses on the maximization of economic benefits through the holistic search for the subjective well-being of their internal clients (Russell, 2008; Baker *et al.*, 2007).

In the same line, in combination with Positive Psychology and Neuroscience, *Neuromanagement* appears as the discipline that uses the tools of the Cognitive Neurosciences capable to manage and to direct organizations (Braidot, 2014). The leader has to pay attention to *Neuromanagement* because there are neurological processes closely linked to tasks inherent to their functions, such as decision-making, the development of individual, and the organizational intelligence, and people's planning and management. The leader, therefore, becomes a *neuroleader*, of who four essential competencies or pillars are required ("*The i4 Model*" by Damiano, 2014), which are as follows:

- Integration: represents the correct balance between body and mind in the performance of their work;
- Inspiration: represents the ability to give answers, decisions, and thoughts away from those of the majority of individuals;
- Imagination, inventiveness, the left side of the reader's brain, and its use to face and solve different situations.
- Intuition: represents the ability that complements the three previous characteristics and allows the leader to detect negative deviations from the team's goals.

Following Neuroscience, ultra-fast brain processes occur in the brain, which is not the same in all individuals, revealing a leader's aptitude (Braidot, 2014).

Derived from the previous studies and reflections, for the present investigation a more extensive survey has been elaborated, from which a set of questions have been extracted, as well as the codes are given to each one of them, which are by what has been commented here, and which appear in Table 2 entitled "Variables used in the study" (see Table 2. Variables used in the study). Although the literature on leadership shows us multiple surveys, the novelty of placing the questions in the current VUCA and digital context has meant that the research began with this first step, with the design of a new questionnaire, which has nevertheless been subjected to several validity tests, both statistical and with a pre-test with experts. The latter was carried out through previous analysis requested from five people who hold Human Resources Management (HRM) positions in their organizations. The writing style of some questions was also refined to ensure that they were intelligible to the respondents.

Table 2. Variables used in the study

	STAFF EMPOWERMENT
DEMOCRAT	A leader must have a democratic/participatory style, as the team members have knowledge and skills that allow them to share decision-making with the leader.
AUTON	Giving employees their autonomy is more efficient for them than supervising their work.
DIVERS	Staff must be composed of a wide diversity of people with different skills and abilities, as it helps create effective leadership.
	INFORMATION AND COMMUNICATION
TRANSP	Transparency – understood as the communication to employees of all information about the company's situation, improves leadership.
OBSOL	The rapid evolution of information technologies (IT) accelerates the obsolescence of some systems used in the organization.
QUALIFY	In the face of the obsolescence caused by technologies, the leader has to pay attention to updating his team members' qualifications.
POWER	To possess knowledge is to possess power.
ICONIC	The leader must know how to differentiate what information he or she needs.
QUENTIN	The leader must know how to use the sources of information available to him/her to find the data he/she needs.
ECONOMIC	The leader must know how to gather knowledge through electronic means.
PROCESS	The leader must know how to handle, process, and re-arrange the information that they obtain through electronic means.
EDIFUND	The leader must disseminate the information obtained through the electronic media freely by the organization.
	CONNECTION AND NETWORKS
ECONEX	Today, the leader's degree of power increases with the social networking and communications connections they can establish.
NETWORK	Nowadays, the leader's degree of power increases with the social and communication connections they can establish, but only professionally.
STAKEHOLDER	The leader has to establish a network of relationships, friendships, and commitments with all the elements that can influence a decision or give him/her interesting, important, and valuable points of view.
WINWIN	The leader must maintain a harmonious relationship with the main groups that influence the organization and seek "win-win" relationships.
EPROF	The leader must maintain a harmonious relationship with the main groups that influence the organization and seek "win-win" relationships, including competitors.
	NEURO LEADERSHIP AND EMOTIONS
INSPIRE	Today's leaders' fundamental pillars to adapt and achieve success in the volatile and changing world people live in are an inspiration. In the New Era, the organizations that are going to be most effective will be those that manage to inspire each of their employees to exercise their leadership.
DESEM	Today's leader's fundamental pillars to adapt and achieve success in the volatile and changing world people live in are related with the integration for performance, which refers to the leader's mental and physical balance when performing tasks.

Continued on following page

Table 2. Continued

COLAB	Today's leader's fundamental pillars to adapt and achieve success in the volatile and changing world in which people live are the following ones: informing workers of the objectives, inspiring in them the necessary commitment to collaboration, and providing *feedback*.
INNOVATES	The fundamental pillars of the current leader to adapt and achieve success in the volatile and changing world people live in are innovation, and introducing the necessary means to achieve the proposed goals.
AGIL	The fundamental pillars of today's leader to adapt and succeed in the volatile and changing world in which people live is Agility, which the leader possesses and with which he or she can detect potential negative deviations in the organization.
DESCONX	It is essential to allow the worker to be disconnected from work once their day is over, even if there is a considerable workload.
SESAC	Today, the management of organizations and their teams has also become a management of the senses and sensations.
EMOTION	When making decisions, the leader also turns to his or her emotional side, i.e., he or she recalls previous emotions or events triggered by the stimulus of making a new decision.
NEWS	Managerial behavior results in inadequate performance only if it creates a stress-free leadership environment.
AMBIENT	With good informal relations between employees and management, a positive working environment improves the latter's leadership, and the impression employees have of them.
EMPATHY	Empathy with employees is vital to building effective leadership.
EXPNEG	Employees may arrive at the workplace after having a negative experience, either personally or at work. It is essential, then, that the leader empathizes with them so that their average performance is not affected.

Source: Authors' own elaboration.

In the prelude of the questionnaire, a series of questions are posed to define the respondents' socio-demographic profile, using a set of nominal qualitative variables, either binomial (Sex) or multinomial (age, sector, and size of the company) (see Appendix 1: Designed Questionnaire). The categories used in the questionnaire are the following ones:

- Sex: Female/Male;
- Age: from 18 to 35 years old/ from 36 to 50 years old/ from 51 to 65 years old/ from 66 years old or more;
- Sectors: Education, training and R&D&I/Food, hotels and restaurants/Recreational, cultural and leisure services/Automotive and transport/Business services/Secondary sector: industry and mining/Commerce/Health and welfare/IT and communications/Artistic and audiovisual production/Banks and financial services/Public sector/Other;
- Size: up to 49 workers/ between 50 and 249 workers/ more than 250 workers.

It should be added that numerous studies are centered on the tremendous power and on the strong influence that happiness possesses towards individuals, in general, and towards Human Resources Management (HRM), in particular (Salas-Vallina *et al.* 2018). In addition, it should be stressed that Happiness Management (HM) represents a novel and a highly powerful instrument that a New Leadership for a New Era should make use of as often as possible, since numerous recent scientific works have successfully proven that individuals' general state of mind, in both personal and professional activities, comes to influence, at an inestimable level, the degree in which the activities are performed and the manner in which an entity, an organization, or a company, performs on the marketplace (Ravina-Ripoll *et al.* 2021).

There should be emphasized that achieving long-term excellence in business is strongly connected with the capacity and degree of performance of individuals as well as with the manner in which individuals receive guidance and motivation from their leaders (Popescu, 2022b).

MAIN FOCUS OF THE CHAPTER

This book chapter presents the importance and the implications of a New Leadership for a New Era, while targeting the most profound and the most relevant effects of association of these days' socio-demographic variables on the leader's competencies. In this new and demanding international business environment, which has been drastically affected by the demanding and energizing effects of the COVID-19 pandemic and of the COVID-19 crisis, entities are the ones that have to adapt their work in order to promptly and to constructively respond to a more challenging environment, where globalization and internationalization, technological advances, and the management of transferring knowledge have become pivotal processes for all inspirational forms of competitiveness, and all types of business process management, that are capable to address in a better and more comprehensive way today's business needs. In continuation, it should be emphasized that this book chapter concentrates the attention of this VUCA environment, in order to determine those particular forces that have the power to provide the entities the necessary strength capable to readjust on a continuous basis. Furthermore, this book chapter centers on discovering the means that organizations possess in order to be capable of attracting and retaining people with adequate and sufficient skills to work in this new context, while showing a deeper and a more reliable form of commitment to management models based on leadership that are capable to contribute now, as never before, to giving visibility, voice, participation, and well-being to all its members. This book chapter successfully demonstrates the powerful belief that the most satisfied collaborators are the most productive, which has also been addressed on numerous occasions in recent scientific studies and which has also been demonstrated by recent literature. In addition, it should be highlighted that this current study is of an empirical, exploratory, and transversal nature, as follows: firstly, the degree of conformity with individual capacities of the new leader was tested among personnel managers in organizations in the Bay of Algeciras Arch – more specially, in the Bay of Algeciras's territory, on the Strait of Gibraltar's northern flank; and secondly, it is analyzed whether these opinions are related to specific socio-demographic characteristics of the respondents.

RESEARCH DESIGN AND METHODOLOGY

This section centers on the research design and methodology specific to this book chapter. This research is carried out in the Bay of Algeciras's territory, on the Strait of Gibraltar's northern flank. This is a territory with unique characteristics at the world level, given its condition as a bridge between two seas, the Mediterranean and the Atlantic, two continents, Europe and Africa, and two cultures. It is an international transit point, characterized in the economic field by having the first port in terms of the volume of the goods traffic in the Mediterranean. In this particular case, it should be noted that for the first period of the year 2020, the accumulated figure of the goods transit for the Port of Algeciras Bay was of 27,432,551 tons. Valencia followed it, with 19,068,969 tons, and Barcelona with 15,170,846 tons (Estadística de Puertos del Estado, 2020). Moreover, the second industrial center of the country, circumstances that force its socio-economic fabric to continuously maintain a high level of competitiveness and efficiency, must continuously adapt to national and international contexts.

Figure 1. Phases of the research process
Source: Authors' own elaboration.

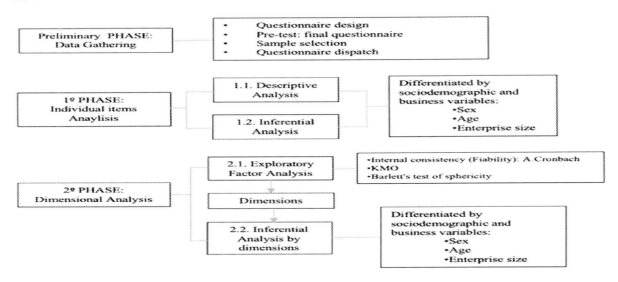

A questionnaire is used as a primary information-gathering instrument (Batjargal, 2007). In a preminninary Phase a first questionnaire is designed and tested with the opinion of a group of experts (human resources managers in organizations in the area). These experts evaluated whether the questions were relevant, whether any were missing, and whether the wording of the questions was adequate (see Figure 1. Phases of the research process). Their comments and suggestions are collected to elaborate the final questionnaire (see Table 2. Variables used in the study).

This is addressed to people in charge of the Human Resources Area (HRA) or similar position, as it is assumed that this is the most sensitive position to the questions posed. The number of recipients was 170, who were sent the questionnaire by email, through a link to it in "Google Forms". The questionnaire consists of several items intended to reflect the degree of respondents' degree of approval for the statements they reflect. This is measured by a Likert scale, where one is "Strongly Disagree", and five is "Strongly Agree".

One hundred twenty-six responses were received, representing 74.11%. After debugging the information, 120 good records remain, 72.72% of the initial sample. This ratio is considered very good in terms of digital means (Internet) surveys, as it is over 70% (Baxter and Babbie, 2004) (see Table 3. Technical data of the fieldwork).

Table 3. Technical data of the fieldwork

Population	Companies, with more than five employees, from the Algeciras Bay Arch.
Sample size	170 units.
Type of sampling	Random stratified by sector of activity.
Territorial scope	Arc of the Bay of Algeciras (Algeciras, Los Barrios, San Roque, La Línea). More than 90% of total companies and population of the region.
Method of data collection	Self-completed questionnaire ("Google Forms").
Initial control parameters:	Sex, age range, activity sector, size of the entity.
Items raised	29 questions, on four dimensions: 1. (1.) Staff empowerment. 2. (2.) Information and Communication. 3. (3.) Connections and Networks. 4. (4.) Neuroleadership and Emotions.
Evaluation of items: Likert Scale	Range: 1: "Strongly disagree" to 5: "Strongly agree".
Data collection period	March-July, 2019.
Statistical program	SPSS 25.00

Source: Authors' own elaboration.

DATA COLLECTION ANALYSIS AND PRESENTATION

The questionnaire's validity is complemented by measuring its reliability and statistical validation through the *Cronbach Alpha* indicator (see Table 4. Reliability Measurement. Cronbach's Alpha). For the selected items, the measure is 0.927, resulting in very high reliability (Alpha's above 0.7 are admitted as high) (Corbetta, 2007). None of the items or variables has had to be eliminated to increase this result, so that the analysis will contain all those elements selected.

Table 4. Reliability measurement; Cronbach's Alpha

Cronbach's Alpha	Cronbach's Alfa based on standardized elements	No. of elements
0,927	0,926	29

Source: Authors' own elaboration.

Main Descriptive Study

After making the crossed tables, or contingency tables, and for more Agile Information Management (AIM), the Sector parameter is renamed in a smaller number of categories, joining the sectors that behave similarly. Six sectors emerge, which are: (1) Public sector/(2) Food, restaurants, hotels and catering, and health and welfare/(3) Education, training and R&D&I/(4) Tourism, culture and artistic and audiovisual production/(5) Trade and automotive and transport/(6) Business services, banking and IT services.

None of the variables studied has an average below 3.49, indicating that the respondents have high regard for the statements they imply. DESCONEX obtains the highest values (4.58), followed by DIV-

ERS and EMPATHY, with 4.48. The score range is full in all the variables (minimum one and maximum 5) except in DESCONX, CALIF, DEMOCRAT, EMPATHY, and DIVERS, where the minimum value recorded is 2; and they are the ones with the lowest standard deviation. The least valued (even exceeding the average value 3) are RED (3.49), EDIFUND (3.74), ECONEX (3.76), and EPROF (3.78), which have deviations more significant than one (see Table 5. Primary descriptors of the variables studied).

When distinguished by Sex, it should be noted that none of the variables have means less than value 3. The standard deviations are small, not exceeding 0.16 in any case. Therefore, the responses are similar for men and women in their averages, although these are usually slightly higher in men's case (except in the case of EDIFUND). The items with the highest averages are those of DESCONEX: 4.67, COLAB: 4.57, EXPNEG: 4.57, DIVERS, and EMPATIA 4.53. The most significant differences by gender are found in ECONEX, INSPIRA, COLAB, NOTENSIO, and EXNEG.

This harmony disappears in part when referring to the categories by age, as the EDIFUND and RED variables are valued with an average of two by respondents belonging to the oldest group, and EPROF with 2.33. It is in this group where the deviations are highest, almost one point. However, in the items OBSOL, DESEMP, COLAB (with an average of 5), and INNOVA with 4.67, it is the group with the highest score. In addition, it should be stated that the rest of the averages equal to or higher than 4.5 are found among the two younger groups, in DESCONX, DEMOCRAT, DIVERS, EXPNEG, and EMPATIA, as well as for the mature age category in NOTENSIO. Figure 2 entitled "Means of variables by Gender", Figure 3 entitled "Means of variables by Age", and Figure 4 entitled "Means of variables by Sector and Size" shows the apparent existing differences between the averages of the first three groups with the last one, that of older people, especially significant in some variables of Information and Communication and Connection and Networks (see Figure 2. Means of variables by Gender; see Figure 3. Means of variables by Age; and, see Figure 4. Means of variables by Sector and Size).

Table 5. Primary descriptors of the variables studied

	Minimum	Maximum	Media	Typical deviation		Minimum	Maximum	Media	Typical deviation
DEMOCRAT	2	5	4,43	0,74	WINWIN	1	5	4,16	0,89
AUTON	1	5	4,04	0,88	EPROF	1	5	3,78	1,01
DIVERS	2	5	4,48	0,77	INSPIRE	1	5	4,15	1,01
TRANSP	1	5	4,33	0,85	DESCONX	2	5	4,58	0,67
OBSOL	1	5	4,24	0,82	DESEM	1	5	4,19	0,99
QUALIFY	2	5	4,39	0,68	COLAB	1	5	4,37	0,89
POWER	1	5	4,10	1,06	INNOVATES	1	5	4,29	0,87
ICONIC	1	5	4,41	0,87	AGIL	1	5	4,16	0,97
QUENTIN	1	5	4,35	0,86	SESAC	1	5	4,00	0,94
ECONOMIC	1	5	4,16	0,92	EMOTION	1	5	3,94	0,90
PROCESS	1	5	4,16	0,95	NEWS	1	5	4,30	0,82
EDIFUND	1	5	3,74	1,10	AMBIENT	1	5	4,40	0,76
ECONEX	1	5	3,76	1,17	EMPATHY	2	5	4,48	0,76
NETWORK	1	5	3,49	1,14	EXPNEG	1	5	4,42	0,86
STAKEHOLDER	1	5	3,92	1,12					

Source: Authors' own elaboration.

About the sector's categories, averages above three are again given in all cases and deviations that barely exceed one-third of a point in some variables and specific categories. The group made up of Trade and Automotive and Transport entities are the one which gives the highest average scores in the majority of questions, followed by Food, catering and hotel management and Health and welfare. It is important to note that practically all sectors give a score of over 4.5 to the DESCONX variable (4.46; 4.60; 4.55; 4.63 and 4.79, respectively).

Figure 2. Means of variables by gender
Source: Authors' own elaboration.

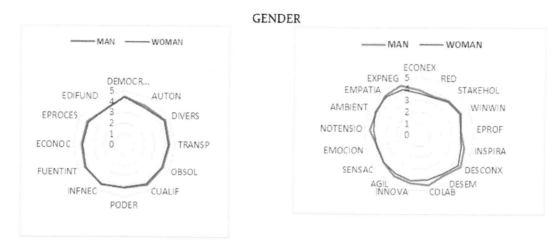

Figure 3. Means of variables by age
Source: Authors' own elaboration.

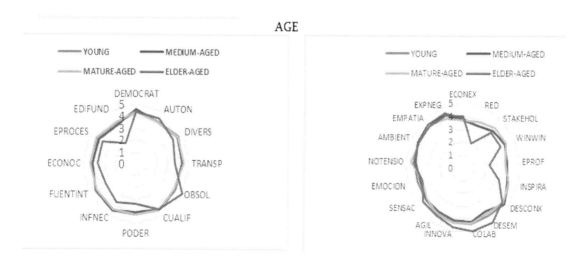

Figure 4. Means of variables by sector and size
Source: Authors' own elaboration.

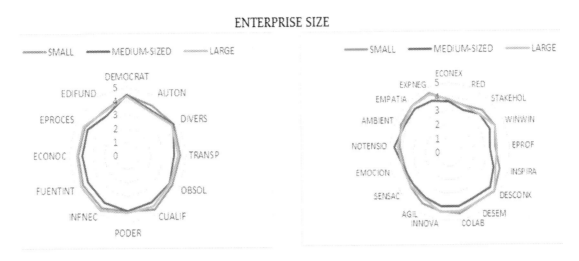

Finally, respondents working in small businesses generally value the various issues raised more highly. Large companies follow this. In particular, in DIVERS, CALIF, DESCONX, EMPATIA, and EXPNEG, small companies' members gave values above 4.5. In continuation, it should be mentioned that those of the large entities are in INFNEC, FUENTINT, DESCONX, EMPATIA, and those of the medium-sized companies are in NOTENSIO. The group of medium-sized organizations scored all the items less highly, except for DEMOCRAT and NOTENSIO.

Analysis of the Association Relations with the Profile Variables

Having detected the differences between the means within the items' distributions for each category of the socio-demographic or profile variables, and given that some of them are relevant, an analysis is proposed to detect possible associations between them.

Null hypotheses are defined as follows below:

- H0Sexoi: There is no association between variable *I* and the variable Sex. The distributions of variable I am similar for the different categories of the variable Sex.
- H0Edadi: There is no association between variable *I* and the variable age. The distributions of variable I am similar for the different categories of the variable age.
- H0Sectori: There is no association between the variable *I* and the Sector variable. The distributions of variable I am similar for the different categories of the Sector variable.
- H0SIZEi: There is no association between variable *I* and the variable size. The distributions of variable I am similar for the different categories of the variable size.

To this end, it is checked beforehand whether the distributions mentioned above behave as usual or as non-normal, or non-parametric. The Kolmogorov-Smirnov (from now on, K-S) and Shapiro-Wilk (from now on, S-W) tests give less than 0.05, and even less than 0.01 in each of the profile variables, in all or most of their distributions, resulting, therefore, in their being non-parametric.

The U Mann-Whitney test is carried out for the Sex binomial and the Kruskal-Wallis test for the multinomial, Age, Sector, and Size. Although slightly the number of records in the sample is more significant than one hundred, it could be assumed that the distributions behave as usual. Therefore, the authors contrast the H0 with the parameters of t-Student, for Sex, and ANOVA for the rest of the profile variables.

Sex

The variables with association with Sex, that is, in which the null hypothesis is rejected, are COLAB and NOTENSIO:

- COLAB: The U-significance of Mann-Whitney is 0.002. According to Levene's test, equal variances are assumed, being sig. In the t-Student test, it is 0.007.
- NOTE: A Mann-Whitney gives a sig. of 0.014. The Levene test assumes equal variances, being sig. of 0.025 in the t-Student test.

Age

There is only one variable associated with age, EDIFUND. Kruskal-Wallis gives a sig. of 0.045. Levene's statistic indicates that equal variances are assumed, being sig. ANOVA of 0.027. Bonferroni is a posthoc test, or of inter category means differences, is applied, being the categories 1 (young) concerning 4 (older) and 3 (mature) concerning 4 (older) where the differences with statistical significance are located at the level of 5% error. The young group's average differs by 1,846 points from that of the older ones and the average for the mature group by 1,950 points.

Sector

About the sector, there is only an association with the variable PODER, with a sig. in Kruskal-Wallis of 0.025. Equal variances are assumed, and the ANOVA turns out to be not significant at the level of 5% (0.080).

Size

In terms of size, there are several variables with which an association is established:

- AUTON: the significance in Kruskal-Wallis is 0.013. The significance in ANOVA is 0.028. Levene indicates that the variances are equal, so the Bonferroni test is applied, with statistically significant differences between groups 1 (small companies) and 3 (large companies), with a distance between their averages of 0.494.
- TRANSP: the following is 0.040 in Kruskal-Wallis, and 0.061 in ANOVA Applying Bonferroni, it is discovered that the group of small companies has an average that differs significantly less error than 5%, from that of the group of medium-sized companies, by 0.470 points.

- QUALIFY: presents a sig. of 0,001 in Kruskal-Wallis and of 0,000 in ANOVA Bonferroni's test indicates that the categories with statistically significant average distributions are those of small enterprises when compared to medium-sized enterprises (0.591) and large enterprises (0.324).
- ICONIC: has a sig. =0.039 in Kruskal-Wallis and of 0.018 in ANOVA Bonferroni points out that the categories in which the differences in averages with an error of less than 5% are shown are those of small enterprises with medium-sized enterprises (0.439), and that of large enterprises with medium-sized enterprises (0.667).
- EXPNEG. Kruskal-Wallis shows a sig. of 0.039, and ANOVA a sig. of 0.021. Bonferroni specifies the difference in statistically significant averages between small and medium-sized companies, with a difference of 0.561 points.

Exploratory Factor Analysis

The correlations between the variables representing the items in this study are mostly higher than 0.3. Therefore, the opportunity arises to work with larger constructs, or "latent variables", that is decided to carry out an Exploratory Factorial Analysis (Ruiz, 2015).

Thus, the Kaiser-Meyer-Olkin (KMO) measure, which is 0.858, confirms that the Partial correlations between the variables are high enough that the set of variables can be subjected to this type of analysis. That is to say, the degree of relationship that exists between two variables once the effect of the remaining variables in the study has been eliminated. A minimum of 0.6 is required (although Kaiser, 1970, only considered it appropriate to carry out this analysis equal to or greater than 0.8). In Barlett's Sphericity Test, which contrasts the null hypothesis that the correlation matrix is an identity matrix, statistical significance is given at the level of 1% (0.000), which makes this hypothesis is rejected and indicates a very high degree of the inter-correlation between the variables.

Thus, it ought to be emphasized that Table 6 entitled "Rotated component matrix" shows both the matrix of correlations and the unilateral critical level (sig. unilateral) associated with each correlation coefficient. It can be seen that most of these are meanings of less than 5% (see Table 6. Rotated component matrix). Also, in this table, it can be seen that the sedimentation graph no longer has an exact inflection from factor 6, so it is decided that the process extracts five factors (see Table 6. Rotated component matrix).

Table 6. Rotated component matrix

	1	2	3	4	5
EMPATIA	0.745				
AMBIENT	0.715				
EXPNEG	0.694				
DIVERS	0.637	0.328			
NOTENSIO	0.599				
AUTON	0.597				
OBSOL	0.560				
DEMOCRAT	0.521				
TRANSP	0.502				
CUALIF	0.461				
EDIFUND	0.455	0.354			0.419
DESCONX	0.419				
INFNEC		0.819			
FUENTINT		0.810			
PODER		0.742			0.329
EPROCES	0.307	0.703		0.344	
ECONOC		0.699		0.392	
INSPIRA	0.307	0.428	0.326	0.340	
DESEM			0.825		
COLAB		0.403	0.703		
AGIL		0.348	0.674		
INNOVA		0.370	0.640		
EPROF				0.787	
STAKEHOL				0.772	
WINWIN		0.511		0.639	
RED				0.377	0.696
SENSAC					0.611
ECONEX		0.372	0.342		0.561
EMOCION			0.460		0.518

Note: Method of extraction: analysis of principal components. Rotation method: Varimax with Kaiser standardization. The rotation has converged in 8 iterations.
Source: Authors' own elaboration.

From the calculation process, in which the primary component extraction method has been used and forced not to admit coefficients lower than 0.3, five factors appear (see Table 6. Rotated component matrix), which explain 61.692% of the variance:

- Factor 1: which is labeled as "management for the digital age" (GESTDIG). It brings together all the characteristics of what management of a leader should be in the current context. It speaks of democratic leadership, which grants autonomy to the collaborators through transparency and access to the necessary information, and training in the management of the same, in the face of the obsolescence created by rapid technological progress (DEMOCRAT, AUTON, TRANSP, EDIFUND, CALIF, and OBSOL). It does so in an open and global environment where diversity, social, cultural, generations, and territories (DIVERS) are valued. Moreover, in which the leader knows, and contemplates, the benefits of establishing an excellent working climate or environment (AMBIENT), without dysfunctional tensions (NOTENSIO), in which he or she shows empathy with his or her workers, allowing them their own space for leisure and disconnection (EMPATHY, EXPNEG, and DESCONX), as elements, all of which increase the effectiveness of his or her leadership.

- Factor 2: called "the leader's tasks towards achievement" (LOGRO). The leader inspires each member of their team to achieve objectives and does so through information and communication. The aged leader knows where to capture information (electronic media, contacts, other sources, etc.), process and interpret it, and, finally, transmit it to their collaborators. The variables that make up this factor are PODER, INFNEC, FUENTINT, ECONOMIC, PROCESS, and INSPIRA.
- Factor 3: labeled "the Neuroleadership" (NEUROLID). This factor includes the four Neuroleadership assets described in Damiano's "*i4 Model*": DESEM, COLAB, INNOVA, AGIL.
- Factor 4: "the leader and his environment" (ENVIRONMENT). Integrated by the leader's relational capital elements: the agents or interest groups, the clients, and even the competitors aggregated in the STAKEHOL, WINWIN, and EPROF variables. The leader must adequately manage relations with the groups above as part of the organization's strategy.
- Factor 5: "the leader as a manager of emotions and sensations" (GESTEMO) The results have confirmed the theory in terms of respondents' conformity with the statement that the leader in the digital age must be focused on adequately managing his own emotions and sensations, as well as those of the other members of his team (SESAC and EMOTION), including in his "digital" relationships, through the networks, whether at a professional or formal level or in his informal relationships within the organization (RED and ECONEX).

Table 7. Component score coefficient matrix

Variable	Componente				
	1	2	3	4	5
DEMOCRAT	0,106	0,026	-0,07	-0,03	0,019
AUTON	0,166	-0,042	0,058	-0,084	-0,009
DIVERS	0,149	0,109	-0,124	-0,11	0,005
TRANSP	0,118	-0,087	0,02	0,059	0,011
OBSOL	0,139	0,026	-0,048	-0,073	0,017
CUALIF	0,081	0,027	-0,013	-0,039	-0,029
PODER	-0,117	0,366	-0,037	-0,300	0,144
INFNEC	-0,007	0,254	-0,037	-0,077	-0,101
FUENTINT	-0,011	0,227	-0,045	-0,041	-0,085
ECONOC	0,028	0,174	-0,047	0,042	-0,095
EPROCES	0,069	0,215	-0,088	0,023	-0,131
EDIFUND	0,136	0,079	-0,178	-0,021	0,206
ECONEX	-0,016	0,055	0,04	-0,141	0,345
RED	-0,158	-0,013	-0,238	0,152	0,542
STAKEHOL	0,007	-0,114	-0,102	0,493	0,014
WINWIN	-0,047	0,044	-0,004	0,209	-0,080
EPROF	-0,067	-0,126	0,001	0,440	-0,046
INSPIRA	0,037	0,040	0,038	0,060	0,019
DESCONX	0,075	0,000	0,034	0,008	-0,091
DESEM	-0,037	-0,088	0,474	-0,052	-0,133
COLAB	-0,045	0,003	0,283	-0,025	-0,09
INNOVA	-0,016	-0,023	0,222	0,016	-0,046
AGIL	-0,054	-0,028	0,302	-0,035	-0,003
SENSAC	0,015	-0,098	-0,026	-0,021	0,312
EMOCION	-0,024	-0,143	0,188	-0,082	0,215
NOTENSIO	0,141	-0,079	-0,021	0,045	0,024
AMBIENT	0,148	-0,104	0,024	0,059	-0,013
EMPATIA	0,178	0,024	-0,077	-0,017	-0,058
EXPNEG	0,205	-0,07	0,031	0,078	-0,149

Note: Method of extraction: analysis of principal components. Rotation method: Varimax with Kaiser standardization. Component scores.
a. The coefficients have been standardized.
Source: Authors' own elaboration.

DISCUSSION AND SYNTHESIS OF RESULTS

This section is particularly centered on carrying out the discussion and the synthesis of results for this book chapter. The matrix of coefficients for the calculation of factorial scores, also called the factor structure matrix (see Table 7. Component score coefficient matrix), provides the information to create the linear equations, with the weights of each variable, which give the respective values in the five factors determined for each respondent (see Table 8. Equations defining the components).

Table 8. Equations defining the components

FACTOR 1 (GESTDIG)=	0,106DEMOCRAT+0,166AUTON+0,149DIVERS+0,118TRANSP+0,139OBSOL+0,081CUALIF+0,117PODER +0,007INFNEC0,011FUENTINT+0,028ECONOC+0,069EPROCES+0,136EDIFND0,016ECONEX0,158RED +0,007STAKEHOL0,047WINWIN0,067EPROF+0,037INSPIRA+0,075DESCONX-0,037DESEM-0,045COLAB +0,016INNOVA+0,054AGIL+0,015SENSAC+0,024EMOCION+0,141NOTENSIO+0,148AMBIENT +0,178EMPATIA+0,205EXPNEG
FACTOR 2 (LOGRO)=	0,026DEMOCRAT-0,042 AUTON+0,109DIVERS-0,089TRANSP+0,026OBSOL+0,027CUALIF-0,366PODER +0,254INFNEC+0,227FUENTINT+0,174ECONOC+0,215EPROCES+0,079EDIFUND+0,055ECONEX-0,013RED -0,114STAKEHOL+0,044WINWIN-0,126EPROF+0,040INSPIRA+0,000DESCONX-0,088DESEM+0,003COLAB -0,023INNOVA-0,028AGIL-0,098SENSAC-0,143EMOCION-0,079NOTENSIO--0,104AMBIENT +0,024EMPATIA-0,070EXPNEG
FACTOR 3 (NEUROLID)=	-0,070DEMOCRAT+0,058 AUTON-0,124DIVERS+0,020TRANSP-0,048OBSOL-0,013CUALIF-0,037PODER -0,037INFNEC-0,045FUENTINT-0,047ECONOC-0,088EPROCES-0,178EDIFUND+0,040ECONEX-0,238RED -0,102STAKEHOL-0,004WINWIN+0,001EPROF+0,038INSPIRA+0,034DESCONX+0,474DESEM+0,283COLAB +0,222INNOVA+0,3028AGIL-0,026SENSAC+0,188EMOCION-0,021NOTENSIO+0,024AMBIENT -0,027EMPATIA+0,031EXPNEG
FACTOR 4 (ENVIRONMENT)=	-0,030DEMOCRAT-0,084 AUTON-0,110DIVERS+0,059TRANSP-0,073OBSOL-0,039CUALIF-0,300PODER -0,077INFNEC-0,041FUENTINT+0,042ECONOC+0,023EPROCES-0,021EDIFUND-0,141ECONEX+0,152RED +0,493STAKEHOL+0,209WINWIN+0,440EPROF+0,060INSPIRA+0,008DESCONX-0,052DESEM-0,025COLAB+0,016INNOVA-0,035AGIL-0,021SENSAC-0,082EMOCION+0,045NOTENSIO+0,059AMBIENT -0,017EMPATIA+0,078EXPNEG
FACTOR 5 (GESTEMO)=	0,019DEMOCRAT-0,009 AUTON+0,005DIVERS+0,011TRANSP+0,0178OBSOL-0,029CUALIF+0,144PODER -0,101INFNEC-0,085FUENTINT-0,095ECONOC-0,131PROCES+0,206EDIFUND+0,345ECONEX+0,542RED +0,014STAKEHOL-0,080WINWIN-0,046EPROF+0,019INSPIRA-0,091DESCONX-0,133DESEM-0,090COLAB -0,046INNOVA-0,003AGIL+0,321SENSAC+0,215EMOCION+0,024NOTENSIO-0,013AMBIENT -0,058EMPATIA-0,149EXPNEG

Source: Authors' own elaboration.

The resulting scores, obtained from the regression method, have zero, as they are calculated in differential format. The covariance's are also zero and indicate that the factors have zero correlations; they are independent of each other (see Table 9. The component score covariance matrix).

Table 9. The component score covariance matrix

Components	1	2	3	4	5
1	1	0	0	0	0
2	0	1	0	0	0
3	0	0	1	0	0
4	0	0	0	1	0
5	0	0	0	0	1

Source: Authors' own elaboration.

Analysis of the Association Relations of the Factors with the Profile Variables

To check whether the scores obtained in these factors are related to the profile variables, a new contrast of the null hypothesis is made, which rejects this option.

- H0SexFactorj: There is no association between Factor *j* and the variable Sex. The distributions of Factor *j* are similar for the different categories of the variable Sex.
- H0AgeFactorj: There is no association between Factor *j* and the Age variable. The distributions of Factor *j* are similar for the different categories of the variable age.
- H0SectorFactorj: There is no association between Factor *j* and the Sector variable. The distributions of Factor *j* are similar for the different categories of the Sector variable.
- H0SizeFactorj: There is no association between Factor *j* and the variable size. The distributions of Factor *j* are similar for the different categories of the variable size.

Sex

It is verified, through the K-S and S-W tests, that the factor distributions for the two categories of the variable Sex are mostly non-parametric. The contrast, carried out using the Mann-Whitney U test, does not show meanings lower than 0.05, so the five null hypotheses are retained. There is no relationship of association of these with the categories of the variable Sex. There are no differences in means between men and women for any of the five factors.

Age

K-S and S-W indicate that most factor distributions by age group are normal. The ANOVA figures are: 0.944 for Factor 1; 0.381 for Factor 2; 0.023 for Factor 3; 0.295 for Factor 4; and 0.441 for Factor 5. Since some of the distributions are non-parametric – especially for categories 1 and 2 (young and middle-aged), Factor 3 is also found to be less than 5% significant in the Kruskal-Wallis test, having the value of 0.045. Having carried out Bonferroni's posthoc test, given that Levene indicates that equal variances are assumed, it turns out that it is group 4, the older age group, which differs in a statistically significant way in its average about age groups 2 (middle-aged, with a difference of 1,671 points) and 3 (mature, with 1,632 points).

Sector

The factor distributions in each of the Sector categories are normal, with a few exceptions. ANOVA has meanings of 0.715 for Factor 1; 0.045 for Factor 2; 0.468 for Factor 3; 0.139 for Factor 4 and 0.468 for Factor 5. To complete this analysis, Kruskal-Wallis confirms it, giving a sig.=0.041. Factor 5 presents a significance of 0.050 precisely. Levene's test indicates that the equality of the variances is assumed, and Bonferroni specifies that the statistically significant differences occur for Factor 2 between category 5 (Trade and Automotive and transport) and category 4 (Tourism, culture and artistic and audiovisual production), with a difference in averages of 1,082 points.

Size

K-W and S-W show mostly non-parametric distributions. The contrast, using Kruskal-Wallis, indicates that the null hypothesis for Factor 1 is rejected, with sig.=0.044. The differences in averages are 0.429 points between small and medium-sized firms, 0.298 between small and medium-sized firms, and 0.130

between large and medium-sized firms. However, the hypothesis cannot be rejected when carrying out the ANOVA test, as the significance is 0.135.

SOLUTIONS AND RECOMMENDATIONS

In terms of solutions of recommendations, it should be pointed out that, in order to ensure, create and maintain a responsible and a sustainable business environment in the Post-COVID-19 Era, all entities at a global level, should be centered on the following key aspects: promoting strong business ethics; becoming more innovative, thus focusing on issues such as creativity, knowledge, human resources, innovation, intangible assets, intellectual capital, and leadership; addressing at a larger and more comprehensive scale the Sustainable Development Goals (SDGs), the individuals' need for well-being and mindfulness in all the daily activities – both in terms of personal and of professional tasks; promoting a VUCA environment, focused on organizational culture and real forms of understanding towards individuals.

What is more, also in terms of solutions of recommendations, organizations need to help and to promote the sustainable development objectives, thus providing a tremendous support in building long-term inclusive global knowledge societies, governed by information and communication, for sustainable development in a world characterized by a rapidly changing business environment.

Furthermore, the New Leadership for a New Era brings a whole new meaning and a completely different dimension to the business opportunities that will govern the Post-COVID-19 Era. In this matter, the management for the digital age becomes crucial and represents the very essence of individuals' daily lives both for personal and for personal interaction and activities. Likewise, the intense competition expected and demanded by the marketplace will continue to be done by achieving high productivity, but intangible assets – such as, human resources, intellectual capital, knowledge, intellectual property, will be the forces that will be capable to make a difference in the Post-COVID-19 Era, and will be able to set in motion and move forward entities, organizations and businesses. In addition, preparing and fostering the New Leadership for a New Era will have the most powerful significance in an open and in an international environment characterized by diversity, where the real values will be the human, ethical, social, and cultural ones, thus establishing an excellent working climate or environment for all employees, like never before.

While addressing the ideas that are specific to this section focus on solutions of recommendations, it should be mentioned that leadership implicates also a subjective approach, like any other component that may be encountered in the area of Human Resources Management (HRM). This subjective approach means that the individuals that get in contact with the leaders of the entities (the employees of the entities, the colleagues having similar ranks and positions in the entities, the partners of the entities, the suppliers, the clients, the stakeholders, the representatives of the competitors, and all the other people that enter into direct contact with the leaders of the entities) are more or less affected, depending on the case, by the leaders approaches, desires, discourse, objectives, requirements, style, type personality, temperament, and so on (Popescu, 2022c). Also, the leaders are influenced, in turn, by the environment in which they activate, and, also, by the individuals they get in contact with, thus being more or less willing to change, to grow, to prosper, and to help their entities, and the people around them grow together with them and become more prosperous, happier, and centered on their well-being, and health. In addition, leaders have the power to motivate, which represents a positive activity, but, also, to demotivate, which represents a less desired form of action and of creating prosperity and happiness in the entities.

Based on all the aspects analyzed, presented, suggested, and recommended in this book chapter, in terms of the New Leadership for a New Era when addressing the challenges and changes derived from the Post-COVID-19 Era, it should also be considered that each person has its own style, its own sensibilities, and its own temperament (Schwartz, 2011; Cieciuch, 2017; Roccas and Sagiv, 2010). Thus, the solutions for a better future for all as well as the solutions for a more positive and productive approach both in the personal and professional lives should be the ones that rely on collective happiness, creativity, knowledge, human resources, innovation, well-being, and mindfulness. In the end, according the authors of this book chapter, *Happiness Management (HM)* may be the very essence and the key to the New Leadership for a New Era, thus enhancing power of leadership expressed so far by individuals far beyond the challenges and changes derived from the Post-COVID-19 Era, and going to the next level, where people are seen as the most important assets of today's society as well as the promoters of the Sustainable Development Goals (SDGs) instruments, methods, and principals.

FUTURE RESEARCH DIRECTIONS

In terms of future research directions this current research could expended in terms of analyzing the New Leadership for a New Era beyond the challenges and changes derived from the Post-COVID-19 Era, by creating and promoting a management model that is capable to maximize its financial results through leadership while focusing on the power derived from the energy of workers in a business environment which revolves around collective happiness, creativity, knowledge, human resources, innovation, well-being, and mindfulness.

In continuation, the patterns and the methodologies and methods used in this research could be used successfully in other regions, countries, and/or group of countries besides the Bay of Algeciras Arch – more specially, in the Bay of Algeciras's territory, on the Strait of Gibraltar's northern flank. It is the authors' strong belief that analyzing the New Leadership for a New Era beyond the challenges and changes derived from the Post-COVID-19 Era can be done with great accomplishments in other regions, countries, and/or group of countries, the results showing the need to improve leadership at all levels, and enable leaders worldwide to become more connected with the needs of their organizations, their employees, and the environment as a whole. In consequence, it should be added that all around the world there is a paramount need to create the portrait of the New Leader for the New Era who has to manage in an open, democratic, participative, and transparent way, in an environment characterized by diversity of collaborators and collaborations, and in an excellent working climate, thus having the power to inspire commitment among the team members, while sharing in the same time the necessary information.

CONCLUSION

From the survey, it should be noted that the statements sustained by the 29 items are appreciated with values above the average, value 3, for the entire sample. Questions, such as the need to allow the worker to disconnect entirely from their tasks once their workday is over, living in the work environment with diverse people with different skills and aptitudes, and the fact that the leader shows empathy with their collaborators are the most valued. Together with the desire for a democratic/participatory style of the leader, and the continuous updating of the qualification in the face of accelerated technological advances, these are the issues where there is the least discrepancy between the respondents.

The men have slightly overestimated the various items, except for referring to the leader's duty to disseminate information obtained through the organization's electronic media freely. Of the variables in which there are more significant differences by gender, only two of them show a relationship of association, in that one of the fundamental pillars of what current leadership should be is sharing objectives with employees and creating in them the commitment to collaborate to achieve them (more significant in men, with an average of 4.57, than in women, 4.11), and in empathizing with employees who have had negative experiences so that it does not affect their regular performance (average in men, 4.47; and in women, 4.13).

When it comes to age categories, people over 65 have the most significant discrepancy in their opinions concerning other groups, giving lower scores, and younger people generally score higher. As there are many variables whose assessments show differences in the various age groups, only one, however, experiences an association with this socio-demographic characteristic, EDIFUND. In this case, young people support the leader freely disseminating information through the organization with greater force than people of mature age or those over 65.

In the study of the sectors, it stands out that, once again, the disconnection of work in hours outside the working day is the issue with the highest average score in all of them. Workers in Trade and Automotive and Transport are generally the ones who most value the items in the questionnaire. The variable POWER shows a relationship of association with the sector, with the Trade, Automotive and Transport group having the highest average (4.86) and Tourism, Culture and Artistic and Audiovisual Production the lowest (3.89).

When analyzed by the enterprise's size, it is found that people working in large enterprises give the highest scores for one set of variables and that respondents in medium-sized enterprises generally give the lowest scores. However, those in small companies stand out as highly valuing most of the study's issues. Thus, when comparing the association relationships, it is found that small enterprises are the ones with the highest average for all the variables in which such a relationship occurs. This means that those responsible for human resources in small companies give greater importance to the fact that the leader of the current era gives the employee his autonomy; knows how to differentiate between useful and necessary information, and communicates it to his collaborators so that everyone knows the situation of the company, with transparency; attends to the actualization of the qualification of the members of his team, and empathizes with them when they have had a negative experience so that their regular performance is not harmed.

When information is extracted from the sample in factors or constructs, independent of each other, the original 29 variables are concentrated in five factors, explaining 61,692 of the variance. These portray a leader for this New Era who has to manage in an open, democratic, participative, and transparent way, in an atmosphere of the diversity of collaborators and an excellent working climate; who has to inspire commitment among the members of his team, sharing the necessary information, in order to achieve the objectives of the organization; that it has to possess the four dimensions of the "*i4 Model*" related to Neuroleadership; that it has to have and expand an internal relational capital, with its team, and external, customers – actual and potential, competitors and other stakeholders of the entity; and that it is aware of the importance of managing sensations and emotions, starting with its own, and knows how to do so.

Men and women have similar opinions on these five factors. However, when they are categorized by age group, there is an association with Factor 3, and it is people over 65 who place the highest value on the four assets of the "*i4 Model*", especially compared to people of average age (36-50) and mature age (51-65). It is striking that in this sample, no association was made between age and the factors that support participatory and open management (GESTDIG) and attention to emotions (GESTEMO) on the part of the leader. This is because it seems to be accepted that the youngest, the "millennials", give priority in their objectives to feel listened to, comfortable and happy in their jobs as opposed to other objectives, such as a high or consolidated salary (Akhavan *et al.*, 2017; Rani and Samuel, 2016).

If this is done by sector, it is the workers in Commerce and the Automotive and Transport sectors which differ in their perceptions, in a statistically significant way, from those in Tourism, culture and artistic and audiovisual production in terms of valuing more highly the factor that deals with the leader who generates commitment among his or her collaborators and thus leads them to the achievement of the objectives, sharing all the information about the entity necessary for this.

It is the people responsible for personnel in small companies who show a statistical difference in their opinions about the duty of the new leader to create an open, diverse and participative working environment, ensuring a good climate among all the members of the team, giving it a more significant endorsement than those who hold the same functions in medium and large companies. In this sense, they are in line with the idea that active participation of the employee in the performance of his or her job generates a more significant commitment from the employee to the organization in the era of Industry 4.0 (Oztemel and Gursev, 2020; Kadir *et al.*, 2019). In recent years, there has been an extensive literature that argues that factors such as active participation, performance, and commitment contribute to increasing the well-being and happiness of the worker in his or her work environment, and, through them, the productivity of the organization (e.g., Böckerman *et al.*, 2020; García-Buades *et al.*, 2020; Foncubierta-Rodríguez and Sánchez-Montero, 2019).

This work presents a double limitation: firstly, that of the territorial scope, concentrated in the Arc of the Bay of Algeciras, and secondly, that of the number of records in the sample. Subsequent analyses in larger areas, with a more significant number of participants, or in the same territory, with larger consecutive samples, obtained and treated periodically to detect evolution in the perceptions of the issues raised, are presented as appropriate. On the other hand, the extraction of factors or constructs from the starting variables has been done on an experimental basis. It would be advisable to carry out a confirmatory study of these.

The questions, competencies, or skills in the 29 variables in this research reflect part of the New Era's human and relational capital's desired leadership model. A company will make an effort to attract and retain this type of leader, as he or she brings value to the company and becomes an element of strategic power (Edvinsson and Malone, 1999). By putting these competencies into practice in an organization, the leader turns them into the organization's structural capital, thus closing the circle of the three essential components of Intellectual Capital. Research on New Leadership under the Intellectual Capital (IC) approach would be complementary and appropriate.

Finally, and as mentioned above, it is also suggested that work be considered under the concept of *Happiness Management (HM),* as a leadership model based on multicultural management, and aimed at encouraging through happiness the resources of creativity, commitment, technological innovation, internal entrepreneurship, and social responsibility. This term is gaining a certain degree of scientific notoriety within the corporate strategies of human resources (Sánchez-Vázquez and Sánchez-Ordóñez, 2019; Iberoamerican *Group of Multidisciplinary Studies on Happiness (IGOMSOH)*, since 2017).

Studies on the influence and importance of these factors are critical in times of economic crisis, such as the recent financial sector crisis or the current one caused by the health crisis of the COVID-19 pandemic. In them, traditionally motivating elements (Hertzberg), such as salary received, bonuses or incentives, job stability, etc., lose their potential. Other motivators have to replace them to encourage the worker to perform adequately, achieve objectives, and lead to productivity.

In addition, it should be mentioned that creating and promoting at a successful level a New Leadership for a New Era, while addressing the effects of association of socio-demographic variables on the leader's competencies represents the very essence of a bright future for all organizations worldwide, since the New Leadership for a New Era especially in the Post-COVID-19 Era implicates a safer business environment for all, with a high desire of committing to a more ethical and a more opened business model, characterized by the influence of the dominant traits of the new economy development and societal change.

ACKNOWLEDGMENT

This research received no specific grant from any funding agency in the public, commercial, or not-for-profit sectors. All authors have equally contributed to the manuscript. All authors have read and agreed to the published version of the manuscript.

REFERENCES

Adamik, A., & Nowicki, M. (2020). Barriers of Creating Competitive Advantage in the Age of Industry 4.0: Conclusions from International Experience. In Contemporary Challenges in Cooperation and Coopetition in the Age of Industry 4.0 (pp:3-42). Springer. doi:10.1007/978-3-030-30549-9_1

Akhavan, A. R., Abzari, M., Isfahani, A. N., & Fathi, S. (2017). Generational differences in job engagement: A case study of an industrial organization in Iran. *Industrial and Commercial Training*, *49*(3), 106–115. doi:10.1108/ICT-10-2016-0068

Baker, D.; Greenberg, C. & Hemingway, C. (2007). *Empresas Felices=Empresas Rentables*. Barcelona: Ediciones Gestión 2000.

Batjargal, B. (2007). Internet Entrepreneurship: Social Capital, Human Capital, and Performance of Internet Ventures in China. *Research Policy*, *36*(5), 605–618. doi:10.1016/j.respol.2006.09.029

Bauer, W., Hämmerle, M., Schlund, S., & Vocke, C. (2015). Transforming to a hyper-connected society and economy-towards an Industry 4.0. *Procedia Manufacturing*, *3*, 417–424. doi:10.1016/j.promfg.2015.07.200

Baxter, L. A., & Babbie, E. R. (2004). *The basics of communication research*. Thomson Learning.

BennettN.LemoineG. J. (2014). What VUCA really means for you. *Harvard Business Review, 92*(1/2). Available at: https://ssrn.com/abstract=2389563

Böckerman, P., Bryson, A., Kauhanen, A., & Kangasniemi, M. (2020). Does job design make workers happy? *Scottish Journal of Political Economy*, *67*(1), 31–52. doi:10.1111jpe.12211

Bolman, L. G., & Deal, T. E. (2015). Think-or sink. Leading in a VUCA world. *Leader to Leader*, *76*(76), 35–40. doi:10.1002/ltl.20176

Bonesso, S., Bruni, E., & Gerli, F. (2020). Emotional and Social Intelligence Competencies in the Digital Era. In S. Bonesso, E. Bruni, & F. Gerli (Eds.), *Behavioral Competencies of Digital Professionals* (pp. 41–62). Palgrave MacMillan. doi:10.1007/978-3-030-33578-6_3

Bostancı, S. H., & Yıldırım, S. (2022). The Role of Municipalities in Achieving Water Security: The Case of Turkey. In R. Castanho (Ed.), *Handbook of Research on Sustainable Development Goals, Climate Change, and Digitalization* (pp. 268–286). IGI Global. doi:10.4018/978-1-7998-8482-8.ch017

Braidot, N. (2014). *Neuromanagement. The neuroscientific revolution in organisations, from management to neuromanagement.* Granica.

Caldwell, C., Dixon, R., Floyd, L., Chaudoin, J., Post, J., & Cheokas, G. (2012). Transformative Leadership: Achieving Unparalleled Excellence. *Journal of Business Ethics, 109*(2), 175–187. Advance online publication. doi:10.100710551-011-1116-2

Cieciuch, J. (2017a). Exploring the complicated relationship between values and behavior. In S. Roccas & L. Sagiv (Eds.), *Values and Behavior. Taking a Cross-Cultural Perspective* (pp. 237–247). Springer International Publishing.

Ciulla, J. B. (2020). The importance of leadership in shaping business values. In J. B. Ciulla (Ed.), *The Search for Ethics in Leadership, Business, and Beyond* (pp. 153–163). Springer. doi:10.1007/978-3-030-38463-0_10

Cobo Romaní, C. (2010). New Literacies, Old Problems: The New World of Work and the Unfinished Business of Education. *Reason and Word, 22*(100), 577–588.

Corbetta, P. (2007). *Metodología y técnicas de investigación social.* McGraw-Hill.

Cornellá, A. (2009). *Infoxication: seeking order in information.* Infonomia Books.

Damiano, S. (2014). *Leadership is upside down.* About My Brain.

Doh, J. P., & Quigley, N. R. (2014). Responsible leadership and stakeholder management: Influence pathways and organizational outcomes. *The Academy of Management Perspectives, 28*(3), 255–274. doi:10.5465/amp.2014.0013

Duháček Šebestová, J. (2021). Crisis Situation and Financial Planning for Sustainability: A Case of the Czech SMEs. In C. Popescu & R. Verma (Eds.), *Sustainable and Responsible Entrepreneurship and Key Drivers of Performance* (pp. 59–82). IGI Global., doi:10.4018/978-1-7998-7951-0.ch003

Edvinsson, L., & Malone, M. S. (1999). *Intellectual Capital.* Barcelona: *Gestion*.

Elkington, R., Pearse, N. J., Moss, J., Van der Steege, M., & Martin, S. (2017). Global leaders' perceptions of elements required for effective leadership development in the twenty-first century. *Leadership and Organization Development Journal, 38*(8), 1038–1056. doi:10.1108/LODJ-06-2016-0145

Estadística de Puertos del Estado. (2020). https://www.puertos.es/es-es/estadisticas/EstadisticaMensual/03%20Marzo%202020.pdf

Foncubierta-Rodríguez, M. J., & Sánchez-Montero, J. M. (2019). Towards happiness in workplace: Taking care of motivations and eliminating "digital fears", *Challenges. Revista de Ciencias de la Administración y Economía, 9*(18), 239–257. doi:10.17163/ret.n18.2019.04

García-Buades, M. E., Peiró, J. M., Montañez-Juan, M. I., Kozusznik, M. W., & Ortiz-Bonnín, S. (2020). Happy-Productive Teams and Work Units: A Systematic Review of the "Happy-Productive Worker Thesis". *International Journal of Environmental Research and Public Health, 17*(1), 69. doi:10.3390/ijerph17010069

Geisler, M., Berthelsen, H., & Muhonen, T. (2019). Retaining social workers: The role of quality of work and psychosocial safety climate for work engagement, job satisfaction, and organizational commitment. *Human Service Organizations, Management, Leadership & Governance, 43*(1), 1–15. doi:10.1080/23303131.2019.1569574

Hall, R. D., & Rowland, C. A. (2016). Leadership development for managers in turbulent times. *Journal of Management Development, 35*(8), 942–955. doi:10.1108/JMD-09-2015-0121

Kadir, B. A., Broberg, O., & da Conceição, C. S. (2019). Current research and future perspectives on human factors and ergonomics in Industry 4.0. *Computers & Industrial Engineering, 137.* doi:10.1016/j.cie.2019.106004

Khan, S. N. (Ed.). (2022). Leadership and Followership in an Organizational Change Context. IGI Global. https://doi.org/10.4018/978-1-7998-2807-5.

Kováč, E., Vinogradov, V., & Žigić, K. (2010). Technological leadership and persistence of monopoly under endogenous entry: Static versus dynamic analysis. *Journal of Economic Dynamics & Control, 34*(8), 1421–1441. https://doi.org/10.1016/j.jedc.2010.03.011

Lagadec, P. (2009). A new cosmology of risks and crises: time for a radical shift in paradigm and practice. *Review of Policy Research, 26*(4), 473-487. Recuperado de https://hal.archives-ouvertes.fr/hal-00338386

Lash, S. (2005). *Critique of Information.* Amorrortu.

López-Regalado, M. E., Ahumada-Tello, E., & Ravina-Ripoll, R. (2020). University Social Responsibility from the perspective of Happiness Management. The case of the Faculty of Accounting and Administration of the Autonomous University of Baja California (Tijuana-Mexico). *Revista ESPACIOS, 41*(4), 26.

Lyman, P., & Varian, H. R. (2003). *How much information.* UC Berkeley.

Manovich, L. (2006). *The language of the new media.* Paidós.

Moles, A., & Costa, J. (1989). *La imagen didáctica.* CEAC.

Núñez-Barriopedro, E., Cuesta-Valiño, P., Rodríguez, P. G., & Ravina-Ripoll, R. (2021). How does happiness influence the loyalty of karate athletes? A model of structural equations from the constructs: Consumer Satisfaction, Engagement, and Meaningful. *Frontiers in Psychology, 12.* doi:10.3389/fpsyg.2021.653034

Ouakouak, M. L., Zaitouni, M. G., & Arya, B. (2020). Ethical leadership, emotional leadership, and quitting intentions in public organizations. *Leadership and Organization Development Journal, 41*(2), 257–279. https://doi.org/10.1108/LODJ-05-2019-0206

Özsungur, F. (2021a). Corporate Elderly Entrepreneurship in the Digital World. In K. Sandhu (Ed.), *Handbook of Research on Management and Strategies for Digital Enterprise Transformation* (pp. 149–172). IGI Global. doi:10.4018/978-1-7998-5015-1.ch008

Özsungur, F. (2021b). Business Management and Strategy in Cybersecurity for Digital Transformation. In K. Sandhu (Ed.), *Handbook of Research on Advancing Cybersecurity for Digital Transformation* (pp. 144–162). IGI Global. doi:10.4018/978-1-7998-6975-7.ch008

Oztemel, E., & Gursev, S. (2020). Literature review of Industry 4.0 and related technologies. *Journal of Intelligent Manufacturing*, *31*(1), 127–182. https://doi.org/10.1007/s10845-018-1433-8

Popescu, C. R. (2022a). Mindfulness at Work, a Sound Business Investment: Focusing on the Employee Well-Being While Increasing Creativity and Innovation. In C. Popescu (Ed.), Handbook of Research on Changing Dynamics in Responsible and Sustainable Business in the Post-COVID-19 Era (pp. 1–34). IGI Global. https://doi.org/10.4018/978-1-6684-2523-7.ch001.

Popescu, C. R. (2022b). Mindfulness Business Principles: Producing Outstanding Value and Encouraging Community Connections. In C. Popescu (Ed.), COVID-19 Pandemic Impact on New Economy Development and Societal Change (pp. 196–228). IGI Global. https://doi.org/10.4018/978-1-6684-3374-4.ch010.

Popescu, C. R. (2022c). Environmental, Social, and Corporate Governance by Avoiding Management Bias and Tax Minimization: Reaching a General Consensus Regarding a Minimum Global Tax Rate. In C. Popescu (Ed.), COVID-19 Pandemic Impact on New Economy Development and Societal Change (pp. 94–132). IGI Global. https://doi.org/10.4018/978-1-6684-3374-4.ch006.

Rago, A., Ribeiro, N., Cunha, M. P., & Jesuino, J. C. (2011). How happiness mediates the organizational virtuousness and affective commitment relationship. *Journal of Business Research*, *64*(5), 524–532. https://doi.org/10.1016/j.jbusres.2010.04.009

Rani, N., & Samuel, A. (2016). A study on generational differences in work values and person-organization fit and its effect on turnover intention of Generation Y in India. *Management Research Review*, *39*(12), 1695–1719. https://doi.org/10.1108/MRR-10-2015-0249

Ravina-Ripoll, R., Nunez-Barriopedro, E., Almorza-Gomar, D., & Tobar-Pesantez, L. B. (2021). Happiness Management: A Culture to Explore from Brand Orientation as a Sign of Responsible and Sustainable Production. *Frontiers in Psychology, 12*. doi:10.3389/fpsyg.2021.727845

Roccas, S., & Sagiv, L. (2010). Personal values and behavior: Taking the cultural context into account. *Social and Personality Psychology Compass*, *4*(1), 30–41. https://www.doi.org/10.1111/j.1751-9004.2009.00234.x

Rodriguez, A., & Rodriguez, Y. (2015). Metaphors for today's leadership: VUCA world, millennial and Cloud Leaders. *Journal of Management Development*, *34*(7), 854–866. https://doi.org/10.1108/JMD-09-2013-0110

Ruiz, A. (2015). *Reliability and Validity: Conceptualization and calculation procedures with Spss*. University of Barcelona. Retrieved from http://diposit.ub.edu/dspace/bitstream/2445/65322/1/Fiabilidad_Validez.pdf

Russell, J. E. (2008). Promoting subjective well-being at work. *Journal of Career Assessment, 16*(1), 117–131. https://doi.org/10.1177/1069072707308142

Salas-Vallina, A., Alegre, J., & Fernández Guerrero, R. (2018). Happiness at work in knowledge-intensive contexts: Opening the research agenda. *European Research on Management and Business Economics, 24*(3), 149–159. https://doi.org/10.1016/j.iedeen.2018.05.003

Salazar Estrada, J. G., Guerrero Pupo, J. C., Machado Rodríguez, Y. B., & Cañedo Andalia, R. (2009). Clima y cultura organizacional: Dos componentes esenciales en la productividad laboral. *Acimed, 20*(4), 67–75.

Sánchez-Vázquez, J. F. (2018). El significado vital en las organizaciones: aportaciones de la economía de la felicidad. *Cauriensia, 13*, 143-156. doi:10.17398/2340-4256.13.143

Sánchez-Vázquez, J. F., & Sánchez-Ordóñez, R. (2019). Happiness Management: Review of scientific literature in the framework of happiness at work. *Retos. Revista de Ciencias de la Administración y Economía, 9*(18), 259-271. doi:10.17163/ret.n18.2019.05

Sarkar, A. (2016). We live in a VUCA World: The importance of responsible leadership. *Development and Learning in Organizations, 30*(3), 9–12. https://dx.doi.org/10.1108/DLO-07-2015-0062

Schwartz, S. H. (2011). Values: Individual and cultural. In F. J. R. Van de Vijver, A. Chasiotis, & S. M. Breugelmans (Eds.), *Fundamental Questions in Cross-Cultural Psychology* (pp. 463–493). Cambridge University Press.

Seligman, M. E. P. (1990). *Learned Optimism*. Knopf. Free Press.

Sherman, A., & Barokas, G. (2019). Are happy people more employable? Evidence from field experiments. *Applied Economics Letters, 26*(17), 1384–1387. https://doi.org/10.1080/13504851.2018.1558345

Shore, L. M., Coyle-Shapiro, J. A.-M., Chen, X.-P., & Tetrick, L. E. (2009). Social exchange in work settings: Content, process, and mixed models. *Management and Organization Review, 5*, 289–302. https://doi.org/10.1111/j.1740-8784.2009.00158.x

Tomprou, M., Xanthopoulou, D., & Vakola, M. (2020). Socio-emotional and monetary employee-organization resource exchanges: Measurement and effects on daily employee functioning. *Work and Stress, 34*(2), 189–214. https://doi.org/10.1080/02678373.2019.1616333

Vandekerkhof, P., Steijvers, T., Hendriks, W., & Voordeckers, W. (2018). Socio-emotional wealth separation and decision-making quality in family firm TMTs: The moderating role of psychological safety. *Journal of Management Studies, 55*(4), 648–676. https://doi.org/10.1111/joms.12277

Vargas-Hernández, J. G. (2021). Socio-Intercultural Entrepreneurship Capability Building and Development. In C. Popescu (Ed.), Handbook of Research on Novel Practices and Current Successes in Achieving the Sustainable Development Goals (pp. 259–276). IGI Global. https://doi.org/10.4018/978-1-7998-8426-2.ch013.

Whiteman, W. E. (1998). *Training and educating army officers for the 21st Century: Implications for the United States Military Academy*. Defense Technical Information Center.

KEY TERMS AND DEFINITIONS

Continuously Changing Environment: Represents the natural reaction and the normal response of any type of environment – and most visibly, of the international business environment, to all the changes and to all the challenges that regularly appear in day to day activities and life; in the Post-COVID-19 Era, the environment will be forced to adapt at a faster and at a more visible rhythm than ever before, since survival of businesses will represent a must for all individuals and for all companies that are interested in their success, productivity, performance, and profitability.

Creativity in Business: Is seen as essential in the Post-COVID-19 Era, especially when willing to create and promote the image of a New Leadership for a New Era, since innovation empowers all individuals to become more opened to change, more willing to adapt to the most recent trends and challenges, by addressing change with optimism, and with constructive vision.

Effects of Association of Socio-Demographic Variables on the Leader's Competencies: Represent the key to building inclusive global knowledge societies for sustainable development (SD), since a well-designed and a well-developed strategy for leadership in the Post-COVID-19 Era has the power to enable Transformational Leaders to become more active and more involved in the day to day tasks, thus promoting New and reliable forms of Leadership for a New Era.

Leadership in the Post-COVID-19 Era: Implicates, on the one hand, facing, and, on the other hand, understanding and coping with the new forms of creativity, communication, innovation, doing business, emphasizing, and, in essence, surviving, while preparing for the changes and challenges that are derived from building the "New Normal" of our society; what is more, the COVID-19 Era has the power to create and to promote a New Leadership for a New Era, that is expected to take active and coherent actions that will be capable to show a deeper and greater concern for people, for the environment, for businesses, for Planet Earth.

New Leadership for a New Era: Is considered the very essence of these days society and the most powerful instrument that the management of organizations possesses in order to make the best of the changes and challenges specific to the Post-COVID-19 Era; is believed to represent the motor that will bring competitiveness, profitability, and productivity at a new scale, while centering on individual's needs, desires and requirements.

Powerful Leaders: Are considered those individuals that will be capable to adapt at a faster pace than the rest of their colleagues and of their competitors in the Post-COVID-19 Era, since the "New Normal" imposes a certain abrupt degree of change, derived from the forms of the COVID-19 crisis that occurred due to the COVID-19 pandemic; in essence, the "New Normal" will create the background and the premises for a New Leadership for a New Era, which will especially and majorly revolve around leaders that will be, on the one hand, more inclined to understand and to react in a prompt manner to their employees' needs, and, on the other hand, more agile in determining the marketplace trends and in anticipating the competitions' position and next moves.

Transformational Leaders: Are considered those individuals that are capable to adapt in the fastest and best way possible in the Post-COVID-19 Era, while embracing new challenges and taking into consideration new tasks, since a New Leadership for a New Era has the power to bring great success to entities and put a paramount accent on happiness management, mindfulness, well-being, and joy with every step of way.

APPENDIX: DESIGNED QUESTIONNAIRE

Presentation:
Dear Sir or Madam,
This questionnaire is part of a research carried out within the framework of the University of Cadiz. The aim is to analyze the importance given by people who, like you, manage or work with other people in groups or teams, to a series of questions on Leadership in the new digital era. The information collected in this questionnaire will not be associated with any name, i.e. the data will be completely anonymous and will be used exclusively for the aforementioned academic research.
In the questionnaire 1 would be "I do not agree at all", and 5 would be "I strongly agree".
We thank you in advance for your collaboration; it will be of great help to our work.

INTRODUCTORY QUESTIONS

1. Sex:
   Female
   Male
2. Age category:
   Between 18 and 35 years old
   Between 36 and 50 years old
   Between 51 and 65 years old
   Over 66 years old
3. Sector of activity to which your company belongs:
   Education, training and R&D&I
   Food, hotels and restaurants
   Recreational, cultural and leisure services
   Automotive and/or transport
   Business services
   Secondary sector: industry and mining
   Trade and commerce Health and welfare
   IT and communications
   Artistic and audiovisual production
   Banking and financial services
   Public sector
   Other:
4. Average size of your workforce:
   Less than 10 employees
   Between 10 and 49 employees
   Between 50 and 249 employees
   More than 250 employees

LEADERSHIP ISSUES

Staff Empowerment

1. A leader must have a democratic/participatory style, as the team members have knowledge and skills that allow them to share decision-making with the leader.
    - ○ 1   ○ 2   ○ 3   ○ 4   ○ 5
2. Giving employees their autonomy is more efficient for them than supervising their work.
    - ○ 1   ○ 2   ○ 3   ○ 4   ○ 5
3. Staff must be composed of a wide diversity of people with different skills and abilities, as it helps create effective leadership.
    - ○ 1   ○ 2   ○ 3   ○ 4   ○ 5

Information and Communication

4. Transparency – understood as the communication to employees of all information about the company's situation, improves leadership.
    - ○ 1   ○ 2   ○ 3   ○ 4   ○ 5
5. The rapid evolution of information technologies (IT) accelerates the obsolescence of some systems used in the organization.
    - ○ 1   ○ 2   ○ 3   ○ 4   ○ 5
6. In the face of the obsolescence caused by technologies, the leader has to pay attention to updating his team members' qualifications.
    - ○ 1   ○ 2   ○ 3   ○ 4   ○ 5
7. To possess knowledge is to possess power.
    - ○ 1   ○ 2   ○ 3   ○ 4   ○ 5
8. The leader must know how to differentiate what information he or she needs.
    - ○ 1   ○ 2   ○ 3   ○ 4   ○ 5
9. The leader must know how to use the sources of information available to him/her to find the data he/she needs.
    - ○ 1   ○ 2   ○ 3   ○ 4   ○ 5
10. The leader must know how to gather knowledge through electronic means.
    - ○ 1   ○ 2   ○ 3   ○ 4   ○ 5
11. The leader must know how to handle, process, and re-arrange the information that they obtain through electronic means.
    - ○ 1   ○ 2   ○ 3   ○ 4   ○ 5
12. The leader must disseminate the information obtained through the electronic media freely by the organization.
    - ○ 1   ○ 2   ○ 3   ○ 4   ○ 5

Connection and Networks

13. Today, the leader's degree of power increases with the social networking and communications connections they can establish.
    ○ 1   ○ 2   ○ 3   ○ 4   ○ 5
14. Nowadays, the leader's degree of power increases with the social and communication connections they can establish, but only professionally.
    ○ 1   ○ 2   ○ 3   ○ 4   ○ 5
15. The leader has to establish a network of relationships, friendships, and commitments with all the elements that can influence a decision or give him/her interesting, important, and valuable points of view.
    ○ 1   ○ 2   ○ 3   ○ 4   ○ 5
16. The leader must maintain a harmonious relationship with the main groups that influence the organization and seek "win-win" relationships.
    ○ 1   ○ 2   ○ 3   ○ 4   ○ 5
17. The leader must maintain a harmonious relationship with the main groups that influence the organization and seek "win-win" relationships, including competitors.
    ○ 1   ○ 2   ○ 3   ○ 4   ○ 5

Neuro Leadership and Emotions

18. Today's leaders' fundamental pillars to adapt and achieve success in the volatile and changing world people live in are an inspiration. In the New Era, the organizations that are going to be most effective will be those that manage to inspire each of their employees to exercise their leadership.
    ○ 1   ○ 2   ○ 3   ○ 4   ○ 5
19. Today's leader's fundamental pillars to adapt and achieve success in the volatile and changing world people live in are related with the integration for performance, which refers to the leader's mental and physical balance when performing tasks.
    ○ 1   ○ 2   ○ 3   ○ 4   ○ 5
20. Today's leader's fundamental pillars to adapt and achieve success in the volatile and changing world in which people live are the following ones: informing workers of the objectives, inspiring in them the necessary commitment to collaboration, and providing *feedback*.
    ○ 1   ○ 2   ○ 3   ○ 4   ○ 5
21. The fundamental pillars of the current leader to adapt and achieve success in the volatile and changing world people live in are innovation, and introducing the necessary means to achieve the proposed goals.
    ○ 1   ○ 2   ○ 3   ○ 4   ○ 5
22. The fundamental pillars of today's leader to adapt and succeed in the volatile and changing world in which people live is Agility, which the leader possesses and with which he or she can detect potential negative deviations in the organization.
    ○ 1   ○ 2   ○ 3   ○ 4   ○ 5

23. It is essential to allow the worker to be disconnected from work once their day is over, even if there is a considerable workload.
    ○ 1   ○ 2   ○ 3   ○ 4   ○ 5
24. Today, the management of organizations and their teams has also become a management of the senses and sensations.
    ○ 1   ○ 2   ○ 3   ○ 4   ○ 5
25. When making decisions, the leader also turns to his or her emotional side, i.e., he or she recalls previous emotions or events triggered by the stimulus of making a new decision.
    ○ 1   ○ 2   ○ 3   ○ 4   ○ 5
26. Managerial behavior results in inadequate performance only if it creates a stress-free leadership environment.
    ○ 1   ○ 2   ○ 3   ○ 4   ○ 5
27. With good informal relations between employees and management, a positive working environment improves the latter's leadership, and the impression employees have of them.
    ○ 1   ○ 2   ○ 3   ○ 4   ○ 5
28. Empathy with employees is vital to building effective leadership.
    ○ 1   ○ 2   ○ 3   ○ 4   ○ 5
29. Employees may arrive at the workplace after having a negative experience, either personally or at work. It is essential, then, that the leader empathizes with them so that their average performance is not affected.
    ○ 1   ○ 2   ○ 3   ○ 4   ○ 5

Chapter 2
A Literature Review on Sustainable Consumption in the COVID Era

Niray Tuncel
https://orcid.org/0000-0002-4299-6462
Hacettepe University, Turkey

Esna Betül Buğday
Hacettepe University, Turkey

ABSTRACT

The COVID-19 pandemic has made significant differences in consumers' sustainable consumption behaviors and their attitudes toward environmental issues. After the global spread of the virus, a growing number of people became more aware of the environmental impact of their consumption habits, and their purchasing decisions shifted to favoring products and brands that place a higher value on environmental issues. Therefore, this chapter aims to introduce what the existing knowledge has presented about the impact of the COVID-19 pandemic on consumers' sustainable consumption practices and presents an overview of the existing literature. For this purpose, the current study focused on the recent research that addressed the changes in the sustainable consumption behaviors of consumers from different aspects, such as consumer spending habits, adopting a voluntarily simple life, consumption of energy and natural resources, the purchase, consumption, and use of environmentally friendly products and participating in sustainable practices.

INTRODUCTION

"We are facing a global health crisis unlike any in the 75-year history of the United Nations — one that is killing people, spreading human suffering, and upending people's lives. But this is much more than a health crisis. It is a human crisis. The coronavirus disease (COVID-19) is attacking societies at their core." (United Nations, 2020).

DOI: 10.4018/978-1-6684-5109-0.ch002

A Literature Review on Sustainable Consumption in the COVID Era

According to the UN report, COVID-19 pandemic has had an adverse effect on some sustainable development goals (SDGs). For instance, it has led to the loss of income (i.e., no poverty), disrupted food production and distribution (i.e., zero hunger), devastated health outcomes (i.e., good health and well-being), and increased unemployment and reduced work time (e.g., decent work and economic growth). On the other hand, after the global spread of the virus, a growing number of people became more aware of the environmental impact of their consumption habits, and their purchasing decisions shifted to favoring products and brands that place a higher value on environmental issues (Barbier & Burgess, 2020). Besides, Perkins et al.'s (2021) study focusing on the lessons taken from COVID-19 addressed the potentiality of decreasing fossil fuel consumption and greenhouse emissions. It is suggested that the COVID-19 pandemic is a significant driver of behavioral change in people, with implications for environmental awareness, sustainability, and social responsibility (Ali et al., 2021; Severo et al., 2021). In addition, people have also changed their way of consumption in the COVID-19 era. At the beginning of the pandemic, panic buying at supermarkets for stockpiling was sparked by the widespread fear of COVID-19's consequences (e.g., death and severe disease) (Naeem, 2020). However, following the pandemic's initial months, one of the most obvious signs of a shift in consumer behavior was the adoption of cautious approaches to purchasing habits (Mehta et al., 2020). According to Hobbs (2020), for example, people avoided unnecessary purchases of luxury goods, and they also limited their major purchases to necessities (Tuncer, 2020).

It is seen that the COVID-19 pandemic has made significant differences in consumers' sustainable consumption behaviors and their attitudes toward environmental issues. In this context, this chapter aims to introduce what the existing knowledge has presented about the impact of the COVID-19 pandemic on consumers' sustainable consumption practices and perspectives so far. For this purpose, this chapter presents an overview of the current literature addressing the studies that have focused on the changes in the sustainable consumption behaviors of individual consumers in the COVID-19 era. Hence, this study will help understand the current information about the link between COVID-19 and sustainability from a consumer perspective and see the avenues of research for future studies.

In this context, the remainder of the paper has the following organizational structure. The first section introduces the concept of sustainable consumption. Then, the second section gives a review of the relevant literature on the relationship between sustainable consumption and the COVID-19 pandemic. After that, the discussion and conclusion part is given. Last, limitations and implications for future research finalize the study.

CONCEPTUAL FRAMEWORK

Sustainable Consumption

Sustainable consumption, as stated in Oslo Symposium's (Norwegian Ministry of the Environment, 1994) working definition, is the use of goods and services that meet basic needs and improve the quality of life while minimizing the use of natural resources, toxic materials, waste, and pollutant emissions over the course of a product's life cycle, so as not to jeopardize the needs of future generations. In addition, sustainable consumption involves and promotes social equity while also fostering technological advancement and economic competitiveness (Tukker et al., 2008). Further, Paavola (2001) stated sustainable consumption is a way of consumption that minimizes people's environmental impact.

Sustainable consumption has received increased attention in recent decades as a result of the United Nations Member States adopting and approving the 2030 Agenda for Sustainable Development. This plan of action comprises 17 SDGs, one of which is to ensure sustainable consumption and production patterns that have become much more important than ever due to the worldwide spread of COVID-19. This pandemic has not only influenced people's health but also their way of living in several aspects. Individuals have changed their consumption, spending, and purchasing habits due to safety, health, financial, and environmental concerns, revealing the necessity of examining the issue of sustainability from a consumer perspective. In this manner, previous research focusing on the impact of COVID-19 has approached sustainable consumption from a variety of angles. For instance; changes in spending (Barua, 2021; Hacıoğlu et al., 2020), adopting a voluntarily simple lifestyle (Çınar, 2021; Cambefort, 2020), alterations in consumption of energy (Abdeen et al., 2021; Cheshmehzangi, 2020) and natural sources (Abu-Bakar et al., 2021; Tyagi et al., 2021; Liu et al., 2020), the purchase, consumption, or use of environmentally friendly goods and services (Cui et al., 2022; Peluso et al., 2021), participating in sustainable practices (e.g., recycle and reuse) (Zhang et al., 2021; Ertz, 2020; Buğday & Tunçel, 2022). Based on these dimensions, the current study presents an overview of COVID-19's effect on sustainable consumption on a theoretical framework under the below headings.

LITERATURE REVIEW

Consumer Spending and Adopting a Simple Lifestyle

COVID-19 is seen as a real-time experiment in consumer economy downsizing and a public health emergency, both of which suggest that it offers a long-term opportunity to reduce the prevalence of lifestyles based on high energy and material throughput (Cohen, 2020). People were forced to alter their consumption habits due to social isolation and lockdown measures. Total consumer spending declined in many countries, and it was most obvious in the earlier phases of the pandemic. Researchers at Harvard University Opportunity Insights used credit card data to monitor US spending during the pandemic (Statista, 2020). Between the middle and end of March 2020, consumer spending took a nosedive, according to this research. Even though it was 0.5% higher on March 13 than it was on the same date in 2019, it had dropped 33% by March 30. As states reopened, the trend was gradually improving, but on June 15, 2020, spending levels remained 10% lower than the previous year. This decrease was sharp for the service spending (Barua, 2021); compared to 2019, there was a 31.8% drop in spending on recreation services, while spending on food services and lodging decreased by 21.8% in 2020. Moreover, the turnover of shopping malls has decreased by 70% in the US (Yelp, 2020)

A similar trend was evident in other economies. For instance, as a result of the COVID-19 crisis, British households' spending decreased 40% to 50%, according to transaction data from a large Fintech company (Hacıoğlu et al., 2020). In addition, between the second half of January and the first half of March in 2020, Japanese total spending decreased by 14%. Most of Japan's economic sectors have been adversely affected by the COVID-19 pandemic, but travel (-57%), accommodation (-38%), and entertainment (-26%) were the most severely hit (Watanabe, 2020). Another study (Carvalho et al., 2020) confirmed that during the lockdown, Spanish consumers' expenditures declined. Those who lived in the most affluent areas saw their spending fall the most, which supported the idea that wealthier people's conspicuous consumption was disproportionately affected by lockdown restrictions. Research by Andersen et al. (2020) used transaction-level consumer data from Denmark's biggest bank revealed that in the seven weeks following the shutdown, aggregate spending was, on average, 27% lower than it would have been in the absence of the pandemic. That study also presented that total online spending decreased considerably less than traditional offline spending (12% vs. 32%), and this finding did not provide support for a massive shift from offline to online retailing.

It is clear that the reason for this shrinkage is a lack of funds or a fear of becoming ill. The scarcity of resources in situations such as pandemics, earthquakes, and disasters can be cited as a cause of this situation (Çınar, 2021). Despite the fact that this appears to be a "natural consequence" of the pandemic, some consumers have expressed a desire to reduce their consumption in the long term, and the pandemic provided an opportunity to experiment with a simpler lifestyle by downsizing consumption (Cambefort, 2020). During the quarantine, some consumers questioned their consumption habits and realized excessive consumption does not make them happy at all, while others noticed its negative effects on the environment and society. In her study, Çınar (2021) investigated the tendency of consumers toward voluntarily simple lifestyles during the COVID-19 pandemic and showed consumers' positive inclination toward planned shopping, simple living, and longevity since the COVID-19 period.

Hence, it would not be wrong to indicate that COVID-19 has led to a general decrease in consumer spending and consumption, especially in the service sector, due to the lockdown measures and decline in consumers' mobility. When it comes to simple living, the COVID-19 pandemic allowed for a chance to adopt a simple life by downsizing consumption.

Energy Consumption Levels

COVID-19 also influenced households' energy consumption, and this effect was mostly addressed in terms of electricity and general energy consumption. Most of the reviewed studies found an increase in energy consumption; however, some found a negative or insignificant effect of COVID-19 on the residential energy demand. Thus, it can be stated that COVID-19's impact has been inconsistent in terms of energy consumption.

Regarding the studies on households' general energy consumption, Khatri and Hayasaka (2021) confirmed that electricity consumption and coal combustion for heating increased in January-June 2020 in the residential sector, and air pollution during the lockdown period was primarily caused by domestic coal-burning activities in China. In addition, Rouleau and Gosselin (2021) measured the electricity and heat consumption in a Canadian social housing building and revealed that electricity consumption increased in the first two months of the lockdown, while space heating demand did not show a significant difference. Besides, according to another study (Kang et al., 2021) addressing the use of electricity and gas in South Korea from January to May 2020, the residential electricity consumption increased by 2.50% for multi and 0.19% for single-family residences. While gas consumption declined 2.30% for multi and 3.06% for single-family residences in the same period compared to the previous year.

Moreover, researchers have been particularly intrigued by the shifts in electricity consumption that occurred during the pandemic. It is seen that most of the studies (e.g., Abdeen et al., 2021; Cheshmehzangi, 2020; Qarnain, 2020) have confirmed an increase in residential electricity consumption due to COVID-19. Of them, Abdeen et al. (2021) found that the average household's daily electricity use went up about 12% in 2020 compared to 2019. In addition, Qarnain (2020) in India performed an analysis of survey participants' one-year electricity consumption from April to June 2020 and found that compared to the same period in 2019, the average amount of electricity consumed was 15% more. Social distancing and quarantine had the greatest impact on the increase of energy consumption in residential homes. Cheshmehzangi (2020) demonstrated that January–May 2020 residential energy bills rose significantly in China; according to the analysis, which compared data from 2019 and 2020 with an average increase of 67% in electricity costs in February 2020, 95% in March 2020, 35% in April 2020, and 22% in May 2020. During both of these years, the price per unit remained constant. A rise in residential electricity consumption due to the pandemic has also been confirmed by some recent research for different countries such as Spain (Santiago et al., 2021), Qatar (Abulibdeh, 2021), Kuwait (Alhajeri et al., 2020), and Poland (Bielecki et al., 2021).

On the other hand, the current knowledge provides some evidence for the negative impact of COVID-19 on electricity consumption. For instance, Aruga et al. (2020) revealed a decrease in electricity consumption for poorer regions in India. Additionally, in Brazil, the first trimester of 2020 saw a decrease in electricity consumption of 0.9% compared to 2019, including a decrease of 0.3% coming from residential areas (Carvalho et al., 2020)

Consequently, with some exceptions, COVID-19 has led to a significant rise in residential energy consumption, electricity in particular, as people spent more time in their houses. Hence, it is worth noting that the pandemic has put people in both sustainable (i.e., decline in consumer spending) and unsustainable (i.e., rise in energy use) consumption practices.

The Consumption Patterns of Natural Sources

Water use trends in families have altered due to health, hygiene, and cleaning concerns, as well as longer stays at home due to COVID-19. Studies (Abu-Bakar et al., 2021; Campos et al., 2021; Dziminska et al., 2021; Elmaslar Özbaşlar et al., 2021; Othman Ahmed et al., 2021; Rizvi et al., 2021) have shown an increase in overall residential water usage. For example, Abu-Bakar et al. (2021) compared household water demand between pre-and post-lockdown periods for distinct clusters, finding that water use increased in each cluster of evening peak (25%), late morning (29%), early morning (11%) and multiple peaks (14%). Additionally, Campos et al. (2021) analyzed the individuals' perceptions of changes regarding water use after a couple of months (in June) the pandemic started and unveiled that approximately 40% of the respondents noticed an increase in their water consumption as a result of the rising frequency of showering, hand washing, food hygiene, laundry, and domestic cleaning. Another study (Elmaslar et al., 2021) found that regardless of socioeconomic status, age, or gender, 57.14% of respondents' water footprint (WF) increased after the COVID-19 pandemic, which was linked to increased showers, laundry, and red meat consumption per week and monthly kitchen expenses. Besides, the percentage of participants whose WF increased was the highest for secondary school educated (100%), had 7000 and more income levels (81%), and were aged between 26 and 30 (75%). Similarly, Rizvi et al. (2021) found that the 'Stay Home, Stay Safe' campaign in Dubai resulted in an increase in daytime occupancy in most buildings, as well as an increase in personal and household cleaning, which led to a rise in daily water consumption.

In addition, people also altered their habits with regard to using other types of natural sources during the pandemic. For instance, according to the findings of a study conducted in Mongolia (Azhgaliyeva et al., 2021), a higher percentage of households made the switch to cleaner heating during the COVID-19 period. The same study also demonstrated that the proportion of households using improved fuel instead of raw coal for their heating rose in 2020. In contrast, Chinese residents increased the amount of solid fuel-burning (i.e., residential burning) for heating and cooking, which was the major reason for haze episodes (Dai et al., 2021) during the COVID-19 shutdown. Similarly, another study in India suggested that even though industry coal consumption declined, residential burning of coal for household cooking boosted, leading to an increase in carbon emission during the pandemic lockdown (Tyagi et al., 2021).

In addition to the changes in residential coal consumption, the previous studies also focused on the variations in natural gas consumption. For instance, it was revealed that Korean residents reduced their gas consumption by 2.68% on average in 2020 (January-May) compared to the previous year, and this decline peaked in April 2020 at 12.04% (Kang et al., 2021). However, Liu et al. (2020) analyzed the natural gas consumption of residential buildings in six countries (France, Italy, Great Britain, Belgium, Netherlands, and Spain) and indicated that the lockdown had only a small impact on gas consumption, which fluctuated mainly due to temperature changes during the time period as the temperature variability was removed, the year-to-year difference in natural gas consumption became insignificant.

To sum up, recent research has shown that COVID-19 influenced people's consumption of natural sources. In addition, a wide range of studies focused on behavioral changes considering water use in households and mostly confirmed an increase in water consumption during the pandemic, which was due to the long stays at home and increased frequency of cleaning and washing. In contrast, first, the current knowledge provides a piece of limited information about alteration in people's consumption of other natural sources, and second, the studies have presented conflicting findings. In some countries (e.g., Mongolia), households decreased their coal consumption for heating and cooking, adopting cleaner energy sources; however, in some others (e.g., China and India), households increased their coal consumption, inducing escalated hazardous substances in the air. Likely, the impact of the pandemic on natural gas consumption was inconsistent as a positive, and at the same time, an insignificant effect was revealed. Hence, similar to energy consumption, people exhibited both sustainable and unsustainable behaviors with regard to consuming natural sources as a result of the pandemic.

Shifts toward Sustainable Practices

Consumers' approaches to sustainable practices have also changed during the pandemic. On the one hand, they have increased/decreased the frequency/number of their sustainable behaviors. On the other hand, some others found new ways of practicing sustainable behaviors. Recent studies have addressed the shifts toward sustainable behaviors in the COVID-19 era with regard to several practices such as recycling, reusing, and do-it-yourself activities. Tchetchik et al. (2021) addressed COVID-19's influence on the change in recycling behaviors and unveiled that 44% of low-intensity recyclers in the pre-pandemic period increased their recycling activities in the post-pandemic period while people who were already engaging in recycling activities at medium and high levels before the pandemic mostly continued to do so. Besides, in a qualitative study (Ikiz et al., 2021) aimed at exploring the impact of the pandemic on garbage, recycling, and organic flows, four of ten participants reported that they rose their recycling amount in their buildings as boosted online shopping by households led to an increase in household packaging waste and, as a result, in recycling. Another study (Zhang et al., 2021) confirmed that people with a high intention for recycling in the pandemic were the ones whose responses to recycling were greatly influenced by the COVID-19 outbreak. In addition, Wendtlandt and Wicker (2021) compared individuals' recycling frequencies before and during the pandemic revealing that recycling frequency rose during COVID-19. In contrast, Sarmento et al. (2022) found a decrease in recycled waste during the lockdown period (March-May 2020), and prior to COVID-19, recycled waste showed an upward trend, but this trend did not return when restrictions were loosened in June 2020, indicating a potential shift in recycling habits. However, Gumilar (2020) did not find any difference in people's recycling behaviors between pre- and post-COVID-19 periods.

Some studies also focused on the changes in reuse behavior, which refers to "using materials more than once in their original form rather than discarding them after each use." Reusing resources allows new resources to be used for a longer period of time while preventing old resources from entering the waste stream. As a post-COVID consumption trend, people have increased the reuse of their clothes by repairing or renting them (Seibel et al., 2021), as well as their participation in the second-hand clothing market. Consumers have not only had to rethink their purchasing habits due to decreased disposable income, but they have also come to realize that they should treat their purchases as investments rather than just necessities. In line with this approach, Kim and Kim (2022) demonstrated that cost-saving and social (i.e., connecting people with similar interests) motivations led to higher second-hand fashion consumption (SFC) among high COVID-19 impacted (e.g., financially, physically, socially) consumers compared to low COVID-19 impacted ones. Although a positive influence of COVID-19 on the SFC was confirmed, a study (Van der Wielen & Barrios, 2021) on the search behavior of 27 European Union countries found that after the COVID-19 outbreak, search intensity for second-hand goods dropped. Similarly, Ertz (2020) reported a decline in second-hand consumption since most second-hand exchanges take place in person or in a physical store and the closure of these stores and prohibition of groupings hindered consumers from shopping from second-hand stores. Further, addressing households' reusing behaviors, Ikiz et al. (2021) revealed that due to COVID-19, the reuse activities were suspended. Specifically, there were reuse rooms and/or shelves in five of the buildings, where residents could leave and exchange unwanted items. These have since been shut down because of concerns about touching items that have been handled by others.

Furthermore, people have isolated themselves from others and spent more time at home due to COVID-19 Pandemic, and as a result, they have begun or increased "do it yourself" (DIY) activities in order to cope with this crisis (Kirk & Rifkin, 2020; Silva et al., 2020). In other words, individuals did/made the things rather than purchasing them pre-made or hiring someone else to do/make them. Thus, the studies examining COVID-19's influence on the variations in consumers' sustainable consumption have also addressed the changes in their DIY activities. For instance, Buğday and Tunçel (2022) found a significant difference in the frequency of consumers' DIY activities (including household activities, services, and crafts, maintenance, repair) before and after the COVID-19 pandemic. The findings of that study also revealed that gender, age, education, and income all have an impact on the frequency with which people engage in DIY activities during a pandemic situation. Additionally, Salzano et al. (2021) revealed that 33.9% of the respondents started cooking and 10.6% other DIY practices during the pandemic. Consumers have not only engaged in DIY activities for themselves but also for others as in some countries, people have joined maker movement activities for the sake of healthcare workers. Tsuda and Sakuragi (2020) introduced grassroots activities in Japan that made use of personal fabrication tools to deal with the COVID-19 crisis, with a particular emphasis on the co-design of DIY face shields for healthcare workers. Some consumer groups and communities participated in the production of DIY personal protective equipment to overcome supply shortages in Malaysia as well (Shaharuddin et al., 2021). However, considering consumers' self-sustaining or DIY activities for themselves, such as at-home baking and cooking that rose to prominence during COVID-19, it is difficult to predict whether the prevalence of these activities will continue (Mohabeer, 2021).

After all, it can be stated that the impact of the pandemic on consumers' sustainable practices (i.e., recycling and reusing) has been contradictory as it was found both positive and negative as well as insignificant. Hence, it seems not possible to come to a conclusion about COVID-19's influence on the change in consumers' recycling and reusing behaviors. On the other hand, when it comes to DIY activities, the studies have presented more consistent findings on COVID-19's effect and confirmed that compared to the pre-pandemic period, consumers increased their DIY practices in the post-pandemic period. However, the permanence of these activities still remains unclear, so it presents an avenue of research for future studies.

Green Consumption

COVID-19 is influencing every aspect of human life around the world. The slowdown in economic activity and the precautions adopted to stop the virus' spread have a substantial impact on the environment. The COVID-19 pandemic was directly linked to ecologically damaging actions, notably the hunting of wild animals. In other words, nature's revenge is pushing humans to rethink their habits because of environmental damage and the destruction of wildlife. As expected, the ongoing COVID-19 pandemic is also bringing about change in consumers' purchasing and consumption behavior. New consumption habits and attitudes have encouraged consumers to consume more sustainably during the COVID-19 pandemic (Degli Esposti et al., 2021). Cohen (2020) and Mende and Misra (2021) indicated that the pandemic may encourage a change toward more environmentally friendly consumption, as consumers realize the importance of issues such as environmental pollution and climate change by which their health and the natural environment may be adversely affected. In line with this, Du et al. (2020) stated that a growing number of consumers with a strong sense of environmental responsibility engage in 'conscientious consumption,' which means consuming in order to minimize environmental harm or promote public welfare. It can be concluded that there is an increased awareness of environmental hazards and society's responsibility to save the planet, which has changed people's shopping habits during the pandemic (Gordon-Wilson, 2021).

In particular, the pandemic has an effect on consumers' views about green product purchases and their behavioral intentions toward green product usage. According to WebMD (2020), the pandemic has led people to reconsider how they plan to maintain the environment and how this will keep their loved ones' health safe. Studies proved that as a result of environmental concerns about the COVID-19 pandemic, consumers have been increasingly interested in buying environmentally friendly and sustainable products (Degli Esposti et al., 2021). In their study, Peluso et al. (2021) revealed that during the COVID-19 epidemic, consumers raised their spending on environmentally sustainable products by about 10% in Italy. According to Cui et al. (2022), most consumers are eager to pay more for the products sustainably produced, resulting in a shift in consumer behavior during the COVID-19 pandemic as they began to prioritize environmentally friendly packaged products. Furthermore, Degli Esposti et al. (2021) mentioned that an increasing number of consumers are paying more attention to the environmental impact of their consumption habits and to the origin of raw materials and favoring the brands that are environmentally conscious. According to Euromonitor (2020), the COVID-19 pandemic is likely to support the appearance of a consumer who is "increasingly aware of the impacts of their lifestyle on both the world and the society." Accenture's (2022) findings also proved that over half (61%) of the consumers said they are buying more ecologically friendly items than they were in the past. Furthermore, the same report showed that of the 61% of consumers, 89% are likely to continue with these sustainable changes post-pandemic.

Some of the studies concentrated on the fear induced by the COVID-19 pandemic and its impact on green consumption behavior. They proved that anxiety and uncertainty about the pandemic had led consumers to want to buy green products (Jian et al., 2020; Sun et al., 2021, Chen et al., 2022). As an example, Chen et al. (2022) looked into the elements that influenced the purchasing habits of green product buyers and their behavioral intentions. According to the study, consumers who are highly conscious about their health are increasingly turning to eco-friendly options because of the unpredictability of the COVID-19 pandemic. This might be associated with the fact that a green product is one that is both environmentally and health-friendly over its full life cycle. Fear of a COVID-19 pandemic might also keep people from making long-term commitments to social communities and the environment.

Jian et al. (2020) proved a link between anxiety and unpredictability about COVID-19 and eco-friendly shopping habits in China. Sun et al. (2021) also revealed that consumers' fear of the pandemic influences their desire to buy environmentally friendly products. They stated that people experiencing positive emotions, such as appreciation, motivation, and positivity, are much more likely to pay attention to the environment, as well as reflect themselves via group membership by increasing green consumption. It is seen that the positive awe of COVID-19 reflects altruistic values that are an internal motivator for valuing nature and the environment, and they have a big impact on how people buy green products. Alternatively, individuals with negative awe, such as anxiety, stress, and despair, are more concerned about their own safety and health, which in turn promotes the consumption of environmentally friendly products (Sun et al., 2021, Chen et al., 2022). On the contrary, in his study, Chae (2021) also explored that the COVID-19 pandemic affects sustainable consumption behavior via perceived threat. He stated that negative emotions increased participants' motivation to protect themselves by making the perceived threat more serious. The findings showed that when faced with a pandemic threat, consumers prioritized immediate concerns in order to protect themselves. As a result of not paying attention to others, they were less likely to buy things that were good for the environment.

Sustainable Packaging

Studies showed that consumer preferences have shifted owing to the safety concerns raised during the COVID-19 pandemic. More and more consumers have started to prefer online shopping and delivery systems, and single-use plastic packaging is seen as the most cost-effective and secure solution for the individual package (Prata et al., 2020; Deka et al., 2020; Silva et al., 2020). This growth has resulted in a rise in the amount of plastic waste and garbage generated. According to Sharma et al. (2020), during COVID-19, solid waste management procedures were reduced, causing increasing pollution, primarily from plastics. As a result, the value of the packaging industry in the world is expected to rise from USD 917 billion in 2019 to USD 1.05 trillion by 2024, calculating an annual rate of increase of 2.08% (Pascuta & Vodnar, 2022). For this reason, some researchers concentrated on active and sustainable packaging during the COVID-19 pandemic (Silva et al., 2021; Barone et al., 2021). Among others, Pascuta and Vodnar (2022) studied the active packaging that helps tackle the COVID-19 pandemic's issues, such as increasing plastic consumption and consumers' need for healthy, safe food with a longer shelf life to minimize food loss and waste. They stated that the main reasons for the evolution of new food packaging are changes in consumer demand and new lifestyles during the COVID-19 pandemic. Also, they offered sustainable biopolymeric-based active packaging, which is environmentally safe, antibacterial, and antioxidant-rich.

To further understand the environmental and economic implications of biodegradable food packaging, Barone et al. (2021) looked beyond COVID-19 to examine other options for food packaging. They stated that the pandemic has brought to light an old issue of plastic overconsumption, and the need for longstanding and environmentally friendly solutions is greater than ever before. They also emphasized that policies that promote the use of bioplastics and circular technologies that are better for the environment should be developed and put into place in order to build a system that can fight future pandemics.

Quabdesselam et al. (2021) conducted a study on the effect of food packaging during the COVID-19 pandemic and consumer expectations regarding food safety. The findings of the field survey revealed that consumers are concerned about the health effects of COVID-19 on their lives. They demanded packaging to be safe and to meet their expectations. The study also showed that consumers are unwilling to sacrifice safety in order to ensure the sustainability of their food packaging. In the pandemic, consumers' concerns about hygiene and food safety may take precedence over the environmental performance of packaging materials in the future. Similarly, Grodzinska-Jurczak et al. (2021) observed that environmental care lost its priority position in the value hierarchy because of the increasing health concerns induced by the COVID-19 pandemic. On the contrary, a study by Kitz et al. (2021) found that Canadians are still very interested in cutting back on single-use plastics. According to the results of the study, the amount of food purchased in plastic packaging has remained constant.

Sustainable Food Consumption

Food consumption is critical to developing a sustainable food sector. Since the final link in the food supply chain is the consumer, their food choices and eating habits have an impact on food systems. The pandemic has wreaked havoc on food production and distribution in a variety of ways. Border restrictions have impeded the ability of mechanisms for the timely delivery of seeds. Lockdowns have resulted in a scarcity of inputs, which has resulted in high input costs (OECD, 2020). Accordingly, a number of studies have focused on the effects of the pandemic on sustainable food production and consumption systems (Babbitt et al., 2021; Nchanji & Lutomia, 2021). Most of the literature emphasized the importance of short food supply chains that can help achieve sustainability in uncertain times. Among others, COVID-19's immediate impact on Eastern and Southern African bean production and consumption was highlighted by Nchanji and Lutomia (2021) to demonstrate the importance of short food supply chains in improving the country's farming mechanisms and contributing to sustainable food production and consumption. Using a short-chain approach to growing vegetables and fruits is predicted to reduce food losses and waste linked with pandemic management techniques, according to the study. According to the findings, localized seed and input delivery systems may also be essential in enhancing agricultural production's resilience to future pandemics.

Other studies focused on food consumption at home and stated that consumers are becoming more adept at reducing food waste and using the food efficiently, such as making shopping lists, using up cupboard staples, freezing food, experimenting with new recipes, and storing leftovers for later consumption (Jribi et al., 2020; Restorick, 2020). Similarly, in their study, Schmitt et al. (2021) reported that long-lasting foods like canned veggies and packaged soups have become more popular with consumers over this time period.

As a result of the severity of the COVID-19 outbreak, people began to think more critically about their own health. They began to adopt a more healthful way of life and changed their dietary habits in a sustainable way. For instance, during confinement in the pandemic period, consumers in Spain reduced their intake of fried foods, snacks, fast foods, red meat, pastries, or sweet beverages while increasing their intake of MedDiet (Mediterranean diet) related foods like olive oil, vegetables, fruits, or legumes

(Rodríguez-P´erez et al., 2020). Along with an increase in vegetable and fruit consumption over the pre-restrictions period, some Chinese people have embraced a healthier diet as well (Wang et al., 2020).

To prevent potentially harmful chemicals and maintain a healthy diet during the COVID-19 pandemic, consumers prefer organic foods. It has fewer toxic materials and more essential minerals than normal food, which makes it a better choice for both consumers' health and the environment (Magistris & Gracia, 2016). Wachyuni and Wiweka (2020) reported that, during the pandemic, there was a significant increase of 17.4% in the intention to consume organic food. This situation may be caused by people becoming more aware of how their food affects their health. Similarly, Wang et al. (2021) revealed that consumers' willingness to participate in organic food purchases is determined by their level of health consciousness. Many people are worried about their health because of the COVID-19 outbreak, so they are taking better care of themselves and prefer to buy more environmentally friendly food products. For instance, Campbell (2021) investigated whether consumers are willing to pay for more sustainable food options in the context of the COVID-19 pandemic. He found that there is an implied positive willingness to pay for sustainability. The study also revealed that consumers would pay more for food if the increase in price helped to protect the environment.

Environmental Effect

COVID-19 pandemic has had a lot of negative effects on the environment and the climate. To a certain extent, the pandemic can be thought of as a result of changes in the world's environment. In other words, it is directly related to environmental problems. The pandemic danger is closely linked to the loss of habitat in such huge proportions (Arora & Mishra, 2020). Ongoing attempts to enhance the earth's ecology are put at risk by the COVID-19 pandemic. The pandemic showed that more emphasis should be placed on enacting strict wildlife trade regulations as well as comprehensive environmental protection measures. Sustainability can only be achieved if humans take a holistic approach to improving their interaction with the earth.

Given the pandemic's relevance to environmental issues, several studies concentrated on the environmental effects of the COVID-19 pandemic (Lucarelli et al., 2020; Cohen, 2020). Chakraborty and Maity (2020) tried to describe the effect of the COVID-19 pandemic on society and the ecosystem. They stated that restricting movement to stop the spread of SARS-CoV-2 has had a big impact on the environment. Because there is less demand for power in industries, the use of fossil energy or other conventional sources of energy has dropped a lot, and ecosystems are regenerating rapidly. Lucarelli et al. (2020) evaluated the impact of COVID-19 on pro-environmental behavior by using the Theory of Planned Behavior to climate change. They found that when people were more aware of the link between the epidemic and global warming, they became more committed to environmental causes. Chakraborty and Maity (2020) also emphasized the pandemic's contradictory effects on human society, as evidenced by the fact that it caused widespread devastation.

Arora and Mishra (2020) mentioned the direct effect of human actions on the environment and stated that the main reason for the pandemic was the exploitation of wildlife. They have also characterized the pandemic as nature's revenge. In their study, Ching and Kajino (2020) discussed the relationship between the pandemic and climate change. They underlined that the climate might influence the dissemination of the pandemic, and global warming may result in the emergence of new contagious illnesses. According to these studies, the COVID-19 pandemic has taught people a few critical lessons (Arora & Mishra, 2020; Ching & Kajino, 2020; Hsu et al., 2020; Perkins et al., 2021). Various types of shutdowns have been shown to be effective in the healing of the environment and ecosystems. Pollution levels in the air and water have decreased in many parts of the world. Greenhouse gas (GHG) emissions have been reduced, and the ecosystem has begun to reassert itself (Rume & Islam, 2020). Environmental noise reduction, cleaner beaches, and better air quality all go hand in hand with COVID-19 pandemic preparedness measures, according to Zambrano-Monserrate et al. (2020). For instance, the water clarity has improved significantly, and the clear waters of Venice allow for the observation of seaweed thanks to Italy's lockdown period restriction on motorboat traffic (Bar, 2021). Jribi et al. (2020) reported that the COVID-19 shutdown has reduced food waste in Tunisia, which has reduced soil and water pollution. This demonstrated that it is still possible to improve the quality of air, water, and soil. Besides, as Zambrano-Monserrate et al. (2020) mentioned, the quarantine procedures made people stay at home and cut down on economic activity and communication around the world, which led to lower noise levels in most cities.

Weakening electricity demand has created an opportunity to enhance the reduction of global emissions from the energy sector, as noted by Bertram et al. (2021). Similarly, Mukherjee et al. (2020) stated that the pandemic had given humans a new chance to think about and change the old development paradigm, which has led to bad things for both nature and human civilization. Hence, they indicated that people should look for more sustainable ways to grow. In the same vein, Arora and Mishra (2020) pointed out that the only way to tackle the pandemic is to make every effort to achieve environmental sustainability goals.

Perkins et al. (2021) also noted that several lessons were learned from the pandemic. They suggested that these lessons may be utilized to guide and promote future engagement in the global climate issue. They pointed to the likelihood of decreasing fossil fuel usage and GHG emissions, tackling climate change with urgency, the necessity to operationalize strong sustainability, and the significance of collective action. Pradhan et al. (2021) explored the potential impacts of the COVID-19 pandemic on sustainable development goals in Nepal. They revealed that the pandemic had added new challenges to achieving sustainable development goals, but it has also opened up new opportunities for sustainable transformation. However, they emphasized, as Perkins et al. (2021) did, that immediate action is required to combat environmental problems.

Some studies argued that there is a link between the environmental behaviors of consumers and the COVID-19 pandemic (Ashaari et al., 2020; Ali et al., 2021; Li & Tartarini, 2020; Severo et al., 2021; Stratoulias & Nuthammachot 2020). Severo et al. (2021) investigated the COVID-19 pandemic's impact on environmental consciousness and sustainable consumption among the Baby Boomers, Generation X, and Generation Y in Brazil and Portugal, and Ali et al. (2021) conducted a similar study in Malaysia. The findings of both studies confirmed that consumers' environmental awareness and concerns have improved as a result of the current COVID-19 pandemic. Besides, consumption patterns have become more sustainable, which may signal a shift toward sustainable consumption.

Jian et al. (2020) also studied the connection between the environmental concerns of consumers and the COVID-19 pandemic. They discovered that COVID-19-related fear and uncertainty had a strong positive effect on consumer worries about the environment and reminded them of the importance of environmental protection. They stressed that while "COVID-19 is being reported as a bat-related epidemic," the interaction between humans and nature is crucial, and humans may benefit from learning from and living in harmony with nature rather than striving to exploit and change it.

In contrast to all of these studies, several researchers concentrated on the negative consequences of the COVID-19 pandemic on the environment (Rume &Islam, 2020). Zambrano-Monserrate et al. (2020) claimed that these impacts begin with a decline in recycling activities and an increase in waste. The decrease in recycling and an increase in waste are putting at physical risk locations where the highest amounts of waste and recycling are generated. Rume and Islam (2020) listed the rise in medical waste, over-abundant usage and disposal of disinfectants, masks, and gloves, and a load of unprocessed rubbish wreaking havoc on the ecosystems as the pandemic's primary negative environmental effects.

DISCUSSION AND CONCLUSION

COVID-19 has impacted people's lives in various ways, and as a result, they have had to change their perceptions and behaviors to adopt this new world order, and some significant changes occurred in how they consume and approach environmental issues. Some of these changes have led to individuals engaging in sustainable consumption practices and environmentally friendly behaviors, while others have had the opposite effect. In this context, this study aimed to reveal the alterations in consumers' sustainable behaviors and environmental effects because of the COVID-19 pandemic. For this purpose, the current chapter presents a comprehensive literature review of the studies addressing the link between the pandemic and sustainable consumption. It also provides valuable knowledge and a snapshot in time concerning consumer behavior throughout the pandemic. In this manner, this review particularly concentrated on the COVID-19 related changes in consumer spending, consumption of energy and natural sources, sustainable practices, and the purchase and use of environmentally friendly products that were the focus of most studies.

In the context of sustainable consumption behaviors, voluntary simple living and consumption reduction were also being investigated. During the pandemic, consumers restricted consumption first to reduce the risk and later only because they did not see it as necessary. Hence, consumer spending and consumption have decreased in general due to the COVID-19 pandemic (e.g., Andersen et al., 2020; Watanabe, 2020), and the service sector was the most affected sector of all. The lockdown measures and the decline in consumer mobility were two important reasons behind this situation. In addition, different consumers showed different trends in their spending (e.g., wealthy-unwealthy); wealthy consumers' spending declined more than unwealthy consumers' (Carvalho et al., 2020). Even though the amount/ percentage have differed in terms of sector, country, or consumers' characteristics, the current literature suggests that consumer spending and consumption have declined during the pandemic. As stated by some previous studies (Çınar, 2021; Cambefort, 2020), the COVID-19 pandemic gives people a chance to change their purchasing habits, move toward a simpler way of life, and adopt a more sustainable lifestyle. However, to what extent consumers are keeping these habits now and will do so in the future needs to be investigated.

When it comes to the studies addressing the changes in energy consumption as a result of the pandemic, it is seen that the vast majority of the studies have addressed the changes in electricity consumption as, in both homes and businesses, electricity is the most common form of energy and is a critical factor in determining economic activity. Thus, if people reduce their energy consumption, they can make an important difference in their impact on the environment. However, except for a few (e.g., Aruga et al., 2020), almost all of the reviewed studies (e.g., Alhajeri et al., 2020; Qarnain, 2020) found a positive impact of COVID-19 on electricity consumption. Thus, it is worth indicating that the pandemic has put individuals in an unsustainable position in this context. On the other hand, COVID-19's influence on energy consumption has not been consistent for heating and gas. For instance, heating demand did not show any difference (Rouleau & Gosselin, 2021), while gas consumption decreased (Kang et al., 2021).

Since the current knowledge presents a very limited number of studies focusing on energy consumption other than electricity, these findings were preliminary, and it is difficult to draw a conclusion about the actual impact of COVID-19. Hence, except for electricity consumption, people's inclination toward sustainable energy consumption remains uncertain during the pandemic.

The studies have also investigated individuals' consumption of natural sources in the COVID-19 era, giving particular prominence to water consumption. Most of these studies (e.g., Dziminska et al., 2021; Othman Ahmed et al., 2021) confirmed an increase in overall household water consumption. Conversely, the previous studies gave inconsistent findings on the impact of COVID-19 on the consumption of other natural sources. For instance, Azhgaliyeva et al. (2021) demonstrated a decrease, while Dai et al. (2021) confirmed an increase in coal consumption. Conflicting findings were also explicit for the change in residential use of natural gas (see Kang et al., 2021; Liu et al., 2020). However, due to the limited number of studies, which addressed the link between COVID-19 and the consumption of gas and coal consumption, it is not possible to generalize any certain COVID-19 related change in consumers' behaviors considering these natural sources. However, when it comes to water consumption, it is observed that the consumers adopted unsustainable behavioral habits.

Moreover, recent studies have examined the shifts toward sustainable behaviors in the COVID-19 era with regard to a variety of practices, including recycling, reusing, and DIY activities. For instance, some studies (e.g., Tchetchik et al., 2021; Ikiz et al., 2021) found an increase, whereas others (e.g., Gumilar, 2020; Sarmento et al., 2022) confirmed a decrease or no difference in recycling behavior during the pandemic. With regard to reuse activities, current literature also presents contradictory approaches as Seibel et al. (2021) reported a rise in consumption of second-hand goods (clothes), whereas some others (e.g., Ertz, 2020) indicated a decline. Last, previous research (e.g., Buğday & Tunçel, 2022; Salzano et al., 2021; Shaharuddin et al., 2021) has demonstrated that consumers have risen their DIY activities after the pandemic. Thus, it can be indicated that for recycling and reusing activities, consumers' behavioral changes are uncertain, while for DIY practices, their behavioral changes are consistently positive. In this context, it is worth noticing that consumers moved toward a more sustainable way of consumption in terms of DIY activities.

Further, according to the studies on the green and environmentally friendly consumption patterns of consumers during the pandemic period, it is seen that the majority of consumers have increased their interest in environmental problems as a result of the pandemic (Mende & Misra, 2021). As health, safety, and environmental issues became more important to people; they started to use more environmentally friendly products. Even some consumers stated that they were willing to pay more for environmentally friendly products during this time.

Some of the research conducted during this period focused on the pandemic's unpredictability and the anxiety it caused in people (Jian et al., 2020; Sun et al., 2021). These studies showed that consumers' positive and negative fears contribute to environmentally friendly and sustainable consumption behavior for different reasons. While positive fears of the COVID-19 pandemic are an internal driving force for individuals to adopt sustainable consumption behaviors, negative fears create health and safety-oriented concerns in individuals and therefore lead consumers to adopt sustainable consumption behaviors.

The increased use of packaged products in food, the rise and accumulation of packaging waste in the environment, and the increased use and waste of disposable materials, are just a few of the negative environmental effects of the pandemic. According to research, more than 25,000 tons of plastic were discharged into the sea during the COVID-19 outbreak. This has exacerbated already out-of-control plastic pollution. This waste has a severe impact on marine life and damages the soil. As a result of this scenario, several scholars have begun to investigate the subject of sustainable packaging (Patricio Silva et al., 2021; Barone et al., 2021). When the studies on sustainable packaging were examined, it was discovered that the majority of them advocate for biodegradable, active packaging as the most environmentally friendly and sustainable option. Consumer perceptions of sustainable packaging have also been investigated in a few studies. It appears that consumers prefer safety over environmental concerns when it comes to packaging.

Since the pandemic began, research has revealed significant changes in consumers' food shopping and consumption behaviors. Consumers strived to meet their basic needs quickly and without social interaction, and they preferred to dine at home. When research on sustainable food consumption during the pandemic period is investigated, it is found that the common factor is a shift in consumer food consumption habits. According to several studies, people are turning to healthier food options due to health concerns, and organic food consumption is on the rise (Babbitt et al., 2021).

During the pandemic, one of the most prominent topics is the pandemic's impact on climate change and global warming. According to studies, at the start of the pandemic, energy consumption reduces, and nature begins to regenerate, as global movement is restricted due to quarantine. As claimed by the studies on the environmental effects of the pandemic, there are crucial lessons to be gained from the pandemic (Arora & Mishra, 2020; Lucarelli et al., 2020). This period has demonstrated that the earth and its ecosystem can still be healed. Therefore, people should reconsider their lifestyles in order to live in a more sustainable environment.

COVID-19 has not been a health-related emergency but also has been a milestone that has dramatically changed people's lives and daily habits. In this manner, the COVID-19 pandemic has evolved as a new paradigm that directs consumers' sustainable consumption behaviors and perceptions of the environment and nature. However, the environmental benefits of COVID-19 are only temporary and are meant to serve as a model for society's efforts to improve their way of life in the future. Additionally, it is still hard to conclude that the pandemic has changed people's behaviors in a less or more sustainable way. As sustainable consumption is a multifaceted concept, the impact of COVID-19 has been found unstable in terms of different types of sustainable consumer behaviors.

LIMITATIONS AND IMPLICATIONS FOR FUTURE RESEARCH

This study has some limitations that offer new avenues for future investigation. First, this research tried to address the impact of COVID-19 on some particular types of sustainable consumption practices (e.g., spending and adoption of a simple life, consumption of energy and natural sources, etc.). Hence, future studies may consider the subject from other aspects not included in this study. Second, the current study gave only a piece of information on how COVID-19 related changes in sustainable consumption have differed in terms of consumers' socioeconomic levels and demographical characteristics. Thus, further studies may address this issue as their focus. Third, this study considered the change in several types of sustainable consumption due to the pandemic and presented a general overview so future research might make an in-depth investigation focusing on the alterations in one specific sustainable consumption area (e.g., collaborative consumption). Additionally, the current research summarized the body of knowledge concentrated on the link between COVID-19 and sustainable consumption in a narrative way aiming to highlight the significant points. Hence, other studies can take the issue with a systematic approach. Last, it is currently not possible to specify to what extent the changes in sustainable consumption practices covered in the study are and will be valid, which may also be discovered by future research.

REFERENCES

Abdeen, A., Kharvari, F., O'Brien, W., & Gunay, B. (2021). The impact of the COVID-19 on households' hourly electricity consumption in Canada. *Energy and Building*, *250*, 111280. doi:10.1016/j.enbuild.2021.111280 PMID:35125633

Abu-Bakar, H., Williams, L., & Hallett, S. H. (2021). Quantifying the impact of the COVID-19 lockdown on household water consumption patterns in England. *NPJ Clean Water*, *4*(1), 1–9. doi:10.103841545-021-00103-8

Abulibdeh, A. (2021). Modeling electricity consumption patterns during the COVID-19 pandemic across six socioeconomic sectors in the State of Qatar. *Energy Strategy Reviews*, *38*, 100733. doi:10.1016/j.esr.2021.100733

Accenture. (2022). *COVID-19: Retail consumer habits shift long-term.* https://www.accenture.com/usen/insights/retail/coronavirus-consumer-habits

Alhajeri, H. M., Almutairi, A., Alenezi, A., & Alshammari, F. (2020). Energy demand in the state of Kuwait during the COVID-19 pandemic: Technical, economic, and environmental perspectives. *Energies*, *13*(17), 4370. doi:10.3390/en13174370

Ali, Q., Parveen, S., Yaacob, H., Zaini, Z., & Sarbini, N. A. (2021). COVID-19 and dynamics of environmental awareness, sustainable consumption and social responsibility in Malaysia. *Environmental Science and Pollution Research International*, *28*(40), 56199–56218. doi:10.100711356-021-14612-z PMID:34050516

Andersen, A. L., Hansen, E. T., Johannesen, N., & Sheridan, A. (2020). *Consumer responses to the COVID-19 crisis: Evidence from bank account transaction data.* https://ideas.repec.org/p/cpr/ceprdp/14809.html

Arora, N. K., & Mishra, J. (2020). COVID-19 and importance of environmental sustainability. *Environmental Sustainability*, *3*(2), 117–119. doi:10.100742398-020-00107-z

Aruga, K., Islam, M., & Jannat, A. (2020). Effects of COVID-19 on Indian energy consumption. *Sustainability*, *12*(14), 5616. doi:10.3390u12145616

Ash'aari, Z. H., Aris, A. Z., Ezani, E., Ahmad Kamal, N. I., Jaafar, N., Jahaya, J. N., Manan, S. A., & Saifuddin, M. F. (2020). Spatiotemporal variations and contributing factors of air pollutant concentrations in Malaysia during movement control order due to pandemic COVID-19. *Aerosol and Air Quality Research*, *20*(10), 2047–2061. doi:10.4209/aaqr.2020.06.0334

Azhgaliyeva, D., Mishra, R., & Karymshakov, K. (2021). *Household energy consumption behaviors during the COVID-19 pandemic in Mongolia* (No. 1292). ADBI Working Paper.

Babbitt, C. W., Babbitt, G. A., & Oehman, J. (2021). Behavioral impacts on residential food provisioning, use, and waste during the COVID-19 pandemic. *Sustainable Production and Consumption*, *28*, 315–325. doi:10.1016/j.spc.2021.04.012 PMID:34722846

Bar, H. (2021). COVID-19 lockdown: Animal life, ecosystem and atmospheric environment. *Environment, Development and Sustainability*, *23*(6), 8161–8178. doi:10.100710668-020-01002-7 PMID:33020695

Barbier, E. B., & Burgess, J. C. (2020). Sustainability and development after COVID-19. *World Development*, *135*, 105082. doi:10.1016/j.worlddev.2020.105082 PMID:32834381

Barone, A. S., Matheus, J. R. V., De Souza, T. S. P., Moreira, R. F. A., & Fai, A. E. C. (2021). Green-based active packaging: Opportunities beyond COVID-19, food applications, and perspectives in circular economy—a brief review. *Comprehensive Reviews in Food Science and Food Safety*, *20*(5), 4881–4905. doi:10.1111/1541-4337.12812 PMID:34355490

Barua, A. (2021). *A spring in consumers' steps: Americans prepare to get back to their spending ways.* https://www2.deloitte.com/us/en/insights/economy/us-consumer-spending-after-covid.html

Bertram, C., Luderer, G., Creutzig, F., Bauer, N., Ueckerdt, F., Malik, A., & Edenhofer, O. (2021). COVID-19-induced low power demand and market forces starkly reduce CO2 emissions. *Nature Climate Change*, *11*(3), 193–196. doi:10.103841558-021-00987-x

Bielecki, S., Skoczkowski, T., Sobczak, L., Buchoski, J., Maciąg, Ł., & Dukat, P. (2021). Impact of the lockdown during the COVID-19 pandemic on electricity use by residential users. *Energies*, *14*(4), 980. doi:10.3390/en14040980

Buğday, E. B., & Tunçel, N. (2022, January). *"Do-It-Yourself" consumer activities in the Covid era and the role of demographics* [Paper presented]. *38th EBES Conference*, University of Warsaw, Warsaw, Poland.

Cambefort, M. (2020). How the COVID-19 pandemic is challenging consumption. *Markets, Globalization &. Developmental Review*, *5*(1), 1–13.

Campbell, N. (2021). *The COVID-19 pandemic: impact on consumers' environmental consciousness and food choices in California* [Unpublished honor thesis]. Berkeley University, CA, United States.

Campos, M. A. S., Carvalho, S. L., Melo, S. K., Gonçalves, G. B. F. R., dos Santos, J. R., Barros, R. L., Morgado, U. T. M. A., da Silva Lopes, E., & Abreu Reis, R. P. (2021). Impact of the COVID-19 pandemic on water consumption behaviour. *Water Supply*, *21*(8), 4058–4067. doi:10.2166/ws.2021.160

Carvalho, V. M., Garcia, J. R., Hansen, S., Ortiz, Á., Rodrigo, T., Rodríguez Mora, J. V., & Ruiz, P. (2020). Tracking the COVID-19 crisis with high-resolution transaction data. *Royal Society Open Science*, *8*(8), 210218. doi:10.1098/rsos.210218 PMID:34401194

Chae, M.-J. (2021). Effects of the COVID-19 pandemic on sustainable consumption. *Social Behavior and Personality*, *49*(6), e10199. doi:10.2224bp.10199

Chakraborty, I., & Maity, P. (2020). COVID-19 Outbreak: Migration, effects on society, global environment and prevention. *The Science of the Total Environment*, *728*, 138882. doi:10.1016/j.scitotenv.2020.138882 PMID:32335410

Chen, X., Rahman, M. K., Rana, M. S., Gazi, M. A. I., Rahaman, M. A., & Nawi, N. C. (2022). Predicting consumer green product purchase attitudes and behavioral intention during COVID-19 pandemic. *Frontiers in Psychology*, *12*, 760051. doi:10.3389/fpsyg.2021.760051 PMID:35145450

Cheshmehzangi, A. (2020). COVID-19 and household energy implications: What are the main impacts on energy use? *Heliyon*, *6*(10), e05202. doi:10.1016/j.heliyon.2020.e05202 PMID:33052318

Ching, J., & Kajino, M. (2020). Rethinking air quality and climate change after COVID-19. *International Journal of Environmental Research and Public Health*, *17*(14), 5167. doi:10.3390/ijerph17145167 PMID:32708953

Çınar, D. (2021). A research on the evaluation of consumers' voluntary simplicity lifestyle tendency in the COVID-19 period. *International Journal of Social Sciences and Education Research*, *7*(1), 12–23.

Cohen, M. J. (2020). Does the COVID-19 outbreak mark the onset of a sustainable consumption transition? *Sustainability: Science. Practice and Policy*, *16*(1), 1–3.

Cui, Y., Lissillour, R., Chebeň, J., Lančarič, D., & Duan, C. (2022). The position of financial prudence, social influence, and environmental satisfaction in the sustainable consumption behavioural model: Cross-market intergenerational investigation during the COVID-19 pandemic. *Corporate Social Responsibility and Environmental Management*, 1–25. doi:10.1002/csr.2250

Dai, Q., Ding, J., Hou, L., Li, L., Cai, Z., Liu, B., Song, C., Bi, X., Wu, J., Zhang, Y., Feng, Y., & Hopke, P. K. (2021). Haze episodes before and during the COVID-19 shutdown in Tianjin, China: Contribution of fireworks and residential burning. *Environmental Pollution*, *286*, 117252. doi:10.1016/j.envpol.2021.117252 PMID:33990050

Degli Esposti, P., Mortara, A., & Roberti, G. (2021). Sharing and sustainable consumption in the era of COVID-19. *Sustainability*, *13*(4), 1903. doi:10.3390u13041903

Deka, B. J., Bohra, V., Alam, W., Sanasam, S., Guo, J., Borana, L., & An, A. K. (2020). Environment impact assessment of COVID-19. In M. K. Goyal & A. K. Gupta (Eds.), *Integrated risk of pandemic: COVID-19 impacts, resilience and recommendations* (pp. 169–195). Springer. doi:10.1007/978-981-15-7679-9_8

Du, Y., Ruan, B., & Zhou, C. (2020). *In the post-epidemic era, focus on sustainable fashion consumers in China*. https://www.sohu.com/a/ 424435411_650547/

Dzimińska, P., Drzewiecki, S., Ruman, M., Kosek, K., Mikołajewski, K., & Licznar, P. (2021). The use of cluster analysis to evaluate the impact of COVID-19 pandemic on daily water demand patterns. *Sustainability*, *13*(11), 5772. doi:10.3390u13115772

Elmaslar Özbaş, E., Akın, Ö., Güneysu, S., Özcan, H. K., & Öngen, A. (2021). Changes occurring in consumption habits of people during COVID-19 pandemic and the water footprint. *Environment, Development and Sustainability*, 1–17. doi:10.100710668-021-01797-z PMID:34483718

Ertz, M. (2020). The COVID-19 pandemic crisis: Catalyst of the reconfiguration of commercial exchanges through responsible consumption? *Revue Organisations & Territoires*, *29*(3), 91–93. doi:10.1522/revueot.v29n3.1203

Euromonitor. (2020). *From Sustainability to Purpose: New Values Driving Purpose-Led Innovation.* Euromonitor International.

Gordon-Wilson, S. (2021). Consumption practices during the COVID-19 crisis. *International Journal of Consumer Studies, 46*(2), 575–588. doi:10.1111/ijcs.12701 PMID:34220342

Grodzinska-Jurczak, M., Krawzyck, A., Jurczak, A., Strzelecka, M., Bockowski, M., & Rechcinski, M. (2020). Environmental choices vs. COVID-19 pandemic fear – plastic governance re-assessment. *Socialist Register, 4*(2), 49–66. doi:10.14746r.2020.4.2.04

Gumilar, V. T. (2020). *Sustainable consumer behavior in times of COVID-19* [Unpublished master thesis]. National Sun Yat-Sen University, Taiwan.

Hacıoğlu, S., Känzig, D., & Surico, P. (2020). *Consumption in the time of COVID-19: Evidence from UK transaction data.* https://papers.ssrn.com/sol3/papers.cfm?abstract_id=3603964

Hobbs, J. E. (2020). Food supply chains during the COVID-19 pandemic. *Canadian Journal of Agricultural Economics/Revue Canadienne D'agroeconomie, 68*(2), 171-176.

Hsu, L. Y., Chia, P. Y., & Vasoo, S. (2020). A midpoint perspective on the COVID-19 pandemic. *Singapore Medical Journal, 61*(7), 381–383. doi:10.11622medj.2020036 PMID:32211911

Ikiz, E., Maclaren, V. W., Alfred, E., & Sivanesan, S. (2021). Impact of COVID-19 on household waste flows, diversion and reuse: The case of multi-residential buildings in Toronto, Canada. *Resources, Conservation and Recycling, 164*, 105111. doi:10.1016/j.resconrec.2020.105111 PMID:32839638

Jian, Y., Yu, I. Y., Yang, M. X., & Zeng, K. J. (2020). The impacts of fear and uncertainty of covid-19 on environmental concerns, brand trust, and behavioral intentions toward green hotels. *Sustainability, 12*(20), 8688. doi:10.3390u12208688

Jribi, S., Ben Ismail, H., Doggui, D., & Debbabi, H. (2020). COVID-19 virus outbreak lockdown: What impacts on household food wastage? *Environment, Development and Sustainability, 22*(5), 3939–3955. doi:10.100710668-020-00740-y PMID:32837271

Kang, H., An, J., Kim, H., Ji, C., Hong, T., & Lee, S. (2021). Changes in energy consumption according to building use type under COVID-19 pandemic in South Korea. *Renewable & Sustainable Energy Reviews, 148*, 111294. doi:10.1016/j.rser.2021.111294 PMID:34234624

Khatri, P., & Hayasaka, T. (2021). Impacts of COVID-19 on air quality over China: Links with meteorological factors and energy consumption. *Aerosol and Air Quality Research, 21*(10), 1–18. doi:10.4209/aaqr.200668

Kim, N. L., & Kim, T. H. (2022). Why buy used clothing during the pandemic? Examining the impact of COVID-19 on consumers' second-hand fashion consumption motivations. *International Review of Retail, Distribution and Consumer Research*, 1–16.

Kirk, C. P., & Rifkin, L. S. (2020). I'll trade you diamonds for toilet paper: Consumer reacting, coping and adapting behaviors in the COVID-19 pandemic. *Journal of Business Research, 117*, 124–131. doi:10.1016/j.jbusres.2020.05.028 PMID:32834208

Kitz, R., Walker, T., Charlebois, S., & Music, S. (2021). Food packaging during the COVID-19 pandemic: Consumer perceptions. *International Journal of Consumer Studies*, *46*(2), 434–448. doi:10.1111/ijcs.12691 PMID:34230811

Li, J., & Tartarini, F. (2020). Changes in air quality during the COVID-19 lockdown in Singapore and associations with human mobility trends. *Aerosol and Air Quality Research*, *20*(8), 1748–1758. doi:10.4209/aaqr.2020.06.0303

Liu, Z., Ciais, P., Deng, Z., Lei, R., Davis, S. J., Feng, S., ... He, P. (2020). Near-real-time data captured record decline in global CO2 emissions due to COVID-19. *Nature Communications*, *11*, 1–12. doi:10.103841467-020-20254-5

Lucarelli, C., Mazzoli, C., & Severini, S. (2020). Applying the theory of planned behavior to examine pro-environmental behavior: The moderating effect of COVID-19 beliefs. *Sustainability*, *12*(24), 10556. doi:10.3390u122410556

Magistris, T., & Gracia, A. (2016). The decision to buy organic food products in Southern Italy. *British Food Journal*, *110*(9), 929–947. doi:10.1108/00070700810900620

Mehta, S., Saxena, T., & Purohit, N. (2020). The new consumer behaviour paradigm amid COVID-19: Permanent or transient? *Journal of Health Management*, *22*(2), 291–301. doi:10.1177/0972063420940834

Mende, M., & Misra, V. (2020). Time to flatten the curves of COVID-19 and climate change. Marketing can help. *Journal of Public Policy & Marketing*, *40*(1), 94–96. doi:10.1177/0743915620930695

Mohabeer, R. N. (2021). COVID bread-porn: Social stratification through displays of self-management. *Cultural Studies*, *35*(2-3), 403–411. doi:10.1080/09502386.2021.1898031

Mukherjee, A., Babu, S. S., & Ghosh, S. (2020). Thinking about water and air to attain sustainable development goals during times of COVID-19 pandemic. *Journal of Earth System Science*, *129*(1), 180. doi:10.100712040-020-01475-0

Naeem, M. (2020). Understanding the customer psychology of impulse buying during COVID-19 pandemic: Implications for retailers. *International Journal of Retail & Distribution Management*, *49*(3), 377–393. doi:10.1108/IJRDM-08-2020-0317

Nchanji, E. B., & Lutomia, C. K. (2021). COVID-19 challenges to sustainable food production and consumption: Future lessons for food systems in eastern and southern Africa from a gender lens. *Sustainable Production and Consumption*, *27*, 2208–2220. doi:10.1016/j.spc.2021.05.016

Norwegian Ministry of the Environment. (1994). *Oslo roundtable on sustainable production and consumption* (Oslo Symposium). Author.

OECD. (2020). *Food supply-chains and COVID-19: Impacts and policy lessons.* https://www.oecd.org/coronavirus/policy-responses/food-supply-chains-and-covid-19-impacts-and-policy-lessons-71b57aea/

Othman Ahmed, K. (2021). Impact of COVID-19 Pandemic on Hand Washing Process and Water Consumption. *Eurasian Journal of Science & Engineering*, *7*(1), 228–245.

Ouabdesselam, L., & Sayad, A. (2021). Food packaging and COVID-19. *European Journal of Basic Medical Science*, *11*(2), 23–26.

Paavola, J. (2001). Towards sustainable consumption: Economics and ethical concerns for the environment in consumer choices. *Review of Social Economy*, *59*(2), 227–248.

Pascuta, M. S., & Vodnar, D. C. (2022). Nanocarriers for sustainable active packaging: An overview during and post COVID-19. *Coatings*, *12*, 102.

Peluso, A. M., Pichierri, M., & Pino, G. (2021). Age-related effects on environmentally sustainable purchases at the time of COVID-19: Evidence from Italy. *Journal of Retailing and Consumer Services*, *60*, 102443.

Perkins, K. M., Munguia, N., Ellenbecker, M., Moure-Eraso, R., & Velazquez, L. (2021). COVID-19 pandemic lessons to facilitate future engagement in the global climate crisis. *Journal of Cleaner Production*, *290*, 125178.

Pradhan, P., Subedi, D. R., Khatiwada, D., Joshi, K. K., Kafle, S., Chhetri, R. P., ... Bhuju, D. R. (2021). The COVID-19 Pandemic Not Only Poses Challenges, but Also Opens Opportunities for Sustainable Transformation. *Earth's Future, 9*(7).

Prata, J. C., Silva, A. L., Walker, T. R., Duarte, A. C., & Rocha-Santos, T. (2020). COVID-19 pandemic repercussions on the use and management of plastics. *Environmental Science & Technology*, *54*(13), 7760–7765.

Qarnain, S. S., Sattanathan, M., Sankaranarayanan, B., & Ali, S. M. (2020). Analyzing energy consumption factors during coronavirus (COVID-19) pandemic outbreak: A case study of residential society. *Energy Sources. Part A, Recovery, Utilization, and Environmental Effects*, 1–20.

Restorick, T. (2020). *How has covid-19 changed our eating habits?* https://www.hubbub.org.uk/ blog/how-has-covid-19-changed-our-eating-habits

Rizvi, S., Rustum, R., Deepak, M., Wright, G. B., & Arthur, S. (2021). Identifying and analyzing residential water demand profile; including the impact of COVID-19 and month of Ramadan, for selected developments in Dubai, United Arab Emirates. *Water Supply*, *21*(3), 1144–1156.

Rodríguez-P'erez, C., Molina-Montes, E., Verardo, V., Artacho, R., García-Villanova, B., Guerra-Hernandez, E. J., & Ruíz-Lopez, ´. M. D. (2020). Changes in dietary behaviours during the COVID-19 outbreak confinement in the Spanish COVIDiet study. *Nutrients*, *12*(6), 1–19.

Rouleau, J., & Gosselin, L. (2021). Impacts of the COVID-19 lockdown on energy consumption in a Canadian social housing building. *Applied Energy*, *287*, 116565.

Rume, T., & Islam, S. D. U. (2020). Environmental effects of COVID-19 pandemic and potential strategies of sustainability. *Heliyon*, *6*(9), e04965.

Salzano, G., Passanisi, S., Pira, F., Sorrenti, L., La Monica, G., Pajno, G. B., ... Lombardo, F. (2021). Quarantine due to the COVID-19 pandemic from the perspective of adolescents: The crucial role of technology. *Italian Journal of Pediatrics*, *47*(1), 1–5.

Santiago, I., Moreno-Munoz, A., Quintero-Jiménez, P., Garcia-Torres, F., & Gonzalez-Redondo, M. J. (2021). Electricity demand during pandemic times: The case of the COVID-19 in Spain. *Energy Policy*, *148*, 111964.

Sarmento, P., Motta, M., Scott, I. J., Pinheiro, F. L., & de Castro Neto, M. (2022). Impact of COVID-19 lockdown measures on waste production behavior in Lisbon. *Waste Management (New York, N.Y.)*, *138*, 189–198.

Schmitt, V. G. H., Cequea, M. M., Vásquez Neyra, J. M., & Ferasso, M. (2021). Consumption behavior and residential food waste during the COVID-19 pandemic outbreak in Brazil. *Sustainability*, *13*(7), 3702.

Seibel, S., Santos, I., & Silveira, I. (2021). COVID-19's Impact on Society, Fashion Trends and Consumption. *Strategic Design Research Journal*, *14*(1), 92–101.

Severo, E. A., De Guimarães, J. C. F., & Dellarmelin, M. L. (2021). Impact of the COVID-19 pandemic on environmental awareness, sustainable consumption and social responsibility: Evidence from generations in Brazil and Portugal. *Journal of Cleaner Production*, *286*, 124947.

Shaharuddin, B., Sany, S., & Hasan, N. N. N. (2021). Challenges and Solutions to Shortage of Personal Protective Equipment during COVID-19 Pandemic: A Case Study on Corporate and Community Response. *Journal of Sustainability Science and Management*, *16*(8), 248–255.

Sharma, H. B., Vanapalli, K. R., Cheela, V. S., Ranjan, V. P., Jaglan, A. K., Dubey, B., ... Bhattacharya, J. (2020). Challenges, opportunities, and innovations for effective solid waste management during and post COVID-19 pandemic. *Resources, Conservation and Recycling*, *162*, 105052.

Silva, A. L. P., Prata, J. C., Walker, T. R., Duarte, A. C., Ouyang, W., Barcelò, D., & Rocha-Santos, T. (2021). Increased plastic pollution due to COVID-19 pandemic: Challenges and recommendations. *Chemical Engineering Journal*, *405*, 126683.

Silva, L. E. N., Neto, M. B. G., da Rocha Grangeiro, R., & de Nadae, J. (2020). COVID-19 pandemic: why does it matter for consumer research? [Paper presentation]. CLAV 2020, Sao Paulo, Brasil.

Statista. (2020, June 24). *How COVID-19 has impacted US spending levels*. https://www.statista.com/chart/22091/change-in-consumer-spending-due-to-coronavirus/

Stratoulias, D., & Nuthammachot, N. (2020). Air quality development during the COVID-19 pandemic over a medium-sized urban area in Thailand. *The Science of the Total Environment*, *746*, 141320.

Sun, X., Su, W., Guo, X., & Tian, Z. (2021). The impact of awe induced by COVID-19 pandemic on green consumption behavior in China. *International Journal of Environmental Research and Public Health*, *18*(2), 543.

Tchetchik, A., Kaplan, S., & Blass, V. (2021). Recycling and consumption reduction following the COVID-19 lockdown: The effect of threat and coping appraisal, past behavior and information. *Resources, Conservation and Recycling*, *167*, 105370.

Tsuda, K., & Sakuragi, M. (2020). Co-design of do-it-yourself face shield in Japan under COVID-19 Pandemic. *Strategic Design Research Journal*, *13*(3), 502–510.

Tukker, A., Cohen, M., De Zoysa, U., Hertwich, E., Hofstetter, P., Inaba, A., ... Sto, E. (2008). The Oslo declaration on sustainable consumption. *Journal of Industrial Ecology*, *10*(1-2), 9–14.

Tuncer, F. F. (2020). The spread of fear in the globalizing world: The case of COVID-19. *Journal of Public Affairs*, *20*(4), e2162.

Tyagi, B., Choudhury, G., Vissa, N. K., Singh, J., & Tesche, M. (2021). Changing air pollution scenario during COVID-19: Redefining the hotspot regions over India. *Environmental Pollution*, *271*, 116354.

Van der Wielen, W., & Barrios, S. (2021). Economic sentiment during the COVID pandemic: Evidence from search behaviour in the EU. *Journal of Economics and Business*, *115*, 105970.

Wachyuni, S. S., & Wiweka, K. (2020). The changes in food consumption behavior: A rapid observational study of COVID-19 pandemic. *International Journal of Management Innovation & Entrepreneurial Research*, *6*(2), 77–87.

Wang, X., Lei, S. M., Le, S., Yang, Y., Zhang, B., Yao, W., ... Cheng, S. (2020). Bidirectional influence of the COVID-19 pandemic lockdowns on health behaviors and quality of life among Chinese adults. *International Journal of Environmental Research and Public Health*, *17*(15), 5575.

Watanabe, T. (2020). *The responses of consumption and prices in Japan to the COVID-19 crisis and the Tohoku Earthquake*. https://academiccommons.columbia.edu/doi/10.7916/d8-qs4v-q792

Web, M. D. (2020). *COVID-19 is giving us a lesson-and a warning-about our environment*. https://blogs.webmd.com/webmd-doctors/20200422/covid19-is-giving-us-a-lession-and-a-warning-about-our-environment

Wendtlandt, M., & Wicker, P. (2021). The effects of sport activities and environmentally sustainable behaviors on subjective well-being: A comparison before and during COVID-19. *Frontiers in Sports and Active Living*, *3*, 659837.

Yelp. (2020). *Yelp: Coronavirus economic impact report*. https://blog.yelp.com/news/yelp-coronavirus-economic-impact-report/

Zambrano-Monserrate, M. A., Ruano, M. A., & Sanchez-Alcalde, L. (2020). Indirect effects of COVID-19 on the environment. *The Science of the Total Environment*, *728*, 138813.

Zhang, X., Shao, X., Jeong, E., & Olson, E. (2021). I am worth more than you think I am: Investigating the effects of upcycling on event attendees' recycling intention. *International Journal of Hospitality Management*, *94*, 102888.

KEY TERMS AND DEFINITIONS

Do It Yourself Activities: Doing/making things yourself instead of purchasing them ready-made or hiring someone else to make/do them.

Recycling: It is the act or process of repurposing waste into usable materials.

Reusing: Using materials more than once in their original form rather than discarding them after each use.

Sustainable Consumption: It is a way of consumption that meets the basic needs of humans while minimizing the use of natural resources, toxic materials, waste, and pollutant emissions so as not to endanger the needs of future generations.

Voluntary Simplicity: It is a way of life that reduces the unnecessary consumption of material goods and the pursuit of wealth for its own sake.

Chapter 3
Impressive, Inspiring, and Profound Mindfulness Movement in Organizations:
Boosting Productivity, Cultivating Joy, and Sharping Awareness

Cristina Raluca Gh. Popescu
https://orcid.org/0000-0002-5876-0550
University of Bucharest, Romania & The Bucharest University of Economic Studies, Romania

ABSTRACT

These days, individuals are part of business environments far more overwhelming than ever before as a result of COVID-19 pandemic and COVID-19 crisis, thus having to deal with competitive, demographic, global, economic, legal, political, social, and technological adjustments, advances, and provocations. The post-COVID-19 era has to find the answers and the solutions derived from the key question: "How can people bring mindfulness into the business environment, in order to make individuals more aware of their inner power and their surroundings, and act towards achieving the Sustainable Development Goals (SDGs)?" This study centers, on the one hand, on analyzing the importance and the role of mindfulness for individuals, thus enhancing the tremendous benefits of the impressive, inspiring, and profound mindfulness movement in organizations, and focuses, on the other hand, on presenting those solutions that empower individuals to proceed to the next stages that represent embracing the mindfulness state of mind, by boosting productivity, cultivating joy, and sharping awareness.

INTRODUCTION

In the "Handbook of research on clinical applications of meditation and mindfulness-based interventions in mental health", Sanjeev Kumar Gupta, from the All India Institute of Speech and Hearing, in India, highlights the importance of mental health for all individuals that are part of our society, pointing

DOI: 10.4018/978-1-6684-5109-0.ch003

out that the COVID-19 pandemic has managed to shed a new light on the manner in which people's mental health needs to be analyzed and needs to be addressed, especially when considering the effects of the COVID-19 pandemic on the "societal well-being" (Gupta, 2022). In continuation, it should be mentioned that Kay Fielden interestingly regards mindfulness as a highly "essential quality of integrated wisdom" in the book chapter entitled "Mindfulness: an essential quality of integrated wisdom" (Fielden, 2005). Also, according to Kay Fielden, there is a very powerful connection and relationship between mindfulness and organizations' level of knowledge, which goes beyond the rational level and reaches new and more profound dimensions, such as the emotional, the psychological, and the spiritual perspectives, which ought to be considered more in-depth in a society continuously challenged and constantly faced with major and core changes (Fielden, 2005). Knowledge Management (KM) seems to represent a decisive component of today's entities, especially when centering the attention on key concepts, such as, mindfulness, wisdom, knowledge-based organizations, knowledge-based societies, learning and inquiring organizations, which require a finer understanding of multilayered development solutions and techniques that are capable to promote the achievement Sustainable Development Goals (SDGs) as well as individuals well-being, mental health, creative and innovative powers and perceptions (Fielden, 2005).

The specialists Nancy Kymn Harvin Rutigliano (State University of New York Empire State College, USA), Roger M. Samson (Texas State University, USA), and Alexandria S. Frye (Texas State University, USA) have mentioned in their scientific work entitled very suggestively "Mindfulness: spiriting effective strategic leadership and management" the fact that mindfulness should be seen as "a cognitive strategy" that might be successfully used by leaders and managers, at the level of their organizations, in order to cope with all the negative energies and, most likely, unbearable pressure that comes with their daily tasks, in a business environment that reaches, sometimes, overwhelming levels of stress, and constant overflowing levels of data and information (Rutigliano *et al. 2017*). In particular, it ought to be emphasized that according to the work of Nancy Kymn Harvin Rutigliano (State University of New York Empire State College, USA), Roger M. Samson (Texas State University, USA), and Alexandria S. Frye (Texas State University, USA), mindfulness should represent an impressive and an immense instrument that could lead entities to obtain the highest levels of "strategic leadership and management", thus accomplishing "individual and organizational success" on the long run (Rutigliano *et al. 2017*) (see, in this matter, Figure 1. Specific Links and Connections between the Impressive, Inspiring, and Profound Mindfulness Movement in Organizations and the Desiderate of Boosting productivity, Cultivating joy, and Sharping awareness, on the Road of Building Inclusive Global Knowledge Societies for Sustainable Development (SD), while Targeting the Sustainable Development Goals (SDGs)).

Figure 1. Specific links and connections between the impressive, inspiring, and profound mindfulness movement in organizations and the desiderate of boosting productivity, cultivating joy, and sharping awareness, on the road of building inclusive global knowledge societies for sustainable development (SD), while targeting the sustainable development goals (SDGs)
Source: The authors, based on the references highlighted above and mentioned in the references section of this book chapter entitled "Impressive, inspiring, and profound mindfulness movement in organizations: boosting productivity, cultivating joy, and sharping awareness", which represents an integrating part of the "Handbook of Research on Building Inclusive Global Knowledge Societies for Sustainable Development"

In the same line, the Organization for Economic Co-operation and Development (OECD) representatives have very suggestively mentioned that the idea of reinforcing individuals' global competences, at a wide level, represents a pivotal target for people, especially in highly demanding times, such as the Post-COVID-19 Era, in order "to thrive in a rapidly changing world" (OECD, 2018, p. 2). Also, OECD points out that the idea of reinforcing individuals' global competences represents a paramount step for the societies that are part of the Post-COVID-19 Era, in this manner being able "to progress without leaving anyone behind" and to focus on accomplishing successfully and gradually the Sustainable Development Goals (SDGs) (OECD, 2018, p. 2) (see, in this matter, Figure 2. Challenges of the Post-COVID-19 Era, in Times in which the Business Environments are Facing Overwhelming and Overpowering Changes, as a Result of Mindfulness Movement in Organizations).

Figure 2. Challenges of the post-COVID-19 era, in times in which the business environments are facing overwhelming and overpowering changes, as a result of mindfulness movement in organizations
Source: The authors, based on the references highlighted above and mentioned in the references section of this book chapter entitled "Impressive, inspiring, and profound mindfulness movement in organizations: boosting productivity, cultivating joy, and sharping awareness", which represents an integrating part of the "Handbook of Research on Building Inclusive Global Knowledge Societies for Sustainable Development"

In addition, OECD highlights the fact that today the world encounters an unprecedented level of continuously "growing openness and connectivity", and in the same time faces new rising challenges, such as, for instance: an increased level of inequalities and radicalism – generated by different backgrounds, different levels of understanding and of coping with a multitude of situations, different levels of knowledge, different cultural backgrounds; a highly demanding level in terms of the individuals' skills that are needed in order "to be competitive and ready for a new world of work" – especially in a highly competitive and an increasingly demanding business environment; a high challenge in terms of finding solutions to develop, at the largest scale possible, individuals and organizations "capacity to analyze and understand global and intercultural issues" – especially when willing to accomplish successfully and gradually the Sustainable Development Goals (SDGs) (OECD, 2018, p. 2). Based on the OECD most recent documents and the growing importance placed by this vital international organization on preparing people for an inclusive and sustainable world, thus managing to be in line with the newest global competence framework, it should be stated that there is a strong and pivotal connection between individuals' mindfulness, well-being, mental health, work climate, and business environment, since "the development of social and emotional skills, as well as values like respect, self-confidence and a sense of belonging, are of the utmost importance to create opportunities for all and advance a shared respect for human dignity", in this way being able to actively work and to constantly promote the assessment of global competence, thus being capable to "foster global competence for more inclusive societies" (OECD, 2018, p. 2).

This book chapter entitled "Impressive, inspiring, and profound mindfulness movement in organizations: boosting productivity, cultivating joy, and sharping awareness" represents an integrating part of the "Handbook of Research on Building Inclusive Global Knowledge Societies for Sustainable Development", and is specially designed by the authors in order nowadays specific issues, controversies, problems, especially under the circumstances in which individuals have become part of business environments far more overwhelming and overpowering than ever before as a result of the implications of the COVID-19 pandemic and COVID-19 crisis. Hence, individuals are in the position in which they have to deal these days with highly competitive adjustments, advances, and provocations in all areas and in all domains, namely: demographic, global, economic, legal, political, social, and technological domains, spheres, and dimensions. Under these given circumstances, it ought to be emphasized that probably one of the most amazing and urgent provocation that belongs to the Post-COVID-19 Era is to find the answers and the solutions derived from the key question: "How can people bring mindfulness into the business environment, in order to make individuals more aware of their inner power and their surroundings, and act towards achieving the Sustainable Development Goals (SDGs)?" That is the reason why, this current study entitled "Impressive, inspiring, and profound mindfulness movement in organizations: boosting productivity, cultivating joy, and sharping awareness" centers, first of all, on analyzing the importance and the role of mindfulness for individuals, thus enhancing the tremendous benefits of the impressive, inspiring, and profound mindfulness movement in organizations. In continuation, it should be highlighted that this current study entitled "Impressive, inspiring, and profound mindfulness movement in organizations: boosting productivity, cultivating joy, and sharping awareness" focuses, second of all, on presenting those solutions that empower individuals to proceed to the next stages that represent embracing the mindfulness state of mind, by boosting productivity, cultivating joy, and sharping awareness. Thus, in terms of general objectives of this book chapter, the following aspects need to be stressed, as follows (see, in this particular matter, the six steps highlighted and commented, in-depth, in the lines below):

Step 1: The book chapter centers on presenting the meaning of the concept of "mindfulness", with a particular emphasis on describing the main characteristics, the importance, and the role of this term for individuals and for organizations.

Step 2: The book chapter focuses on introducing the concept of "mindfulness movement", while addressing the most important challenges that are derived from introducing the term of "mindfulness movement" in organizations worldwide.

Step 3: The book chapter concentrates on presenting and describing the most significant adjustments, alternations, changes, fluctuations, and modifications that have occurred in people's day-to-day lives as well as in organizations' activities as a result of introducing the concept of "mindfulness" to the employees of different organizations, thus enabling them to become an integrating and an influential part of the mindfulness movement in entities.

Step 4: The book chapter tackles the manner in which people are able to bring mindfulness into the business environment, in order to become gradually aware of their inner power and their surroundings, and act towards achieving the Sustainable Development Goals (SDGs) – which represent a major priority these days for the entire humanity, especially due to the constant and constant challenges that are specific to the demographic, global, economic, legal, political, social, and technological domains, spheres, and dimensions.

Step 5: The book chapter analyzes the importance and the role of mindfulness for individuals, thus enhancing the tremendous benefits of the impressive, inspiring, and profound mindfulness movement in organizations, especially in the context in which human resources (HRs) and intellectual capital (IC) have become the most important and the most precious intangible assets (IA) that organizations possess these days.

Step 6: The book chapter presents those solutions that empower individuals to proceed to the next stages that represent embracing the mindfulness state of mind, by boosting productivity, cultivating joy, and sharping awareness, zeroing in on dynamic and powerful key concepts, such as: business, knowledge, human resource (HR), innovation, intangible asset (IA), intellectual capital (IC), leadership, Sustainable Development Goals (SDGs), well-being, mindfulness, environment, organizational culture, and creativity.

Background

The background section of this book chapter suggestively entitled "Impressive, inspiring, and profound mindfulness movement in organizations: boosting productivity, cultivating joy, and sharping awareness", which represents an integrating part of the "Handbook of Research on Building Inclusive Global Knowledge Societies for Sustainable Development", focuses on presenting a literature review containing the most significant and up-to-date elements which are specific to the theme chosen for analysis. This section successfully covers and analysis in-depth several essential key terms, such as the following ones: business, business environment or business surroundings, knowledge, Knowledge Management (KM), knowledge-based organizations, knowledge-based societies, learning and inquiring organizations, human resource (HR), human resources (HRs), innovation, intangible asset (IA), intellectual capital (IC), leadership, Sustainable Development Goals (SDGs), well-being, mindfulness, mindfulness movement in organizations, mindfulness movement in society, mental health, people's health, environment, organizational culture, creativity, creation, sustainable economic growth (SEG), and competitiveness. In continuation to the aspects underlined above, it needs to be emphasized that nowadays individuals all around the globe are becoming part of business environments far more overwhelming than ever before in history, in particular, as a result of today's new situations that occurred mainly due to the COVID-19 pandemic and the COVID-19 crisis. Also, these days, individuals are being confronted at a larger and more dynamic scale with competitive, demographic, global, economic, legal, political, social, and technological adjustments, advances, and provocations, in order to be able to find the necessary solutions in order to better, more actively, more efficiently, and more successfully, cope with the situations that were inevitably derived from the COVID-19 pandemic and the COVID-19 crisis. In this matter, this background section has the purpose of helping the authors to pencil in the most decisive issues that will become an integrating part of the Post-COVID-19 Era, while trying to find the answers and the solutions derived from the key question represented by "How can people bring mindfulness into the business environment, in order to make individuals more aware of their inner power and their surroundings, and act towards achieving the Sustainable Development Goals (SDGs)?" Since this current study centers, on the one hand, on analyzing the importance and the role of mindfulness for individuals, thus enhancing the tremendous benefits of the impressive, inspiring, and profound mindfulness movement in organizations, and focuses, on the other hand, on presenting those solutions that empower individuals to proceed to the next stages that represent embracing the mindfulness state of mind, by boosting productivity, cultivating joy, and sharping awareness, the background section of this book chapter suggestively entitled "Impressive, inspiring, and profound mindfulness movement in organizations: boosting productivity, cultivating joy, and sharping awareness", familiarizes the reader with the main concepts of the research on building inclusive global knowledge societies (GKS) for sustainable development (SD), and, in the same time, prepares the reader for a profound analysis which ought to be done in order to create an adequate, representative, and timely research on building inclusive global knowledge societies (GKS) for sustainable development (SD) (see, in this matter, Table 1. Key Concepts and Definitions for the Key Concepts).

The first concept that was chosen for this analysis by the authors of this book chapter is represented by the global knowledge societies (GKS) for sustainable development (SD), since both global knowledge societies (GKS) and sustainable development (SD) are deeply and profoundly interconnected and interrelated. Thus, it should be stressed that according to the authors, global knowledge societies (GKS) for sustainable development (SD) represent, on the one hand, a defining feature of the Post-COVID-19 Era, and constitute, on the other hand, a valuable characteristic of the continuously developing and constantly growing societies which have successfully placed a high degree of importance on preparing people for an inclusive and sustainable future and world, that ought to be governed by the Sustainable Development Goals (SDGs), thus managing to be in line with the newest global competence frameworks that are generated with the aid of individuals' which need to become more and more aware of their potential in terms of mindfulness, well-being, mental health, work climate, and business environment. In continuation to the aspects highlighted in the lines above, it should be emphasized that these days, the development of people's social and emotional skills represents a crucial asset for our society, since values such as respect, self-confidence and a sense of belonging, are rapidly growing in importance, and are meant to generate new and impressive opportunities for all individuals, thus contributing to the advancement of our society and to the promotion of the assessment of individuals' global competence, which enables the processes of fostering global competence for more inclusive, more robust, and more resilient societies for all. In this manner, it is essential to understand that the global knowledge societies (GKS) for sustainable development (SD) will be part of the agenda of numerous influential figures worldwide due to the power that resides in creating, gathering, and using knowledge at the highest levels possible and in a way that will contribute successfully and unequivocally to the well-being of all nations and all businesses worldwide. Even though, according to the 2019 report published by the Eurasian Economic Commission (EEC), the United Nations Conference on Trade and Development (UNCTAD), and the Interstate Bank (IB), and suggestively entitled "Inclusive growth of the Eurasian Economic Union Member States: assessments and opportunities", "development of the world economy over the last thirty years has been characterized by extensive deregulation of markets – particularly financial and currency markets – in rich and poor countries alike", it could be easily remarked "the attrition of the public realm, and the extension of profitmaking opportunities to an ever-widening range of spheres, among which not only economic, but also social, cultural and political life" came to contribute and to make a difference, especially in terms of global knowledge societies (GKS) for sustainable development (SD) (Eurasian Economic Commission (EEC) *et al.* 2019, p. 5).

The second concept that was chosen for this analysis by the authors of this book chapter makes reference to the green, resilient, and inclusive development (GRID), which according to renowned specialists these days, are meant, on the one hand, to address the global challenge of social inequality at a large and extensive scale, and are expected to promote, on the other hand, financial inclusion at a wide level (Thomas & Hedrick-Wong, 2019). What is more, based on the 2019 article published by Howard Thomas –professor emeritus of Strategic Management and Management Education at Singapore Management University, and special advisor at the EFMD Business Magazine, and Yuwa Hedrick-Wong – visiting scholar and senior fellow at Lee Kuan Yew School of Public Policy at the National University of Singapore, and suggestively entitled "Enabling models of inclusive growth: Addressing the need for financial and social inclusion", green, resilient, and inclusive development (GRID) has to look into the problems derived from the increasing level of poverty, while finding solutions to diminish the constantly growing gap between the rich and poor individuals (Thomas & Hedrick-Wong, 2019). Also, these days, all the international organizations worldwide and all the prominent leaders worldwide are turning their attention to accomplishing green, resilient, and inclusive development (GRID) for all individuals and for all societies, due to the overwhelming and highly alarming levels of air pollution, land pollution, and water pollution, due to the pollution-related deaths – which are usually believed to occur, according to the most recent statistics, in low-income, and middle-income countries, and, also, due to climate change, immigration stresses, poverty, and homelessness challenges. In continuation, it should be brought to the attention that, according to specialists, long-term sustainability is based on fostering green, resilient, and inclusive development (GRID) which represent healthier solutions and healthier ways that different societies have to adopt in order to encompass the major problems with which they have confronted themselves with and which lead to growing structural weaknesses over the last decades – especially lately, due to the new changes, challenges, and perspectives that were brought by the COVID-19 pandemic and the COVID-19 crisis. In the light of the issues underlined above, the International Labor Organization (ILO) mentioned in 2018, in the publication entitled "New business models for inclusive growth", the fact that "the future of work is to be one that provides security, equality and prosperity", which prompted the attention to the need of individuals to have the opportunity to find adequate places of work in order to ensure for themselves and for their family members security, equality and prosperity on the medium-run and long-run (International Labor Organization (ILO), 2018, p. 1).

The third concept that was chosen for this analysis by the authors of this book chapter is represented by mindfulness, which is believed to be a highly influential concept today. Under these given context, it ought to be stated that more and more individuals, and more and more specialists worldwide are recommending the exercises, meditation, and practices which are specific to maintaining moment-by-moment awareness of people's thoughts, feelings, sensations, in accordance to the surroundings and the environment where the people try to be part of, in order to foster both well-being and mental health, at home, at the work climate, and, at a general level, in the business environment. What is more, in essence, the vital characteristic of mindfulness that ought to be highlighted is that all the situations that individuals are facing should be taken without any form of judgment, should be accepted as such, in order for the individuals to be able to find the inner strength and the inner solutions to cope with those situations and be able to go to the next levels of their lives, their carriers, their proposed stages in terms of goals, objectives, and targets. Furthermore, the International Labor Organization (ILO) mentioned in 2018, in the publication entitled "New business models for inclusive growth", the fact that "the future of work is to be one that provides security, equality and prosperity", the fact that "business enterprises are the engine of our economies, the generators of prosperity and the creators of jobs", while leaders and managers worldwide are facing "the challenge as to how best to utilize the potential of business to contribute to society", especially in those situations in which there is a raising interest in creating and developing "new business models in order to better understand how we can harness the productive capacity of business to optimally contribute to inclusive and sustainable growth" (International Labor Organization (ILO), 2018, p. 3).

The fourth concept that was chosen for this analysis by the authors of this book chapter is represented by mindfulness into the business environment. According to the authors, mindfulness into the business environment represents probably the most challenging and the most novel approach that can be provided these days in organizations, in terms of creating, ensuring, and fostering long-term individual awareness, well-being, and mental health while referring to the people's work climate and business surroundings. In continuation to the aspects just mentioned, it should be highlighted that the approach and analysis of mindfulness into the business environment departs from the necessity of ensuring resilient, robust, and sustainable development (SD) strategies at the level of entities worldwide, in order to promote global knowledge societies (GKS) for sustainable development (SD), as well as green, resilient, and inclusive development (GRID), while targeting the accomplishment of the Sustainable Development Goals (SDGs) on the long-run. Furthermore, by introducing and maintaining mindfulness into the business environment, especially in the times governed by the COVID-19 pandemic and the COVID-19 crisis, entities worldwide are helped to deal with competitive, demographic, global, economic, legal, political, social, and technological adjustments, advances, and provocations, which will essentially come to represent one of the best and, probably, one of the most successful, solutions to ensuring high levels of financial well-being, performance, and profitability of businesses in the Post-COVID-19 Era.

The fifth concept that was chosen for this analysis by the authors of this book chapter is represented by the mindfulness movement in organizations. According to the authors of this book chapter, mindfulness movement in organizations represents a very powerful manner in which, these days, individuals become integrating part of mindfulness practices all around the world, learning to center – in a peaceful and non-judgmental way – on the present moment. In addition, in essence, the importance of mindfulness practices resides in learning how to achieve inner calm, how to develop a positive mindset, how to acquire the targeted goals while managing to heal from the day to day stress and inevitable pressure that both society and entities put on people. Under this particular context, Daniel W. Grupe (University of Wisconsin, Madison, USA), Chris Smith (Academy for Mindfulness, LLC, USA), and Chad McGehee (University of Wisconsin, Madison, USA) mentioned in the book chapter entitled "Introducing mindfulness training and research into policing: strategies for successful implementation" the fact that by introducing mindfulness practices in different activities – such as, for instance, into law enforcement – confers our society with an inestimable potential that could be represented by broad benefits for employees and the community members alike – or, more concrete, based on the example of the law enforcement environment, by ensuring benefits to both police officers and the general community in an equal manner (Grupe *et al.* 2021). Hence, according to Kimber O. Underdown (Grand Canyon University, USA), Crystal L. McCabe (Grand Canyon University, USA), and Michael F. McCabe (Grand Canyon Education, USA), in the scientific work entitled "Creating and maintaining balance: work-life balance, self-care, and mindfulness", mindfulness could be a good and viable solutions that individuals might get to rely on over time in order to be able to "avoid stress, burnout, and leaving the professions" (Underdown *et al.* 2022).

The sixth concept that was chosen for this analysis by the authors of this book chapter is represented by the resilience and inclusive growth. While analyzing the notion of the resilience and inclusive growth, the authors would like to stress the fact that these are two of the most important issues targeted by the agenda of highly influential and major international organizations, such as the Organization for Economic Co-operation and Development (OECD), the United Nations (UN) agency, and the Climate Change Committee (CCC), thorough different types of programs, like the United Nations Development Program (UNDP) or the United Nations (UN) Sustainable Development Goals (SDGs) in the framework of the 2030 Agenda. Also, based on the most recent literature in the field, resilience and inclusive growth make reference to the most popular and the most successful instruments, methods, models, and tools that are capable to empower regions and countries at a global level to create and to foster inclusive growth models (such as, for instance, the European inclusive growth model, or the OECD Inclusive Growth Project), which have become, over time, essential to supporting the economic development (ED). In continuation to the aspects already brought into discussion, in essence, according to prominent economic, political, and social leaders worldwide, inclusive growth stands for economic growth that has been distributed in a fair way across society and which has the power to generate new opportunities for all individuals and for all entities, since it is based on several main pillars, among which could be mentioned the following ones: (a) fostering high, efficient, and sustained growth meant to create, on the one hand, productive jobs for all, and, on the other hand, economic opportunities for all; (b) investing in the most relevant domains of our society, such as education, health, other social services, thus expanding people's capacity to be healthy, productive, and have an adequate state of well-being, and either diminishing or eliminating market and institutional failures and social exclusion at all levels of the society; and (c) establishing social safety nets which would become capable to protect the poor individuals of our society and to mitigate the risks of different but inevitable societal shocks (economic, financial, demographic shocks, which could be associated with different types of crisis, such as, the COVID-19 pandemic and the COVID-19 crisis) (Eurasian Economic Commission (EEC) *et al.* 2019). Also, the COVID-19 pandemic and the COVID-19 crisis have introduced in our society "additional stressors", which are felt by all individuals at an international level, but at a different degree, which imposes people's need to cope with the current situation by addressing, in the best way possible, the "life-work balance, self-care, and mindfulness", in order to better prepare for the changes that will animate the Post-COVID-19 Era (Underdown *et al.* 2022).

The seventh concept that was chosen for this analysis by the authors of this book chapter is represented by the Sustainable Development Goals (SDGs).

Table 1. Key concepts and definitions for the key concepts

Key Concepts	Definitions for the Key Concepts
Global Knowledge Societies (GKS) for Sustainable Development (SD)	• Represent, on the one hand, a defining feature of the Post-COVID-19 Era, and constitute, on the other hand, a valuable characteristic of the continuously developing and constantly growing societies which have successfully placed a high degree of importance on preparing people for an inclusive and sustainable future and world, that ought to be governed by the Sustainable Development Goals (SDGs), thus managing to be in line with the newest global competence frameworks that are generated with the aid of individuals' which need to become more and more aware of their potential in terms of mindfulness, well-being, mental health, work climate, and business environment; what is more, these days, the development of people's social and emotional skills represents a crucial asset for our society, since values such as respect, self-confidence and a sense of belonging, are rapidly growing in importance, and are meant to generate new and impressive opportunities for all individuals, thus contributing to the advancement of our society and to the promotion of the assessment of individuals' global competence, which enables the processes of fostering global competence for more inclusive, more robust, and more resilient societies for all.
Green, Resilient, and Inclusive Development (GRID)	• These days, all the international organizations worldwide and all the prominent leaders worldwide are turning their attention to accomplishing green, resilient, and inclusive development (GRID) for all individuals and for all societies, due to the overwhelming and highly alarming levels of air pollution, land pollution, and water pollution, due to the pollution-related deaths – which are usually believed to occur, according to the most recent statistics, in low-income, and middle-income countries, and, also, due to climate change, immigration stresses, poverty, and homelessness challenges; according to specialists, long-term sustainability is based on fostering green, resilient, and inclusive development (GRID) which represent healthier solutions and healthier ways that different societies have to adopt in order to encompass the major problems with which they have confronted themselves with and which lead to growing structural weaknesses over the last decades – especially lately, due to the new changes, challenges, and perspectives that were brought by the COVID-19 pandemic and the COVID-19 crisis.
Mindfulness	• Represents a highly influential concept today, since more and more individuals, and more and more specialists worldwide recommend the exercises, meditation, and practices which are specific to maintaining moment-by-moment awareness of people's thoughts, feelings, sensations, in accordance to the surroundings and the environment where the people try to be part of; in essence, the vital characteristic of mindfulness that ought to be highlighted is that all the situations that individuals are facing should be taken without any form of judgment, should be accepted as such, in order for the individuals to be able to find the inner strength and the inner solutions to cope with those situations and be able to go to the next levels of their lives, their carriers, their proposed stages in terms of goals, objectives, and targets.

Continued on following page

Table 1. Continued

Key Concepts	Definitions for the Key Concepts
Mindfulness into the Business Environment	• Represents probably the most challenging and the most novel approach that can be provided these days in organizations, in terms of creating, ensuring, and fostering long-term individual awareness, well-being, and mental health while referring to the people's work climate and business surroundings; in continuation, it should be highlighted that the approach and analysis of mindfulness into the business environment departs from the necessity of ensuring resilient, robust, and sustainable development (SD) strategies at the level of entities worldwide, in order to promote global knowledge societies (GKS) for sustainable development (SD), as well as green, resilient, and inclusive development (GRID), while targeting the accomplishment of the Sustainable Development Goals (SDGs) on the long-run; furthermore, by introducing and maintaining mindfulness into the business environment, especially in the times governed by the COVID-19 pandemic and the COVID-19 crisis, entities worldwide are helped to deal with competitive, demographic, global, economic, legal, political, social, and technological adjustments, advances, and provocations, which will essentially come to represent one of the best and, probably, one of the most successful, solutions to ensuring high levels of financial well-being, performance, and profitability of businesses in the Post-COVID-19 Era.
Mindfulness Movement in Organizations	• Represents a very powerful manner in which, these days, individuals become integrating part of mindfulness practices all around the world, learning to center – in a peaceful and non-judgmental way – on the present moment; in essence, the importance of mindfulness practices resides in learning how to achieve inner calm, how to develop a positive mindset, how to acquire the targeted goals while managing to heal from the day to day stress and inevitable pressure that both society and entities put on people.
Promoting Mental Health	• Represents, on the one hand, a real challenge for specialists these days, and, in the same time, on the other hand, an essential step for a better and more safer environment for all individuals, especially in the context in which several prominent organizations, among which could be successfully mentioned the Organization for Economic Co-operation and Development (OECD), the United Nations (UN) agency, and the World Health Organization (WHO) have shown more and more interest in understanding the causes that lead to mental illnesses and the actions and the solutions due to be taken in order to promote human development and to obtain human development indicators that "may help describe the effectiveness of macro policies on mental health" (World Health Organization (WHO), 2005, p. 200).
Resilience and Inclusive Growth	• Are two of the most important issues targeted by the agenda of highly influential and major international organizations, such as the Organization for Economic Co-operation and Development (OECD), the United Nations (UN) agency, and the Climate Change Committee (CCC), thorough different types of programs, like the United Nations Development Program (UNDP) or the United Nations (UN) Sustainable Development Goals (SDGs) in the framework of the 2030 Agenda; based on the most recent literature in the field, resilience and inclusive growth make reference to the most popular and the most successful instruments, methods, models, and tools that are capable to empower regions and countries at a global level to create and to foster inclusive growth models (such as, for instance, the European inclusive growth model, or the OECD Inclusive Growth Project), which have become, over time, essential to supporting the economic development (ED); in essence, according to prominent economic, political, and social leaders worldwide, inclusive growth stands for economic growth that has been distributed in a fair way across society and which has the power to generate new opportunities for all individuals and for all entities, since it is based on several main pillars, among which could be mentioned the following ones: (a) fostering high, efficient, and sustained growth meant to create, on the one hand, productive jobs for all, and, on the other hand, economic opportunities for all; (b) investing in the most relevant domains of our society, such as education, health, other social services, thus expanding people's capacity to be healthy, productive, and have an adequate state of well-being, and either diminishing or eliminating market and institutional failures and social exclusion at all levels of the society; and (c) establishing social safety nets which would become capable to protect the poor individuals of our society and to mitigate the risks of different but inevitable societal shocks (economic, financial, demographic shocks, which could be associated with different types of crisis, such as, the COVID-19 pandemic and the COVID-19 crisis).
Sustainable Development Goals (SDGs)	• Represent an integrating part of the "2030 Agenda for Sustainable Development (SD)", which has been adopted by all United Nations (UN) Member States in 2015, and have the capacity to provide a common blueprint that mainly focuses on world peace and global prosperity for all the people worldwide as well as the planet, now and into the future (United Nations (UN), 2015); in continuation, it should be highlighted that the 17 Sustainable Development Goals (SDGs), represent according to the "2030 Agenda for Sustainable Development (SD)" an important and urgent desiderate for action due to be taken by all developed and developing countries all around the world, as a result of "a global partnership", having as key priorities "ending poverty and other deprivations", while addressing common and strong "strategies that improve health and education, reduce inequality, and spur economic growth – all while tackling climate change and working to preserve our oceans and forests" (United Nations (UN), 2015).

Continued on following page

Table 1. Continued

Source: The authors, based on the references highlighted above and mentioned in the references section of this book chapter entitled "Impressive, inspiring, and profound mindfulness movement in organizations: boosting productivity, cultivating joy, and sharping awareness", which represents an integrating part of the "Handbook of Research on Building Inclusive Global Knowledge Societies for Sustainable Development"; these key terms are presented also in the section entitled "Key Terms and Definitions", due to be encountered at the end of this book chapter, being considered of great value for this current scientific work, since they are believed to present, in a synthetically form, the very essence of individuals' desire and struggle to create global knowledge societies for sustainable development, while promoting the worlds' Sustainable Development Goals (SDGs)

The United Nations (UN) 2015 document entitled "Transforming Our World: The 2030 Agenda for Sustainable Development" represents a very powerful "plan of action for people, planet and prosperity", which "seeks to strengthen universal peace in larger freedom" (United Nations (UN), 2021, p. 5). In continuation, according to the United Nations Development Program (UNDP), one of the most important Sustainable Development Goals (SDGs) is represented by the third objective which is ensuring "healthy lives and promote well-being for all at all ages", which shows the importance that our society these days puts on being "in good health", since "our health affects everything from how much we enjoy life to what work we can perform" (United Nations Development Program (UNDP), 2020, p. 6). This third objective which may be found among the worlds' Sustainable Development Goals (SDGs), could be associated with the sixth objective which focuses on ensuring "availability and sustainable management of water and sanitation for all", starting from the belief that "everyone on earth should have access to safe and affordable drinking water" (United Nations Development Program (UNDP), 2020, p. 9). When analyzing the case of the impressive, inspiring, and profound mindfulness movement in organizations, by finding new ways of boosting productivity, cultivating joy, and sharping awareness, it should be illustrated that the worlds' Sustainable Development Goals (SDGs) make also reference to promoting "sustained, inclusive and sustainable economic growth, full and productive employment and decent work for all", which is represented by the eight objective on the 2030 Agenda for Sustainable Development (SD) (United Nations Development Program (UNDP), 2020, p. 11). Since the concept of mindfulness in organizations is analyzed by specialists together with other related terms, such as, business, knowledge, human resource (HR), innovation, intangible asset (IA), intellectual capital (IC), leadership, Sustainable Development Goals (SDGs), well-being, mindfulness, environment, organizational culture, and creativity, it needs to be brought to light that the ninth objective on the 2030 Agenda for Sustainable Development (SD) is building "resilient infrastructure, promote inclusive and sustainable industrialization and foster innovation" (United Nations Development Program (UNDP), 2020, p. 12). All in all, building inclusive global knowledge societies (GKS) for sustainable development (SD) represent a real provocation for today's society and business environment (Eurasian Economic Commission (EEC) *et al.* 2019).

MAIN FOCUS OF THE CHAPTER

This current section that constitutes, in essence, the main focus of the current book chapter presents the main part of the scientific work entitled the "Impressive, inspiring, and profound mindfulness movement in organizations: boosting productivity, cultivating joy, and sharping awareness", as an integrating part of the "Handbook of Research on Building Inclusive Global Knowledge Societies for Sustainable Development".

In a recent document published by the European Commission (EC) in 2022 called "Joint European Roadmap towards lifting COVID-19 containment measures", it has been highlighted that the Members of the European Council have declared the fact that they are fully "committed to do everything that is necessary to protect the EU's citizens and overcome the crisis while preserving the European values and way of life", and it has been brought to the attention the fact that "beyond the urgency of fighting the COVID-19 pandemic and its immediate consequences, the Members of the European Council called for preparing the measures necessary to get Europe's societies and economies back to a normal functioning and to sustainable growth, integrating inter alia the green transition and the digital transformation, and drawing all lessons from the crisis" (European Commission (EC), 2022, p. 1). In this matter, while addressing the case of Europe's societies and economies, it has been noted that all the European Union's Member States must "prepare the ground for a comprehensive recovery plan and unprecedented investment" (European Commission (EC), 2022, p. 1), which could offer us the unprecedented opportunity to value all the lessons learned during this time period, as a result of COVID-19 pandemic and COVID-19 crisis, and become more aware of the importance of living in the present moment, being more empathetic towards the needs of the individuals around us, more inclined to become more understanding and less judgmental, and more motivated to act in the spirit of mindfulness, health, well-being, in the attempt to promote a general successful mindfulness movement in organizations that would be capable to boosting productivity, cultivating joy, and sharping awareness for all individuals.

In continuation to all the aspects presented in the lines above, it ought to be stressed that these days individuals that are part of the business environments at an international level are facing far more overwhelming changes and challenges than ever before, mainly, as a result of COVID-19 pandemic and COVID-19 crisis. In this matter, specialists have noted that "the fast evolving nature of the COVID-19 pandemic and the significant unknowns coming with a new virus and the disease it causes have led to unprecedented challenges for health care systems as well as to dramatic socio-economic impacts in Europe and the whole world", while, in the same time, "the crisis has already claimed thousands of lives and continues to put health care systems under enormous strain", and, also, "extraordinary and unprecedented measures – both economic and social – have been taken" (European Commission (EC), 2022, p. 2).

In this matter, the authors of this book chapter strongly believe that introducing and promoting mindfulness movement in organizations represents a vital component that individuals possess and that could help our society cope better with the implications of the COVID-19 pandemic and COVID-19 crisis, facilitating a smoother shift towards the Post-COVID-19 Era. What is more, it needs to be highlighted that several restrictive measures have been implemented by the authorities since they were believed to be "necessary to slow down the spread of the virus", thus saving "tens of thousands of lives", but it implicated, in the same, "a high social and economic cost", since all these steps "put a strain on mental health and force citizens to radically change their day-to-day lives" (European Commission (EC), 2022, p. 2). The economic pressure that has been created has led in a very short time period to "huge shocks to the economy and seriously impacted the functioning of the Single Market", while "whole sectors" have been "closed down", and connectivity was "significantly limited and international supply chains and people's freedom of movement have been severely disrupted" for longer periods of time than before (European Commission (EC), 2022, p. 2). So, our society as whole had to deal with competitive, demographic, global, economic, legal, political, social, and technological adjustments, advances, and provocations.

In our opinion, the Post-COVID-19 Era has to find the answers and the solutions derived from the key question: "How can people bring mindfulness into the business environment, in order to make individuals more aware of their inner power and their surroundings, and act towards achieving the Sustainable

Development Goals (SDGs)?" (see, in this matter, Figure 3. Priorities of the Post-COVID-19 Era, in Times in which the Business Environments are Facing Overwhelming and Overpowering Changes, as a Result of Mindfulness Movement in Organizations).

Figure 3. Priorities of the post-COVID-19 era, in times in which the business environments are facing overwhelming and overpowering changes, as a result of mindfulness movement in organizations
Source: The authors, based on the references highlighted above and mentioned in the references section of this book chapter entitled "Impressive, inspiring, and profound mindfulness movement in organizations: boosting productivity, cultivating joy, and sharping awareness", which represents an integrating part of the "Handbook of Research on Building Inclusive Global Knowledge Societies for Sustainable Development"

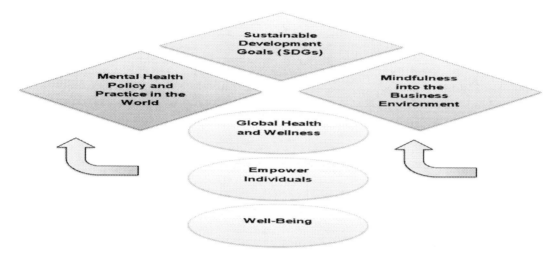

That is a key argument for this current scientific work, given our strong belief that this study centers, on the one hand, on analyzing the importance and the role of mindfulness for individuals, thus enhancing the tremendous benefits of the impressive, inspiring, and profound mindfulness movement in organizations, and focuses, on the other hand, on presenting those solutions that empower individuals to proceed to the next stages that represent embracing the mindfulness state of mind, by boosting productivity, cultivating joy, and sharping awareness. In the same time, based on recent reports, "successfully coordinating the lifting of containment measures at EU level will also positively impact the EU's recovery", especially under the circumstances in which it has been acknowledged that "there is a need to strategically plan the recovery that is mindful of citizens' needs, in which the economy needs to pick up pace and get back on a path of sustainable growth, integrating the twin green and digital transition and drawing all lessons from the current crisis for the EU's preparedness and resilience" (European Commission (EC), 2022, p. 15).

Also, based on the most recent literature review analyzed in the previous section, namely the background section, today's society revolves around several keywords and key concepts, such as, business, knowledge, human resource, innovation, intangible asset, intellectual capital, leadership, sustainable development goals, well-being, mindfulness, environment, organizational culture, and the process of creating a better and a more aware society and economy.

In this matter, the meaning of the concept of "mindfulness" is becoming more and more important for all individuals worldwide, and it can be remarked that there exists a particular emphasis on describing and understanding the main characteristics, the importance, and the role of this term for individuals and for organizations.

For instance, while referring to the mindful and mindfulness movements, in general, an important study on "Move to be Well: The Global Economy of Physical Activity", published in October 2019, by the Global Wellness Institute (GWI), has mentioned that "mindful movement includes activities such as yoga, tai chi, qigong, Pilates, stretch, and barre, as well as other less mainstream somatic, bodywork, and energy-based methods such as Gyrotonic and Gyrokinesis, Nia Technique, Feldenkrais Method, and 5Rhythms", and, in the same time, stressed the fact that "while these classes are increasingly offered at gyms and fitness studios as part of a comprehensive fitness class offering, consumers usually turn to them with the intentions of improving mind-body health and mental focus, and for stress-relief and mindfulness, in addition to physical exercise" (Global Wellness Institute (GWI), 2019, p. 16). Also, in the same cited source, it has been brought to the attention that "the participants in this market are primarily (but not exclusively) adults" (Global Wellness Institute (GWI), 2019, p. 16). The Global Wellness Institute (GWI) is a non-profit organization that "positively impacts global health and wellness by advocating for both public institutions and businesses that are working to help prevent disease, reduce stress, and enhance overall quality of life", having as key declared aim "to empower wellness worldwide" (Global Wellness Institute (GWI), 2019, p. 12).

In order to introduce the concept of "mindfulness movement", while addressing the most important challenges that are derived from introducing the term of "mindfulness movement" in organizations worldwide, the authors of this book chapter would like to make reference to an important study that belongs to The European Observatory on Health Systems and Policies, which represents "a partnership between the World Health Organization Regional Office for Europe, the Governments of Belgium, Finland, Greece, Norway, Slovenia, Spain and Sweden, the Veneto Region of Italy, the European Investment Bank, the Open Society Institute, the World Bank, CRP-Santé Luxembourg, the London School of Economics and Political Science and the London School of Hygiene & Tropical Medicine" (European Observatory on Health Systems and Policies & World Health Organization (WHO), 2007, p. 3). This important study is entitled "Mental Health Policy and Practice across Europe. The future direction of mental health care", published by European Observatory on Health Systems and Policies and World Health Organization, in 2007, mentions the following dominant characteristics concerning individuals' mental health: (a) "Mental health may be the most neglected public health issue. In much of Europe it remains a taboo to discuss the challenges that mental health raises for governments, societies, and particularly for people with mental health problems themselves."; (b) "Mental health issues remain a low priority among international donors as well as policy-makers."; and (c) "It is an important time for the development of mental health policy and practice across Europe. There has never been so much visibility or recognition of the need to tackle mental health problems and promote good mental health. Now it is time to act" (European Observatory on Health Systems and Policies & World Health Organization (WHO), 2007, pp. 23-25).

What is more, it is our opinion that these days, the decisions that need to be taken in terms of mindfulness movement, at a general level, should mainly concentrate on presenting and describing the most significant adjustments, alternations, changes, fluctuations, and modifications that have occurred in people's day-to-day lives as well as in organizations' activities as a result of introducing the concept of "mindfulness" to the employees of different organizations, thus enabling them to become an integrating and an influential part of the mindfulness movement in entities. Also, it is a great concern as well as a pivotal point of analysis and discussion the manner in which people are able to bring mindfulness into the business environment, in order to become gradually aware of their inner power and their surroundings, and act towards achieving the Sustainable Development Goals (SDGs) – which represent a major priority these days for the entire humanity, especially due to the constant and constant challenges that are specific to the demographic, global, economic, legal, political, social, and technological domains, spheres, and dimensions. In continuations, the specialists ought to further their research to the in-depth analysis of the importance and the role of mindfulness for individuals, thus enhancing the tremendous benefits of the impressive, inspiring, and profound mindfulness movement in organizations, especially in the context in which human resources (HRs) and intellectual capital (IC) have become the most important and the most precious intangible assets (IA) that organizations possess these days.

Furthermore, there remains the need to present those solutions that empower individuals to proceed to the next stages that represent embracing the mindfulness state of mind, by boosting productivity, cultivating joy, and sharping awareness, zeroing in on dynamic and powerful key concepts, such as: business, knowledge, human resource (HR), innovation, intangible asset (IA), intellectual capital (IC), leadership, Sustainable Development Goals (SDGs), well-being, mindfulness, environment, organizational culture, and creativity.

Thus, there are several vital concepts that have prompted our attention and that are believed to have a strong connection with the process of enhancing the impressive, inspiring, and profound mindfulness movement in organizations, while boosting productivity, cultivating joy, and sharping awareness, while focusing on building inclusive global knowledge societies for sustainable development, as follows: global knowledge societies (GKS) for sustainable development (SD); green, resilient, and inclusive development (GRID); mindfulness; mindfulness into the business environment; mindfulness movement in organizations; promoting mental health; resilience and inclusive growth; and Sustainable Development Goals (SDGs).

All these key concepts as well as the links between these pivotal concepts and the mindfulness movement in organizations are presented in the lines below.

The first concept under analysis is the global knowledge societies (GKS) for sustainable development (SD) and represents, on the one hand, a defining feature of the Post-COVID-19 Era, and constitute, on the other hand, a valuable characteristic of the continuously developing and constantly growing societies which have successfully placed a high degree of importance on preparing people for an inclusive and sustainable future and world, that ought to be governed by the Sustainable Development Goals (SDGs), thus managing to be in line with the newest global competence frameworks that are generated with the aid of individuals' which need to become more and more aware of their potential in terms of mindfulness, well-being, mental health, work climate, and business environment. In continuation, these days, the development of people's social and emotional skills represents a crucial asset for our society, since values such as respect, self-confidence and a sense of belonging, are rapidly growing in importance, and are meant to generate new and impressive opportunities for all individuals, thus contributing to the advancement of our society and to the promotion of the assessment of individuals' global competence, which enables the processes of fostering global competence for more inclusive, more robust, and more resilient societies for all.

The second concept under analysis is the green, resilient, and inclusive development (GRID) which refers to the fact that, these days, all the international organizations worldwide and all the prominent leaders worldwide are turning their attention to accomplishing green, resilient, and inclusive development (GRID) for all individuals and for all societies, due to the overwhelming and highly alarming levels of air pollution, land pollution, and water pollution, due to the pollution-related deaths – which are usually believed to occur, according to the most recent statistics, in low-income, and middle-income countries, and, also, due to climate change, immigration stresses, poverty, and homelessness challenges. Also, according to specialists, long-term sustainability is based on fostering green, resilient, and inclusive development (GRID) which represent healthier solutions and healthier ways that different societies have to adopt in order to encompass the major problems with which they have confronted themselves with and which lead to growing structural weaknesses over the last decades – especially lately, due to the new changes, challenges, and perspectives that were brought by the COVID-19 pandemic and the COVID-19 crisis.

The third concept under analysis is represented by mindfulness, which according to specialists is a highly influential concept today, since more and more individuals, and more and more specialists worldwide recommend the exercises, meditation, and practices which are specific to maintaining moment-by-moment awareness of people's thoughts, feelings, sensations, in accordance to the surroundings and the environment where the people try to be part of. While going more in-depth with our analysis, it should be stated that, in essence, the vital characteristic of mindfulness that ought to be highlighted is that all the situations that individuals are facing should be taken without any form of judgment, should be accepted as such, in order for the individuals to be able to find the inner strength and the inner solutions to cope with those situations and be able to go to the next levels of their lives, their carriers, their proposed stages in terms of goals, objectives, and targets.

The fourth concept under analysis is represented by mindfulness into the business environment, which according to the studies represents probably the most challenging and the most novel approach that can be provided these days in organizations, in terms of creating, ensuring, and fostering long-term individual awareness, well-being, and mental health while referring to the people's work climate and business surroundings. Furthermore, it should be highlighted that the approach and analysis of mindfulness into the business environment departs from the necessity of ensuring resilient, robust, and sustainable development (SD) strategies at the level of entities worldwide, in order to promote global knowledge societies (GKS) for sustainable development (SD), as well as green, resilient, and inclusive development (GRID), while targeting the accomplishment of the Sustainable Development Goals (SDGs) on the long-run; furthermore, by introducing and maintaining mindfulness into the business environment, especially in the times governed by the COVID-19 pandemic and the COVID-19 crisis, entities worldwide are helped to deal with competitive, demographic, global, economic, legal, political, social, and technological adjustments, advances, and provocations, which will essentially come to represent one of the best and, probably, one of the most successful, solutions to ensuring high levels of financial well-being, performance, and profitability of businesses in the Post-COVID-19 Era.

The fifth concept under analysis is represented by mindfulness movement in organizations, which represents a very powerful manner in which, these days, individuals become integrating part of mindfulness practices all around the world, learning to center – in a peaceful and non-judgmental way – on the present moment; in essence, the importance of mindfulness practices resides in learning how to achieve inner calm, how to develop a positive mindset, how to acquire the targeted goals while managing to heal from the day to day stress and inevitable pressure that both society and entities put on people.

The sixth concept under analysis is represented by the activities and the measures taken by promoting mental health, which represent, on the one hand, a real challenge for specialists these days, and, in the same time, on the other hand, an essential step for a better and more safer environment for all individuals, especially in the context in which several prominent organizations, among which could be successfully mentioned the Organization for Economic Co-operation and Development (OECD), the United Nations (UN) agency, and the World Health Organization (WHO) have shown more and more interest in understanding the causes that lead to mental illnesses and the actions and the solutions due to be taken in order to promote human development and to obtain human development indicators that "may help describe the effectiveness of macro policies on mental health" (World Health Organization (WHO), 2005, p. 200).

The seventh set of concepts under analysis is represented by resilience and inclusive growth, which are believed to be two of the most important issues targeted by the agenda of highly influential and major international organizations, such as the Organization for Economic Co-operation and Development (OECD), the United Nations (UN) agency, and the Climate Change Committee (CCC), thorough different types of programs, like the United Nations Development Program (UNDP) or the United Nations (UN) Sustainable Development Goals (SDGs) in the framework of the 2030 Agenda. Moreover, based on the most recent literature in the field, resilience and inclusive growth make reference to the most popular and the most successful instruments, methods, models, and tools that are capable to empower regions and countries at a global level to create and to foster inclusive growth models (such as, for instance, the European inclusive growth model, or the OECD Inclusive Growth Project), which have become, over time, essential to supporting the economic development (ED). Furthermore, in essence, according to prominent economic, political, and social leaders worldwide, inclusive growth stands for economic growth that has been distributed in a fair way across society and which has the power to generate new opportunities for all individuals and for all entities, since it is based on several main pillars, among which could be mentioned the following ones: (a) fostering high, efficient, and sustained growth meant to create, on the one hand, productive jobs for all, and, on the other hand, economic opportunities for all; (b) investing in the most relevant domains of our society, such as education, health, other social services, thus expanding people's capacity to be healthy, productive, and have an adequate state of well-being, and either diminishing or eliminating market and institutional failures and social exclusion at all levels of the society; and (c) establishing social safety nets which would become capable to protect the poor individuals of our society and to mitigate the risks of different but inevitable societal shocks (economic, financial, demographic shocks, which could be associated with different types of crisis, such as, the COVID-19 pandemic and the COVID-19 crisis).

The eight concept under analysis is represented by Sustainable Development Goals (SDGs) which represents an integrating part of the "2030 Agenda for Sustainable Development (SD)", which has been adopted by all United Nations (UN) Member States in 2015, and have the capacity to provide a common blueprint that mainly focuses on world peace and global prosperity for all the people worldwide as well as the planet, now and into the future (United Nations (UN), 2015). In continuation to the aforementioned issues, it should be highlighted that the 17 Sustainable Development Goals (SDGs), represent according to the "2030 Agenda for Sustainable Development (SD)" an important and urgent desiderate for action due to be taken by all developed and developing countries all around the world, as a result of "a global partnership", having as key priorities "ending poverty and other deprivations", while addressing common and strong "strategies that improve health and education, reduce inequality, and spur economic growth – all while tackling climate change and working to preserve our oceans and forests" (United Nations (UN), 2015).

The idea proposed by nations worldwide of reaching the "national growth through regional prosperity", especially as countries' response to the COVID-19 pandemic and the COVID-19 crisis, leads to the following key ideas: "A region's economic assets are crucial to its ability to compete, but intangible factors such as the time it takes to commute to a job, the proximity of universities and health services, and personal and vehicular safety considerations. In many countries, there is a marked region-to-region difference in all these factors" (Organization for Economic Co-operation and Development (OECD), 2022a). Also, the Post-COVID-19 Era brings with it the promise of better coping with the effects of the

COVID-19 pandemic and the COVID-19 crisis, by finding solutions to increase growth and enhance national and regional prosperity, while focusing on individuals' well-being, health, and bright future (Popescu, 2017; Popescu, 2018; Popescu, 2019a; 2019b; 2019c; 2019d; 2019e; 2019f; 2019g). In continuation, the United Nations (UN) Sustainable Development Goals (SDGs) come to support people's need to find solutions to increase growth and enhance national and regional prosperity, while focusing on individuals' well-being, health, and bright future, and, also, shed a new light on the importance of reaching a balance between individuals' actions and activities, while seeking solutions to preserve the ecosystems and the biodiversity at a large scale (Popescu, 2020a; 2020b; 2020c; 2020d; Popescu, 2021a; 2021b; 2021c; 2021d).

Thus this current section has shown that nowadays there exists a profound need to support the mindfulness movement in organizations, since specialists consider the mindfulness movement in organizations as highly impressive and particularly inspiring, since the mindfulness movement in organizations has the power to boost productivity, cultivate joy, and shape awareness among people, offering the common basis for a better future for all, on the road of building inclusive global knowledge societies for sustainable development (SD), while addressing the changes and the challenges targeted by the United Nations (UN) Sustainable Development Goals (SDGs).

DISCUSSION AND SYNTHESIS OF RESULTS

The discussion and synthesis of results section of the book chapter entitled "Impressive, inspiring, and profound mindfulness movement in organizations: boosting productivity, cultivating joy, and sharping awareness", as an integrating part of the "Handbook of Research on Building Inclusive Global Knowledge Societies for Sustainable Development", emphasizes the need to take specific actions and steps in order to ensure "joint action on mental health and well-being" as well as a better understanding and a better implementation of "mindfulness-based interventions and learning" at all levels and in all domains worldwide (European Union (EU), 2017; Organization for Economic Co-operation and Development (OECD), 2019).

Step 1: The first step that requires close consideration refers to the individuals' need to know more about the benefits and the opportunities offered by practicing mindfulness and being part of mindfulness movement in day-to-day lives as well as in organizations. In this particular matter, it should be highlighted that the documentation on "Joint Action on Mental Health and Well-being (MH-WB): Mental Health and Schools. Situation analysis and recommendations for action", published by the European Union, in the framework of the Health Program, as part of the Second Program for Community Action for Health 2008-2013, has demonstrated that "inter-sectorial collaboration was found to be consistently lacking" in terms of presenting the "interventions, evaluation of coverage and outcomes" as well as "the findings of the review and analysis carried out by 9 European Countries (Croatia, England, Estonia, Finland, Italy, Iceland, Malta, Norway, Slovak Republic), one Region (Galicia Region, Spain) and one Municipality based in Sweden (Botkyrka) in the area of the mental health and well-being of children and adolescents", which practically raises the crucial importance of the involvement of mindfulness in certain fields and domains at a global level (European Union (EU), 2017, pp. 13-14). The same aforementioned documentation has successfully emphasized the fact that there exists the need for "a structural framework for the collaboration between the health, education, social and significant other sectors for the promotion of mental well-being, prevention and treatment of mental and behavioral disorders of children and adolescents, with a special focus on the interventions carried out in the school setting", which may lead, in due time, to "the promotion of mental well-being, prevention and treatment of mental and behavioral disorders of" adult population and facilitate the interaction of people in specific environments, such as, for instance, the business environment, where different entities, companies, and organizations should learn how to interact and how to perform better, more efficiently, and more humanly, especially when referring to the addressing and accomplishing the Sustainable Development Goals (SDGs) (European Union (EU), 2017, p. 14).

Step 2: The second step that requires close consideration refers to the fact that mindfulness and other well-being interventions "may uniquely contribute to a well-rounded education in concert with other SEL interventions" (where the acronym SEL stands for "Social-Emotional Learning") "have the potential to improve student well-being, health, and learning", which would lead to the need to further address and value the potential of mindfulness and other well-being interventions into the daily lives of individuals, into their normal routine, and at the places of work (Organization for Economic Co-operation and Development (OECD), 2019, p. 8, p. 21). In this case, recent studies focused on "Mindfulness and Learning in the Laboratory" have shown that the application of mindfulness techniques "are particularly relevant to key aspects of cognition for learning, such as mind-wandering, cognitive flexibility, emotion regulation, executive functioning, and stress reduction" (Organization for Economic Co-operation and Development (OECD), 2019, p. 9).

Step 3: The third step that requires close consideration refers to the fact that "the interventions most likely to promote mental health are those that are set up with no specific mental health goal, such as interventions aimed at empowerment of specific groups in the population", as noted by the World Health Organization (WHO) in the 2005 documentation on "Promoting Mental Health. Concepts. Emerging Evidence. Practice. A Report of the World Health Organization, Department of Mental Health and Substance Abuse in collaboration with the Victorian Health Promotion Foundation and The University of Melbourne", published in Geneva, Switzerland (World Health Organization (WHO), 2005, p. 200). To some extent, specialists have managed to promote the idea that, on the one hand, they "believe that the best action for promotion of mental health in developing countries will come not from evidence-based programs, but from our acknowledgement that human development and mental health are inextricably linked", and, on the other hand, that "the strategies most likely to promote mental health are likely to be those found within existing human development initiatives that combat the core social and economic inequities that are ultimately the basis of much human suffering today" (World Health Organization (WHO), 2005, p. 200). In continuation to the aspects highlighted above, it should be stressed that by promoting mental health at a worldwide level the specialists are facing, on the one hand, a real challenge these days, and, in the same time, on the other hand, the specialists are in front of an essential step for a better and more safer environment for all individuals, especially in the context in which several prominent organizations, among which could be successfully mentioned the Organization for Economic Co-operation and Development (OECD), the United Nations (UN) agency, and the World Health Organization (WHO) have shown more and more interest in understanding the causes that lead to mental illnesses and the actions and the solutions due to be taken in order to promote human development and to obtain human development indicators that "may help describe the effectiveness of macro policies on mental health" (World Health Organization (WHO), 2005, p. 200).

SOLUTIONS AND RECOMMENDATIONS

The solutions of recommendations section of the book chapter entitled "Impressive, inspiring, and profound mindfulness movement in organizations: boosting productivity, cultivating joy, and sharping awareness", as an integrating part of the "Handbook of Research on Building Inclusive Global Knowledge Societies for Sustainable Development", addresses the implications of mindfulness movement in organizations, in terms of boosting productivity, cultivating joy, and sharping awareness, reaching a wide range of topics and wide range of opportunities and possibilities, especially in the new context that is currently represented by the challenges of the Post-COVID-19 Era.

Based on the documents analyzed, mindfulness movement in organizations represents a key solution and a major opportunity in the Post-COVID-19 Era, since it shows the need for specialists to start promoting and implementing mindfulness programs in schools, in order to make individuals more and more aware of the importance of their mental health and well-being as well as of the way in which boosting productivity, cultivating joy, and sharping awareness might be accomplished successfully with the aid of programs that reach out to the people's needs, desires, and inner balance.

In this matter, for instance, the documentation belonging to the Organization for Economic Co-operation and Development (OECD), 2019, prepared by the Directorate for education and Skills Education Policy Committee, and entitled "Future of Education and Skills 2030: Curriculum Analysis. Draft - The Science of Mindfulness-Based Interventions and Learning: A Review for Educators (EDU/EDPC(2019)15)", which has been presented during the 10th Informal Working Group, between the 23rd and the 25th of October 2019, in Ilsan and Seoul, Korea, has indicated that "mindfulness may improve cognitive abilities that are key to learning outcomes, and may have a complementary relationship with other interventions such as retrieval practice", while the field experiments showed promising findings, being a relevant "indicative of high feasibility, low risk, and suggest generalizability across diverse groups, ages, genders, and cultures" (Organization for Economic Co-operation and Development (OECD), 2019, p. 4). In continuation, the same documentation cited above has managed to provide "practical advice and best practices for the implementation of mindfulness training in schools, and highlight the promising future of digital mindfulness-based interventions as a scalable and affordable way to implement mindfulness in educational contexts", which leads us to the conclusion that mindfulness in organizations represents a valuable asset for individuals, which could treasure much better the opportunities that might encounter in terms of learning the mindfulness techniques, instruments, and methods especially if having the change to learn them in school (Organization for Economic Co-operation and Development (OECD), 2019, p. 4).

In the same line with the aspects highlighted above, the documentation on "Joint Action on Mental Health and Well-being (MH-WB): Mental Health and Schools. Situation analysis and recommendations for action", published by the European Union, in the framework of the Health Program, as part of the Second Program for Community Action for Health 2008-2013, brings to the attention the following aspects: "The Policy Recommendations included at the end of this report are constructed on the premise that the school and pre-school educational contexts represent the core setting both in terms of reaching the target (i.e., children and adolescents) as well as in terms of promoting interaction with the significant other sectors", being "intended to provide a structural framework for the collaboration between the health, education, social and significant other sectors for the promotion of mental well-being, prevention and treatment of mental and behavioral disorders of children and adolescents, with a special focus on the interventions carried out in the school setting" (European Union (EU), 2017). For example, among the solutions of recommendations due to be encountered in "Joint Action on Mental

Health and Well-being (MH-WB): Mental Health and Schools. Situation analysis and recommendations for action", published by the European Union, in the framework of the Health Program, as part of the Second Program for Community Action for Health 2008-2013, the following key issues might be brought to light, as follows: (1) "Strengthen information and research on mental health and well-being among children and adolescents"; (2) "Promote schools as a setting where health promotion and prevention of mental and behavioral disorders and early identification can reach all children and young people"; (3) "Enhance training for all school staff on mental health"; and (4) "Consider schools as part of a wider network with other stakeholders and institutions involved in mental health of children and adolescents in local communities" (European Union (EU), 2017, pp. 14-15).

In terms of solutions of recommendations due to be found in this context, it should be mentioned that responsibility represents the key for taking better actions and for making better decisions when it comes to providing a power message through the mindfulness movement in organizations, in order to be able to boost productivity, cultivate joy, and sharp awareness among all individuals (Popescu, 2022a; 2022b; 2022c; 2022d; 2022e; 2022f; 2022g). In this matter, a very good example is provided by the "Organization for Economic Co-operation and Development (OECD)-FAO Guidance for Responsible Agricultural Supply Chains", in which it has been successfully highlighted that the "agricultural enterprises are a major source of growth and development", especially in the context in which these entities are responsible for offering "expertise, technology, and financing capacities to provide safe and nutritious food to a growing population and meet our changing energy demands", and, also, are believed to be "critical for the fulfillment of the Sustainable Development Goals (SDGs)", since these organizations act as key players having "a key role in generating quality investment, decent employment, and supply chains that benefit producers and consumers" (Organization for Economic Co-operation and Development (OECD), 2022). Also, it should be remembered that creating and maintaining "the framework on risk-based due diligence" in terms of responsible agricultural enterprises is essential according to the Organization for Economic Co-operation and Development (OECD), due to the fact that "companies can systematically identify, assess and mitigate potential negative impacts associated with their business" and, in the same time, "companies can implement into their business models and processes" the practical approaches that proved to be successful over time (Organization for Economic Co-operation and Development (OECD), 2022). According to specialists, taking the right and the responsible decisions and, in the same time, being aware and mindful about the future of our society, represents the very essence of ensuring a stable and secure future for the generations due to come, thus constantly concentrating on the objectives promoted by the Sustainable Development Goals (SDGs) (Popescu & Dumitrescu, 2019; Popescu & Popescu, 2014; Popescu & Popescu, 2015; Popescu & Popescu, 2018; Popescu & Popescu, 2019a; 2019b; 2019c).

FUTURE RESEARCH DIRECTIONS

The future research directions section of the book chapter entitled "Impressive, inspiring, and profound mindfulness movement in organizations: boosting productivity, cultivating joy, and sharping awareness", as an integrating part of the "Handbook of Research on Building Inclusive Global Knowledge Societies for Sustainable Development", takes into consideration the forms in which this current scientific work might be further continued and the information highlighted here might be further enhanced, analyzed, and disseminated.

In the authors' opinion, the impressive, inspiring, and profound mindfulness movement in organizations might be successfully linked to "the science of mindfulness-based interventions and learning", thus boosting productivity, cultivating joy, and sharping awareness at a wide, more complex, and highly comprehensive level (Organization for Economic Co-operation and Development (OECD), 2019, p. 1). This particular idea came after a thorough analysis of the documentation belonging to the Organization for Economic Co-operation and Development (OECD), 2019, prepared by the Directorate for education and Skills Education Policy Committee, and entitled "Future of Education and Skills 2030: Curriculum Analysis. Draft - The Science of Mindfulness-Based Interventions and Learning: A Review for Educators (EDU/EDPC(2019)15)", which has been presented during the 10th Informal Working Group, between the 23rd and the 25th of October 2019, in Ilsan and Seoul, Korea. The major question that has been addressed in the aforementioned documentation is represented by "Is there sufficient evidence that mindfulness training is ready to be implemented in schools?", and the purpose of challenging specialists in the field to go "beyond the relatively comprehensive literature on mindfulness and mental health", in order to "investigate whether mindfulness can help students learn" (Organization for Economic Co-operation and Development (OECD), 2019, p. 4). In this context, the study on the "Future of Education and Skills 2030: Curriculum Analysis. Draft - The Science of Mindfulness-Based Interventions and Learning: A Review for Educators (EDU/EDPC(2019)15)" began "by drawing on laboratory studies in experimental psychology and cognitive science", and then reflected "on research conducted in schools and other applied contexts", briefly discussed "key insights from the neuroscience of mindfulness, and compare mindfulness to other well-known learning interventions", and has successfully shown "that mindfulness interventions have the potential to make students more focused, to help them regulate their emotions, to be more flexible and creative, and to change their brains in a way that encourages greater conscious control of their thoughts, feelings, and actions" (Organization for Economic Co-operation and Development (OECD), 2019, p. 4). In this matter, a future research direction that could be considered could be the one that should focus on finding the present and the future benefits and the present and the future opportunities between promoting mindfulness movement in organizations by better understanding "the science of mindfulness-based interventions and learning", and by starting to use "mindfulness-based interventions and learning" for individuals in schools (Organization for Economic Co-operation and Development (OECD), 2019, p. 4).

Also, in the authors' opinion, the impressive, inspiring, and profound mindfulness movement in organizations might be successfully linked to the process of taking "joint action on mental health and well-being", as recommended in the documentation on "Joint Action on Mental Health and Well-being (MH-WB): Mental Health and Schools. Situation analysis and recommendations for action", published by the European Union, in the framework of the Health Program, as part of the Second Program for Community Action for Health 2008-2013 (European Union (EU), 2017). In general lines, it should be brought to the attention that the report on "Joint Action on Mental Health and Well-being (MH-WB): Mental Health and Schools. Situation analysis and recommendations for action", published by the European Union "has been prepared in the framework of the Joint Action on Mental Health and Well-being funded under the Second Programme for Community Action for Health 2008-2013" and "presents the findings of the review and analysis carried out by 9 European Countries (Croatia, England, Estonia, Finland, Italy, Iceland, Malta, Norway, Slovak Republic), one Region (Galicia Region, Spain) and one Municipality based in Sweden (Botkyrka) in the area of the mental health and well-being of children and adolescents" (European Union (EU), 2017, p. 13). It is our opinion that the subject of the impressive, inspiring, and profound mindfulness movement in organizations might be successfully linked to the process of taking "joint action on mental health and well-being", in the context in which "the economic impact of mental disorders and well-being, the potential economic savings of public mental health interventions, the issue as pertaining specifically to children and adolescents, the relevance of the school setting for promotion and prevention initiatives and finally the importance of inter-sectorial collaboration as a key to achieving more effective and sustainable health outcomes" have been regarded by specialists as major subjects of concern in the current context at a large level (European Union (EU), 2017, p. 13).

In terms of future research directions, there should be pointed out that there are numerous analysis and connections that could be made between different types of international guides and frameworks, such as, for example, the Organization for Economic Co-operation and Development (OECD) Due Diligence Guidance for different domains and fields of activities (Popescu *et al.*, 2015; Popescu *et al.*, 2017a; 2017b, 2017c, 2017d, 2017e; Popescu & Popescu, 2014; Popescu & Popescu, 2015). In this regard, the Organization for Economic Co-operation and Development (OECD) Due Diligence Guidance for Meaningful Stakeholder Engagement in the Extractive Sector represents "a guide for practitioners in the mining, oil and gas industries" and it has the purpose of providing "a practical framework for identifying and managing risks with regard to stakeholder engagement activities to ensure companies play a role in avoiding and addressing adverse impacts as defined in the OECD Guidelines for Multinational Enterprises" (Organization for Economic Co-operation and Development (OECD), 2022c; Organization for Economic Co-operation and Development (OECD), 2022b). In addition, by taking the actions and the measures mentioned in the lines above, forecasting the future of our society will have to take into account the evolutions of all major trends that will be identified, over time, in all the major sectors (Popescu *et. al*, 2009; Popescu *et. al*, 2011; Popescu *et. al*, 2014; Popescu *et. al*, 2015; Popescu *et. al*, 2017; Popescu *et. al*, 2009; Popescu *et. al*, 2016a).

Thus, on the desire to build inclusive global knowledge societies for sustainable development (SD) has led to the belief that these days there is a tremendous need to focus on the impressive, inspiring, and profound mindfulness movement in organizations, in the attempt of boosting productivity, cultivating joy, and sharping awareness for all people, at a general level, and, in the same time, to become more and more concerned about the impact that the abrupt disruptions and changes in our society (such as, pandemics, crisis, wars) might have on individuals' mental-health, well-being, inner balance, and inner state of awareness (Popescu *et. al*, 2016b; Popescu *et. al*, 2017; Popescu *et. al*, 2009; Popescu *et. al*, 2013; Popescu *et. al*, 2009a; Popescu *et. al*, 2009b; Popescu *et. al*, 2010).

CONCLUSION

The conclusions section of the book chapter entitled "Impressive, inspiring, and profound mindfulness movement in organizations: boosting productivity, cultivating joy, and sharping awareness", as an integrating part of the "Handbook of Research on Building Inclusive Global Knowledge Societies for Sustainable Development", has the power to show the importance of mindfulness movement in organizations, while emphasizing the ways in which boosting productivity, cultivating joy, and sharping awareness can be accomplished successfully in challenging and complex times such as the ones that humanity faces currently.

First of all, it should be remembered at all times, that individuals' state of mind and general health are responsible for the individuals capacity to perform better, for longer time periods, be more productive, and accomplish higher objectives, targets, and aims. Thus, it should be noted that the book chapter centers on presenting the meaning of the concept of "mindfulness", with a particular emphasis on describing the main characteristics, the importance, and the role of this term for individuals and for organizations, particularly since according to specialists, the concept of "mindfulness" has become lately more and more popular among entities worldwide. Also, it should be taken into consideration that based on the ideas of specialists highlighted in this scientific work, the concept of "mindfulness" comes hand in hand with individuals' ability and capacity to be more productive especially in the context in which the working environment is inclined towards cultivating joy, and sharping awareness, even in the context of sometimes overwhelming and overpowering competition among colleagues, clients, and organizations.

Second of all, it should be stated that the book chapter focuses on introducing the concept of "mindfulness movement", while addressing the most important challenges that are derived from introducing the term of "mindfulness movement" in organizations worldwide, starting from the fact that today's "mindfulness movement" in organizations worldwide targets individuals' well-being, mental health, and will to become better, stronger, more balanced, and more aware of the personal needs as well as the need of others and the planet. In other words, the term of "mindfulness movement" in organizations worldwide should be analyzed together with other noteworthy concepts, such as: Global Knowledge Societies (GKS) for Sustainable Development (SD), Green, Resilient, and Inclusive Development (GRID), Resilience and Inclusive Growth, and Sustainable Development Goals (SDGs) (see, in this matter, the correlations done by the authors of this current book chapter in the section "Key Terms and Definitions", due to be encountered at the end of this scientific work).

Third of all, the book chapter concentrates on presenting and describing the most significant adjustments, alternations, changes, fluctuations, and modifications that have occurred in people's day-to-day lives as well as in organizations' activities as a result of introducing the concept of "mindfulness" to the employees of different organizations, thus enabling them to become an integrating and an influential part of the mindfulness movement in entities. In this particular matter, it ought to be stressed that by introducing the concept of "mindfulness" to the employees of different organizations worldwide, people are offered a tremendous opportunity as well as a great chance and support to be part of something greater than the individuals' own thoughts, needs, desires, and objectives in this live. For instance, according to this current study, the concept of "mindfulness" of the employees of different organizations worldwide offers individuals the opportunity to be more connected with their inner needs and inner selves, while addressing, in the same time, the global objectives represented by sustainability and sustainable development, in a society that revolves around three main pillars, namely the economic, the environmental, and the social pillars. However, it has been more and more highlighted that, in this particular case, the emphasis should be more on people and on our planet, rather than on productivity and profits, since the planets resources are limited and subject to constant sources of pollution. What is more, specialists worldwide strongly believe that the use natural resources and energy must be done in such a way that it should offer the future generations the change to a healthy, robust, and sustainable ecosystems, well conserved and preserved, thus centering on the planet's sustainable development (SD). Furthermore, the authors of this book chapter strongly believe that "mindfulness" of people, in general, and of organizations' employees, in particular, should be done in accordance to the sustainable development (SD) desiderates, thus, on the one hand, limiting "the usage of natural resources", and, on the other hand, giving these natural resources the "proper time for their refreshment" (United Nations (UN), 2015).

Fourth of all, it should be stressed that the book chapter tackles the manner in which people are able to bring mindfulness into the business environment, in order to become gradually aware of their inner power and their surroundings, and act towards achieving the Sustainable Development Goals (SDGs) –

which represent a major priority these days for the entire humanity, especially due to the constant and constant challenges that are specific to the demographic, global, economic, legal, political, social, and technological domains, spheres, and dimensions. In this matter, it should be emphasized that the concept of "mindfulness" has a paramount influence and power when it comes to addressing individuals' state of mind, state of health, inner balance in terms of inner thoughts, desires, aims, and general state of well-being in direct relation with the environment. That is precisely why, according to the authors of this book chapter, acting towards achieving the Sustainable Development Goals (SDGs) should be seen also as a form of finding viable solutions to support live on this planet, the preservation of all live forms, as well as robust heath for all. When focusing on the Sustainable Development Goals (SDGs), one should take into account that the Sustainable Development Goals (SDGs) represent an integrating part of the "2030 Agenda for Sustainable Development (SD)", which has been adopted by all United Nations (UN) Member States in 2015. Also, in the same line, one should take into consideration the fact that the Sustainable Development Goals (SDGs) have the capacity to provide a common blueprint that mainly focuses on world peace and global prosperity for all the people worldwide as well as the planet, now and into the future (United Nations (UN), 2015). In continuation to all the aspects highlighted in the lines above, it should be highlighted that the 17 Sustainable Development Goals (SDGs), represent according to the "2030 Agenda for Sustainable Development (SD)" an important and urgent desiderate for action due to be taken by all developed and developing countries all around the world, as a result of "a global partnership", having as key priorities "ending poverty and other deprivations", while addressing common and strong "strategies that improve health and education, reduce inequality, and spur economic growth – all while tackling climate change and working to preserve our oceans and forests" (United Nations (UN), 2015).

Fifth of all, the book chapter analyzes the importance and the role of mindfulness for individuals, thus enhancing the tremendous benefits of the impressive, inspiring, and profound mindfulness movement in organizations, especially in the context in which human resources (HRs) and intellectual capital (IC) have become the most important and the most precious intangible assets (IA) that organizations possess these days. In addition, mindfulness movement in organizations comes to support the idea that individuals have to find solutions in order to be able to cope better "with stress, study problems, time management", as well as with their "anxiety, and depression", thus specialists have prompted the fact that it has been "well-established that mindfulness can improve well-being, and reduce stress, anxiety, and depression" (Organization for Economic Co-operation and Development (OECD), 2019, p. 5). For instance, in this regard, specialists have reached the following dominant conclusions: "Mindfulness interventions in education may provide one fruitful approach", and "(…) the range of positive outcomes associated with mindfulness practice is striking" (Organization for Economic Co-operation and Development (OECD), 2019, p. 5).

Sixth of all, the book chapter presents those solutions that empower individuals to proceed to the next stages that represent embracing the mindfulness state of mind, by boosting productivity, cultivating joy, and sharpening awareness, zeroing in on dynamic and powerful key concepts, such as: business, knowledge, human resource (HR), innovation, intangible asset (IA), intellectual capital (IC), leadership, Sustainable Development Goals (SDGs), well-being, mindfulness, environment, organizational culture, and creativity. In context, it should be noted that "the scientific literature provides many examples of mindfulness-related changes in brain function and structure", however, "these findings should be interpreted carefully, as while the field has certainly matured (…), longitudinal studies that track the same individual over longer periods of time with active controls are necessary to provide more direct evidence for the effects of mindfulness and a full understanding of the neural mechanisms underlying these effects", while "most of the neuroscientific studies on mindfulness have so far been conducted in adults, and currently, relatively less is known about how mindfulness may affect the developing brain (…)" (Organization for Economic Co-operation and Development (OECD), 2019, p. 20).

It has been recognized by specialists, at a global level, that the power of decision-making represents a strong engagement towards engagement performance, sound business management practices, and robust business operations (Popescu *et. al*, 2011; Popescu *et. al*, 2012a; 2012b; Popescu *et. al*, 2013; Popescu *et. al*, 2014; Popescu *et. al*, 2015a; 2015b; 2015c). Also, while focusing on the issues highlighted in the lines above, it should be considered that "companies can contribute to positive social and economic development when they involve stakeholders, such as local communities, in their planning and decision making", especially in the case of those particular entities that have been, over time, "associated with extensive social, economic and environmental impacts" (Organization for Economic Co-operation and Development (OECD), 2022c).

ACKNOWLEDGMENT

This research received no specific grant from any funding agency in the public, commercial, or not-for-profit sectors.

REFERENCES

Eurasian Economic Commission (EEC), United Nations Conference on Trade and Development (UNCTAD), & Interstate Bank (IB). (2019). *Inclusive growth of the Eurasian Economic Union Member States: Assessments and opportunities.* http://www.eurasiancommission.org/ru/act/integr_i_makroec/dep_makroec_pol/Documents/Inclusive_growth_in_EAEU_Member.pdf

European Commission (EC). (2022). *Joint European Roadmap towards lifting COVID-19 containment measures.* https://ec.europa.eu/info/sites/default/files/communication_-_a_european_roadmap_to_lifting_coronavirus_containment_measures_0.pdf

European Observatory on Health Systems and Policies & World Health Organization. (2007). *Mental Health Policy and Practice across Europe. The future direction of mental health care.* Open University Press. https://www.euro.who.int/__data/assets/pdf_file/0007/96451/E89814.pdf

European Union (EU). (2017). *Joint Action on Mental Health and Well-being (MH-WB): Mental Health and Schools. Situation analysis and recommendations for action, published by the European Union, in the framework of the Health Program.* The Second Programme for Community Action for Health 2008-2013. https://ec.europa.eu/health/system/files/2017-07/2017_mh_schools_en_0.pdf

Fielden, K. (2005). Mindfulness: An Essential Quality of Integrated Wisdom. In J. Courtney, J. Haynes, & D. Paradice (Eds.), *Inquiring Organizations: Moving from Knowledge Management to Wisdom* (pp. 211–228). IGI Global. doi:10.4018/978-1-59140-309-8.ch011

Global Wellness Institute (GWI). (2019). *Move to be Well: The Global Economy of Physical Activity*. https://globalwellnessinstitute.org/wp-content/uploads/2019/10/2019-Physical-Activity-Economy-FINAL-NEW-101019.pdf

Grupe, D. W., Smith, C., & McGehee, C. (2021). Introducing Mindfulness Training and Research Into Policing: Strategies for Successful Implementation. In E. Arble & B. Arnetz (Eds.), *Interventions, Training, and Technologies for Improved Police Well-Being and Performance* (pp. 125–149). IGI Global. doi:10.4018/978-1-7998-6820-0.ch007

Gupta, S. K. (Ed.). (2022). *Handbook of Research on Clinical Applications of Meditation and Mindfulness-Based Interventions in Mental Health*. IGI Global. doi:10.4018/978-1-7998-8682-2

International Labor Organization (ILO). (2018). *Global Commission on the future of work. New business models for inclusive growth. Issue Brief.* Prepared for the 2nd Meeting of the Global Commission on the Future of Work. https://www.ilo.org/wcmsp5/groups/public/---dgreports/---cabinet/documents/publication/wcms_618172.pdf

Organisation for Economic Co-operation and Development (OECD). (2018). *Preparing Our Youth for an Inclusive and Sustainable World: The OECD PISA global competence framework*. https://www.oecd.org/education/Global-competency-for-an-inclusive-world.pdf

Organisation for Economic Co-operation and Development (OECD). (2019). *Future of Education and Skills 2030: Curriculum Analysis. Draft - The Science of Mindfulness-Based Interventions and Learning: A Review for Educators.* 10th Informal Working Group. 23 – 25 October 2019. Ilsan and Seoul, Korea. EDU/EDPC(2019)15. Directorate For Education And Skills Education Policy Committee. https://www.oecd.org/officialdocuments/publicdisplaydocumentpdf/?cote=EDU/EDPC(2019)15&docLanguage=En

Organization for Economic Co-operation and Development (OECD). (2022a). *National growth through regional prosperity: OECD Regions at a Glance*. https://www.oecd.org/newsroom/nationalgrowththroughregionalprosperityoecdregionsataglance.htm

Organization for Economic Co-operation and Development (OECD). (2022b). *OECD-FAO Guidance for Responsible Agricultural Supply Chains*. http://mneguidelines.oecd.org/rbc-agriculture-supply-chains.htm

Organization for Economic Co-operation and Development (OECD). (2022c). *OECD Due Diligence Guidance for Meaningful Stakeholder Engagement in the Extractive Sector*. http://mneguidelines.oecd.org/stakeholder-engagement-extractive-industries.htm

Popescu, C. R. (2021a). Sustainable and Responsible Entrepreneurship for Value-Based Cultures, Economies, and Societies: Increasing Performance Through Intellectual Capital in Challenging Times. In C. Popescu & R. Verma (Eds.), *Sustainable and Responsible Entrepreneurship and Key Drivers of Performance* (pp. 33–58). IGI Global. doi:10.4018/978-1-7998-7951-0.ch002

Popescu, C. R. (2021b). Measuring Progress Towards the Sustainable Development Goals: Creativity, Intellectual Capital, and Innovation. In C. Popescu (Ed.), *Handbook of Research on Novel Practices and Current Successes in Achieving the Sustainable Development Goals* (pp. 125–136). IGI Global. doi:10.4018/978-1-7998-8426-2.ch006

Popescu, C. R. (2022a). Mindfulness at Work, a Sound Business Investment: Focusing on the Employee Well-Being While Increasing Creativity and Innovation. In C. Popescu (Ed.), *Handbook of Research on Changing Dynamics in Responsible and Sustainable Business in the Post-COVID-19 Era* (pp. 1–34). IGI Global. doi:10.4018/978-1-6684-2523-7.ch001

Popescu, C. R. (2022b). Impact of Innovative Capital on the Global Performance of the European Union: Implications on Sustainability Assessment. In C. Popescu (Ed.), *Handbook of Research on Novel Practices and Current Successes in Achieving the Sustainable Development Goals* (pp. 90–124). IGI Global. doi:10.4018/978-1-7998-8426-2.ch005

Popescu, C. R. (2022c). Mindfulness Business Principles: Producing Outstanding Value and Encouraging Community Connections. In C. Popescu (Ed.), *COVID-19 Pandemic Impact on New Economy Development and Societal Change* (pp. 196–228). IGI Global. doi:10.4018/978-1-6684-3374-4.ch010

Popescu, C. R. (2022d). Environmental, Social, and Corporate Governance by Avoiding Management Bias and Tax Minimization: Reaching a General Consensus Regarding a Minimum Global Tax Rate. In C. Popescu (Ed.), *COVID-19 Pandemic Impact on New Economy Development and Societal Change* (pp. 94–132). IGI Global. doi:10.4018/978-1-6684-3374-4.ch006

Popescu, C. R. G. (2017). The Role Of Total Quality Management In Developing The Concept Of Social Responsibility To Protect Public Interest In Associations Of Liberal Professions. *Amfiteatru Economic, 19*, 1091-1106.

Popescu, C. R. G. (2018). "Intellectual Capital" - Role, Importance, Components and Influences on the Performance of Organizations - A Theoretical Approach. *32nd Conference of the International-Business-Information-Management-Association (IBIMA). Vision 2020: Sustainable Economic Development And Application Of Innovation Management.*

Popescu, C. R. G. (2019b). Business Development Opportunities: Demonstrating Present And Future Performance, Auditing Intellectual Capital: A Case Study On Romanian Organizations. *33rd International-Business-Information-Management-Association (IBIMA) Conference. Vision 2025: Education Excellence and Management of Innovations through Sustainable Economic Competitive Advantage.*

Popescu, C. R. G. (2019c). Intellectual Capital, Integrated Strategy and Performance: Focusing on Companies' Unique Value Creation Mechanism and Promoting Better Organizational Reporting In Romania: A Framework Dominated By the Impact of Green Marketing and Green Marketing Strategies. *33rd International-Business-Information-Management-Association (IBIMA) Conference. Vision 2025: Education Excellence and Management of Innovations through Sustainable Economic Competitive Advantage.*

Popescu, C. R. G. (2019d). Demonstrating How Universities Extend Value Creation And Performance: Convergence Between Intellectual Capital Contributions And Research Quality - A Romanian Collective Intelligence Framework. *11th International Conference on Education and New Learning Technologies (EDULEARN). EDULEARN19: 11th International Conference On Education And New Learning Technologies.*

Popescu, C. R. G. (2019e). Using Intellectual Capital Measurements In Universities To Assess Performance - Evidence From The Romanian Education System. *11th International Conference on Education and New Learning Technologies (EDULEARN). EDULEARN19: 11th International Conference On Education And New Learning Technologies.*

Popescu, C. R. G. (2019f). Intellectual Capital Evaluation And Measuring Effectiveness - A Case Study On Romania's Experience In Terms Of Performance And Excellence. *13th International Technology, Education And Development Conference (INTED2019). 13th International Technology, Education and Development Conference (INTED).*

Popescu, C. R. G. (2019g). Evaluating Intellectual Capital And Its Influence On Companies' Performance - A Case Study On Romania's Experience. *13th International Technology, Education And Development Conference (INTED2019). 13th International Technology, Education and Development Conference (INTED).*

Popescu, C. R. G. (2020a). Developing a Model for Entrepreneurship Competencies: Innovation, Knowledge Management, and Intellectual Capital – Success Competences for Building Inclusive Entrepreneurship and Organizational Performance. In J. Šebestová (Ed.), *Developing Entrepreneurial Competencies for Start-Ups and Small Business* (pp. 1–22). IGI Global. doi:10.4018/978-1-7998-2714-6.ch001

Popescu, C. R. G. (2020b). Analyzing the Impact of Green Marketing Strategies on the Financial and Non-Financial Performance of Organizations: The Intellectual Capital Factor. In V. Naidoo & R. Verma (Eds.), *Green Marketing as a Positive Driver Toward Business Sustainability* (pp. 186–218). IGI Global. doi:10.4018/978-1-5225-9558-8.ch008

Popescu, C. R. G. (2020c). Approaches to Sustainable and Responsible Entrepreneurship: Creativity, Innovation, and Intellectual Capital as Drivers for Organization Performance. In B. Hernández-Sánchez, J. Sánchez-García, & A. Moreira (Eds.), *Building an Entrepreneurial and Sustainable Society* (pp. 75–95). IGI Global. doi:10.4018/978-1-7998-2704-7.ch004

Popescu, C. R. G. (2020d). Sustainability Assessment: Does the OECD/G20 Inclusive Framework for BEPS (Base Erosion and Profit Shifting Project) Put an End to Disputes Over The Recognition and Measurement of Intellectual Capital? *Sustainability, 12*(23), 10004. . doi:10.3390/su122310004

Popescu, C. R. G. (2021c). Impact of Innovative Capital on the Global Performance of the European Union: Implications on Sustainability Assessment. In C. Popescu (Ed.), *Handbook of Research on Novel Practices and Current Successes in Achieving the Sustainable Development Goals* (pp. 90–124). IGI Global. doi:10.4018/978-1-7998-8426-2.ch005

Popescu, C. R. G. (Ed.). (2021d). *Handbook of Research on Novel Practices and Current Successes in Achieving the Sustainable Development Goals*. IGI Global. doi:10.4018/978-1-7998-8426-2

Popescu, C. R. G. (2022e). Fostering Creativity in Business: Empowering Strong Transformational Leaders. In C. Popescu (Ed.), *Handbook of Research on Changing Dynamics in Responsible and Sustainable Business in the Post-COVID-19 Era* (pp. 349–381). IGI Global. doi:10.4018/978-1-6684-2523-7.ch017

Popescu, C. R. G. (Ed.). (2022f). *COVID-19 Pandemic Impact on New Economy Development and Societal Change*. IGI Global. doi:10.4018/978-1-6684-3374-4

Popescu, C. R. G. (Ed.). (2022g). *Handbook of Research on Changing Dynamics in Responsible and Sustainable Business in the Post-COVID-19 Era*. IGI Global. doi:10.4018/978-1-6684-2523-7

Popescu, C. R. G., & Dumitrescu, M. (2019). About Decisions: International Environment For Business And Perspectives Before And After The Financial Crisis - Roles Played By Corporate Governance, Knowledge Asymmetry And Intellectual Capital In The Romanian Business Environment. *34th International-Business-Information-Management-Association (IBIMA) Conference. Vision 2025: Education Excellence and Management of Innovations through Sustainable Economic Competitive Advantage.*

Popescu, C. R. G., & Popescu, G. N. (2014). Theoretical contributions concerning performance - the way to achieve excellence. *24th International-Business-Information-Management-Association Conference (IBIMA) Conference. Crafting Global Competitive Economies: 2020 Vision Strategic Planning & Smart Implementation.*

Popescu, C. R. G., & Popescu, G. N. (2015). What is Total Quality Management and how Can It Be Used in the Development of an Economy - A Case Study on Romania's Experience. *6th LUMEN International Conference on Rethinking Social Action Core Values. Rethinking Social Action. Core Values.*

Popescu, C. R. G., & Popescu, G. N. (2018). Methods of Evaluating "Intellectual capital" of an Organization and Ways of Enhancing Performance in the Knowledge-based Economy - A Synthetically Approach. *32nd Conference of the International-Business-Information-Management-Association (IBIMA). Vision 2020: Sustainable Economic Development And Application Of Innovation Management.*

Popescu, C. R. G., & Popescu, G. N. (2019a). The Social, Economic, and Environmental Impact of Ecological Beekeeping in Romania. In G. Popescu (Ed.), Agrifood Economics and Sustainable Development in Contemporary Society (pp. 75-96). IGI Global. doi:10.4018/978-1-5225-5739-5.ch004

Popescu, C. R. G. & Popescu, G. N. (2019b). An Exploratory Study Based on a Questionnaire Concerning Green and Sustainable Finance, Corporate Social Responsibility, and Performance: Evidence from the Romanian Business Environment. *Journal of Risk and Financial Management, 12*(4), 162. . doi:10.3390/jrfm12040162

Popescu, C. R. G., & Popescu, G. N. (2019c). International Environment For Business: Economic Growth, Sustainable Development, Competitiveness And The Power Of Intellectual Capital - Focus On Romanian Business Environment. *34th International-Business-Information-Management-Association (IBIMA) Conference. Vision 2025: Education Excellence and Management of Innovations through Sustainable Economic Competitive Advantage.*

Popescu, C. R. G., Popescu, G. N., & Popescu, V. A. (2015). Corporate Governance in Romania: Theories and Practices. In Corporate Governance And Corporate Social Responsibility: Emerging Markets Focus (pp. 375-401). World Scientific Publ Co Pte Ltd.

Popescu, C. R. G., Popescu, G. N., & Popescu, V. A. (2017a). Assessment Of The State Of Implementation Of Excellence Model Common Assessment Framework (CAF) 2013 By The National Institutes Of Research - Development - Innovation In Romania. *Amfiteatru Economic, 19*(44), 41-60.

Popescu, C. R. G., Popescu, G. N., & Popescu, V. A. (2017b). Sustainability Leadership, the Key to a Better World - A Case Study on Romania's Situation. *29th International-Business-Information-Management-Association Conference (IBIMA). Sustainable Economic Growth, Education Excellence, And Innovation Management Through Vision 2020.*

Popescu, C. R. G., Popescu, G. N., & Popescu, V. A. (2017c). International Migration, Attempting To Create a Better World - A Case Study on Romania's Situation. *29th International-Business-Information-Management-Association Conference (IBIMA). Sustainable Economic Growth, Education Excellence, And Innovation Management Through Vision 2020.*

Popescu, C. R. G., Popescu, G. N., & Popescu, V. A. (2017d). Illusion of Diversity and Certitude of ChangeIn Buyers Tastes - Soft Drinks Industry Global Overview: Nowadays Key Trends. *30th International Business-Information-Management-Association Conference (IBIMA). Vision 2020: Sustainable Economic Development, Innovation Management, And Global Growth.*

Popescu, C. R. G., Popescu, G. N., & Popescu, V. A. (2017e). The What, Why and How of Performance-Driven Funding In Sports Industry - Economics and Management of Sports Industry's Competitive Strategy. *30th International Business-Information-Management-Association Conference (IBIMA). Vision 2020: Sustainable Economic Development, Innovation Management, And Global Growth.*

Popescu, C. R. G., & Popescu, V. A. (2014). The concept of excellence in business organizations - Case of Romania. *24th International-Business-Information-Management-Association Conference (IBIMA) Conference. Crafting Global Competitive Economies: 2020 Vision Strategic Planning & Smart Implementation.*

Popescu, C. R. G., & Popescu, V. A. (2015). Enhancing Learning by Improving Organizational Performance in the Quality Field - A Case Study on Romania's Experience on Business Process Management. *6th LUMEN International Conference on Rethinking Social Action Core Values. Rethinking Social Action.*

Popescu, C. R. G., Popescu, V. A., & Popescu, G. N. (2009). New Economy From Supremacy - To The Sudden Crisis. *Metalurgia International, 14,* 109-112.

Popescu, C. R. G., Popescu, V. A., & Popescu, G. N. (2011). Alternative Fuels - New Perspectives For A Bright Future. In *Crises After The Crisis: Inquiries From A National, European And Global Perspective, Vol. IV. 18th International Economic Conference on Crisis After the Crisis - Inquiries from a National European and Global Perspective.*

Popescu, C. R. G., Popescu, V. A., & Popescu, G. N. (2014). Excellence models for performance management: Case study: The evolution of "quality concept" in Japan - the Japanese model of excellence. Academic Press.

Popescu, C. R. G., Popescu, V. A., & Popescu, G. N. (2015). The Entrepreneur's Role In The Performance Growth Of The Financial Audit Activity In Romania. *Amfiteatru Economic, 17*(38), 228-246.

Popescu, C. R. G., Popescu, V. A., & Popescu, G. N. (2017). Forecasting Of Labour Market And Skill Needs In Nowadays Society - A Case Study On Romania's Situation Facing The Challenges Of The New Economy. *11th International Conference on Technology, Education and Development (INTED). INTED2017: 11th International Technology, Education And Development Conference.*

Popescu, C. R. G., Roman, C., & Popescu, V. A. (2009). Study On The Costs Of Implementing The European Union's Environmental Policy And The Results Of Applying The European Environmental Standards On Competitiveness In Romania. *Metalurgia International, 14*(4), 149-153.

Popescu, G. N., Popescu, C. R. G., & Popescu, V. A. (2016a). The Challenges Of Nowadays Companies, As Economic Organizations - A Case Study On Romania's Situation. *10th International Management Conference (IMC) - Challenges of Modern Management. Proceedings Of The 10th International Management Conference: Challenges Of Modern Management (IMC 2016).*

Popescu, G. N., Popescu, C. R. G., & Popescu, V. A. (2016b). The Textile Industry in the Context of Economic Growth, Economic Development and Sustainable Development - A Nowadays Economic and Managerial Approach. *28th International Business-Information-Management-Association Conference (IBIMA).*

Popescu, G. N., Popescu, C. R. G., & Popescu, V. A. (2017). The Role And The Importance Of The University- Industry Collaboration - A Case Study On Romania's Situation Concerning Today's Educational Trends. *11th International Conference on Technology, Education and Development (INTED). INTED2017: 11th International Technology, Education And Development Conference.*

Popescu, G. N., Popescu, V. A., & Popescu, C. R. G. (2009). Research For Defining The Standards And Identifying The Opportunities For Increasing The Role Of The Green It In The Context Of Improving The Global Economy Management And Monitoring. *Metalurgia International, 14*(8), 48-53.

Popescu, G. N., Popescu, V. A., & Popescu, C. R. G. (2013). What Is Business Intelligence And How Can It Be Used In The Development Of An Economy - A Case Study On Romania's Experience. *7th International Technology, Education And Development Conference (INTED2013).*

Popescu, V. A., Popescu, G. N., & Popescu, C. R. G. (2009a). The Effects Of Informatics Revolution On Organizing The Modern Management, Accounting, Control And Financial Audit. *Metalurgia International, 14*(9), 156-164.

Popescu, V. A., Popescu, G. N., & Popescu, C. R. G. (2010). Global Trends - How Countries Can Learn From History. *Metalurgia International, 14*(5), 186-193.

Popescu, V. A., Popescu, G. N., & Popescu, C. R. G. (2011). "Liquid Assets" Or Turning Fine Wines In A Very Profitable Investment. In Crises After The Crisis: Inquiries From A National, European And Global Perspective, Vol. IV. *18th International Economic Conference on Crisis After the Crisis - Inquiries from a National European and Global Perspective.*

Popescu, V. A., Popescu, G. N., & Popescu, C. R. G. (2012a). Building a culture for innovation through competitive intelligence and accountability: case of Romania. *Innovation And Sustainable Competitive Advantage: From Regional Development To World Economies, Vols. 1-5. 18th International-Business-Information-Management-Association Conference (IBIMA).*

Popescu, V. A., Popescu, G. N., & Popescu, C. R. G. (2012b). Knowledge And Knowledge Management - New Challenges And Future Perspectives. *EDULEARN12: 4th International Conference On Education And New Learning Technologies. Book Series: EDULEARN Proceedings. 4th International Conference on Education and New Learning Technologies (EDULEARN).*

Popescu, V. A., Popescu, G. N., & Popescu, C. R. G. (2013). The Impact Of Higher Education On The Development Of Nowadays Society - A Case Study On Romania's Experience. *7th International Technology, Education And Development Conference (INTED2013). Book Series: INTED Proceedings. 7th International Technology, Education and Development Conference (INTED)*.

Popescu, V. A., Popescu, G. N., & Popescu, C. R. G. (2014). The Economic And Social Dimensions Of Romania's Metallurgical Industry. *Metalurgija, 53*(1), 113-115.

Popescu, V. A., Popescu, G. N., & Popescu, C. R. G. (2015a). The Relation Productivity - Environment In The Context Of Sustainable Development - Case Study On The Romanian Industry. *Metalurgija, 54*(1), 286-288.

Popescu, V. A., Popescu, G. N., & Popescu, C. R. G. (2015b). Competitiveness And Sustainability - A Modern Economic Approach To The Industrial Policy. *Metalurgija, 54*(2), 426-428.

Popescu, V. A., Popescu, G. N., & Popescu, C. R. G. (2015c). The Impact Of Global Crisis On The Dominant Sectors Of The Economy At The Romanian Industry. *Metalurgija, 54*(2), 289-291.

Popescu, V. A., Popescu, G. N., Roman, C., & Popescu, C. R. G. (2009b). From Creative Accounting To The Moral And Financial Crisis. *Metalurgia International, 14*(9), 141-149.

Popescu C. R. G. (2019a). Corporate Social Responsibility, Corporate Governance and Business Performance: Limits and Challenges Imposed by the Implementation of Directive 2013/34/EU in Romania. *Sustainability, 11*(19), 5146.

Rutigliano, N. K., Samson, R. M., & Frye, A. S. (2017). Mindfulness: Spiriting Effective Strategic Leadership and Management. In V. Wang (Ed.), *Encyclopedia of Strategic Leadership and Management* (pp. 460–469). IGI Global. doi:10.4018/978-1-5225-1049-9.ch033

Thomas, H., & Hedrick-Wong, Y. (2019). Enabling models of inclusive growth: Addressing the need for financial and social inclusion. *Global Focus Magazine. The EFMD Business Magazine*. https://www.globalfocusmagazine.com/enabling-models-of-inclusive-growth-addressing-the-need-for-financial-and-social-inclusion/

Underdown, K. O., McCabe, C. L., & McCabe, M. F. (2022). Creating and Maintaining Balance: Work-Life Balance, Self-Care, and Mindfulness. In S. Ramlall, T. Cross, & M. Love (Eds.), *Handbook of Research on Future of Work and Education: Implications for Curriculum Delivery and Work Design* (pp. 533–545). IGI Global. doi:10.4018/978-1-7998-8275-6.ch031

United Nations Development Program (UNDP). (2020). *Sustainable Development Goals (SDGs)*. Booklet. United Nations Development Program.

United Nations (UN). (2015). *Transforming Our World: The 2030 Agenda for Sustainable Development A/RES/70/1*. sustainabledevelopment.un.org. https://sustainabledevelopment.un.org/content/documents/21252030%20Agenda%20for%20Sustainable%20Development%20web.pdf

United Nations (UN). (2021). *The Sustainable Development Goals Report 2021*. https://unstats.un.org/sdgs/report/2021/The-Sustainable-Development-Goals-Report-2021.pdf

World Health Organization (WHO). (2005). *Promoting Mental Health. Concepts. Emerging Evidence. Practice*. A Report of the World Health Organization, Department of Mental Health and Substance Abuse in collaboration with the Victorian Health Promotion Foundation and The University of Melbourne. https://www.who.int/mental_health/evidence/MH_Promotion_Book.pdf

KEY TERMS AND DEFINITIONS

Global Knowledge Societies (GKS) for Sustainable Development (SD): Represent, on the one hand, a defining feature of the Post-COVID-19 Era, and constitute, on the other hand, a valuable characteristic of the continuously developing and constantly growing societies which have successfully placed a high degree of importance on preparing people for an inclusive and sustainable future and world, that ought to be governed by the Sustainable Development Goals (SDGs), thus managing to be in line with the newest global competence frameworks that are generated with the aid of individuals' which need to become more and more aware of their potential in terms of mindfulness, well-being, mental health, work climate, and business environment; what is more, these days, the development of people's social and emotional skills represents a crucial asset for our society, since values such as respect, self-confidence and a sense of belonging, are rapidly growing in importance, and are meant to generate new and impressive opportunities for all individuals, thus contributing to the advancement of our society and to the promotion of the assessment of individuals' global competence, which enables the processes of fostering global competence for more inclusive, more robust, and more resilient societies for all.

Green, Resilient, and Inclusive Development (GRID): These days, all the international organizations worldwide and all the prominent leaders worldwide are turning their attention to accomplishing green, resilient, and inclusive development (GRID) for all individuals and for all societies, due to the overwhelming and highly alarming levels of air pollution, land pollution, and water pollution, due to the pollution-related deaths – which are usually believed to occur, according to the most recent statistics, in low-income, and middle-income countries, and, also, due to climate change, immigration stresses, poverty, and homelessness challenges; according to specialists, long-term sustainability is based on fostering green, resilient, and inclusive development (GRID) which represent healthier solutions and healthier ways that different societies have to adopt in order to encompass the major problems with which they have confronted themselves with and which lead to growing structural weaknesses over the last decades – especially lately, due to the new changes, challenges, and perspectives that were brought by the COVID-19 pandemic and the COVID-19 crisis.

Mindfulness: Represents a highly influential concept today, since more and more individuals, and more and more specialists worldwide recommend the exercises, meditation, and practices which are specific to maintaining moment-by-moment awareness of people's thoughts, feelings, sensations, in accordance to the surroundings and the environment where the people try to be part of; in essence, the vital characteristic of mindfulness that ought to be highlighted is that all the situations that individuals are facing should be taken without any form of judgment, should be accepted as such, in order for the individuals to be able to find the inner strength and the inner solutions to cope with those situations and be able to go to the next levels of their lives, their carriers, their proposed stages in terms of goals, objectives, and targets.

Mindfulness Into the Business Environment: Represents probably the most challenging and the most novel approach that can be provided these days in organizations, in terms of creating, ensuring, and fostering long-term individual awareness, well-being, and mental health while referring to the people's work climate and business surroundings; in continuation, it should be highlighted that the approach and analysis of mindfulness into the business environment departs from the necessity of ensuring resilient, robust, and sustainable development (SD) strategies at the level of entities worldwide, in order to promote global knowledge societies (GKS) for sustainable development (SD), as well as green, resilient, and inclusive development (GRID), while targeting the accomplishment of the Sustainable Development Goals (SDGs) on the long-run; furthermore, by introducing and maintaining mindfulness into the business environment, especially in the times governed by the COVID-19 pandemic and the COVID-19 crisis, entities worldwide are helped to deal with competitive, demographic, global, economic, legal, political, social, and technological adjustments, advances, and provocations, which will essentially come to represent one of the best and, probably, one of the most successful, solutions to ensuring high levels of financial well-being, performance, and profitability of businesses in the Post-COVID-19 Era.

Mindfulness Movement in Organizations: Represents a very powerful manner in which, these days, individuals become integrating part of mindfulness practices all around the world, learning to center – in a peaceful and non-judgmental way – on the present moment; in essence, the importance of mindfulness practices resides in learning how to achieve inner calm, how to develop a positive mindset, how to acquire the targeted goals while managing to heal from the day to day stress and inevitable pressure that both society and entities put on people.

Promoting Mental Health: Represents, on the one hand, a real challenge for specialists these days, and, in the same time, on the other hand, an essential step for a better and more safer environment for all individuals, especially in the context in which several prominent organizations, among which could be successfully mentioned the Organization for Economic Co-operation and Development (OECD), the United Nations (UN) agency, and the World Health Organization (WHO) have shown more and more interest in understanding the causes that lead to mental illnesses and the actions and the solutions due to be taken in order to promote human development and to obtain human development indicators that "may help describe the effectiveness of macro policies on mental health" (World Health Organization (WHO), 2005, p. 200).

Resilience and Inclusive Growth: Are two of the most important issues targeted by the agenda of highly influential and major international organizations, such as the Organization for Economic Co-operation and Development (OECD), the United Nations (UN) agency, and the Climate Change Committee (CCC), thorough different types of programs, like the United Nations Development Program (UNDP) or the United Nations (UN) Sustainable Development Goals (SDGs) in the framework of the 2030 Agenda; based on the most recent literature in the field, resilience and inclusive growth make reference to the most popular and the most successful instruments, methods, models, and tools that are capable to empower regions and countries at a global level to create and to foster inclusive growth models (such as, for instance, the European inclusive growth model, or the OECD Inclusive Growth Project), which have become, over time, essential to supporting the economic development (ED); in essence, according to prominent economic, political, and social leaders worldwide, inclusive growth stands for economic growth that has been distributed in a fair way across society and which has the power to generate new opportunities for all individuals and for all entities, since it is based on several main pillars, among which could be mentioned the following ones: (a) fostering high, efficient, and sustained growth meant to create, on the one hand, productive jobs for all, and, on the other hand, economic opportunities for all; (b) investing in the most relevant domains of our society, such as education, health, other social services, thus expanding people's capacity to be healthy, productive, and have an adequate state of well-being, and either diminishing or eliminating market and institutional failures and social exclusion at all levels of the society; and (c) establishing social safety nets which would become capable to protect the poor individuals of our society and to mitigate the risks of different but inevitable societal shocks (economic, financial, demographic shocks, which could be associated with different types of crisis, such as, the COVID-19 pandemic and the COVID-19 crisis).

Sustainable Development Goals (SDGs): Represent an integrating part of the "2030 Agenda for Sustainable Development (SD)", which has been adopted by all United Nations (UN) Member States in 2015, and have the capacity to provide a common blueprint that mainly focuses on world peace and global prosperity for all the people worldwide as well as the planet, now and into the future (United Nations (UN), 2015); in continuation, it should be highlighted that the 17 Sustainable Development Goals (SDGs), represent according to the "2030 Agenda for Sustainable Development (SD)" an important and urgent desiderate for action due to be taken by all developed and developing countries all around the world, as a result of "a global partnership", having as key priorities "ending poverty and other deprivations", while addressing common and strong "strategies that improve health and education, reduce inequality, and spur economic growth – all while tackling climate change and working to preserve our oceans and forests" (United Nations (UN), 2015).

Chapter 4
An Analysis of the Health Economic Impacts of COVID-19 and Government Financial Packages in Its Management

Nima Norouzi
https://orcid.org/0000-0002-2546-4288
Bournemouth University, UK

Sajedeh Rabipour
https://orcid.org/0000-0001-8450-1723
Islamic Azad University, UAE

ABSTRACT

This chapter focuses on the extent of government intervention against COVID-19 and compares and evaluates support packages in different countries based on available statistical evidence. Economic interventions were described by collecting statistical data from government reports and international organizations. The statistical sample includes 46 countries with the highest number of patients as of May 20, 2021. Comparing the success rate of the health system (net ratio of the number of recovered to the number of patients with COVID-19) and the share of government support in countries affected by the COVID-19 virus shows a positive correlation coefficient of 0.26. The high recovery rate of COVID-19 patients in Iran has been achieved while the Iranian economy is under inhumane US sanctions. The experience of COVID-19 crisis management in Iran shows that the general mobilization of facilities and capabilities can turn any threat into an opportunity for the country's progress, growth, and excellence.

INTRODUCTION

Covid-19 viruses form an extensive family of enveloped, positive-stranded RNA viruses. Micro components of Covid-19 viruses infect many mammals and birds and cause diseases of the upper respiratory

DOI: 10.4018/978-1-6684-5109-0.ch004

tract, gastrointestinal tract, liver, and central nervous system (Gallagher & Buchmeier,2001). Covid-19 viruses infect the upper respiratory tract in humans and birds, while Covid-19 viruses in pigs and cattle cause intestinal infections that ultimately lead to severe economic losses (Perlman et al, 1999).

The first human Covid-19 viruses were isolated by different the United States and Great Britain techniques almost simultaneously. The British Research Council, Joint Cold Research Unit, has studied the secretions of people with natural respiratory infections using standard methods of cell culture isolation or by inoculating them into human volunteers (Reed, 1984).

It has been more than four and a half months since the official announcement of the Covid-19 virus outbreak in the Chinese city of Wahan. During this period, various hypotheses such as inadvertent or intentional leakage from the Wuhan Institute of Virology or natural genetic mutation of the virus have been proposed by researchers, politicians, and intelligence agencies on how this deadly virus works. However, these hypotheses and opinions are not certain and have not been proven.

On the other hand, statistical evidence from different countries shows that the risk and rate of spread of this virus, contrary to initial assumptions, is very high, and it has a higher rate of spread among large populations, and men are more vulnerable to the virus than women

Other countries that have officially reported Covid-19 outbreaks after China have attributed the outbreak, usually to the human-to-human transmission through air travel and border crossings. By the end of May 2021, according to Worldometers data, the number of patients has exceeded 170 million, and the number of deaths has exceeded 3.86M (Deb et al., 2021). Thus, the mortality rate of this disease in the world is close to 6.5 percent. Iran officially confirmed the occurrence of Covid-19 with the official confirmation of two cases in the city of Qom on February 20, 2020. Since then, according to the official statistics of the Ministry of Health, Treatment and Medical Education, the number of patients has reached 3.1M, the number of deaths is 82965, and the number of recovered people has reached 2.75M. Thus, the mortality rate of Covid-19 in Iran is slightly lower than the global average (~6%), and the recovery rate is approximately 78%. Given that Iran is subject to unfair and inhumane US sanctions in various economic, commercial, and medical dimensions, Iran's achievements in managing and dealing with the Covid-19 crisis are remarkable and show the dedication of the medical staff and the mobilization of all facilities inside the country.

Different countries have implemented various short-term plans to deal with the Covid-19. These programs have affected various economic, social, and cultural dimensions. In this article, the extent of government intervention in the fight against Covid-19 is examined, and support packages in different countries are compared and evaluated according to statistical evidence.

Background

One of the main challenges in health is identifying the factors that determine the number of resources that the country allocates for health care. The literature (Deng & Huang, 2009; Etokakpan et al., 2020) in this field confirm the direct and significant relationship between environmental quality and community health in the long run. In other words, although environmental degradation does not pose a significant threat to public health in the short term, it poses a serious threat to public health in the long run. Countries that have inadvertently caused more damage to the environment have been fined for heavy health care costs in the long run. Finally, the environment's quality can be considered one of the determinants of health costs in the short and long term.

The definition of health from the perspective of the World Health Organization is to enjoy complete physical, mental, and social well-being and not just to have no disease or disability (Franklin et al., 2015).

According to this definition, it is considered that the issue of health in society is a multidimensional category that encompasses a wide range of aspects of human life. Therefore, a country can be considered at an acceptable level of health that has an acceptable status in various aspects involved (effective) in this issue (Fazli & Abbasi, 2018).

As a result, in the comparison between countries in this field, a set of indicators should be considered, or use indicators calculated as a result of other indicators in the fields of disease and health, welfare, social indicators, etc., which will be addressed in the following(Grossman & Krueger, 1995).

On the other hand, in the economic literature, it has been proven that a country with a higher level of production and productivity will inevitably have a higher level of savings and investment, and more investment will mean more production and national income. This cycle can go on continuously. This is well evident in developed countries with high per capita incomes(Danish & Wang, 2018) . On the other hand, higher per capita income means higher purchasing power (and spending) in various areas, including (purchase) of consumer goods, durable goods, welfare, recreational services, health services, environmental expenditures, cultural affairs, etc. Therefore, it is obvious that in a country with a higher national (or per capita) income, the expenditures on consumer goods, recreation, health, environmental services, etc. (compared to other countries) are higher than in a developing country. Therefore, it can be said that the relationship between economic growth and health is a direct relationship. This means that the higher the level of economic growth, the better one can expect to be in terms of health indicators. Obviously, in this case, along with economic growth in its general sense, factors such as increasing health awareness of citizens, the quality of health services, etc., for example, using the capabilities of information and communication technology and in the electronic field, in particular, are involved (Grossman & Krueger, 1996).

Based on theoretical foundations and empirical observations, the importance of health expenditure challenge in health economics is due to the relationship between health expenditure and growth, examined directly and indirectly. In the direct effect approach, if health expenditure is seen as an investment in the accumulation of human capital, then by considering human capital as the engine of economic growth, any increase in health expenditure through an improvement in human capital stock will increase revenue. Will follow. In the indirect effect approach, the increase in health expenditures leads to an increase in life expectancy and longevity and a reduction in working days, which loses the workforce and increases the supply of labor and production(Huang & Chen, 2020).

Also, because a healthier workforce has higher motivation and productivity, health expenditures can lead to increased production if it promotes health in the community. Meanwhile, some economists believe that government health spending can harm output growth because it is part of consumer spending and reduces investment opportunities. On the other hand, improving health if other conditions are stable means fewer resources will be spent on treatment in the future. Therefore, some resources that should be spent on treatment in the future can be used for other purposes (Hao et al., 2018; Jalil & Feridun, 2011).In this regard, it seems that countries are seeking to reduce environmental waste as the development process simultaneously, and in other words, they are pursuing different approaches to sustainable development. But what is common in different development approaches is the observance of environmental considerations and the reduction of various types of pollution. Because the first consequence of pollution is an increase in some diseases and endangering human health, however, this phenomenon seems to have a long-term nature. Among all types of pollution, air pollution, which has recently become one of the main problems of life in large cities, is a complex problem that requires national and even international determination to solve. Cases such as pulmonary respiratory diseases, pediatric anesthesia, decreased intellectual and worked efficiency of the community, nervous stress, and physical and mental fatigue are the effects of this type of infection on the economic and mental health of the community and reciprocally medical costs of the community. In Iran, pollution in different wards affects factors such as mortality, increased respiratory disease, suicide, the increased occupancy rate of hospital beds, other social costs, etc. has negative effects on the economy and the community's health(Kaput & Roschelle, 2013).

The relationship between economic growth and inverted U-quality is known as the Kuznets environmental curve. In the early years of economic growth, environmental degradation increases, but after reaching a certain level of growth, the environment improves. In other words, in the high stages of growth, environmental degradation decreases (Kurt, 2015).

Researchers have proposed various methods to study the relationship between economic growth and the environment. One of these methods is EKC, which examines the impact of economic growth on various aspects of environmental quality. This method is based on the U-curve of Kuznets (Li & Fang, 2011).

Researchers (Li et al., 2021) explain the relationship between economic growth and environmental pollution in an experimental study based on the Simon Kuznets curve. According to this curve, Kuznets concludes that economic growth in a developing country does not increase uniformly over time, but rather that income increases to a certain level and then enters a downward trend. By generalizing the Kuznets curve to the relationship between economic growth and environmental quality, two main points can be made: First, the environment is like a commodity. In underdeveloped and less developed economies, the demand for tangible goods is more important than the demand for the environment. When an economy develops and reaches a certain level, the demand for a good quality environment increases. The second is the impact of economics and technology on the environment. As the economy grows, more natural resources are consumed, and carbon and waste production increase. But when the scale of the economy reaches a certain threshold, more technologically advanced sectors replace the consumption resources of the industrial sector. In this situation, the emission of pollution and waste is reduced, and in parallel, policies to protect environmental health and the use of appropriate technologies improve the environmental situation. When a country specializes in producing one or more goods due to the special conditions of trade and the international division of labor, it can export the said goods and exchange them for goods that other countries produce at lower costs and with better quality. In this case, the country with a relative advantage in producing that product will increase its national income. Researchers have shown that unbalanced economic growth and various factors such as trade liberalization and environmental policies create curves like the Kuznets curve (Meadows & Randers, 2012).

Based on theoretical foundations and empirical observations, the importance of health expenditure challenge in health economics is due to the relationship between health expenditure and growth, examined directly and indirectly. In the direct effect approach, if health expenditure is seen as an investment in the accumulation of human capital, then by considering human capital as the engine of economic growth, any increase in health expenditure through an improvement in human capital stock will increase revenue. In the indirect effect approach, an increase in health expenditures leads to an increase in life expectancy, longevity, and a reduction in working days that the workforce loses due to illness or that of its relatives, and will increase labor supply and production. Also, because a healthier workforce has higher motivation and productivity, health expenditures can lead to increased production if it promotes health in the community. Meanwhile, some economists believe that government health spending can harm output growth because it is part of consumer spending and reduces investment opportunities. On the other hand, improving health if other conditions are stable means fewer resources will be spent on treatment in the future(Olulu et al., 2014; Pelletier et al., 2014).

Therefore, some resources that should be spent on medical expenses in the future can be used for other purposes (Ricci, 2007).

In a study, authors(Tamazian & Rao, 2010) examined the relationship between air pollution and heart disease and the costs to patients. They found that air pollution impacts cardiovascular disease and the spread of acute heart disease and has high costs for these individuals and the community. Accordingly, people with known or suspected cardiovascular disease, including the elderly, diabetics, pregnant women, and lung disease, are advised to exercise their leisure activities outdoors when air pollution is high. In the long run, this will harm economic growth and reduce society's efficient workforce(Solaymani, 2021).

In a study, researchers examined data from 213 countries, including low-, middle- and high-income countries, between 1970 and 2008. The results indicate a positive relationship between per capita income and per capita pressure on nature, and this effect is more pronounced in middle-income countries than in low-income and high-income countries. Also, the use of various institutional and structural auxiliary variables showed the existence of this positive effect. The researchers recognized the negative impact of increased trade on the environment and confirmed the instability of economic growth, especially in middle-income countries(Tamazian & Rao, 2010). A study examined the effects of air pollutant abuse on health. They found that exposure to air pollutants increased mortality and hospitalization due to cardiovascular and respiratory diseases(Zhang & Meihan, 2020). In another study, due to high consumption and growing demand for coal in China, short-term and long-term relationships between coal consumption and national income were examined in a two-way supply-demand pattern to find economic effects and air pollution(Zhang et al, 2017). For this purpose, they used econometric models for vector error correction and collective. The results show a direct two-way relationship between coal consumption, carbon dioxide emissions, and pollution emissions in the short and long term. It was also concluded that there is an indirect relationship between coal consumption and GDP on the supply side, while on the demand side, the opposite is true(Zafar et al., 2019; Liu & Ao, 2021).

A study investigated the impact of economic growth and energy consumption on environmental pollution using the ARDL method in China from 1995-2011. The results indicate that China's negative financial development rate does not increase carbon dioxide emissions and reduce pollution. Also, in the long run, carbon dioxide emissions are mainly explained by national income, energy consumption, and trade liberalization(Yazdi et al., 2014).

In their study of 24 economies in transition, researchers examine that it can be detrimental to the environment if financial liberalization is not placed in a strong institutional framework. Also, according to the study results, the EKC hypothesis is valid for the target countries(Coccia, 2021).

Using the panel data method, a study investigated the impact of air pollution (as an indicator of environmental quality) on health economics in the group of selected middle-income countries and countries with the highest air pollution. Estimating the models using the fixed effects method in the group of selected countries in 2000-2016 shows that air pollution has a positive and significant effect on health in developing countries (Blázquez-Fernández et al,. 2019).

A novel study using Johansson and Joselius co-integration method 1995-2014 or considering carbon dioxide emissions and arable land for environmental quality, concluded that in addition to the long-term balance between exports and Environmental quality indicators, export variables and foreign direct investment have a significant negative impact on environmental quality indicators(Zhang et al., 2020).

The relationship between energy consumption, economic growth, and carbon dioxide emissions as a measure of environmental pollution worldwide is studied. For this purpose, they used time-series data for 1990-2015 and used the error correction model. This study indicates a positive relationship between independent variables such as energy consumption, economic growth, trade liberalization, population, and carbon dioxide emissions (kubatko & Kubatko, 2019). An article examined the causal relationship between variables using the Toda and Yamato methods. They result from three one-way causal relationships: carbon dioxide emissions to per capita income, carbon dioxide emissions to per capita energy consumption, and per capita energy consumption to water pollution(Apergis et al., 2020)

A study examined the Granger causality relationship between energy consumption, national income, and carbon dioxide emissions by adding labor and capital variables. Their results indicate a one-way causal relationship between national income, energy consumption, and carbon dioxide emissions, but the causality between national income and carbon dioxide emissions is not confirmed(Zhang et al., 2018).

METHODS AND MATERIALS

This is a descriptive-analytical study. Given that the documents and complete reports on the consequences of the actions and programs of countries against Covid-19 have not yet been officially presented, the description of their programs and outputs is based on the best information available. For this purpose, international organizations such as the World Health Organization, the World Bank, the International Labor Organization, the International Monetary Fund, and the country's initial reports of various organizations and ministries have been studied. Thus, the method of data collection is documentary and library.The statistical population of the study is 215 UN member states. The statistical sample includes 46 countries with several cases above 1M (including China as the source of Covid-19 prevalence, USA, Spain, Italy, France, Germany, England, Turkey, Iran, Russia, Brazil, India, Peru, Canada, Saudi Arabia, Belgium, Mexico, Chile, Pakistan, Netherlands, Qatar, Ecuador, Belarus, Sweden, Switzerland, Portugal, Singapore, Bangladesh, UAE, Ireland, Poland, Ukraine, Indonesia, Romania, South Africa, Colombia, Kuwait, Israel, Japan, Austria, Egypt, Dominican Republic, Philippines, Denmark, South Korea, and Serbia) until May 31, 2021.

RESULTS AND DISCUSSION

The ratio of the number of deaths and the number of recoveries to the total number of patients are two very important indicators for evaluating the success rate of the health system of countries, with the difference that the ratio of deaths should be kept to a minimum and the ratio of recovered to a maximum. These ratios are calculated in table 1 for the top 15 countries with the highest incidence. In this table, Iran ranks third in terms of recoveries (excluding Britain) and eighth in terms of deaths, while the United States has the worst position in terms of recoveries. Countries can also be ranked according to the number of Covid-19 patients and the number of recoveries per 10,000 population. Accordingly, among 215 small and large countries, Iran ranks 141st regarding the number of patients and 82nd regarding mortalities. Figure (1) shows the distribution of Covid-19 deaths versus per capita income logarithm (IMF, 2020). According to this figure, there is no regular pattern between the two variables. In other words, there is no clear relationship between the level of development and economic well-being of countries and the degree of success in controlling Covid-19 disease. The selected sample also confirms this fact. In the study sample, industrialized countries and oil countries- It is located in the Middle East and Eastern Europe, and these countries have been selected from the four major continents of the world. The simple correlation coefficient between the per capita income logarithm and the death ratio is weak (+ 0.28).

The spread of the Covid-19 virus in the shadow of global communications and business and travel tourism and cultural, artistic, and sports communities and low estimates of its effects compared to cases of SARS, Ebola, and Morse disease, caused that after China, Italy, and Iran, Asian countries And then European and American countries quickly become infected with this deadly virus.

The procedures adopted to reduce the rate of transmission of the disease have been similar almost everywhere. Reduction of workers' working hours, forced dismissal of workers and reduction of the level of high-risk production and service activities in areas affected by the disease and prohibition of religious ceremonies, sports competitions, and cultural-artistic events and in some cases, short and medium-term quarantine of the first government measures It has been in most of the countries studied. According to the reports of the International Labor Organization, the International Monetary Fund, the World Food and Agriculture Organization, and the World Bank, the effects of these measures (rising unemployment and thus increasing unemployment insurance claims), a sharp decline in prices and global oil demand, figure Negative expectations for the future of world economic growth, the fall of major stock indices and the increase in government spending have been expressed.

The occurrence of Covid-19, policies to control it, countermeasures and management measures, as well as related economic consequences, indicate that in the economic analysis of the Covid-19 epidemic, we must look for causation from the outbreak of Covid-19 virus and the occurrence of Covid-19 to policies. Consider the economics of governments and, in particular, financial support and incentive packages. In other words, it was Covid-19 that led to the prevailing expansionary fiscal and monetary policies in most countries in the Covid-19 crisis and vice versa.

On the other hand, in influencing government measures and policies to control the Covid-19, it is reasonable to assume that increased government intervention would cause a relative reduction in the death rate from Covid-19 disease and a relative increase in the recovery rate. However, it should be remembered that in the occurrence of epidemics, effective- Most government policies, without public cooperation and social participation, will not be enough to contain the epidemic.

The most important economic indicators to assess the relative success of economies are the unemployment rate (labor market and employment variables), the inflation rate (a measure of economic stability and the general level of prices), and the economic growth rate (indicating changes in GDP). In the continuation of the discussion, based on official reports, the status of these indicators will be briefly evaluated.

Table 1. Performance ratios of health systems of 51 selected countries against Covid-19

Country	Recovery rate	Rank	Mortality Rate	Rank
China	94.31	1	5.59	7
Germany	88.22	2	4.61	6
Iran	77.99	3	5.71	8
Turkey	74.46	4	2.77	3
Spain	70.64	5	9.96	12
Italy	57.08	6	14.19	13
Saudi Arabia	52.85	7	0.55	1
Canada	50.62	8	7.47	11
India	39.58	9	3.09	5
Brazil	39.28	10	6.61	10
Peru	36.71	11	2.93	4
France	34.60	12	15.50	15
Russia	27.66	13	0.96	2
USA	22.99	14	5.95	9
UK	n.a.	15	14.2	14

Figure 1. Distribution of ratio in the past of Covid-19 against per capita income logarithm

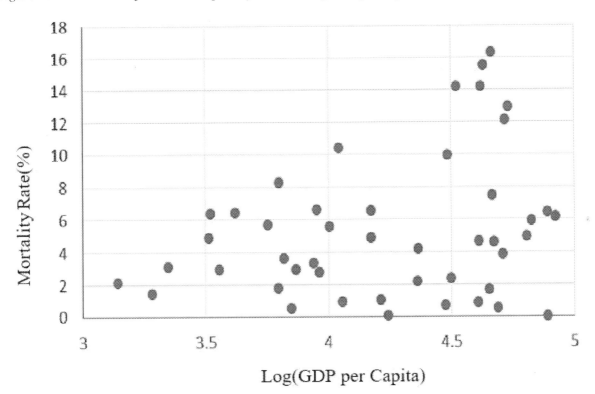

An Analysis of the Health Economic Impacts of COVID-19

The International Labor Organization, in its April 2020 report on Global Labor Market Monitoring, Lost Hours of Work (Compulsory Unemployment Index), Ratio of Closed Businesses, Covid-19 -Affected Trades, and Activities, and Impact of the Covid-19 Crisis on Informal Employment, has examined. According to the report, the average "reduction in working hours" in the world, which was about 4.5 hours in the first half of 2020, will increase to 10.5 hours in the second half of 2020 (i.e., more labor will be voluntarily unemployed). Among them, the largest reduction in working hours is projected in North America (from 1.3 hours to 9.6 hours) and then the Arab countries from 1.8 to 10.3 hours) and in the next place in Europe and Central Asia (from 1.9 to 11.8 hours). The effect of the Covid-19 crisis on the employment market by production and service activities is presented in Table 2. According to the table, the most impact of this crisis on retail and wholesale activities, repair of motor vehicles and motorcycles with 232 million injured people (21 million employers and 211 million self-employed workers) and the least vulnerable sector, the field of public administration, It will be defense and social security. Also, in informal employment, the International Labor Organization estimates that 47% of all employment in reference countries is affected. In low-income countries, about 68 percent, and in high-income countries, about 15 percent of total employment will be affected by informal employment as Covid-19.

Table 2. The effect of the Covid-19 crisis on the employment market by production and service activities

Sector	Total affected by the crisis (million)	self-employed workers (million)	Employers (million)
Retail and wholesale activities, repair of motor vehicles and motorcycles	212	211	21
Factory production	111	99	12
Accommodation and food services	51	44	7
Real estate, business, and office activities	42	35	7
Art, entertainment, recreation, and other services	61	57	4
Transportation, warehousing and transportation	80	76	4
Building	112	103	9
Finance and insurance	4	3	1
Mining and mining	<4	3	<1
Agriculture, forestry, and fisheries	489	470	19
Health and social activities	13	11	2
Education	8	7	1
Water, bar, gas	<4	3	<1
Defense and government management, social security	<1	0	<1

The disease has affected the supply of goods and ultimately their prices through disruption of the supply chain. With declining economic growth and declining supply, inflation seems to be a natural phenomenon. The World Bank forecasts that the average oil price will drop to $ 35 a barrel in 2020 (down 43% from the average $ 61 a barrel in 2019) due to declining tourism, passenger transportation, delays in industrial orders, and increased crude oil storage (Abedi et al., 2021). Energy prices (including crude oil, natural gas, and coal are projected to average 40 percent lower in 2020 than in 2019. The cessation of economic activity has upset the balance of supply and demand for mineral goods. It is expected to Metal prices fall, slowing economic growth in China, which accounts for half of the global metal demand, will affect industrial metal prices, but gold has risen as the portfolio changes from stocks to precious metals. Following the outbreak of the Covid-19, global rice prices have reached a seven-year high, and wheat prices have risen 15 percent since the second half of March(Agba et al., 2020).

Covid-19 was initially a local shock to the Chinese economy, but it has shocked the global economy due to the epidemic. In an economic study, a standard computable general equilibrium (CGE) model is used to simulate the potential impact of Covid-19 on GDP (8). In this study, Covid-19 economic shocks are divided into four categories: employment reduction shock by up to 3%, international trade spending increase shock by up to 25%, international tourism reduction shock (50% reduction in consumption tax on related services). Tourism) and the shock of a 15% drop in household demand. In the baseline scenario of the Covid-19 global epidemic, GDP falls 2% below the global average, 2.5% for developing countries, and 1.8% for industrialized countries. In the scenario of the spread of the epidemic and with a long period of control, global GDP will fall by almost 4%. This decrease in GDP has had the greatest effect on the negative shock in the production of domestic services affected by this disease and tourism services.

Figure 2. Share of government support for the Covid-19) Percentage of GDP

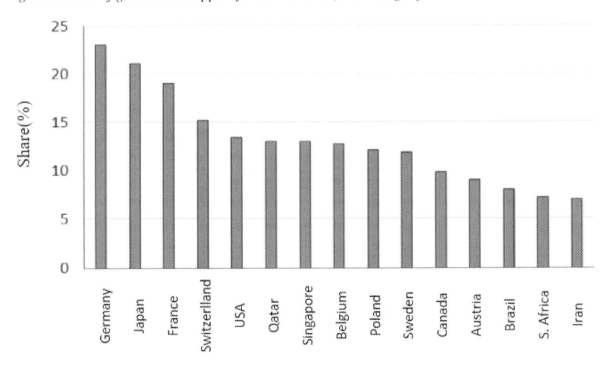

Different countries have designed different measures and executive programs to curb the spread of the Covid-19. But the International Monetary Fund has highlighted the common features of all of these programs in one or more of the following cases (IMF, 2020):

1. Financing the costs of prevention, diagnosis, treatment, and control of epidemic diseases, including the increase of Covid-19 diagnostic tests, production of medical equipment, research on the development of effective drugs and vaccines,
2. Accelerate the payment of unemployment insurance and renew the contracts of employed workers
3. Delay or deferral of taxes and repayment of bank loans
4. Payment of direct assistance to households and enterprises, including wage subsidies, working capital of small and medium-sized companies, gratuitous assistance, payment of salaries without sick leave, employment insurance, an increase of tax credits, and child care assistance
5. Suspension of the payment of the employer and worker's contribution to social security
6. Tariff and VAT exemptions for the import of strategic health products (personal protective equipment and laboratory kits) and food industries and services
7. Financing the health care system, long-term care, short-term work
8. Compensation for income from illness among people - employment, family businesses, and small businesses
9. Guarantee the export funds of companies, including exporters
10. Relative reduction of working hours
11. Deferment of housing rent payment by tenants and extension of rental contracts, payment of housing allowance
12. Providing facilities for the purchase of strategic food products
13. Facilitate health insurance for government employees
14. Guarantee of new bank loans to companies and self-employed by governments
15. Direct financial support to vulnerable households, cash and non-cash grants to informal workers and the unemployed

To compare the amount of government support based on the IMF reports and the release of the multiplicity of currencies of countries, the share of this support in GDP is calculated and shown for the top 15 countries in Figure (2). Among the 46 selected countries, the average share of government support (GDP) was 6.3%, with Ecuador accounting for 0.05% and Germany for 23%, respectively. Meanwhile, the share of financial support for GDP in Iran is about 7%.

In epidemics, the speed of reaction of people and health systems is an important factor in controlling and combating the disease. If the general public does not pay close attention to health advice, each person can get the disease because of social interactions at work or home or in public places. The desire to hold social events is not limited to a particular country. Various cultural, sporting, religious, educational, political, and economic events are held on various local, national, or international occasions. Especially during the World Sports Championships, the number of interactions between people increases sharply and, of course, has its economic benefits and costs.

The capacity of health care systems in different communities also has a large impact on mortality from epidemics. When the number of critically ill patients exceeds the number of intensive care beds and ventilators, not all people with acute illnesses can receive adequate treatment, and the number of deaths naturally increases. As the number of clients increases, physicians must decide which patients will most likely recover and provide them with treatment first.

Therefore, economic power is one of the important components affecting the capacity of health care systems in controlling the epidemic. Countries with free trade and advanced market economies can produce or supply shortages of diagnostic equipment and medicines more quickly. High economic power also increases government support for affected industries and businesses.

A "health system success rate" has been defined to measure the relationship between economic strength and the success of countries' health systems in curbing or slowing the spread of Covid-19 disease. This coefficient is obtained based on the net ratio of the number of recovered (number of recovered to the number of dead) to the total number of patients and is expressed as a percentage. Obviously, in this coefficient, the larger the fraction, the higher the coefficient and the more success it shows. The share of government support (GDP) with the success rate of the health system against the Covid-19 epidemic was examined for all countries studied (46 countries with the highest number of patients) and compared to the top 15 countries in the table (3). Meanwhile, the success rate of 72.3 for Iran shows that for every 100 cases of Covid-19, the net number of recoveries is about 72.

On the other hand, according to this table, the correlation coefficient between the level of support against Covid-19 and the success rate of health systems is positive and equal to 0.26. Therefore, in addition to the share of financial support, the effectiveness of this share should also be considered.

The International Monetary Fund expects the global economy to experience its worst year since the Great Depression of the 1930s as the Covid-19 continues to erupt. The global economy is projected to shrink by 3% this year (ILO, 2020). The Organization for Economic Co-operation and Development (OECD) has also predicted that the global economy will likely experience a 1.5% slowdown in the economic impact of the Covid-19. On the other hand, according to the International Labor Organization (ILO), the Covid-19 outbreak affects about 2.7 billion people in the world labor force (Yang; et al, 2009; Wormer et al., 2013). Prolonged and widespread outbreaks of Covid-19 virus may cause various economies to stagnate. The economic shock caused by the Covid-19 outbreak affects the service sector more than agriculture and industry, as the capacity for informal employment in the service sector is high. Therefore, the Covid-19 crisis will lead to the spread of poverty in the world and will cause the most damage to small and medium enterprises(Carlsson-Szlezak et al., 2020).

CONCLUSION

Iran has special and unnatural conditions in the face of Covid-19 compared to other countries. The covid-19 disease has spread in different provinces and within 3 months of its spread, the health system has been able to achieve valuable successes in controlling and combating this ominous phenomenon. The high recovery rate of Covid-19 patients in Iran compared to other countries, including European countries, has been achieved while the Iranian economy is under inhumane US sanctions in all aspects of banking and trade. Under these circumstances, the supply of medical supplies and equipment, Covid-19 diagnostic kits, and effective drugs for the treatment of the disease will be provided to the government and the Ministry of Health at great expense; Nevertheless, Iran ranks 8th out of 46 countries with a success rate of 72.3% and is among the top 15 countries in terms of the share of financial support for measures against Covid-19 with a share of about 7% of GDP. Given that the correlation coefficient between financial support measures and the success rate of countries against Covid-19 is only about 0.26, it can be said that other influential factors such as coordination of the pillars of the system, different capacities of the people, academia, health, and even military and law enforcement they play against. In the case of Iran, the results of the policy showed that increasing the efforts and actions of the government and the people in the form of public mobilization of facilities and capabilities can potentially turn threats into an opportunity for progress, growth, and excellence of the country. Although economic activity was disrupted and the pace of educational activities in schools and universities slowed down, the decline in production and economic benefits, and academic backwardness can be offset. The important point is that with appropriate measures, the country's health and long-term human capital can be prevented from being affected by negative shocks of production and economic growth in the short term.

REFERENCES

Abedi, V., Olulana, O., Avula, V., Chaudhary, D., Khan, A., Shahjouei, S., Li, J., & Zand, R. (2021). Racial, economic, and health inequality and COVID-19 infection in the United States. *Journal of Racial and Ethnic Health Disparities*, *8*(3), 732–742. doi:10.100740615-020-00833-4 PMID:32875535

Agba, A. O., Ocheni, S. I., & Agba, M. S. (2020). COVID-19 and the world of work dynamics: A critical review. *Journal of Educational and Social Research*, *10*(5), 119–119. doi:10.36941/jesr-2020-0093

Carlsson-Szlezak, P., Reeves, M., & Swartz, P. (2020). What coronavirus could mean for the global economy. *Harvard Business Review*, *3*(10).

Deb, P., Furceri, D., Ostry, J. D., & Tawk, N. (2021). The economic effects of Covid-19 containment measures. *Open Economies Review*, 1–32.

Gallagher, T. M., & Buchmeier, M. J. (2001). Coronavirus spike proteins in viral entry and pathogenesis. *Virology*, *279*(2), 371–374. doi:10.1006/viro.2000.0757 PMID:11162792

ILO (International Labour Organization). (2020). ILO Monitor: COVID-19 and the world of work. Available at: ilo.org/global

IMF (International Monetary Fund), World Economic Outlook Database. (2020). Available at: http://www.imf.org.

Maliszewska, M., Mattoo, A., & Van Der Mensbrugghe, D. (2020). *The potential impact of COVID-19 on GDP and trade: A preliminary assessment*. World Bank Policy Research Working Paper, (9211).

Perlman, S. R., Lane, T. E., & Buchmeier, M. J. (1999). Coronaviruses: Hepatitis, peritonitis, and central nervous system disease. *Effects of Microbes on the Immune System*, *1*, 331-348.

Reed, S. E. (1984). The behaviour of recent isolates of human respiratory coronavirus in vitro and in volunteers: Evidence of heterogeneity among 229E-related strains. *Journal of Medical Virology*, *13*(2), 179–192. doi:10.1002/jmv.1890130208 PMID:6319590

Wormer, B. A., Augenstein, V. A., Carpenter, C. L., Burton, P. V., Yokeley, W. T., Prabhu, A. S., Harris, B., Norton, S., Klima, D. A., Lincourt, A. E., & Heniford, B. T. (2013). The green operating room: Simple changes to reduce cost and our carbon footprint. *The American Surgeon*, *79*(7), 666–671. doi:10.1177/000313481307900708 PMID:23815997

Wosik, J., Fudim, M., Cameron, B., Gellad, Z. F., Cho, A., Phinney, D., Curtis, S., Roman, M., Poon, E. G., Ferranti, J., Katz, J. N., & Tcheng, J. (2020). Telehealth transformation: COVID-19 and the rise of virtual care. *Journal of the American Medical Informatics Association: JAMIA*, *27*(6), 957–962. doi:10.1093/jamia/ocaa067 PMID:32311034

Xiao, Y., & Torok, M. E. (2020). Taking the right measures to control COVID-19. *The Lancet. Infectious Diseases*, *20*(5), 523–524. doi:10.1016/S1473-3099(20)30152-3 PMID:32145766

Yang, C., Peijun, L., Lupi, C., Yangzhao, S., Diandou, X., Qian, F., & Shasha, F. (2009). Sustainable management measures for healthcare waste in China. *Waste Management (New York, N.Y.)*, *29*(6), 1996–2004. doi:10.1016/j.wasman.2008.11.031 PMID:19157834

Zambrano-Monserrate, M. A., Silva-Zambrano, C. A., & Ruano, M. A. (2018). The economic value of natural protected areas in Ecuador: A case of Villamil Beach National Recreation Area. *Ocean and Coastal Management*, *157*, 193–202. doi:10.1016/j.ocecoaman.2018.02.020

ADDITIONAL READING

Coccia, M. (2021). High health expenditures and low exposure of population to air pollution as critical factors that can reduce fatality rate in COVID-19 pandemic crisis: A global analysis. *Environmental Research*, *199*, 111339. doi:10.1016/j.envres.2021.111339 PMID:34029545

Cristea, A., Hummels, D., Puzzello, L., & Avetisyan, M. (2013). Trade and the greenhouse gas emissions from international freight transport. *Journal of Environmental Economics and Management*, *65*(1), 153–173. doi:10.1016/j.jeem.2012.06.002

Danish, & Wang, Z. (2018). Dynamic relationship between tourism, economic growth, and environmental quality. *Journal of Sustainable Tourism, 26*(11), 1928-1943.

Deng, H., & Huang, J. (2009). Environmental Pollution and Endogenous Growth: Models and Evidence from China. In *2009 International Conference on Environmental Science and Information Application Technology* (Vol. 1, pp. 72-79). IEEE. 10.1109/ESIAT.2009.467

Etokakpan, M. U., Adedoyin, F. F., Vedat, Y., & Bekun, F. V. (2020). Does globalization in Turkey induce increased energy consumption: Insights into its environmental pros and cons. *Environmental Science and Pollution Research International*, *27*(21), 26125–26140. doi:10.100711356-020-08714-3 PMID:32358749

Fazli, P., & Abbasi, E. (2018). Analysis of the validity of Kuznets curve of energy intensity among D-8 countries: panel-ARDL approach. International Letters of Social and Humanistic Sciences, 81.

Franklin, B. A., Brook, R., & Pope, C. A. III. (2015). Air pollution and cardiovascular disease. *Current Problems in Cardiology*, *40*(5), 207–238. doi:10.1016/j.cpcardiol.2015.01.003 PMID:25882781

Grossman, G. M., & Krueger, A. B. (1995). Economic growth and the environment. *The Quarterly Journal of Economics*, *110*(2), 353–377. doi:10.2307/2118443

Chapter 5
Analysing the Relationship Between Green Intellectual Capital and the Achievement of the Sustainable Development Goals

Bartolomé Marco-Lajara
https://orcid.org/0000-0001-8811-9118
University of Alicante, Spain

Patrocinio Zaragoza-Saez
University of Alicante, Spain

Javier Martínez Falcó
https://orcid.org/0000-0001-9004-5816
University of Alicante, Spain

Luis A. Millan-Tudela
https://orcid.org/0000-0003-3669-9960
University of Alicante, Spain

ABSTRACT

The research aims to analyze the link between the green intellectual capital (GIC) and the Sustainable Development Goals (SDGs) in the wine industry, contributing to the academic literature in a remarkable way, since, to the authors' knowledge, there is no previous research that has addressed this relationship. To achieve the proposed objective, the research follows a qualitative approach, given that the case study method was used. The research results show the positive effect of the three dimensions of the GIC (green human capital, green structural capital, green relational capital) on the achievement of SDGs 5, 6, 7, 9, 11, 12, 13, 15, and 17.

DOI: 10.4018/978-1-6684-5109-0.ch005

INTRODUCTION

Growing customer awareness of environmental challenges and strict environmental regulations mean that sustainability has become a business paradigm present in various economic sectors. There is a certain consensus in considering sustainability as a necessary challenge given the negative externalities that organizations generate to the environment. Thus, although the intellectual background of this debate dates back to the 1950s, it is still necessary to continue advancing in this direction.

In the wine industry, sustainability is an extremely important issue for two main reasons. On the one hand, the industry faces serious threats as a consequence of climate change, as well as water and energy scarcity (Gilinsky et al., 2016; Marco-Lajara et al., 2022). On the other hand, proper environmental management of wineries can mean obtaining a competitive advantage, by allowing increasing market share and organizational innovation processes (Fiore et al., 2016). In this sense, previous works have shown that customers tend to select wines that have been developed following sustainable practices, despite not knowing what they imply in practice (Schäufele & Hamm, 2017). From the producers' point of view, it has been shown that the implementation of environmental practices improves the quality and economic efficiency of employees (Szolnoki, 2013).

The concept of sustainability in the wine industry is supported by official documents of the International Organization of Vine and Wine (OIV), defining what sustainable viticulture is (OIV, 2004), what its guidelines are (OIV, 2008) and its general principles (OIV, 2016). Similarly, the main wine regions have developed their own national programs in order to implement the principles of sustainability in their contexts (Marco-Lajara et al., 2021a; Marco-Lajara et al., 2021b). For the case of Spain, the Spanish Wine Federation (FEV, for its acronym in Spanish) developed the Strategic Plan 2019-2024 (FEV, 2019) with the aim of guaranteeing the future production of wine and its legitimacy in society through a comprehensive sustainability strategy. This document establishes the set of policies that can be developed by the wine industry value chain to achieve the Sustainable Development Goals (SDGs) established by the United Nations (UN). These goals were established in 2015 in the framework of the 2030 Agenda with the aim of promoting sustainable development.

According to this strategic plan, the 11 SDGs related to the wine industry and, therefore, those in which the sector can have a relevant impact, are the following: SDG 3 -health and well-being-, SDG 5 -gender equality-, SDG 6 -clean water and sanitation-, SDG 7 -affordable and clean energy-, SDG 8 -decent work and economic growth-, SDG 9 -industry, innovation and infrastructure-, SDG 11 -sustainable cities and communities-, SDG 12 -responsible production and consumption-, SDG 13 -climate action-, SDG 15 -living terrestrial ecosystems-, SDG 17 -partnerships to achieve the goals-.

Compliance with the SDGs by organizations allows them to balance their economic, social and environmental objectives. In order to meet these objectives, companies must generate new knowledge that allows them to develop their activities through a sustainable approach (Boons et al., 2013), and they can adopt to increase their endowment of intangibles in its three aspects: human capital, structural capital and relational capital (Davenport & Prusak, 1998). In this sense, the Intellectual Capital (IC) that incorporates environmental aspects, i.e., Green Intellectual Capital (GIC), takes on special relevance as it represents an essential element for achieving corporate sustainability.

The motivation for this research stems from two premises. First, a higher GIC enables companies to better meet their environmental challenges. Secondly, the GIC allows the transformation of the organization through the knowledge achieved. Based on these arguments and using the case study applied to a winery, this study aims to answer the following research question: does GIC have a positive effect on the fulfillment of the SDGs promoted by the UN?

To answer the question posed, the research is structured as follows. First, after this brief introduction, section 2 presents the theoretical framework, providing a theoretical review of the GIC and the SDGs. Section 3 explains the methodology followed in the empirical part to address the stated objective. Section 4 presents the main results obtained in the research. Finally, section 5 presents the conclusions obtained from the study, highlighting the most relevant contributions, its limitations and future lines of research in section 6.

BACKGROUND

Intellectual Capital (IC) encompasses the set of intangibles that an organization possesses and that allow it to achieve a competitive advantage over its competitors (Edvinsson & Malone, 1997). This set of intangibles includes the individual knowledge of employees as well as the collective knowledge of the organization. According to tradition, IC has been classified into three major blocks: human, structural and relational capital (Edvinsson, 1997). These blocks include intangible assets corresponding to individuals (human capital), to the firm (structural capital) and to those that arise as a consequence of the organization's relationships with its environment (relational capital).

Scientific production has traditionally focused on the study of IC. However, little research has addressed IC from an environmental perspective. In fact, until the publication of Chen's (2008) seminal article, in which he introduces the GIC construct, no researcher had investigated IC under the premises of sustainable development. In his study, Chen (2008) classified GIC into three blocks: Green Human Capital (GHC), Green Structural Capital (GSC) and Green Relational Capital (GRC), opening a new field of research within the study of IC, since through his research he found a positive relationship between the three dimensions of GIC and the attainment of competitive advantage. Later, Huang & Kung (2011) demonstrated that GIC represented an essential element for the company's adaptation to strict environmental regulations, as well as for the creation of value in the organization. In recent years, there has been an intensification of the study of GIC, with several papers addressing the effect of this set of environmental intangible assets on other green constructs (Yusoff et al., 2019). However, to the best of our knowledge, the link between GIC and SDGs has not been addressed in the literature previously, highlighting the need to address this relationship.

Since the creation by the UN of the 2030 Agenda in 2015, companies started to take an interest in how they could adhere to these goals, given that they play a key role in the achievement of the SDGs. Thus, although the goals have a global scope and all actors must be involved in their achievement, organizations play a key role in achieving the social, economic and environmental goals set out in the SDGs (Van der Waal and Thijssens, 2020). Indeed, in 2015 the UN stated, "We call on all businesses to apply their creativity and innovation to solving sustainable development challenges" (Shakoury, 2018).

The growing interest in the SDGs on the part of organizations has aroused the interest of many academics specialized in environmental management, and there are two main streams of research on the subject of these goals. On the one hand, several researchers have analyzed the catalytic factors that lead to greater compliance with the SDGs (Rosati & Faria, 2019; Van der Waal & Thijssens, 2020). On the other hand, other researchers explore the relationship between SDG compliance and gaining competitive advantage (Boiral et al., 2019; Pineda-Escobar, 2019). The present study contributes to the first typology of research, given that GIC is conceived as a catalytic variable for the adequate fulfillment of the SDGs.

GHC increases when employees acquire green knowledge, thus improving the sustainable performance of organizations. This green knowledge possessed by workers makes it possible to overcome the problems arising from international environmental regulations and increasing customer awareness of environmental issues (Chang & Chen, 2012). In this sense, it is of utmost importance to explore the potential effect of GHC on organizations' adherence to the SDGs, since the stock of green knowledge possessed by the organization's members makes a difference in achieving the organization's sustainable goals (Jirakraisiri et al., 2021). The effect of GHC on other environmental variables, such as green innovation, green supply chain or environmental performance, among others, has been demonstrated in the academic literature (Yadiati et al., 2019; Yong et al., 2019; Yusliza et al., 2020; Mansoor et al., 2021). However, the link between GHC and SDGs has not yet been empirically addressed. On the basis of these arguments, we formulate the following proposition.

Proposition 1: GHC is positively related to the achievement of the SDGs.

Several studies have recognized the role played by the GSC in achieving sustainable development (Zameer et al., 2020). This typology of ecological intangibles allows obtaining lasting competitive advantages over time, as well as reducing the negative externalities generated by organizations (Liu, 2010; Chang & Chen, 2012; Delgado-Verde et al., 2014; Malik et al., 2020). In the same way as GSC, several publications show the positive relationship between GSC and other variables such as green culture, green innovation or green performance. However, the relationship between GSC and SDGs has not been addressed in the academic literature previously. For this reason, we pose the following hypothesis:

Proposition 2: GSC is positively related to the achievement of the SDGs.

The organization's relationships with its different stakeholders, such as suppliers, customers or shareholders, can contribute to the achievement of environmental performance by the organization (Dal Mas & Paoloni, 2019). In fact, some research suggests that sustainable organizations emerge as a consequence of their links with the other stakeholders involved in their activity (Zhang et al., 2020). Moreover, the exchange of knowledge between the organization and its stakeholders has been considered a key element in the implementation of a sustainable approach by the organization. There is a vast scientific production that analyzes the relationship of GRC with green competitive advantage, environmental practices and green human resource management, among other aspects (Thiagarajan & Sekkizhar, 2017; Febrianti et al., 2020; Asiaei et al., 2021; Ulla et al., 2021). Based on these arguments, we propose the following hypothesis.

Proposition 3: GRC is positively related to the achievement of the SDGs

METHODOLOGY

This study follows a qualitative approach, given that the case study method has been used for its realization. This is conceived as an appropriate tool to deepen the understanding of the case under study (Chetty, 1996).

There are three reasons why the case study method was selected for this research. First, the case study technique allows the testing of propositions, thus contributing to the process of building new theory. Secondly, a revealing case has been selected as it develops a high degree of environmental practices. Third, the study allows acquiring a deep understanding of the phenomenon under study.

Sample

The purpose of sampling when conducting a case study is to collect those cases that improve the understanding of the phenomenon under study, in our case the link between GIC and the SDGs. In this sense, as Ishak et al. (2013) point out, "it is about finding cases or units of analysis that enhance what other researchers have learned about a particular phenomenon."

The case study method involves the use of non-probability sampling. However, despite being this type of sampling, three criteria were followed to select the sample. First, it had to be a winery with ISO 14001 and Wineries for Climate Protection (WfCP) certification as a reflection of its proactivity in environmental issues. Secondly, it had to be a pioneer in the integration of environmental practices in the wine sector. Thirdly, it had to be a winery with wide national and international recognition in the environmental field. After an initial screening, it was decided to select Bodegas Luzón for meeting the three established criteria.

Data Collection and Analysis

The case study conducted consisted of three phases: (1) literature review, (2) data collection, and (3) case study analysis. The first phase consisted of exploring the literature related to GIC and the SDGs. Second, a comprehensive description of the Bodegas Luzon case was conducted to identify its suitability for the present research and data were collected. Finally, we proceeded to the analysis and subsequent writing of the present research.

Given the qualitative nature of the research, triangulation was used for data collection in order to increase the validity and reliability of the conclusions drawn from the study (Denzin, 1978). To carry out the triangulation, three sources of data were used (1) in-depth interview with the winery's winemaker and environmental manager; (2) direct observation (visit to the winery and contact with employees); (3) access to the winery's internal documentation (environmental statements, bulletins, acknowledgments, etc.) and external documentation (corporate videos, website, the Iberian Balance Sheet Analysis System database, etc.).

The interview was structured in three blocks (see Appendix 1). The first block of questions aimed to learn about the winery's origins, as well as its commitment to the environment in general. In the second block, questions were asked about the dimensions of the GIC and their relationship with the winery's environmental management. Finally, the third block of questions addressed those issues related to the company's degree of compliance with the SDGs that had not been asked in the other blocks.

The interview was conducted on August 15, 2021, lasted one hour and was recorded in its entirety for later transcription. The use of transcripts to create theoretical frameworks has been widely used in the management literature (Lawrence, 2010). This process involves identifying key words and phrases from the interviews to determine areas of convergence and potential knowledge gaps that remain to be filled.

During the visit to the facilities, it was possible to speak with other members of the winery staff in addition to the winemaker and the environmental manager, who emphasized the organization's commitment to sustainable development. Data collection was interrupted when additional data provided a minimal understanding of the phenomenon under study. Once the transcription was completed, the interviewees' opinions on the first draft were analyzed for validity. Both interviewees reviewed and accepted the transcripts of their interviews.

RESULTS

Green Intellectual Capital in Bodegas Luzón

The origins of Bodegas Luzón date back to 1841, the year in which Don José de Molina, commander of the Royal Army in the Spanish colony of Manila (Philippines), decided to return to his homeland: Jumilla. It was then that he took over the responsibility for the lands inherited from his father, providing them with the necessary infrastructure for wine production. The land was christened by Don José de Molina as Finca Luzón, in memory of the island where he was stationed for so long. This estate would later be inherited by his daughter Doña Ana Josefa Molina Gil, who did the same with her first-born daughter, Doña Carmen Guillén, leaving the winery linked to the female branch of the family from then onwards. In 2005, the Fuertes family took over the winery's historical legacy by acquiring it, one of the major milestones since its foundation. As the winemaker of Bodegas Luzón points out, "the acquisition of the winery by the Fuertes family was a great step forward in the development of both the winery and the Jumilla Denomination of Origin".

The winery currently has around 450 hectares of its own vineyards and another 1,000 hectares of vineyards managed by farmers, 80% of which are organically grown. The main grape variety they work with is Monastrell, a characteristic grape mainly in the Denominations of Origin (DOs) of the Region of Murcia (DO Jumilla, DO Yecla, DO Bullas) and in the DOs of Alicante and Almansa, as this type of grape needs a warm climate and good sunlight to ripen. Among the wines produced by Bodegas Luzón, the following stand out: Altos de Luzón, Alma de Luzón, Por Ti, Luzón Colección Blanco, Luzón Colección Rosado, Luzón Colección Monastrell, Luzón Colección Garnacha Tintorera, Luzón Colección Roble and Luzón Colección Crianza. They have also recently committed to the production of organic wines such as Verdecillo, Verdecillo Blanco, Luzón Ecológico Blanco and Luzón Organic, making them a benchmark winery in terms of sustainability. Thus, in 2009 they obtained the ISO 14000 certificate, becoming one of the first Spanish wineries to hold this environmental quality label and a national benchmark in sustainability due to their proactive attitude to initiate such sustainable practices. In the words of the winemaker:

"All the sustainable practices we have done in the winery are proactive, it is a long-term investment, because if you do it well and you execute it properly, the money comes back. Everything is returnable, whether in sales or image, but it is not short term, it is very long term. Therefore, if you don't develop sustainable actions with the long term in mind, they won't work. You need a very strong initial investment

Analysing the Relationship

without knowing when it will be returnable. In fact, neither at the beginning nor now do we know with certainty the exact return. But we do know that it gives us an added quality in terms of image, organization, work, cleanliness, hygiene, improvement, and costs. But we have internalized all these actions after ten years of work. You can't do this to get money back the next day, because you don't even know when it's going to come back, and you might lose it."

As explained above, the blocks that make up the GIC are: the GHC, the GSC and the GRC. The factors that influence the formation of the three blocks of environmental intangibles for the case studied are set out below (see Table 1). On the one hand, as far as the GHC is concerned, it is worth highlighting the efforts made by the winery to integrate environmental values among its workers. Bodegas Luzón invests in training courses to provide its workers with green knowledge that allows the organization to reduce costs (through the efficient use of resources) and differentiate itself (through its high specialization in sustainable practices), attends trade fairs in the sector to detect new trends in the wine industry, makes the codified knowledge of the organization available to its workers through the code of conduct and good practices, and fosters motivation, job satisfaction and a sense of belonging to the group among its workers through managerial integrity, as its good environmental practices enable it to activate a transformative mechanism among workers: learning by imitation.

As far as the GSC is concerned, there are different factors that influence its construction. The winery has annual circular economy programmes to achieve the Triple R premises: reduce, reuse and recycle, it has its own computer systems to measure its water footprint and carbon footprint, it has eco-efficient facilities, it has prestigious certifications that endorse its commitment to the environment, such as the ISO 14000 and the Wineries for Climate Protection certificates, it has a brand with wide international recognition for its environmental work and its organic wines, has a flat organizational structure that facilitates the transmission of green knowledge, the values of its organizational culture are framed within the pillars of sustainability and it carries out annual R&D&I projects to improve the sustainability of the winery, which are subsequently translated into tangible results for the organization, such as the launch of wine without added sulphites and wine with low levels of sulphur.

As far as the GRC is concerned, Bodegas Luzón is part of a large number of associations and agreements that enable the organisation's environmental knowledge to be obtained and updated, such as: its membership of the Jumilla DO, the Jumilla Wine Business Association (ASEVIN, for its acronym in Spanish), the Jumilla Wine Route, the Murcia Institute for Agricultural and Food Research and Development (IMIDA, for its acronym in Spanish), the Integrated Centre for Agricultural Training and Experiences (CIFEA, for its acronym in Spanish) in Jumilla or the research and training agreements with Spanish universities such as the University of Cartagena, the University of Murcia and the University of Valencia. The winery also requires green certificates from its suppliers to be able to work with it, with the aim of establishing a green supply chain.

Table 1. Dimensions of green intellectual capital in Bodegas Luzón.

		GREEN INTELLECTUAL CAPITAL
GREEN HUMAN CAPITAL	Training courses	Environmental Manager – "The winery offers annual training to all its employees. On an environmental level, they are trained in good environmental practices in order to save resources." Winemaker- "At the company level it is very important to have these environmental awareness programmes because imagine the waste of resources if, for example, a worker were to leave the lights on in the winery. All the awareness-raising work that the organization does adds up to achieve our annual targets."
	Trade fairs	Environmental Manager – "We have a national and international sales team that is in charge of trade fairs and other commercial actions." Winemaker – "We participate in what we see as most interesting for our business in order to progress."
	Good practice manuals	Environmental Manager – "When a worker is hired, he/she is given initial training and, subsequently, the code of conduct and the code of good environmental practices are handed over to him/her."
	Motivation, job satisfaction and sense of belonging	Winemaker – "The workers are motivated and satisfied in the winery because we care about the things that are happening, in water consumption, in electricity consumption... Things as simple as throwing a piece of paper on the floor and picking it up make us all feel that sustainability is ours. If the workers see that I arrive and throw a piece of paper on the floor, that I leave the light on or that I have the tap running, they will do the same."

Continued on following page

Table 1. Continued

		GREEN INTELLECTUAL CAPITAL
GREEN STRUCTURAL CAPITAL	Circular Economy Programme	Winemaker – "We have a circular economy programme through which we develop different practices. For example, the stalks are reused for bedding, cattle feed and even as fertiliser for the vineyards. The wastewater that comes out goes to irrigate the vineyard, to the entrance garden, etc." Environmental Manager – "The last circular economy project we have carried out relates to the wastewater that is generated when the tanks are cleaned with soda. Previously, this water with soda was stored and taken away, and now we have a tank where this water is introduced, and this water then goes to the winery's treatment plant."
	IT systems to measure carbon and water footprints	Winemaker- "We have our own programmes created by the winery's IT team. There are people dedicated every day to measuring and counting the waste that is generated."
	Eco-efficient facilities	Winemaker – "We currently have solar panels, and we are going to install more. We are going to be self-sufficient in solar energy when we do the installation in September." Environmental Manager – "Our energy right now comes from wind power; we have the guarantee from our distributor that it is renewable. However, a study has been carried out and the process of installing the solar panels is underway."
	Brand	Winemaker – "At the user level I think that people, especially in Spain, still don't link the Bodegas Luzón brand with sustainable wine. On the other hand, in the European and American markets they do value it. In Spain, the value is being given by the distributor, but I think that the end consumer still does not associate Bodegas Luzón with sustainability. This is a task that we still have to develop."
	Certifications	Environmental Manager – "We are ISO 14000 and WineriesforClimateProtection (WfCP) certified, plus certified organic wine and vegan."
	Organisational structure	Winemaker – "The structure is quite flat, the management encourages us to develop new ideas on all environmental issues. Also, when we knock on their door it is always open."
	Proposal box	Winemaker – "We have a formal and informal suggestion box, because we have an APP where we have a suggestion box and a message button. But, in the end, everything formal is difficult to use, or at least people don't use it. In the warehouse we listen to everyone, because in the end we are a small company where the manager has coffee with us and is just one of us."
	Organisational culture	Winemaker – "The values at the winery have been clear from the beginning: improvement, innovation and excellence. We are a food company whose forte is constant improvement through the pillars of sustainability."
	Investments in R&D&I	Winemaker – "We take part in all the R&D&I projects that add value to us. Many of these projects have helped us to launch new products on the market, which today are an important pillar to sustain the structure of the winery."
	Innovation performance	Environmental Manager- "The latest innovation has been the wine without added sulphites. An ecological wine, totally natural. We have been developing the necessary technology to be able to market sulphite-free wine for some time and it is now a reality. In addition, at the beginning of the year we did a study of the purification plant which has allowed us to consume less energy." Winemaker – "For example, we did a study for organic wines with low levels of sulphites and we are currently making our 12-month organic crianza wine. This study, in particular, has helped us to know why we were combining so much sulphur, why we were oxidizing the wine so much, and so on. We are now selling wine with twelve months of ageing with sulphur dioxide of 70 million matches when before it was 130."

Continued on following page

Table 1. Continued

		GREEN INTELLECTUAL CAPITAL
GREEN RELATIONAL CAPITAL	Relations with institutions	Environmental Manager- "We are in ASEVIN, the Jumilla Wine Route, the DO JUMILLA, the IMIDA and the CIFEA. We also receive students from the University of Valencia, from Murcia, and we are currently developing a research project with the University of Cartagena."
	Relations with customers and suppliers	Environmental Manager – "In the winery we have suppliers who have ecological certificates and we have much more peace of mind and security. Also, as we calculate our carbon footprint, we try to buy from the closest suppliers, because of the transport issue. For cardboard we ask that they have their forest sustainability certificates, for paper and ink we ask that the suppliers certify that the inks are non-toxic, we use the lightest bottles possible, etc. We ask for a series of requirements that are related to the triple dimension of sustainability." Winemaker – "To engage with our customers we use all kinds of media, from trade fairs, LinkedIn, Instagram, to face-to-face meetings. Everything is valid if the customer is serious."

Source: own elaboration

Sustainable Development Goals in Bodegas Luzón

Bodegas Luzón contributes to the fulfillment of the Sustainable Development Goals related to the wine industry. Despite being a traditionally male sector in its origin, the winery has been making progress in gender equality in recent years, with the increasing incorporation of women in all areas of work related to the sector. As the winemaker points out, "currently 35% of the people working in the winery are women. However, we are working to achieve parity." This underscores its commitment to improving its contribution to SDG 5 related to gender equality.

The WfCP certification also enables the winery to comply with SDGs 6, 7 and 13. On the one hand, water management is one of the requirements to obtain the certifications, including specific actions such as calculating the water footprint or implementing a plan to reduce consumption and improve discharges. On the other hand, using alternative energy sources to cover part of the winery's thermal needs and implementing energy auditing systems to save consumption in the production activity is also another of the essential pillars to obtain both awards. Likewise, wineries with these certifications must follow the action plan drawn up by the certifying body to address climate change.

The organization is capable of generating 50 jobs, exerting a tractor effect on other activities in the auxiliary industry and related sectors. It also contributes to the growth, internationalization and international projection of the Spanish economy, through a consolidated trade surplus and export network, as well as the presence of Spanish wine products in more than 40 countries, thus contributing to SDG 8. As the winemaker points out: "I am proud to see how our wines are in the best restaurants in New York and Tokyo and how you are part of that brand."

The wine sector is closely linked to the land and is therefore particularly aware that it can only continue to guarantee the quality of its products through respect for the environment and the conservation of the natural resources on which it depends so much. Bodegas Luzón is aware of the importance of the land and respect for the environment, which is reflected in the statements of the environmental manager, "we have to leave a good future for our children. We cannot lose the wine culture of the region, we have to fight against that, be sustainable and return to artisanal agriculture", and in the importance of organic vineyards, since 80% of the vineyard area owned by the winery is organic, thus contributing to

Analysing the Relationship

the fulfillment of SDG 12- Similarly, the wine tourism activities carried out by the winery contribute significantly to the protection of the cultural and natural heritage of Jumilla through its close historical link not only with gastronomy but also with the cultural heritage of the region, allowing the construction and development of sustainable cities and communities (SDG 11).

CONCLUSION

The purpose of this research is to analyze the different effects of the GIC of wine companies on the fulfillment of the SDGs, contributing to the academic literature in a remarkable way, since, to our knowledge, there is no previous research that has addressed this relationship.

The origins of Bodegas Luzón date back to 1841, the year in which Don José de Molina decided to return to his homeland: Jumilla. It was then when he took over the lands inherited from his father, providing them with the necessary infrastructure for wine production. In 2005, the Fuertes family took over the historical legacy of the winery by acquiring it, one of the biggest milestones since its foundation as one of the most important business groups in Spain. These milestones have enabled the generation of employment and wealth in the region where it is located, as well as exerting a tractor effect on other activities in the auxiliary industry and related sectors (fulfilling SDG 8).

Regarding the GHC, the results indicate that Bodegas Luzon employees are in a constant process of acquiring environmental knowledge, since the members of the organization attend courses on environmental awareness and management organized by the company, participate in industry fairs to detect new trends in sustainability in the sector and codify their knowledge through codes of conduct and good environmental practices so that all members can access this stock of green knowledge. This acquired knowledge has allowed them to be involved in pioneering projects in the industry, such as the development of green process innovations, such as making their own compost from grape stalks (meeting SDG 9), as well as developing a sustainable production system based on a reduction of pesticides and fertilizers, soil conservation, rational use of water resources and proper waste management (meeting SDG 12). This allows us to confirm Proposition 1.

As regards GSC, the winery has its own circular economy program, ISO 14001 and WfCP certification to endorse its environmental commitment, a brand linked to sustainable production, a flat organizational structure, a green organizational culture, as well as R&D&I projects to improve the winery's sustainability. This set of green organizational intangibles has enabled the organization to promote gender equality in the organization (meeting SDG 5), develop strategies for efficient water management and to reduce pollution and waste (meeting SDG 6), to make a clear commitment to self-consumption and clean energy (meeting SDG 7), to implement climate change adaptation and mitigation initiatives (meeting SDG 13), to develop a wine tourism model aimed at enhancing the value of the territory (meeting SDG 11), and to promote organic farming and local grape varieties: Monastrell (meeting SDG 15). This allows us to confirm Proposition 2.

As for the GRC, Bodegas Luzón is part of numerous associations that allow it to acquire and transfer its environmental knowledge, such as the DO Jumilla, ASEVIN, the Jumilla Wine Route, IMIDA, CIFEA or the research agreements with several Spanish universities. The winery also requires green certificates from its suppliers in order to work with it. This allows us to guarantee the construction of public-private alliances to promote policies consistent with the different aspects that affect the wine industry in terms of sustainability (complying with SDG17). This allows us to confirm Proposition 3. By way of conclusion, Figure 1 attempts to summarize the relationships found between the GIC and the SDGs through the case study conducted.

Figure 1. Relationship between the GIC and the SDGs.
Source: own elaboration

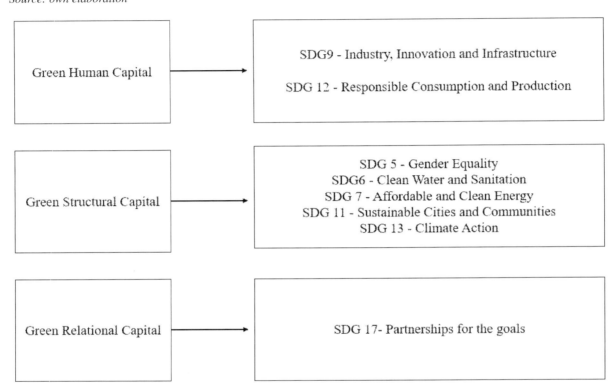

FUTURE RESEARCH DIRECTIONS

Despite the relevant contributions made in this research, the study suffers from certain limitations. The main limitation is related to the impossibility of establishing comparisons in the single case study and to the fact that the winery analyzed stands out as an environmental benchmark within the wine industry. To overcome this limitation, as a future line of research we intend to carry out a multiple case study to analyze the GIC-SDG link both in wineries that stand out for their environmental work and those that are not guaranteed by this feature.

ACKNOWLEDGMENT

This research has not received any specific subsidy from any public, commercial or non-profit sector funding agency. However, we would like to sincerely thank Bodegas Luzón for allowing us to enter their facilities, for allowing us to conduct an in-depth interview with their quality manager and for providing us with all the necessary documentation to carry out the research.

REFERENCES

Asiaei, K., Bontis, N., Alizadeh, R., & Yaghoubi, M. (2021). Green intellectual capital and environmental management accounting: Natural resource orchestration in favor of environmental performance. *Business Strategy and the Environment, 31*(1), 76–93. doi:10.1002/bse.2875

Boiral, O., Heras-Saizarbitoria, I., & Brotherton, M. (2019). Corporate sustainability and indigenous community engagement in the extractive industry. *Journal of Cleaner Production, 235*, 701–711. doi:10.1016/j.jclepro.2019.06.311

Boons, F., Montalvo, C., Quist, J., & Wagner, M. (2013). Sustainable innovation, business models and economic performance: An overview. *Journal of Cleaner Production, 45*, 1–8. doi:10.1016/j.jclepro.2012.08.013

Chang, C. H., & Chen, Y. (2012). The determinants of green intellectual capital. *Management Decision, 50*(1), 74–94. doi:10.1108/00251741211194886

Chen, Y. (2008). The positive effect of green intellectual capital on competitive advantages of firms. *Journal of Business Ethics, 77*(3), 271–286. doi:10.100710551-006-9349-1

Chetty, S. (1996). The case study method for research in small-and medium-sized firms. *International Small Business Journal, 15*(1), 73–85. doi:10.1177/0266242696151005

Dal Mas, F., & Paoloni, P. (2019). A relational capital perspective on social sustainability; the case of female entrepreneurship in Italy. *Measuring Business Excellence, 24*(1), 114–130. doi:10.1108/MBE-08-2019-0086

Davenport, T., & Prusak, L. (1998). *Working knowledge: How organizations manage what they know*. Harvard Business Press.

Delgado-Verde, M., Amores-Salvadó, J., Martín-de Castro, G., & Navas-López, J. (2014). Green intellectual capital and environmental product innovation: The mediating role of green social capital. *Knowledge Management Research and Practice, 12*(3), 261–275. doi:10.1057/kmrp.2014.1

Edvinsson, L. (1997). Developing intellectual capital at Skandia. *Long Range Planning, 30*(3), 366–373. doi:10.1016/S0024-6301(97)90248-X

Edvinsson, L., & Malone, M. (1997). *Intellectual Capital: Realizing your company's true value by finding its hidden brainpower*. Oxford University Press, New York.

Febrianti, F. D., Sugiyanto, S., & Fitria, J. R. (2020). Green Intellectual Capital Conservatism Earning Management, To Future Stock Return As Moderating Stock Return (Study Of Mining Companies In Indonesia Listed On Idx For The Period Of 2014-2019). *The Accounting Journal Of Binaniaga, 5*(2), 141–154. doi:10.33062/ajb.v5i2.407

FEV. (2019). *El sector del vino y el papel de la FEV en los Objetivos de Desarrollo Sostenible*. Disponible en: http://www.fev.es/fev/sostenibilidad-y-responsabilidad/objetivos-de-desarrollo-sostenible_122_1_ap.html

Fiore, M., Silvestri, R., Contò, F., & Pellegrini, G. (2017). Understanding the relationship between green approach and marketing innovations tools in the wine sector. *Journal of Cleaner Production, 142*, 4085–4091. doi:10.1016/j.jclepro.2016.10.026

Gilinsky, A. Jr, Newton, S., & Vega, R. (2016). Sustainability in the global wine industry: Concepts and cases. *Agriculture and Agricultural Science Procedia, 8*, 37–49. doi:10.1016/j.aaspro.2016.02.006

Huang, C., & Kung, F. (2011). Environmental consciousness and intellectual capital management: Evidence from Taiwan's manufacturing industry. *Management Decision, 49*(9), 1405–1425. doi:10.1108/00251741111173916

Ishak, N. M., Bakar, A., & Yazid, A. (2014). Developing Sampling Frame for Case Study: Challenges and Conditions. *World Journal of Education, 4*(3), 29–35.

Jirakraisiri, J., Badir, Y., & Frank, B. (2021). Translating green strategic intent into green process innovation performance: The role of green intellectual capital. *Journal of Intellectual Capital, 22*(7), 43–67. doi:10.1108/JIC-08-2020-0277

Lawrence, A. (2010). Managing disputes with nonmarket stakeholders: Wage a fight, withdraw, wait, or work it out? *California Management Review, 53*(1), 90–113. doi:10.1525/cmr.2010.53.1.90

Liu, C. (2010). Developing green intellectual capital in companies by AHP. In *2010 8th International Conference on Supply Chain Management and Information* (pp. 1-5). IEEE.

Malik, S., Cao, Y., Mughal, Y., Kundi, G., Mughal, M., & Ramayah, T. (2020). Pathways towards sustainability in organizations: Empirical evidence on the role of green human resource management practices and green intellectual capital. *Sustainability, 12*(8), 3228. doi:10.3390u12083228

Mansoor, A., Jahan, S., & Riaz, M. (2021). Does green intellectual capital spur corporate environmental performance through green workforce? *Journal of Intellectual Capital, 22*(5), 823–839. doi:10.1108/JIC-06-2020-0181

Marco-Lajara, B., Seva-Larrosa, P., Martínez-Falcó, J., & Sánchez-García, E. (2021a). How Has COVID-19 Affected The Spanish Wine Industry? An Exploratory Analysis. *Natural Volatiles & Essential Oils Journal, 8*(6), 2722–2731.

Marco-Lajara, B., Seva-Larrosa, P., Ruiz-Fernández, L., & Martínez-Falcó, J. (2021b). The Effect of COVID-19 on the Spanish Wine Industry. In A. Coşkun (Ed.), *Impact of Global Issues on International Trade* (pp. 211–232). IGI Global.

Marco-Lajara, B., Zaragoza-Sáez, P., Martínez-Falcó, J., & Sánchez-García, E. (2022). Green Intellectual Capital in the Spanish Wine Industry. In C. Goi (Ed.), *Innovative Economic, Social, and Environmental Practices for Progressing Future Sustainability* (pp. 102–120). IGI Global.

OIV. (2004). *Resolution CST 1/2004-Develpment of Sustainable Vitivinivulture*. Pareis.

OIV. (2008). *Resolution CST/2008-OIV Guidelines for Sustainable Vitiviniculture: Production, Processing and Packaging of Products*. Verone/it.

OIV. (2016). *Resolution CST 518/2016-OIV General Principles of Sustainable Vitiviniculture – Environmental - Social - Economic and Cultural Aspects*. Brento Gonçalves.

Pineda-Escobar, M. (2019). Moving the 2030 agenda forward: SDG implementation in Colombia. *Corporate Governance: The International Journal of Business in Society, 19*(1), 176–188. doi:10.1108/CG-11-2017-0268

Rosati, F., & Faria, L. (2019). Addressing the SDGs in sustainability reports: The relationship with institutional factors. *Journal of Cleaner Production, 215*, 1312–1326. doi:10.1016/j.jclepro.2018.12.107

Schäufele, I., & Hamm, U. (2017). Consumers' perceptions, preferences and willingness-to-pay for wine with sustainability characteristics: A review. *Journal of Cleaner Production, 147*, 379–394. doi:10.1016/j.jclepro.2017.01.118

Shakoury, K. (2018). *Critical discourse analysis of Iranian Presidents' Addresses to the United Nations General Assembly (2007-2016)* (Doctoral dissertation). University of Saskatchewan.

Szolnoki, G. (2013). A cross-national comparison of sustainability in the wine industry. *Journal of Cleaner Production, 53*, 243–251. doi:10.1016/j.jclepro.2013.03.045

Thiagarajan, A., & Sekkizhar, J. (2017). The Impact of Green Intellectual Capital on Integrated Sustainability Performance in the Indian Auto-component Industry. *Journal of Contemporary Research in Management, 12*(4), 21–78.

Ullah, H., Wang, Z., Bashir, S., Khan, A., Riaz, M., & Syed, N. (2021). Nexus between IT capability and green intellectual capital on sustainable businesses: Evidence from emerging economies. *Environmental Science and Pollution Research International, 28*(22), 27825–27843. doi:10.100711356-020-12245-2 PMID:33515153

Van der Waal, J., & Thijssens, T. (2020). Corporate involvement in sustainable development goals: Exploring the territory. *Journal of Cleaner Production, 252*, 119625. doi:10.1016/j.jclepro.2019.119625

Yadiati, W., Nissa, N., Paulus, S., Suharman, H., & Meiryani, M. (2019). The role of green intellectual capital and organizational reputation in influencing environmental performance. *International Journal of Energy Economics and Policy, 9*(3), 261–267. doi:10.32479/ijeep.7752

Yong, J., Yusliza, M., Ramayah, T., & Fawehinmi, O. (2019). Nexus between green intellectual capital and green human resource management. *Journal of Cleaner Production, 215*, 364–374. doi:10.1016/j.jclepro.2018.12.306

Yusliza, M., Yong, J., Tanveer, M., Ramayah, T., Faezah, J., & Muhammad, Z. (2020). A structural model of the impact of green intellectual capital on sustainable performance. *Journal of Cleaner Production, 249*, 119334. doi:10.1016/j.jclepro.2019.119334

Yusoff, Y., Omar, M., Zaman, M., & Samad, S. (2019). Do all elements of green intellectual capital contribute toward business sustainability? Evidence from the Malaysian context using the Partial Least Squares method. *Journal of Cleaner Production, 234*, 626–637. doi:10.1016/j.jclepro.2019.06.153

Zhang, Y., Sun, J., Yang, Z., & Wang, Y. (2020). Critical success factors of green innovation: Technology, organization and environment readiness. *Journal of Cleaner Production*, *264*, 121701. doi:10.1016/j.jclepro.2020.121701

ADDITIONAL READING

Atkin, T., Gilinsky, A. Jr, & Newton, S. K. (2012). Environmental strategy: Does it lead to competitive advantage in the US wine industry? *International Journal of Wine Business Research*, *24*(2), 115–133. doi:10.1108/17511061211238911

Atkin, T., Wilson, D., Thach, L., & Olsen, J. (2017). Analyzing the impact of conjunctive labeling as part of a regional wine branding strategy. *Wine Economics and Policy*, *6*(2), 155–164. doi:10.1016/j.wep.2017.10.003

Baiano, A. (2021). An Overview on Sustainability in the Wine Production Chain. *Beverages*, *7*(1), 15. doi:10.3390/beverages7010015

Gilinsky, A., Santini, C., Lazzeretti, L., & Eyler, R. (2008). Desperately seeking serendipity: Exploring the impact of country location on innovation in the wine industry. *International Journal of Wine Business Research*, *20*(4), 302–320. doi:10.1108/17511060810919425

Merli, R., Preziosi, M., & Acampora, A. (2018). Sustainability experiences in the wine sector: Toward the development of an international indicators system. *Journal of Cleaner Production*, *172*, 3791–3805. doi:10.1016/j.jclepro.2017.06.129

Montella, M. (2017). Wine tourism and sustainability: A review. *Sustainability*, *9*(1), 113. doi:10.3390u9010113

Mozell, M. R., & Thach, L. (2014). The impact of climate change on the global wine industry: Challenges & solutions. *Wine Economics and Policy*, *3*(2), 81–89. doi:10.1016/j.wep.2014.08.001

KEY TERMS AND DEFINITIONS

Green Human Capital: A set of knowledge, skills, and abilities of employees related to environmental protection and green innovation.

Green Intellectual Capital: A set of intangible assets held by both individuals and the organization that are intended to protect the environment and foster green innovation in the organization.

Green Relational Capital: Intangible assets based on the existing relationships between the organization and its stakeholders.

Green Structural Capital: Intangible assets owned by the organization and aimed at environmental protection and eco-innovation in the company.

ISO 14000: A set of rules governing the environmental management of companies.

Sustainability: Development that meets the needs of the present without compromising the ability of future generations, ensuring a balance between economic growth, environmental care, and social well-being.

Wineries for Climate Protection: Distinctive label that guarantees the wineries' protection of the environment.

APPENDIX

Block 1: History and Generic Data

1. When was the winery founded?
2. What do you consider to be the most important milestones of the organization?
3. Do you have other wineries in the national or international territory? How has the expansion/internationalization strategy been?
4. How many hectares of vineyards does the winery manage?
5. What is the surface area of organic vineyards and how long has there been organic vineyards?
6. What grape varieties do you work with?
7. How are the different distribution channels of the winery distributed? To which countries are they mainly exported?
8. Is organic, natural or biodynamic wine produced and to which countries is it mainly exported?
9. Is the wine distributed under the same brand or are there different brands within the group? Which ones?
10. What is the current situation of the winery?
11. How have you been able to combat the difficulties arising from COVID-19?

Block 2: Green Intellectual Capital

Green Human Capital

12. Do the employees attend seminars, workshops, events to improve their knowledge about sustainability in the industry?
13. Does the organization participate in industry fairs?
14. Does the organization have a manual of good practices, environmental statements, explicit commitments to improve its environmental performance?
15. How would you rate the motivation of employees in the winery to make it a benchmark for sustainability?
16. Do you consider that being a sustainable winery improves the employee's working situation?
17. Since when has the organization been firmly committed to the sustainability of the winery?

Green Structural Capital

18. Are there any recycling programs in the organization? Which ones?
19. Are there any emission control programs in the winery? Which ones?

20. Through which systems is the carbon footprint and water footprint measured?
21. Are there waste and energy reduction plans?
22. How is the waste generated in the winery reused? Are any products made from the by-products?
23. Do you have circular economy programs?
24. How do the winery facilities facilitate the efficient use of energy? Are there solar panels?
25. Do you consider that there is a link between the Bodegas Luzón brand and sustainability on the part of the customer?
26. Is there a department or person in charge of sustainability in the winery?
27. Does the winery have certificates that endorse its commitment to sustainability?
28. What is the organizational structure like? Is it hierarchical or flat?
29. What values of the organization do you consider that favor the sustainability of the winery?
30. Does the winery invest in R&D? Examples?

Green Relational Capital

31. Does the winery participate with other associations to improve the environment?
32. Does the winery collaborate with its suppliers to improve its environmental objectives?
33. Do you take into account green certifications when collaborating with your suppliers?
34. Do you have collaboration agreements with universities?
35. How do you relate to your customers? Do you organize events to get to know their tastes and their preference for organic wine?

Block 3: Sustainable Development Objectives

36. How many employees does the winery currently have? Is there parity between men and women?
37. Do you develop wine tourism activities and to what extent do you consider that these activities contribute to the territorial development of Jumilla?
38. What is the link between the winery and the land where it was born (Jumilla)?
39. What are the winery's future challenges in terms of sustainability?

Chapter 6
Green Economics and Urbanization in OIC Member Countries

Nima Norouzi
https://orcid.org/0000-0002-2546-4288
Bournemouth University, UK

ABSTRACT

Although urbanization is often discussed in the context of economic modernization, it is nevertheless a population indicator that increases urban density and changes the structure of human behavior and, as a result, affects household energy consumption patterns. Accordingly, the purpose of this study is to investigate the effect of urbanization on carbon dioxide emissions in the member countries of the Organization of the Islamic Conference using the Paneldita approach and the application of the STIRPAT model. The method used in the present study is scientific-analytical and the purpose of the research is applied. Statistics and information about the variables used in the research are extracted from the WDI2014 CD. The econometric tools used in the research are EViews software and the econometric method used in the research is the Paneldita method. The research period is 2000 to 2020 and the research area is 43 countries selected from the member countries of the Islamic conference.

INTRODUCTION

2010 was an important milestone in urbanization, with global urbanization exceeding 50%. Although urbanization is on the rise in developed countries, developing countries are expected to experience the greatest increase in urbanization, with the United Nations Population Division predicting that by 2025, urbanization in less developed areas will exceed 50 Percent will pass. In addition, urbanization in the less developed regions of the world is expected to more than triple, rising from 18 percent in 1950 to 67 percent in 2050(Alam et al., 2007). Although urbanization is often discussed in the context of economic modernization, it is nevertheless a demographic indicator that increases urban density and changes the structure of human behavior. As a result, it affects household energy consumption patterns.

DOI: 10.4018/978-1-6684-5109-0.ch006

Three theories of ecological modernization, environmental change to urban space, and urban density are used to explain how urbanization can affect the natural environment, according to Pumani Wong and Kanko. The theory of ecological modernization explains how urbanization is a process of social transformation that is also an important indicator of modernization. According to this theory, as societies move from the lower stages of development to the middle stages of development, environmental problems may increase(Barnes et al., 2010). Because in these stages of development, economic growth takes precedence over environmental sustainability. As societies reach higher stages of development, environmental damage becomes more important and societies look for ways to make their societies more environmentally sustainable. The detrimental impact of economic growth on the environment may be reduced by technological innovation, urbanization, and the shift from a production-based economy to a knowledge-based economy. The theory of environmental change to urban space relates environmental issues to urban change at the city level. According to this theory, in the modern age, cities often become richer (more powerful) by increasing their production base, and this causes industrial pollution problems that affect land, air, and water.

As cities become more empowered, industrial pollution may be reduced through environmental regulation, technological innovation, or changes in the structure of the economic sector.

More affluent cities are creating more residual residences, and resilient residences are demanding more energy production, putting more pressure on the environment. Urban congestion theory also addresses the benefits of increasing urbanization. Higher urban density helps facilitate economies of scale for public infrastructures such as public transportation, water supply, electricity generation, schools, and hospitals, and these savings Economies of scale cause less environmental damage. Theories of ecological modernization and urban environmental change both show that urbanization can have negative and positive effects on the natural environment with a net impact, so that if urbanization has a positive and significant effect on carbon dioxide emissions, then it can Climate change forecasting policies and policies will be effective, and as a result, carbon dioxide emission forecasting models that are unable to calculate the impact of urbanization on carbon dioxide emissions will be able to predict carbon dioxide emissions(Burton, 2000).

If urbanization has a significant negative impact on carbon dioxide emissions, then it will make it easier to achieve sustainable development goals. Also, if urbanization has a statistically significant effect on carbon dioxide emissions, then it will not have a significant effect on carbon dioxide emissions, which with the negative and positive effects of urbanization on carbon dioxide emissions that neutralize each other, Is compatible. Therefore, considering that urbanization can have a different effect on carbon dioxide emissions, the present study seeks to investigate this issue in 34 selected countries of the Organization of the Islamic Conference using the STIRPAT0 model and using the distance panel data method. The time is 2000 to 2020. The hypothesis presented in the research is based on the existence of the effect of urbanization on carbon dioxide emissions in the member countries of the Organization of the Islamic Conference.

Based on the organization of the topics of the article, after the introduction, in the second part, the theoretical foundations and research background are reviewed and in the third part, the geographical map of the member countries of the Organization of the Islamic Conference is given. In the fourth part, the research method is introduced and the fifth part is dedicated to the findings and the discussion and conclusion is the final part of the research.

BACKGROUND

Although urbanization is mostly discussed in the form of economic modernization, but it is a demographic phenomenon that increases urban density, changes the framework of human behavior and thus affects the pattern of household energy consumption. However, the area in which the effects of urban growth on energy consumption nationally and carbon dioxide emissions are fully explored is not clearly explained in a single theory. In contrast, some of the possible effects of urbanization on the environment have been discussed in detail and separately in three related theories: 1) The theory of ecological modernization 2) The theory of the transformation of the environment into the city And 3) The theory of urban density. The first theory focuses on effects at the national level, the other two theories focus on effects at the city level.
The following three theories are explained(Baltagi, 2021):

Theory of Ecological Modernization

This theory was developed in the early 1980s in a small group of Western European countries, especially Germany, the Netherlands, and the United Kingdom. Social scientists such as Martin Janick of Germany and Arthur P. J. Mol from the Netherlands and Joseph Murphy from the UK have made significant contributions to this theory. The purpose of ecological modernization theory is to analyze how industrial societies deal with environmental crises. The general purpose of studies in line with the traditional theory of environmental modernization is to focus on existing and planned environmental adjustments as a result of social activities, socio-institutional plans, as well as political discourses to protect the livelihood of communities(Mol & Spaargaren, 2000). Thus, the theory of ecological modernization emphasizes not only economic modernization but also socio-institutional change, in which urbanization is a process of social transformation, researchers argue that environmental problems may range from low to medium stages of development. However, modernization can further minimize such problems, for example, communities that are moving towards the realization of the importance of environmental sustainability, seeking to eliminate the destructive effects of the environment. Due to economic growth, due to technological innovations, urban density and change of direction towards knowledge-based industries and services(Capello & Camagni, 2000).

Theory of Changing the Environment to Urban Space

It is a powerful tool to answer the question, "What are the environmental challenges that cities are affected by?" This theory mainly discusses the types of environmental-urban issues and their evolution. . McGranahan et al. And McGranahan & Sungsor argue that urban-environmental pressures lead to more fragmentation and delays in resource regulation(McGranahan & Songsore, 1994). As a result, environmental-urban issues are different at different stages of economic development. The lower stages of development are often faced with environmental problems related to poverty (lack of safe water supply and poor sanitation). However, as income levels increase, these problems gradually subside. The increase in wealth in cities is mostly accompanied by an increase in productive activities that lead to significant industrial pollution, such as climate pollution. Such problems are reduced in wealthy cities due to improvements in environmental regulations, technological advances, and structural changes in the economy. Consumption patterns and lifestyles in wealthy cities tend to use more resources than in lower-income cities, so wealthy cities are more prone to consumption-related environmental issues. In other words, in cities that are becoming richer, the demand for urban infrastructure, transportation, and the consumption of personal resources is increasing. As a result, consumption issues, such as energy consumption and CO_2 emissions, become important(Crenshaw & Jenkins, 1996).

The Theory of Urban Density

This theory discusses the environmental benefits of urban congestion, arguing that high urban density leads to economies of scale for urban public infrastructure (e.g., public transportation, schools, and Reduces water supply, dependence on cars, long transportation routes and losses due to electricity distribution, and ultimately leads to reduced energy consumption and reduced CO_2 emissions from energy consumption. However, some Critics say the damage from urban sprawl is likely to outweigh the benefits of traffic congestion, overcrowding and air pollution. In principle, without the support of proper urban infrastructure, high urban density can lead to significant environmental problems.

A number of researchers have studied the relationship between urbanization and carbon dioxide emissions. In one of the first studies, Parikh and Shokla developed the impact of urbanization on energy consumption and toxic greenhouse gas emissions using data from 83 developed and developing countries for 1986. The results showed a positive and significant effect of urbanization on greenhouse gas emissions of CH_4, CO_2 and CFC and the elasticity of CO_2 emissions to urbanization was 0.036(Parikh & Shukla, 1995). York et al. (2003) And have released carbon dioxide greenhouse gas emissions. According to the study, increasing urbanization increases carbon dioxide emissions. Cole & Neumayer (2004) studied 86 countries between 1975 and 1998 and concluded that there was a positive relationship between urbanization and carbon dioxide emissions. A 10 percent increase in urbanization leads to a 7 percent increase in carbon dioxide emissions. Fan et al. (2006) A study examined the impact of environmental determinants in Pakistan between 1971 and 2005. The research findings indicate that the increase in GDP and the intensity of energy use increase environmental pollution (carbon dioxide emissions). Five years ago, they concluded that when using the total carbon dioxide emission variable as a dependent variable, urbanization had a positive but insignificant effect on carbon dioxide emissions, but when transported carbon dioxide was used as a dependent variable. Urbanization has a positive and significant effect on carbon dioxide emissions. Pumani Wong and Kanko used the STIRPAT model to study the impact of urbanization on carbon dioxide emissions in 99 countries between 1975 and 2005. In this study, a large number of panel regression methods have been used, but the experimental methods are all static in nature. The results of the study show that urbanization has a positive and significant effect on carbon dioxide emissions for each income group, but its greatest impact is for the middle income group of countries, so that for low income groups, the estimated coefficient of urbanization between 0.43 and 0.61 changed and for the average income groups, the estimated coefficient on urbanization varies between 0.21 and 0.51. For high-income groups, the estimated coefficient on urbanization varies between 0.04 and 0.35(World Bank, 2012; McGranahan & Songsore, 1994).

Sharma studied a large panel of 69 countries, including high-income, middle-income and low-income countries, and concluded that in the global panel, urbanization has a significant negative impact on carbon emissions, so that for Global panel, one percent increase in urbanization reduces 0.7 percent in carbon dioxide emissions(Sharma, 2011). Heilig (2012) studied the nine newly industrialized countries of Brazil, China, India, Malaysia, Mexico, the Philippines, South Africa, Thailand, and Turkey from 1971 to 2007, and as a result of the existence of a long-term accumulator between gas emissions(Kim et al., 2020). Carbon dioxide has reached production, energy consumption, commercial openness and urbanization, so that in the long run, a 1% increase in energy consumption and revenue has caused a 1.2 and 0.2% increase in carbon dioxide emissions, respectively, and a 1% increase in urbanization. 0.6% reduction in carbon dioxide emissions. Lina et al. (2013) Used STIRPAT model to analyze The impact of various factors, especially urbanization, on carbon dioxide emissions in Tianjin, China, has been addressed between 1990 and 2010. The results indicate that population and transportation structure have an important effect on carbon dioxide emissions and urbanization directly increases carbon emissions in Tianjin. Ponce and Marshall have also empirically examined how carbon dioxide emissions are affected nationally by urbanization and environmental policies. For this purpose, the data panel model was used for 80 countries between 1983 and 2005. The results of the random and fixed effects model show that at the global average, the emission elasticity of carbon dioxide relative to urbanization is 0.95. Meaning that one percent increase in urbanization increases 0.95 percent in carbon dioxide emissions(Newman & Kenworthy, 1989; Jacobi et al., 2010).

METHODS AND MATERIAL

The purpose of this study is to investigate the effect of urbanization on carbon dioxide emissions in selected member countries of the Organization of the Islamic Conference in the annual period 2000 to 2020. Accordingly, using the data panel method and using the model used by Saderski in the form of STIRPT model, this issue is investigated. Many researchers have a model of random effects with population, resources and technology regression (STIRPAT) Have been used to investigate the relationship between urbanization and greenhouse gas emissions of carbon dioxide, including the study of Liddle & Lung (2010), Poumanyvong & Kaneko, and Martinez-Zarzosu and Marotti(Martínez-Zarzoso & Maruotti, 2011; Poumanyvong & Kaneko, 2010; Jenks et al., 1996).

$$I = P \times A \times T \tag{1}$$

STIRPAT is based on the IPAT model developed by Ehrlich and Holdern. The IPAT model links environmental impact to population, resource abundance and technology. There are two criticisms of the IPAT model: First, it is a mathematical equation or arithmetic identity that is not suitable for testing a hypothesis. Second, it assumes a strict fit between the variables. Hence, Dietz & Rosa (1997) present a random version of IPAT:

$$I_{it} = a_i P_{it}^b A_{it}^c T_{it}^d e_{it} \tag{2}$$

In the above relation P: population, A: abundance of resources, T: technology and I: shows environmental change. Also, the subtitle i = 1,..., N specifies the countries and the subtitle t = 1,..., T also specifies the time period. Country-specific effects are also denoted by ai, and ε_{it} indicates a random error. The natural logarithms of equation (2) provide a good linear diagnosis for panel estimation, and since logarithms are taken from variables, the estimated coefficients can also be considered as elastic.

$$Ln(I_{it}) = bLn(P_{it}) + cLn(A_{it}) + Ln(T_{it}) + v_i + \varepsilon_{it} \qquad (3)$$

Accordingly, by modeling the model used by Saderski in the form of STIRPAT model, according to Equation (4) to study the impact of urbanization on carbon dioxide emissions in 43 selected countries of the Organization of the Islamic Conference with the names of Iran, Yemen, Nigeria, Mozambique, Morocco, Egypt, Malaysia, Maldives, Libya, Lebanon, Kuwait, Ivory Coast, Kazakhstan, Qatar, Kyrgyzstan, Comoros, Guinea-Bissau, Guyana, Gambia, Gabon, Oman, Iraq, Suriname, Syria, Sudan, Senegal, Saudi Arabia, Djibouti, Algeria, Tunisia, Togo, Turkmenistan, Turkey, Tajikistan, Bangladesh, Brunei, Pakistan, Uzbekistan, Indonesia, UAE, Albania, Jordan and Azerbaijan are covered annually from 2000 to 2020. The data used in the study are extracted from the WDI2020 CD and it should be noted that in the WDI2020 version, for most selected countries, statistics and information on urbanization variables by 2020, GDP per capita by year 2020 and energy consumption are available until 2020, but due to the existence of statistics and information on the carbon dioxide emission variable until 2021, the time period until 2020 is limited(Ponce de Leon Barido & Marshall, 2014; Gouldson & Murphy, J. 1997). The reason for selecting 43 countries out of 57 member countries of the Islamic Conference was the lack of complete and coherent information for the remaining 14 countries. Also, in the field of researchers' research, many studies have been done on the subject of research in Iran, but the studies that have been done as a panel using the STIRPAT model are the study of Fitras and the victim of nature, which he examined the effect. Urban growth has focused on energy consumption and carbon dioxide emissions in 18 countries in the Middle East and North Africa between 1990 and 2007. Also in his study, in the STIRPAT model used, the technology variable has been decomposed into the added value of the industry and services sector. Marotti, the technology variable is estimated using the energy intensity variable(Sadorsky, 2014).

$$Ln(CO2_{it}) = a_1 + a_2 LUPOP_{it} + a_3 LGDPP_{it} + a_4 LENIN_{it} + U_{it} \qquad (4)$$

In Equation (4) CO2: per capita emissions of carbon dioxide (in metric tons), UPOP: urban population (percentage of total population), GDPP: real per capita GDP (based on base year 2005), ENIN: Energy intensity defined as the energy consumption equivalent to kilograms of oil divided by real GDP at constant price in 2005, following the study by Martinez-Zarzosu, Marotti and Saderski, L: is the logarithm sign and U: is the model waste statement.

Combined data is a set of data based on which observations are examined by a large number of cross-sectional variables (N), often randomly selected, over a specified period of time (T). In this case, this NxT is called statistical data combined data or cross-sectional data-time series. In this way, there will be two types of dimensions: time dimension and sections dimension (individuals), which is also called group-time data(Ehrlich & Holdren, 1971).

Since hybrid data includes both aspects of time series data and cross-sectional data, the use of models should be noted that in the STIRPAT model used by Saderski according to Equation (3), the real per capita GDP variable as a proxy for The affluence variable and the energy intensity variable are used as proxies for the technology variable.

A good statistical descriptor that describes the characteristics of those variables is more complex than the models used in cross-sectional data and time series. Panel data sets have many advantages over cross-sectional or time-series data, some of the most important of which are: 1) By considering individual variables, this inequality is taken into account. 2) By combining time series and cross-sectional observations, panel data with higher information, higher flexibility, less alignment between variables, and greater degree of freedom provide higher performance. 3) By studying repetitive cross-sectional observations, panel data are better suited to study changes dynamically (e.g., periods of unemployment and labor mobility are better assessed with panel data), 4) panel data show effects that cannot be Simplicity observed in cross-sectional and time series data is better determined (e.g., the effects of minimum wage rules on employment are better examined with panel data), 5) Panel data enables us to study more complex behavioral models (For example: technology changes and cost-effectiveness with your panel data), 6) The panel data eliminates bias by providing large amounts of data(Parikh & Shukla, 1995).

RESULTS AND DISCUSSION

Checking the Reliability of Variables

Before estimating the model, it is necessary to test the reliability of the variables used in the model, because the instability of the variables, both in the case of time series data and panel data, causes the problem of false regression. Contrary to what is common with time series data, in the case of panel data, generalized Dickey-Fuller and Dickey-Fuller tests cannot be used for reliability testing, but the variability of variables must be tested collectively.

Levin, Lin and Chou (LLC) tests were used to evaluate the reliability of the variables. Based on the test results given in Table (1), due to the fact that the probability values are less than 0.05, the H0 hypothesis that there is a single root at the 95% confidence level is rejected and the model variables are stable at the level or In other words, they are I(0).

Table 1. Results of the reliability test of variables using Levin, Lin and Chou unit root test

Parameter	Without Trend Analysis		With Trend Analysis	
	Stat.	Prob.	Stat.	Prob.
LCO2	-7.79	0.000	-13.88	0.000
LUPOP	-3.89	0.000	-9.87	0.000
LGDPP	-2.18	0.014	-6.76	0.000
LENIN	-3.04	0.001	-10.12	0.000

Model Estimation

In the following, the model introduced in Equation (4) is estimated. The question that is often asked in applied studies is whether it is possible to integrate the data or whether the model gives different results at different times. In other words, are the slopes and widths of the origins different in the model for different sections or not? In the presence of individual heterogeneities and differences, the combined data method should be used. For this purpose, the significance of individual effects should be tested before any kind of estimation. The statistic used to test whether individual effects are significant or not is F-Limer. If at a certain significance level, the calculated F is greater than the value of the table F with degrees of face freedom (1-N) and denominator (NT-NK), hypothesis H0 that the individual effects are not significant is rejected and therefore the model should be paneldita. To be estimated. But if the calculated F is smaller than the corresponding F in the table, then hypothesis H0 cannot be rejected.

Table (2) shows the results of the fixed effects test for Equation (4). As can be seen in the table, in the mentioned model, according to the probability value related to F statistic, at 95% confidence level, the calculated F statistic is larger than the F statistic value of the table and indicates the rejection of H0 hypothesis and confirmation of data panel estimation method. In the research model.

Table 2. Results related to the fixed effects test

Parameter	Statistic	Prob.
Cross-Section F	117.89	0.000
Cross-Section Chi-square	1113.44	0.000

In the next step, the Hausman test is used to answer whether the difference in width from the origin of the cross-sectional units is constant or whether random operations can express this difference between the units more clearly. We test H0 hypothesis on the consistency of random effect estimates against H1 hypothesis on the inconsistency of random effect estimates or fixed effect compatibility.

Table (3) shows the results of the Hausman test. According to the table, it can be seen that at 95% confidence level, H0 hypothesis based on the consistency of random effect estimates is not rejected and random estimation should be used to estimate the model.

Table 3. Results related to Hausman test

Parameter	Chi-sq.Statistic	Prob.
Cross-Section random	6.97	0.070

Equation (5) shows the results of model estimation. As can be seen, the sign of the coefficients is in accordance with the expected theoretical foundations and is also statistically significant, so that a one percent increase in urbanization variables. Real GDP per capita and energy intensity increase by 0.57, 0.74 and 0.58% respectively in carbon dioxide emissions.

$$Ln(CO2_{it}) = -10.17 + 0.57 LUPOP_{it} + 0.74 LGDPP_{it} + 0.55 LENIN_{it} \tag{5}$$

CONCLUSION

The purpose of this study is to investigate the effect of urbanization on carbon dioxide emissions in a selection of member countries of the Organization of the Islamic Conference between 2000 and 2020. Based on the research findings, the coefficient sign was in accordance with the expected theoretical foundations and was also statistically significant, so that all three variables of urbanization, GDP per capita and energy intensity had a positive and significant effect on carbon dioxide emissions. The amount of carbon dioxide emission elasticity relative to the variables of urbanization, GDP per capita and energy intensity are 0.57, 0.74 and 0.55, respectively. In interpreting the positive effect of urbanization variable on carbon dioxide emissions, it can be said that because most of the member countries of the Organization of the Islamic Conference are low-developing or developing countries, therefore, based on two theories of ecological modernization. And the change of environment to urban space, due to the increase in urbanization and the structure of urban life, which requires the use of more energy and fuel resources, especially in transportation, with increasing energy consumption increases carbon dioxide emissions in these countries. This result can be seen in the study of Parikh and Shokla, York, Cole and Neumayer, Liddell and Lang, Lina, Ponce Also approved. In interpreting the positive effect of GDP per capita on carbon dioxide emissions, it can be stated that because with the increase in GDP and the study countries are on the path of growth, these countries need high energy consumption and the increase in production itself requires more use. Wet production inputs, energy is also one of those production inputs, and because this energy consumption is more supplied by fossil fuels such as gasoline and diesel, it increases carbon dioxide emissions and also as another reason. It can be said that since most of the member countries of the Organization of the Islamic Conference have problems such as lack of human skills, inefficiency in production and lack of technological developments, so increasing production in these countries can increase carbon dioxide emissions. This result has been confirmed in the study of Alam et al., Hossein, Fitras and Barati, and Behboodi et al. Regarding the positive effect of energy intensity on carbon dioxide emissions, it can be said that excessive energy consumption and inefficiency in its consumption can increase environmental pollution, including carbon dioxide emissions, which is the result of this study. Alam et al., Hussein, Fitras et al., Fitras et al. And Behboodi et al. Have also been approved. Therefore, in line with the results of the research, it is suggested that in the member countries of the Organization of the Islamic Conference, by optimizing energy consumption and increasing the use of new energy sources that cause less pollution, as well as energy efficiency in production and technology development Production and distribution of energy in countries, realization of energy prices, promotion of technical and environmental standards of industrial production, increase of energy consumption efficiency and expansion of cultural education, environmental protection and providing suitable bases and development of villages, while establishing a demographic balance, Reduce air pollution and carbon dioxide emissions.

REFERENCES

Alam, S., Fatima, A., & Butt, M. S. (2007). Sustainable development in Pakistan in the context of energy consumption demand and environmental degradation. *Journal of Asian Economics*, *18*(5), 825–837. doi:10.1016/j.asieco.2007.07.005

Baltagi, B. H. (2021). *Econometric analysis of panel data*. Springer Nature. doi:10.1007/978-3-030-53953-5

Barnes, D. F., Krutilla, K., & Hyde, W. F. (2010). *The urban household energy transition: social and environmental impacts in the developing world*. Routledge. doi:10.4324/9781936331000

Burton, E. (2000). The compact city: Just or just compact? A preliminary analysis. *Urban Studies (Edinburgh, Scotland)*, *37*(11), 1969–2006. doi:10.1080/00420980050162184

Capello, R., & Camagni, R. (2000). Beyond optimal city size: An evaluation of alternative urban growth patterns. *Urban Studies (Edinburgh, Scotland)*, *37*(9), 1479–1496. doi:10.1080/00420980020080221

Cole, M. A., & Neumayer, E. (2004). Examining the impact of demographic factors on air pollution. *Population and Environment*, *26*(1), 5–21. doi:10.1023/B:POEN.0000039950.85422.eb

Crenshaw, E. M., & Jenkins, J. C. (1996). Social structure and global climate change: Sociological propositions concerning the greenhouse effect. *Sociological Focus*, *29*(4), 341–358. doi:10.1080/00380237.1996.10570650

Dietz, T., & Rosa, E. A. (1997). Effects of population and affluence on CO2 emissions. *Proceedings of the National Academy of Sciences of the United States of America*, *94*(1), 175–179. doi:10.1073/pnas.94.1.175 PMID:8990181

Ehrlich, P. R., & Holdren, J. P. (1971). Impact of population growth. *Science*, *171*(3977), 1212–1217. doi:10.1126cience.171.3977.1212 PMID:5545198

Fan, Y., Liu, L. C., Wu, G., & Wei, Y. M. (2006). Analyzing impact factors of CO2 emissions using the STIRPAT model. *Environmental Impact Assessment Review*, *26*(4), 377–395. doi:10.1016/j.eiar.2005.11.007

Gouldson, A., & Murphy, J. (1997). *Ecological modernisation: Economic restructuring and the environment*. Academic Press.

Heilig, G. K. (2012). World urbanization prospects: The 2011 revision. United Nations, Department of Economic and Social Affairs (DESA), Population Division. *Population Estimates and Projections Section, New York*, *14*, 555.

Jacobi, P., Kjellen, M., McGranahan, G., Songsore, J., & Surjadi, C. (2010). *The citizens at risk: from urban sanitation to sustainable cities*. Routledge. doi:10.4324/9781849776097

Jenks, M., Burton, E., & Williams, K. (1996). Compact cities and sustainability: an introduction. *The compact city: A sustainable urban form*, 11-12.

Kim, H., Shoji, Y., Tsuge, T., Aikoh, T., & Kuriyama, K. (2020). Understanding services from ecosystem and facilities provided by urban green spaces: A use of partial profile choice experiment. *Forest Policy and Economics*, *111*, 102086. doi:10.1016/j.forpol.2019.102086

Li-na, X., Tao, Z., Xiao-feng, Y., & Yan-dong, Z. (2013). Analysis the Impact of Urbanization on Carbon Emissions Using the Stirpat Model in Tianjin, China. *Journal of Applied Sciences*, *13*(21), 4608–4611. doi:10.3923/jas.2013.4608.4611

Liddle, B., & Lung, S. (2010). Age-structure, urbanization, and climate change in developed countries: Revisiting STIRPAT for disaggregated population and consumption-related environmental impacts. *Population and Environment*, *31*(5), 317–343. doi:10.100711111-010-0101-5

Martínez-Zarzoso, I., & Maruotti, A. (2011). The impact of urbanization on CO2 emissions: Evidence from developing countries. *Ecological Economics*, *70*(7), 1344–1353. doi:10.1016/j.ecolecon.2011.02.009

McGranahan, G., & Songsore, J. (1994). Wealth, health, and the urban household: Weighing environmental burdens in…. *Environment*, *36*(6), 4–45. doi:10.1080/00139157.1994.9929172

Mol, A. P., & Spaargaren, G. (2000). Ecological modernisation theory in debate: A review. *Environmental Politics*, *9*(1), 17–49. doi:10.1080/09644010008414511

Newman, P. G., & Kenworthy, J. R. (1989). *Cities and automobile dependence: An international sourcebook*. Academic Press.

Parikh, J., & Shukla, V. (1995). Urbanization, energy use and greenhouse effects in economic development: Results from a cross-national study of developing countries. *Global Environmental Change*, *5*(2), 87–103. doi:10.1016/0959-3780(95)00015-G

Ponce de Leon Barido, D., & Marshall, J. D. (2014). Relationship between urbanization and CO2 emissions depends on income level and policy. *Environmental Science & Technology*, *48*(7), 3632–3639. doi:10.1021/es405117n PMID:24422489

Poumanyvong, P., & Kaneko, S. (2010). Does urbanization lead to less energy use and lower CO2 emissions? A cross-country analysis. *Ecological Economics*, *70*(2), 434–444. doi:10.1016/j.ecolecon.2010.09.029

Sadorsky, P. (2014). The effect of urbanization on CO2 emissions in emerging economies. *Energy Economics*, *41*, 147–153. doi:10.1016/j.eneco.2013.11.007

Sharma, S. S. (2011). Determinants of carbon dioxide emissions: Empirical evidence from 69 countries. *Applied Energy*, *88*(1), 376–382. doi:10.1016/j.apenergy.2010.07.022

World Bank. (2012). *Inclusive green growth: The pathway to sustainable development*. The World Bank.

York, R., Rosa, E. A., & Dietz, T. (2003). STIRPAT, IPAT and ImPACT: Analytic tools for unpacking the driving forces of environmental impacts. *Ecological Economics*, *46*(3), 351–365. doi:10.1016/S0921-8009(03)00188-5

ADDITIONAL READING

Anderson, V. (2006). Turning economics inside out. *International Journal of Green Economics*, *1*(1-2), 11–22. doi:10.1504/IJGE.2006.009334

Cato, M. S. (2012). *Green economics: an introduction to theory, policy and practice*. Routledge. doi:10.4324/9781849771528

Eichholtz, P., Kok, N., & Quigley, J. M. (2013). The economics of green building. *The Review of Economics and Statistics*, 95(1), 50–63. doi:10.1162/REST_a_00291

Green, D. (2003). *Silent revolution: The rise and crisis of market economics in Latin America*. NYU Press.

Hahnel, R. (2014). *Green economics: Confronting the ecological crisis*. Routledge. doi:10.4324/9781315703947

Hydes, K. R., & Creech, L. (2000). Reducing mechanical equipment cost: The economics of green design. *Building Research and Information*, 28(5-6), 403–407. doi:10.1080/096132100418555

Pearce, D. (1992). Green economics. *Environmental Values*, 1(1), 3–13. doi:10.3197/096327192776680179

Smith, R., & World Economics Association. (2016). *Green capitalism: the god that failed*. London: College Publications.

KEY TERMS AND DEFINITIONS

Circularity: A circular economy (also referred to as "circularity") is an economic system that tackles global challenges like climate change, biodiversity loss, waste, and pollution. Most linear economy businesses take a natural resource and turn it into a product that is ultimately destined to become waste because it has been designed and made. This process is often summarised by "take, make, waste." By contrast, a circular economy uses reuse, sharing, repair, refurbishment, remanufacturing, and recycling to create a closed-loop system, minimize resource inputs, and create waste, pollution, and carbon emissions. The circular economy aims to keep products, materials, equipment, and infrastructure in use for longer, thus improving the productivity of these resources. Waste materials and energy should become input for other processes through waste valorization: either as a component or recovered resource for another industrial process or as regenerative resources for nature (e.g., compost). This regenerative approach contrasts with the traditional linear economy, which has a "take, make, dispose of" production model.

Eco Commerce: Eco commerce is a business, investment, and technology-development model that employs market-based solutions to balancing the world's energy needs and environmental integrity. Through green trading and green finance, eco-commerce promotes the further development of "clean technologies" such as wind power, solar power, biomass, and hydropower.

Eco-Tariffs: An Eco-tariff, also known as an environmental tariff, is a trade barrier erected to reduce pollution and improve the environment. These trade barriers may take the form of import or export taxes on products with a large carbon footprint or imported from countries with lax environmental regulations.

Emissions Trading: Emissions trading (also known as cap and trade, emissions trading scheme, or ETS) is a market-based approach to controlling pollution by providing economic incentives for reducing the emissions of pollutants.

Environmental Enterprise: An environmental enterprise is an environmentally friendly/compatible business. Specifically, an environmental enterprise is a business that produces value in the same manner which an ecosystem does, neither producing waste nor consuming unsustainable resources. In addition, an environmental enterprise rather finds alternative ways to produce one's products instead of taking advantage of animals for the sake of human profits. To be closer to being an environmentally friendly company, some environmental enterprises invest their money to develop or improve their technologies which are also environmentally friendly. In addition, environmental enterprises usually try to reduce global warming, so some companies use environmentally friendly materials to build their stores. They also set in environmentally friendly place regulations. All these efforts of the environmental enterprises can bring positive effects both for nature and people. The concept is rooted in the well-enumerated theories of natural capital, the eco-economy, and cradle-to-cradle design. Examples of environmental enterprises would be Seventh Generation, Inc., and Whole Foods.

Green Economy: A green economy is an economy that aims at reducing environmental risks and ecological scarcities and that aims for sustainable development without degrading the environment. It is closely related to ecological economics but has a more politically applied focus. The 2011 UNEP Green Economy Report argues "that to be green, and an economy must be not only efficient but also fair. Fairness implies recognizing global and country-level equity dimensions, particularly in assuring a Just Transition to an economy that is low-carbon, resource-efficient, and socially inclusive."

Green Politics: Green politics, or ecopolitics, is a political ideology that aims to foster an ecologically sustainable society often, but not always, rooted in environmentalism, nonviolence, social justice, and grassroots democracy. It began taking shape in the western world in the 1970s; since then, Green parties have developed and established themselves in many countries around the globe and have achieved some electoral success.

Low-Carbon Economy: A low-carbon economy (LCE) or decarbonized economy is based on low-carbon power sources with minimal greenhouse gas (GHG) emissions into the atmosphere, specifically carbon dioxide. GHG emissions due to anthropogenic (human) activity are the dominant cause of observed climate change since the mid-20th century. Continued emission of greenhouse gases may cause long-lasting changes worldwide, increasing the likelihood of severe, pervasive, and irreversible effects for people and ecosystems.

Natural Resource Economics: Natural resource economics deals with the supply, demand, and allocation of the Earth's natural resources. One main objective of natural resource economics is to understand better the role of natural resources in the economy to develop more sustainable methods of managing those resources to ensure their future generations. Resource economists study interactions between economic and natural systems intending to develop a sustainable and efficient economy.

Sustainable Development: Sustainable development is an organizing principle for meeting human development goals while simultaneously sustaining the ability of natural systems to provide the natural resources and ecosystem services on which the economy and society depend. The desired result is a state of society where living conditions and resources are used to continue to meet human needs without undermining the integrity and stability of the natural system. Sustainable development can be defined as development that meets the needs of the present without compromising the ability of future generations to meet their own needs. Sustainability goals, such as the current UN-level Sustainable Development Goals, address the global challenges, including poverty, inequality, climate change, environmental degradation, peace, and justice.

Chapter 7
Mathematics of the Circular Economics:
A Case Study for the MENA Region

Nima Norouzi
https://orcid.org/0000-0002-2546-4288
Bournemouth University, UK

ABSTRACT

Based on the findings of economic studies on the consequences of industrialization in emerging economies, this study aims to evaluate rotational economy processes in the Middle East and North Africa (MENA) using a Shannon entropy algorithm. An entropy-based analysis was performed for 19 MENA countries in the period 2000-2020. The modeling process involves constructing a hybrid index that consists of a weighted sum of all the indices developed by an algorithm based on Shannon's entropy. The weight assigned to each index in the analysis measures the importance of each index involved in developing the composite index. The results are similar to the international balancing, which combines and confirms the precision and reliability of this method.

INTRODUCTION

The use of limited spatial resources raises many concerns for both governments and academics searching for the optimal solution to face the challenges of climate change or the growing demand in the consumer economy. The ratification of the Kyoto Protocol and its implementation in as many countries as possible will pave the way to combat pollution caused by industrial processes(Andersen, 2007). The transformation of a linear economy, based on the production-consumption-waste model, into circular economies, with the definition of revitalization and the production-consumption-reuse of resources, seems a mystery that does not exist today. Consumption pattern structure (Andersen, 2007; Bernstad Saraiva et al., 2018) investing in innovative equipment to protect the environment plays a key role in a rotating economy. Beyond the evolution of the classical model of economic growth (Baravalle et al., 2018), Anderson conceptualized an economic growth model to determine the main influencing factors,

DOI: 10.4018/978-1-6684-5109-0.ch007

then using empirical data in an attempt to determine the economic factors that stimulate or inhibit the transition to a circular pattern(Andersen, 2007). The economic literature of the last ten years is abundant in the presentation of econometrics to determine the impact of waste management processes on economic activities in the context of the general equilibrium model (Cobo et al., 2018). For example, in Sweden, Ljunggren Söderman and others. (Cleary, 2009) To find the correct answer to the request of the Swedish Parliament to reduce the percentage of waste concerning the growth rate, he analyzed the relationship between the management of the solid waste program. It should be noted here that Sweden is among the countries with the highest rates of waste reuse and is among the EU member states in terms of classification. Cannon et al. (2018) examined the impact on GDP of hazardous waste from mining activities in South Africa. It should be noted that the two continents of Africa and Asia are in the last place in terms of waste reuse, while North America and Europe are at the top of the ranking and among the most industrialized countries. The impact of environmental policies on growth prospects has been studied by international organizations such as the Statistical Office of the European Union (OECD) (De Almeida & Borsato, 2019) and by European institutions, for example, the European Commission (EC). Highly industrialized and developed agricultural countries inevitably face environmental challenges. The preservation of ecosystems around the world is or should be a political priority. The United Nations Environment Program reflects these concerns. A prestigious organization with a valuable contribution to evaluating European environmental policies is the Allen MacArthur Foundation, established in 2010 to accelerate the transition to a circular economy. The Allen MacArthur Foundation report "Economic Growth - Circular Economy, Europe's Competitive Outlook" (Georgescu-Roegen, 2013) shows that a high-tech circular economy enables Europe to increase productivity by up to 3% per year. According to this study, this initial benefit in 2030 will generate 0.6 trillion euros compared to current European economies, which will mean a GDP growth of 7% compared to the current scenario and positively impact employment.

The concept of "cradle to cradle" (C2C) was introduced by Mc Donough and Braungart and is specific to the regenerative circular economy (Hussain & Haque, 2016). This concept applies to the sustainable energy production process and includes converting waste into new products, natural energy resources, and the diversity of ecosystems. On the contrary, Morrison (2011) criticizes the "cradle to grave" equation used in the industrial process, in which the products are transferred to the trash, often without the possibility of reuse.

The extent of China's economic development over the past two decades is well known. The destruction of the environment inevitably led to an economic miracle. Therefore, the circular economy is a strategy for sustainable development and has been proposed by the Beijing-based government to improve energy efficiency and materials. This strategy, formally adopted in 2002, was implemented and developed in pilot areas in China (Kronborg, 2014). National laws and regulations have been adopted to facilitate the implementation of rotational economy projects. China is the first globally to provide objective and credible information on the implementation status of circular economy processes based on a single index system for political decision-making. The work of Chinese economists (Kopnina, 2017) critically analyzes China's applied circular economy model. The indicators provided by the Chinese government can be widely used by other countries and being aware of the risk of environmental degradation as a reference point to know the state of development of the circular economy. The circular economy can also be related to the pattern of the community economy (Ljunggren Söderman et al., 2016). This method can be considered a closed loop of material flow rather than the linear "production-use-disposal" view. Closing the loop through energy recovery or recycling is only part of modifying the linear economic model.

Repair, reuse, or remanufacturing circuits are preferred over energy recovery, recycling, or landfilling (Luo et al., 2018). The rapid development of digital technology is the key to enabling organizations to scale business models of the circular economy (Liu, 2013). When a value chain moves towards circular economy practices, the dynamics of power and competition change through destructive technologies such as recycling, analytics, and mobile technology (Lahti et al., 2018). The research question here is whether there is a direct and positive relationship between R&D costs for the Middle East and North Africa (MENA) circular economy processes and their economic efficiency. We measure this using the composite index. This chapter is organized as follows. In the first part, we present a composite indicator elaborated on Shannon entropy. The weight of our analysis assigned to each index measures the importance of each index involved in developing the composite index. Then, an entropy-based analysis was performed for 19 countries of the MENA basin based on an algorithm constructed using a composite index. The Mena country rankings become more apparent, and the results are discussed in the analysis section.

Background

The economic system is conventionally conceived as an open model (Molina-Sánchez et al., 2018). Production produces P, capital goods, K, and consumer goods, C; conversely, capital goods produce consumption in the future. Purpose of Consumption is the Well-being or Utility, U. Sometimes, this linear landscape also includes the natural resources R (see Figure 1).

Figure 1. Conventional linear economic processes

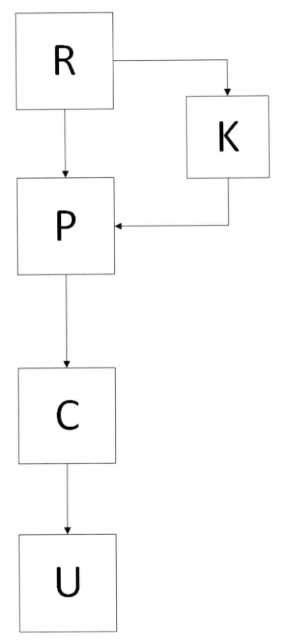

The linear economy process is becoming a circular economy in which the relationship between resource use and waste is considered. The result is that the total amount of waste generated in a cycle must equal the number of depleted resources. Capital goods can be used as temporary sources of resources, but they become waste systems in the environmental system after being consumed. Energy cannot be wasted, but it can be wasted or converted. However, the relationship between natural resources and waste in each cycle is somewhat more complex due to the reserves of capital goods (Núñez-Cacho et al., 2018a). In the linear process, the box r is for recycling. Waste can, to some extent, become a resource and change the economy. Unfortunately, not all waste is recyclable (Núñez-Cacho et al., 2018b), partly due to physical limitations and missed opportunities (see Figure 2). While this cycle is very evident for fossil fuels that form carbon dioxide molecules in the atmosphere, entropy growth also applies to most metals (Norouzi et al., 2020a). Liu (2013), in his dissertation, believes that the more energy and matter a person extracts for the economy, the higher the level of entropy. The circulation of energy and materials helps delay the increase in entropy and thus reduce the need for new inputs in the economic process.

Figure 2. Circular economy processes(in which R is recycling, and W is waste, Source: Andersen (2007))

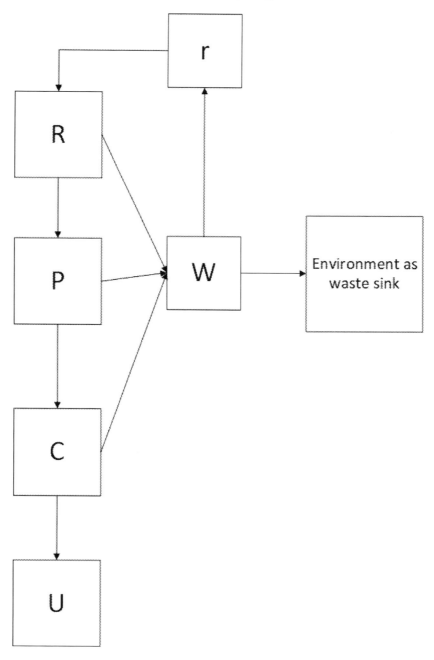

The environment can be assumed to perform four main economic welfare functions: (1) a basic resource for the economy. (2) comfort values, (3) a residual current sink; And (4) a life support system (Norouzi et al., 2020b). In Figure 3, we can see the relationship between the environment and its four basic economic functions. Waste transferred to the environment has great potential for harm by affecting life support performance and comfort levels and has also been eliminated from economic trends. In a circular economy that uses reuse and recycling, waste loss from the economic process may be delayed for non-renewable resources (Norouzi et al., 2021a). However, there may be additional problems with minimizing residual returns. Some economists think that the resources needed for the economy and material inputs should be limited, and that minimization should be a prerequisite for the remaining cycle.

Figure 3. Circular economy processes(Source: Pearce and Turner (1990), in which r is the recycling, P is the production, C is the consumption, U is the Utility, K is the capital goods, R is the natural resources, ER is the finite resources, RR is the recyclable resources, A is the absorption capacity, W is the waste, h is the harvest, and y is the yield)

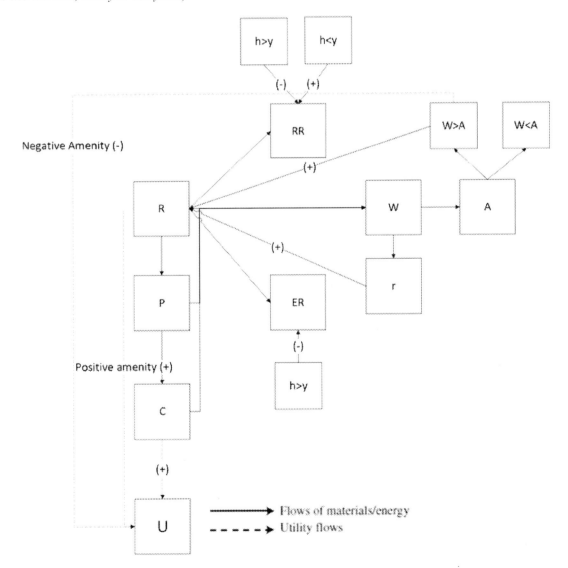

A circular economy formed through efficient recycling and reusing resources can create jobs, encourage entrepreneurs to invest in the context of their support programs, and, last but not least, sustainable economic growth. Contributes to investment and resource efficiency (Rada et al., 2018; Norouzi & Kalantari, 2020)

The use of entropy in environmental and biological processes was first proposed by Shannon (1948), who proposed entropy to quantify the information provided by a random variable or a possible experiment. This use of entropy evolved rapidly, and its application expanded to other fields such as biology, physics, economics, culture, and sociology. Develop theories based on the usefulness of information and measure information based on research by renowned researchers, including Xie & Saltzman (2000)., Von Neumann & Morgenstern (2007), Kolmogorov & Tikhomirov (1959), Tsallis (1988), and Norouzi (2021a). The level of uncertainty can be measured using the concept of entropy and can be interpreted as fuzzy or random. Different techniques have been developed to analyze the randomness of decision problems applied in different contexts that use risk criteria or information criteria(Norouzi & Fani, 2020a).

RESULTS AND DISCUSSION

The modeling of circular economy processes has been analyzed in various research papers. It has been shown that there is a close relationship between the use of the periodic economy and economic growth (Norouzi & Fani, 2021a). Other authors such as Norouzi & Fani (2021b), Perman et al. (2003), Rada et al. (2018), and Romero-Hernández & Romero (2018) concluded that human capital and innovation for the benefit of the environment have a positive effect on economic growth. The chapter will now use entropy measures to assess the returns of a rotating economy for 19 MENA countries. The data is collected from the world bank and is shown in Table 1. For the circular economy, the percentage of municipal waste recycling as a proxy has been used, while economic growth has been defined as the increase in the percentage of GDP in each country per capita in member countries(Norouzi et al., 2021b).

Table 1. Recycling rate and economic growth of the MENA countries

Country	GDP Per Capita,($)	Recycling (%)
Bahrain	50,700	6.7
Egypt	12,600	3.7
Iran	18,100	29.6
Iraq	17,900	8.7
Israel	35,200	31.1
Jordan	12,300	16.8
Kuwait	71,900	21.8
Lebanon	18,500	6.7
Oman	46,700	27.3
State of Palestine	4,300	6.4
Qatar	127,700	9.5
Saudi Arabia	55,200	16.5
Syria	2,900	0.5
Libya	7,685	5.2
United Arab Emirates	67,900	15.3
Yemen	2,400	0.2
Djbouti	3,414	4.5
Algeria	3,973	2.3
Sudan	1,480	0.9

The weights were determined after calculating the following steps.

Step 1

(A) Data standardization. The original matrix $X=(x_{ij})$ is standardized with the equation

$$y_{ij} = \frac{x_{ij} - \min x_{ij}}{\max x_{ij} - \min x_{ij}}, j=1,2 \tag{1}$$

(B) (B) Equation:

$$z_{ij} = \frac{y_{ij} - \min y_{ij}}{S_j}, j=1,2 \tag{2}$$

Mathematics of the Circular Economics

It is used to finalize the standard, where S_j and y_j show the standard deviation and the mean value of the index j.

(C) The entropy equation contains a natural logarithm, so the index value cannot be negative.

$$u_{it} = d + z_{ij} \qquad (3)$$

Where d is a number greater than the value, d is obtained 0.789623, and Table 2 shows the results after step 1.

Table 2. Results obtained when performing step 1

Country	Y_1	Y_2	Z_1	Z_2	U_1	U_2
Country	0.1259	0.1259	0.1259	0.1259	0.1259	0.1259
Bahrain	0.5611	0.64	129.0337	173.2444	209.0654	253.2761
Egypt	0.4885	0.4342	102.9794	0.9183	183.0111	171.8616
Iran	0.1123	0.1019	-0.3194	-0.397	0.4809	0.4033
Iraq	0.089	0.0824	-0.403	-0.4743	0.3973	0.3261
Israel	0.0225	0.0309	-0.6418	-0.6781	0.1585	0.1222
Jordan	0.1851	0.1589	-0.0586	-0.1713	0.7417	0.629
Kuwait	0.1259	0.1259	0.1259	0.1259	0.1259	0.1259
Lebanon	0.5611	0.64	76.9251	173.2444	156.9568	90.4471
Oman	0.4885	0.4342	50.8708	0.9183	130.9025	9.0327
State of Palestine	0.1123	0.1019	-0.3194	-0.397	0.4809	0.4033
Qatar	0.089	0.0824	-0.403	-0.4743	0.3973	0.3261
Saudi Arabia	0.0225	0.0309	-0.6418	-0.6781	0.1585	0.1222
Syria	0.1851	0.1589	-0.0586	-0.1713	0.7417	0.629
Libya	0.1259	0.1259	0.1259	0.1259	0.1259	0.1259
United Arab Emirates	0.5611	0.64	24.8165	173.2444	104.8482	-72.3818
Yemen	0.4885	0.4342	-1.2377	0.9183	78.794	-153.796
Djibouti	0.1123	0.1019	-0.3194	-0.397	0.4809	0.4033
Algeria	0.089	0.0824	-0.403	-0.4743	0.3973	0.3261
Sudan	0.0225	0.0309	-0.6418	-0.6781	0.1585	0.1222

Step 2

In this step, we calculate the weight values of the indicators.

(A) The probabilities of the jth index of the i-th sample are calculated by the equation

$$P_{ij} = \frac{u_{ij}}{\sum_{i=1}^{m} u_{ij}} \quad (4)$$

Where j = 1, n and i = 1, m and the final results after using step 2 can be seen in Table 3.

Table 3. Calculation of the weight of the indicators

Country	P1	P2
Bahrain	0.1123	0.1019
Egypt	0.089	0.0824
Iran	0.0225	0.0309
Iraq	0.1851	0.1589
Israel	0.1259	0.1259
Jordan	0.5611	0.64
Kuwait	0.4885	0.4342
Lebanon	0.1123	0.1019
Oman	0.089	0.0824
State of Palestine	0.089	0.0824
Qatar	0.0225	0.0309
Saudi Arabia	0.1851	0.1589
Syria	0.1259	0.1259
Libya	0.5611	0.64
United Arab Emirates	0.4885	0.4342
Yemen	0.1123	0.1019
Djbouti	0.089	0.0824
Algeria	0.0225	0.0309
Sudan	0.1851	0.1589

(B) (B)   Now, we calculate the entropy ej, which corresponds to the index j, using the equation

$$e_j = \frac{-1}{\ln(m)} \sum_{i=1}^{m} p_{ij} \ln(p_{ij}), \text{ where } j = 1, n \quad (5)$$

Therefore, results is obtained as $e_1 = 0.8434$ and $e_2 = 0.8722$.

(C) The utility function corresponding to the j-th index can be calculated using the equation $d_j = 1 - e_j$, which results give us $d_1 = 0.1566$ and $d_2 = 0.1278$.

(D) (D)   Now, we use standardization to standardize the weight of j indices

Mathematics of the Circular Economics

$$w_j = \frac{d_j}{\sum_{i=1}^{n} d_j}, Where\ j = 1, n$$

(6) Therefore, we have the results $w_1 = 0.5506$ and $w_2 = 0.4494$.

Step 3

In this step, the samples will be evaluated. The equation gives the value of j indices in the i-th sample

$f_{ij} = w_j.y_{ij}$, where $j=1,n$ (7)

Therefore, the total value of the i-th sample is given by equation (7)

$$f_i = \sum_{j=1}^{m} f_{ij} = w_j.y_{ij}, Where\ j = 1, m \qquad (8)$$

Table 4 shows the results obtained when performing step 3.

Table 4. Results obtained when performing step 3

Country	F1	F2	Score
Bahrain	0.089	0.0824	0.1714
Egypt	0.0225	0.0309	0.0534
Iran	0.1851	0.1589	0.344
Iraq	0.1123	0.1019	0.2143
Israel	0.089	0.0824	0.1714
Jordan	0.0225	0.0309	0.0534
Kuwait	0.1851	0.1589	0.344
Lebanon	0.4885	0.4342	0.9227
Oman	0.089	0.0824	0.1714
State of Palestine	0.0225	0.0309	0.0534
Qatar	0.1851	0.1589	0.344
Saudi Arabia	0.1259	0.1259	0.2518
Syria	0.5611	0.64	120.1098
Libya	0.089	0.0824	0.1714
United Arab Emirates	0.0225	0.0309	0.0534
Yemen	0.1851	0.1589	0.344
Djbouti	0.1259	0.1259	0.2518
Algeria	0.5611	0.64	120.1098
Sudan	0.4885	0.4342	0.9227

Now, we get the country ranking by running the data through the four steps of the algorithm above. The results are shown in Table 5 in descending order. The country with the first place has the highest score.

Table 5. Classification of countries after using the algorithm

Country	Outcome
Bahrain	0.98
Egypt	0.7639
Iran	0.7018
Iraq	0.5982
Israel	0.463
Jordan	0.2903
Kuwait	0.2406
Lebanon	0.1921
Oman	0.1503
State of Palestine	0.136
Qatar	0.1264
Saudi Arabia	0.1229
Syria	0.1087
Libya	0.1074
United Arab Emirates	0.0859
Yemen	0.0647
Djbouti	0.0463
Algeria	0.0463
Sudan	0.0299

An investment index is calculated as the 10-year average government investment in R&D for a circular economy. The efficiency index for all EU countries is calculated as the ratio between the result presented in Table 5 and the investment index (Norouzi & Fani, 2020b, Norouzi, 2021b). The results can be seen in Table 6.

Table 6. Circular economy productivity index

Country	Outcome	R&D Investment	Efficiency Index
Bahrain	0.2903	0.9678	0.294
Egypt	0.1503	0.795	0.1853
Iran	0.0008	0.0087	0.0837
Iraq	0.0859	0.0189	4.4512
Israel	0.0463	0.2671	0.1698
Jordan	0.7018	1.0158	0.6771
Kuwait	0.0299	0.0513	0.5711
Lebanon	0.2406	0.6198	0.3804
Oman	0.1264	4.1716	0.0297
State of Palestine	0.1922	5.8264	0.0323
Qatar	0.0349	0.2699	0.1266
Saudi Arabia	0.0028	0.1103	0.025
Syria	0.7639	0.3246	2.3065
Libya	0.1229	2.6672	0.0452
United Arab Emirates	0.0034	0.0313	0.1088
Yemen	0.0149	0.0698	0.2095
Djibouti	0.98	0.1293	7.4299
Algeria	0.1074	0.0473	2.2246
Sudan	0.4631	1.8615	0.2437

The above results show interesting results: countries with higher research and development costs for the circular economy have higher efficiency scores. At the same time, countries with a higher level of utilization of the rotating economy have a higher efficiency index(Norouzi & Ataei, 2021). The World Bank report on environmental policies shows some cases of resource reuse in MENA countries. The implementation of circular economy processes requires significant investment in environmental infrastructure so that member countries can develop smoothly and achieve their environmental objectives (Rényi, 1961; Ragazzi et al., 2017). There are deficiencies in the efficiency of resources and human resources working in the field of environmental protection. Beyond the current state of the circular economy, this work presents the benefits of using a conceptual model in sustainable economic growth based on an efficient and responsible consumption of resources.

Studies from advanced economies have shown the many benefits of educating civil society about environmental protection when investing in collecting, sorting, and recycling infrastructure (Stahel). The positive effects of the circular economy process proportionally increase municipal income, the labor force employed, and the earnings of entrepreneurs who provide environmental infrastructure (Sherwin, 2018).

Probably the most important advantage of using the circular economy process is felt separately. Due to the similarity between the life of products (through reuse or lengthening the life of the product) and human life, we can see how environmental factors are diffused in the quality of our daily life. The results of our analysis confirm the results of the economic literature (Tseng et al., 2018) that the processes related to the circular economy have positive effects on economic growth and resource productivity and are consistent with increasing the productivity of resources by 15% by 2030, which can lead to GDP growth of almost 1% (Shaheen et al., 2012). This study can also be for regional, local, and national government officials involved in drafting the legislative background and companies that can develop their business plans based on the expected effects of the circular economy on each member. Important(Baars et al., 2021). Furthermore, this study highlights a simple, reliable, and practical tool to evaluate a productivity index to produce a circular economy using a hybrid index. It should be noted that when the relationship between the number of results obtained by entropy measurements and the average value of the ten years relevant for research and development is calculated, the cost of research and development for circular economic processes is calculated for each country, the results show that countries have a higher level of investment in more efficient circular economy processes(Xiao et al., 2018).

As mentioned in the introduction, the research orientation has been created due to the growing interest in evaluating research and circular economy processes at the Mena level. The rating based on entropy analysis shown in Table 6 is similar to the international rating, confirming our entropy analysis as an efficient tool. The findings are consistent with other studies in this field (Zhao et al., 2018); when different data sets are analyzed, they show significant and consistent results. Given that the macroeconomic indicators obtained from the analysis are related to 20 years, one of the main limitations of this research is the time database used for factor analysis. Another limitation is the availability of data and the time frame. Future research will take longer to provide a more accurate picture of circular economy trends in the EU. In addition to adding to the dataset for analysis using information metrics, further research should also examine what kinds of entropy measures lead to more complete and reliable findings. This study was carried out based on a composite index modeled by Shannon's entropy. Therefore, future studies can model circular economy processes using other measures of entropy. Last but not least, the future analysis could extend this research to other countries or the world.

SOLUTIONS AND RECOMMENDATIONS

The Covid-19 crisis, along with environmental crises, has taught us many lessons. The speed and casualties of learning Covid-19 had far-reaching consequences for the economy. This crisis, first of all, exposed our vulnerability. A virus has quarantined almost every human being in the world for several weeks. Due to this situation, economic activities were interrupted. With this virus, nature has shown us that we are neither above it nor in control of it. Many ecologists point out that the current health crisis is, first and foremost, an ecological crisis, and if we can not adapt our activities to the current situation, we will have to wait for other crises. In addition, this crisis showed us that the destiny of all human beings depends on each other, and in the meantime, geographical boundaries do not matter. We all live in a global village. Goods and people are moving rapidly to different parts of the world, which can be a testament to our unity. But viruses are transmitted at the same rate; Therefore, it must be said that our unbridled trade exchanges have direct effects on our lives, and these effects can not be summed up only in positive effects(Núñez-Cacho et al., 2018b).

The crisis has also led more people to pay attention to the problems caused by the geographical distance between producer and consumer. The gap between being more profitable and taking advantage of competitive and relative advantages (for example, many American companies prefer to build factories in China or India to use cheaper labor) has led to dependency. These dependencies made it difficult to access foreign products such as masks, test chemicals, and various medications. To these can be added environmental damage, including deviation from the norm. At the moment, our priority is health and wellness problems, but energy costs and environmental consequences will also gradually become more prominent(Bag et al., 2021). Environmental problems can still be seen today more vividly than ever before in the wake of the Great Depression. Both environmental and health crises have an important feature in common. Both advise the world to take a more local approach. Both warn of the need for change. In addition, vigilant and fundamental goals must be set to pay more attention to climate and biodiversity issues. These two crises also make us think more about human integration and new forms of cooperation between different economic actors from different regions and generations(Ibn-Mohammed et al., 2021). These crises have shown us that it is time to prepare for the "post-Corona world." However, to properly understand this new reality, we must be careful in choosing the right answers to the right questions. One might argue that the most important question is supplying (in the case of the global shortage of masks), and the answer must be sought in increasing supply and diversification to suppliers so that we no longer see dependency and scarcity. From the point of view of economics and classical strategy, it is a good solution, but forgetting the environmental question is a big mistake. The real question, therefore, seems to be defined as: "How can we bring production closer to demand so that we can take a more holistic view of global warming and natural resource constraints?" This is the question posed by the French philosopher and sociologist Edgar Moran(Rényi, 1961; Ragazzi et al., 2017). From the perspective of microeconomics, Robert Boyer invites economists to "return to the resources of political economy in the use of concepts and methods that make it possible to overcome the most fundamental problems of any society(De Pascale et al., 2021)." His invitation makes us think about a rotating economy that seems to be a promising model for sustainable development. But achieving a rotational economy requires redesigning the current model of linear economics. The new economic model (rotational economy) is a regenerative system in which the input of resources and waste, the emission of greenhouse gases, and its waste are reduced by reducing consumption and shrinking cycles of materials and energy consumption(Nandi et al., 2021). This goal can be achieved through sustainable design, maintenance, repair, reuse, reproduction, and recycling. In other words, by reducing waste, waste and raw materials, and energy consumption, less pressure is put on the earth's natural resources. Recycling, maximizing the use of resources and reducing unnecessary costs are among the most important strategies to achieve the goals of this economic model and make it a good model for dealing with the problems we are currently struggling with(Rényi, 1961; Ragazzi et al., 2017).

Governmental and international organizations, along with policymakers, have a great responsibility to drive these changes. Hence, the priority of change to have a bright future belongs to these areas. It may be argued that such changes are needed to achieve sustainable development. But the reality is that without a return to nature and respect for its order. This is exactly what we experienced during the Corona. The economy alone cannot do everything. In addition, the costs imposed on communities have delayed their economic development for months and perhaps years. Therefore, we need to adopt a development strategy tailored to environmental issues that can move towards growth sustainably and reasonably. This means that some sectors of the economy will decline so that other sectors can develop. The issue of externalities is a topic that should be included in these considerations (the issue of side effects states that any economic activity has hidden costs paid for by the development of other members of society instead of being paid by the enterprise in question. Subtracting the side costs from the profit of the enterprise, we can discuss its real economic benefits (for example, these side effects can be increased health costs of society following the activities of polluting industries) (Núñez-Cacho et al., 2018b; Hartley et al., 2020).

Moving towards a rotating economy also means the geographical location of some industries. In the meantime, more strategic industries (food, healthcare) are a priority. This shift in a geographical location not only reduces dependence but also reduces carbon emissions from transportation(Yadav et al., 2020). Reducing transportation and waste costs in this way can offset some of the short-term benefits (due to reduced comparative benefits) and all long-term benefits. Increasing the use of renewable energy is also in the category of priority industries, which still need to have a short geographical distance between producer and consumer(Bag et al., 2020).

The new economic model has many opportunities for various economic actors and businesses. In addition to the fact that some green industries, such as digital and renewable energy, have a more promising future, general solutions can be introduced for all businesses. As mentioned, reducing the gap between production and consumption is the first case. This reduces shipping costs, waste, and delivery time. In addition, it increases the resilience of businesses to deal with disruptions such as those seen with corona prevalence. Naturally, when discussing the reduction of geographical distances, the use of the potential of local suppliers is also considered. Reducing waste and consuming raw materials are other measures that businesses can include in their plans. Reducing waste has always been one of the most important ways to reduce production costs. However, increasing natural constraints and resource scarcity are increasing attention to this approach. Another issue is reducing the use of natural resources, one of the most important methods of increasing recycling. When a raw material enters the production process, it should be used as much as possible and sometimes returned to the production and consumption cycle. In addition to reducing production costs, these measures increase resilience to raw material shortages(Norouzi et al., 2021c; Ferasso et al., 2020). Changing consumption and finding new functionality for existing products and tools is another solution that businesses can consider. This is especially true when recycling is not possible. Finally, there is the move to a low-consumption economy. Many sociologists consider today's economy to be a luxury and consumerist economy, but luxury also has a great lesson for us in addition to its negative social and environmental aspects(Harris et al., 2021). Many luxury products are very high quality and durable. When the products of society are of good quality, durable and versatile, all the benefits of the rotational economy model can be seen in it; Including reducing total costs, reducing waste, reducing side effects, increasing flexibility, and of course, increasing customer satisfaction(Perman et al., 2003; Morseletto, 2020).

CONCLUSION

As mentioned in the introduction, the research orientation has been created due to the growing interest in evaluating research and circular economy processes at the Mena level. The rating based on entropy analysis shown in the results section is similar to the international rating, confirming our entropy analysis as an efficient tool. The findings are consistent with other studies in this field; when different data sets are analyzed, they show significant and consistent results. Given that the macroeconomic indicators obtained from the analysis are related to 20 years, one of the main limitations of this research is the time database used for factor analysis. Another limitation is the availability of data and the time frame. Future research will take longer to provide a more accurate picture of circular economy trends in the EU. In addition to adding to the dataset for analysis using information metrics, further research should also examine what kinds of entropy measures lead to more complete and reliable findings. This study was carried out based on a composite index modeled by Shannon's entropy. Therefore, future studies can model circular economy processes using other measures of entropy. Last but not least, the future analysis could extend this research to other countries or the world.

ACKNOWLEDGMENT

This research received no specific grant or funding from any funding agency in the public, commercial, or not-for-profit sectors.

REFERENCES

Andersen, M. S. (2007). An introductory note on the environmental economics of the circular economy. *Sustainability Science*, 2(1), 133–140. doi:10.100711625-006-0013-6

Andersen, P. (2007). What is web 2.0. *Ideas, technologies and implications for education*, 1(1), 1-64.

Baars, J., Domenech, T., Bleischwitz, R., Melin, H. E., & Heidrich, O. (2021). Circular economy strategies for electric vehicle batteries reduce reliance on raw materials. *Nature Sustainability*, 4(1), 71–79. doi:10.103841893-020-00607-0

Bag, S., Pretorius, J. H. C., Gupta, S., & Dwivedi, Y. K. (2021). Role of institutional pressures and resources in the adoption of big data analytics powered artificial intelligence, sustainable manufacturing practices and circular economy capabilities. *Technological Forecasting and Social Change*, 163, 120420. doi:10.1016/j.techfore.2020.120420

Bag, S., Wood, L. C., Mangla, S. K., & Luthra, S. (2020). Procurement 4.0 and its implications on business process performance in a circular economy. *Resources, Conservation and Recycling*, 152, 104502. doi:10.1016/j.resconrec.2019.104502

Baravalle, R., Rosso, O. A., & Montani, F. (2018). Causal shannon–fisher characterization of motor/imagery movements in eeg. *Entropy (Basel, Switzerland)*, 20(9), 660. doi:10.3390/e20090660 PMID:33265749

Bernstad Saraiva, A., Souza, R. G., Mahler, C. F., & Valle, R. A. B. (2018). Consequential lifecycle modelling of solid waste management systems–Reviewing choices and exploring their consequences. *Journal of Cleaner Production*, 202, 488–496. doi:10.1016/j.jclepro.2018.08.038

Cannon, W. R., Zucker, J. D., Baxter, D. J., Kumar, N., Baker, S. E., Hurley, J. M., & Dunlap, J. C. (2018). Prediction of metabolite concentrations, rate constants and post-translational regulation using maximum entropy-based simulations with application to central metabolism of neurospora crassa. *Processes (Basel, Switzerland)*, 6(6), 63. doi:10.3390/pr6060063 PMID:33824861

Cleary, J. (2009). Life cycle assessments of municipal solid waste management systems: A comparative analysis of selected peer-reviewed literature. *Environment International*, 35(8), 1256–1266. doi:10.1016/j.envint.2009.07.009 PMID:19682746

Cobo, S., Dominguez-Ramos, A., & Irabien, A. (2018). From linear to circular integrated waste management systems: A review of methodological approaches. *Resources, Conservation and Recycling, 135*, 279–295. doi:10.1016/j.resconrec.2017.08.003

De Almeida, S. T., & Borsato, M. (2019). Assessing the efficiency of End of Life technology in waste treatment—A bibliometric literature review. *Resources, Conservation and Recycling, 140*, 189–208. doi:10.1016/j.resconrec.2018.09.020

De Pascale, A., Arbolino, R., Szopik-Depczyńska, K., Limosani, M., & Ioppolo, G. (2021). A systematic review for measuring circular economy: The 61 indicators. *Journal of Cleaner Production, 281*, 124942. doi:10.1016/j.jclepro.2020.124942

Ferasso, M., Beliaeva, T., Kraus, S., Clauss, T., & Ribeiro-Soriano, D. (2020). Circular economy business models: The state of research and avenues ahead. *Business Strategy and the Environment, 29*(8), 3006–3024. doi:10.1002/bse.2554

Georgescu-Roegen, N. (2013). *The entropy law and the economic process*. Harvard University Press.

Harris, S., Martin, M., & Diener, D. (2021). Circularity for circularity's sake? Scoping review of assessment methods for environmental performance in the circular economy. *Sustainable Production and Consumption, 26*, 172–186. doi:10.1016/j.spc.2020.09.018

Hartley, K., van Santen, R., & Kirchherr, J. (2020). Policies for transitioning towards a circular economy: Expectations from the European Union (EU). *Resources, Conservation and Recycling, 155*, 104634. doi:10.1016/j.resconrec.2019.104634

Hussain, M. E., & Haque, M. (2016). Impact of economic freedom on the growth rate: A panel data analysis. *Economies, 4*(2), 5. doi:10.3390/economies4020005

Ibn-Mohammed, T., Mustapha, K. B., Godsell, J., Adamu, Z., Babatunde, K. A., Akintade, D. D., Acquaye, A., Fujii, H., Ndiaye, M. M., Yamoah, F. A., & Koh, S. C. L. (2021). A critical analysis of the impacts of COVID-19 on the global economy and ecosystems and opportunities for circular economy strategies. *Resources, Conservation and Recycling, 164*, 105169. doi:10.1016/j.resconrec.2020.105169 PMID:32982059

Kolmogorov, A. N., & Tikhomirov, V. M. (1959). ε-entropy and ε-capacity of sets in function spaces. *Uspekhi Matematicheskhi Nauk, 14*(2), 3–86.

Kopnina, H. (2017). Sustainability: New strategic thinking for business. *Environment, Development and Sustainability, 19*(1), 27–43. doi:10.100710668-015-9723-1

Kronborg, M. T. (2014). Optimal consumption and investment with labor income and European/American capital guarantee. *Risks, 2*(2), 171–194. doi:10.3390/risks2020171

Lahti, T., Wincent, J., & Parida, V. (2018). A definition and theoretical review of the circular economy, value creation, and sustainable business models: Where are we now and where should research move in the future? *Sustainability, 10*(8), 2799. doi:10.3390u10082799

Liu, Y. (2013). Energy production and regional economic growth in China: A more comprehensive analysis using a panel model. *Energies, 6*(3), 1409–1420. doi:10.3390/en6031409

Ljunggren Söderman, M., Eriksson, O., Björklund, A., Östblom, G., Ekvall, T., Finnveden, G., Arushanyan, Y., & Sundqvist, J. O. (2016). Integrated economic and environmental assessment of waste policy instruments. *Sustainability*, *8*(5), 411. doi:10.3390u8050411

Luo, Z., Xie, F., Zhang, B., & Qiu, D. (2018). Quantifying the Nonlinear Dynamic Behavior of the DC-DC Converter via Permutation Entropy. *Energies*, *11*(10), 2747. doi:10.3390/en11102747

Molina-Sánchez, E., Leyva-Díaz, J. C., Cortés-García, F. J., & Molina-Moreno, V. (2018). Proposal of sustainability indicators for the waste management from the paper industry within the circular economy model. *Water (Basel)*, *10*(8), 1014. doi:10.3390/w10081014

Morrison, P. (2011). Meeting the Environmental Challenge with Technology. In SPE Digital Energy Conference and Exhibition. OnePetro. doi:10.2118/143837-MS

Morseletto, P. (2020). Targets for a circular economy. *Resources, Conservation and Recycling*, *153*, 104553. doi:10.1016/j.resconrec.2019.104553

Nandi, S., Sarkis, J., Hervani, A. A., & Helms, M. M. (2021). Redesigning supply chains using blockchain-enabled circular economy and COVID-19 experiences. *Sustainable Production and Consumption*, *27*, 10–22. doi:10.1016/j.spc.2020.10.019 PMID:33102671

Norouzi, N. (2021a). The Pahlev Reliability Index: A measurement for the resilience of power generation technologies versus climate change. *Nuclear Engineering and Technology*, *53*(5), 1658–1663. doi:10.1016/j.net.2020.10.013

Norouzi, N. (2021b). Post-COVID-19 and globalization of oil and natural gas trade: Challenges, opportunities, lessons, regulations, and strategies. *International Journal of Energy Research*, *45*(10), 14338–14356. doi:10.1002/er.6762 PMID:34219899

Norouzi, N., & Ataei, E. (2021). Covid-19 Crisis and Environmental law: Opportunities and challenges. *Hasanuddin Law Review*, *7*(1), 46–60. doi:10.20956/halrev.v7i1.2772

Norouzi, N., de Rubens, G. Z., Choupanpiesheh, S., & Enevoldsen, P. (2020a). When pandemics impact economies and climate change: Exploring the impacts of COVID-19 on oil and electricity demand in China. *Energy Research & Social Science*, *68*, 101654. doi:10.1016/j.erss.2020.101654 PMID:32839693

Norouzi, N., & Fani, M. (2020a). The impacts of the novel corona virus on the oil and electricity demand in Iran and China. *Journal of Energy Management and Technology*, *4*(4), 36–48.

Norouzi, N., & Fani, M. (2020b). Black gold falls, black plague arise-An Opec crude oil price forecast using a gray prediction model. *Upstream Oil and Gas Technology*, *5*, 100015. doi:10.1016/j.upstre.2020.100015

Norouzi, N., & Fani, M. (2021a). The prioritization and feasibility study over renewable technologies using fuzzy logic: A case study for Takestan plains. *Journal of Energy Management and Technology*, *5*(2), 12–22.

Norouzi, N., & Fani, M. (2021b). Environmental Sustainability and Coal: The Role of Financial Development and Globalization in South Africa. Iranian (Iranica). *Journal of Energy & Environment*, *12*(1), 68–80. doi:10.5829/IJEE.2021.12.01.09

Norouzi, N., Fani, M., Hashemi Bahramani, E., Hemmati, M. H., & Bashash Jafarabadi, Z. (2021c). Behavioral Economics and Energy consumption: Investigating the Role of Attitudes and Beliefs on Household Electricity Consumption in Iran. *Journal of Artificial Intelligence and Big Data*, *1*(1).

Norouzi, N., Fani, M., & Ziarani, Z. K. (2020b). The fall of oil Age: A scenario planning approach over the last peak oil of human history by 2040. *Journal of Petroleum Science Engineering*, *188*, 106827. doi:10.1016/j.petrol.2019.106827

Norouzi, N., & Kalantari, G. (2020). The sun food-water-energy nexus governance model a case study for Iran. *Water-Energy Nexus*, *3*, 72–80. doi:10.1016/j.wen.2020.05.005

Norouzi, N., Khanmohammadi, H. U., & Ataei, E. (2021b). The Law in the Face of the COVID-19 Pandemic: Early Lessons from Uruguay. *Hasanuddin Law Review*, *7*(2), 75–88. doi:10.20956/halrev.v7i2.2827

Norouzi, N., Zarazua de Rubens, G. Z., Enevoldsen, P., & Behzadi Forough, A. (2021a). The impact of COVID-19 on the electricity sector in Spain: An econometric approach based on prices. *International Journal of Energy Research*, *45*(4), 6320–6332. doi:10.1002/er.6259

Nuñez-Cacho, P., Górecki, J., Molina-Moreno, V., & Corpas-Iglesias, F. A. (2018b). What gets measured, gets done: Development of a circular economy measurement scale for building industry. *Sustainability*, *10*(7), 2340. doi:10.3390u10072340

Núñez-Cacho, P., Molina-Moreno, V., Corpas-Iglesias, F. A., & Cortés-García, F. J. (2018a). Family businesses transitioning to a circular economy model: The case of "Mercadona". *Sustainability*, *10*(2), 538. doi:10.3390u10020538

Pearce, D. W., & Turner, R. K. (1990). *Economics of natural resources and the environment*. JHU press.

Perman, R., Ma, Y., McGilvray, J., & Common, M. (2003). *Natural resource and environmental economics*. Pearson Education.

Rada, E. C., Ragazzi, M., Torretta, V., Castagna, G., Adami, L., & Cioca, L. I. (2018). Circular economy and waste to energy. In AIP Conference Proceedings (Vol. 1968, No. 1, p. 030050). AIP Publishing LLC. doi:10.1063/1.5039237

Ragazzi, M., Fedrizzi, S., Rada, E. C., Ionescu, G., Ciudin, R., & Cioca, L. I. (2017). Experiencing urban mining in an Italian municipality towards a circular economy vision. *Energy Procedia*, *119*, 192–200. doi:10.1016/j.egypro.2017.07.068

Rényi, A. (1961). On measures of entropy and information. In *Proceedings of the Fourth Berkeley Symposium on Mathematical Statistics and Probability*, Volume 1: *Contributions to the Theory of Statistics* (pp. 547-561). University of California Press.

Romero-Hernández, O., & Romero, S. (2018). Maximizing the value of waste: From waste management to the circular economy. *Thunderbird International Business Review*, *60*(5), 757–764. doi:10.1002/tie.21968

Shaheen, S. A., Mallery, M. A., & Kingsley, K. J. (2012). Personal vehicle sharing services in North America. *Research in Transportation Business & Management*, *3*, 71–81. doi:10.1016/j.rtbm.2012.04.005

Shannon, C. E. (1948). A mathematical theory of communication. *The Bell System Technical Journal*, *27*(3), 379–423. doi:10.1002/j.1538-7305.1948.tb01338.x

Sherwin, W. B. (2018). Entropy, or information, unifies ecology and evolution and beyond. *Entropy (Basel, Switzerland)*, *20*(10), 727. doi:10.3390/e20100727 PMID:33265816

Stahel, W. R. (2017). Analysis of the structure and values of the European Commission's Circular Economy Package. In *Proceedings of the Institution of Civil Engineers-Waste and Resource Management* (Vol. 170, No. 1, pp. 41-44). Thomas Telford Ltd. 10.1680/jwarm.17.00009

Tsallis, C. (1988). Possible generalization of Boltzmann-Gibbs statistics. *Journal of Statistical Physics*, *52*(1), 479–487. doi:10.1007/BF01016429

Tseng, M. L., Wong, W. P., & Soh, K. L. (2018). An overview of the substance of resource, conservation and recycling. *Resources, Conservation and Recycling*, *136*, 367–375. doi:10.1016/j.resconrec.2018.05.010

Von Neumann, J., & Morgenstern, O. (2007). *Theory of games and economic behavior*. Princeton university press.

Xiao, S., Dong, H., Geng, Y., & Brander, M. (2018). An overview of China's recyclable waste recycling and recommendations for integrated solutions. *Resources, Conservation and Recycling*, *134*, 112–120. doi:10.1016/j.resconrec.2018.02.032

Xie, J., & Saltzman, S. (2000). Environmental policy analysis: An environmental computable general-equilibrium approach for developing countries. *Journal of Policy Modeling*, *22*(4), 453–489. doi:10.1016/S0161-8938(97)00076-8

Yadav, G., Luthra, S., Jakhar, S. K., Mangla, S. K., & Rai, D. P. (2020). A framework to overcome sustainable supply chain challenges through solution measures of industry 4.0 and circular economy: An automotive case. *Journal of Cleaner Production*, *254*, 120112. doi:10.1016/j.jclepro.2020.120112

Zhao, H., Guo, S., & Zhao, H. (2018). Impacts of GDP, fossil fuel energy consumption, energy consumption intensity, and economic structure on SO2 emissions: A multi-variate panel data model analysis on selected Chinese provinces. *Sustainability*, *10*(3), 657. doi:10.3390u10030657

ADDITIONAL READING

Aguilar-Hernandez, G. A., Rodrigues, J. F. D., & Tukker, A. (2021). Macroeconomic, social and environmental impacts of a circular economy up to 2050: A meta-analysis of prospective studies. *Journal of Cleaner Production*, *278*, 123421. doi:10.1016/j.jclepro.2020.123421

Anderson, V. (2006). Turning economics inside out. *International Journal of Green Economics*, *1*(1-2), 11–22. doi:10.1504/IJGE.2006.009334

Baars, J., Domenech, T., Bleischwitz, R., Melin, H. E., & Heidrich, O. (2021). Circular economy strategies for electric vehicle batteries reduce reliance on raw materials. *Nature Sustainability*, *4*(1), 71–79. doi:10.103841893-020-00607-0

Cato, M. S. (2012). *Green economics: an introduction to theory, policy and practice*. Routledge. doi:10.4324/9781849771528

Eichholtz, P., Kok, N., & Quigley, J. M. (2013). The economics of green building. *The Review of Economics and Statistics*, 95(1), 50–63. doi:10.1162/REST_a_00291

Green, D. (2003). *Silent revolution: The rise and crisis of market economics in Latin America*. NYU Press.

Hahnel, R. (2014). *Green economics: Confronting the ecological crisis*. Routledge. doi:10.4324/9781315703947

Hydes, K. R., & Creech, L. (2000). Reducing mechanical equipment cost: The economics of green design. *Building Research and Information*, 28(5-6), 403–407. doi:10.1080/096132100418555

Mhatre, P., Panchal, R., Singh, A., & Bibyan, S. (2021). A systematic literature review on the circular economy initiatives in the European Union. *Sustainable Production and Consumption*, 26, 187–202. doi:10.1016/j.spc.2020.09.008

Pearce, D. (1992). Green economics. *Environmental Values*, 1(1), 3–13. doi:10.3197/096327192776680179

KEY TERMS AND DEFINITIONS

Circular Economy: A circular economy is an economic system of closed loops in which raw materials, components, and products lose their value as little as possible, renewable energy sources are used, and systems thinking is at the core.

Circularity: A circular economy (also called "circularity") is an economic system that tackles global challenges like climate change, biodiversity loss, waste, and pollution. Most linear economy businesses take a natural resource and turn it into a product destined to become waste because it has been designed and made. This process is often summarised by "take, make, waste." By contrast, a circular economy uses reuse, sharing, repair, refurbishment, remanufacturing, and recycling to create a closed-loop system, minimize resource inputs, and create waste, pollution, and carbon emissions. The circular economy aims to keep products, materials, equipment, and infrastructure in use for longer, thus improving the productivity of these resources. Waste materials and energy should become input for other processes through waste valorization: either as a component or recovered resource for another industrial process or as regenerative resources for nature (e.g., compost). This regenerative approach contrasts with the traditional linear economy, which has a "take, make, dispose of" production model.

Natural Resource Economics: Natural resource economics deals with the supply, demand, and allocation of the earth's natural resources. One main objective of natural resource economics is to understand better the role of natural resources in the economy to develop more sustainable methods of managing those resources to ensure their future generations. Resource economists study interactions between economic and natural systems intending to develop a sustainable and efficient economy.

Natural Resources: Natural resources are resources that exist without any actions of humankind. This includes the sources of valued characteristics such as commercial and industrial use, aesthetic value, scientific interest, and cultural value. It includes sunlight, atmosphere, water, land, all minerals, and all vegetation and animal life on earth. Natural resources can be part of our natural heritage or protected in nature reserves.

Recycling: Recycling is the process of converting waste materials into new materials and objects. The recovery of energy from waste materials is often included in this concept. The recyclability of a material depends on its ability to reacquire the properties it had in its original state. It is an alternative to "conventional" waste disposal that can save material and help lower greenhouse gas emissions. It can also prevent the waste of potentially useful materials and reduce the consumption of fresh raw materials, reducing energy use, air pollution (from incineration), and water pollution (from landfilling).

Sustainable Development: Sustainable development is an organizing principle for meeting human development goals while simultaneously sustaining the ability of natural systems to provide the natural resources and ecosystem services on which the economy and society depend. The desired result is a state of society where living conditions and resources are used to meet human needs without undermining the integrity and stability of the natural system. Sustainable development can be defined as development that meets the needs of the present without compromising the ability of future generations to meet their own needs. Sustainability goals, such as the current UN-level Sustainable Development Goals, address the global challenges, including poverty, inequality, climate change, environmental degradation, peace, and justice.

Waste Valorization: Waste valorization, beneficial reuse, value recovery, or waste reclamation is the process of waste products or residues from an economic process being valorized (given economic value) by reuse or recycling to create economically useful materials. The term comes from practices in sustainable manufacturing, economics: industrial ecology, and waste management. The term is usually applied in industrial processes where residue from creating or processing one good is used as a raw material or energy feedstock for another industrial process. Industrial wastes, in particular, are good candidates for valorization because they tend to be more consistent and predictable than other waste, such as household waste.

Chapter 8
Legendary, Life-Changing, and Memorable Benefits of Digitalization to Restart the Economy:
Impact of COVID-19 on Global Economic Environment for Sustainable Development

Cristina Raluca Gh. Popescu
https://orcid.org/0000-0002-5876-0550
University of Bucharest, Romania & The Bucharest University of Economic Studies, Romania

Arturo Luque González
Universidad Técnica de Manabí, Ecuador & Observatorio Euromediterráneo de Espacio Público y Democraca, Ecuador

ABSTRACT

The COVID-19 pandemic and COVID-19 crisis suddenly, abruptly accentuated both individual and business needs to move at an accelerated rate to digital activities like never before in history of mankind, which led to increased importance of digitalization in terms of use of digital technologies. The post-COVID-19 era seeks to create novel communication patterns and business models capable to ensure new revenue and value-producing benefits and opportunities in accordance to the Sustainable Development Goals by launching tremendous provocations on global economic environment for sustainable development: How can people and entities adapt, implement digitalization in their daily lives, in order to restart the economy? What will the world's digital business transformation roadmap look like, in order to find a balance between individuals' expectations and planet's needs? Will the digital skills transformation enhance the role of human resources in society, or will these new acquired skills create an even larger gap between people than ever before? Is artificial intelligence the future?

DOI: 10.4018/978-1-6684-5109-0.ch008

Legendary, Life-Changing, and Memorable Benefits

INTRODUCTION

These days, the accent that is put in our society on digital transformation is unprecedented, which makes the authors of this current book chapter seek to address in a wide and comprehensive manner the legendary, life-changing, and memorable benefits of digitalization to restart the economy, with the profound desire to understand at a better level the impact of the COVID-19 on the global economic environment for the sustainable development (SD). In continuation, it ought to be mentioned that there are several key concepts and vital terms that are strongly connected with all the forms of digitalization and digital transformation, as follows: business, knowledge, human resources (HR), innovation, intangible assets (IA), intellectual capital (IC), Sustainable Development Goals (SDGs), global economic environment, restart the economy, COVID-19 pandemic, and COVID-19 crisis.

In the European Commission's (EC) "Proposal for a Decision of the European Parliament and of the Council establishing the 2030 Policy Program "Path to the Digital Decade"", published in September 2021, the importance of the digitalization process as well as the role of the digital decade are clearly acknowledged by specialists in the statements that mentioned the support of the European Union (EU) towards the "transformation" and "the transition towards a climate neutral, circular and resilient economy. The EU's ambition is to be digitally sovereign in an open and interconnected world, and to pursue digital policies that empower people and businesses to seize a human centered, sustainable and more prosperous digital future. This includes addressing vulnerabilities and dependencies as well as accelerating investment" (European Commission (EC), 2021, p.1). The document continues with new vital issues in the same line and on the same topics, as follows: "(…) digital training and education should support a workforce in which people can acquire specialized digital skills to get quality jobs and rewarding careers. In addition, addressing the major shortage of cyber security skills in the EU workforce will be essential, as an important component of protecting the EU against cyber threats. Therefore, in addition to the target on basic digital skills established in the European Pillar of Social Rights Action Plan, the EU shall have a target of 20 million employed Information and Communication Technologies specialists in the EU, with convergence between women and men" (European Commission (EC), 2021, p.2).

The creation of the current book chapter on "Legendary, life-changing, and memorable benefits of digitalization to restart the economy: Impact of COVID-19 on global economic environment for sustainable development" comes as a result of the influence of the COVID-19 pandemic and the COVID-19 crisis on people's daily lives and business activities, based on these days' current circumstances in which the COVID-19 pandemic and the COVID-19 crisis have suddenly and abruptly accentuated both individuals and businesses need to move at an accelerated rate to digital activities like never before in history of mankind. In this matter, it can be remarked that the COVID-19 pandemic and the COVID-19 crisis have led to increased importance of digitalization in terms of use of digital technologies. That is the reason why the European Commission stated in the document entitled "Shaping Europe's Digital Future", published in February 2020, the following aspects: "Digital technologies are profoundly changing our daily life, our way of working and doing business, and the way people travel, communicate and relate with each other. Digital communication, social media interaction, e-commerce, and digital enterprises are steadily transforming our world (Luque, 2021). They are generating an ever-increasing amount of data, which, if pooled and used, can lead to a completely new means and levels of value creation. It is a transformation as fundamental as that caused by the industrial revolution" (European Commission (EC), 2020a, p.2).

Hence, the Post-COVID-19 Era seeks to create novel communication patterns and business models capable to ensure new revenue and value-producing benefits and opportunities in accordance to the

Sustainable Development Goals (SDGs) (Luque et al., 2021), by launching tremendous provocations on global economic environment for sustainable development, such as, for instance, the following ones (please see, in this matter, the next four pivotal steps presented and explained):

Step 1: The book chapter centers on finding an answer to the key question (research question RQ1): "How can people and entities adapt and implement digitalization in their daily lives, in order to restart the economy?" In this precise context, it has been noted that in the case of the European Commission (EC) the target is to create and to ensure "a European society powered by digital solutions that are strongly rooted in our common values, and that enrich the lives of all of us: people must have the opportunity to develop personally, to choose freely and safely, to engage in society, regardless of their age, gender or professional background. Businesses need a framework that allows them to start up, scale up, pool and use data, to innovate and compete or cooperate on fair terms. And Europe needs to have a choice and pursue the digital transformation in its own way" (European Commission (EC), 2020a, p.3).

Step 2: The book chapter focuses on better understanding (research question RQ2: "How will the world's digital business transformation roadmap look like, in order to find a balance between individuals' expectations and planet's needs?" In this matter, the specialists have noted the following vital aspects, as follows: "A digital revolution is transforming the world as we know it at unprecedented speed. Digital technologies have changed the way businesses operate, how people connect and exchange information, and how they interact with the public and private sectors. European businesses and citizens' alike need an adequate policy framework and appropriate skills and infrastructures to capture the enormous value created by the digital economy and make a success of digital transformation" (European Parliament (EP), 2019, p.1).

Step 3: The book chapter concentrates on presenting and describing the implications of the following pivotal question, as follows (research question RQ3): "Will the digital skills transformation enhance the role of human resources in society, or will these new acquired skills create an even larger gap between people than ever before?" While addressing this point, the Organization for Economic Co-operation and Development (OECD) position should be emphasized, namely: "As digitalization creates both opportunities and challenges that transcend borders, international cooperation is a key dimension to make the most out of the digital transformation at local, national and international levels" (OECD *et al.*, 2020, p.1). In continuation, it ought to be highlighted that countries worldwide "harness the digital transformation to foster their sustainable development", while being preoccupied to "build their domestic capacities to overcome the interlinked challenges of the development traps, thus promoting a multi-dimensional approach to development and aligning national and international priorities" (OECD *et al.*, 2020, p.1), which are represented by human resources and their importance and place in today's society, "connectivity, digital inclusion, digital public goods, digital human rights and capacity building" (OECD *et al.*, 2020, p.5).

Step 4: The book chapter seeks to address the following major provocation, namely (research question RQ4): "Is artificial intelligence (AI) the future?" The discussion on this sensible topic, has its roots in the following issues raised by the European Commission (EC) and the European Parliament (EP): "(…) the Parliament stressed the potential for economic growth stemming from technological transformation and called for the EU budget to have an appropriate role in supporting the digitalization of European industry and the promotion of digital skills and entrepreneurship. The Parliament has also called for the promotion of and support to women entrepreneurs in the framework of the digital transformation of industry in particular. Already in January 2017, leading the debate at EU level, the Parliament had called on the European Commission to assess the impact of artificial intelligence, and made wide-ranging recommendations for setting a legal and ethical EU framework for robotics and AI. In February 2019, the Parliament also adopted a resolution on how to foster a comprehensive European industrial policy on artificial intelligence and robotics" (European Parliament (EP), 2019, p.8).

The matters that accompany the international process of digitalization on the road to restart the economy are very important, so that is the reason why this book chapter focuses on these aspects in particular. In this matter, it should be stressed that on the one hand, digitalization to restart the economy represents, according to world known specialists, a possible and plausible solution for today's highly challenged economy, as a result of the influence of the COVID-19 pandemic and the COVID-19 crisis on our society, in overbearing times in which both individuals and businesses are expected to move, suddenly, abruptly, and at an accelerated rate to the digital activities, like never before in the history of mankind. Nevertheless, on the other hand, digitalization to restart the economy represents, according to most recent studies, a valuable and longtime expected step due to be taken by both people and organizations, which is capable to lead to the increased importance of digitalization in terms of use of digital technologies in the Post-COVID-19 Era which is responsible for targeting to create novel communication patterns and pivotal business models in our society, capable to ensure new revenue and value-producing benefits and opportunities, while ensuring the United Nations' (UN) Sustainable Development Goals (SDGs). Besides, "at the multilateral level, despite becoming increasingly complex, the global architecture on digital co-operation has not necessarily become more effective", so that is the reason why the general focus ought to address "three main, interrelated components of a new model of international co-operation" in order to "contribute to sustainable development" in the world (OECD *et al.*, 2020, p.5). According to the published documents on "Latin American Economic Outlook 2019: Development in Transition" and on "Latin American Economic Outlook 2020: Digital Transformation for Building Back Better" (in the chapter entitled "The role of international co-operation in the digital age"), the "new model of international co-operation" prompters are highly encouraging: "1) nationally driven development processes by strengthening institutional capacities; 2) inclusive multilateral governance platforms to facilitate exchange on an equal footing; and 3) inclusion of new tools and actors within instruments to co-ordinate policies at the international level" (OECD *et al.*, 2019; OECD *et al.*, 2020, p.5).

What is more, the digital skills transformation (DST) in the Post-COVID-19 Era is seen as one of the most interesting and novel provocations that characterizes at present the global economic environment for the sustainable development (SD) and, in the same time, one of the most expected actions due to be taken by people and organizations in order to support the countries' ambitions to facilitate the economic recovery and help reshape the economy, while concentrating on finding valuable answers to vital questions, such as the following ones: "How can people and entities adapt and implement digitalization in their daily lives, in order to restart the economy?", "How will the world's digital business transformation roadmap look like, in order to find a balance between the individuals' expectations and the planet's needs?", "Will the digital skills transformation enhance the role of human resources in society, or will these new acquired skills create an even larger gap between people than ever before?", and "Is artificial intelligence (AI) the future?". Thus, the United Nations (UN) Secretary General's Roadmap for Digital Cooperation mentions and centers on eight key areas for action, as follows: (1) "achieving universal connectivity by 2030"; (2) "promoting digital public goods to create a more equitable world"; (3) "ensuring digital inclusion for all, including the most vulnerable"; (4) "strengthening digital capacity-building"; (5) "ensuring the protection of human rights in the digital era"; (6) "supporting global cooperation on artificial intelligence"; (7) "promoting trust and security in the digital environment"; (8) "building a more effective architecture for digital cooperation" (United Nations (UN), 2020a).

In addition, the digital business processes (DBP) in these days society have been encountered and have been used long before the appearance of the COVID-19 pandemic and the COVID-19 crisis, not representing at all a buzzword in our society, since these types of activities are believed to be a pivotal solution to a bright future for all individuals, being fully customizable, highly intuitive, and very fast, making them a must, also, for the Post-COVID-19 Era. Also, these activities are believed to empower individuals and organizations at a very high extent in terms of data digitalization and technology, facilitating the process of encoding information, and aiming to increase the lifecycle value of businesses through better use of information, knowledge, data, and digital technology. In the European Commission's (EC) document on "Assessment and roadmap for the digital transformation of the energy sector towards an innovative internal energy market", the following issues have been brought into analysis: "(…) the EU energy system is going through increasing decentralization and decarbonization processes. Digitalization, in this context, is a key enabler, as it unlocks opportunities for actors across the value chain (i.e. consumers, prosumers, retailers, traders, producers, network operators), providing them with new solutions. At the moment, digital technologies are already playing an important role in the energy sector. Internet of Things, Artificial Intelligence, Big Data, Cloud, 5G and Blockchain technologies are influencing changes both in energy companies' value creation strategies and in customer behavior. They are expected to have an impact on long-time established roles, particularly by creating trust and empowering consumers. In addition to this, digital technologies also provide the opportunity to integrate more renewable energy into grids and use energy more efficiently in households, industry and the whole system. They thus contribute to the creation of favorable conditions for tackling the sustainable low carbon economy challenge" (European Commission (EC), 2020b, p.33).

In continuation to the aspects aforementioned, the Digital Business Process Management (DBPM) represents a vital step in any activity that relies on digital transformation, since the integration of the digital technology into all areas of business is regarded as the immediate consequence of the COVID-19 pandemic and the COVID-19 crisis and as the wide range solution in the Post-COVID-19 Era, since it makes reference to the manner in which digital transformation changes how entities operate and how they are able to deliver value in the present days and in the future, thus meeting the customers preferences with tailor-made offers and suitable digital products. There are several challenges that have been mentioned by the Organization for Economic Co-operation and Development (OECD) in the document entitled "A measurement roadmap for the future", in "Measuring the Digital Transformation: A Roadmap for the Future", such as: (1) "In the shorter term, the challenge is to improve the international comparability of current indicators and make statistical systems more flexible and responsive to the introduction of new and rapidly evolving concepts driven by the digital transformation" (OECD, 2019, p.4); (2) "In the longer term, the challenge for the statistical community will be to design new and interdisciplinary approaches to data collection and to leverage the information captured by digital systems" (OECD, 2019, p.5); and (3) "The next generation of data infrastructure for policy making in the digital era needs to build partnerships with the private sector and engage with stakeholders to bring publicly available, reliable data into the policy-making process" (OECD, 2019, p.5).

Besides all these, the digital organization (DO) in the Post-COVID-19 Era makes reference, these days, to the business process (BP) transformation that takes place in all entities, at an international level, especially when organizations are inclined to seek success in all areas of activities in accordance to the sustainable development (SD) requirements and targets, while centering on very specific and highly targeted forms of processes – namely, the scope processes, addressing the need of individuals to reinvent the activities at a faster pace, and creating and implementing more evolved, more comprehensive, and more reliable digital business models (DBM). In like manner, it should be prompted that organizations are using these days a number of digital tools that are giving tribute to technology and ecosystems, thus enhancing the most wanted process of providing greater value to the customers and clients through new experiences, new products and services, new business models, and new solutions to their problems.

Furthermore, the implications of the Global Economic Environment (GEE) for Sustainable Development (SD) and of the Sustainable Development Goals (SDGs) for Building Inclusive Global Knowledge Societies are brought into discussion.

First of all, the Global Economic Environment (GEE) for Sustainable Development (SD) is believed to be the result of the individuals' continuous struggle to maintain an appropriate balance between the unrivalled benefits offered by taking care of the planet, so that the planet will take care, in turn, of the people, and individuals and organizations amplified desire to ensure economic growth, seek financial stability, and evolve with the aid of advanced digital technologies, in order to make the most of the benefits and the opportunities that the Post-COVID-19 Era are due to be brought in terms of the incredible amount of information due to be processed, encoded, and valued as knowledge, the world's business environment and the newest digital trends, the digital transformation of the local and the international markets, the competitive landscape, the rapid response of the entities' human resources (HR) facing the perspective of the artificial intelligence (AI) today and in the future.

Second of all, the Sustainable Development Goals (SDGs) for Building Inclusive Global Knowledge Societies is a worldwide desiderate promoted assiduously by the United Nations (UN), in the spirit of calling all countries (developed and developing) to take action in reaching the Global Goals, with the tremendous desire to end poverty, the paramount need to protect the Planet Earth, and the overpowering desire to ensure that all individuals are capable to enjoy both peace and prosperity now and in the future. Thus, these Global Goals have their profound roots implemented in the overbearing desire to foster sustainability at three main levels, namely economic, environmental, and social, due to their immediate and unequivocal relationship together with the people, our planet, and the profits.

The next sections of this book chapter that are coming to support and to complete this current introductory section are represented by: (a) the background section, where the authors have made an in-depth literature review analysis on the topics of interest for this current research; (b) the main focus of the chapter, which intends to clarify the purpose of this scientific work and highlight the legendary, life-changing, and memorable benefits of digitalization to restart the economy, while centering on the crucial impact of the COVID-19 on the global economic environment for the world's sustainable development; (c) the discussion and synthesis of results, where the authors have emphasized there main findings; the solutions and recommendations, where the authors have focused on showing the importance of being part of the digital era and adapting to its challenges, having in mind that: "In the world of tomorrow, digital skills, basic and advanced, will be essential to reinforce our collective resilience as a society: only digitally empowered and capable citizens and a highly skilled digital workforce can be the masters of their own destiny, confident and assertive in their means, value and choices" (European Commission (EC), 2021, p.2); (d) the future research directions, where the authors have centered there energy and attention on showing what other ideas might be valued in the next scientific works (other book chapters in international volumes, articles for international journals, and papers for international conferences); (e) the conclusion section which is intended to present the main ideas derived from this current highly important research; (f) the references section which illustrates the authors' preoccupation towards identifying the most important international sources that have been prepared and that have been published so far in the area of this current book chapter; and (g) the key terms and definitions which come to pencil the most relevant concepts due to be considered in order to provide a better understanding of this current scientific work.

Background

The background section of this book chapter suggestively entitled "Legendary, life-changing, and memorable benefits of digitalization to restart the economy: Impact of COVID-19 on global economic environment for sustainable development", as an integrating part of the "Handbook of Research on Building Inclusive Global Knowledge Societies for Sustainable Development", focuses on presenting the literature review on the most dominant concepts for this book chapter, such as, for example: business; international and European business environment; knowledge; human resources; innovation; intangible assets (IA); intellectual capital (IC); Sustainable Development Goals (SDGs); digitalization, global economic environment; restart the economy (Luque, 2022); and COVID-19. Also, it should be stressed that this particular section revolves around the following major questions that are considered a tremendous provocation for the authors of this book chapter, as follows: "How can people and entities adapt and implement digitalization in their daily lives, in order to restart the economy?", "How will the world's digital business transformation roadmap look like, in order to find a balance between individuals' expectations and planet's needs?", "Will the digital skills transformation enhance the role of human resources in society, or will these new acquired skills create an even larger gap between people than ever before?", and "Is artificial intelligence the future?"

The European Commission (EC) is closely interested in the benefits and in the implications of digitalization at all levels, highlighting the following aspects: "Digitalization is taking place at a fast pace in all European countries. The COVID-19 pandemic is also accelerating digitalization at many levels. Digitalization is transforming the economies, societies, forms of communication, jobs and the necessary skills for the workplace and everyday life. The great challenges resulting from this are addressed by a number of newly launched European policies that have strong links to digitalization and for a transformation towards an innovative and sustainable society" (European Commission (EC), 2020c, p.6).

Moreover, the European Commission (EC) has taken serious action towards reaching the worlds Sustainable Development Goals (SDGs), especially in the context in which the general vision is the one of "a digitalized and a sustainable society", in which "the various strategies and action plans" are centered on accomplishing "a large portfolio of measures, instruments and milestones that are always linked to digital technologies" (European Commission (EC), 2020c, p.6). In continuation, it ought to be noted that, according to the European Commission (EC) document on "Eco-Innovation and Digitalization Case studies, environmental and policy lessons from EU Member States for the EU Green Deal and the Circular Economy EIO Biennial report 2020", all the measures, instruments and milestones that were proposed by specialists "are eco-innovative and sustainable", so they all should "contribute to improving living conditions in Europe", since digitalization clearly represents "a major opportunity to accelerate the transition to a circular Europe, which, however, should not create new avoidable short- or longer-term environmental pressures or shift problems" (European Commission (EC), 2020c, p.6).

Legendary, Life-Changing, and Memorable Benefits

Nevertheless, the COVID-19 pandemic has proven that the implications and the involvement of digitalization are going far beyond the usual concepts and the usual strategies, which enables us to see the importance of digitalization worldwide as well as its ramifications. In this matter, for instance, the United Nations (UN) (2020b) – in the document published on "United Nations E-Government Survey 2020. Digital Government in the Decade of Action for Sustainable Development" – have closely focused their efforts on presenting the changes and the challenges of digitalization in the public sector, in terms of the "e-government" and the "digital government", at a global level, demonstrating that "the role of e-government" and the "efforts to achieve digital equity have been amplified by the nexus of digitalization and the societal impact of the pandemic" (United Nations (UN), 2020b, p.26).

Furthermore, the importance of digitalization for our society has implications in the education domains as well, aiming "to improve the full continuum of teacher education" (Organization for Economic Co-operation and Development (OECD), 2020, p.15). In this matter, countries all over the world are now "(…) committed to developing a network of tutor-teachers for basic education. The role is carried out by a teacher who embraces new pedagogies and promotes the digitalization of teaching. Actions may include organizing training on digital pedagogy, conducting competence surveys, providing technical guidance or networking with peers (…)" (Organization for Economic Co-operation and Development (OECD), 2020, p.15). The case of Finland – presented in these lines – might prove to be similar to the case of other countries. Hence, while referring to the impact of the COVID-19 on the global economic environment for the sustainable development recent figures have managed to show the following aspects: "considerable improvements in teachers' digital competencies" were noted, but, in the same time, "ongoing disparities in the integration of digital tools in the classroom" were discovered (Organization for Economic Co-operation and Development (OECD), p.15). Also, "as countries moved to online learning during the COVID-19 pandemic, this policy may have proved beneficial in both having raised digital competencies among teachers and providing an established support network within and between schools" (Organization for Economic Co-operation and Development (OECD), p.15).

The document on "Shaping the Digital Transformation in Europe", prepared in the form of a "Final Report: A study prepared for the European Commission DG Communications Networks, Content and Technology", published in September 2020 by the European Commission (EC), focuses on "Nine Signature Initiatives to Lead the Way" in terms of addressing the world's economy and the desiderate to ensure competitiveness at all levels, facing successfully societal change as well as climate changes and provocations, while centering on finding constant solutions to ensure "democracy, trust and diversity" as well as "sovereignty and security" (European Commission (EC), 2020d, p.6).

In continuation to the aspects highlighted in the lines above, several specialists have acknowledged the fact that by becoming more and more dependent on technology and on digitalization, the risk of cyber-attacks becomes much higher than in usual circumstances and in environments not so dependent on technology, on informatics, and on artificial intelligence (AI) (Popescu & Popescu, 2018; Popescu, 2018). In this matter, for instance, there are several professions and several professionals that have become increasingly dependent on very elaborate and sophisticated computer programs and software's, such as in the case of the accounting and the audit specialists, which puts these experts at high cyber-attacks risks (Popescu *et al.*, 2015; Popescu & Popescu, 2018). Also, these cyber-attacks risks have not only increased, but they have diversify their range of action, which prompted to the need of management specialists to be more alert when it comes to finding and offering solutions in terms of the appropriate management of information systems security (Popescu, 2019a). Based on the aforementioned ideas and arguments, specialists these days have turned their attention to very pressing issues, such as finding answers to major questions (Popescu, 2019b): "How can people and entities adapt, implement digitalization in their daily lives, in order to restart the economy?", "How will the world's digital business transformation roadmap look like, in order to find a balance between individuals' expectations and planet's needs?", "Will the digital skills transformation enhance the role of human resources in society, or will these new acquired skills create an even larger gap between people than ever before?", "Is artificial intelligence the future?" There is indeed the need to understand the manner in which people and entities might adapt and could implement digitalization in their daily lives, in order to restart the economy, especially in turbulent times, which are mostly characterized by conflict, disorder, unstable, and unsettled situations (Popescu, 2019c). Also, these are times in which it is highly understandable to asks ourselves how will the world's digital business transformation roadmap is going to look like, in order to find a balance between individuals' expectations and planet's needs, especially when tackling the turmoil that may be encountered as a result of the impact of COVID-19 on global economic environment for the quest to foster sustainable development (SD) (Popescu, 2019d). Hence, the new accompanying step that comes as a result of the steps mentioned in the lines above, is represented by weather or not the digital skills transformation will manage to enhance the role of human resources in society, or these new acquired skills will, in fact, create an even larger gap between people than ever before, raising the inequalities among individuals and increasing the degree of poverty at a global level (Popescu, 2019e). So, artificial intelligence (AI) could indeed represent the future of mankind and of businesses at a global level, but in the context in which will be able to ensure stability, and not to create chaos and insecurity (Popescu & Popescu, 2018).

MAIN FOCUS OF THE CHAPTER

This current section that constitutes, in essence, the main focus of the current book chapter presents the main part of the scientific work entitled the "Legendary, life-changing, and memorable benefits of digitalization to restart the economy: Impact of COVID-19 on global economic environment for sustainable development", as an integrating part of the "Handbook of Research on Building Inclusive Global Knowledge Societies for Sustainable Development".

In the lines below, the authors have analyzed and discussed the "Nine Signature Initiatives to Lead the Way" in terms of addressing the world's economy and the desiderate to ensure competitiveness at all levels, facing successfully societal change as well as climate changes and provocations, while centering on finding constant solutions to ensure "democracy, trust and diversity" as well as "sovereignty and security" which were referred to the previous section (European Commission (EC), 2020d, p.6).

These nine initiatives are believed to be extremely relevant for this book chapter, since they are capable to provide an in-depth image of our society to focus more on digitalization in order to restart the economy, while centering on key attributes such as performance, excellence, and competitiveness, in a highly challenged and a highly challenging business environment.

The first initiative mentioned by the European Commission (EC) (2020d) is represented by "developing and scaling EU tech ecosystems to match the global best", which intends to place Europe at the top, "as a leader in key new frontier digital technologies around Centers of Excellence enabled by the collaboration between Super-Universities, Public Authorities, established Industries and vibrant Start-ups", in this way showing the important connections that might be encountered between the governmental agencies, the education system, and the innovative sectors that mainly depend on technology and its development (European Commission (EC), 2020d, p.6). A successful correlation could be made in this particular

Legendary, Life-Changing, and Memorable Benefits

context with implications of the artificial intelligence (AI), in the authors' attempt to find pertinent and useful answers to the key question "Is artificial intelligence the future?" In the case of the European Union's (EU) countries, the answer to this important question is strongly connected with the countries scope to "(i) boosting the EU's technological and industrial capacity and AI uptake across the economy, (ii) preparing for the socio-economic changes brought about by AI, by encouraging the modernization of education and training systems, nurturing talent, anticipating changes in the labor market, supporting labor market transitions and adapting social protection systems, and (iii) ensuring an appropriate ethical and legal framework (Luque and Herrero-García, 2019), based on the Union's values and in line with the EU Charter of Fundamental Rights" (European Parliament (EP), 2021, p.1). In like manner, these days the European Union's (EU) countries are expected to take "concrete and complementary actions at EU, national and regional level aiming at maximizing the impact of investments at EU and national levels, encouraging synergies and cooperation across the EU, fostering the exchange of best practices and collectively defining the way forward on AI", which determines the importance of AI at all levels and all around the globe especially when it comes to promoting the values of the knowledge-based society and the digital era (European Parliament (EP), 2021, p.1).

The second initiative highlighted by the European Commission (EC) (2020d) is represented by "creating a Digital leadership instrument for innovation procurement of digital technologies of European strategic importance, combining innovation funding and public procurement" (European Commission (EC), 2020d, p.6). In this matter, the European Commission (EC) is keen on supporting "innovation procurement as a tool to deliver solutions to economic and societal challenges", based on the fact that it follows the existing demand trends that may be encountered in our society, it promises to center at all times on innovation step-by-step and at all stages, and it makes use of "cutting edge digital solutions" (European Commission (EC), 2022).

The third initiative emphasized by the European Commission (EC) (2020d) is represented by "building EU data platforms for strategic B2B sectors", which are intended to contribute substantially to the management businesses processes at the EU level (European Commission (EC), 2020d, p.6). Under these circumstances, an example could be represented by "the Europe-wide sharing of health data (or similarly utilities or transport data) to improve healthcare outcomes, research and fuel innovation while respecting privacy and citizen trust", since supporting people's health and well-being is a very strong motivation for leaders and health specialists at the national and the international levels (European Commission (EC), 2020d, p.6).

The fourth initiative emphasized by the European Commission (EC) (2020d) is represented by "leading the way towards trustworthy AI worldwide by both promoting AI based innovation to fuel economic growth and social innovations while ensuring transparency and a positive social impact, which can include social measures to counter potential adverse effects" (European Commission (EC), 2020d, p.6). The main purpose of these measures is intended to make the difference between the European AI solution and other international AI solution, while attempting to maintain the European AI solution "as ethical and trustworthy", while actively serving the purposes of the individuals, the entities, and the society, in general (European Commission (EC), 2020d, p.6).

The fifth initiative stressed by the European Commission (EC) (2020d) is represented by "empowering cities and communities across Europe by promoting and enabling development and equal access to citizen-centric smart city technologies" in order to ensure "better public and private services across transport, health, energy, social and community services" for the municipalities that belong to the EU (European Commission (EC), 2020d, p.6). In order to support the importance of this initiative promoted by the European Commission (EC), there is the strong need to mention the crucial role of digital technologies on all sectors of our society, in order to be able to enhance the benefits that information technologies and electronics could bring to our economies and our societies.

The sixth initiative brought to light by the European Commission (EC) (2020d) is represented by "raising a cyber-security shield for Europe to protect EU citizens, businesses and Member States from attacks on their data and data systems" (European Commission (EC), 2020d, p.6). The use of information technologies as well as digital technologies has raised serious security risks in terms of a wide range of activities and that is the reason why "protecting end-to-end technology supply chains including foreign technology and increasing strategic autonomy for key technologies" represents a major priority the European Commission (EC) (European Commission (EC), 2020d, p.6).

The seventh initiative analyzed by the European Commission (EC) (2020d) is represented by "advancing citizen control of their personal data" and "building on the General Data Protection Regulation" so that "understanding, user-centricity, control and effective enforcement of citizens' data rights and enable innovation and new business models based on data portability" could be enhanced and improved at a wide scale (European Commission (EC), 2020d, p.6). Innovation has a high impact in our society, especially when addressing the circumstances that are surrounding the information technologies and the digital technologies, so the impact that both the information technologies and the digital technologies have on our economy and our businesses has the purpose of accelerating prosperity and of finding solutions capable to solve the economic and social disruptions that are occurring in our daily lives due to the specific information and technology risks and increased levels of inequalities.

The eight form of initiative on which the European Commission (EC) (2020d) focuses the discussions is represented by "promoting digital solutions for climate risks by both promoting the positive potential of digital technologies to reduce CO2 emissions and resource use in other industries as well as reducing the growing contribution of ICT to CO2 emissions and material use (particularly rare metals) due to both infrastructure (e.g. data centers) and ICT devices" (European Commission (EC), 2020d, p.6). In this matter, it ought to be mentioned that pollution represents a great reason for concern for all countries at a global level, not solely for the countries that are part of the EU. The next wave of digital transformations might come with new and enhanced solutions for a better future for all individuals, which would create the possibility for Europe (in this case) to position itself much better and deeper in the global process that is due to create a durable, robust, resilient, and sustainable society.

The ninth form of initiative on which the European Commission (EC) (2020d) focuses the discussions is represented by "supporting lifelong learning for the future of work, to enable at-scale reskilling of citizens (particularly populations at risk of unemployment) and equip all citizens with the digital and cognitive skills they need to succeed in a future of work context" (European Commission (EC), 2020d, p.6). Lifelong learning represents a desiderate for the future and is expected to provide constant benefits for all Europeans, especially when proactive measures and solutions are expected to be taken in order to foster the development of our society and to boost the addition of high technologies.

DISCUSSION AND SYNTHESIS OF RESULTS

The discussion and synthesis of results section of this book chapter is believed to be of outmost importance especially when targeting the analysis of the COVID-19 implications on the digital transformation of business.

Legendary, Life-Changing, and Memorable Benefits

As it can be noticed, the digital transformation of business as a result of the COVID-19 pandemic and the COVID-19 crisis implicates these days more than ever before the idea of creating new values in terms of businesses as well as enabling new experiences for the consumers, while basing the perchance decisions on the immense power of digital models and digital interfaces.

The roles of leaders and of leadership are essential in times that are surrounding the Post-COVID-19 Era, since successful actions are due to be found in the new opportunities that the digital transformation of our economy and of our society relies on. Hence, the decision-making process in the Post-COVID-19 Era will come to implicate taking actions as a result of the impact of the COVID-19 in order to hinder countries' efforts to become much powerful and much stronger, while helping their economies to take advantage of the information and the communication technologies (ICTs) (see, in this matter, Figure 1. Specific links and connections between the legendary, life-changing, and memorable benefits of digitalization to restart the economy, while centering on the implications of the impact of COVID-19 on global economic environment for sustainable development).

Figure 1. Specific links and connections between the legendary, life-changing, and memorable benefits of digitalization to restart the economy, while centering on the implications of the impact of COVID-19 on global economic environment for sustainable development
Source: The authors, based on the references of this book chapter

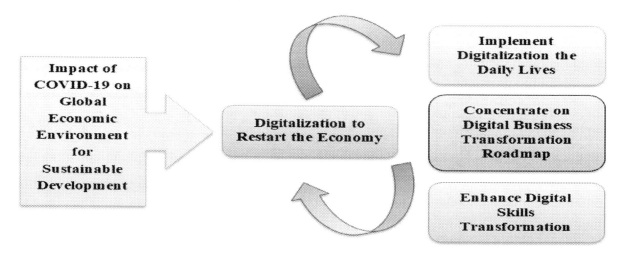

Also, this book chapter has managed to demonstrate the fact that the potential of the digital economy is immense and has no boundaries – unless referring to the individuals' minds boundaries, which prompts us to acknowledge that by helping the countries to maximize their potential in terms of the digital economy, it will lead to finding innovative solutions for a bright future as well as ensure inclusive growth for the restart of the economy so deeply affected by the measures taken due to the COVID-19 pandemic and the COVID-19 crisis.

All in all, high-quality connectivity in the Post-COVID-19 Era comes to support the need of individuals and of entities to be part of a powerfully digital economy and society, where it can clearly be acknowledged that the power of business transactions will rely on accomplishing the necessary skills for the digital intensive sectors.

SOLUTIONS AND RECOMMENDATIONS

The solutions and recommendations section of this book chapter surround the topic addressing the benefits of digitalization to restart the economy, while centering on the impact of the COVID-19 on global economic environment for sustainable development, in order to ensure the premises for fostering sustainable development in the Post-COVID-19 Era, on the challenging road of building inclusive global knowledge societies.

In this matter, the next waves of the digital transformations are due to complete and to complement the road already taken by our society and by our economy as a result of the COVID-19 pandemic as well as the COVID-19 crisis. A vital solution and a clear recommendation would be to align the investments in the digitalization processes with the investments the digital skills of individuals. In continuation to this, it should be mentioned that the digital transformation should be analyzed and regarded together with the green transformation, since these two forms – namely, the digital transformation and the green transformation, are believed to be the most important ones for our society these days (see, in this matter, Figure 2. Specific solutions for ensuring a bright future for all in the Post-COVID-19 era).

Figure 2. Specific solutions for ensuring a bright future for all in the Post-COVID-19 era
Source: The authors, based on the references of this book chapter

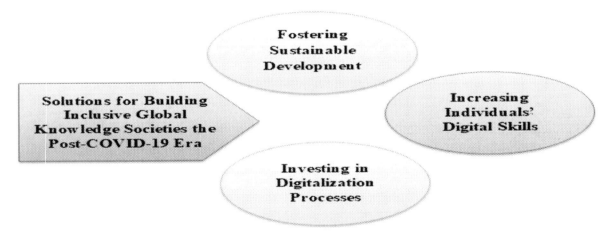

Moreover, these are times in which recovery, growth, and competitiveness have reached one of their highest peaks, at a global level, which raises the matters that are surrounding the implications and the problems that need to be faced and absorbed in terms of leadership, digital value changes, business process management in times of increased preoccupation towards the digitalization processes and the artificial intelligence (AI) implementation consequences.

Furthermore, according to the aspects highlighted in this book chapter, the most recent statistics have shown that the COVID-19 pandemic is believed to be responsible for the most acute and accentuate economic crisis in post-war times. As a result, on the one hand, the need for social distancing has promoted the need to ensure the digital transformations in our society, while, on the other hand, the businesses paused or slower their pace, while the usual rhythm of consumption and investment dropped significantly and alarmingly. In this matter, a possible solution could be represented by identifying new sources of investments capable to support businesses in order to be able to help them change their existing patterns to the new ones that surround a society and an economy inclined more towards digitalization and information technologies.

FUTURE RESEARCH DIRECTIONS

The future research directions section of this book chapter aims at providing new research dimensions in terms of digital technologies and digitalization, while addressing the implications of the COVID-19 on our society and on our economy, in the quest for finding solutions to support a global economic environment due to successfully foster sustainable development for the benefit of all individuals.

In this matter, one possible future direction might be represented by presenting the next waves of digital transformations expected by specialists especially in developing and developed countries, with a particular emphasis on the values that could be expected to surround these next waves of digital transformations. High-potential technologies represent a clear preoccupation for all major business players on the marketplace these days, and that is the reason why shaping the digital transformation of our economy and of our society as a whole may clearly be considered a very important subject of analysis and debate now and in the future.

In continuation, another possible future direction could be represented by finding viable solutions capable to correlate the society's need to constantly innovate with the strategic decision to make investment decisions in potentially successful projects, capable to boost productivity, profitability and sustainability, and take an active role in the digitalization process of our economy and of our society.

Also, since digital transformation represents a top priority for all, a possible future direction might be represented by presenting the future of mankind in relation with advanced digital skills, artificial intelligence (AI), and cyber-security transformations and risks. In this regard, numerous correlations and analysis could be made by including references to the digital infrastructure and the digital infrastructure investments.

CONCLUSION

The conclusion section of the book chapter entitled "Legendary, life-changing, and memorable benefits of digitalization to restart the economy: Impact of COVID-19 on global economic environment for sustainable development", as an integrating part of the "Handbook of Research on Building Inclusive Global Knowledge Societies for Sustainable Development", is centered on the immense power of digitalization – as main solution capable to restart the economy, in challenging times such as the ones that people are currently living. The impact of the COVID-19 on the global economic environment is believed to be enormous when referring to individuals' and countries' continuous struggle to ensure the sustainable development (SD) of our planet.

First of all, while emphasizing the most important aspects related to digitalization to restart the economy, while addressing the impact of the COVID-19 on the global economic environment for sustainable development (SD), it should be prompted that specialists see the aspects related with the "digital eco-innovation as a means to reach a circular economy in Europe" (European Commission (EC), 2020c, p.6). Also, by understanding today's "trends in technological digital eco-innovations" and by illustrating these trends "by good technology and policy practices", the circular economy together with the innovations that are capable "to make digital products, hardware and infrastructures more sustainable in Member States" will further our society and will ensure the accomplishment of the Sustainable Development Goals (SDGs) for building inclusive global knowledge societies (GKSs) (European Commission (EC), 2020c, p.6).

Second of all, the importance of digitalization to restart the economy comes from the countries and regions need to address "eco-innovation performance of countries", which could be assiduously and strenuously centered on "the value of green early stage investments", while "potentially pointing to more eco-innovative start-ups in future markets" (European Commission (EC), 2020c, p.6). In this matter, this book chapter has highlighted the believes of several major international organizations, such as, for instance the United Nations Economic Commission for Europe, which has focused on showing that the "development of sustainable transport systems and connectivity are important factors of achieving" and for maintaining the Sustainable Development Goals (SDGs) (United Nations Economic Commission for Europe (UNECE), 2021).

Third of all, the importance of digitalization to restart the economy has profound links and deep connections with the education system of nations. A close analysis of different education systems has shown that the process of digitalization in the education systems has started long before the COVID-19 pandemic. An example a good practices in terms of digitalization in the education systems is represented by "the Finnish matriculation examination", where the forms examination are "fully electronic and traditional paper tests were no longer available" starting with the year 2019 (Organization for Economic Co-operation and Development (OECD), p.17). In this way, the digital advancement in the Finnish education system permitted "the tests to incorporate enhanced digital and visual tools, requiring students to complete computation, editing or graphic presentation tasks", while the students were "supported in becoming familiar with such tools" through different digital platforms which act as "an electronic examination systems" used in different schools, high schools, and universities (Organization for Economic Co-operation and Development (OECD), p.17).

ACKNOWLEDGMENT

This research received no specific grant from any funding agency in the public, commercial, or not-for-profit sectors.

REFERENCES

European Commission (EC). (2020a). *Shaping Europe's Digital Future*. Luxembourg: Publications Office of the European Union. https://ec.europa.eu/info/sites/default/files/communication-shaping-europes-digital-future-feb2020_en_4.pdf doi:10.2759/48191

European Commission (EC). (2020b). *Assessment and Roadmap for the Digital Transformation of the Energy Sector Towards an Innovative Internal Energy Market*. Luxembourg: Publications Office of the European Union. https://www.euneighbours.eu/sites/default/files/publications/2020-03/MJ0220185ENN.en_.pdf doi:10.2833/36433

European Commission (EC). (2020c). *Eco-Innovation and Digitalisation Case studies, environmental and policy lessons from EU Member States for the EU Green Deal and the Circular Economy EIO Biennial report 2020*. https://ec.europa.eu/environment/ecoap/sites/default/files/eio5_eco-innovation_and_digitalisation_nov2020.pdf

European Commission (EC). (2020d). *Shaping the Digital Transformation in Europe. European Commission DG Communications Networks, Content & Technology. Final Report: A study prepared for the European Commission DG Communications Networks, Content and Technology*. https://www.ospi.es/export/sites/ospi/documentos/documentos/Sstudy_Shaping_the_digital_transformation_in_Europe_Final_report_202009.pdf

European Commission (EC). (2021). *Proposal for a Decision Of The European Parliament And Of The Council establishing the 2030 Policy Programme "Path to the Digital Decade" (Text with EEA relevance) {SWD(2021) 247 final}. Brussels, 15.9.2021 COM(2021) 574 final 2021/0293 (COD)*. https://www.digitales.es/wp-content/uploads/2021/11/COM_2021_574_final_act_EN_v8_ptPK7Tb1DRDE-7515KeapWlChi8_79300.pdf

European Commission (EC). (2022). *Shaping Europe's digital future. Procurement of ICT innovation*. https://digital-strategy.ec.europa.eu/en/policies/innovation-procurement

European Parliament (EP). (2019). *Briefing. EU policies – Delivering for citizens EPRS*. European Parliamentary Research Service. https://www.europarl.europa.eu/RegData/etudes/BRIE/2019/633171/EPRS_BRI(2019)633171_EN.pdf

European Parliament (EP). (2021). *Briefing. Initial Appraisal of a European Commission Impact Assessment. Artificial intelligence act Impact assessment (SWD(2021) 84, SWD(2021) 85 (summary)) accompanying a Commission proposal for a regulation of the European Parliament and of the Council laying down harmonized rules on artificial intelligence (Artificial Intelligence Act) and amending certain Union legislative acts(COM(2021) 206)*. EPRS. European Parliamentary Research Service. https://www.europarl.europa.eu/RegData/etudes/BRIE/2021/694212/EPRS_BRI(2021)694212_EN.pdf

Luque, A. (2021). Practicality, support or premeditated calculation in the digital age: The case of Ecuador. *Revista Venezolana de Gerencia, 26*(6), 29–46. doi:10.52080/rvgluz.26.e6.3

Luque, A. (2022). Analysis of the concept of informal economy through 102 definitions: Legality or necessity. *Open Research Europe, 2022*(1), 134. doi:10.12688/openreseurope.13990.2

Luque, A., & Herrero-García, N. (2019). How corporate social (ir)responsibility in the textile sector is defined, and its impact on ethical sustainability: An analysis of 133 concepts. *Corporate Social Responsibility and Environmental Management, 26*(6), 1–22. doi:10.1002/csr.1747

Luque González, A., Coronado Martín, J. Á., Vaca-Tapia, A. C., & Rivas, F. (2021). How Sustainability Is Defined: An Analysis of 100 Theoretical Approximations. *Mathematics, 2021*(9), 1308. doi:10.3390/math9111308

Organization for Economic Co-operation and Development (OECD). (2019). *A measurement roadmap for the future, in Measuring the Digital Transformation: A Roadmap for the Future*. OECD Publishing. www.oecd.org/going-digital/measurement-roadmap.pdf. https://www.oecd.org/digital/measurement-roadmap.pdf

Organization for Economic Co-operation and Development (OECD). (2019). *Latin American Economic Outlook 2019: Development in Transition*. OECD Publishing. doi:10.1787/g2g9ff18-

Organization for Economic Co-operation and Development (OECD). (2020). *Education Policy Outlook*. https://www.oecd.org/education/policy-outlook/country-profile-Finland-2020.pdf

Organization for Economic Co-operation and Development (OECD). (2020). *The role of international co-operation in the digital age, in Latin American Economic Outlook 2020: Digital Transformation for Building Back Better*. OECD Publishing. https://www.oecd-ilibrary.org/docserver/7d3929e1-en.pdf?expires=1648890283&id=id&accname=guest&checksum=8B23F2183B460C897B762B09B9065C3E

Popescu, C. R. G. (2018). "Intellectual Capital" - Role, Importance, Components and Influences on the Performance of Organizations - A Theoretical Approach. *32nd Conference of the International-Business-Information-Management-Association (IBIMA). Vision 2020: Sustainable Economic Development And Application Of Innovation Management*.

Popescu, C. R. G. (2019a). Business Development Opportunities: Demonstrating Present And Future Performance, Auditing Intellectual Capital: A Case Study On Romanian Organizations. *33rd International-Business-Information-Management-Association (IBIMA) Conference. Vision 2025: Education Excellence and Management of Innovations through Sustainable Economic Competitive Advantage*.

Popescu, C. R. G. (2019b). Intellectual Capital, Integrated Strategy and Performance: Focusing on Companies' Unique Value Creation Mechanism and Promoting Better Organizational Reporting In Romania: A Framework Dominated By the Impact of Green Marketing and Green Marketing Strategies. *33rd International-Business-Information-Management-Association (IBIMA) Conference. Vision 2025: Education Excellence and Management of Innovations through Sustainable Economic Competitive Advantage*.

Popescu, C. R. G. (2019c). Demonstrating How Universities Extend Value Creation And Performance: Convergence Between Intellectual Capital Contributions And Research Quality - A Romanian Collective Intelligence Framework. *11th International Conference on Education and New Learning Technologies (EDULEARN). EDULEARN19: 11th International Conference On Education And New Learning Technologies*.

Popescu, C. R. G. (2019d). Using Intellectual Capital Measurements In Universities To Assess Performance - Evidence From The Romanian Education System. *11th International Conference on Education and New Learning Technologies (EDULEARN). EDULEARN19: 11th International Conference On Education And New Learning Technologies*.

Popescu, C. R. G. (2019e). Intellectual Capital Evaluation And Measuring Effectiveness - A Case Study On Romania's Experience In Terms Of Performance And Excellence. *13th International Technology, Education And Development Conference (INTED2019). 13th International Technology, Education and Development Conference (INTED)*.

Popescu, C. R. G., & Popescu, G. N. (2018). Risks of cyber attacks on financial audit activity. *The Audit Financiar Journal, 16*(149), 140-140. https://ideas.repec.org/a/aud/audfin/v16y2018i149p140.html

Popescu, C. R. G., Popescu, G. N., & Popescu, V. A. (2015). Corporate Governance in Romania: Theories and Practices. In *Corporate Governance And Corporate Social Responsibility: Emerging Markets Focus* (pp. 375-401). World Scientific Publ Co Pte Ltd. https://www.worldscientific.com/doi/abs/10.1142/9789814520386_0014 doi:10.1142/9789814520386_0014

United Nations Economic Commission for Europe (UNECE). (2021). *SPECA Workshop on digitalization of transport services (eTIR and eCMR)*. https://unece.org/transport/events/speca-workshop-digitalization-transport-services-etir-and-ecmr-nur-sultan

United Nations (UN). (2020a). *Secretary General's Roadmap for Digital Cooperation*. https://www.un.org/en/content/digital-cooperation-roadmap/assets/pdf/Roadmap_for_Digital_Cooperation_EN.pdf

United Nations (UN). (2020b). *United Nations E-Government Survey 2020. Digital Government in the Decade of Action for Sustainable Development*. The Department of Economic and Social Affairs of the United Nations Secretariat. United Nations. https://publicadministration.un.org/egovkb/Portals/egovkb/Documents/un/2020-Survey/2020%20UN%20E-Government%20Survey%20(Full%20Report).pdf

KEY TERMS AND DEFINITIONS

Digital Business Process Management (DBPM): Represents a vital step in any activity that relies on digital transformation, since the integration of the digital technology into all areas of business is regarded as the immediate consequence of the COVID-19 pandemic and the COVID-19 crisis and as the wide range solution in the Post-COVID-19 Era, since it makes reference to the manner in which digital transformation changes how entities operate and how they are able to deliver value in the present days and in the future, thus meeting the customers preferences with tailor-made offers and suitable digital products.

Digital Business Processes (DBP): Have been encountered and have been used long before the appearance of the COVID-19 pandemic and the COVID-19 crisis, not representing at all a buzzword in our society, since these types of activities are believed to be a pivotal solution to a bright future for all individuals, being fully customizable, highly intuitive, and very fast, making them a must, also, for the Post-COVID-19 Era; these activities are believed to empower individuals and organizations at a very high extent in terms of data digitalization and technology, facilitating the process of encoding information, and aiming to increase the lifecycle value of businesses through better use of information, knowledge, data, and digital technology.

Digital Organization (DO) in the Post-COVID-19 Era: Makes reference, these days, to the business process (BP) transformation that takes place in all entities, at an international level, especially when organizations are inclined to seek success in all areas of activities in accordance to the sustainable development (SD) requirements and targets, while centering on very specific and highly targeted forms of processes – namely, the scope processes, addressing the need of individuals to reinvent the activities at a faster pace, and creating and implementing more evolved, more comprehensive, and more reliable digital business models (DBM); in like manner, it should be prompted that organizations are using these days a number of digital tools that are giving tribute to technology and ecosystems, thus enhancing the most wanted process of providing greater value to the customers and clients through new experiences, new products and services, new business models, and new solutions to their problems.

Digital Skills Transformation (DST) in the Post-COVID-19 Era: Is considered to be one of the most interesting and novel provocations that characterizes at present the global economic environment for the sustainable development (SD) and, in the same time, one of the most expected actions due to be taken by people and organizations in order to support the countries' ambitions to facilitate the economic recovery and help reshape the economy, while concentrating on finding valuable answers to vital questions, such as the following ones: "How can people and entities adapt and implement digitalization in their daily lives, in order to restart the economy?", "How will the world's digital business transformation roadmap look like, in order to find a balance between the individuals' expectations and the planet's needs?", "Will the digital skills transformation enhance the role of human resources in society, or will these new acquired skills create an even larger gap between people than ever before?", and "Is artificial intelligence (AI) the future?".

Digitalization to Restart the Economy: On the one hand, represents, according to world known specialists, a possible and plausible solution for today's highly challenged economy, as a result of the influence of the COVID-19 pandemic and the COVID-19 crisis on our society, in overbearing times in which both individuals and businesses are expected to move, suddenly, abruptly, and at an accelerated rate to the digital activities, like never before in the history of mankind; on the other hand, represents, according to most recent studies, a valuable and longtime expected step due to be taken by both people and organizations, which is capable to lead to the increased importance of digitalization in terms of use of digital technologies in the Post-COVID-19 Era which is responsible for targeting to create novel communication patterns and pivotal business models in our society, capable to ensure new revenue and value-producing benefits and opportunities, while ensuring the United Nations' (UN) Sustainable Development Goals (SDGs).

Global Economic Environment (GEE) for Sustainable Development (SD): Is believed to be the result of the individuals' continuous struggle to maintain an appropriate balance between the unrivalled benefits offered by taking care of the planet, so that the planet will take care, in turn, of the people, and individuals and organizations amplified desire to ensure economic growth, seek financial stability, and evolve with the aid of advanced digital technologies, in order to make the most of the benefits and the opportunities that the Post-COVID-19 Era are due to be brought in terms of the incredible amount of information due to be processed, encoded, and valued as knowledge, the world's business environment and the newest digital trends, the digital transformation of the local and the international markets, the competitive landscape, the rapid response of the entities' human resources (HR) facing the perspective of the artificial intelligence (AI) today and in the future.

Sustainable Development Goals (SDGs) for Building Inclusive Global Knowledge Societies: Is a worldwide desiderate promoted assiduously by the United Nations (UN), in the spirit of calling all countries (developed and developing) to take action in reaching the Global Goals, with the tremendous desire to end poverty, the paramount need to protect the Planet Earth, and the overpowering desire to ensure that all individuals are capable to enjoy both peace and prosperity now and in the future; in continuation, these Global Goals have their profound roots implemented in the overbearing desire to foster sustainability at three main levels, namely economic, environmental, and social, due to their immediate and unequivocal relationship together with the people, our planet, and the profits.

Chapter 9
Role of Training Transfer in the Aftermath of the COVID-19 Pandemic

Ramnath Dixit
https://orcid.org/0000-0002-7131-5857
Symbiosis International University (Deemed), India

Vinita Sinha
Symbiosis Centre for Management and Human Resource Development, Symbiosis International University (Deemed), India

ABSTRACT

This chapter aims to highlight the significance of training transfer in organizations in the aftermath of the COVID-19 pandemic. Transfer of training has always been sidelined in companies for various reasons, and this problem aggravates during situations such as the pandemic or economic upheavals. It is imperative that workplace transfer is given its due credit in the learning and development framework to ensure successful implementation of trained skills and knowledge thereby justifying the training investments made. The chapter highlights the bottlenecks that need to be addressed towards training transfer in the context of a post-pandemic scenario and also suggests practical recommendations to overcome these challenges.

INTRODUCTION

In 2020, the COVID-19 pandemic expanded quickly, moving from a local, then regional, worry to the cause of utter disruption in the daily lives of individuals in hundreds of countries throughout the world in just a few months (Bryan et al., 2020). The Covid-19 pandemic has had devastating consequences on businesses and organizations. Even for educational institutions, the Covid-19 has posed a massive challenge (Daniel, 2020). The influence of COVID-19 on education and training at all levels has been extraordinary (Kanwar & Mishra, 2021). Organizations are witnessing challenging times to keep their

DOI: 10.4018/978-1-6684-5109-0.ch009

businesses afloat and are constantly looking for new ways to do so (Diab-Bahman & Al-Enzi, 2020). The Covid-19 lockdowns have changed the way we manage our schools, communicate with our loved ones, teach and learn, work, shop, travel, obtain medical treatment, spend leisure time, engage in trade, and carry out many of life's normal activities (Sneader & Sternfels, 2020). The human resources function has been struggling to ensure survival and continuity of training initiatives in the wake of such adverse circumstances. Evidence from the healthcare domain concerning medical fraternity clearly indicates the negative impact of Covid-19 pandemic on the training initiatives (Edigin et al., 2020; Ferrara et al, 2020; Amparore et al., 2020, Sneyd et al., 2020; Crosby & Sharma, 2020; Hall et al., 2020; Mishra et al., 2020). Training and development is a critical organizational task as it provides the personnel with pertinent insights on ways to perform their roles and the resources to deliver performance in their field of work (Suazo et al., 2009). Training is not only important in large corporation but it is also a game-changer in Small & Medium Enterprises (SMEs) (Dixit & Sinha, 2021). Results from study conducted by Dixit (2019) reveal that training of healthcare professionals ensured superior service performers by learners.

The entire training landscape has shifted drastically and is unlikely to regain normalcy in the immediate near future. Organizations that are willing to continue investing resources in learning interventions, thereby need to ensure successful application of trained knowledge and skills back at the workplace. An increasing number of organizations have realized that merely conducting training programs without implementation measures, is insufficient in causing desired behavior change at the workplace. Change management interventions at the workplace therefore, need to focus on getting their employees to implement learnings in a post-training scenario to justify training costs. Training transfer or learning transfer is thus pivotal to employee development and business growth as it focuses on-ground implementation of knowledge interventions. The post Covid-19 scenario, especially in the context of learning and development is fragile and merely increasing training programs, without complimenting them with effective training transfer strategies is likely to be an unsuccessful venture. This chapter aims to highlight the role of training transfer in driving business growth and influencing behavior change in the aftermath of the pandemic. The key elements of concerning training transfer in the aftermath of Covid-19 pandemic, involve the following:

1. Impact of the pandemic on the training transfer landscape in organizations
2. Challenges concerning online training dissemination
3. Barriers related to transfer of training in a virtual environment
4. Financial constraints and infrastructural bottlenecks to support transfer
5. Absence of strategic approach for training transfer during crisis situations

BACKGROUND

Transfer of training is one of the most underestimated domains as far as learning interventions in organizations is concerned. An enormous amount of money is spent by organizations to train their personnel, yet a fraction of that is diverted towards training transfer which is often the logical conclusion of a training program. According to a recent survey, worldwide organizations spent $356 billion on training interventions in 2015 (Baldwin & Ford, 2017). Even more abysmal is to witness the state of transfer of training during times of business upheavals caused by macro-economic factors or global scenarios such as the pandemic. According to empirical evidence, around 40% of trainees fail to transfer knowledge and abilities immediately following training, and 70% fail to transfer one year later (Saks, 2002). If training is not transferred through proper application of newly gained information and learnings, not only will performance remain at the pre-training level, but the company will also see no return on its investment (Mozammel, 2019). Training transfer is critical to ensuring a return on training investments; otherwise, firms will see only a small percentage of workers returning to work with the knowledge and skills they received during the training, resulting in enormous losses (Lim & Nowell, 2014).

Learning transfer benefits both employees and organizations since it results in learning retention over a longer period of time (Soerensen, 2017). In the literature on human resource development, the notion of transfer of training has recently gotten a lot of attention (Chauhan et al., 2016). Poor training transfer methods result in wastage of a large portion of training investments (Dhaka et al., 2018). Since the success or failure of a training programme is determined by trainees' ability to apply skills taught in the classroom on the job, the concept of transfer becomes critical (Rahyuda et al., 2018). It is critical to recognize that organizations must describe and assure that trainees effectively use newly taught skills and behaviors in the workplace upon their return (Sangkala et al., 2016). Grossman & Salas (2011) rightly state that individuals and organizations will benefit little from a training programme if trainees do not retain the acquired abilities over time. Results of study conducted by Shen & Tang (2018) demonstrate that through the mediation of training transfer and job happiness, training has an indirect impact on customer service quality. Also, employees are more satisfied if they can successfully transfer training outcomes to the workplace, according to empirical research (Pineda, 2010; Strand & Bosco-Ruggiero, 2011).

KEY DIMENSIONS IMPACTING TRAINING TRANSFER IN PANDEMIC TIMES

On account of several bottlenecks in the organization, the training and development function frequently turns out to be ineffective (Dixit & Sinha, 2020). Some of the key dimensions that have impacted the transfer of training in organizations, in the post-pandemic period are explained in detail below:

1. Impact of the Pandemic on the Training Transfer Landscape in Organizations

The Covid-19 pandemic has brought about a paradigm shift in the way organizations view learning and development in the workplace context. The new way of working is characterized by remote working or what is commonly known as "work from home" concept. The learning landscape has been adversely impacted, causing irreversible damage to training infrastructure in case of certain organizations. With workplaces being shut for a substantial period, both during and after the pandemic, classroom training programs have been badly hit. Companies are still working to assist their staff by giving laptops and other required infrastructural and technical support, as well as ensuring cybersecurity, monitoring, and company online access (Mehrotra 2020; Majumdar 2020). Even when employees use their mobile hotspot to attach their devices, the speed is still slow, making even simple tasks difficult (Kagti, 2020).

Although, several organizations have transitioned from a physical classroom format to an online medium to address their employee training needs, the shift hasn't been easy for a vast majority of businesses. Given these barriers associated with training dissemination, the impact has been even worse with regards to workplace transfer of training. Transfer of training or learning transfer refers to the application of acquired skills and knowledge from the training program back in the workplace context. On account of the absence of post-training implementation plans in place, sixty to ninety percent of organizations perform poorly (Sookhai & Budworth, 2010). Another bottleneck that organizations are facing is the hesitancy of employees in attending training programs during the pandemic and in its aftermath. This is owing to the fact that there is an environment of fear due to job losses, pay-cuts and unpredictability in the overall business environment. So in such situations where dissemination of training itself is uncertain, transfer of training becomes an increasingly challenging phenomenon. Learning and development teams in organizations further face an uphill task of motivating employees to attend programs and also encourage them to apply their learnings in a post-training scenario.

2. Challenges Concerning Online Training Dissemination

Since the advent of the pandemic, learners in the corporate environment have been compelled to meet their training needs in an online mode. Dependence on technology has further augmented certain challenges in the context of training dissemination. These include absence of appropriate infrastructure to partake in online training programs, technology hesitancy amongst learners, lack of personal touch in the learning process, financial constraints to fund technological platforms. Evidence from online clinical trainings in virtual remote environments exhibits various barriers for learners (Chen et al., 2020). Similar sentiments are echoed in another study related to blended learning which shows that challenges associated with online learning for both students and teachers (Rasheed et al., 2020). Educators have expresses their concerns about their capacity to convert clinical abilities into an online context (Minton, 2019). Snow et al. (2018) observed that modeling, evaluating, and analyzing students' interpersonal and counselling abilities may not be possible with asynchronous online teaching. Also, learners who are habituated to classroom format of training, often find it difficult to transition to an online mode of training. There are also further concerns with regards to effectiveness of online sessions in providing the necessary insights as it is difficult to engage leaners through experiential learning methods and other activity driven learning aids.

Online training also heavily depends on the facilitator's ability to engage the audience, which is a skill that needs to be nurtured and mastered over a period of time. The currently pandemic has exposed several facilitators on account of their lack of ability to deliver online trainings with the same efficacy as they would delivery classroom programs. Furthermore, classroom sessions usually are conducted in the form of full day interventions, which is practically difficult to replicate in an online format as there is the presence of learning fatigue during online sessions. Several learners find it difficult to attend sessions with longer durations as there is hardly any scope for physical movement or even active involvement. In a research involving students from an Indian University, it was discovered that online education was stressful and adversely impacted both social and emotional well-being (Chakraborty et al., 2021). In addition to these, there are other supplementary issues such as the fact that several learners are reluctant to switch on their cameras during the course of online sessions. In many cases, it is also observed that the learners do not participant wholeheartedly during online programs which further derides the purpose of conducting training. Facilitators are often found to be complaining about the fact that participants also exhibit a tendency to undertake other routine responsibilities while attending online sessions. It is also observed that on many occasions the participants attend online sessions from their homes which usually is a location full of distractions and causes deviation from serious and active learning. The amount of control that the facilitator can exercise in an online session is comparatively lesser than the control a facilitator has in a conventional classroom format. As a result of these limitations, several facilitators have expressed serious reservations of conducting online sessions during the pandemic scenario.

3. Barriers Related to Transfer of Training in a Virtual Environment

Transfer of training heavily relies on the opportunity of application extended by organizations to its employees to practice the learnings from a training program. Since the beginning of the pandemic and also in the recovery periods, employees have been operating from the confines of their homes. This has deprived employees of the opportunity to implement their acquired knowledge and skills from the training program back at the workplace. Also, virtual environments make it further difficult to receive both supervisor support and peer support which are essential conditions for successful workplace transfer to happen. Since online learning thrives on the availability of (Information and Communications Technology, ICT) facilities, one of the challenges connected with online learning is access to ICT resources (Arthur-Nyarko & Kariuki, 2019). Employee training is transferred to a large extent as a result of post-training behaviors (Burke & Baldwin, 1999). It is important for the learners to strike transfer conversation with their respective supervisor. These conversations usually are productive when they happen at the actual workplace. The current pandemic situation had shifted these physical conversations to virtual mode. There are some inherent factors which make these transfer conversations difficult in a virtual mode. Firstly, the supervisor and/ or the subordinate who has undergone the training, might experience discomfort in conducting virtual conversations discussing about the application efforts and necessary support to make transfer happen. Secondly, it is also difficult for the learner to reach out to the peers in a virtual mode and seek their support on ensuring successful transfer post-training.

4. Financial Constraints and Infrastructural Bottlenecks Concerning Transfer

Past experiences reveal that during crisis situations such as the pandemic or other business upheavals, training interventions often end up being the scapegoat as they are denied the necessary financial support. In times of economic crisis, it is widely considered that training is one of the first victims (Felstead et al., 2012). According to the Training Industry Report, overall training expenditures in the United States dropped significantly during and after the Great Recession in 2009 and 2010, followed by a surge in 2011 and a drop back to 2008 levels in 2012. One of primary reasons for this is that resources are usually diverted to serve other business exigencies rather than investing in learning and development projects. This adversely impacts the frequency and the continuity of training interventions in the organizations. In such precarious scenarios, the learning and development function is forced to look for cheaper options, which often leads to compromise on training quality and in worst cases the entire training intervention might be stalled for an indefinite period till the business regains normalcy.

Training is a long-term investment, not a one-time cost. Regardless of the economy, it should be maintained as a continual process to keep businesses competitive and productive (Rao, 2009). It is thus clear that when organizations are demotivated to invest on training interventions, there is still scope for funding transfer of training activities. Surprisingly, several organizations do not even budget for transfer activities while planning their training requirements. Even in well-performing organizations, there is only a miniscule portion of the financial budgets consumed for training transfer, while majority of funds in focused on design and delivery of training. In some cases, organizations may have financial strength to fund their transfer initiatives but may lack the necessary infrastructure to ensure successful implementation. For instance, organizations that may want to employ coaches to support employee transfer efforts may not have access to effective coaches who can deliver performance. Similarly, training transfer tools such as live projects that present the learners with an opportunity for application require the selection of appropriate projects, else the whole enterprise may fail to deliver the desired transfer results.

5. Absence of Strategic Approach for Training Transfer During Crisis Situations

The issue for today's enterprises is to manage improvisation processes at all levels at the same time (Bailey & Breslin, 2021). Organizational willingness is of prime importance to ensure continual training transfer at the workplace. There is a need to develop organizational resilience in the face of external uncertainties (Linnenluecke, 2017). According to research, occupational environments can play a significant role in enabling individuals and organizations to develop resilience and effective coping methods (Liu et al., 2019). This assumes greater even greater importance during crisis situations such as the pandemic or the period thereafter. In several instances, organizations have been guilty of not ensuring a strategic approach towards training transfer. A myopic view towards training interventions often gets exposed during crisis situations. Business crisis could be on account of recessionary trends in the market, economic upheavals or even pandemic situations. Absence of strategic approach towards transfer of training or the lack of transfer planning is a malaise that leaves learners in a complicated situation where the onus of application is solely on the learners without any support from organizational stakeholders. This often hampers on-the-job application of trained knowledge, especially during crisis periods where the emphasis is more on survival than knowledge acquisition and subsequent implementation.

Table 1. Key dimensions impacting training transfer

Training Transfer Challenges	Underlying Causes
Impact of the pandemic on the training transfer landscape in organizations	• Learner hesitancy towards participating in training interventions • Unpredictability in the business environment
Challenges concerning online training dissemination	• Technological challenges related to online trainings • Challenges related to learner engagement and involvement
Barriers related to transfer of training in a virtual environment	• Difficult to receive transfer support from Supervisors and Peers • Lack of opportunity to apply learnings in actual environment
Financial constraints and infrastructural bottlenecks concerning transfer	• Diversion of resources from training and learning transfer to other areas • Absence of infrastructural support
Absence of strategic approach for training transfer during crisis situations	• Myopic view of organizations towards learning and subsequent transfer • Onus on transfer solely on learners, thereby lacking support from other organizational stakeholders

SOLUTIONS AND RECOMMENDATIONS

1. Systemic Overhaul of Learning and Development Ecosystem in Organizations

It is pertinent that organizations redefine their learning and development strategies from a new perspective in the aftermath of Covid-19 pandemic. Additionally, in a pandemic scenario, activities concerning training evaluation often face several bottlenecks (Laksono, 2021). There needs to be a holistic approach towards training employees on key skills. Furthermore, learning interventions need to be designed in a manner that support knowledge dissemination cutting across geographical barriers. Virtual sessions should be developed and conducted to enable both training delivery as well as training transfer. Research conducted by Yaw (2008) emphasizes the need for using effective tools to ensure transfer. Emphasis should be laid upon providing learning transfer tools such as one-on-one coaching, live projects on the job as well as knowledge sharing sessions in a post-training environment to aid successful implementation. Burke & Saks (2009) believe that several stakeholders in the organization are and should be held accountable for training transfer efforts. Broad & Newstrom (1992) suggest several recommendations on strengthening accountability towards training transfer in organizations such as incorporating training transfer into supervisory performance standards (i.e., performance standards include an expectation that supervisors will support training and will be held accountable for the results), create a supervisor–trainee contract that outlines each party's commitment to maximizing training results, action preparation for the transfer (i.e., commitment to behavioral change by the trainee and support by the supervisor), planning transfer assessments (i.e., a mechanism for providing objective feedback to the supervisor and employee on the application of training-related knowledge and abilities), and performing evaluation surveys and providing feedback (for instance, reminding employees of what they learned and that they need to apply it).

Employees and supervisors must understand what precise actions are required of them, how those actions will be monitored, and what punishments or rewards will be given for good or bad transfer performance (Santos & Stuart, 2003). It is important to note that following up after the training and/or building awareness in learners that there will be a follow-up is useful in ensuring effective transfer (Saks & Belcourt, 2006). Furthermore, learners display superior transfer results when it is embedded as a reward system in their work environment (Taylor et al., 2005). A recent study by Hughes et al. (2020) demonstrates that work environment support factors viz. peer, supervisor and organizational support have a positive impact training transfer and use of knowledge, skills and attitudes (KSAs) over a long-term duration. Workplace support is an important factor to consider when implementing any training programme (Chiaburu & Lindsay, 2008). Similarly, the presence of Supervisor's support and involvement is also a critical factor in ensuring successful transfer (Bhatti et al., 2018). Hughes et al. (2020) also posit that supporting training at all levels of the workplace can account for 32% of the variation in training transfer, which is excellent news for practitioners hoping to reap the benefits of training.

2. Transitioning From Training Dissemination to Training Transfer

Transfer is central to all learning (Marini & Genereux, 1995). Although gradually, decision-makers in the learning and development function in organizations need to shift from mere training design and delivery to ensuring a self-sustaining transfer ecosystem. It is therefore relevant that facilitators employed under various interventions are chosen not only for their facilitation skills but also for their ability to drive transfer efforts in a post-training environment. Additionally, trainees either nominated by respective supervisors for training programs as well as self-nominated trainees should be clearly instructed about demonstrate transfer efforts after having attended the training intervention. In their study, Rahyuda et al. (2018) show how using post-training transfer interventions improves trainees' readiness and motivation to employ newly learned abilities in the workplace, allowing them to retain and apply the new skills on the job.

3. Leveraging Technology Led Tools to Support Transfer of Training Initiatives

Several developing technologies have already aided in the digital transformation of many businesses and industries, but in a post-COVID-19 future, they will assume greater significance (Almeida et al., 2020). In many circumstances, digital transformation will no longer be a cliché, but a requirement for everybody (Singhal & Sneader 2020). Digital training initiatives will need to be accelerated by businesses and build 'an ecosystem of learning partners to produce and deliver digital content rapidly to a broad base of employees' (Agrawal et al. 2020). Furthermore, Chief Learning Officers (CLOs) can revitalize their learning organizations by developing digital training programs and forming an ecosystem of learning partners to produce and distribute digital content to a large number of employees quickly. Technology is a key driver in the post Covid-19 scenario and hence needs to be leveraged appropriately with respect to both conducting learning initiatives as well as ensuring post-training transfer. There is ample scope for harnessing technology led training transfer tools such as Augmented Reality (AR), Gamification, E-learning, Mobile Applications and other related ones to facilitate transfer efforts in the organization. Research pertaining to healthcare sector undertaken by (Dixit & Sinha, 2019) provides encouraging results in transfer efforts on account of using tools like Augmented Reality in facilitating transfer. There is also an opportunity to include Gamification as part of training activities to enhance motivation and engagement amongst learners (Larson, 2020). Evidence from a study undertaken by Vigersky et al., (2021) shows encouraging results of using virtual learning, at par with in-person training.

4. Incorporating Training Transfer as Part of Organizational Learning and Development Strategy

Training transfer can be adjudged as the Achilles heel of the training process (Botke et al., 2018). It is imperative that learning and development personnel in organizations focuses on establishing adequate and appropriate transfer mechanisms to ensure on-the-job application of trained knowledge and skills. Organizations must take into account the fact that budgets for learning interventions include transfer initiatives along-with training design and delivery. Systems should be set up to ensure that both learners and training enablers are accountable for learning transfer at the workplace. Organizations must cater to ensuring that reporting managers or supervisors of trainees take responsibility of overseeing transfer efforts and consistently support practical execution of training concepts. It is equally important for the top management of the organization to facilitate a congenial environment under which learners are motivated and have sufficient opportunities to apply their learnings at the workplace. It is also recommended that annual performance appraisals focus on transfer initiatives undertaken by learners along-with number of training man-days for which trainings have been attended. Evidence from healthcare sector shows that there is a need to focus on post-training interventions to encourage application of classroom trainings back at the workplace (Dixit, 2021). Specific best practices for aiding training transfer include supervisory support activities, coaching, providing opportunities to perform, using interactive activities in training, monitoring transfer, and making training content job-relevant (Burke et al., 2013). Some recommendations by Burke & Saks (2009) towards strengthening training transfer in organizations include conducting a training transfer accountability audit to identify where and for whom accountability lapses exist in an organization, developing and clearly communicating prescriptions and expectations for training transfer for each stakeholder group, and evaluating training transfer outcomes across training programs.

According to the study by Burke & Hutchins (2008), a trainer's job accounts for roughly 48% of the total training process, work climate accounts for 49%, and training design and delivery and involvement account for 46%. However, the study found that learner characteristics had a substantial low impact of only 2%. At the same time, the study found that supervisory support contributed 25% to training transfer, with trainees contributing roughly 23% to training transfer before and after training, respectively. Previous studies have also indicated a positive relationship between support from supervisor and the results of post-training transfer (Laker & Powell, 2011; Massenberg et al., 2015; Sieberling & Kauffeld, 2017). The creation of a congenial climate prior to training is quintessential for transfer to happen (Salas et al., 2012), however it is pertinent to note that the period of time immediate after training is also crucial for transfer to take place (Noe, 1986). A study by Botke et al. (2018) refers to three categories of transfer-enhancing interventions viz. goal-setting, relapse prevention and programme framing.

5. Contingency Plan to Counter Crisis and Ensure Sustenance of Training Initiatives

When nations and economies are affected by a crisis, new ideas emerge, paving the way for innovative solutions that can be implemented to secure the organization's existence (Davis, 2009). Organizations need to assume greater responsibility in ensuring sustenance of training initiatives through effective crisis management strategies. The ability to actively adapt to unanticipated occurrences is the most important problem for organizations working in uncertain environments (Dobrowolski, 2020). There is a need to adopt Strategic Flexibility that aims to enforce the ideal plan of action in a given situation to counter unpredictable environment (Yawson & Greiman, 2016). Decision-makers in the learning and development teams exercise adequate measures to provide for consistent training opportunities during crisis situations. Crisis situations often deprive learning and development initiatives of necessary capital as it often gets diverted to other business priorities, leaving learning interventions in a precarious situation. This warrants the necessity to have adequate contingency measures towards learning and development initiatives to facilitate long-term survival of training initiatives and their successful workplace application. Managers must focus not only focus on providing feedback but also resort to using feedforward as a potent mechanism to drive employee performance at the workplace (Dixit & Sinha, 2021). Training design strategies based on variation theory can aid in the transfer of specialized skill training (McMahon, 2021). The transfer of training-specific organizational support aids in the development of an organizational training climate that encourages and inspires employees to apply their new skills and knowledge on the job (Sturges et al., 2010). There is also a need for "Training Transfer Accountability Audit" (TTAA), which could reveal the extent to which accountability is an issue and where solutions are most needed (Burke & Saks, 2009). Throughout the training lifecycle, including before (e.g., motivation to participate), during (e.g., incentive to learn), and after training, trainee motivation is critical (e.g., motivation to transfer) (Beier & Kanfer, 2010; Chiaburu & Lindsay, 2008). Self-initiated autonomous motivation to transfer is a desire to put newly acquired talents to use and is likely to be effective when trainees use self-managed intervention (Gegenfurtner et al., 2009) as compared to controlled motivation which is less likely to be impactful on transfer performance (Gegenfurtner, 2013).

To ensure business sustenance post the pandemic and simultaneously build essential workforce skills, Agarwal et al., (2020) recommend six steps to reskilling as below:

- Step 1: Rapidly identify the skills your recovery business model depends on

- Step 2: Build employee skills critical to your new business model
- Step 3: Launch tailored learning journeys to close critical skill gaps
- Step 4: Start now, test rapidly, and iterate
- Step 5: Act like a small company to have a big impact
- Step 6: Protect learning budgets (or regret it later)

With many firms travelling towards the Work from Home (WFH) model, the future of work, or what is being referred to as the "new normal," will be about networking, virtual interactions, crossfunctional and decentralised teams, and newer skills and knowledge. To enable such functioning, HRD professionals must seize this chance now and respond to this pandemic or any other crises in a sophisticated manner in order to create an effective and responsive organization that is well-prepared to handle the new normal whenever a crisis arises (Arora & Suri, 2020).

Table 2. Recommended solutions to address training transfer challenges

Recommended Solutions	Expected Benefit for Training Transfer
Systemic overhaul of learning and development ecosystem in organizations	• Enhancing the online training infrastructure in organizations • Ensuring stakeholder support and necessary implementation tools to enable transfer
Transitioning from training dissemination to training transfer	• Focusing on training transfer and just merely on training design and delivery • Creating post-training transfer interventions
Leveraging technology led tools to support transfer of training initiatives	• Harnessing technology as a potent tool to enable effective transfer • Investing in tools such as Augmented Reality (AR) and Gamification to ensure transfer
Incorporating training transfer as part of organizational learning and development strategy	• Budgeting for training transfer as part of the organizational learning strategy • Enhancing role of supervisors in supporting on the job application
Contingency plan to counter crisis and ensure sustenance of training initiatives	• Ensuring continuance of training initiatives in the wake of crisis • Building learner motivation to facilitate transfer efforts

FUTURE RESEARCH DIRECTIONS

Several businesses are losing money as a result of their failure to properly implement training transfer. As a result, it's critical to guarantee that transfer training is properly implemented in order to protect investment and boost work performance and productivity (Mozammel, 2019). Not only can an organization assist growth and motivate its human resources by concentrating on transfer difficulties, but it can also get a strong return on its training expenditure (Blume et al., 2010; Stenling & Tafvelin, 2016). The transfer of training is successful when employees implement their training contents at work after receiving training intervention (Ahmed et al., 2016). Hence, efforts must be made to address workplace transfer barriers, and either eliminate them wherever possible, or at least minimize their negative influence that hampers transfer. It is especially imperative in the aftermath of Covid-19 pandemic that organization exhibit additional emphasis on the area concerning training transfer. This will not only ensure successful application of training concepts back on the job, but will also ensure positive repercussions in terms of business results, which will further impact both business survival and sustainability.

CONCLUSION

The consequences of the pandemic demands organizational leaders to adopt novel approaches to withstand the challenges arising in a post-pandemic scenario (D'Auria & De Smet, 2020). Managers must coach more, and HR and training departments must be more creative in their planning, in the post-covid world (Thilagaraj, 2021). Raynor (2007) suggests a four-pronged framework Strategic Flexibility Analysis (SFA) as a tool to counter unpredictable scenarios such as the Covid-19 pandemic that ensures strategic implementation through concrete steps including Anticipation, Accumulation, Formulation, and Operation. Yawson (2020) opines four possible scenarios in a post-Covid-19 pandemic viz. 'Meaning of work,' 'Leadership,' 'Contactless Commerce & Education,' and 'Volunteerism.' On similar lines, researchers Arora & Suri (2020) recommend the adoption of a 4-R Crisis Normalcy Model that can be leveraged by HRD professionals in the aftermath of the Covid-19 pandemic to redefine, relook, redesign, and reincorporate HRD Interventions. 'HRD needs to become more predictive – to develop the ability to understand how human capital systems and organizations will behave' in the wake of post-COVID-19 pandemic (Yawson & Greiman 2017).

Despite breakthroughs in our understanding of the transfer problem and best practices for training transfer, transfer remains a chronic problem in businesses (Burke & Hutchins, 2008). The literature on training transfer has been more focused on post-training transfer initiatives, however, few studies have sought to capture the specific mechanism through which these treatments affect training transfer (Rahyuda et al., 2018). The post Covid-19 era has exposed the lack of seriousness prevailing towards learning infrastructure in organizations. There is an urgent need to address the training related challenges in organizations. Training transfer is a critical factor that can ensure effective implementation of trained skills and knowledge as well as justify enormous training investments. Research reveals that organizations have a better opportunity of gaining superior returns on training investment provided they facilitate effective learning transfer (Nazli & Khairudin, 2018). Decision-makers need to focus on long-term sustainability of learning interventions to facilitate both business survival and expansion. Focusing on training initiatives with emphasis on transfer of training would therefore be a necessary step in the right direction.

REFERENCES

Agrawal, S., De Smet, A., Lacroix, S., & Reich, A. (2020). *To Emerge Stronger from the COVID-19 Crisis, Companies Should Start Reskilling Their Workforces Now*. McKinsey & Company.

Ahmed, U., Abdul Majid, A. H., Mohd Zin, M. L., Phulpoto, W., & Umrani, W. A. (2016). Role and impact of reward and accountability on training transfer. *Business and Economics Journal*, 7(1), 1–6.

Almeida, F., Santos, J. D., & Monteiro, J. A. (2020). The challenges and opportunities in the digitalization of companies in a post-COVID-19 World. *IEEE Engineering Management Review*, 48(3), 97–103. doi:10.1109/EMR.2020.3013206

Amparore, D., Claps, F., Cacciamani, G. E., Esperto, F., Fiori, C., Liguori, G., Serni, S., Trombetta, C., Carini, M., Porpiglia, F., Checcucci, E., & Campi, R. (2020). Impact of the COVID-19 pandemic on urology residency training in Italy. *Minerva Urologica e Nefrologica*, 72(4), 505–509. doi:10.23736/S0393-2249.20.03868-0 PMID:32253371

Arora, P., & Suri, D. (2020). Redefining, relooking, redesigning, and reincorporating HRD in the post Covid 19 context and thereafter. *Human Resource Development International, 23*(4), 438–451. doi:10.1080/13678868.2020.1780077

Arthur-Nyarko, E., & Kariuki, M. G. (2019). Learner Access to Resources for eLearning and Preference for Elearning Delivery Mode in Distance Education Programs in Ghana. *International Journal of Educational Technology, 6*(2), 1–8.

Bailey, K., & Breslin, D. (2021). The COVID-19 Pandemic: What can we learn from past research in organizations and management? *International Journal of Management Reviews, 23*(1), 3–6. doi:10.1111/ijmr.12237

Baldwin, T. T., Kevin Ford, J., & Blume, B. D. (2017). The state of transfer of training research: Moving toward more consumer-centric inquiry. *Human Resource Development Quarterly, 28*(1), 17–28. doi:10.1002/hrdq.21278

Beier, M. E., & Kanfer, R. (2009). Motivation in training and development: A phase perspective. In Learning, Training, and Development in Organizations (pp. 90-122). Routledge.

Bhatti, M. A., Juhari, A. S., & Umrani, W. A. (2018). Addressing generational issues in training and development at Aerospace Composites Malaysia. *Global Business and Organizational Excellence, 38*(1), 47–52. doi:10.1002/joe.21900

Blume, B. D., Ford, J. K., Baldwin, T. T., & Huang, J. L. (2010). Transfer of training: A meta-analytic review. *Journal of Management, 36*(4), 1065–1105. doi:10.1177/0149206309352880

Botke, J. A., Jansen, P. G., Khapova, S. N., & Tims, M. (2018). Work factors influencing the transfer stages of soft skills training: A literature review. *Educational Research Review, 24*, 130–147. doi:10.1016/j.edurev.2018.04.001

Broad, M. L., & Newstrom, J. W. (1992). *Transfer of training: Action Packed Strategies to Ensure High Payoff from Training Investments*. Addison-Wesley.

Burke, L. A., & Baldwin, T. T. (1999). Workforce training transfer: A study of the effect of relapse prevention training and transfer climate. *Human Resource Management, 38*(3), 227-241.

Burke, L. A., & Hutchins, H. M. (2008). A study of best practices in training transfer and proposed model of transfer. *Human Resource Development Quarterly, 19*(2), 107–128. doi:10.1002/hrdq.1230

Burke, L. A., Hutchins, H. M., & Saks, A. M. (2013). Best practices in training transfer. In M. A. Paludi (Ed.), Psychology for Business Success (pp. 115–132). Praeger/ABC-CLIO.

Burke, L. A., & Saks, A. M. (2009). Accountability in training transfer: Adapting Schlenker's model of responsibility to a persistent but solvable problem. *Human Resource Development Review, 8*(3), 382–402. doi:10.1177/1534484309336732

Chakraborty, P., Mittal, P., Gupta, M. S., Yadav, S., & Arora, A. (2021). Opinion of students on online education during the COVID-19 pandemic. *Human Behavior and Emerging Technologies, 3*(3), 357–365. doi:10.1002/hbe2.240

Chauhan, R., Ghosh, P., Rai, A., & Shukla, D. (2016). The impact of support at the workplace on transfer of training: A study of an Indian manufacturing unit. *International Journal of Training and Development*, *20*(3), 200–213. doi:10.1111/ijtd.12083

Chen, S. Y., Wathen, C., & Speciale, M. (2020). Online Clinical Training in the Virtual Remote Environment: Challenges, Opportunities, and Solutions. *The Professional Counselor*, *10*(1), 78–91. doi:10.15241yc.10.1.78

Chiaburu, D. S., & Lindsay, D. R. (2008). Can do or will do? The importance of self-efficacy and instrumentality for training transfer. *Human Resource Development International*, *11*(2), 199–206. doi:10.1080/13678860801933004

Crosby, D. L., & Sharma, A. (2020). Insights on otolaryngology residency training during the COVID-19 pandemic. *Otolaryngology - Head and Neck Surgery*, *163*(1), 38–41. doi:10.1177/0194599820922502 PMID:32312158

D'Auria, G., & De Smet, A. (2020). Leadership in a crisis: Responding to the coronavirus outbreak and future challenges. *Psychology (Irvine, Calif.)*, *22*(2), 273–287.

Daniel, J. (2020). Education and the COVID-19 pandemic. *Prospects*, *49*(1), 91–96. doi:10.100711125-020-09464-3 PMID:32313309

Davis, I. (2009). The New Normal. *The McKinsey Quarterly*. https://www.mckinsey.com/ business-functions/strategy-and-corporate-finance/our-insights/the-new-normal

Dhaka, B. L., Vatta, L., & Chayal, K. (2018). Workplace Factors Affecting Training Transfer–A Meta Evaluation. *Indian Research Journal of Extension Education*, *18*(2), 91–92.

Diab-Bahman, R., & Al-Enzi, A. (2020). The impact of COVID-19 pandemic on conventional work settings. *The International Journal of Sociology and Social Policy*, *40*(9/10), 909–927. doi:10.1108/IJSSP-07-2020-0262

Dixit, R. (2021). Facilitating Training Transfer of Patient Service Skills through Healthcare Learning Champion (HLC) Interventions. *Psychology and Education Journal*, *58*(4), 4468–4474.

Dixit, R., & Sinha, V. (2019). Leveraging augmented reality for training transfer: A case of healthcare service providers in ophthalmology. *Development and Learning in Organizations*, *34*(6), 33–36. doi:10.1108/DLO-09-2019-0211

Dixit, R., & Sinha, V. (2020). Addressing Training and Development Bottlenecks in HRM: Facilitating a Paradigm Shift in Building Human Capital in Global Organizations. In *Contemporary Global Issues in Human Resource Management*. Emerald Publishing Limited. doi:10.1108/978-1-80043-392-220201012

Dixit, R., & Sinha, V. (2021). Is feedforward the way forward? A case of managers in a manufacturing firm. *Development and Learning in Organizations*, *35*(2), 7–10. doi:10.1108/DLO-10-2019-0254

Dixit, R., & Sinha, V. (2021). Training as a Strategic HRM Tool to Foster Employee Development in SMEs. In *Handbook of Research on Strategies and Interventions to Mitigate COVID-19 Impact on SMEs* (pp. 609–628). IGI Global. doi:10.4018/978-1-7998-7436-2.ch030

Dixit, R. R. (2019). Enhancing service experience through excellence in patient relationship (EPR) training programs. *Indian Journal of Public Health Research & Development, 10*(5), 771–776. doi:10.5958/0976-5506.2019.01105.7

Dobrowolski, Z. (2020). The supreme audit institutions readiness to uncertainty. *Entrepreneurship and Sustainability Issues, 8*(1), 513–525. doi:10.9770/jesi.2020.8.1(36)

Edigin, E., Eseaton, P. O., Shaka, H., Ojemolon, P. E., Asemota, I. R., & Akuna, E. (2020). Impact of COVID-19 pandemic on medical postgraduate training in the United States. *Medical Education Online, 25*(1), 1774318. doi:10.1080/10872981.2020.1774318 PMID:32493181

Felstead, A., Green, F., & Jewson, N. (2012). An analysis of the impact of the 2008–9 recession on the provision of training in the UK. *Work, Employment and Society, 26*(6), 968–986. doi:10.1177/0950017012458016

Ferrara, M., Romano, V., Steel, D. H., Gupta, R., Iovino, C., van Dijk, E. H., & Romano, M. R. (2020). Reshaping ophthalmology training after COVID-19 pandemic. *Eye (London, England), 34*(11), 2089–2097. doi:10.103841433-020-1061-3 PMID:32612174

Gegenfurtner, A. (2013). Dimensions of motivation to transfer: A longitudinal analysis of their influence on retention, transfer, and attitude change. *Vocations and Learning, 6*(2), 187–205. doi:10.100712186-012-9084-y

Gegenfurtner, A., Festner, D., Gallenberger, W., Lehtinen, E., & Gruber, H. (2009). Predicting autonomous and controlled motivation to transfer training. *International Journal of Training and Development, 13*(2), 124–138. doi:10.1111/j.1468-2419.2009.00322.x

Grossman, R., & Salas, E. (2011). The transfer of training: What really matters. *International Journal of Training and Development, 15*(2), 103–120. doi:10.1111/j.1468-2419.2011.00373.x

Hall, A. K., Nousiainen, M. T., Campisi, P., Dagnone, J. D., Frank, J. R., Kroeker, K. I., Brzezina, S., Purdy, E., & Oswald, A. (2020). Training disrupted: Practical tips for supporting competency-based medical education during the COVID-19 pandemic. *Medical Teacher, 42*(7), 756–761. doi:10.1080/0142159X.2020.1766669 PMID:32450049

Hughes, A. M., Zajac, S., Woods, A. L., & Salas, E. (2020). The role of work environment in training sustainment: A meta-analysis. *Human Factors, 62*(1), 166–183. doi:10.1177/0018720819845988 PMID:31136198

Kagti, S. (2020). *When You Work from a PG, It's a Fight for Internet*. Accessed 5 November 2021. https://www.livemint.com/mint-lounge/business-of-life/when-you-work-from-a-pg-it-s-a-fight-for-internet-11586186976325.html

Kanwar, A., & Mishra, S. (2021). *Research in Open Learning: Lessons for a Post-COVID World*. Academic Press.

Laker, D. R., & Powell, J. L. (2011). The differences between hard and soft skills and their relative impact on training transfer. *Human Resource Development Quarterly, 22*(1), 111–122. doi:10.1002/hrdq.20063

Laksono, B. A. (2021). The Strategy of Education and Training During The Covid-19 Pandemic. *Aksara: Jurnal Ilmu Pendidikan Nonformal, 7*(3), 855–864.

Larson, K. (2020). Serious games and gamification in the corporate training environment: A literature review. *TechTrends, 64*(2), 319–328. doi:10.100711528-019-00446-7

Lim, D. H., & Nowell, B. (2014). Integration for training transfer: Learning, knowledge, organizational culture, and technology. In *Transfer of Learning in Organizations* (pp. 81–98). Springer. doi:10.1007/978-3-319-02093-8_6

Linnenluecke, M. K. (2017). Resilience in business and management research: A review of influential publications and a research agenda. *International Journal of Management Reviews, 19*(1), 4–30. doi:10.1111/ijmr.12076

Liu, Y., Cooper, C. L., & Tarba, S. Y. (2019). Resilience, wellbeing and HRM: A multidisciplinary perspective. *International Journal of Human Resource Management, 30*(8), 1227–1238. doi:10.1080/09585192.2019.1565370

Majumdar, R. (2020). *Firms Need Built-In Anti-Phishing Solutions for Employees: Microsoft*. Accessed 5 November 2021. https://www.livemint.com/industry/infotech/firms-need-built-in-antiphishing-solutions-for-employees-microsoft-11589349297916.html

Marini, A., & Genereux, R. (1995). The challenge of teaching for transfer. In A. McKeough, J. Lupart, & A. Marini (Eds.), *Teaching for Transfer: Fostering Generalization in Learning* (pp. 1–19). Lawrence Erlbaum Associates, Inc.

Massenberg, A. C., Spurk, D., & Kauffeld, S. (2015). Social support at the workplace, motivation to transfer and training transfer: A multilevel indirect effects model. *International Journal of Training and Development, 19*(3), 161–178. doi:10.1111/ijtd.12054

McMahon, C. J., Gallagher, S., James, A., Deery, A., Rhodes, M., & van Merriënboer, J. J. (2021). Does high-variation training facilitate transfer of training in paediatric transthoracic echocardiography? *Cardiology in the Young, 31*(4), 602–608. doi:10.1017/S1047951120004412 PMID:33300481

Mehrotra, K. (2020). *Is Your Organization Ready for Work from Home (WFH)?* Accessed 5 November 2021. https://cio.economictimes.indiatimes.com/news/corporate-news/is-yourorganization-ready-for-work-from-home-wfh/74644617

Minton, C. A. B. (2019). Counselor Education and Supervision: 2017 inaugural review. *Counselor Education and Supervision, 58*(1), 4–17. doi:10.1002/ceas.12120

Mishra, D., Nair, A. G., Gandhi, R. A., Gogate, P. J., Mathur, S., Bhushan, P., ... Singh, M. K. (2020). The impact of COVID-19 related lockdown on ophthalmology training programs in India–Outcomes of a survey. *Indian Journal of Ophthalmology, 68*(6), 999. doi:10.4103/ijo.IJO_1067_20 PMID:32461413

Mozammel, S. (2019). Understanding Post-Training Factors and Job Performance Relationship: Review of Literature for Transfer of Training Enthusiasts. *Annals of Contemporary Developments in Management & HR, 1*(3), 33–38. doi:10.33166/ACDMHR.2019.03.004

Nazli, N. N. N. N., & Khairudin, S. M. H. S. (2018). The factors that influence transfer of training and its effect on organizational citizenship behaviour. *Journal of Workplace Learning, 30*(2), 121–146. doi:10.1108/JWL-09-2017-0080

Noe, R. A. (1986). Trainees' attributes and attitudes: Neglected influences on training effectiveness. *Academy of Management Review, 11*(4), 736–749. doi:10.2307/258393

Pineda, P. (2010). Evaluation of training in organisations: A proposal for an integrated model. *Journal of European Industrial Training, 34*(7), 673–693. doi:10.1108/03090591011070789

Rahyuda, A. G., Soltani, E., & Syed, J. (2018). Preventing a relapse or setting goals? Elucidating the impact of post-training transfer interventions on training transfer performance. *International Journal of Training Research, 16*(1), 61–82. doi:10.1080/14480220.2017.1411287

Rao, M. S. (2009). Is cutting development and training in a recession a good idea? Looking at the IT and ITeS sector in India. *Development and Learning in Organizations, 23*(5), 7–9. doi:10.1108/14777280910982915

Rasheed, R. A., Kamsin, A., & Abdullah, N. A. (2020). Challenges in the online component of blended learning: A systematic review. *Computers & Education, 144*, 103701. doi:10.1016/j.compedu.2019.103701

Raynor, M. E. (2007). Solving the strategy paradox: How to reach for the fruit without going out on a limb. *Strategy and Leadership, 35*(4), 4–10. doi:10.1108/10878570710761327

Saks, A. M. (2002). So what is a good transfer of training estimate? A reply to Fitzpatrick. *The Industrial-Organizational Psychologist, 39*(3), 29–30.

Saks, A. M., & Belcourt, M. (2006). An investigation of training activities and transfer of training in organizations. *Human Resource Management, 45*(4), 629–648. doi:10.1002/hrm.20135

Salas, E., Tannenbaum, S. I., Kraiger, K., & Smith-Jentsch, K. A. (2012). The science of training and development in organizations: What matters in practice. *Psychological Science in the Public Interest, 13*(2), 74–101. doi:10.1177/1529100612436661 PMID:26173283

Sangkala, M., Ahmed, U., & Pahi, H. M. (2016). Empirical investigating on the role of supervisor support, job clarity, employee training and performance appraisal in addressing job satisfaction of nurses. *International Business Management, 10*(23), 5481–5486.

Santos, A., & Stuart, M. (2003). Employee perceptions and their influence on training effectiveness. *Human Resource Management Journal, 13*(1), 27–45. doi:10.1111/j.1748-8583.2003.tb00082.x

Seiberling, C., & Kauffeld, S. (2017). Volition to transfer: Mastering obstacles in training transfer. *Personnel Review, 46*(4), 809–823. doi:10.1108/PR-08-2015-0202

Shen, J., & Tang, C. (2018). How does training improve customer service quality? The roles of transfer of training and job satisfaction. *European Management Journal, 36*(6), 708–716. doi:10.1016/j.emj.2018.02.002

Sneader, K., & Singhal, S. (2020). *From Thinking about the Next Normal to Making it Work: What to Stop, Start, and Accelerate*. McKinsey & Company.

Sneader, K., & Sternfels, R. A. (2020). *From surviving to thriving: Reimagining the Post-COVID-19 Return*. McKinsey & Company.

Sneyd, J. R., Mathoulin, S. E., O'Sullivan, E. P., So, V. C., Roberts, F. R., Paul, A. A., ... & Balkisson, M. A. (2020). The impact of the COVID-19 pandemic on anaesthesia trainees and their training. *British Journal of Anesthesia*. doi:10.1016/j.bja.2020.07.011

Snow, W. H., Lamar, M. R., Hinkle, J. S., & Speciale, M. (2018). Current Practices in Online Counselor Education. *The Professional Counselor*, *8*(2), 131–145. doi:10.15241/whs.8.2.131

Soerensen, P., Stegeager, N., & Bates, R. (2017). Applying a Danish version of the Learning Transfer System Inventory and testing it for different types of education. *International Journal of Training and Development*, *21*(3), 177–194. doi:10.1111/ijtd.12102

Sookhai, F., & Budworth, M. H. (2010). The trainee in context: Examining the relationship between self-efficacy and transfer climate for transfer of training. *Human Resource Development Quarterly*, *21*(3), 257–272. doi:10.1002/hrdq.20044

Stenling, A., & Tafvelin, S. (2016). Transfer of training after an organizational intervention in Swedish sports clubs: A self-determination theory perspective. *Journal of Sport & Exercise Psychology*, *38*(5), 493–504. doi:10.1123/jsep.2016-0084 PMID:27736273

Strand, V., & Bosco-Ruggiero, S. (2011). Implementing transfer of learning in training and professional development in a US public child welfare agency: What works? *Professional Development in Education*, *37*(3), 373–387. doi:10.1080/19415257.2010.509675

Sturges, J., Conway, N., & Liefooghe, A. (2010). Organizational support, individual attributes, and the practice of career self-management behavior. *Group & Organization Management*, *35*(1), 108–141. doi:10.1177/1059601109354837

Suazo, M. M., Martínez, P. G., & Sandoval, R. (2009). Creating psychological and legal contracts through human resource practices: A signaling theory perspective. *Human Resource Management Review*, *19*(2), 154–166. doi:10.1016/j.hrmr.2008.11.002

Taylor, P. J., Russ-Eft, D. F., & Chan, D. W. (2005). A meta-analytic review of behavior modeling training. *The Journal of Applied Psychology*, *90*(4), 692–709. doi:10.1037/0021-9010.90.4.692 PMID:16060787

Thilagaraj, A. (2021). Training and Development in a Post-Covid-19 Workplace. *Utkal Historical Research Journal*, *34*(19), 77-80.

Vigersky, R. A., Velado, K., Zhong, A., Agrawal, P., & Cordero, T. L. (2021). The effectiveness of virtual training on the MiniMed™ 670G system in people with type 1 diabetes during the COVID-19 pandemic. *Diabetes Technology & Therapeutics*, *23*(2), 104–109. doi:10.1089/dia.2020.0234 PMID:32678672

Yaw, D. C. (2008). Tools for transfer. *Industrial and Commercial Training*, *40*(3), 152–155. doi:10.1108/00197850810868658

Yawson, R. (2020). Strategic flexibility analysis of HRD research and practice post COVID-19 pandemic. *Human Resource Development International*, *23*(4), 406–417. doi:10.1080/13678868.2020.1779169

Yawson, R. M., & Greiman, B. C. (2016). A systems approach to identify skill needs for agrifood nanotechnology: A multiphase mixed methods study. *Human Resource Development Quarterly*, *27*(4), 517–545. doi:10.1002/hrdq.21266

Yawson, R. M., & Greiman, B. C. (2017). Strategic flexibility analysis of agrifood nanotechnology skill needs identification. *Technological Forecasting and Social Change*, *118*, 184–194. doi:10.1016/j.techfore.2017.02.019

ADDITIONAL READING

Baldwin, T. T., & Ford, J. K. (1988). Transfer of training: A review and directions for future research. *Personnel Psychology*, *41*(1), 63–105. doi:10.1111/j.1744-6570.1988.tb00632.x

Baldwin, T. T., Ford, J. K., & Blume, B. D. (2009). Transfer of training 1988–2008: An updated review and agenda for future research. *International Review of Industrial and Organizational Psychology*, *24*(1), 41–70. doi:10.1002/9780470745267.ch2

Broad, M. L. (2005). *Beyond Transfer of Training: Engaging Systems to Improve Performance*. John Wiley & Sons.

Ford, J. K., Baldwin, T. T., & Prasad, J. (2018). Transfer of training: The known and the unknown. *Annual Review of Organizational Psychology and Organizational Behavior*, *5*(1), 201–225. doi:10.1146/annurev-orgpsych-032117-104443

Holton, E. F. III, & Baldwin, T. T. (2003). *Improving Learning Transfer in Organizations*. John Wiley & Sons.

Kirwan, C. (2016). *Improving Learning Transfer: A Guide to Getting More out of What You Put into Your Training*. Routledge. doi:10.4324/9781315588063

Leberman, S., & McDonald, L. (2016). *The Transfer of Learning: Participants' Perspectives of Adult Education and Training*. CRC Press. doi:10.4324/9781315552118

Matthews, P. (2018). *Learning Transfer at Work: How to Ensure Training Performance*. Three Faces Publishing.

Weber, E. (2014). *Turning Learning into Action: A Proven Methodology for Effective Transfer of Learning*. Kogan Page Publishers.

KEY TERMS AND DEFINITIONS

Human Resource Development (HRD): Human Resource Development refers to the holistic measures adopted by organizations that involves training and other developmental efforts to enable employees perform effectively at the workplace.

Information and Communications Technology (ICT): Information and Communications Technology is an inclusive term that comprises all forms of communication and computing infrastructure.

Pandemic: A pandemic is defined as an epidemic of an infectious disease that spreads worldwide and impacts multiple continents (e.g., Spanish flu, SARS, COVID-19, etc.).

Training Intervention: A training intervention is a process in learning and development that involves training need assessment, training design, training delivery, training transfer as well as training evaluation.

Training Investment: Training investment is the monetary equivalent spent by an organization on training its personnel.

Training Transfer: Training transfer or learning transfer refers to the on-the-job application of skills and knowledge acquired during a training program, back at the workplace.

Work From Home (WFH): Work from home, also referred to as remote working is a concept that allows employees to perform their regular duties from the confines of their homes, instead of an office.

Chapter 10
Water Utilization Rate:
Impact on Iranian Economic Growth

Nima Norouzi
https://orcid.org/0000-0002-2546-4288
Bournemouth University, UK

ABSTRACT

In economic growth models, less attention is paid to natural resources and their importance on economic growth. The decline of the world's water resources, especially in countries with inherently limited water resources, such as Iran, has caused a water supply and demand crisis. This chapter deals with the effect of water utilization rate on economic growth. The hypothesis of this research is based on Barrow and Sala's Martin model developed by Barber. According to this model, the effect of the water utilization rate on economic growth can be nonlinear. The tool for measuring the amount of water in this study is the water utilization rate. Other explanatory variables used in the model include the share of water exports, the share of water activities, and the share of gross capital. This chapter uses a self-regression model with distributive interruption with the shore test approach for 1990-2020 for Iran. The estimation results indicate that the relationship between water utilization rate and economic growth for Iran is inversely U-shaped.

INTRODUCTION

Everyone in the community is aware of the importance of having water. Water is a common treasure trove of human beings, a treasure that has become one of the greatest challenges of the present century. In recent decades, the water supply and demand gap has been in crisis due to declining world water resources. Meanwhile, countries with inherent limitations in their water resources are more seriously involved in this crisis. Iran is no exception to this rule and is one of the countries facing a physical shortage of water due to the number of resources and per capita water withdrawal. According to Falcon Mark, Iran will face a physical shortage of water by 2025. Proper use and utilization of the country's water resources can be the first step to deal with this crisis.

DOI: 10.4018/978-1-6684-5109-0.ch010

Water is an element on which human life depends, so how can it not impact its economy. At first glance, it may be said that a country that has more water resources and, by its nature, more exploitation of its water resources also has higher economic growth; in other words, there is a positive relationship between economic growth and water efficiency rates. Because Iran has a hot and dry climate, population growth and declining per capita renewable water have been further reduced so that the annual per capita amount of renewable water in the country has been reduced from 13,000 cubic meters in 1300 to about 1400 cubic meters in 2013. Therefore, to deal with the current water crisis and its consequences on the country's economic growth, we need to examine the relationship between water utilization rate and economic growth as closely as possible. For this purpose, the present article has been organized into five specific sections. In the second part of the theoretical framework, the third part provides an overview of the studies performed, data analysis and estimation methods in the fourth part, and conclusions and suggestions in the fifth part.

Background

Hydrological imagery of the world's freshwater sources shows an emerging global threat in which declining freshwater resources are reflected in increasing global water demand. But for a better understanding of this issue, we will mention a brief history of water resources in the world. Of all the world's water resources, freshwater reserves alone account for 2.6 percent of total surface water reserves, of which 1.98 percent are polar ice caps and glaciers, and 0.59 percent are water bodies. Undergrounds are inaccessible, of which only 0.14% of water is available and usable. Therefore, water resources are less than the amount that can meet the world's water demand.

According to the United Nations, if we assume that per capita water demand does not change and the world's population reaches 9 billion by 2050, about 82 percent of the world's freshwater will be extracted. Therefore, the water crisis is an international issue that can concern all developed and developing countries.

The water crisis, both at the micro and macro levels, is causing serious damage to the economies of countries and the world as a whole. As the water crisis threatens the world's economic growth, this doubles the importance of examining the relationship between water utilization rate and economic growth. But this relationship can be different in different countries, and this difference is due to the abundance and scarcity of water resources in countries. Therefore, the relationship between water utilization rate and economic growth can be examined from two perspectives: countries facing forced water restrictions. Second, countries that do not face mandatory water restrictions.

This research is done for Iran. Iran is geographically located in the warm and dry region of the world, and it is natural to face a shortage of water resources. Here, we will clarify water scarcity in the country and move towards the water crisis with more reasons. Iran is a desert country with a large area in appearance, but its useful area is very small. In addition, Iran's geographical location has caused water poverty, so that the average annual rainfall in Iran is one-third of other geographical areas (Zanouz, 2014). The water crisis is a serious problem not only for the country but also for the world. In this study, water is considered one of several variables affecting economic growth because in all programs of the country, achieving higher economic growth has always been on the government's agenda. However, water scarcity must be considered, and therefore it is necessary to portray the effect of water utilization rate on economic growth in the form of a growth model; in other words, water as an input from the government to producers.

All human beings are aware of the importance of water in their lives, but over time, we see that the need for water due to population growth, urban development, expansion of industrial and agricultural activities are increasing day by day. The issue of water and the concern about the water crisis has become one of the most important global challenges in the third millennium, and this concern about the water future of Iran, which has a hot and dry climate, doubles. In the case of Iran, population growth has been the most important factor in reducing the per capita renewable water in the last century. The population of Iran during the past decades has increased from 8 million in 1926 to 78 million by the end of 2013. As mentioned earlier, the per capita amount of renewable water in the country has been significantly reduced. In addition to increasing the population of Iran, it has increased the demand for water in all major areas of water harvesting (agriculture, wine, and industry). Therefore, increasing demand for water on the one hand and water constraints and scarcity, on the other hand, have made the water crisis even more dramatic. On this basis, it can be said that the water crisis in Iran has been affected by three main factors that can be controlled by human beings, including population growth, inefficient agriculture, and poor management, and the thirst for development.

A. Population growth: The population of Iran in the last century has increased significantly so that in the 1900s, the population of Iran was less than 10 million people. And at the time of the revolution (1978), the population reached 35 million; after the revolution, the population almost doubled in the last two decades due to economic and social development. However, despite the significant increase in population and, consequently, the decrease in per capita water availability, water withdrawal not only did not decrease but, on average, reached 204 liters per person per day. In some provinces, this amount reached 400 liters per day, which shows that water withdrawal Water in Iran is twice the world standard, and we now have access to 70% of the water resources at our disposal, while the extraction of more than 40% of freshwater resources means entering the water stress stage.

B. Inefficient agriculture: Iran's agriculture has always been severely inefficient and relies heavily on irrigation and over-harvesting of limited water resources. Only 15 percent of Iran's area can be cultivated, but 97 percent of the country's water abstraction is related to agriculture. It accounts for 22% of the country's employment, and its share of GDP in 2016 was only 13%.

Figure 1. The role of agriculture in the economy, water consumption, and Employment rate (in 2016)

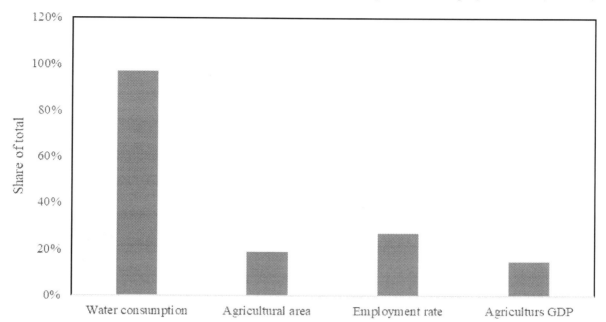

C. Mismanagement and development thirst: After the Islamic Revolution in Iran, international pressures have strengthened the development thirst and desire to prove Iran's independence to the world. But more than anything, the water crisis in Iran is due to the improper and inefficient management of water resources. The Environmental Protection Agency estimates that the use rate of groundwater resources in Iran is three times higher than the international standard.

Numerous studies have examined the empirical relationship between water and economic growth. The results of the studies can be divided into two categories: 1) the existence of a significant relationship between water utilization rate and economic growth 2) the lack of a significant relationship between water utilization rate and economic growth. Koksu et al. (1971) surveyed the Northeastern United States, where major water development projects are underway, for 61 cities during 1948-1948. The findings show no significant relationship between the variables as water resources development has been a weak tool to accelerate economic growth for the northeastern United States.

Howe (1976) presented four conditions, the fulfillment of each of which causes water to be a limiting factor for economic growth. 1) When the amount of water used in the economy is constant relative to the production process. 2) When water resources are stable, the expansion of these resources and the exploitation of new water resources are slow or costly. 3) Excessive use of water resources. 4) When water is a factor in controlling human health. That is, human health is affected by water.

Rock (1998) analyzed the role of water as a tool for economic development and growth using cross-sectional panel data from 1992 for OECD countries. His findings show an inverse U relationship between water use and national income, also that this relationship is also affected by water use efficiency in agriculture.

Goklani (2002) examined the qualitative evaluation of water consumption in agricultural water abstraction during the years 1998-1998. His research findings show that with increasing water consumption in the agricultural sector, agricultural production increases, but with more water consumption, this amount decreases. Bihatari (2004) examined the relationship between irrigation rates and national income for 66 countries in Asia, Africa, and Latin America from 1972 to 1991. The study results confirmed the existence of an inverse U relationship between irrigation rate and national income. Gatto and Lanzafam (2005), using panel data for 38 countries from 1960-2000, obtained a significant relationship between freshwater production and harvesting. Katz (2008) examined the existence of an inverse U-correlation between water consumption and economic growth for the United States during the years 1998-2002, excluding 30 OECD countries, and for the United States during the years 2000-1960. The results indicate an inverse U relationship between water efficiency and economic growth.

Duarte, Pinilla, and Serrano (2013) analyzed the relationship between water per capita and per capita income of 65 countries in 1962-2008 in the context of the Kuznets curve. The results show a significant relationship between per capita water abstraction and per capita gross domestic product in the framework of a nonlinear relationship similar to the inverse U curve.

Khalilabadi and Abrishami (2004) studied the role of water in the development of agriculture. The findings of their study show that the water sector is a fundamental part of the economy and can be used as an engine of economic growth in the economy. Also, the agricultural sector and related activities are very effective in economic growth, so that each investment unit in the agricultural sector leads to direct and indirect employment of 29 people.

Momeni et al. (2013) examined the effect of cold storage in the water sector on national production using the time data of the national accounts for the years 1980-2009 for the three sectors of agriculture, industry, mining, and services. The results show that the attractiveness of water investment in the agricultural sector is significant and positive and is not significant for other sectors. The results also confirm the short-term and long-term causal relationship between economic growth and investment in water resources.

Mohammad Khani and Yazdanian (2014) examined the water crisis and its management requirements from supply and demand. Findings show that in a situation where the agricultural sector accounts for more than 90% of water consumption in the country, due to structural problems in this sector and the growing trend of population and food consumption, despite the pressure on the country's groundwater resources, The trade deficit of this sector has reached more than $ 8 billion in 2014. According to these results, Iran is currently in a severe water crisis.

METHODS AND MATERIAL

There must be a distinction between environmental issues such as natural resources and land for which property rights exist and clean climates for which there are no property rights. Two important reasons for the existence of property rights for an environmental commodity have been suggested: The market first provides valuable indications of how the commodity is used. Second, from the price of environmental goods, evidence can be obtained about its importance in production. Before addressing the relationship between water and economic growth, it is necessary to determine the economic nature of water. Although there is a strong dependence on the private sector to participate in some water services in some countries, the main institution of water supply for the industrial, agricultural, and drinking sectors can be considered the government.

Water Utilization Rate

According to Barrow (1990) and Salai-Martin (1992), the growth model, which includes publicly produced goods, can be defined as effective input for the private producers of an economy. If water has the characteristics of an irreplaceable commodity, then water scarcity can affect economic growth in two ways. First, as the amount of water in the economy is increasingly declining, the government must divert freshwater resources that are less available by exploiting and purchasing a larger share of the total economic resources, including dams, pumping stations, and so on—extract supply infrastructure, etc. Second, water abstraction in an economy may be limited due to limited water resources. Therefore, how water utilization affects economic growth may be different for an economy with limited water resources.

As a result, it is necessary to distinguish between models of forced restriction and non-mandatory restriction of water resources. In this section, we enter the water variable as an irreplaceable commodity in the economic growth model. Then, this model is applied to cases where water shortage is mandatory and cases that do not face limited water resources. We test the hypothesis of an inverse U relationship between economic growth and water utilization rate using a global data set.

Hydrologists' most common freshwater access measurement method is the FAO definition of total renewable water resources, including the average annual and groundwater flow from domestic rainfall, and usually includes inflows from other countries. In the following analysis, we consider the amount of water flows as a tool for measuring the country's total renewable freshwater resources. It should be noted that hydrologists have provided different definitions for the two concepts of water abstraction and water consumption.

Water abstraction means water that has been removed or extracted from freshwater sources and is used by humans (industrial, agricultural or domestic water consumption). However, some of this water, although with a slight change in quality and quantity, may return to the source. Conversely, water consumption is water taken out of the source; in fact, water consumed either due to pollution or "settling" in a place that is not economically reusable is lost. As a result, water consumption is withdrawn water that has been irreversibly lost after human use. For example, in 1995, the amount of freshwater extracted in the world reached 3,800 cubic kilometers, of which 2,100 cubic kilometers were consumed. This study uses annual water harvesting (billion cubic meters per year) to measure freshwater demand. There are two reasons for this. First, globally available information on water abstraction is more reliable and accurate than water consumption. Second, hydrologists measure water pressure and scarcity, usually by access to water per person (cubic meters per person per year) or water withdrawal rate (ratio of water intake to freshwater resources per year). When the second tool is used, hydrologists usually consider a country's water pressure between 0.2 and 0.4, with values above 0.4 indicating severe water shortages.

Because the present study was conducted in Iran and since the amount of water pressure in Iran has not been studied, citing reasons such as the geographical location of Iran, which is located in a hot and dry region, and a sharp decrease in per capita water available over time We consider the amount of rainfall in Iran among the countries with limited water resources and use the annual water harvest to measure the use of freshwater. In the following analysis, suppose w is the total amount of freshwater resources in the country (in the form of billion cubic meters per year), and r is the total amount of fresh water in the country (in the form of billion cubic meters per year). In other words, w represents the concept of hydrologists of all available water resources annually for an economy, while r's water resources have been removed.

As Barrow (1990) and Salai-Martin (1992) suggested, the amount of water harvested by a country for domestic, agricultural, and industrial purposes is characterized by irreplaceable government goods prone to condensation. The effect of water uptake (r) on economic growth can be presented as a growth model that includes such dense government goods as effective inputs for private producers. The rate of water uptake (r) per capita production of the producer i, or y_i can be shown as follows:

$$y_i = Ak_i f\left(\frac{r}{y}\right) \tag{1}$$

According to Rebelo, part of private production depends on the fixed per capita income of capital (k_i) for the producer, including physical and human capital. 0<A is also a parameter that indicates the level of technology. In addition, production increases concerning water uptake. However, due to the density, the amount of water flow available to the first producer is necessarily limited to water use by all producers in the economy. Total per capita production in the economy depends on the production of all producers, i.e., y_i=Ny, which must increase the ratio of water harvest to production to increase the amount of water available to the ith producer. In contrast, any increase in per capita production that depends on the perception in the economy reduces the water available to each producer, resulting in y_i in equation (1). However, equation (1) shows only the irreplaceable aspect of water harvesting among producers.

In addition, how water is harvested in the economy is not considered in equation (1), which can reduce the feedback of its effects throughout environmental services and, consequently, total production. Also, environmental damage and lack of hydrological functions resulting from total water utilization may affect freshwater availability, and the impact of those years or even decades will affect production in the form of reproduction. The total water resources may not only have the characteristics of an irreplaceable commodity, but the provision of these resources may also be affected by physical availability or water scarcity. We will continue to discuss how such a situation arises.

First, it can generally be assumed that the government provides a share of water to all private production in the economy. For example, in modeling the supply of public goods, Barrow (1990) argued that a state might be the sole purchaser of private-sector output, for example, warships and highways, in which case Providing harvested water (r) In that economy, an individual can imagine that the government buys a share of z, or takes over the total economic output that is specifically earmarked for water resources, such as dams, irrigation networks., Water pipes, pumping stations, etc. This shows that r = zy. However, as freshwater abstraction in the economy (r) increases relative to the number of renewable water resources available w, it is expected that total production will be allocated to the water supply. As water becomes scarcer, water abstraction increases relative to existing freshwater resources, and the government must extract less available freshwater resources.

To do this, it is necessary to buy a larger share of the economy's total production in terms of dams, pumping stations, infrastructure resources, etc. By specifying that $\rho = r/w$ as the rate of water withdrawal relative to the total freshwater available, the continuation will be as follows:

$$r = z(\rho)y \quad z' > 0 \quad z'' > 0 \quad z(0) = 0 \tag{2}$$

$$z(1) = \alpha \quad z'(0) = 0 \quad z'(1) = \beta \quad \beta < inf$$

Water Utilization Rate

Where $\beta>0$, $0<\alpha<1$ and $z(\rho)<1$ are the proportion of the total output of the economy allocated by the government to water supply and are thought to be a function of the increase in water abstraction by the economy relative to freshwater resources(ρ). In addition, as total output, y, increases in the economy, so does water harvest, r. Finally, as water is severely depleted, i.e., $\rho \to 1$, the ratio of production allocated by the government to water supply by α is limited by β. Water scarcity can also affect water abstraction by limiting the total amount of water available in an economy. This means that even if all the freshwater sources are removed, i.e., $\rho=1$, the rate of water use is limited. Therefore, all freshwater in the economy is limited.

$$r = z(\rho)y \leq w \tag{3}$$

Where $r=z(\rho)y<w$ if $0< \rho <1$ or $\rho=0$ and $r=z(\rho)y=w$ if $\rho=1$.

By establishing the standard theory that labor supply and population are the same and that the population is growing at a constant rate n, per capita output in the economy is shown to be:

$$y = c + r + \dot{k} + (w + n)k \quad k(0)=k0 \tag{4}$$

Where c is per capita consumption, $\dot{K}$ is the change in per capita capital over time, and ω is the rate of capital decline. Finally, it seems that all consumers in the economy have the same preferences in the long run, which is achieved by:

$$W = \int_0^{inf} e^{-\delta t} \left[\frac{c^{1-\theta} -1}{1-\theta} \right] dt \quad \delta = v - n \geq 0 \tag{5}$$

Where υ is the temporal preference rate, the maximization of W concerning the choice of c and ρ in Equations (1) to (4) gives us the Lagrangian expression L, which includes the current Hamiltonian value for the problem specified by Equation (4) as well as the control constraint of the variable r in the equation. (3) is given, is.

$$L = \frac{c^{1-\theta} -1}{1-\theta} + \lambda \left[(1-z(\rho)) Akf(z(\rho)) - c - (\omega+n)k \right] + \mu \left[w - z(\rho) Akf(z(\rho)) \right] \tag{6}$$

With the first-order derivative, we will have:

$$c^{-\theta} = \lambda \tag{7}$$

$$\lambda \left[(1-z(\rho)) Akfz' \right] - \lambda Akf(z(\rho))z' = \mu \left[Akf(z(\rho))z' + z(\rho) Akfz' \right] \tag{8}$$

$$\mu(t) \geq 0 w - z(\rho) Akf(z(\rho)) . = 0 \mu \left[w - z(\rho) Akf(z(\rho)) \right] = 0 \qquad (9)$$

$$\lim_{t \to \inf} \left[e^{-\delta t} \lambda(t) k(t) = 0 \right] \qquad (10)$$

Equation (7) is a standard condition that refers to the equity of the final utility of consumption (λ) with the shadow price of capital. Equation (8) states that the optimal allocation of water abstraction in the economy involves poor complementary conditions imposed by the constraint of water scarcity. In addition, the Lagrangian coefficient μ can be interpreted as the value of freshwater scarcity in the economy. Equation (9) shows the change over time in the final value attributed to the capital stock in the economy. Equation (10) is the measurement condition for the long-run time horizon problem. Derivation of Equation (7) concerning time and substituting it in equation (9) yields returns (production):

$$g_s = \frac{\dot{c}}{c} = \frac{1}{\theta} \left[(1 - z(\rho)) Af(z(\rho)) - (\omega + n + \delta) - \mu \left(\frac{z(\rho) Af(z(\rho))}{c^{-\theta}} \right) \right] \qquad (11)$$

The above equation shows that growth in per capita consumption is inversely related to the allocation of water supply by the government $z(\rho)$, and to the share of water participation in the final production of capital, $Af(z(\rho))-(\omega+n+\delta)$ is positively related and, conversely, under the influence of water scarcity conditions of ($\mu \left(\frac{z(\rho) Af(z(\rho))}{c^{-\theta}} \right)$). Another main aim is to consider the impacts of water scarcity. For this purpose, we first look at an economy that does not have limited water resources.

Case 1. Water scarcity is not vital in the economy:

If water scarcity (Equation (3)) is not critical, then it is necessary to have w>r and $\mu(t)=0$ for all times to obtain the complimentary conditions. Therefore, equation (11) is changed as follows:

$$g = \frac{1}{\theta} \left[(1 - z(\rho)) Af(z(\rho)) - (\omega + n + \delta) \right] \qquad (12)$$

Although the effects of water scarcity growth on water consumption are not long-lasting, g is also affected by water use in the economy. Growth is inversely related to the allocation of water resources by the government $z(\rho)$ and is positively affected by water consumption to generate net final capital $Af(z(\rho))-(\omega+n+\delta)$. It can be easily shown that in this economy, per capita consumption, capital, and total production all grow at the same rate of g, and there is no dynamic transition for this steady-state growth path. Which was used in equation (8) for $\mu(0)=0$, is selected along with the initial values for consumption and production. They also show that at the optimal water productivity rate ρ^*, growth in the economy reaches its maximum by deriving equation (12):

Water Utilization Rate

$$\frac{\partial g}{\partial \rho} \gtreqless 0 \ if \ f(z(\rho)) \gtreqless (1-z(\rho))f'(z(\rho)) \tag{13}$$

As a result, the rate of water utilization is expressed by Equation (8), in which the rate of growth is at its maximum in g*. In addition, just as z(ρ) is strongly convex, the slope of equation (12) is positive for ρ<ρ* and concerning water utilization and negative for ρ>ρ*. Inversely. As shown in Figure 2, the relationship between growth and utilization of water is concave.

Figure 2. Growth rate and water utilization rate (ρ = r/w)

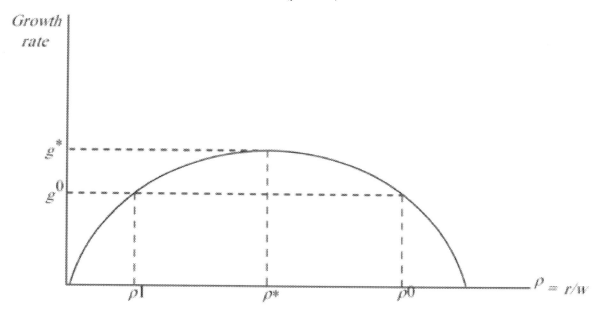

However, current water supply policies are not very effective in most countries, even water restrictions. For example, water management in some countries may increase water utilization, shown in Figure 2 as ρ^0. There are two implications of this conclusion. First, as shown in Figure (2), uncontrolled water exploitation will lead to lower economic growth, i.e., $g^0 < g^*$. This means that at the level of operation ρ^0 the amount of economic growth is g^0, which is less than the maximum growth rate. Second, private producers who profit from the existence of water do not pay enough to produce this irreplaceable commodity. If the rate of water utilization is very low, i.e., in the amount of ρ^1 ($\rho^1 < \rho^*$), economic growth will be g^1 and it is still less than the maximum economic growth rate, i.e., ($g^0 < g^*$). An economy in such conditions may continue to grow by exploiting more freshwater resources.

Case 2. We are facing limited water resources

We now turn to a situation in which water scarcity is critical in equation (3). Therefore, to obtain the complementary conditions, it is necessary that w=r and 0<μ(t) for all times. Equation (2) also holds that z(1)=r/y=w/y=az'(1)=β<inf, meaning that the ratio of total economic output allocated by the govern-

ment to water supply is currently limited by the ratio of renewable water sources to total output indicated by the maximum budget allocation rate α. Limited to water, per capita consumption growth is provided by the revised version of equation (11), in which the rate of government-allocated production for water supply in the maximum case is α:

$$g_s = \frac{\dot{c}}{c} = \frac{1}{\theta}\left[(1-a)Af(a) - (\omega+n+\delta) - \mu\left(\frac{aAf(a)}{\lambda}\right)\right] \tag{14}$$

Growth in a water-limited economy (g_s) is positively affected by the final net productivity of capital which is $Af(a)-(\omega+n+\delta)$, which includes the amount of water consumed for this productivity, but significantly reversely influenced by government allocation of production to supply water resources (a), and conditions set for water shortages ($\frac{\mu(aAf(a))}{\lambda}$). Also, remember that it will always be in the government's best interest to select the highest production allocation over freshwater resources in a water-limited economy. For a water-limited economy, equation (8) is shown as follows:

$$\mu = \lambda\left(\frac{f'(a)}{f(a)+af'(a)} - 1\right) > 0 \tag{15}$$

Using the following expression, equation (14) can be simplified as follows:

$$g_s = \frac{1}{\theta}\left[f(a) - (\omega+n+\delta) - aAf(a)\left(\frac{f'(a)}{f(a)+af'(a)}\right)\right] \tag{16}$$

Equation (16) shows that in an economy with limited water resources, consumption, capital, and production all grow at a constant rate of g_s. In the initial period, the government selects the maximum allocation of economic production for the supply of freshwater, αy =r= w, along with the initial values for consumption and production. After the initial period, y(t), c(t), and k(t) all grow at the fixed rate specified in equation (16). However, in an economy with limited water resources, it will always be profitable for the government to Allocate the largest amount of allocated α production to freshwater resources, but this does not necessarily mean that economic growth will occur.

$$g_s \gtreqless 0 \text{ if } Af(a) - (\omega+n+\delta) \gtreqless aAf(a)\left(\frac{f'(a)}{f(a)+af'(a)}\right) \tag{17}$$

Growth in the economy with limited water resources occurred only when the net final productivity of capital outweighed the negative effects of water scarcity on the economy. In general, in an economy with limited water resources, water is always valuable. Thus, the ultimate benefit of water in terms of its share in final productivity will always outweigh its supply cost. In other words, it will always be optimal to allocate as much production as possible to extract the available freshwater resources. However, whether this leads to growth or stagnation depends on whether the net benefit of the utilities outweighs the cost of resources for water supply. A water-limited economy can still provide sufficient water resources for producers to increase their net productivity in the economy without allocating too much of their output to do so and thus lead to economic growth.

RESULTS AND DISCUSSION

In the present study, time-series data during the period 1990-2020 have been used. The dependent variable of economic growth and independent variables is the share of water exports in GDP and the share of water activities in the Iranian economy from GDP in the economic time series database of the Central Bank of the Islamic Republic of Iran. Information from the Ministry of Energy and the Water Consumption Management Organization has been collected. Descriptions of the variables used in the econometric model are reported in Table (1).

Table 1. Definition and source of data

Variable	Description
GDP growth rate	Per capita growth of real GDP per capita at the base year of 2004
Water utilization rate (ρ)	The water utilization rate variable is the main explanatory variable in the model, and the results of our study for this study are about this variable and its relationship with the GDP per capita growth variable, which is the ratio of the total annual water harvest of the country (r) to total Annually water resources of the country (w).
The share of water exports on GDP (EX)	The share of water exports is based on GDP, obtained from the export of traditional agricultural goods to GDP at current prices because most of the water harvested in the country is related to the agricultural sector, which accounts for about 93% of water harvest. Has given and the goods exported as exports of this sector are interpreted as water goods, and in a way, EX can be considered the share of water goods exports in GDP.
The share of water activities on Iran's economy from GDP (SW)	The share of water activities in the Iranian economy from GDP as a variable that can show the effect of water abstraction in economic sectors on per capita GDP growth. We have identified agricultural, chemical, basic metals, paper, cardboard, printing, binding, food, beverage, and tobacco industries (Ministry of Energy). Then, using the ratio of the total value added of these industries to GDP to current prices, we obtained the share of water industries in the Iranian economy.

As mentioned in the Theoretical Framework section, the relationship between water efficiency and economic growth for countries that did not face limited water resources was shown as an inverse U-curve, which is the result of a negative coefficient of ρ^2, a positive coefficient ρ, which means that in the first stages of development, with water exploitation, economic growth increases, but over time and more water exploitation, economic growth will decrease. Because water is a limited resource, and over time, it will have to incur higher and heavier costs to exploit new water resources, resulting in more economic growth and less economic growth.

Due to the sample size and the need for short-term and long-term tensions to investigate the inverse U relationship, we use the self-regression method with a distributive interval with the limit test approach proposed by Sons, Shane, and Smith (2001). This cointegration approach has many advantages over other cointegration methods such as Johansen (1988), Engel and Granger (1987), and Johansen and Josilius (1990): First, the applicability of this method regardless of I(0) or I(1) being the second variables, calculating short-term and long-term coefficients during the third co-existence test, being an efficient estimator even for small samples IV, being able to have different optimal intervals for the variables. However, if the order of accumulation of each variable is greater than one, for example, a variable with the degree I(2), the critical values presented by the sons and colleagues will not be invoked. For this purpose, it is necessary to use the unit root test to identify the properties of the model variables.

As mentioned, the self-regression method with distributed interrupt with the edge test approach can be used for variables I(0) and I(1), but the unit root test to determine the time series characteristics of variables and ensure the absence of variables I(2). The results of Table (2) show that all variables will be stable with a maximum of one degree of differentiation, so the maximum order of accumulation is one I(1).

Table 2. Generalized Dickey-Fuller test

Parameter	Variable level	First-order difference
Growth	-1.102	-2.072
ρ	-0.412	-7.016
ρ^2	0.541	-3.091
SW	4.933	-2.923
EX	3.621	-4.089

At this stage, the research model is specified as follows:

$$\Delta Growth_t = \beta_0 + \sum_{i=1}^{k} x_{1i} \Delta Growth_{t-1} + \sum_{i=0}^{k} x_{2i} \Delta \rho_{t-1} + \sum_{i=0}^{k} x_{3i} \Delta \rho_{t-1}^2 + \sum_{i=0}^{k} x_{4i} \Delta EX_{t-1}$$
$$+ \sum_{i=0}^{k} x_{5i} \Delta SW_{t-1} + \lambda_1" Growth_{t-1} + \lambda_2 \rho_t + \lambda_3 \rho_{t-1}^2 + \lambda_4 EX_{t-1} + \lambda_5 SW_{t-1} + \varepsilon_t$$

(18)

Where ε_t are perturbations, x_{1i}, x_{2i}, x_{3i}, x_{4i} and x_{5i} are short-term coefficients, and λ_1, λ_2, λ_3, λ_4 and λ_5 are long-term coefficients. The selection of the optimal interrupt is based on the Akaike information criterion. The boundary test process is based on F or Wald statistics, the null hypothesis of which is that there is no accumulation, $\lambda_1 = \lambda_2 = \lambda_3 = \lambda_4 = \lambda_5$, relative to the alternative hypothesis, i.e., $\lambda_1 \neq \lambda_2 \neq \lambda_3 \neq \lambda_4 \neq \lambda_5$. If F is less than the lower bound, it means that there is no correlation. If the F-value is greater than the upper limit, the existence of saturation is also confirmed. If F is between two boundaries, the test will be accompanied by uncertainty. If the accumulation between variables is confirmed in this stage, then long-term and short-term models can be estimated in the next stage. According to Table (3), the results of the F-edge test show evidence of a long-term relationship between model variables at a significance level of 5%.

Water Utilization Rate

Table 3. Border test results

Critical margins	95% low margin	95% high margin	90% low margin	90% high margin
F-stat	3.41	4.76	2.88	3.99
W-stat	16.72	23.74	13.69	19.86

Note: Critical edges are calculated using Microfit 5 software.

The diagnostic tests use the ARDL interrupt estimation model: 1) Lagrange coefficient test for sequential autocorrelation of perturbations; 2) cryptographic test for the square-based pattern of fitted values. 3) Residual normality test based on skewness and residual elongation. Heterogeneity analysis of variance based on the remaining square regression to ensure the correct fit of the model. The results of the diagnostic tests in Table (4) show that the estimated model has successfully passed all diagnostic tests.

Table 4. Diagnostic tests - ARDL method

Test type	LM version	p-value	F version	p-value
Serial correlation	$X^2(1) = 0.074$	(0.811)	$F(1.21) = 0.044$	(0.872)
Functional form	$X^2(1) = 1.855$	(0.187)	$F(1.21) = 1.552$	(0.352)
Normality	$X^2(2) = 0.298$	(0.896)	Not applicable	
Heteroscedasticity	$X^2(1) = 0.005$	(0.977)	$F(1.33) = 0.005$	(0.972)
ARDL lag estimates test statistics				
R-squared	0.992		R-Bar-Squared 0.987	
S. E. of regression	0.017		F-Stat. F(5.22) 163.232	(0.000)
Mean of the dependent variable	0.021		S. D. if dependent variable 0.092	
Residual sum of squares	0.005		Equation Log-likelihood 102.742	
Akaike Info. Criterion	91.721		Schwarz Bayesian Criterion 82.154	
DW-statistic	2.127		Durbin's h-statistic -0.398	(0.701)

Table 5. Estimation of long-term and short-term models

Variable	T-stat	Error	Coefficient
Growth: Long-term growth			
ρ	5.122	2.212	11.077
ρ^2	-4.944	1.723	-7.986
EX	-9.521	0.000	-0.011
SW	7.892	0.297	2.389
constant	-5.389	0.723	-3.894
$\Delta Growth$: *Reevaluation model*			
$\Delta\rho$	4.775	0.944	4.341
$\Delta\rho_{t-1}$	-1.894	0.995	-1.884
$\Delta\rho^2$	-4.542	0.671	-3.132
$\Delta\rho^2_{t-1}$	1.997	0.721	1.453
ΔEX	-4.361	0.005	-0.009
ΔSW	3.711	0.289	1.073
ΔSW_{t-1}	-4.821	0.167	-0.842
ECT_{t-1}	-4.554	0.154	-0.742

Note: The optimal intervals are selected based on the Akaic information criterion.

After confirming the correlation between the variables, short-term and long-term models are estimated, according to the results reported in Table (5), the variable of water utilization rate (ρ) has a long-term coefficient of 11.067 at a significant level of 1%, which indicates a positive relationship with per capita GDP growth.

As expected, the variable 2ρ at a significance level of 1% has a long-term coefficient of 7.964, which indicates an inverse relationship between this water utilization rate and economic growth in the country. In other words, with the increase in water utilization, the country's economic growth continuously decreases. The share of water exports in GDP has a significant negative coefficient. The coefficient -0.009 (EX) can be interpreted so that the water goods included in this research are agricultural goods, have low elasticity and low flexibility. Therefore, with the increase in exports, such goods are exported as water, which due to the country's limited water, causes a decrease in economic growth. The variable of the share of water economic activities has a significant coefficient of 2.310 in the long run.

The positive contribution of 5 economic activities on water (chemical industries, paper industries, water and food and beverage, basic metals, and agriculture), which are key sectors of the economy, means that water efficiency in these areas should be given serious attention. In fact, by increasing the optimal utilization of water and using it in these sectors, economic growth can be brought to the country's economy. The error correction component (ECT_{t-1}), which measures the speed of correction of deviations from equilibrium, is expected to be $-1 < ECTt-1 = 0.66 < 0$ (with a sig. of 0.000), which shows a high value and a relative significance level of 1%. In other words, approximately 66% of the deviations from the previous period in the current period are corrected.

Figure 3. Cumulative sum of recursive residuals or CUSUM test

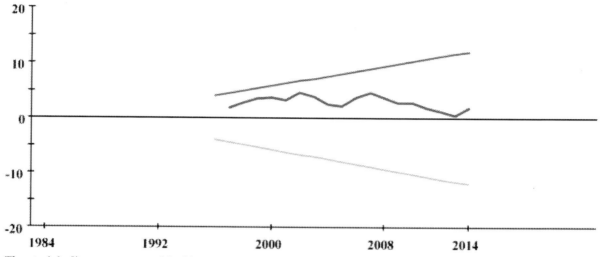

The straight lines represent critical bounds at 5% significance level

Figure 4. Cumulative sum of squares of recursive Residuals or CUSUMSQ test

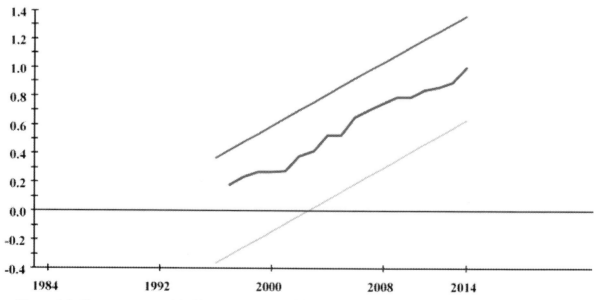

The straight lines represent critical bounds at 5% significance level

Finally, it should be noted that even with confirming the correlation between the variables, the estimated coefficients are not necessarily stable. Therefore, CUSUM and CUSUMSQ Brown et al. (1975) experiments are examined to ensure the stability of the coefficients. These two tests are very simple to use and only need to check the CUSUM and CUSUMSQ diagrams, which should only be placed between two confidence lines. In this case, it can be ensured that the model coefficients are stable. Figures (3) and (4) show the confirmation of the stability of the ARDL model.

CONCLUSION

The present article examines the impact of water management on Iran's economic growth. As a country with limited water resources, Iran is facing a huge harvest of water resources. Thus, the agricultural sector accounts for about 93% of the total water harvest, while agricultural production is very low compared to water consumption. According to Barber (2004), the relationship between water use and economic growth in countries can be reversed. According to the argument presented in his article, with the increase of water utilization, economic growth increases, but with more exploitation, economic growth decreases. In other words, when countries are in the early stages of economic growth, with the increase in the exploitation of water resources, economic growth increases rapidly, but if the extraction of water resources continues, economic growth will decrease. Therefore, the study of such a relationship is very important for Iran. Therefore, using the annual time series data from 1990 to 2020, we investigated the inverse U relation for Iran using the self-regulatory method with distributed interruption with the edge test approach. The research findings show a nonlinear relationship between water use per capita and economic growth, meaning that the inverse U relationship has been confirmed for Iran as a country with severe water resource constraints.

REFERENCES

Babran, S., & Honarbakhsh, N. (2007). Water Crisis in Iran and the World. Environment and Sustainable Development Studies Research Journal. *Time*, 1.

Bahmani-Oskooee, M., & Chomsisengphet, S. (2002). Stability of M2 money demand function in industrial countries. *Applied Economics*, 34(16), 2075–2083. doi:10.1080/00036840210128744

Barbier, E. B. (2004). Water and economic growth. *The Economic Record*, 80(248), 1–16. doi:10.1111/j.1475-4932.2004.00121.x

Barro, R. J. (1990). Government spending in a simple model of endogenous growth. *Journal of Political Economy*, 98(5, Part 2), S103–S125. doi:10.1086/261726

Barro, R. J., & Sala-i-Martin, X. (1992). Public finance in models of economic growth. *The Review of Economic Studies*, 59(4), 645–661. doi:10.2307/2297991

Bhattarai, M. (2004). *Irrigation Kuznets Curve, governance and dynamics of irrigation development: a global cross-country analysis from 1972 to 1991* (Vol. 78). IWMI.

Cosgrove, W. J., & Rijsberman, F. R. (2014). *World water vision: making water everybody's business*. Routledge. doi:10.4324/9781315071763

Cox, P. T., Grover, C. W., & Siskin, B. (1971). Effect of water resource investment on economic growth. *Water Resources Research*, 7(1), 32–38. doi:10.1029/WR007i001p00032

Dosi, C., & Easter, K. W. (2002). Water scarcity: institutional change, water markets, and privatization. In *Economic Studies on Food, Agriculture, and the Environment* (pp. 91–115). Springer. doi:10.1007/978-1-4615-0609-6_6

Duarte, R., Pinilla, V., & Serrano, A. (2013). Is there an environmental Kuznets curve for water use? A panel smooth transition regression approach. *Economic Modelling, 31*, 518–527. doi:10.1016/j.econmod.2012.12.010

Engle, R. F., & Granger, C. W. (1987). Co-integration and error correction: Representation, estimation, and testing. *Econometrica, 55*(2), 251–276. doi:10.2307/1913236

Falkenmark, M., Lundqvist, J., Klohn, W., Postel, S., Wallace, J., Shuval, H., ... Rockström, J. (1998). Water scarcity as a key factor behind global food insecurity: Round table discussion. *Ambio*, ●●●, 148–154.

Faurés, J. M., Vallée, D., Eliasson, Ă., & Hoogeveen, J. (2001). *Statistics on Water Resources by Country in FAO's AQUASTAT Programme*. Joint ECE/EUROSTAT Work Session on Methodological Ossues of Environmental Statistics.

Gatto, E., & Lanzafame, M. (2005). *Water resource as a factor of production: water use and economic growth*. Paper presented at the 45th ERSA Conference, Amsterdam.

Gleick, P. H. (1998). *The world's water 1998-1999: the biennial report on freshwater resources*. Island Press.

Gleick, P. H. (2000). Water conflict chronology. *The World's Water 2008-2009: The Biennial Report on Freshwater Resources*, 151-196.

Goklany, I. M. (2002). Comparing 20th century trends in US and global agricultural water and land use. *Water International, 27*(3), 321–329. doi:10.1080/02508060208687012

Howe, C. W. (1976). The effects of water resource development on economic growth the conditions for success. *Natural Resources Journal, 16*(4), 939–955.

Johansen, S. (1988). Statistical analysis of cointegration vectors. *Journal of Economic Dynamics & Control, 12*(2-3), 231–254. doi:10.1016/0165-1889(88)90041-3

Katouzian, M. A. (1978). Oil versus agriculture a case of dual resource depletion in Iran. *The Journal of Peasant Studies, 5*(3), 347–369. doi:10.1080/03066157808438052

Katz, D. (2015). Water use and economic growth: Reconsidering the Environmental Kuznets Curve relationship. *Journal of Cleaner Production, 88*, 205–213. doi:10.1016/j.jclepro.2014.08.017

Madani, K. (2014). Water management in Iran: What is causing the looming crisis? *Journal of Environmental Studies and Sciences, 4*(4), 315–328. doi:10.100713412-014-0182-z

Madani, K., AghaKouchak, A., & Mirchi, A. (2016). Iran's socio-economic drought: Challenges of a water-bankrupt nation. *Iranian Studies, 49*(6), 997–1016. doi:10.1080/00210862.2016.1259286

Mirzaei Khalilabadi, H., & Abrishami, H. (2004). *The role of water in the development of the agricultural sector*. University of Tehran, Faculty of Economics.

Mohammadjani, E., & Yazdanian, N. (2014). Analysis of the state of the water crisis in the country and its management requirements. *Quarterly Trend, 21*, 117–144.

Narayan, P. K., & Narayan, S. (2010). Carbon dioxide emissions and economic growth: Panel data evidence from developing countries. *Energy Policy, 38*(1), 661–666. doi:10.1016/j.enpol.2009.09.005

Nattagh, N. (1986). *Agriculture and regional development in Iran*. Middle East and North African Studies Press.

Pesaran, M. H., Shin, Y., & Smith, R. J. (2001). Bounds testing approaches to the analysis of level relationships. *Journal of Applied Econometrics, 16*(3), 289–326. doi:10.1002/jae.616

Rebelo, S. (1991). Long-run policy analysis and long-run growth. *Journal of Political Economy, 99*(3), 500–521. doi:10.1086/261764

Rock, M. T. (1998). Freshwater use, freshwater scarcity, and socioeconomic development. *Journal of Environment & Development, 7*(3), 278–301. doi:10.1177/107049659800700304

Romer, D. (2018). *Macroeconomic theory*. University of California.

Seyf, A. (2009). Population and agricultural development in Iran, 1800–1906. *Middle Eastern Studies, 45*(3), 447–460. doi:10.1080/00263200902853439

Sullivan, C. (2002). Calculating a water poverty index. *World Development, 30*(7), 1195–1210. doi:10.1016/S0305-750X(02)00035-9

Tir, N. A., Momeni, F., & Boboevich, G. T. (2014). Exploring the effects of water sector investment in economic development in Iran. *Procedia: Social and Behavioral Sciences, 131*, 396–405. doi:10.1016/j.sbspro.2014.04.137

Vörösmarty, C. J., Green, P., Salisbury, J., & Lammers, R. B. (2000). Global water resources: vulnerability from climate change and population growth. *Science, 289*(5477), 284-288.

ADDITIONAL READING

Gleick, P. H. (1998). *The world's water 1998-1999: the biennial report on freshwater resources*. Island Press.

Goklany, I. M. (2002). Comparing 20th century trends in US and global agricultural water and land use. *Water International, 27*(3), 321–329. doi:10.1080/02508060208687012

Howe, C. W. (1976). The effects of water resource development on economic growth the conditions for success. *Natural Resources Journal, 16*(4), 939–955.

Johansen, S. (1988). Statistical analysis of cointegration vectors. *Journal of Economic Dynamics & Control, 12*(2-3), 231–254. doi:10.1016/0165-1889(88)90041-3

Katouzian, M. A. (1978). Oil versus agriculture a case of dual resource depletion in Iran. *The Journal of Peasant Studies, 5*(3), 347–369. doi:10.1080/03066157808438052

Katz, D. (2015). Water use and economic growth: Reconsidering the Environmental Kuznets Curve relationship. *Journal of Cleaner Production*, *88*, 205–213. doi:10.1016/j.jclepro.2014.08.017

Madani, K. (2014). Water management in Iran: What is causing the looming crisis? *Journal of Environmental Studies and Sciences*, *4*(4), 315–328. doi:10.100713412-014-0182-z

Madani, K., AghaKouchak, A., & Mirchi, A. (2016). Iran's socio-economic drought: Challenges of a water-bankrupt nation. *Iranian Studies*, *49*(6), 997–1016. doi:10.1080/00210862.2016.1259286

Mohammadjani, E., & Yazdanian, N. (2014). Analysis of the state of the water crisis in the country and its management requirements. *Quarterly Trend*, *21*, 117–144.

KEY TERMS AND DEFINITIONS

Circularity: A circular economy (also referred to as "circularity") is an economic system that tackles global challenges like climate change, biodiversity loss, waste, and pollution. Most linear economy businesses take a natural resource and turn it into a product that is ultimately destined to become waste because it has been designed and made. This process is often summarised by "take, make, waste." By contrast, a circular economy uses reuse, sharing, repair, refurbishment, remanufacturing, and recycling to create a closed-loop system, minimize resource inputs, and create waste, pollution, and carbon emissions. The circular economy aims to keep products, materials, equipment, and infrastructure in use for longer, thus improving the productivity of these resources. Waste materials and energy should become input for other processes through waste valorization: either as a component or recovered resource for another industrial process or as regenerative resources for nature (e.g., compost). This regenerative approach contrasts with the traditional linear economy, which has a "take, make, dispose of" production model.

Eco Commerce: Eco commerce is a business, investment, and technology-development model that employs market-based solutions to balancing the world's energy needs and environmental integrity. Through green trading and green finance, eco-commerce promotes the further development of "clean technologies" such as wind power, solar power, biomass, and hydropower.

Eco-Tariffs: An Eco-tariff, also known as an environmental tariff, is a trade barrier erected to reduce pollution and improve the environment. These trade barriers may take the form of import or export taxes on products with a large carbon footprint or imported from countries with lax environmental regulations.

Emissions Trading: Emissions trading (also known as cap and trade, emissions trading scheme, or ETS) is a market-based approach to controlling pollution by providing economic incentives for reducing the emissions of pollutants.

Environmental Enterprise: An environmental enterprise is an environmentally friendly/compatible business. Specifically, an environmental enterprise is a business that produces value in the same manner which an ecosystem does, neither producing waste nor consuming unsustainable resources. In addition, an environmental enterprise rather finds alternative ways to produce one's products instead of taking advantage of animals for the sake of human profits. To be closer to being an environmentally friendly company, some environmental enterprises invest their money to develop or improve their technologies which are also environmentally friendly. In addition, environmental enterprises usually try to reduce global warming, so some companies use environmentally friendly materials to build their stores. They also set in environmentally friendly place regulations. All these efforts of the environmental enterprises can bring positive effects both for nature and people. The concept is rooted in the well-enumerated theories of natural capital, the eco-economy, and cradle-to-cradle design. Examples of environmental enterprises would be Seventh Generation, Inc., and Whole Foods.

Green Economy: A green economy is an economy that aims at reducing environmental risks and ecological scarcities and that aims for sustainable development without degrading the environment. It is closely related to ecological economics but has a more politically applied focus. The 2011 UNEP Green Economy Report argues "that to be green, and an economy must be not only efficient but also fair. Fairness implies recognizing global and country-level equity dimensions, particularly in assuring a Just Transition to an economy that is low-carbon, resource-efficient, and socially inclusive."

Green Politics: Green politics, or ecopolitics, is a political ideology that aims to foster an ecologically sustainable society often, but not always, rooted in environmentalism, nonviolence, social justice, and grassroots democracy. It began taking shape in the western world in the 1970s; since then, Green parties have developed and established themselves in many countries around the globe and have achieved some electoral success.

Low-Carbon Economy: A low-carbon economy (LCE) or decarbonized economy is based on low-carbon power sources with minimal greenhouse gas (GHG) emissions into the atmosphere, specifically carbon dioxide. GHG emissions due to anthropogenic (human) activity are the dominant cause of observed climate change since the mid-20th century. Continued emission of greenhouse gases may cause long-lasting changes worldwide, increasing the likelihood of severe, pervasive, and irreversible effects for people and ecosystems.

Natural Resource Economics: Natural resource economics deals with the supply, demand, and allocation of the Earth's natural resources. One main objective of natural resource economics is to understand better the role of natural resources in the economy to develop more sustainable methods of managing those resources to ensure their future generations. Resource economists study interactions between economic and natural systems intending to develop a sustainable and efficient economy.

Sustainable Development: Sustainable development is an organizing principle for meeting human development goals while simultaneously sustaining the ability of natural systems to provide the natural resources and ecosystem services on which the economy and society depend. The desired result is a state of society where living conditions and resources are used to continue to meet human needs without undermining the integrity and stability of the natural system. Sustainable development can be defined as development that meets the needs of the present without compromising the ability of future generations to meet their own needs. Sustainability goals, such as the current UN-level Sustainable Development Goals, address the global challenges, including poverty, inequality, climate change, environmental degradation, peace, and justice.

Chapter 11
Structure of Gas-Exporting Countries Forum:
Heterogeneity of Members and Their Ranking Criteria in Influencing the Global Gas Market

Nima Norouzi
https://orcid.org/0000-0002-2546-4288
Bournemouth University, UK

ABSTRACT

The main focus of the studies, which have been conducted mainly by experts from gas-consuming countries, is to evaluate and measure the impact of this forum on the price of natural gas in the main consumer markets. Unfortunately, the issue of homogeneity or heterogeneity of members and the role that this issue can play in the success of the policies and goals of this organization has received less attention. In this chapter, the authors first show the heterogeneity of members and then, with the help of appropriate indicators, rank member countries in influencing policies and achieving the goals of the assembly in the short, medium, and long term. Based on the presented indicators, it can be concluded that Russia, Qatar, and Algeria are the countries that play the most important role in influencing the policies of the assembly in the short and medium-term, while Russia, Qatar, and Iran, respectively, are three influential members in the long-term policies of the assembly.

INTRODUCTION

Currently, the Assembly of Gas Exporting Countries consists of 13 gas producing and exporting countries in alphabetical order: Algeria, UAE, Iran, Bolivia, Trinidad and Tobago, Russia, Oman, Qatar, Equatorial Guinea, Libya, Egypt, Nigeria. And Venezuela. Iraq, Kazakhstan, Norway, and the Netherlands are observer members of the forum. It can be seen that with such a set of countries, this forum can be a powerful organization in the global gas market and play a more active role in the global energy mar-

DOI: 10.4018/978-1-6684-5109-0.ch011

ket compared to international energy organizations. At present, the strong position of the assembly is due solely to the large reserves of natural gas that its members hold. About 63% of the world's natural gas reserves are geographically located in the member states of the assembly. It also owns 39% of the natural gas trade by pipeline and 65% of global LNG production and trade. The three main members of the forum, Iran, Russia, and Qatar, hold about 50% of the world's natural gas reserves(Lu et al., 2019).

This forum is a group of large natural gas producers formed with the characteristics of an international and governmental organization to improve coordination and strengthen the cooperation of the member countries. Another goal of this forum is to design a mechanism for the fruitfulness of the dialogue between gas producers and consumers to ensure the stability and security of supply and demand in natural gas markets. According to the Statute of the Assembly, the mission and purpose of the assembly are defined as follows: "To protect the sovereignty of member states over their natural gas reserves and the capabilities of each member in independent planning and management for sustainable development, Exploitation and protection of natural gas reserves for the benefit of the people of each member state."

This chapter has tried to examine the appropriate conditions for achieving this goal according to the assembly structure. In other words, the key question in this chapter is whether this organization has a homogeneous and homogeneous structure to achieve this common goal? After reviewing the research background in the second part, we examine the position of the member countries of the assembly in terms of key indicators in the oil and gas sectors, which is the subject of the third part of this chapter. In the fourth section, we introduce the indicators related to the classification of countries, and in the fifth section, we examine the member countries in terms of their impact on the assembly policies and provide an integrated analysis in this regard. The conclusion of this chapter is the subject of the sixth section.

Background

Studies on the behavior of the assembly have mainly focused on analyzing the behavior of members to maximize profits. These studies are typically similar to the models based on the dominant firm theory in the oil market, which operates in a competitive environment governing the activities of a set of small firms. The design of such models for OPEC behavior was very common in the 1970s and 1990s, although a wide range of models designed to explain OPEC behavior at different historical stages and in line with global oil market developments can be identified and categorized. The dominant firm model was first used by Yafeh and Soligo (2006) to analyze assembly behavior. This article shows how dominant countries such as Russia can influence the performance of other gas producers operating in a competitive environment and thus influence the direction of the assembly. Another hypothesis that is put forward in this context is that it is possible to achieve the goals of this institution by formulating an appropriate strategy for cooperation between the member states of the assembly without using the tool of increasing prices and imposing it on natural gas importers (Masoul and Chongming, 2010).

Vagbara (2007) examines the impact of the assembly's policies from an economic, political, and at the same time, comparative perspective on OPEC's historical behavior in the form of a cartel. Bahagat (2008), by examining the fundamental factors in the formation and behavior of oil and gas markets and identifying the parameters that determine the differences between the two markets, concludes that this forum is fundamentally different from OPEC and, therefore, at least in the future. Nearly can not become a gas OPEC.

Using a "large energy balance model," Gabriel et al. (2012) investigated the possibility of forming a gas cartel in the future and assessed its impact on gas markets in different parts of the world. Willerton et al. (2015) examined Russia's special position in the assembly in the context of OPEC and emphasized that Russia, with its huge reserves and high capacity to produce and export natural gas, is in a position to coordinate with Other member states will lead the cartel. Wood et al. (2016) have studied the formation of gas cartels on the extraction process from game theory.

The assembly's policies in the form of natural gas exports through the pipeline can be found in the studies of Schaefer (2008), Constantini et al. (2007), Finon (2011), Konoplianik (2012), and Lotfi et al. (2016) observed. Mahdavi Hao et al. (2020) have studied gas export through the pipeline concerning its limitations and the natural gas market structure among the member countries of the assembly from the perspective of cooperation in gas transit. Roson & Hubert (2015) has examined countries' interests related to the peace pipeline in two modes of cooperation and non-cooperation in the form of a game theory model.

In analyzing the behavior of gas exporting countries through game theory, we can refer to the study of Amin et al. (2021). In this paper, the gas exports of Iran and Russia to India and Pakistan are investigated in a hypothetical scenario and the framework of cooperative games using the Muskin method. This study shows that the optimal position for both countries is not to export gas to India and Pakistan. Klein (2018) has examined the feasibility of cooperation between the member countries of the assembly in exporting natural gas through pipelines.

Das et al. (2021) have made a comparative study of the position of the natural gas industry in the three countries of Iran, Russia, and Qatar and have explained the importance of this issue from the perspective of Iran's national security. Ahmad et al. (2016) examine the trade policies of major oil or gas exporting countries such as Iran, Russia, and Qatar and examine the ineffectiveness of EU sanctions due to the growing energy demand growth, especially in Europe in the long run. Dźwigoł et al. (2019) studied transmission pipelines' role in increasing Iran's authority by linking interests with neighboring countries and the relationship between Iranian authority and regional security. This article emphasizes cooperation with neighboring countries and the role of oil and gas pipelines in establishing peace.

The general policy of the assembly is to increase the members to have more power in the relations governing the energy markets, especially the natural gas markets. Analyzing the status and importance of the current members of the assembly is very important to examine the cooperation policies of the members. The topics discussed in this section provide a basis for understanding each assembly member's role in designing a model of cooperation between members. One of the main axes of this evaluation is to study the situation of oil and gas sectors and consider the variables that reveal the impact of these sectors on the national economy of each member country. Hence, the oil and gas sectors in these countries and the impact that these sectors have on the national economy have been studied(Leitch et al., 2019).

A. The situation of the oil sector: Considering that until the foreseeable future, the situation of the gas industry can not be examined independently of the oil industry, so understanding the position of each member state should be concerning the conditions governing the oil sector in those countries. Therefore, to understand the position and importance of the gas sector in each of the member countries, the following variables in the oil sector should be considered to affect the domestic market and according to the ability to meet global demand: Volume of proven crude oil reserves, volume Crude oil production, crude oil refining capacity, production of petroleum products, consumption of petroleum products, export of petroleum products and export of crude oil(Visenescu, 2018).

B. Situation of the gas sector: According to what was mentioned in paragraph A of the above, the following variables in the natural gas sector in each of the member countries should be considered: the volume of proven natural gas reserves, production of natural gas supplied to the market, consumption Domestic dry natural gas and natural gas exports(Sovacool, 2009).

C. The impact of the oil and gas sector on the national economy: The development of a strategy for the cooperation of the members of the assembly in gas exports can not be considered independently of the restrictions and restrictions in the national economy of each member country in terms of their national economy depends on oil and gas revenues. Therefore, it is reasonable to assume that each member state prefers its national interests to those of the assembly and therefore considers the assembly's policies on natural gas exports bound by its national interests. Thus, one cannot expect that gas export policies for a country that currently enjoys foreign exchange earnings from crude oil and natural gas exports will be the same as for a country that relies solely on gas export earnings, while there are restrictions. A large amount of natural gas or crude oil production allocated to domestic consumption will be very different from a country with enough capacity to export a very high share of crude oil or natural gas production due to the small national economy.

Therefore, in analyzing the position and importance of each member country in formulating the optimal strategy for natural gas exports by the assembly, in addition to the indicators listed in paragraphs A and B above, the following variables should be considered: total export value, the ratio of crude oil export value Total exports, the balance of payments, GDP per capita and population. The above information, which can effectively analyze the pattern of cooperation of the Assembly members in gas exports, is prepared for the member countries in the table (1 and 2).

Table 1. Key variables of oil and gas sectors and national economy of the member countries of the assembly (2018) (Part 1)

Variable (unit)	Algeria	Trinidad and Tobago	Bolivia	Iran	UAE	Equatorial Guinea
Proven crude oil reserves (billion barrels)	12.2	0.7	0.2	157.3	97.8	1.1
Crude oil and condensate production (million barrels per day)	1.7	0.2	0.1	3.8	2.7	0.3
Refining capacity (million barrels per day)	0.7	0.1	n/a	1.7	0.7	n/a
Consumption of petroleum products (million barrels per day)	0.4	0.1	0.1	1.8	0.2	0.01
Exports of petroleum products (million barrels per day)	0.3	0.1	0.1	0.5	0.3	0.01
Crude oil exports (million barrels per day)	0.7	0.1	n/a	2.1	2.5	0.3

Continued on following page

Table 1. Continued

Variable (unit)	Algeria	Trinidad and Tobago	Bolivia	Iran	UAE	Equatorial Guinea
Proven natural gas reserves (trillion cubic meters)	4.5	0.5	0.3	33.8	6.1	0.04
Production of natural gas supplied to the market (billion cubic meters per year)	86.0	41.2	16.1	160.6	52.7	7.3
Domestic consumption of dry natural gas (billion cubic meters per year)	31.0	22.9	2.5	152.0	61.0	1.7
Natural gas exports (billion cubic meters per year)	52.0	17.6	13.3	9.15	5.2	5.2
Population (million people)	38.0	1.3	10.0	75.8	8.2	1.3
GDP per capita (US dollar)	5525.0	16699.0	2421.0	7713.0	41382.0	27478.0
Total value of exports (billion dollars)	73.0	12.1	9.1	133.3	252.6	n/a
Crude oil export value (billion dollars)	48.0	4.8	0.2	101.5	104.6	9.9
Share of crude oil exports in total exports (share)	65.8	39.6	1.6	76.2	41.4	n/a
Balance of payments (billion dollars)	15.5	4.2	0.6	26.8	33.4	n/a

Table 2. Key variables of oil and gas sectors and national economy of the member countries of the assembly (2018) (Part 2)

Variable (unit)	Qatar	Oman	Russia	Venezuela	Nigeria	Egypt	Libya
Proven crude oil reserves (billion barrels)	25.4	5.5	60.0	297.6	37.2	4.4	47.1
Crude oil and condensate production (million barrels per day)	1.7	0.9	1.3	2.5	2.6	0.8	0.5
Refining capacity (million barrels per day)	0.1	0.3	5.5	1.1	0.5	0.04	0.4
Consumption of petroleum products (million barrels per day)	0.2	0.1	2.8	1.0	0.3	0.7	0.3
Exports of petroleum products (million barrels per day)	0.2	0.1	2.3	0.5	0.02	0.1	0.1
Crude oil exports (million barrels per day)	0.6	0.8	4.9	1.6	2.4	0.1	1.4
Proven natural gas reserves (trillion cubic meters)	25.5	0.9	48.0	5.5	5.2	2.2	1.6
Production of natural gas supplied to the market (billion cubic meters per year)	123.0	29.0	676.0	35.8	40.9	65.0	7.9
Domestic consumption of dry natural gas (billion cubic meters per year)	21.8	17.5	509.0	27.2	7.2	51.1	6.8
Natural gas exports (billion cubic meters per year)	113.7	10.9	221.0	n/a	25.9	10.5	3.7
Population (million people)	1.8	2.8	143.0	29.0	154.7	83.0	6.5
GDP per capita (US dollar)	98144.0	52221.0	13089.0	10864.0	1443.0	2781.0	5691.0
Total value of exports (billion dollars)	107.1	49.2	576.0	92.7	108.3	48.8	49.3

Continued on following page

Table 2. Continued

Variable (unit)	Qatar	Oman	Russia	Venezuela	Nigeria	Egypt	Libya
Crude oil export value (billion dollars)	72.6	25.2	206.2	88.2	86.2	8.0	45.4
Share of crude oil exports in total exports (share)	67.8	51.2	35.8	95.2	79.6	16.4	92.1
Balance of payments (billion dollars)	53.6	10.3	98.8	27.3	17.9	n/a	16.8

Source: Association of Gas Exporting Countries (www.gecf.org) - It should be noted that the statistics in this table are for the years 2016 and 2017, which were reported to the Secretariat of the Assembly in 2018.

METHODS AND MATERIAL

Define Indicators Related to the Classification of Countries

The information provided in this section provides a good basis for comparatively comparing member countries, assessing the impact of each on the collective policies of the assembly, and then classifying member countries based on this model. Such a classification makes it possible to identify the real centers of power in the assembly and call them key assembly members because their role in adopting the assembly's policies is undeniable. Our method of comparative comparison of member countries is based on the following criteria:

A. Paying attention to the indicators that can distinguish these countries from the other in natural gas production. Therefore, we must first calculate the production volume in all the member countries of the assembly and then obtain the production ratio of each member state to total production.

B. In addition to the production index (paragraph A above), it should be noted that potential production is the same as the proven volume of natural gas reserves in each of the member countries. Naturally, a country with higher proven reserves has a higher production capacity and, therefore, can play a more important role in the future of the assembly's exports. A country with low reserves will certainly have more advantage and power in the assembly's decisions and policies. Because in the future, it will have more power to influence the global natural gas market. Therefore, we have to make two indicators: 1- The ratio of proven natural gas reserves in each member country to the total proven natural gas reserves in the assembly and 2- The ratio of annual natural gas production in each member drawer to the volume of proven reserves in the same country. The second index is, in fact, the same annual discharge coefficient of proven reserves, which works in the opposite direction of the index of proven reserves, because the higher the discharge coefficient, the sooner the volume of proven reserves expires, despite the high ratio of proven reserves.

C. In classifying countries, it is necessary to distinguish between a country that, despite a very high volume of natural gas production, a significant share of which goes to domestic consumption, and a country that has low domestic consumption but high reserves, because the former, despite its very high volume. Production has little export potential and, therefore, will play a lesser role in the assembly's export policies. In contrast, with limited domestic consumption and assuming considerable production capacity, the latter will have a very high impact on the assembly's macro policies on gas exports. Since the difference between the production and consumption of natural gas is usually allocated for exports, the ratio of natural gas exports of each member country to the total natural gas exports of the assembly should be calculated. It is also necessary to obtain the exports of each member country to the total world export of natural gas to determine the position of each member country and the extent of its influence in the total world gas trade. These two indicators are the most important in the short and medium-term for ranking member countries in terms of the degree of impact of each on the design of the optimal model of export policies of the assembly. Obviously, in the long run, what determines the volume of proven natural gas reserves determines each member's potential production.

Macro Variables of Oil and Gas and their Ranking Indicators

To calculate the indicators defined in paragraphs A to C of Sections (4.1), the following quantitative information is required for members of the Assembly: Proven natural gas reserves, natural gas production, and natural gas exports. Quantitative information of the above variables and similar variables in the oil sector is summarized in table (3).

First, we calculate the five indicators for the gas sector in the member countries of the assembly. The volume of natural gas exports in 2017 through pipelines and LNG for all exporting countries in the world (based on BPP estimates in 2018) is about 1.03434 billion cubic meters, which is used in the calculations of the fifth index. Table (4) shows the five indicators related to the gas sector of the member countries of the assembly.

Table 3. Macro variables of oil and gas member countries (2018)

Member countries	Crude oil exports (million barrels per day)	Natural gas exports (billion cubic meters per year)	Crude oil and condensate production (million barrels per day)	Natural gas production (billion cubic meters per year)	Proven crude oil reserves (billion barrels)	Proven natural gas reserves (trillion cubic meters)
Algeria	0.7	52.9	1.7	86.0	12.2	4.5
UAE	2.5	5.2	2.6	52.7	97.8	6.1
Iran	2.1	9.2	3.7	160.6	157.3	33.8
Bolivia	~0	13.3	0.05	16.1	0.2	0.3
Trinidad and Tobago	0.08	17.6	0.2	41.2	0.7	0.4
Russia	4.9	221.0	10.2	676.0	60.0	48.0
Oman	0.7	10.9	0.9	29.0	5.5	0.9
Qatar	0.6	113.7	1.6	123.0	25.4	25.5
Guinea	0.3	5.2	0.3	7.3	1.1	0.04
Libya	1.4	3.7	0.5	7.9	47.1	1.5
Egypt	0.1	10.5	0.7	65.0	4.4	2.2
Nigeria	2.4	25.9	2.5	40.9	37.2	5.2
Venezuela	1.6	~0	2.4	35.8	297.6	5.5
Total	17.2	488.2	27.5	1341.5	746.5	133.9

Source: Association of Gas Exporting Countries (www.gecf.org) - It should be noted that the statistics in this table are for the years 2016 and 2017, which were reported to the Secretariat of the Assembly in 2018.

Table 4. Five ranking indicators of the member countries of the assembly in the gas sector (in %-2018)

	Member countries	The export ratio of each member to total world exports	The export ratio of each member to the total export of the assembly	The annual discharge rate of each member	Production ratio of each member to the total production of the assembly	The ratio of proven reserves of each member to total proven reserves of the assembly
1	Algeria	5.0	10.7	1.9	6.4	3.4
2	UAE	0.5	1.1	0.9	3.9	4.6
3	Iran	0.9	1.9	0.5	12.0	25.2
4	Bolivia	1.3	2.7	5.8	1.2	0.2
5	Trinidad and Tobago	1.7	3.6	10.0	3.1	0.3
6	Russia	21.4	45.3	1.4	50.4	35.8
7	Oman	1.0	2.2	3.4	2.2	0.6
8	Qatar	11.0	23.3	0.5	9.2	19.0
9	Guinea	0.5	1.1	19.7	0.5	~0
10	Libya	0.4	0.7	0.5	0.6	1.1
11	Egypt	1.0	2.1	2.9	4.8	1.6
12	Nigeria	2.5	5.3	0.8	3.1	3.9
13	Venezuela	~0	~0	0.7	2.7	4.1

Source: Author calculations

RESULTS AND DISCUSSION

Ranking in Terms of Impact in the Short and Medium-Term

As mentioned earlier, the ratio of the volume of natural gas exports of each member country to the total natural gas exports of the assembly can be a good indicator to determine the impact of that member on the decisions and strategy of the assembly. We know that large exporters such as the United States, Canada, Mexico, Brunei, the Netherlands, Norway, the United Kingdom, Kazakhstan, Turkmenistan, Indonesia, and Myanmar affect the global gas market but are not members of the forum. Therefore, the question arises whether the main member states of the assembly, which can play a leading role in the assembly's policies, are of particular importance in the global gas market in a similar way? To answer this question, the last column of Table 4, which shows the ratio of exports of each member of the assembly to total global exports of natural gas, has been calculated. We now rank the member countries of the assembly according to the ratio of each member's exports to the total exports of the assembly. Table (5) shows this ranking. This table shows the ranking of the Assemblymember countries in making decisions and determining the assembly's strategies for influencing the global natural gas market in the short and medium-term.

Table 5. Ranking of Assemblymember countries in terms of short-term and medium-term market effects (2018)

	Member countries	The export ratio of each member to total world exports (%)	The export ratio of each member to the total export of the assembly (%)
1	Russia	21.4	45.3
2	Qatar	11.0	23.3
3	Algeria	5.0	10.6
4	Nigeria	2.5	5.3
5	Trinidad and Tobago	1.7	3.6
6	Bolivia	1.3	2.7
7	Oman	1.0	2.2
8	Egypt	1.0	2.1
9	Iran	0.9	1.9
10	Guinea	0.5	1.1
11	UAE	0.5	1.1
12	Libya	0.4	0.8
13	Venezuela	~0	~0

Source: Researcher calculations

Referring to Table 5, it is clear that Russia, Qatar, and Algeria account for about 45%, 23%, and 10% of the assembly's exports, respectively, and therefore these three countries can be classified as "strong" countries. Nigeria, Trinidad and Tobago, Bolivia, Oman, and Egypt, which account for about 5.31, 3.60, 2.72, 2.23, and 2.15% of the assembly's natural gas exports, are among the "medium" countries. Finally, Iran, Guinea, UAE, and Libya, with about 1.87, 1.07, 1.06, and 0.75% of the total natural gas exports of the assembly, along with Venezuela, are classified as "weak" countries, respectively.

Ranking in Terms of Long-Term Impact on the Natural Gas Market

The role that a natural gas producer and exporter can play in the long run in regional and global natural gas markets is directly a function of the proven natural gas reserves of that country on the one hand and the volume of natural gas production and exports on the other. A country's gas exports are the difference between domestic production and consumption. Hence, the larger the domestic consumer market, the lower the level of exports, despite high production. Therefore, the position of the Assembly members in the regional and global natural gas markets depends on the production capacity, the volume of the domestic consumer market, and the proven natural gas reserves of each of them.

It should also be noted that as the rate of discharge from a country's gas reservoirs increases, the country's exports will naturally increase, assuming domestic consumption is stable, and therefore the impact of that country as a member of the assembly will be strengthened in the assembly's policies. But this is only true in the short and medium-term because the high rate of reservoir depletion causes the volume of reserves and consequently the reservoir pressure to decrease rapidly, which means a reduction in the expected supply in the future. Therefore, those members of the assembly who currently have a high discharge rate can play an important role in the assembly's policy-making process in the short and

Structure of Gas-Exporting Countries Forum

medium-term with more exports. Still, in the long run, their role will diminish due to reduced expected supply unless The volume of their proven reserves is very high, which, of course, is true of some members of the assembly, as we shall see.

We now rank the member countries of the assembly according to the ratio of proven reserves of each member to the total proven reserves of the assembly, the ratio of production of each member to the total production of the assembly, the annual discharge coefficient, and the ratio of reserves to annual production. Table (6) shows this ranking.

Table 6. Ranking of forum member countries in terms of long-term market impacts (2018)

	Ratio of reserve to annual production		Annual discharge coefficient		Ratio of the production of each member to the total production of the assembly		Ratio of proven reserves of each member to total proven reserves of the assembly	
	Rank	Time, yr	Rank	Share,%	Rank	Share,%	Rank	Share,%
Russia	7	71.0	7	1.4	1	50.4	1	35.8
Iran	1	210.0	1	0.5	2	12.0	2	25.2
Qatar	2	207.0	2	0.5	3	9.2	3	19.0
UAE	6	116.0	6	0.9	6	3.9	4	4.6
Venezuela	4	154.0	4	0.7	9	2.7	5	4.1
Nigeria	5	52.0	5	0.8	8	3.0	6	3.8
Algeria	8	52.0	8	1.9	4	6.4	7	3.4
Egypt	9	34.0	9	2.9	5	4.8	8	1.7
Libya	3	196.0	3	0.5	12	0.6	9	1.1
Oman	10	30.0	10	3.4	10	2.2	10	0.6
Trinidad and Tobago	12	10.0	12	10.0	7	3.1	11	0.3
Bolivia	11	17.0	11	5.7	11	1.2	12	0.2
Guinea	13	5.0	13	19.7	13	0.5	13	0.1

It is necessary to explain some points about table 6 as follows:

A. The ratio of proven natural gas reserves to the annual production of natural gas in each member country shows the time of depletion of reservoirs, assuming the continuation of production at the current level. This time is in terms of years. This ratio, which R/P usually indicates in energy economics studies, is a not very accurate approximation of reality. Suppose R is the volume of reservoir reserves, and P is the annual output from that reservoir. In that case, R/P is not an exact expression of the discharge time because the reservoirs' hydrocarbon material (oil or natural gas) is not the same as the hydrocarbon material in reservoirs built on the land. R/P for onshore tanks for storing hydrocarbons indicates the exact time it takes to empty the tank, but draining from natural oil or gas reservoirs deep underground is a function of reservoir pressure that allows hydrocarbons to be extracted naturally be done. Natural discharge or primary recycling is the volume of gas or fluid in the reservoir that can be extracted from production wells under the initial reservoir pressure. The average natural discharge from gas reservoirs in our country under initial recycling conditions is usually 70 to 80%, but this figure is not more than 20 to 25% on average in our country's oil reservoirs. A share of the remaining fluid in the tank can be extracted by secondary recycling or tertiary recycling [26].

However, as production from a gas or oil tank continues, and the reservoir pressure decreases, the production level also decreases. Hence, the production process from oil or gas fields is not linear but has a curve shape. Therefore, maintaining the level of production and its continuity is possible only by digging an increasing number of production wells during the operation of the reservoir. Still, in any case, there comes a time when the per capita production of all production wells will decrease at the same time—preventing a reduction in production. Over-harvesting methods, including secondary and tertiary recycling, which typically involve oil reservoirs, should be used to prevent this from happening. The calculations performed in the last column of table (6) ignore these reservoir engineering facts for ease of calculation. Hence, the figures in the last column are only an approximation of the facts, which, of course, is sufficient to classify the assembly countries.

B. As shown in table (6), the figures in the annual discharge coefficient column vary from 0.47 to 19.73%. This indicates the heterogeneity of the member states of the assembly in terms of the status of gas tanks and production policies from those tanks. It is important to note that the lower the annual discharge rate of a reservoir, which is the ratio of the annual production from the reservoir to the volume of proven reserves, the longer the extraction time, the higher the share of extraction recovered in situ.

It can be seen that according to the evacuation coefficient, Iran is in the first place with 0.47%, Qatar is in second place with 0.48%, and Libya is in third place with 0.51%. The duration of production at the current level for these three countries is 210 years (Iran), 207 years (Qatar), and 196 years (Libya), respectively.

Similarly, it can be seen from the last two columns of table (6) that according to the annual discharge coefficient and the number of years of continuous production at the current level, Venezuela ranks fourth (0.65% and 154 years), Nigeria. In fifth place (0.79% and 126 years), UAE in sixth place (0.86% and 116 years), Russia in seventh place (1.40% and 71 years), Algeria in eighth place (1.91%), And 52 years) and Egypt is in ninth place (2.93% and 34 years). Production continuity figures for other member states of the assembly are less than 30 years old, which has been ignored in the analysis of long-term impacts.

C. Special effects of Guinea (19.73% and 5 years), Trinidad and Tobago (10.04% and 10 years), Bolivia (5.75% and 17 years), and Oman (3.37% and 30 years) In the long run (more than 30 years) they will not have access to the global gas market. Therefore, these countries can be ignored in the considerations and analyses related to the forum's long-term impact on regional and global natural gas markets. In the most optimistic scenario, these countries can be called a weak group, and their impact, in the long run, can be considered positive only if discoveries are made.

D. 9 countries of the first group can be divided into strong and medium groups. In this classification, the ratio of the proven reserves of each member to the total proven reserves of the assembly must also

Structure of Gas-Exporting Countries Forum

be taken into account. By this measure, Russia, which has about 36% of the proven reserves of the assembly, despite being ranked seventh in terms of the reserve to production ratio and seventh in terms of annual discharge coefficient, is especially high, especially because of the high annual production ratio of natural gas. In Russia, of the total production of the assembly (approximately 49%), the discoverer of the country's high capacity in production engineering, which will certainly continue in the future, and therefore puts Russia in first place in terms of long-term impact on regional and global natural gas markets.

Iran with more than 25% of proven natural gas reserves in the assembly (second place) and high ratio of annual natural gas production to the total production of the assembly (11.97% equivalent to second place) and the ratio of reserves to annual production (210 years equivalent) First place, of course, should be second to the long-term impact of the member states of the assembly. Nevertheless, the large domestic consumption market and our country's weak share in gas exports at the Assembly level (1.87%) and the global level (0.88%) make it impossible to classify Iran as the second long-term influence of the assembly.

With a similar argument and taking into account the ratio of one member gas export to total assembly exports on the one hand and total global gas exports on the other hand and considering the ratio of proven member reserves to total proven assembly reserves and annual discharge coefficient and reserve ratio to Production, Qatar is ranked second, and Iran is ranked third as "strong" countries. Similarly, it is easy to see that Venezuela is in fifth place, Nigeria is in sixth place, Algeria and Egypt and Libya are in seventh, eighth, and ninth place, respectively, classified as "medium" countries in terms of long-term impact.

Table (7) classifies the member states of the assembly into three groups: strong, medium, and weak, according to the long-term impact criterion.

It is now possible to combine the general results from Tables (6) and (7) in Table (8) and show the impact of the Assemblymember countries on the regional and global natural gas markets in the short, medium, and long term.

Table 7. Consolidated ranking of Assemblymember countries in terms of long-term effects on the market

State	Rank	Influence type
Russia	1	Strong
Qatar	2	
Iran	3	
UAE	4	Intermidiate
Venezuela	5	
Nigeria	6	
Algeria	7	
Egypt	8	
Libya	9	
Oman	10	Weak
Bolivia	11	
Trinidad and Tobago	12	
Guinea	13	

Source: Researcher calculations and analyzes

Table 8. Consolidated ranking of Assemblymember countries in terms of market impact

Long term			Short/medium term		
State	Rank	Type	State	Rank	Type
Russia	1	Strong	Russia	1	Strong
Qatar	2		Qatar	2	
Iran	3		Algeria	3	
UAE	4	Intermidiate	Nigeria	4	Intermidiate
Venezuela	5		Trinidad and Tobago	5	
Nigeria	6		Bolivia	6	
Algeria	7		Oman	7	
Egypt	8		Egypt	8	
Libya	9		Iran	9	Weak
Oman	10	Weak	Guinea	10	
Bolivia	11		UAE	11	
Trinidad and Tobago	12		Libya	12	
Guinea	13		Venezuela	13	

Source: Researcher calculations and analyzes

CONCLUSION

Iran proposed establishing the assembly in 2001, but its charter was adopted on December 23, 2008, at the Seventh Ministerial Meeting in Moscow. From the beginning of January 2010, the first Secretary-General of the Assembly officially began his work and made the establishment of the Secretariat a priority in his plans. Analyzing the position and importance of each member of the assembly from the perspective of members' cooperation policies requires understanding the role that each assembly member can play in designing a model of cooperation. In this paper, the key variables in the oil and gas sectors of each member country that affect their national economies were evaluated and five indicators were introduced to rank members in terms of impact on natural gas trade in the short, medium, and long term. An integrated analysis of the classification of member states in terms of their degree of influence on the policies of the assembly is another key topic of this article, which of course allows us to categorize the members of the assembly to identify real centers of power in the assembly because their role in The policies of the assembly is undeniable.

According to these five criteria, in the short and medium-term Russia, Qatar and Algeria are among the strong countries of the assembly, but in the long run, Russia, Qatar, and Iran will be strong members of the assembly. It is important to note that each member state seeks to maximize its interests. For this reason, the success of their policies in the short and medium-term depends on their access to consumer markets and the appropriate infrastructure for transmission lines and LNG production and transportation facilities, and the existence of conversion terminals in destination markets. The impact factor, in the long run, is also a function of the facilities and prospects for the development of gas fields, the construction of pipelines, and the construction of facilities and equipment for the production of LNG and related industries. Therefore, according to the issues raised, the following points can be considered regarding the general principles governing how the members of the assembly cooperate:

A. Each member of the assembly seeks to maximize the benefits of its presence in regional and global natural gas markets.
B. The strategy referred to in paragraph A shall be designed at the short-term and medium-term levels as well as at the long-term level.
C. The strategy of the members of the assembly in the framework of short-term and medium-term cooperation is based on current production and exports, which is a function of access to consumer markets, appropriate infrastructure, especially transmission lines, facilities, and equipment for production and transmission of LNG and LNG to natural gas transmission terminals. To distribution networks in destination countries.
D. The strategy of the members of the assembly in the framework of long-term cooperation relies on the long-term impact coefficient of each member on the regional markets, which is a function of the proven natural gas reserves and annual discharge coefficient on the one hand and facilities and prospects of construction of pipelines LNG and related industries on the other hand.
E. The favorable strategies of the assembly members in the Jim and Dahl paragraphs mentioned above are strongly influenced by the geographical location of the member countries. Access to existing transmission lines on the one hand and access to international waters to enter the LNG business are key variables in formulating these strategies. For example, Table 7 shows that Russia and Qatar rank first and second in terms of short-term, medium-term, and long-term impacts in regional and global markets, respectively, but the natural gas export and trade pattern of each of these two countries are strongly influenced by their geographical location. Taking advantage of its access to international waters, Qatar has naturally focused its interests on heavy investment in the development of the LNG industry and entry into the regional and global LNG trade market, while Russia's interests require that its natural gas exports and trade be based on Focus pipeline. Thus, according to BPI statistics in 2018, Russia's natural gas exports through the pipeline amounted to 186 billion cubic meters, while the figure for Qatar is more than 19 billion cubic meters. On the other hand, in the same year, Russia's volume of LNG exports was about 15 billion cubic meters, while Qatar exported more than 105 billion cubic meters of LNG in the same year, which reveals Qatar's comparative advantage in accessing international open waters.

The Islamic Republic of Iran is in a much better position than Qatar because, in terms of access to open waters, it can export natural gas in the form of LNG and due to its special geographical location, it can easily deliver natural gas to the pipeline. Export to Asia and Europe. Hence, the role of the Islamic Republic of Iran in the long-term effects of the assembly is definite.

REFERENCES

Ahmad, W. N. K. W., Rezaei, J., de Brito, M. P., & Tavasszy, L. A. (2016). The influence of external factors on supply chain sustainability goals of the oil and gas industry. *Resources Policy, 49*, 302–314. doi:10.1016/j.resourpol.2016.06.006

Amin, Z. S., Hossein, I. S., & Mohammadreza, M. (2021). Introducing a new market-based system using game theory approach to promote energy efficiency: Case of Iranian energy market. *Energy Efficiency, 14*(6), 1–16. doi:10.100712053-021-09977-6

Apokin, A. (2019). LNG Trade Flows In The Case Of Oversupplied Markets And Its Consequent Impact On Prices And Investment. In *Local Energy, Global Markets, 42nd IAEE International Conference*. International Association for Energy Economics.

Bahgat, G. (2008). Gas OPEC? Rhetoric Versus Reality. *The Journal of Social, Political, and Economic Studies, 33*(3), 281.

Costantini, V., Gracceva, F., Markandya, A., & Vicini, G. (2007). Security of energy supply: Comparing scenarios from a European perspective. *Energy Policy, 35*(1), 210–226. doi:10.1016/j.enpol.2005.11.002

Cremer, J., & Weitzman, M. L. (1976). OPEC and the monopoly price of world oil. *European Economic Review, 8*(2), 155–164. doi:10.1016/0014-2921(76)90010-6

Das, N., Dasgupta, S., Roy, J., Langhelle, O., & Assadi, M. (2021). Emission Mitigation and Energy Security Trade-Off: Role of Natural Gas in the Indian Power Sector. *Energies, 14*(13), 3787. doi:10.3390/en14133787

Dudley, B. (2018). BP statistical review of world energy. *BP Statistical Review, 6*(2018), 00116.

Dźwigoł, H., Dźwigoł-Barosz, M., Zhyvko, Z., Miśkiewicz, R., & Pushak, H. (2019). Evaluation of the energy security as a component of national security of the country. *Journal of Security & Sustainability Issues, 8*(3), 307–317. doi:10.9770/jssi.2019.8.3(2)

Finon, D. (2007). Russia and the 'Gas-OPEC': Real or Perceived Threat?. *Russie. Nei. Visions,* 24.

Finon, D. (2011). The EU foreign gas policy of transit corridors: Autopsy of the stillborn Nabucco project. *OPEC Energy Review, 35*(1), 47–69. doi:10.1111/j.1753-0237.2010.00185.x

Gabriel, S. A., Rosendahl, K. E., Egging, R., Avetisyan, H. G., & Siddiqui, S. (2012). Cartelization in gas markets: Studying the potential for a "Gas OPEC". *Energy Economics, 34*(1), 137–152. doi:10.1016/j.eneco.2011.05.014

GECF Secretariat. (2018). *Energy and Gas Market Analysis.* www.gecf.org

Hao, W., Shah, S. M. A., Nawaz, A., Asad, A., Iqbal, S., Zahoor, H., & Maqsoom, A. (2020). The impact of energy cooperation and the role of the one belt and road initiative in revolutionizing the geopolitics of energy among regional economic powers: An analysis of infrastructure development and project management. *Complexity, 2020*, 2020. doi:10.1155/2020/8820021

Jaffe, A. M., & Soligo, R. (1970). Market structure in the new gas economy: is cartelization possible? *Natural Gas and Geopolitics,* 439-464.

Klein, T. (2018). Trends and contagion in WTI and Brent crude oil spot and futures markets-The role of OPEC in the last decade. *Energy Economics, 75,* 636–646. doi:10.1016/j.eneco.2018.09.013

Konoplyanik, A. A. (2012). Russian gas at European energy market: Why adaptation is inevitable. *Energy Strategy Reviews, 1*(1), 42–56. doi:10.1016/j.esr.2012.02.001

Leitch, A., Haley, B., & Hastings-Simon, S. (2019). Can the oil and gas sector enable geothermal technologies? Socio-technical opportunities and complementarity failures in Alberta, Canada. *Energy Policy*, *125*, 384–395. doi:10.1016/j.enpol.2018.10.046

Lotfi, T., Golmohammadi, V., & Sarmadi, H. (2016). Political Consideration and Development of Economic Relations, Economic Cooperation Capacities of Iran and the Republic of Azerbaijan. *Mediterranean Journal of Social Sciences, 7*(3), 72.

Lu, H., Guo, L., Azimi, M., & Huang, K. (2019). Oil and Gas 4.0 era: A systematic review and outlook. *Computers in Industry*, *111*, 68–90. doi:10.1016/j.compind.2019.06.007

Maskin, E. (2003). Coalitional bargaining with externalities. *Keynote lecture for the European Economic Association Conference.*

Massol, O., & Tchung-Ming, S. (2010). Cooperation among liquefied natural gas suppliers: Is rationalization the sole objective? *Energy Economics*, *32*(4), 933–947. doi:10.1016/j.eneco.2010.02.008

Roson, R., & Hubert, F. (2015). Bargaining power and value sharing in distribution networks: A cooperative game theory approach. *Networks and Spatial Economics*, *15*(1), 71–87. doi:10.100711067-014-9270-6

Schaffer, M. B. (2008). The great gas pipeline game: Monopolistic expansion of Russia's Gazprom into European markets. *Foresight*, *10*(5), 11–23. doi:10.1108/14636680810918478

Sovacool, B. K. (2009). Energy policy and cooperation in Southeast Asia: The history, challenges, and implications of the trans-ASEAN gas pipeline (TAGP) network. *Energy Policy*, *37*(6), 2356–2367. doi:10.1016/j.enpol.2009.02.014

Visenescu, R. S. (2018). Russian-ASEAN cooperation in the natural gas sector. Lessons from the Russian-Vietnamese relation. *Energy Policy*, *119*, 515–517. doi:10.1016/j.enpol.2018.05.006

Wagbara, O. N. (2007). How would the gas exporting countries forum influence gas trade? *Energy Policy*, *35*(2), 1224–1237. doi:10.1016/j.enpol.2006.03.017

Willerton, J. P., Goertz, G., & Slobodchikoff, M. O. (2015). Mistrust and hegemony: Regional institutional design, the FSU-CIS, and Russia. *International Area Studies Review*, *18*(1), 26–52. doi:10.1177/2233865914562256

Wood, A. D., Mason, C. F., & Finnoff, D. (2016). OPEC, the Seven Sisters, and oil market dominance: An evolutionary game theory and agent-based modeling approach. *Journal of Economic Behavior & Organization*, *132*, 66–78. doi:10.1016/j.jebo.2016.06.011

ADDITIONAL READING

Lu, H., Guo, L., Azimi, M., & Huang, K. (2019). Oil and Gas 4.0 era: A systematic review and outlook. *Computers in Industry*, *111*, 68–90. doi:10.1016/j.compind.2019.06.007

Massol, O., & Tchung-Ming, S. (2010). Cooperation among liquefied natural gas suppliers: Is rationalization the sole objective? *Energy Economics*, *32*(4), 933–947. doi:10.1016/j.eneco.2010.02.008

Roson, R., & Hubert, F. (2015). Bargaining power and value sharing in distribution networks: A cooperative game theory approach. *Networks and Spatial Economics*, *15*(1), 71–87. doi:10.100711067-014-9270-6

Schaffer, M. B. (2008). The great gas pipeline game: Monopolistic expansion of Russia's Gazprom into European markets. *Foresight*, *10*(5), 11–23. doi:10.1108/14636680810918478

Sovacool, B. K. (2009). Energy policy and cooperation in Southeast Asia: The history, challenges, and implications of the trans-ASEAN gas pipeline (TAGP) network. *Energy Policy*, *37*(6), 2356–2367. doi:10.1016/j.enpol.2009.02.014

Visenescu, R. S. (2018). Russian-ASEAN cooperation in the natural gas sector. Lessons from the Russian-Vietnamese relation. *Energy Policy*, *119*, 515–517. doi:10.1016/j.enpol.2018.05.006

Willerton, J. P., Goertz, G., & Slobodchikoff, M. O. (2015). Mistrust and hegemony: Regional institutional design, the FSU-CIS, and Russia. *International Area Studies Review*, *18*(1), 26–52. doi:10.1177/2233865914562256

KEY TERMS AND DEFINITIONS

Circularity: A circular economy (also referred to as "circularity") is an economic system that tackles global challenges like climate change, biodiversity loss, waste, and pollution. Most linear economy businesses take a natural resource and turn it into a product that is ultimately destined to become waste because it has been designed and made. This process is often summarised by "take, make, waste." By contrast, a circular economy uses reuse, sharing, repair, refurbishment, remanufacturing, and recycling to create a closed-loop system, minimize resource inputs, and create waste, pollution, and carbon emissions. The circular economy aims to keep products, materials, equipment, and infrastructure in use for longer, thus improving the productivity of these resources. Waste materials and energy should become input for other processes through waste valorization: either as a component or recovered resource for another industrial process or as regenerative resources for nature (e.g., compost). This regenerative approach contrasts with the traditional linear economy, which has a "take, make, dispose of" production model.

Eco Commerce: Eco commerce is a business, investment, and technology-development model that employs market-based solutions to balance the world's energy needs and environmental integrity. Through green trading and green finance, eco-commerce promotes the further development of "clean technologies" such as wind power, solar power, biomass, and hydropower.

Eco-Tariffs: An Eco-tariff, also known as an environmental tariff, is a trade barrier erected to reduce pollution and improve the environment. These trade barriers may take the form of import or export taxes on products with a large carbon footprint or imported from countries with lax environmental regulations.

Emissions Trading: Emissions trading (also known as cap and trade, emissions trading scheme, or ETS) is a market-based approach to controlling pollution by providing economic incentives for reducing the emissions of pollutants.

Environmental Enterprise: An environmental enterprise is an environmentally friendly/compatible business. Specifically, an environmental enterprise is a business that produces value in the same manner which an ecosystem does, neither producing waste nor consuming unsustainable resources. In addition, an environmental enterprise rather finds alternative ways to produce one's products instead of taking advantage of animals for the sake of human profits. To be closer to being an environmentally friendly company, some environmental enterprises invest their money to develop or improve their technologies which are also environmentally friendly. In addition, environmental enterprises usually try to reduce global warming, so some companies use environmentally friendly materials to build their stores. They also set in environmentally friendly place regulations. All these efforts of the environmental enterprises can bring positive effects both for nature and people. The concept is rooted in the well-enumerated theories of natural capital, the eco-economy, and cradle-to-cradle design. Examples of environmental enterprises would be Seventh Generation, Inc., and Whole Foods.

Green Economy: A green economy is an economy that aims at reducing environmental risks and ecological scarcities and that aims for sustainable development without degrading the environment. It is closely related to ecological economics but has a more politically applied focus. The 2011 UNEP Green Economy Report argues "that to be green, and an economy must be not only efficient but also fair. Fairness implies recognizing global and country-level equity dimensions, particularly in assuring a Just Transition to an economy that is low-carbon, resource-efficient, and socially inclusive."

Green Politics: Green politics, or ecopolitics, is a political ideology that aims to foster an ecologically sustainable society often, but not always, rooted in environmentalism, nonviolence, social justice, and grassroots democracy. It began taking shape in the western world in the 1970s; since then, Green parties have developed and established themselves in many countries around the globe and have achieved some electoral success.

Low-Carbon Economy: A low-carbon economy (LCE) or decarbonized economy is based on low-carbon power sources with minimal greenhouse gas (GHG) emissions into the atmosphere, specifically carbon dioxide. GHG emissions due to anthropogenic (human) activity are the dominant cause of observed climate change since the mid-20th century. Continued emission of greenhouse gases may cause long-lasting changes worldwide, increasing the likelihood of severe, pervasive, and irreversible effects for people and ecosystems.

Natural Resource Economics: Natural resource economics deals with the supply, demand, and allocation of the Earth's natural resources. One main objective of natural resource economics is to understand better the role of natural resources in the economy to develop more sustainable methods of managing those resources to ensure their future generations. Resource economists study interactions between economic and natural systems intending to develop a sustainable and efficient economy.

Sustainable Development: Sustainable development is an organizing principle for meeting human development goals while simultaneously sustaining the ability of natural systems to provide the natural resources and ecosystem services on which the economy and society depend. The desired result is a state of society where living conditions and resources are used to continue to meet human needs without undermining the integrity and stability of the natural system. Sustainable development can be defined as development that meets the needs of the present without compromising the ability of future generations to meet their own needs. Sustainability goals, such as the current UN-level Sustainable Development Goals, address the global challenges, including poverty, inequality, climate change, environmental degradation, peace, and justice.

Chapter 12
Would You Pay for the Environment?
An Application of the Environmental Preferences

Esra Karapınar Kocağ
https://orcid.org/0000-0002-2239-0519
Gümüşhane University, Turkey

ABSTRACT

Environmental degradation is a rising global concern. Many countries aim a sustainable development that could reduce the pressure on the environment. Macro-level actions are mostly investigated in the literature. However, micro-level components to ensure a sustainable future are very limited. This chapter argues that individuals as micro-level actors in the system are extremely important actors to stop the depletion of the nature and to help restoring it. Who is more supportive to protect the environment? What kind of factors influence this behaviour? This chapter aims to shed light on individual determinants of environmentally friendly preferences. To do so, the WVS was used, and findings indicate that gender and unemployment status have no significant effect. However, age, income level, and education level of individuals significantly influence preferences of individuals. Bearing in mind potential limitations, this chapter nevertheless acknowledges the importance of individual characteristics that can help protect the environment.

INTRODUCTION

Global environmental concerns have been recognised by most of the countries across the world. The United Nations Environment Programme (UNEP) as an international organisation focus on global environment and promotes practical implementations of the environmental aspects of sustainable development in the United Nations (UNEP, n.d.) like many other organisations. The Australian National Disaster Risk Reduction Framework emphasizes the importance of developing resilient communities in responding to

DOI: 10.4018/978-1-6684-5109-0.ch012

disasters and adapting to climate change (UNEP, 2022). This resilience of communities are likely to be achieved via a combination of macro and micro level measures, although most targeted indicators are at the national level and they are implemented by the governmental actions (Dahl, 2012). Macro level indicators that are to be top-down and micro level indicators that are to be bottom-up (Zainudin et al., 2020) need to work together to achieve sustainability goals of each country.

Environmental preference of individuals is a micro level key element that would reduce the pressure on the planet. Detrimental alteration on the planet has mostly occurred by human action. As human being is the most important element of this damage on the earth, restoration of the damage and protection of the environment must be the responsibility of humanity. Acting in a responsible way depends on an individual's socio-economic, political, and cultural context (Fahlquist, 2009). *CountUsIn,* an organisation in cooperation with UNEP, offers sixteen steps that individuals could do to reduce personal carbon emission and to influence leaders, which are *fly less, cut your waste, insulate your home, clothes that last, walk and cycle more, seasonal and local, dial it down, talk to friends, drive electric, switch your energy, green your money, speak up at work, eat more plants, get solar, repair and re-use,* and *tell your politicians.* Taking all these steps this project aims to reach to a billion individuals that could reduce carbon pollution by almost 20 per cent of the total reduction need. As proposed by Count Us In project, individual action matters in combatting detrimental effects of the climate change. Dahl (2012:15) highlights that "..*A complete set of multilevel sustainability indicators would aim to capture key factors for success from individual motivation and behaviour through to respect for planetary limits as a complex integrated system. No indicator system has yet aimed at this level of complexity, but without it, significant parts of the sustainability challenge will go unrecognized and unmanaged..*". Therefore, individual action or preferences as part of this complex integrated system need to be taken into account.

This chapter, in this respect, focuses on micro level actors and aims to shed some light on what factors influence individual preferences on the environment. To measure the environmental preference, willingness to pay for the environment was used in the empirical investigation. Three waves of the World Values Survey (WVS) which are Wave 2 (1989-1993), Wave 4 (1999-2004), and Wave 5 (2005-2009) with 93,131 individuals from 63 countries were included in this analysis. Considering a wide range of countries over years in this investigation, the current chapter seems to be a significant contribution to the relevant literature on the subject that could help understanding the reasoning of human action/preference.

This chapter is structured as follows. First, the author provides a brief background on the issue of global concerns about environmental degradation, along with macro and micro level roots of the problem. The next section offers an empirical investigation of the environmental preference. The data set and methodological choice were introduced in this section. Last but not least, the future research directions, limitations of the chapter, and conclusion sections were presented in the following section.

Background

Global concerns about climate change that has mostly occurred due to harmful human action have hotly debated in the public, as well as in scientific researches and policy agendas. Widespread damaging effects of climate change on the environment and human wellbeing have clearly been observed by many countries across the globe. Increased pressure on countries to fulfil their development goals leads to overuse of resources which eventually negatively affect the ecosystem, and this negative effect is not only exposed by a particular country where harmful action has taken place but also several other countries are exposed through negative externality that spreads into other places.

Because economic, social, and environmental resources are damaged and these resources are interconnected, societies face considerable challenges (Flint, 2013). These challenges over years have made countries to think and act on the sustainable development. Sustainability refers to "…an ecosystem's potential for subsisting over time, with almost no alteration" (Jabareen, 2008:181). Current economic systems that produce intensively to get a higher level of output which subsequently means increased Gross Domestic Product (GDP) do not seem to be in line with what sustainability refers. Natural capital that are not creatable by humans (Jabareen, 2008) has been depreciated by human action in this production process. Twentieth century has witnessed huge human population growth together with increased industrial output by 40 times, energy use by 16 times, fish catch by 35 times, and carbon and sulphur dioxide emissions by 10 times (Dasgupta, 2007). That is to say, all changes in the way human beings live cause to an unavoidable alteration on the planet.

Renewable energy, in this respect, is seen as an alternative to polluting and diminishing energy sources such as fossil fuels (Abdelwahab, 2012). As opposed to fossil fuels, renewable energy sources (e.g., solar energy, biomass energy, wind energy) are used in the production process recursively with no emissions that harm the environment (Panwar et al., 2011). Environmental literature provides a wide range of studies focusing renewable energy sources to combat global concerns (see for example Bull (2001); Lund (2007); Moriarty and Honnery (2012); Olabi and Abdelkareem (2022)). Even though clean energy is a very crucial and maybe the most visible step through a sustainable future, there exist other steps to take such as food security and hunger, waste management, land use, and more (see Sachs et al. (2019) for more detail). International, national, regional, local, and individual actors need to tackle with these issues all together.

Micro level factors such as individual preferences matter for a sustainable environment. As highlighted by Spangenberg (2002:306) *"..Although normative through its ethical fundament, the concept of sustainability is not dogmatic but open to be shaped by political decisions and citizens' as well as customers' preferences..."* From an economic point of view high income households, ceteris paribus, are likely to be more willing to contribute to the environmental protection than low income households, if the quality of environment is a normal good (Ivanova & Tranter, 2008). Income level, therefore, is an important constraint on individual preferences. Because of the fact that only individuals with a certain level of income can afford to buy environmentally friendly product, or to invest into greener energy, or in general to choose a greener life. However, the relationship between income and environmental preference may not be as expected. In this manner, Roca (2003) emphasises the importance of individual preferences on the environmental quality. Amongst several individual factors, income and demand for a better environment is expected to be associated. On the contrary to the general expectations, individual preferences of high income people might not be environment-friendly since environmental costs are displaced into a far future or a far place. That means higher level of income may not always translate into a lower level of consumption preferences to reduce environmental degradation. In another study in the literature, Lekakis and Kousis (2001) investigated whether there is a relationship between income and environmental actions. Authors used environmental actions per capita to examine the relationship between these actions and income for three Southern European countries, Greece, Spain, and Portugal during 1974-1994. Findings revealed that increased income do not lead to an increase in the environmental actions. Accordingly, it is hard to conclude a clear relationship between individual characteristics and the environmental preferences.

Contributing to the restoration actually combines two different disciplines that have different concerns and methods (Holl & Howarth, 2000). Even though causes of the environmental degradation is very complicated, it is known that the massive economic growth in recent decades has been reached at the cost of the natural health (UNEP, 2021). Therefore, a sustainable future necessitates a good balance between economic considerations and environmental considerations. Individual responsibility for paying for the restoration of the environment, in that respect, depends on various social and ecological contexts (Holl & Howarth, 2000).

Unlike the actual payment for the environment, this chapter draws attention to whether an individual would agree or disagree the idea of paying for the environment which is different from paying a certain amount of money for it. One can argue that individual preferences, feelings, and thoughts are not always solid evidence to show those people will act in favour of the environment. Nevertheless, it can be said that even if individuals might be less likely to engage in environment-protective behaviour than those who express support for it, still individuals who have positive attitudes are more likely to act to protect the environment (Scott & Willits, 1994). From this point of view, individuals' preferences or attitudes towards environment is as important as their actions in a protective way. Apart from a few attempts (see for example Holl & Howarth (2000); Ivanova & Tranter (2008); Sun (2001)), there is no extensive researches to explain individual factors on the environmental preferences. This chapter, in this respect, provides useful insights on the individual determinants of environmental preferences.

AN EMPIRICAL INVESTIGATION OF ENVIRONMENTAL PREFERENCE

In this section of the chapter, author offers an empirical investigation of the individual preferences on the environment. For this purpose, first, the data set that were utilised for empirical test were introduced. The data set were obtained from the World Values Survey Database and it covers considerable numbers of countries over years.

Along with the introduction of the data set, this section also provides information the methodological preference and reasoning on choosing this particular methodology. Besides, descriptive statistics and intuitive figures were also presented to give a better idea on the selected topic.

This section ends with the findings of the empirical investigation. Raw coefficients of the ordered probit model was given in the first column. Because of the nature of the ordered probit model, coefficients are not directly interpretable. Therefore, the marginal effects in each category is calculated and presented in the following columns to make the interpretation easier.

Data and Methodology

In this chapter, the author utilizes V2.0 version of the World Values Survey (WVS) which is an international research programme providing extensive set of data to help analysing various topics. WVS data is available upon a registration process and it is offered free of charge. The version used in this chapter is a time series dataset for 1981-2020 time period which is a combination of WVS survey waves of Wave 1 (1981-1983), Wave 2 (1990-1992), Wave 3 (1995-1998), Wave 4 (2000-2004), Wave 5 (2005-2008), Wave 6 (2010-2014), and Wave 7 (2017-2020) (Inglehart, R., C. Haerpfer, A. Moreno, C. Welzel, K. Kizilova, J. Diez-Medrano, M. Lagos, P. Norris, 2014). This is a time series data file that shows the changes in the values across countries over time, but it is not a panel data set in which there is continuity between samples over waves. In the data file, there are originally 106 countries and 432,482 individual observations. It should be noted that each wave does not include the same countries. More precisely, there exist data for some countries in particular waves, but not for all countries across waves. More information on the data set is provided by the official website of the organisation (see https://www.worldvaluessurvey.org/WVSDocumentationWVL.jsp).

Dependent variable in this empirical investigation is a categorical variable, which is *"Would give part of my income for the environment?"*. There are four ordered answer categories that respondents chose: 1. Strongly agree, 2. Agree, 3. Disagree, and 4. Strongly disagree. This question was only asked in Wave 2 (1989-1993), Wave 4 (1999-2004), and Wave 5 (2005-2009). Therefore, only these waves were kept in the sample and rest of it was dropped from the sample. Besides, all of the missing observations along with responses such as no answer, and don't know options were dropped. Eventually, this empirical analysis end up with 93,131 individuals from 63 countries. More details on the sampled countries were provided in the appendix section.

Percentage shares of the answers given by respondents are presented in Figure 1 below. According to the table, it can be said that almost half of the sample (i.e., 48.56 per cent) agrees to give part of their income for the environment. About 23 per cent of the sample disagree the idea of giving money for the environment, while 20 per cent of the sample strongly agree to give. Only about 9 per cent of the sample reported that they strongly disagreed to pay for the environment.

Figure 1. Distribution of answer categories, percentages
Source: *Own calculations using WVS data.*

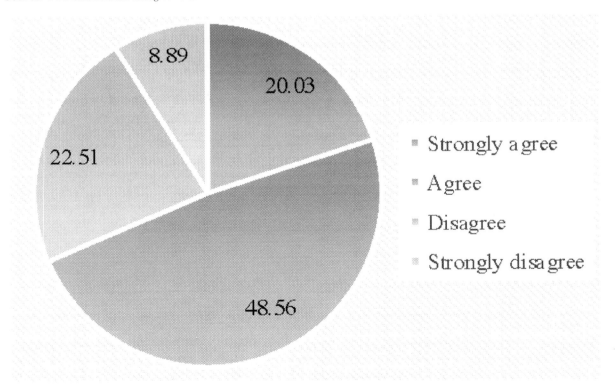

In terms of country-specific distributions of the responses, Figure 2 shows the percentage distribution of the answer category of strongly agree for top 20 countries. According to the figure, respondents from

India seem to be the most willing to pay for the environment, with 7.46 per cent. Brazil and Vietnam were followed with slightly more than 5 per cent of the sample strongly agreed to pay. In the rest of the countries, it is seen that they are mostly less developed or developing countries. The reason behind supportive preferences of individuals from these countries might be relatively higher dependency on agricultural products. Climate change and unpredictability of natural conditions makes agricultural sector which depends upon the natural sources vulnerable (Hanif et al., 2010). Only Canada is an exception on that list of countries. This might be due to higher level of awareness and more disposable income to sacrifice for the environment in Canada as developed country.

Figure 2. Top 20 countries that strongly agreed to give part of income for the environment, percentage
Source: *Own calculations using WVS data.*

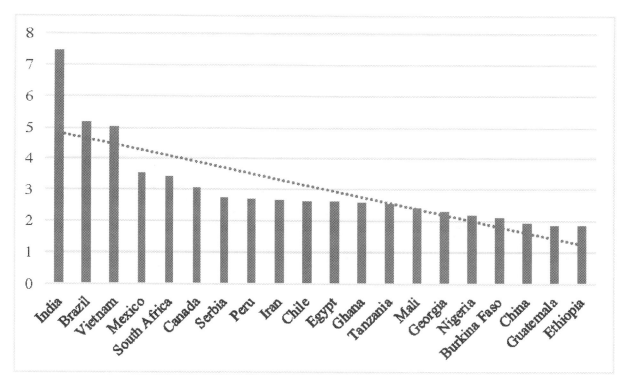

The author also thought it would be useful to see which countries mostly marked they would strongly disagree to pay for the environment. They are given in Figure 3 as percentage share. It is seen that there are more developed countries in this list than the previous one. Germany (with 6.71 per cent), Canada (with 2.69 per cent), United States of America (with 2.2 per cent), and Norway (with 1.87 per cent) are examples of the developed countries where respondents strongly disagreed to give part of their income for the environment. In developed countries, people might think that the depletion of the environment is mostly caused by developing countries where mass production with lower level of green standards and consumption of individuals who do not consider the natural capacity takes place. Hence, they may blame those individuals for this problem and may not be willing to pay for them. Additionally, individuals in the developed countries are likely to pay higher taxes to contribute their welfare states. Thereby, they may think natural restoration should already be comprised within those taxes. These and probably other reasons might people less willing to pay for the environment. However, respondents from South Africa presented the highest unwillingness to pay for the environment with almost 11 per cent. This very high unwillingness of individuals from South Africa might be explained by low level of income which make a financial contribution to the environment unbearable.

Figure 3. Top 20 countries that strongly disagreed to give part of income for the environment, percentage
Source: *Own calculations using WVS data.*

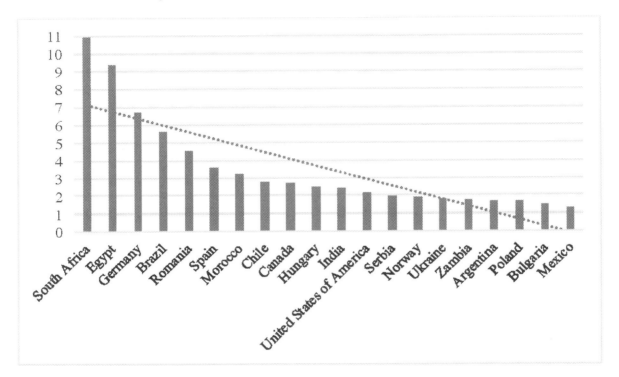

In the construction of independent variables that are expected to explain individual willingness to pay for the environment, several survey questions that constitutes a standard set of socio-economic indicators were utilised. Table 1 presents summary statistics of those variables used in the analysis.

Table 1. Summary statistics of the variables of interest

Variable		Obs	Mean	Std. Dev.	Min	Max
pay_environment	Would give part of my income for the environment					
Strongly agree		93131	(base)			
Agree		93131	0.4856	0.4998	0	1
Disagree		93131	0.2251	0.4177	0	1
Strongly disagree		93131	0.0889	0.2846	0	1
female	Gender					
0		93131	(base)			
1		93131	0.5072	0.5000	0	1
agecat	Age category					
15-24		93131	(base)			
25-39		93131	0.3484	0.4765	0	1
40-54		93131	0.2662	0.4420	0	1
55-69		93131	0.1560	0.3629	0	1
70 +		93131	0.0563	0.2304	0	1
incomecat	Income category					
Low income		93131	(base)			
Mid income		93131	0.5351	0.4988	0	1
High income		93131	0.1203	0.3254	0	1
education	Education level					
Lower		93131	(base)			
Middle		93131	0.4217	0.4938	0	1
Upper		93131	0.3063	0.4610	0	1
unemployed	Unemployment status					
0		93131	(base)			
1		93131	0.1074	0.3096	0	1

Source: Own calculations using WVS data.

The independent variables used in the analysis are standard set of socio-economic indicators which are in a categorical order. Age variable is given in five age categories. Using categories rather than particular ages was thought to be more intuitive in the interpretation of the coefficients. Income categories in the survey were originally scaled in ten steps, however the author preferred to generate three broader categories to have more observations in each category which makes the analysis more meaningful and to make the presentation simpler. Education also has three categories. Finally gender and unemployment status are dichotomous variables, taking 1 if a person is female and/or unemployed.

Weighing is an important issue in the empirical studies to have valid results. Unweighted analysis might be misleading. Therefore, the empirical analysis in this chapter considers original country weights that are provided in WVS dataset to compensate small deviations from target figures in each country.

Further information on weighting the sample can be found at organisations' website (see https://www.worldvaluessurvey.org/WVSContents.jsp?CMSID=WEIGHT&CMSID=WEIGHT).

In order to test the individual preferences towards giving part of income for the environment, an ordered probit model as specified in Equation 1 is estimated. Let E_i be the outcome to observe about preferences towards the environment by an individual i (e.g., strongly agree, agree, disagree, and strongly disagree.). When selecting among those categorical answers, the respondent will evaluate her/his level of preference on what could be considered a continuous scale and select the category that best approximates her/his personal evaluation. The stated categorical preference can therefore be interpreted as the outcome of an underlying latent continuous variable $E_{icy}*$ which measures the continuous level of environmental preferences.

Let's assume that latent $E_{icy}*$ variable is determined by the following equation:

$$E^*_{icy} = \beta_0 + \beta_1 X_{icy} + \varepsilon_{ict} \qquad (1)$$

where X_{ict} includes individual's i socio-economic and demographic characteristics in country c in year y. ε_i is a zero mean random error term reflecting unobserved factors related with individual preferences about the environment. Time period in the analysis, so the variable y, covers Wave 2 (1989-1993), Wave 4 (1999-2004), and Wave 5 (2005-2009).

FINDINGS

This section reports estimation results of the ordered probit model of environmental preferences of individuals. Dependent variable that measures this preference is "Would give part of my income for the environment?".

Interpretation of the coefficients is different in this kind of ordered probit models than a standard OLS estimation. While the sign and significance of the probit coefficients can be interpreted, it is difficult to interpret magnitude of the probit coefficients. Therefore, to make the interpretation easier and more meaningful, the author prefers calculating marginal effects. Table 2 presents the empirical findings of this investigation. First column of the table shows raw coefficients and it is followed by marginal effects that are obtained for each answer category.

As seen in the table, sum of the coefficients across the answer categories is equal to 1. This is because the probability is measure on a scale of 0 to 1. These marginal effects show the change in the probability of individuals having a particular environmental preference when the independent variable increases by one unit.

Would You Pay for the Environment?

Table 2. Findings, raw coefficients and marginal effects for each answer category

VARIABLES	Raw coefficients	Marginal effects in each category			
		Strongly agree	Agree	Disagree	Strongly disagree
Female	0.005	-0.001	-0.000	0.001	0.001
	(0.008)	(0.002)	(0.001)	(0.001)	(0.001)
Age: 25-39	0.047***	-0.012***	-0.003***	0.009***	0.007***
	(0.012)	(0.003)	(0.001)	(0.002)	(0.002)
Age: 40-54	0.028**	-0.007**	-0.002**	0.005**	0.004**
	(0.013)	(0.003)	(0.001)	(0.002)	(0.002)
Age: 55-69	0.005	-0.001	-0.000	0.001	0.001
	(0.015)	(0.004)	(0.001)	(0.003)	(0.002)
Age: 70+	0.055***	-0.014***	-0.004***	0.010***	0.008***
	(0.020)	(0.005)	(0.001)	(0.004)	(0.003)
Mid income	-0.078***	0.020***	0.006***	-0.014***	-0.012***
	(0.010)	(0.002)	(0.001)	(0.002)	(0.001)
High income	-0.158***	0.042***	0.010***	-0.029***	-0.023***
	(0.015)	(0.004)	(0.001)	(0.003)	(0.002)
Education: Middle	-0.140***	0.034***	0.014***	-0.025***	-0.023***
	(0.011)	(0.003)	(0.001)	(0.002)	(0.002)
Education: Upper	-0.289***	0.075***	0.021***	-0.053***	-0.043***
	(0.013)	(0.003)	(0.001)	(0.002)	(0.002)
Unemployed	0.005	-0.001	-0.000	0.001	0.001
	(0.015)	(0.004)	(0.001)	(0.003)	(0.002)
Constant cut1	-0.931***				
	(0.041)				
Constant cut2	0.488***				
	(0.041)				
Constant cut3	1.421***				
	(0.042)				
Observations	93,130				
Pseudo R-squared	0.0465				

Note: Dependent variable is "Would give part of my income for the environment?". There are four ordered answer categories that respondents chose: 1. Strongly agree, 2. Agree, 3. Disagree, and 4. Strongly disagree.
Robust standard errors in parentheses
*** $p<0.01$, ** $p<0.05$, * $p<0.1$

Environmental behaviour or preference may depend upon an individual's gender. Some researches in the field report that females are more concerned for the environment than males (Zelezny et al., 2000). Thereby, one can expect a gender difference in this particular preference as well. However, according to Table 2, the coefficient of female is not statistically significant, which means there is no gender difference on the willingness to pay for the environment. Age categories are also included in the specification to see if there exists any age effect (i.e. whether being younger or older has any affect) on this environmental preference. It is expected that younger individuals to hold more pro-environmental preferences since they have relatively longer life expectancy and they probably face environmental degradation faster (Sarigöllü, 2008), despite the contradictory evidence from the literature (Mainieri et al., 1997; Sarigöllü, 2008). Empirical investigation in this chapter provided evidence that younger people do not show a higher level of pro-environmental preference (i.e., willingness to pay for the environment). Being in the age category of 25-39 rather than the base category of 15-24 decreases the probability of being in outcome 1 or 2 (strongly agree or agree) and increases the probability of being in the outcome 3 or 4 (disagree or strongly disagree). More precisely, being in ages of 25-39 decreases the probability of reporting she/he would strongly agree to give part of her/his income for the environment by 1.2 percentage points. This finding is statistically significant at 1 percent significance level. Findings in the age category of 40-54 is similar to the first one though significance and magnitudes of the coefficients are slightly lower. The marginal effects in the age group of 55-69 are very small and not statistically significant. In the oldest age category, coefficients are larger and statistically significant at 1 percent level. This means elderly people are the most unwilling group to pay for the environment. Nevertheless, it should be noted that the reference group is age group of 15-24. Therefore, signs and magnitudes of the coefficients should be considered within this respect.

Income is an important indicator to explain this particular environmental preference that is directly related to individual income. The literature of environmental economics has widely discuss the relationship between income and environmental pollution, so called "*Environmental Kuznets Curve (EKC)*" which argues a U shape relationship between income growth and pollution (see for example, Grossman & Krueger (1991); Iwata et al. (2010); Narayan & Narayan (2010); Saboori et al. (2012)). Despite the existence of a wide range research across different parts of the world over years, there is no clear evidence amongst them.

Environmental behaviour of individuals might be weakened by income constraints due to the fact that economic priorities may shift this behaviour in favour of or against the environment depending on the tolerability of the financial sacrifice (Eden, 1993). Therefore, one can expect that individuals with relatively high level of disposable income are to be more likely to sacrifice some part of their income for the environment. However, individuals with relatively very limited disposable income may feel that environmental quality is not a prior concern in their life which eventually translates into less willingness to pay for the environment. Coefficients of the empirical analysis of this chapter show that having mid or high income rather than low income increases the probability of strongly agreeing or agreeing the idea of giving part of income for the environment. The magnitude is higher for high income group as expected. This finding is in line with the expected behaviour of a bearable sacrifice for relatively high income individuals.

In the next step, education is thought to be an important factor to shape the environmental preferences through higher awareness as a result of education process. Even if type of education may affect differently the environmental preferences or attitudes at some point, education itself is implicitly assumed to be linked to the environmental concerns (Gifford & Sussman, 2012). In this respect, current and future behaviour may also be different. Borden & Schettino (1979) found that what an individual says what she or he would be willing to do in the future is based on her or his emotional reaction, however, current commitment of individuals is a combination of emotional involvement and high knowledge. Even though this empirical investigation do not distinguish current and future behavioural preferences, as seen, education is found to be significantly associated with the environmental preferences. That is to say, having a mid-level of education rather than low level increases the probability of being in the category of strongly agree by 3.4 percentage points and agree by 1.4 percentage points to give part of the income for the environment. Magnitudes are higher for individuals with upper level of education as expected. This finding is statistically significant at 1 per cent significance level. Therefore, higher education which is implicitly assumed to provide higher level of environmental knowledge and awareness is found to be linked to the higher willingness to support the environment.

Finally, unemployment variable is included in the specification to see whether unemployment status has any effect on this preference. Behaviours that require financial contributions are likely to decrease with unemployment as income decreases during unemployment (Meyer, 2016). Findings of this study show that even if the sign of the coefficients of unemployment are negative for strongly agree and agree categories, they are very small and not statistically significant. Hence, surprisingly there could not be found any significant association between unemployment status and willingness to pay for the environment in this sample of observations.

FUTURE RESEARCH DIRECTIONS

Environmental system is extremely important to sustain the welfare of societies. In the most part of the world, goals to reduce detrimental effects of the climate change and to protect the environment find place on the political agendas of the governments. It should be accepted that macro level indicators such as sustainability performance at the national level are important to see the big picture of which countries contribute more or less into a greener future. However, it must be borne in mind that micro level indicators are an inseparable core of that future. Therefore, these micro indicators need to be understood deeper.

In this chapter, the author investigated individual behaviour on the willingness to pay for the environment. This constitutes a small piece of a huge range of preferences or attitudes. In this respect, having more environmental indicators on different aspects of environmentally protective behaviour would be useful to get a clearer picture. Additionally, because environmental degradation has been caused by developed countries through modernisation process, and the problem is generally being underdeveloped for other countries (Zeus & Reif, 1990), a comparison of individual preferences from developed, developing, and least developed countries would help to understand the difference in terms of development level which could help to offer more specific policy recommendations to implement on the particular countries. Furthermore, interactions of the current explanatory variables such as age and education, age and income, education and income, and other explanatory variables that are likely to influence this preference might be included in the specification to see whether being young and educated has any significant effect, for example.

CONCLUSION

This chapter overviews macro and micro level factors affecting the environmental degradation in an age of alarming global climate change. International, national, regional, local, and individual actors need to tackle with these issues all together. Amongst all those actors, this chapter primarily focuses on individual preferences as they are extremely important to protect the environment and to achieve a sustainable future. The author measured individual preferences through a World Values Survey (WVS) question that asks a respondent whether she/he would give part of her/his income for the environment. Based on four answers given to this question (e.g. strongly agree, agree, disagree, strongly disagree), 93,131 survey respondents from 63 countries were investigated on what factors influence their answers, so the environmental preference. A standard set of socio-economic explanatory variables were used to explain this preference. Since the dependent variable in this chapter is a categorical variable, considering four answer categories for the above survey question, the author preferred to apply an ordered probit model in the analysis, as widely used. Differently from a standard OLS estimation, coefficients of the ordered probit model are not directly interpretable. Therefore, marginal effects for each answer categories were calculated separately to interpret the findings more specifically.

Empirical findings showed that there is significant age effect on this preference. Elderly people who are 70 or older are less likely to support a monetary contribution for the environment than young people whose age is between 25 and 39. Besides, there was found no significant effect for age group of 55-69. This group of people might be those in early retirement age group. Age effect, therefore, did not provide clear evidence on environmentally supportive behaviour of young people. This finding do not support the expectation of younger individuals' higher pro-environmental preferences through longer life expectancy and their probably faster environmental degradation experience as stated by (Sarigöllü, 2008).

Income is thought to be an important indicator to explain willingness to pay for the environment because of the fact that it enables individuals for such a protective behaviour. Findings of this chapter support this view since a higher level of income was found to increase the probability of agreeing the idea of paying for the environment. Nonetheless, unemployment was found not to be significant on this particular environmental behaviour on the contrary to the expectations. As disposable income decreases during unemployment, monetary support for the environment was expected to be unlikely. Even though the signs of the first two outcomes (i.e., strongly agree and agree) are negative, they are very small in magnitude and not statistically significant. Nevertheless, it should be noted that the survey question used is a hypothetical question which does not expect a direct action from people. Hence, this may soften individuals' reported preference.

Education, on the other hand, is found to be a significant indicator to explain pro-environmental behaviour. Individuals with higher level of education are more likely to support the idea of paying for the environment. Education may directly affect pro-environmental behaviour via a higher level of environmental awareness as a result education process. Besides that, it can indirectly affect this behaviour because of the fact that high educated individuals are likely to be high income earners, and individuals with higher disposable income my sacrifice part of their income easier than those with low level of disposable income. Nonetheless, whether it is direct or indirect, education is still a significant indicator to explain environmental behaviour.

Findings of this chapter have important implications for policy interventions. It is seen that education is very important factor to shape the environmental attitudes. Therefore, it should be accessible for everyone. This may not be an issue for the developed countries, but educational standards in several developing countries are not well enough to provide service for everyone in the society. Not only the education itself but also content of it matters. If educational institutions offer a higher level of awareness on the effects of climate change which has been caused mostly by human action, and necessitated restoration process, young generations might be more willing to pay attention and to act in favour of the environment. Moreover, financial difficulty can make people ignore the environmental degradation through maybe higher costs of greener choices or priorities of urgent cost of living. In such cases across many regions, poverty seems to be a serious obstacle to deal with. When people are freed from this kind of constraints, they are more likely to care about the place they live in.

REFERENCES

Abdelwahab, Z. (2012). Renewable Energy, Sustainable Development and Environmental Protection in Ksours (Case of Algeria). *Energy Procedia*, *18*, 666–671. doi:10.1016/j.egypro.2012.05.081

Borden, R. J., & Schettino, A. P. (1979). Determinants of Environmentally Responsible Behavior. *The Journal of Environmental Education*, *10*(4), 35–39. doi:10.1080/00958964.1979.9941906

Bull, S. R. (2001). Renewable energy today and tomorrow. *Proceedings of the IEEE*, *89*(8), 1216–1226. doi:10.1109/5.940290

CountUsIn. (n.d.). *Making Changes That Matter*. Retrieved March 9, 2022, from https://www.count-us-in.org/en-gb/

Dahl, A. L. (2012). Achievements and gaps in indicators for sustainability. *Ecological Indicators*, *17*, 14–19. doi:10.1016/j.ecolind.2011.04.032

Dasgupta, P. (2007). The idea of sustainable development. *Sustainability Science*, *2*(1), 5–11. doi:10.100711625-007-0024-y

Eden, S. E. (1993). Individual Environmental Responsibility and its Role in Public Environmentalism. *Environment and Planning A. Economy and Space*, *25*(12), 1743–1758. doi:10.1068/a251743

Fahlquist, J. N. (2009). Moral Responsibility for Environmental Problems—Individual or Institutional? *Journal of Agricultural & Environmental Ethics*, *22*(2), 109–124. doi:10.100710806-008-9134-5

Flint, R. W. (2013). *Basics of Sustainable Development BT - Practice of Sustainable Community Development: A Participatory Framework for Change*. Springer. doi:10.1007/978-1-4614-5100-6_2

Gifford, R., & Sussman, R. (2012). Environmental attitudes. In *The Oxford handbook of environmental and conservation psychology* (pp. 65–88). Oxford University Press. doi:10.1093/oxfordhb/9780199733026.013.0004

Hanif, U., Syed, S. H., Ahmad, R., Malik, K. A., & Nasir, M. (2010). Economic Impact of Climate Change on the Agricultural Sector of Punjab. *Pakistan Development Review*, *49*(4), 771–798. doi:10.30541/v49i4IIpp.771-798

Holl, K. D., & Howarth, R. B. (2000). Paying for Restoration. *Restoration Ecology*, *8*(3), 260–267. doi:10.1046/j.1526-100x.2000.80037.x

Inglehart, R., Haerpfer, C., Moreno, A., Welzel, C., Kizilova, K., Diez-Medrano, J., Lagos, M., & Norris, P. E. P., & B. P. (Eds.). (2014). *World Values Survey: All Rounds - Country-Pooled Datafile Version*. https://www.worldvaluessurvey.org/WVSDocumentationWVL.jsp

Ivanova, G., & Tranter, B. (2008). Paying for Environmental Protection in a Cross-national Perspective. *Australian Journal of Political Science*, *43*(2), 169–188. doi:10.1080/10361140802035705

Iwata, H., Okada, K., & Samreth, S. (2010). Empirical study on the environmental Kuznets curve for CO2 in France: The role of nuclear energy. *Energy Policy*, *38*(8), 4057–4063. doi:10.1016/j.enpol.2010.03.031

Jabareen, Y. (2008). A New Conceptual Framework for Sustainable Development. *Environment, Development and Sustainability*, *10*(2), 179–192. doi:10.100710668-006-9058-z

Lekakis, J. N., & Kousis, M. (2001). Demand for and supply of environmental quality in the environmental Kuznets curve hypothesis. *Applied Economics Letters*, *8*(3), 169–172. doi:10.1080/13504850150504531

Lund, H. (2007). Renewable energy strategies for sustainable development. *Energy*, *32*(6), 912–919. doi:10.1016/j.energy.2006.10.017

Mainieri, T., Barnett, E. G., Valdero, T. R., Unipan, J. B., & Oskamp, S. (1997). Green Buying: The Influence of Environmental Concern on Consumer Behavior. *The Journal of Social Psychology*, *137*(2), 189–204. doi:10.1080/00224549709595430

Meyer, A. (2016). Is unemployment good for the environment? *Resource and Energy Economics*, *45*, 18–30. doi:10.1016/j.reseneeco.2016.04.001

Moriarty, P., & Honnery, D. (2012). What is the global potential for renewable energy? *Renewable & Sustainable Energy Reviews*, *16*(1), 244–252. doi:10.1016/j.rser.2011.07.151

Narayan, P. K., & Narayan, S. (2010). Carbon dioxide emissions and economic growth: Panel data evidence from developing countries. *Energy Policy*, *38*(1), 661–666. doi:10.1016/j.enpol.2009.09.005

Olabi, A. G., & Abdelkareem, M. A. (2022). Renewable energy and climate change. *Renewable & Sustainable Energy Reviews*, *158*, 112111. doi:10.1016/j.rser.2022.112111

Panwar, N. L., Kaushik, S. C., & Kothari, S. (2011). Role of renewable energy sources in environmental protection: A review. *Renewable & Sustainable Energy Reviews*, *15*(3), 1513–1524. doi:10.1016/j.rser.2010.11.037

Roca, J. (2003). Do individual preferences explain the Environmental Kuznets curve? *Ecological Economics*, *45*(1), 3–10. doi:10.1016/S0921-8009(02)00263-X

Saboori, B., Sulaiman, J., & Mohd, S. (2012). Economic growth and CO2 emissions in Malaysia: A cointegration analysis of the Environmental Kuznets Curve. *Energy Policy*, *51*, 184–191. doi:10.1016/j.enpol.2012.08.065

Sachs, J. D., Schmidt-Traub, G., Mazzucato, M., Messner, D., Nakicenovic, N., & Rockström, J. (2019). Six Transformations to achieve the Sustainable Development Goals. *Nature Sustainability*, *2*(9), 805–814. doi:10.103841893-019-0352-9

Sarigöllü, E. (2008). A Cross-Country Exploration of Environmental Attitudes. *Environment and Behavior*, *41*(3), 365–386. doi:10.1177/0013916507313920

Scott, D., & Willits, F. K. (1994). Environmental Attitudes and Behavior: A Pennsylvania Survey. *Environment and Behavior*, *26*(2), 239–260. doi:10.1177/001391659402600206

Spangenberg, J. H. (2002). Environmental space and the prism of sustainability: Frameworks for indicators measuring sustainable development. *Ecological Indicators, 2*(3), 295–309. doi:10.1016/S1470-160X(02)00065-1

Sun, C. (2001). Paying for the Environment in China: The Growing Role of the Market. *China Environment Series, 4*, 32–42. http://citeseerx.ist.psu.edu/viewdoc/download?doi=10.1.1.201.7949&rep=rep1&type=pdf

UNEP. (2021). *Ecosystem restoration for people, nature and climate.* https://wedocs.unep.org/bitstream/handle/20.500.11822/36251/ERPNC.pdf

UNEP. (2022). *Noise, Blazes and Mismatches-Emerging Issues of Environmental Concern.* https://www.unep.org/frontiers

UNEP. (n.d.). *About UN Environment Programme.* Retrieved March 8, 2022, from https://www.unep.org/about-un-environment

Zainudin, N., Lau, J. L., & Munusami, C. (2020). Micro-Macro Measurements of Sustainability BT - Affordable and Clean Energy. Springer International Publishing. doi:10.1007/978-3-319-71057-0_91-1

Zelezny, L. C., Chua, P. P., & Aldrich, C. (2000). Elaborating on gender differences in environmentalism. *The Journal of Social Issues, 56*(3), 443–457. doi:10.1111/0022-4537.00177

Zeus, J. H., & Reif, K. (1990). Evolution of Environmental Attitudes in the European Community. *Scandinavian Political Studies, 13*(2), 119–146. doi:10.1111/j.1467-9477.1990.tb00433.x

ADDITIONAL READING

Borden, R. J., & Schettino, A. P. (1979). Determinants of Environmentally Responsible Behavior. *The Journal of Environmental Education, 10*(4), 35–39. doi:10.1080/00958964.1979.9941906

Dahl, A. L. (2012). Achievements and gaps in indicators for sustainability. *Ecological Indicators, 17*, 14–19. doi:10.1016/j.ecolind.2011.04.032

Eden, S. E. (1993). Individual Environmental Responsibility and its Role in Public Environmentalism. *Environment and Planning A. Economy and Space, 25*(12), 1743–1758. doi:10.1068/a251743

Gifford, R., & Sussman, R. (2012). Environmental attitudes. In *The Oxford handbook of environmental and conservation psychology* (pp. 65–88). Oxford University Press. doi:10.1093/oxfordhb/9780199733026.013.0004

Holl, K. D., & Howarth, R. B. (2000). Paying for Restoration. *Restoration Ecology, 8*(3), 260–267. doi:10.1046/j.1526-100x.2000.80037.x

Jabareen, Y. (2008). A New Conceptual Framework for Sustainable Development. *Environment, Development and Sustainability, 10*(2), 179–192. doi:10.100710668-006-9058-z

Sarigöllü, E. (2008). A Cross-Country Exploration of Environmental Attitudes. *Environment and Behavior, 41*(3), 365–386. doi:10.1177/0013916507313920

UNEP. (2021). *Ecosystem restoration for people, nature and climate.* https://wedocs.unep.org/bitstream/handle/20.500.11822/36251/ERPNC.pdf

Zeus, J. H., & Reif, K. (1990). Evolution of Environmental Attitudes in the European Community. *Scandinavian Political Studies, 13*(2), 119–146. doi:10.1111/j.1467-9477.1990.tb00433.x

KEY TERMS AND DEFINITIONS

Environmental Degradation: Deterioration in the quality of the environment.

Ordered Probit Model: This is an ordinal regression model in which the dependent variable has more than two outcomes.

Pro-Environmental Behaviour: A way of behaviour that supports the environment.

APPENDIX

Table 3. Countries included in the sample

Country Name	Freq.	Percent	Cum.
United States of America	2,260	2.43	2.43
Puerto Rico	663	0.71	3.14
Canada	3,405	3.66	6.79
Trinidad and Tobago	969	1.04	7.84
Mexico	2,517	2.7	10.54
Guatemala	924	0.99	11.53
Peru	2,750	2.95	14.48
Brazil	3,062	3.29	17.77
Chile	2,000	2.15	19.92
Argentina	1,209	1.3	21.22
Uruguay	899	0.97	22.18
Switzerland	1,067	1.15	23.33
Spain	1,790	1.92	25.25
Andorra	931	1	26.25
Germany	1,700	1.83	28.07
Poland	849	0.91	28.99
Hungary	943	1.01	30
Italy	624	0.67	30.67
Albania	895	0.96	31.63
Montenegro	722	0.78	32.4
Macedonia	967	1.04	33.44
Bosnia and Herzegovina	1,094	1.17	34.62
Serbia	1,938	2.08	36.7
Slovenia	935	1	37.7
Cyprus	1,018	1.09	38.8
Bulgaria	814	0.87	39.67
Moldova	1,765	1.9	41.57
Romania	1,430	1.54	43.1
Ukraine	847	0.91	44.01
Georgia	1,289	1.38	45.39
Finland	913	0.98	46.37
Sweden	932	1	47.38
Norway	934	1	48.38
Mali	965	1.04	49.41
Burkina Faso	1,079	1.16	50.57

Continued on following page

Table 3. Continued

Country Name	Freq.	Percent	Cum.
Ghana	1,406	1.51	52.08
Nigeria	855	0.92	53
Uganda	529	0.57	53.57
Tanzania	964	1.04	54.6
Rwanda	1,017	1.09	55.7
Ethiopia	1,426	1.53	57.23
Zambia	1,029	1.1	58.33
Zimbabwe	778	0.84	59.17
South Africa	4,854	5.21	64.38
Morocco	1,153	1.24	65.62
Iran	2,518	2.7	68.32
Turkey	1,263	1.36	69.68
Egypt	3,039	3.26	72.94
Kyrgyzstan	987	1.06	74
China	2,101	2.26	76.26
Taiwan ROC	1,220	1.31	77.57
Hong Kong SAR	1,030	1.11	78.67
South Korea	2,219	2.38	81.05
Japan	1,657	1.78	82.83
India	4,969	5.34	88.17
Bangladesh	1,269	1.36	89.53
Thailand	1,464	1.57	91.1
Vietnam	2,318	2.49	93.59
Malaysia	1,196	1.28	94.88
Philippines	1,166	1.25	96.13
Indonesia	1,678	1.8	97.93
Australia	1,239	1.33	99.26
New Zealand	688	0.74	100
Total	**93,131**	**100**	

Chapter 13
Strategies of Green Economics:
Analyzing the Renewable Energy Impact in Making the Economy Green

Nima Norouzi
https://orcid.org/0000-0002-2546-4288
Bournemouth University, UK

ABSTRACT

The crises that threaten countries and human societies are the limited resources of non-renewable (fossil) energy sources and the increasing environmental pollution caused by the excessive consumption of fossil fuels, which are necessary for paying attention to energy resources. The close relationship between economic and environmental issues has led to the emergence of new approaches in international environmental law, one of the most important of which is the green economy. Since one of the most important goals of the green economy is to reduce greenhouse gas emissions, the use of renewable energy sources is a shortcut to the green economy. In this regard, the main purpose of this chapter is to compare the impact of renewable energy on the green economy in selected middle-income and high-income countries.

INTRODUCTION

The close connection between economic and environmental issues has led to the emergence of new approaches in international environmental law, one of the most prominent of which is the green economy. It is possible to move beyond the traditional economics approach and achieve a green economy by observing the principle of fairness and environmental integration. In other words, the traditional economy is based more on the excessive use of natural resources and disregard for the rights of present and future generations. The effects of such an economy can be irreversible in practice. Meeting the environmental challenges of the world requires moving towards a green economy. Therefore, turning to a green and ecological economy should be to reduce greenhouse gas emissions (Aldieri & Vinci, 2018), protection of natural resources, the realization of social and individual justice to fight inequalities that reducing

DOI: 10.4018/978-1-6684-5109-0.ch013

greenhouse gas emissions is one of the most important goals of the green economy (Bovenberg & van der Ploeg, 1994).

Increasing the supply of energy from renewable sources, in addition to the benefits of reducing greenhouse gas emissions, reduces the risks of rising fossil fuel prices. The energy sector is responsible for two-thirds of greenhouse gas emissions. Estimates show that by 2030, the cost of climate change in terms of climate adaptation will increase from $ 50 billion to $ 170 billion, only half of which can be borne by developing countries. Many countries, as importers of crude oil, have also been challenged by rising fossil fuel prices. For example, oil accounts for 10 to 15% of total African imports and more than 30% of the average. Attracts export revenue. Some African countries, such as Kenya and Senegal, spend more than half of their export earnings on energy imports. Investment in renewable resources, which are also locally available, can in many cases significantly increase energy security along with development, economic and financial security (Bailey & Caprotti, 2014).

In recent years, various countries, both developed and developing, have paid much attention to renewable energy, and rising fossil fuel prices, environmental considerations, energy security, petrochemical use, technological advances, and economic justification are largely decisive. The future has been renewable energy. Renewable energy is essentially environmentally friendly and keeps the environment healthy, and as a result, can reduce the major greenhouse gas emissions that impose high costs on society (Barbier, 2011). Therefore, we should look for alternatives to fossil fuels, such as renewable energy. Renewable energies (new energies) such as wind, solar, hydropower, geothermal, biogas and biomass are compatible with nature and do not pollute the environment, and from the major greenhouse gas emissions impose many costs on society, Prevent. In summary, the top three characteristics of renewable energy are (Bordeianu, 1995):

Renewable energy sources have a long life and natural cycles and, unlike non-renewable energy sources, such as fossil fuels, are not finite, which ensures the continuity of energy consumption for future generations; Renewable energy sources, especially wind and solar energy, have significant potential in energy production due to their abundance and convenient geographical facilities, and their use can save fossil fuel consumption; The unique use of fossil fuel power plants will create a focus on energy production areas, while renewable energy sources can easily be used to generate energy in any location with suitable geographical conditions. This leads to decentralized energy production in sparsely populated areas such as villages(Cuomo et al., 2016).

With the increase in world population and limited energy resources, all countries face energy consumption. The crises that threaten countries and human societies are the limited resources of non-renewable or fossil energy sources such as oil, gas, and coal, and the other is the increase in environmental pollution caused by excessive consumption of fossil fuels. Destructive and irreversible effects of the greenhouse effect, acid rain, have increased carbon dioxide emissions, which have endangered human life and living organisms (Claessens & Yurtoglu, 2013). Preventing excessive degradation of the environment and subsequent ozone depletion, climate change and changing the rhythm of the seasons, global warming, reduction of agricultural areas and reduction of non-renewable natural resources, protection of natural resources for future generations is essential and shows the importance of paying attention to the use of renewable energy sources.

Therefore, the main purpose of this study is to compare the impact of renewable energy consumption on the green economy in selected middle-income and high-income countries in the period 2016-2005 using data panel models. In this regard, these hypotheses are raised that renewable energy consumption has a negative and significant effect on carbon dioxide emissions as an indicator of a green economy

Strategies of Green Economics

in the group of selected countries. Also, the impact of renewable energy on the green economy in the group of selected middle-income countries is higher than the group of selected high-income countries. Then, after reviewing the theoretical foundations and research history, the structure of the model used is introduced and estimated, and finally, conclusions and suggestions are presented.

Background

Environmental protection is one of the major concerns of the international community. To protect non-renewable natural resources and respect the rights of current and future generations, the issue of sustainable development has been considered by governments and international organizations(Djankov et al., 2004). The goal of sustainable development is to strike a balance between economic, social, and environmental dimensions. The traditional approach of the brown economy and the maximum use of natural resources, regardless of the rights of current and future generations, leads to the destruction and pollution of the environment, in contrast to the green economy option that some governments and international institutions consider, not only It is a response to the challenges facing the international community, but it has also helped to realize the concept of sustainable development. On the other hand, the greenness of the economy and reasonable and fair productivity of resources will help their sustainability and renewability. The third dimension of the concept of sustainable development, which is environmental protection, will be strengthened (Fani & Norouzi, 2020). The green economy is a type of economy in which economic growth and development are based on the ecological balance of the environment, assuming that the two goals of economic development and environmental protection can be achieved simultaneously.

Since one of the most important goals of the green economy is to reduce greenhouse gas emissions, the use of renewable energy sources is a shortcut to the green economy. The green economy is recognized as the key to sustainable development. In other words, achieving sustainable development is impossible without a green economy. Therefore, the transition to a green economy is one of the requirements for sustainable development (Hamdouch & Depret, 2010).

The United Nations Environment Program (UNEP) has recently expanded the concept of clean production, including resource efficiency, which is a key element in the transition to a green economy (Guo et al., 2020). The development and expansion of renewable energy help achieve economic, social, and environmental development of countries, which is one of the key factors in achieving sustainable development. The use of renewable energy can reduce dependence on fossil fuels, reduce emissions from energy production and consumption, and reduce greenhouse gas emissions, which significantly impact global warming. Renewable, clean (clean), abundant and reliable energy, and, if properly developed, can play an important role as a sustainable energy source in achieving the goals of sustainable development of countries (Hu & Wang, 2020).

The use of renewable energy and low carbon technologies is the most important sub-sector of the green economy. Because on the one hand, most of the emissions occur during energy production, and on the other hand, resources are needed to invest in this sector.

It is a big financial thing that is difficult or impossible without the support of the public sector. The cost of producing energy from renewable sources is much higher compared to fossil fuels. As a result, recognizing the existing capacities, evaluating the optimal option, and appropriate policy in the energy sector can help accelerate the movement towards low carbon products and processes (Hayek, 1945).

The approach of the green economy is to pay attention to environmental constraints and its vulnerabilities while addressing the traditional and main goals of economics, the use of renewable resources and non-excessive use of non-renewable resources and consequently the irreparable damage to the environment, etc. have been gradually considered with the pervasiveness of the green economy. Since a green economy is an economic development based on sustainable development and is based on environmental compatibility, its goal is to reduce environmental risks. Enables the peaceful coexistence of human beings with nature, which requires increasing the optimal use of renewable energy. The use of renewable energy reduces dependence on fossil resources and reduces the greenhouse effect, which is one of the goals of the green economy to reduce greenhouse gas emissions(Jalilian et al., 2007).

In this regard, studies in the field of renewable energy and green economy can be classified into three categories:

The first group of studies that have addressed the importance of renewable energy and the green economy. Such as Khoshnava et al. (2019), Kiviaho et al. (2004), Kaufmann et al. (2014), Kaufmann et al. (2005), Li & Lin (2016), La Porta et al. (1997).

La Porta et al. (2002) and Milani (2000) explained that the green economy framework has helped harmonize environmental and socio-economic goals. The environmental dimension covers various environmental issues (e.g., climate change, renewables, energy, natural capital), while the economic dimension includes various economic aspects such as development, growth, cost, or competition. The social dimension is less visible. Emphasis on these three aspects of sustainability shows the strong link between a green economy and sustainability. The green economy can often be used to reduce resource pressures, climate change, and emissions while guaranteeing economic growth and employment(Norouzi et al., 2020a). In this regard, the role of governments in implementing the framework of long-term green economy regulations It is very important that the development of renewable resources can create short-term socio-economic benefits that indicate green growth (Norouzi et al., 2020b).

Norouzi (2021a), Norouzi & Kalantari (2020), and Norouzi et al. (2021) explained in studies that renewable and clean energy could be the first option due to limited fossil fuel resources and environmental pollution. Be converted to produce energy. The use of renewable energy plays an important role in preserving the natural and human environment, reducing global warming, and achieving sustainable development goals (Norouzi & Fani, 2020). Renewable energy is more compatible with nature and the environment, and its production leads to little environmental pollution; due to their renewability, the resources of this type of energy are not limited and depleted. In general, it is recommended that communities seeking sustainable development use renewable energy sources.

Norouzi & Fani (2021a) and Norouzi et al. (2021b) described in studies that after the Rio Conference in 1992; Sustainable development has become one of the main goals of the international community. Green growth requires programs to achieve economic growth and prosperity with less consumption of resources and waste for food production, transportation, construction, housing, and energy. Green growth is a precondition for building a green economy. Sustainable environmental development in Iran can be provided by introducing the green economy versus the brown economy and the green productivity approach.

The second category of studies examines the causal relationship between renewable energy and green economy using the Granger causality test. Such as the studies of Norouzi & Ataei (2021), and Norouzi & Fani (2020b).

Porter & Van der Linde (1995) examined the causal relationship between renewable energy and carbon dioxide emissions in Pakistan in the period 1970-1990, found that there is a two-way causal relationship between renewable energy consumption and CO_2 emissions. Stiglitz (1998) examined this relationship in Denmark during the period 1972-1995. The results showed a one-way causal relationship between renewable energy consumption and greenhouse gas emissions. Szyja et al. (2016) also showed that in 19 countries in 1984-2007, there is a two-way causal relationship between renewable energy consumption and carbon dioxide emissions.

The third group of studies examined the impact of renewable energy on the green economy and other economic variables using time series methods. In this regard, we can refer to the studies of Vuola et al. (2020).

Vukovic et al. (2019) explained that renewable energy consumption had harmed pollution in Central and Eastern Europe, Western Europe, East Asia, the Pacific, South Asia, and the United States. At the same time, renewable energy consumption has no significant effect on pollution in the Middle East, North Africa, and sub-Saharan Africa. Zhao et al.'s (2020) study in China in 1975-2005 showed a direct relationship between economic growth and carbon dioxide emissions. Pahle et al.(2016), in the period 2003-2004, explained that the increase in per capita income has a positive and significant effect on per capita renewable energy consumption and the long-term price elasticity of per capita renewable energy consumption is -0.70 (23). Loiseau et al. (2016), in a study in Germany in the period 1971-1999, described Germany as the largest economy in Europe and the leader in the consumption of renewable energy throughout the continent. Also, the consumption of renewable energy has had a significant impact on the economic growth of Germany, so that a 1% increase in the consumption of renewable energy has increased the economic growth of Germany by 0.2194% (Zhang et al., 2017).

METHODS AND MATERIALS

In this paper, using theoretical foundations and empirical study of Apergis et al. (2010) to investigate the impact of renewable energy on the green economy in the group of selected countries with modifications, model (1) has been used.

$$(LCO_2)_{it} = \beta_0 + \beta_1 LRENEWABLE_{it} + \beta_2 LGDP_{it} + \beta_3 LHU_{CA_{it}} + \beta_4 LICT_{it} + \beta_5 LOPENNESS_{it} + \beta_6 RU\_LAW_{it} + U_{it} \quad (1)$$

In the regression equation (1), LCO2 is the logarithm of carbon dioxide emissions (the main greenhouse gas) as an indicator of green economy, LRENEWABLE logarithm of renewable energy consumption, LGDP is the logarithm of GDP changes Fixed per capita price in 2010 as an indicator of economic growth, LHU_CA stands for the logarithm of gross enrollment rate in higher education as an indicator of human capital, LICT is the logarithm of Internet penetration coefficient as an indicator Indicates information and communication technology (ICT), LOPENNESS is the logarithm of the ratio of total exports and imports of goods and services to GDP as an indicator of the degree of openness of the economy, the RU_LAW is the rule of law, including equation error and, i and t represent the country and time(Al-Mulali et al., 2016).

In terms of identifying and collecting information and statistical sources, the method used in this article is written documentation, library, receipt, and electronic information. This article collects data from the statistical information available in the World Bank at www.worldbank.org, governance site at www.govindicators.org, BP energy data site at www.bp.com, and the International Renewable Energy

Agency (IRENA) at www.irena.org. The statistical population is selected according to the criteria of the World Bank. The World Bank classifies countries by geographical area or by income level. The countries selected in this study are selected based on income level. The World Bank classifies countries into low-income, middle-income, and high-income countries based on per capita income. In the World Bank classification, Iran is a middle-income country(Akin, 2014).

Therefore, in this article, middle-income countries (including Iran) have been selected. This group includes Argentina, South Africa, Ukraine, Ecuador, Indonesia, Iran, Brazil, Peru, Thailand, Turkey, China, Russia, Romania, Philippines, Kazakhstan, Colombia, Malaysia, Egypt, Mexico, Venezuela, Vietnam, India.

Also, to compare the impact of renewable energy on the green economy in two different structures, another group has been selected in this article. This group includes countries with high incomes. Includes Germany, Austria, Australia, Spain, United Kingdom, USA, Italy, Belgium, Portugal, Czech Republic, Denmark, Japan, Sweden, Switzerland, Chile, France, Finland, Canada, South Korea, Poland, Norway, New Zealand, The Netherlands, Casta Rica, and Greece.

In selecting the selected countries, middle-income and high-income countries have been selected that produce and consume renewable energy. Statistical data of the variables used in this paper were also available in the period under review(Ollo-López & Aramendía-Muneta, 2012).

RESULTS AND DISCUSSION

To estimate the model, it is first necessary to determine the type of estimation method for the specific type of panel data. Therefore, the F-Limer statistic was first used to determine the presence (absence) of width from a separate origin for each country. According to the amount of F-Limer statistics calculated in Table 1, the null hypothesis of the test based on the use of the ordinary least squares method is rejected. As a result, constrained regression (ordinary least squares) is not valid, and the width of different sources (fixed or random effects method) should be considered in the model. Then, the Hausman test was used to test the model using the fixed or random effects method. According to the number of statistics obtained in Table 1, the fixed effects method was used to estimate the model.

Strategies of Green Economics

Table 1. Results of estimating the effect of renewable energy consumption on the green economy in the group of selected countries (Dependent variables: logarithm of carbon dioxide emissions)

Variable	High-income countries	Mid-income countries
	Coefficient [t-stat](prob.)	Coefficient [t-stat](prob.)
C	93.653 [3.812] (0.000)	136.224 [4.881] (0.000)
LRENEWABLE	-1.413[-14.523](0.000)	-2.303[-5.536](0.000)
LGDP	2.861E-10[13.892](0.000)	4.192E-9[14.443](0.000)
LHU_CA	1.304E-5[-1.754](0.077)	-2.278[-10.096](0.000)
LICT	-0.778[-4.474](0.000)	-0.963[-2.732](0.006)
LOPENNESS	36.962[1.775](0.077)	0.576[2.773](0.006)
RU_LAW	-34.654[-2.489](0.013)	-110.122[-3.956](0.000)
R^2	0.996	0.997
D-W	1.134	0.663
F-statistic(Prob.)	243.291(0.000)	508.642(0.000)
F-limer stat	422.331(0.000)	5.286(0.000)
Hausman stat	36.245(0.000)	38.864(0.000)

Estimating the regression model using the fixed effects method in the group of selected middle-income and high-income countries in 2000-2020 is shown in Table 1.

The logarithm of renewable energy consumption has a negative and significant effect on carbon dioxide emissions as an indicator of the green economy in selected countries. Therefore, the hypothesis about the negative and significant impact of renewable energy consumption on the green economy in the group of selected countries can not be rejected.

The impact of renewable energy consumption on the green economy in middle-income countries is higher than that of high-income countries. Therefore, the hypothesis about the greater impact of renewable energy consumption on the green economy in middle-income countries than in the group of high-income countries can not be rejected.

Economic growth has a positive and significant effect on carbon dioxide emissions as an indicator of the green economy in selected countries. Increasing economic growth requires more natural resources and energy, especially fossil fuels, followed by releasing large amounts of pollutants that cause environmental degradation and serious damage to the environment. The results of this study are consistent with the studies of Cole (2004) and Cuomo et al. (2016).

The logarithm of the gross rate of enrollment in higher education as an indicator of human capital has a negative and significant effect on carbon dioxide emissions as an indicator of the green economy in the group of selected countries. Human resources are literate and aware of the rules and regulations, with the correct use of energy resources and the protection of the environment around it, reduces environmental pollution, and maintains its quality.

The logarithm of Internet penetration coefficient as an indicator of information and communication technology (ICT) has a negative and significant effect on carbon dioxide emissions as an indicator of the green economy in the group of selected countries. Proper use of ICT services will reduce traffic and consequently reduce the consumption of transportation fuels and greenhouse gas emissions, as well as the use of ICT services, useful information, and access to various issues raised in communities; it increases people's awareness and then implements effective strategies to improve the quality of the environment and reduce pollutants. Alopez and Aramandia Monta (2012) showed that information and communication technology reduces greenhouse gas emissions (Cristea et al., 2013).

The logarithm of the ratio of total exports and imports of goods and services to GDP as an indicator of the degree of openness of the economy has a positive and significant effect on carbon dioxide emissions as an indicator of the green economy in the selected countries. Environmental pollution has received a lot of attention in recent years. On the other hand, trade liberalization can affect the emission of pollution by increasing productivity by increasing the productivity of products, according to the principle of comparative advantage of countries in the production of goods in which they have a comparative advantage(Barbier, 2011). Increasing trade affects pollution emissions in two ways: 1) by increasing carbon dioxide emissions from international transportation, and 2) by transferring carbon dioxide emissions from the importing country to the exporting country, while Increasing the production of polluting goods in exporting countries may increase pollution in these countries (Hamdouch & Depret, 2010).

The rule of law has a significant negative impact on carbon dioxide emissions as an indicator of the green economy in the group of selected countries. The rule of law makes the transparency of actions and

The activities of governments and the improvement of the decision-making process of governments are done through popular participation. The transparency of the laws related to the activities of companies and economic institutions and the proper functioning of the government increase investment and economic growth (Guo et al., 2020).

The value of the coefficient of determination in the model shows that more than 90% of the changes in carbon dioxide emissions as an indicator of the green economy in the group of selected countries are explained by the explanatory variables of the model.

Climate change due to increased greenhouse gas emissions is one of the important factors in climate change and events, environmental hazards, natural disasters, and serious damage to the economy, which expands renewable energy as a source of clean energy. It can play an important role in reducing environmental pollution and the major emissions of polluting gases such as carbon dioxide and other greenhouse gases and prevent the imposition of high costs on society. In other words, renewable energy, clean (clean), abundant and reliable, and if properly developed, can play an important role as a sustainable energy source in achieving sustainable development goals. The main reason for emphasizing renewable energy and helping to solve environmental problems and prevent the loss of fossil fuels is the protection of natural resources for future generations, which undoubtedly is renewable energy due to the simplicity of its technology. They are important in the green economy and sustainable economic development. The results of this study are consistent with the studies of Khoshnava et al. (2019), Kiviaho et al. (2014), and Loiseau et al. (2016). However, it is not consistent with the results of the study of Vuola et al. (2020) in the Middle East, North Africa, and sub-Saharan Africa. Ollo-López et al. (2012) in Pakistan in 1970-1990 showed that renewable energy had played an important role in reducing carbon dioxide emissions. Pahle et al. (2016) In 1996-2014 showed that the intensity of carbon dioxide emissions had decreased significantly due to the use of more efficient and cleaner technologies and the tendency to use cleaner fuels. Barbier (2011) in Denmark 1972-2007 showed a one-way causal relationship between the consumption of renewable energy and greenhouse gas emissions. The study by Cristea et al. (2013) Also showed that renewable energy consumption had not had a significant impact on reducing pollution in the Middle East, North Africa, and sub-Saharan Africa. Therefore, based on empirical evidence, there is no consensus on how renewable energy affects carbon dioxide emissions as an indicator of the green economy in different countries. This study also showed that the impact of renewable energy consumption on the green economy in selected middle-income countries is higher than the group of selected high-income countries. This indicates the lack of adequate and efficient use of renewable energy in the group of selected middle-income countries. The expansion of its use compared with the group of selected high-income countries has been able to have more effects on reducing carbon dioxide emissions as an indicator of a green economy.

SUCCESSFUL EXPERIENCES IN THE GREE ECONOMICS

Green economics or environmental economics has come to the attention of many governments in recent decades. The interactions between economics and the environment have become an undeniable reality; Just as economic policies affect the environment, the economy is also affected by environmental change. Environmental pollution is one of the most important challenges of societies. In developed countries, by investing in renewable energy, new technologies in controlling environmental pollution, and improving energy efficiency, steps have been taken to improve it, but it has not been considered in developing countries. The GGEI is the first green economy index introduced in 2010 and is widely used today by policymakers, international organizations, civil society, and the private sector. A leading report compiled by the Deputy Minister of Economic Affairs of the Ministry of Economic examines the experience of five countries - Sweden, Norway, Costa Rica, Germany, and Denmark - in the green economy and, in particular, the development of renewable energy(Nima, 2021).

Green Economics in Sweden

According to the Global Green Economic Index in 2014, Sweden ranked first to have the best performance among countries in the world. Sweden currently has the highest rate of renewable energy use in the European Union; More than 45% of Sweden's energy supply is renewable, relying on hydropower and biofuels. More than 12 percent of electricity generation comes from cogeneration plants and 2 percent from wind farms. Since 2013, Sweden has helped to encourage the use of second-generation biofuels with a tax exemption on hydrogenated vegetable and animal fats and oils up to 15% by volume of diesel fuel. Diesel provided sustainable conditions for biofuel producers and distributors and helped promote the use of renewable energy. Other strengths of Sweden include developing environmentally friendly technologies in recycling, renewable energy (wind, solar, hydropower, biofuels), information technology, green transport, electric motors, green chemistry, lighting, and many energy-efficient industries.

The government invested in environmental technologies from 2011 to 2014, thus supporting its commitment to working with China, India, and Russia on environmental technologies. In general, Sweden has been a leader in organic farming, renewable energy use, per capita investment in green technologies, and sustainable development research. Given that Sweden was the first country in the world to impose a heavy tax on fossil fuels in 1991 to develop green energy resources and to increase the efficiency of this type of tax, it reduced its exemption in 2013 and 2015, the government of this country To further protect the environment, it intends to eliminate fossil fuels from all cars by 2030 and to eliminate carbon by 2050. The country was able to take effective steps to increase energy efficiency by enacting a new planning and construction law in 2011 and working on smart grids(Guo et al., 2020).

Given the scarcity of raw materials and the need to increase resource efficiency, Sweden implements a minerals and resource efficiency strategy. Sweden has also made significant changes in waste recycling in recent decades; More than 99% of household waste is recycled. In 1975, only 38% of household waste was recycled. Because fuel waste is relatively cheap, the Swedes use it efficiently and profitably. Overall, Sweden is a leader in reducing environmental impact compared to neighboring countries and is unique in converting waste into electricity using high-power incinerators, which has led to the import of waste from other countries. The Swedish Environmental Protection Agency has also developed a practical plan to prevent waste, including encouraging manufacturers to make products with longer lifespans and is considering offering tax breaks to repair some goods.

Green Economics in Norway

Norway has set ambitious environmental policy goals for sustainable development. These goals are supported by a strong analytical framework on environmental, social, and economic issues that focus on managing human, natural, productive, and financial capital. Measures such as simplification of regulations, decentralization of environmental responsibilities, and intelligent use of economic tools have contributed to the successful implementation of many Norwegian environmental policies. Also, the requirement of all projects to conduct environmental impact assessments and better inform the affected people about these projects, special attention to issues such as air pollution, water and sewage infrastructure, and river management are among the most important environmental measures in Norway. Norway is also one of the world leaders in financing clean climate projects. It helps developing countries reduce deforestation, expand renewable energy and adapt to climate change(Hu & Wang, 2020).

Green Economics in Costa Rica

Costa Rica is one of the countries in Central America and is ranked third in terms of best performance in the global green economy index in 2014, committed to becoming a carbon-free country by 2021. To increase the use of renewable energy, the country is offering new incentives for the construction of renewable energy plants of seven megawatts or larger, including the import of materials without customs duties, exemption from operating taxes for some time, and the possibility of issuing carbon offsets. Pointed to be of considerable value for increasing investment attractiveness. Doing so has generated more than 90 percent of Costa Rica's electricity from renewable energy sources such as hydropower, geothermal energy, and wind power. Costa Rica also provides tax incentives to the biofuel industry. With the high supply of palm oil, biodiesel production is expected to become the leading biofuel in the country(Khoshnava et al., 2019).

Green Economics in Germany

According to the Global Green Economy Performance Index in 2014, Germany ranks fourth. It is one of the pioneers in promoting renewable energy protection policies. The Renewable Energy Law, first implemented in Germany in 2000, is one of the factors in the country's success in the environment. Within the framework of this law, the policy of encouraging cogeneration power plants, limited emission exchange system, energy tax reform, etc., are included. The enactment of the Renewable Energy Law and the development of incentive tariffs for wind, solar, hydro, geothermal, and biomass energy

Strategies of Green Economics

in this law have been effective in forming a 29% share of net electricity consumption from renewable energies. Nevertheless, Germany is reviewing the Renewable Energy Act to motivate access to and expand electricity networks, marine wind energy, and technologies for peak consumption management and storage. Energy pricing through taxes and other financial instruments plays an important role in the composition of German energy policy.

The German parliament passed the Environmental Tax Reform Act in 1999, which gradually increased oil and gas tax rates and introduced a new electricity tax. Germany also has a good position in exporting green technologies. According to the German Solar Energy Association, photovoltaic exports increased from 14% in 2004 to 55% in 2011 and 65% in 2013, with 80% targeting 2020. Also, according to the German Wind Energy Association, the share of current exports of the wind industry is between 65 and 70%. Germany plays a key role in the renewable energy market and in the market for products that increase energy efficiency; In 2004, Germany accounted for 17% of the global efficiency market and even larger shares than the United States, Japan, and Italy. One of Germany's goals is to increase renewable energy consumption to 18% of final energy consumption by 2020 and 80% of electricity consumption by 2050(Kiviaho et al., 2014).

Green Economics in Denmark

Denmark is one of the pioneers in the implementation of appropriate policies in the field of renewable energy, energy efficiency, and climate change in the member countries of the Organization for Economic Cooperation and Development (OECD); According to the Global Green Economy Index (GGEI) in 2014, the country ranked fifth among countries in the world. Enacting appropriate tax laws in the field of environment is one of the factors influencing the proper position of this country in the green economy; In 1992, Denmark was the second country after Sweden to impose a carbon tax on some types of energy consumption by households and industries, and in 2012 it collected the highest energy tax among EU countries. Carbon tax rates in Denmark vary for different purposes; In such a way that the home sector pays the highest taxes and the energy industries pay the lowest carbon tax in addition to tax rebates to facilitate competition. To develop environmental innovations, the country has allocated carbon tax revenue to subsidize the area.

In addition, incentive tariffs on the wind, biomass, geothermal, hydroelectric, and solar energy are another action taken by the Danish government to reduce carbon emissions. Denmark is one of the pioneers in the development of wind energy in Europe. On average, the country's wind farms supply more than a quarter of Denmark's electricity needs. Electricity generation from renewable sources is supported at a price above market price. Total market price and surplus price guarantee a stable income for the producer. All subsidy costs are transferred to the consumer as equal public service requirements. Under Denmark's energy program, the Danish government, as the first European country, provided many subsidies to the fledgling wind industry, which was also successfully implemented in Germany. The rapid decline in lead emissions in Denmark in the early 1990s due to laws banning the sale of lead fuels for transportation resulted from regulations for catalytic converters in automobile exhaust systems and nitrate-free units in thermal power plants(Loiseau et al., 2016).

In 2001, Denmark introduced a limited emission exchange system for electricity generation, according to which free licenses were granted to firms in proportion to the number of pollutants emitted by firms in the past. Denmark's limited edition exchange system was developed in 2003 and replaced in 2005 by the EU Emissions Exchange Scheme. Denmark has also transformed its car power system to eliminate fossil fuels by 2050 and supply all renewable energy sources. In general, the most important measures taken in Denmark to improve performance in the field of the green economy can be such as environmental impact assessment and attention in policy decisions in all sectors, funding for the use of new technologies, providing information to consumers on how to influence Their choices focused on the environment and the regulation of resource use and pollution mitigation through price and tax tools.

CONCLUSION

According to the results obtained in line with this study, it can be concluded that measures to provide access to renewable and clean energy in remote and rural areas create job opportunities, reduce poverty and establish social justice. Creating appropriate educational and advertising fields in expanding the use of renewable energy Allocating sufficient funds to implement renewable energy technologies for electricity generation of residential, commercial buildings, factories, transportation industries, and water treatment that reduce environmental pollution Followed by the achievement of a green economy. Government policies and investments to use environmentally friendly technologies, renewable energy, implement and finance industrial research projects, train efficient staff and comply with existing laws and regulations, and implement treaties and agreements International will create a green economy in the communities. As a strategic policy, environmental taxes can require producers to use environmental laws and standards and prevent environmental degradation. Creating suitable grounds for using software and hardware in line with environmental goals and creating the necessary culture can significantly impact environmental degradation.

ACKNOWLEDGMENT

This research received no specific grant from any funding agency in the public, commercial, or not-for-profit sectors.

REFERENCES

Akin, C. S. (2014). The impact of foreign trade, energy consumption and income on CO2 emissions. *International Journal of Energy Economics and Policy*, *4*(3), 465.

Al-Mulali, U., Ozturk, I., & Solarin, S. A. (2016). Investigating the environmental Kuznets curve hypothesis in seven regions: The role of renewable energy. *Ecological Indicators*, *67*, 267–282. doi:10.1016/j.ecolind.2016.02.059

Aldieri, L., & Vinci, C. P. (2018). Green economy and sustainable development: The economic impact of innovation on employment. *Sustainability*, *10*(10), 3541. doi:10.3390u10103541

Apergis, N., Payne, J. E., Menyah, K., & Wolde-Rufael, Y. (2010). On the causal dynamics between emissions, nuclear energy, renewable energy, and economic growth. *Ecological Economics*, *69*(11), 2255–2260. doi:10.1016/j.ecolecon.2010.06.014

Bailey, I., & Caprotti, F. (2014). The green economy: Functional domains and theoretical directions of enquiry. *Environment & Planning A*, *46*(8), 1797–1813. doi:10.1068/a130102p

Barbier, E. (2011). The policy challenges for green economy and sustainable economic development. *Natural Resources Forum*, *35*(3), 233–245. doi:10.1111/j.1477-8947.2011.01397.x

Bordeianu, S. (1995). Political risk services and political risk yearbook: Edited William D. Coplin and Michael K. O'Leary. Syracuse, NY: Political Risk Services, 1994. 7 vols. $5,570.00 commercial subscribers (to the services), $750.00 (to the Yearbook). Journal of Government Information, 22(2), 186-188.

Bovenberg, A. L., & van der Ploeg, F. (1994). Environmental policy, public finance and the labour market in a second-best world. *Journal of Public Economics*, *55*(3), 349–390. doi:10.1016/0047-2727(93)01398-T

Claessens, S., & Yurtoglu, B. B. (2013). Corporate governance in emerging markets: A survey. *Emerging Markets Review*, *15*, 1–33. doi:10.1016/j.ememar.2012.03.002

Cole, M. A. (2004). Trade, the pollution haven hypothesis and the environmental Kuznets curve: Examining the linkages. *Ecological Economics*, *48*(1), 71–81. doi:10.1016/j.ecolecon.2003.09.007

Cristea, A., Hummels, D., Puzzello, L., & Avetisyan, M. (2013). Trade and the greenhouse gas emissions from international freight transport. *Journal of Environmental Economics and Management*, *65*(1), 153–173. doi:10.1016/j.jeem.2012.06.002

Cuomo, F., Mallin, C., & Zattoni, A. (2016). Corporate governance codes: A review and research agenda. *Corporate Governance*, *24*(3), 222–241. doi:10.1111/corg.12148

Djankov, S., McLiesh, C., & Klein, M. U. (Eds.). (2004). *Doing business in 2004: understanding regulation* (Vol. 1). World Bank Publications.

Fani, M., & Norouzi, N. (2020). Using Social and Economic Indicators for Modeling, Sensitivity Analysis and Forecasting the Gasoline Demand in the Transportation Sector: An ANN Approach in case study for Tehran metropolis. *Iranian Journal of Energy*, *23*(2), 71–91.

Guo, M., Nowakowska-Grunt, J., Gorbanyov, V., & Egorova, M. (2020). Green technology and sustainable development: Assessment and green growth frameworks. *Sustainability*, *12*(16), 6571. doi:10.3390u12166571

Hamdouch, A., & Depret, M. H. (2010). Policy integration strategy and the development of the 'green economy': Foundations and implementation patterns. *Journal of Environmental Planning and Management*, *53*(4), 473–490. doi:10.1080/09640561003703889

Hayek, F. A. (1945). The use of knowledge in society. *The American Economic Review*, *35*(4), 519–530.

Hu, W., & Wang, D. (2020). How does environmental regulation influence China's carbon productivity? An empirical analysis based on the spatial spillover effect. *Journal of Cleaner Production*, *257*, 120484. doi:10.1016/j.jclepro.2020.120484

Jalilian, H., Kirkpatrick, C., & Parker, D. (2007). The impact of regulation on economic growth in developing countries: A cross-country analysis. *World Development*, *35*(1), 87–103. doi:10.1016/j.worlddev.2006.09.005

Kaufmann, D., Kraay, A., & Mastruzzi, M. (2004). Governance matters III: Governance indicators for 1996, 1998, 2000, and 2002. *The World Bank Economic Review, 18*(2), 253–287. doi:10.1093/wber/lhh041

Kaufmann, D., Kraay, A., & Mastruzzi, M. (2005). *Governance matters IV: governance indicators for 1996-2004*. World bank policy research working paper series, (3630).

Khoshnava, S. M., Rostami, R., Zin, R. M., Štreimikienė, D., Yousefpour, A., Strielkowski, W., & Mardani, A. (2019). Aligning the criteria of green economy (GE) and sustainable development goals (SDGs) to implement sustainable development. *Sustainability, 11*(17), 4615. doi:10.3390u11174615

Kiviaho, J., Nikkinen, J., Piljak, V., & Rothovius, T. (2014). The co-movement dynamics of European frontier stock markets. *European Financial Management, 20*(3), 574–595. doi:10.1111/j.1468-036X.2012.00646.x

La Porta, R., Lopez-de-Silanes, F., Shleifer, A., & Vishny, R. (2002). Investor protection and corporate valuation. *The Journal of Finance, 57*(3), 1147–1170. doi:10.1111/1540-6261.00457

La Porta, R., Lopez-de-Silanes, F., Shleifer, A., & Vishny, R. W. (1997). Legal determinants of external finance. *The Journal of Finance, 52*(3), 1131–1150. doi:10.1111/j.1540-6261.1997.tb02727.x

Li, J., & Lin, B. (2016). Green economy performance and green productivity growth in China's cities: Measures and policy implication. *Sustainability, 8*(9), 947. doi:10.3390u8090947

Loiseau, E., Saikku, L., Antikainen, R., Droste, N., Hansjürgens, B., Pitkänen, K., Leskinen, P., Kuikman, P., & Thomsen, M. (2016). Green economy and related concepts: An overview. *Journal of Cleaner Production, 139*, 361–371. doi:10.1016/j.jclepro.2016.08.024

Milani, B. (2000). *Designing the green economy: The postindustrial alternative to corporate globalization*. Rowman & Littlefield.

Norouzi, N. (2021a). The Pahlev Reliability Index: A measurement for the resilience of power generation technologies versus climate change. *Nuclear Engineering and Technology, 53*(5), 1658–1663. doi:10.1016/j.net.2020.10.013

Norouzi, N. (2021b). Post-COVID-19 and globalization of oil and natural gas trade: Challenges, opportunities, lessons, regulations, and strategies. *International Journal of Energy Research, 45*(10), 14338–14356. doi:10.1002/er.6762 PMID:34219899

Norouzi, N., & Ataei, E. (2021). Covid-19 Crisis and Environmental law: Opportunities and challenges. *Hasanuddin Law Review, 7*(1), 46–60. doi:10.20956/halrev.v7i1.2772

Norouzi, N., de Rubens, G. Z., Choupanpiesheh, S., & Enevoldsen, P. (2020a). When pandemics impact economies and climate change: Exploring the impacts of COVID-19 on oil and electricity demand in China. *Energy Research & Social Science, 68*, 101654. doi:10.1016/j.erss.2020.101654 PMID:32839693

Norouzi, N., & Fani, M. (2020a). The impacts of the novel corona virus on the oil and electricity demand in Iran and China. *Journal of Energy Management and Technology, 4*(4), 36–48.

Norouzi, N., & Fani, M. (2020b). Black gold falls, black plague arise-An Opec crude oil price forecast using a gray prediction model. *Upstream Oil and Gas Technology, 5*, 100015. doi:10.1016/j.upstre.2020.100015

Norouzi, N., & Fani, M. (2021). The prioritization and feasibility study over renewable technologies using fuzzy logic: A case study for Takestan plains. *Journal of Energy Management and Technology*, *5*(2), 12–22.

Norouzi, N., Fani, M., & Ziarani, Z. K. (2020b). The fall of oil Age: A scenario planning approach over the last peak oil of human history by 2040. *Journal of Petroleum Science Engineering*, *188*, 106827. doi:10.1016/j.petrol.2019.106827

Norouzi, N., & Kalantari, G. (2020). The sun food-water-energy nexus governance model a case study for Iran. *Water-Energy Nexus*, *3*, 72–80. doi:10.1016/j.wen.2020.05.005

Norouzi, N., Khanmohammadi, H. U., & Ataei, E. (2021b). The Law in the Face of the COVID-19 Pandemic: Early Lessons from Uruguay. *Hasanuddin Law Review*, *7*(2), 75–88. doi:10.20956/halrev.v7i2.2827

Norouzi, N., Zarazua de Rubens, G. Z., Enevoldsen, P., & Behzadi Forough, A. (2021a). The impact of COVID-19 on the electricity sector in Spain: An econometric approach based on prices. *International Journal of Energy Research*, *45*(4), 6320–6332. doi:10.1002/er.6259

Ollo-López, A., & Aramendía-Muneta, M. E. (2012). ICT impact on competitiveness, innovation and environment. *Telematics and Informatics*, *29*(2), 204–210. doi:10.1016/j.tele.2011.08.002

Pahle, M., Pachauri, S., & Steinbacher, K. (2016). Can the Green Economy deliver it all? Experiences of renewable energy policies with socio-economic objectives. *Applied Energy*, *179*, 1331–1341. doi:10.1016/j.apenergy.2016.06.073

Porter, M. E., & Van der Linde, C. (1995). Toward a new conception of the environment-competitiveness relationship. *The Journal of Economic Perspectives*, *9*(4), 97–118. doi:10.1257/jep.9.4.97

Stiglitz, J. (1998). The private uses of public interests: Incentives and institutions. *The Journal of Economic Perspectives*, *12*(2), 3–22. doi:10.1257/jep.12.2.3

Szyja, P. (2016). The role of the state in creating green economy. *Oeconomia Copernicana*, *7*(2), 207–222. doi:10.12775/OeC.2016.013

Vukovic, N., Pobedinsky, V., Mityagin, S., Drozhzhin, A., & Mingaleva, Z. (2019). A study on green economy indicators and modeling: Russian context. *Sustainability*, *11*(17), 4629. doi:10.3390u11174629

Vuola, M., Korkeakoski, M., Vähäkari, N., Dwyer, M. B., Hogarth, N. J., Kaivo-oja, J., Luukkanen, J., Chea, E., Thuon, T., & Phonhalath, K. (2020). What is a green economy? Review of national-level green economy policies in Cambodia and Lao PDR. *Sustainability*, *12*(16), 6664. doi:10.3390u12166664

Zhang, B., Wang, B., & Wang, Z. (2017). Role of renewable energy and non-renewable energy consumption on EKC: Evidence from Pakistan. *Journal of Cleaner Production*, *156*, 855–864. doi:10.1016/j.jclepro.2017.03.203

Zhao, M., Liu, F., Song, Y., & Geng, J. (2020). Impact of air pollution regulation and technological investment on sustainable development of green economy in Eastern China: Empirical analysis with panel data approach. *Sustainability*, *12*(8), 3073. doi:10.3390u12083073

ADDITIONAL READING

Anderson, V. (2006). Turning economics inside out. *International Journal of Green Economics*, *1*(1-2), 11–22. doi:10.1504/IJGE.2006.009334

Cato, M. S. (2012). *Green economics: an introduction to theory, policy and practice*. Routledge. doi:10.4324/9781849771528

Eichholtz, P., Kok, N., & Quigley, J. M. (2013). The economics of green building. *The Review of Economics and Statistics*, *95*(1), 50–63. doi:10.1162/REST_a_00291

Green, D. (2003). *Silent revolution: The rise and crisis of market economics in Latin America*. NYU Press.

Hahnel, R. (2014). *Green economics: Confronting the ecological crisis*. Routledge. doi:10.4324/9781315703947

Hydes, K. R., & Creech, L. (2000). Reducing mechanical equipment cost: The economics of green design. *Building Research and Information*, *28*(5-6), 403–407. doi:10.1080/096132100418555

Pearce, D. (1992). Green economics. *Environmental Values*, *1*(1), 3–13. doi:10.3197/096327192776680179

Smith, R., & World Economics Association. (2016). *Green capitalism: the god that failed*. London: College Publications.

KEY TERMS AND DEFINITIONS

Circularity: A circular economy (also referred to as "circularity") is an economic system that tackles global challenges like climate change, biodiversity loss, waste, and pollution. Most linear economy businesses take a natural resource and turn it into a product that is ultimately destined to become waste because it has been designed and made. This process is often summarised by "take, make, waste." By contrast, a circular economy uses reuse, sharing, repair, refurbishment, remanufacturing, and recycling to create a closed-loop system, minimize resource inputs, and create waste, pollution, and carbon emissions. The circular economy aims to keep products, materials, equipment, and infrastructure in use for longer, thus improving the productivity of these resources. Waste materials and energy should become input for other processes through waste valorization: either as a component or recovered resource for another industrial process or as regenerative resources for nature (e.g., compost). This regenerative approach contrasts with the traditional linear economy, which has a "take, make, dispose of" production model.

Eco Commerce: Eco commerce is a business, investment, and technology-development model that employs market-based solutions to balancing the world's energy needs and environmental integrity. Through green trading and green finance, eco-commerce promotes the further development of "clean technologies" such as wind power, solar power, biomass, and hydropower.

Eco-Tariffs: An Eco-tariff, also known as an environmental tariff, is a trade barrier erected to reduce pollution and improve the environment. These trade barriers may take the form of import or export taxes on products with a large carbon footprint or imported from countries with lax environmental regulations.

Emissions Trading: Emissions trading (also known as cap and trade, emissions trading scheme, or ETS) is a market-based approach to controlling pollution by providing economic incentives for reducing the emissions of pollutants.

Environmental Enterprise: An environmental enterprise is an environmentally friendly/compatible business. Specifically, an environmental enterprise is a business that produces value in the same manner which an ecosystem does, neither producing waste nor consuming unsustainable resources. In addition, an environmental enterprise rather finds alternative ways to produce one's products instead of taking advantage of animals for the sake of human profits. To be closer to being an environmentally friendly company, some environmental enterprises invest their money to develop or improve their technologies which are also environmentally friendly. In addition, environmental enterprises usually try to reduce global warming, so some companies use environmentally friendly materials to build their stores. They also set in environmentally friendly place regulations. All these efforts of the environmental enterprises can bring positive effects both for nature and people. The concept is rooted in the well-enumerated theories of natural capital, the eco-economy, and cradle-to-cradle design. Examples of environmental enterprises would be Seventh Generation, Inc., and Whole Foods.

Green Economy: A green economy is an economy that aims at reducing environmental risks and ecological scarcities and that aims for sustainable development without degrading the environment. It is closely related to ecological economics but has a more politically applied focus. The 2011 UNEP Green Economy Report argues "that to be green, and an economy must be not only efficient but also fair. Fairness implies recognizing global and country-level equity dimensions, particularly in assuring a Just Transition to an economy that is low-carbon, resource-efficient, and socially inclusive."

Green Politics: Green politics, or ecopolitics, is a political ideology that aims to foster an ecologically sustainable society often, but not always, rooted in environmentalism, nonviolence, social justice, and grassroots democracy. It began taking shape in the western world in the 1970s; since then, Green parties have developed and established themselves in many countries around the globe and have achieved some electoral success.

Low-Carbon Economy: A low-carbon economy (LCE) or decarbonized economy is based on low-carbon power sources with minimal greenhouse gas (GHG) emissions into the atmosphere, specifically carbon dioxide. GHG emissions due to anthropogenic (human) activity are the dominant cause of observed climate change since the mid-20th century. Continued emission of greenhouse gases may cause long-lasting changes worldwide, increasing the likelihood of severe, pervasive, and irreversible effects for people and ecosystems.

Natural Resource Economics: Natural resource economics deals with the supply, demand, and allocation of the Earth's natural resources. One main objective of natural resource economics is to understand better the role of natural resources in the economy to develop more sustainable methods of managing those resources to ensure their future generations. Resource economists study interactions between economic and natural systems intending to develop a sustainable and efficient economy.

Sustainable Development: Sustainable development is an organizing principle for meeting human development goals while simultaneously sustaining the ability of natural systems to provide the natural resources and ecosystem services on which the economy and society depend. The desired result is a state of society where living conditions and resources are used to continue to meet human needs without undermining the integrity and stability of the natural system. Sustainable development can be defined as development that meets the needs of the present without compromising the ability of future generations to meet their own needs. Sustainability goals, such as the current UN-level Sustainable Development Goals, address the global challenges, including poverty, inequality, climate change, environmental degradation, peace, and justice.

Chapter 14
Strategic Organizational Resilience as a Response to the Crisis:
Towards a Recovery of SMEs

José G. Vargas-Hernández
https://orcid.org/0000-0003-0938-4197
Posgraduate and Research Department, Tecnológico Mario Molina Unidad Zapopan, Mexico

María Fernanda F. Higuera Cota
https://orcid.org/0000-0001-8285-1076
Autonomous University of Baja California, Mexico

ABSTRACT

SMEs, like other organizations, are subject to risk and change in an uncertain environment today more than ever with the economic effects of the COVID-19 pandemic. That is why this study aims to analyze resilience at a strategic level in organizations and the factors that make up organizational resilience. The analysis starts from the assumption that SMEs need to implement a cultural change to respond to crises and disruptions. From a strategic perspective, the chapter provides the concept of organizational resilience, the elements that make it up, and identifies the necessary actions to carry out more flexible and progressive strategies. The study concludes that SMEs require a cultural change, where the main objective is the creation of innovative and creative environments to face crises, through an adaptation and response system based on strategies that consider the resources and capacities of each productive unit.

INTRODUCTION

The world is experiencing changes in all areas - cultural, economic, geopolitical, social, technological, among others - which increase for some countries the possibilities of growth, while they generate new economic scenarios that can be exploited. However, the situation described above does not impact in

DOI: 10.4018/978-1-6684-5109-0.ch014

the same way for all countries, especially for developing countries. Rather, in some cases it aggravates pre-existing problems of poverty, unemployment, underemployment, violence, etc. and if to that are added the crises experienced worldwide in recent decades:

The 1937 recession during the recovery from the Great Depression, characterized by a contraction in the money supply caused by the policies of the Federal Reserve and the Treasury Department by contractionary fiscal policies, which included reduced public spending and increased tax collection through tax revenue from citizens (Ocampo, Stallings, Belloso & Frenkel, 2017).

The 1945 recession was a direct result of the post-war period, a conflict that involved more than 70 countries and caused great damage to the world economy, especially in Europe and the United States (Rapoport & Brenta, 2010).

In 1975 another recession arose called the recession of the 70s, considered as a period of economic stagnation, derived from a combination of recession and high inflation and an oil crisis that took place in 1973 and the collapse of the management system Bretton Woods international economy with the famous "Nixon Shock". It consisted of the implementation of changes to the economic and foreign relations policies of the United States government in 1971, under the mandate of then-President Richard Nixon, which included ending the convertibility of the dollar to gold.

Another crisis of great magnitude was the one that arose in late 2008 and early 2009, the collapse of the United States real estate market due to the financial crisis and the subprime mortgage crisis (Jaramillo & Jaramillo, 2016).

The most current crisis is the health crisis that began in the city of Wuhan, China, at the end of 2019, generated by the COVID-19 virus, which has an important impact worldwide, by hitting the productive and business structure. And although it is very difficult to predict the intensity and duration of the current crisis, it is possible to identify some of its specificities.

As can be seen, the crises described above are global phenomena that affect all the countries of the world, although the impact is different in each region. However, all of them are characterized by slow economic growth, less dynamism in international trade, and changes in consumption and production patterns.

In a scenario like the one presented, it is usual for many people to think about creating small and medium-sized enterprises (SMEs). In addition to being of great importance for the productive fabric, because on a global scale according to figures from the International Council for Small Enterprises, SMEs represent between 96 and 99 percent of all formal companies and generate between 60 and 70 percent of employment, while contributing close to 50 percent of GDP (Romero, 2006), that is why they cannot be left out of this process.

Unfortunately, the COVID-19 pandemic since 2020 is having a very profound impact on the economy and society. ECLAC estimated that by the end of 2020 2.7 million companies, equivalent to 19% of all companies in the region, closed. In the case of microenterprises, this percentage reached 21%. And although the concept of resilience has gained importance in the study of organizations for a few decades, it is necessary to review from a strategic perspective the approach to organizational resilience, to face the challenges posed by the effects of COVID-19 for the SMEs. In addition to other obstacles that SMEs face such as disorder, disasters, catastrophes, possible failures, cycle of decline or collapse, among others.

Thus, the following question arises, what are the key elements for the development of organizational resilience at a strategic level? And from a strategic perspective, what actions are necessary for SMEs to develop in a resilient way? The previous two questions are essential to understand what the actions are that SMEs should take in the face of crises and disruptions.

HISTORY OF THE PROBLEM

Countries, communities, organizations, and individuals are prone to a diverse and changing environment; The threats posed by this sometimes-turbulent environment can vary in severity and frequency and can originate internally or externally (Quiñonez & Prado-Solís, 2017). In the business context, organizations today face a higher level of pressure from the external environment due to the rapid evolution of business circumstances, the environment in which they compete is increasingly dynamic; Today's increasingly chaotic business environments require organizations to be more resilient (Kantur & Iseri-Say, 2012).

The environment has challenged companies to create and implement strategies to face risks and compete in an environment of uncertainty. Those organizations that can survive over time in the face of current and future challenges are known as "resilient organizations". "Organizations will only be able to improve their resilience if there is clarity about the concept and the variables that determine resilience so that they can be continuously evaluated, developed and improved over time" (Hillmann & Guenther, 2020: 26).

Resilience, "the ability of a dynamic system to successfully adapt to disturbances that threaten the functioning, viability or development of the system" (Masten, 2014: 10). The scarce use of organizational resilience terms prevails and the lack of common understanding about essential concepts, organizational resilience adaptability, adaptive innovation and engineering resilience, adaptive innovation strategies, among others.

JUSTIFICATION

Although there are innumerable approaches to the study of organizational resilience within academic publications, the concepts, characteristics and uses have remained largely undefined and ambiguous until now (Quiñonez & Prado-Solis, 2017). Resilience is considered as "the ability of a system to absorb shocks and reorganize while undergoing changes to continue to market essentially the same feedback function, structure and identity (Folke, 2016: 44).

The concept of "resilience" as the archetype of organizations is relatively young, but it continues to gain importance in academia. There is a growing literature on what resilience means for individuals, communities and countries, the academic literature has been particularly abundant in providing different interpretations of the term.

However, the debate on the use of the term resilience in the business environment arises from the need for organizations to be constantly aware of the challenges that could erode their entire existence and thus take the appropriate measures to anticipate such events. For this reason, and due to the current challenges faced by SMEs because of the COVID-19 crisis, in this research we opted to deepen organizational resilience from a strategic approach, seeking to take advantage of and develop strategic options.

CONCEPTUAL AND THEORICAL FRAMEWORK

After reviewing some concepts of organizational resilience, for this research work, the concept used is organizational resilience, it is the capacity of organizations based on cultural change to make sense of the environment and thus manage the available resources to take advantage of and develop strategic options (Ates & Bititci 2011).

Organizational Resilience

Organizational resilience is defined as capacity, behavior, strategy, result, performance, among other concepts. Organizational resilience has a strategic role (Carmeli & Markman,2011; by Oliveira-Teixeira & Werther,2013; Hamel & Välikangas,2003) and also has a relevant role at the operational level, such as the supply chain, to maintain the provision and functionality of the service (Jüttner & Maklan, 2011; Pettit, Fiksel & Croxton2010; Ponomarov & Holcomb,2009; Sheffi & Rice,2005; Zsidisin & Wagner,2010). Organizational resilience is being analyzed from the perspectives of systemic, psychological, social, and strategic management.

Resilience is the capacity of strategic awareness linked to management to face in advance any disruption from internal and external shocks and unexpected events (Annarelli & Nonino 2016). At the organizational level, resilience can be adjusted in challenging conditions (Sutcliffe & Vogus, 2003) that involve the ability to recover from the event of risk and disorder to maintain the ability to function, in turn, it is considered a strategic advantage (Gittel *et al.* 2006). Strategic organizational resilience is an imperative for survivable data entry applications to address and mitigate risks.

Resilience from the Psychological Perspective and Systemic Management

Resilience theories assume that resilience is an inherent trait of personality (Fletcher & Sarkar, 2013) and includes protective factors for a coping strategy that allows recovery from any psychological stressor (Earvolino-Ramirez, 2007). The resilience literature is based on theories of resource-based vision (RBV), based on capabilities and strategy (Barney 2001, 2001a).

Resilience as a property is related to negative events such as surviving and adapting to interruptions (Bell, 2002; Horne III & Orr, 1998; Hu, Li & Holloway, 2008; Lengnick-Hall & Beck 2009; Sheffi & Rice, 2005), threats (Bhamidipaty et al., 2007; Dewald & Bowen, 2010) disasters and catastrophes (Alblas & Jayaram, 2015); challenging conditions (Sutcliffe & Vogus, 2003; Vogus & Sutcliffe, 2007); disturbances (Hollnagel, 2010; Linnenluecke & Griffiths, 2012; Mamouni-Limnios et al., 2014); or changes (Fiksel, 2006; Grøtan & Asbjørnslett, 2007; Mafabi et al., 2015), as is the case of SMEs, given the prolonged closure from the COVID-19 pandemic, as a result of confinement, where not all companies were able to cover the accumulated costs due to the fall in sales and were pushed beyond their survival thresholds.

Resilience is more than the property of an adaptive and response system. Adaptation and resilience as responses depend on the type of change. Resilience leads to accelerated change (Linnenluecke &

Griffiths, 2012). Organizational resilience has as potential sources of effective responses in the event of unexpected events DIY, wisdom, virtual role systems and interactions.

Resilience is the ability of a company to survive, adapt and grow even in times of turbulent change (Pettit et al. 2010, 2013). Resilience is the ability of systems to anticipate and adapt to potential failures. Resilience is the ability to adapt to new and complex problems without interrupting the functioning of the system (Borges & Menegon 2012). Resilience is defined as the ability to focus on adaptation and derive the resilience dimension from flexibility, vulnerability, adaptability, efficiency, and other indicators.

Resilience is the ability to adapt and change behavior by focusing on adaptation (Huber et al. 2012; Øien 2013; Bhamra et al. 2011). Organizational adaptation to environmental changes requires resilience (Collis 1991). Resilience is also a desirable strategic organization. Resilience is positive adaptation despite diversity (Fleming & Ledogar, 2008). Resilience should reflect social and human factors such as agility, adaptation, and rapid response of organizations in developing a diverse and enduring portfolio despite a stressful and turbulent environment (Coullahan & Pastor, 2008). Resilience is the ability to recognize, adapt and face the unexpected (Woods & Hollnagel, 2006).

Resilience is the ability of a system to anticipate and manage risk (Hollnagel *et al.* 2006; McDonald 2006) through the adaptation of actions and processes to ensure operation in disruptive events (Dalziell & McManus, 2004). Resilience is the ability to face and adapt to stress from risks, disasters, or crises to survive and reduce damage (Pelling, 2003). The safety and reliability perspective are related to the concepts of anticipation or awareness and adaptability to resilience.

Increasing organizational resilience requires innovation and creativity to generate new ideas characterized by originality of thought and imagination. There are factors and mechanisms that contribute to resilience despite the use of different terms such as creativity and innovation, improvisation, building awareness of the situation, vulnerabilities, improvisation capacity, people's resilience, flexibility, robustness, and redundancy. Organizational resilience is a strategy designed and implemented to promote the resilience of the organizational community to survive and achieve success after a disaster (Bhamra *et al.*, 2011; Lee *et al.*, 2013).

Organizational Resilience and its Relationship with Innovation

The concept of resilience has been treated from multiple disciplinary perspectives including ecology, engineering, safety, reliability, positive psychology, organizational development, strategic management, among others. The interesting thing here is that, regardless of which discipline is approached, organizational resilience always points to the capacities that companies must absorb unexpected events, the development of specific responses in certain situations, and the participation in transformative activities.

Along the same lines of the disciplines, there are various theories that strengthen organizational resilience, for example, from the theory of resources and capacities, this is used as a strategy to strengthen the phenomena of organizational resilience during and after facing a crisis and achieving higher rates of organizational development and growth. It should be noted that the principles that support organizational resilience are leadership, strategic and operational planning, performance, among others. "The most important factors of organizational resilience in the emergency response of an organization are the development and development of knowledge" (Gečienė, 2021: 41).

Additionally, organizational resilience is a framework for managing resources in a coherent strategy aimed at developing organizational capabilities. The organizational resistance framework is formed by the linking of principles, components and attributes destined to design, develop, and implement organizational strategies to achieve growth and continuous improvement. The construction of organizational resilience capacities requires the adjustment of strategies during the cycle of decline, collapse, and reconstruction, where the organizational resilience framework increases the capacity for adaptability and agility to respond to disruptive events.

Resilience promotes development, transformation and innovation while generating new configurations under internal and external shocks (Folke, 2006). Some of the indicators of organizational resilience are the capacity for innovation, creativity, improvisation, collaboration, monitoring the situation and reporting (Lee et al., 2013; Ates & Bititci, 2011). Hence, it is considered that organizational resilience is linked to innovation, in the words of Akgün and Halit (2014) innovation influences organizational resilience conceived as the ability to absorb and develop responses to participate in transformative activities that lead to a better performance and capitalize on disruptions that threaten the organization.

Likewise, for Mafabi *et al.* (2012) organizational resilience is linked to innovation, but, in turn, is linked to knowledge management responding to the environmental demands of organizational adaptation, effective and efficient service provision, promoting competitiveness and value respectable. Another element in common between organizational innovation and resilience is that both approaches work in collaboration with all stakeholders and stakeholders cannot separate their functions and processes to face risks and mitigate threats through empowerment to take advantage of all the opportunities. Organizational resilience transgresses the guidelines and becomes a tool of disruptive innovation in practice. Likewise, Reinmoeller & Dardwiik (2005) consider organizational resilience as the ability to self-renew through innovation over time.

Along these lines, the response of organizational resilience is adaptation and openness to preserve long-term survival and the functioning of systems (Handmer & Dovers, 1996). Placing adaptability as another element of great importance for the development of organizational resilience. Authors such as Sullivan-Taylor & Branicki (2011) consider that the most resilient organizations are those that are adapted and formed by people who trust and support each other. They also point out that resilience risk and protective factors must be based on capabilities, such as the ability to become flexible and adaptable to respond to changes.

Similarly, Daneses *et al.* (2009) define organizational resilience as the ability of owners to respond and adapt to stressful events to solve problems, again highlighting adaptability as a key element for organizational resilience.

Adaptive Innovation and Organizational Resilience

Resilience is the individual, organizational and community capacity to resist, absorb, adapt, and recover a better state after a disruptive event (McManus et al, 2008). "Resilience is contextually specific, much as evolving thinking in the field of public health now emphasizes - precision public health - identifying the most at-risk localities and then targeting interventions to their unique contexts, rather than always seeking generalizable mechanisms that support well-being. being of entire populations (Ungar, 2021: 10).

Organizational resilience is formed by the balance of preventive control, conscious action, performance optimization and adaptive innovation. According to Nemeth (2009: 3), organizational resilience focuses on organizational recovery from irregular variations and unstable operations. That is, preventive actions are related to the ability to detect environmental and organizational disturbances and critical developments, adapt, and react proactively to future changes. Adaptive innovation in organizational resilience is created through the exploration and invention of new technologies and markets. Organizations respond to failures through resilience actions to reinforce preventive control, training, and participation in adaptive innovation and conscious action (Denver & Pilbeam, 2015).

Thus, an adaptive innovation approach is necessary for the design of organizational resilience, as well as the implementation of more flexible strategies to create, invest and discover new products and markets in a market environment competitive (Denver, 2017). In the words of Hoffmann (2016) ecosystems increase resilience through access and adaptation to new technologies, flexibility and the exchange of assets and cost reduction, while organizations can increase resilience through managerial efforts that assess internal and external challenges with collaborative partnerships and strategic alliances and deployment of resources.

Returning to the contributions of Denver and Pilbeam (2015) where they express the importance of invention and new technologies in the development of organizational resilience, there is a vast literature that agrees that organizational resilience is also influenced by resilience engineering. For resilience engineering anchors the concept of resilience and its development of characteristics in the operational means for its evaluation (McDonald, 2006, Patterson & Dutch, 2015).

Resilience Engineering and its Influence on Organizational Resilience

Resilience engineering is a new concept of thinking about a problem, security, opportunities, methods, and tools to assess organizational capacity and build strong and flexible processes (Pellissier, 2011; Omidvar et al. 2017). Organizational resilience is based on resilience engineering principles that provide the basis for designing, improving, and controlling resilience (Huber et al. 2012; Øien 2013; Pellissier 2011; Erol *et al.* 2010).

Organizational resilience is formed by the balance of preventive control, conscious action, performance optimization and adaptive innovation. And as engineering resilience is the construction of systems to maintain normal function under a variety of conditions and recover it after external forces return to a desired range (Woods & Hollnagel, 2006), engineering resilience becomes another. decisive element to anticipate responses from the system.

Resilience engineering has been studied from various perspectives, from the ecosystem perspective, it seeks persistence and rebound to the previous state before the crisis until it is robust (Pimm, 1984). While, from ergonomic studies, resilience engineering focuses on the ability of the system to recover, adjust, preserve, monitor, and maintain its operation, in the short term to minimize damage costs (Hollnagel, Woods & Leveson, 2006; Kikuchi & Yamaguchi, 2012). "In summary, engineering resilience illustrated the stability foundation of ecosystem science, while also serving as an objective that could complement efficiency- management based on efficiency or misguided conservation efforts" (Cañizarez, Copeland & Doorn, 2021: 8).

Thus, the resilience of systems engineering operates in a reliable pattern defined on a variety of independent parameters. That is, the organization can maintain adequate organizational performance aimed at limiting the number of organizational errors (Bieńkowska, Tworek and Zablocka-klucza, 2020). For Di Gravio, Mancini, Patriarca and Constantino (2015), engineering resilience seeks the design and implementation of models that respond to emerging conditions that cause system failures. In other words, preventive actions are related to the ability to detect environmental and organizational disturbances, critical developments and to react proactively to future changes.

The resilience engineering perspective designs systems based on redundancy, flexibility, and adaptability. That is why resilience engineering is considered a new paradigm of organizational innovation

(Pellissier, 2011), it seeks to maintain a competitive advantage through the ability to deliver performance while, paradoxically, innovating and adapting to turbulent changes. Thus, the resilience approach to nonlinearity is proactive adaptability rather than reactive changes (Howard-Grenville *et al.*, 2014).

The foundation of the organizational resilience engineering perspective is in the security domain and focuses on people at all levels of organizations who create security through their practices and view security as the positive presence of something (Dekker *et al.*, 2008). Like Dekker *et al.* (2008) Bergstrom et al. (2015) consider that organizational resilience has implications for security resulting from interactions at different levels, especially in complex systems even when there are external concerns.

STRATEGIC ORGANIZATIONAL RESILIENCE

Resilience is defined as an organizational and operational and strategic capacity using different research methods, focused on specific problems in different contexts (Ismail *et al.* 2011). In turn, organizational resilience is understood as an essential quality developed to achieve a competitive advantage through the strategic use of resources and capabilities aimed at strategically challenging and facing adverse events and conditions and avoiding the collapse of resources (Manfield & Newey, 2015). For Acquaah *et al.* (2011) resilience is the result of various mechanisms of family and non-family equifinality, considered as the ability of organizations to align strategies in competitive advantages. That is, organizational resilience is a strategic initiative to change operations and increase competitiveness (Sheffi & Rice 2005).

Recent approaches to organizational resilience focus on strategies as sources (Reinmoeller & van Baardwijk, 2005; Carmeli & Markman, 2011) or processes (Alesi, 2008; Ates & Bititci2011;). Available resources and strategy have an impact on the development of organizational resilience to maintain in a variety of operating conditions. Organizations operating on the edge develop resilience and exploration capacities, among others, and pursue external search and rotation strategies (Marcus & Nichols, 1999). Hence, the interest in deepening strategic organizational resilience, which is considered a form of strategic response capacity (Burnard & Bhamra, 2011) that is achieved through the development and adjustments of new and existing resources in response to the condition's unstable economics (Suire & Vicente, 2014).

In the context of organizations, synchronization of communications and messaging strategies facilitate organizational resilience and influence subsequent behavioral outcomes, including job performance during crisis situations. Organizational resilience is the ability of the company to make sense of its environment, generate strategic options and realign its resources faster than its rivals to obtain a decisive advantage (Ates & Bititci, 2001).

Another contextual factor in the domain of organizational resilience behavior is the influence of national culture on shared purpose and value that influences strategic choice and leadership styles (Acar & Winfrey, 1994; Colisión, 1991). A methodological approach Organizational culture embedded in continuous management that incorporates strategic planning can improve organizational resilience in the pursuit of risk mitigation (IBM Corporation, 2004). Companies establish corporate cultures that facilitate information, establish organizational goals, design, and implement strategies empowered by better vision, foresight, and knowledge.

Culture development and strategy for resilience vary between organizations and have a greater impact than engineering for resilience. Other factors suggested by other authors are organizational transparency, risk interdependencies, the development of viability in the organization, alignment between strategy and objectives, organizational knowledge on resilience, awareness of the situation, the uses of situational awareness and measures to assess resilience (Starr *et al.*, 2003).

Organizational leadership that demonstrates qualities and commitment to managing risk and preparing for unexpected disruptions to implement collaborative strategies in a collaborative effort to improve and increase healthy organizational culture and resilience. Leadership and culture of service, relationships prepared for change and networks are independent attributes. Networks of internal and external relationships are identified by indicators of effective partnerships, leverage of knowledge, breaking silos, and internal resources.

Actions to Improve Organizational Resilience

Organizational resilience requires sufficient resources and strategic coherence considering operational stability. Resilience resources are those with little or no sustained dependency during a collapse and recovery of strategic resources. Organizational resilience is concerned with intervention, responsiveness, strategic formalization of activities, planned interventions, and informed experiences to support survival, growth, and maturity through crisis events.

Resilience systems have been linked to some functionalities capable of responding to any type of events, anticipating future threats and opportunities, learning from the past, monitoring solutions and being able to promote proactive strategies (Rankin, Lundberg & Woltier, 2014). Organizational resilience is viewed as a positive and forward-looking rather than defensive strategic enabler for more flexible, anticipatory, and proactive organizations that seize opportunities.

Increasing organizational resilience is achieved by seeking mitigation strategies aimed at balancing competition objectives, reducing costs, in disruptive events, addressing vulnerability and the impact of known and unknown risks, and strengthening the organizational system against the threats. Ensuring resilience requires robust creativity such as the ability to anticipate and adapt to critical strategic change (Marwa & Milner, 2013). It is through contingency planning that the organization will be able to respond to an emergency.

Planning enables change in the organization identified by the indicator's unit of purpose, proactive stance, planning strategies, and stress test plans. That is, business planning is a strategy to promote and improve organizational resilience capacities to resist and maintain operations during a crisis (Speight, 2011). Strategic planning and development planning and crisis management can improve the resilience of the organization. Strategic management must include organizational stability, change and resilience.

Even with strategic planning, some organizations may be limited in the resources to implement planning activities. Furthermore, planning activities do not necessarily result in the social capital necessary for organizational resilience. However, the development of organizational resilience can be strengthened through strategic human resource management practices. According to Lengnick-Hall *et al.* (2011) the strategic development of human resources improves organizational resilience.

Another important aspect within organizational resilience is operational management, for Annarelli & Nonino (2016) organizational resilience faces internal and external disruptions of unexpected events by linking operational management. That is, by aligning your manufacturing strategies with the competitive strategy, resulting in a competitive advantage and superior performance. On the other hand, Kiuchi & Shireman (1999) consider that organizational resilience is a performance indicator, which considers and emphasizes the stage of the organization's life cycle and, consequently, the strategies developed by it. In other words, organizational resilience is associated with business responses in strategic renewal (Chan, 2011; Suire & Vicente, 2014).

Local companies implement different resilience strategies after crises and disruptions depending on their resources, considering the ability to survive, adapt and grow in turbulent times (Lengnick-Hall et al., 2011; Stucliffe & Vongus, 2003; Dahles & Susilowati, 2015). The concept of resilience is used by organizations to precipitate the development of capacities for the strategic formalization of the business context.

Due to their innovative nature, SMEs - by adapting to various functions, being flexible in the face of certain market changes, the ability to serve small markets, limited production capacity, usually informal distribution channels, among other challenges - share characteristics such as a potential strategically resilient formalization. planning activities. Resilience is determined by historical, developmental, and strategic factors associated with operational disruptions, crisis recovery, and strategic renewal and develops growth-survival-maturity (Herbane, 2019; Blundel, 2013; Doern, 2016).

THE RELEVANT FINDIGNS OF THEORICAL STUDIES

To identify the actions to take advantage of and develop strategic options to respond to the current challenges faced by SMEs because of the COVID-19 pandemic, this research opted to deepen organizational resilience. The objective of this paper is to analyze resilience at a strategic level in organizations, and the factors that compose it. In other words, the study seeks to identify the actions that allow designing, creating, investing, and discovering new products and markets in a competitive environment.

Organizational resilience experiences in organizations conceptualized in strategic planning and the conditions that configure entrepreneurial activities lead to survival, transformation, and growth. Strategic planning is linked to organizational resilience and performance associated with improving responses to any acute disruption.

Strategic renewal and organizational resilience in organizations in general and SMEs contribute to analyzing entrepreneurial activities in relation to the crisis, between resilience and social capital (Gao, Sung & Zhang, 2013). The strategic renewal of the resilience of organizations is characterized by reinvention (Demmer, Vickery & Calantone, 2011).

Strategic and resilience planning in organizations can be measured in different dimensions and functional areas and vision and mission statements (O'Reagan & Ghobadian, 2007; Peyrefitte, 2012). Organizational resilience is being analyzed from the perspectives of systemic, psychological, social, and strategic management.

Figure 1.

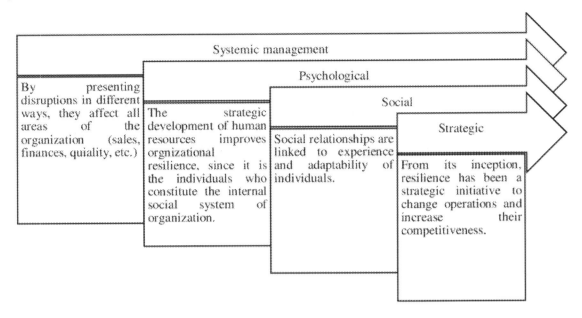

As can be seen in Figure 1, there are multiple perspectives from which organizational resilience can be approached, but it is the study of them together that leads us to the desired results, since they are all interrelated, especially when analyzed from a strategic level, because through this it is able to face adverse events and conditions to avoid the collapse of resources.

On the other hand, more tactical methods, and approaches to strengthening organizational resilience in specific areas, such as the supply chain, are not well developed, as demonstrated during the recent COVID-19 crisis, in part due to a lack of data. and collaboration between functional areas, high costs, and the inability to measure strategic benefits (Marchese & O'Dwyer, 2014). Organizing and planning activities are necessary before, during and after the disaster. The indicators of these activities to measure organizational resilience, proposed by Stephenson (2010), are planning strategies, participation in exercises, proactive posture, external resources, and recovery priorities.

In addition, organizational resilience must be linked to innovation and knowledge management from an adaptive approach, considering that organizational resilience points to the capacities that SMEs possess to absorb unexpected events. Another element that should not be forgotten to include is engineering as it is the basis for the design, improvement, and control of the resilience of organizations, all this through two actions, operational management, and strategic planning as observed in Figure 2.

Figure 2.

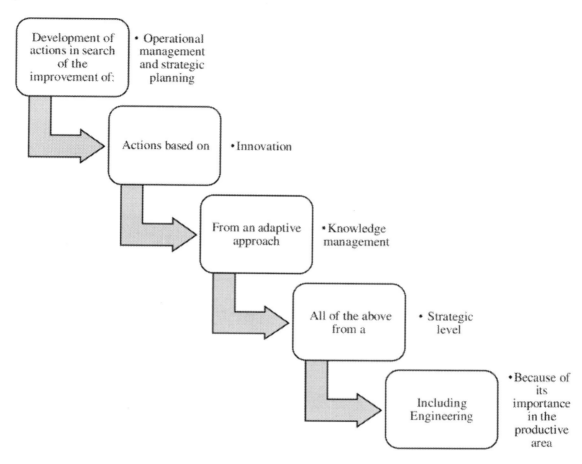

Thus, organizational resilience develops to resurface from unexpected events that lead to declines in market share and earnings and disrupt its ability to continue operations necessary to meet shareholder expectations. In addition, it was found that advances in the measurement of organizational resilience can be based on resilience engineering, moving from the conceptualization of the resilience of indicators to measurement.

Lastly, organizational resilience requires strategic agility aimed at seizing unexpected opportunities. Resilience is itself strategic and operational agility. The development of this strategic organizational agility leads to capabilities that meet market demands and alternative options for growth (Ismail, *et al.*, 2011).

CONCLUSION

This analysis concludes that organizational resilience and innovation developed from an adaptive approach achieve organizational resilience as the ability to self-renew at a strategic level. Also, organizational resilience is seen as an imperative for survivability imputation applications to address and mitigate risks. The shift to organizational resilience as recovery from adversity unlocks new value to focus on organizational transformation and driven innovation to help in adverse conditions. While engineering resilience is related to system stability, evolution focuses on the change and growth of a system.

Organizational resilience theory explains that adaptation and response systems will largely depend on the type of change. And when it comes to crises or disruptions, great ideas are required to deal with these adverse conditions. That is why innovation and engineering are necessary to address organizational resilience. Given that by using both, we postulate the congruence between innovation from an adaptive approach and resilience in engineering that converge in making analytical decisions that enable the development of strategies after crises and disruptions, through organizational contingency planning.

Finally, although the results presented here are encouraging, by providing a guideline of the elements that are needed for proper operational management and strategic planning in a crisis scenario. More empirical research on organizational resilience is needed to demonstrate the value of a contingency planning strategy that emphasizes the risks and vulnerabilities of the organization rather than the availability of assets and resources (Speight, 2011).

REFERENCES

Acar, W., & Winfrey, F. (1994). The resilient organization: Maintaining organizational renewal and performance. *J Strateg Change.*, *3*(3), 165–173. doi:10.1002/jsc.4240030307

Acquaah, M., Amoako-Gyampah, K., & Jayaram, J. (2011). Resilience in Family and Non-Family Businesses: An Examination of the Relationships Between Manufacturing Strategy, Competitive Strategy, and Business Performance. *International Journal of Production Research*, *49*(18), 5527–5544. doi:10.1080/00207543.2011.563834

Akgün, M., & Halit, K. (2014). Organizational resilience and firm product innovation and performance. *International Journal of Production Research*, *52*(23), 6918–6937. doi:10.1080/00207543.2014.910624

Alblas, A. & Jayaram, J. (2015). Designing resilience in the context of the fuzzy interface (FFE): an empirical examination. *International Journal of Research on Production*, *53*(22), 6820-6838.

Alesi, P. (2008). Build resilience across the company by integrating business continuity capability into day-to-day business culture and technology. *Journal of Business Continuity & Emergency Planning*, *2*, 214–220. PMID:21339108

Annarelli, A., & Nonino, F. (2016). Strategic and Operational Management of Organizational Resilience: Current Status of Research and Future Directions. *Omega*, *62*, 1–18. doi:10.1016/j.omega.2015.08.004

Ates, A., & Bititci, U. (2011). Change Process: A Key Enabler for Building Resilient SMEs. *International Journal of Production Research*, *49*(18), 5601–5618. doi:10.1080/00207543.2011.563825

Barney, J. (2001). Resource-Based Theories of Competitive Advantage: A Ten-Year Retrospective on the Resource-Based View. *Journal of Management*, *6*(6), 643–650. doi:10.1177/014920630102700602

Barney, J. (2001a). Is the resource-based "vision" a useful perspective for strategic management research? Yes. *Academy of Management Review*, *26*(1), 41–56.

Bell, M. (2002). *The five principles of organizational resilience*. Gartner Research.

Bergstrom, J., van Winsen, R., & Henriqson, E. (2015). On the justification of resilience in the field of security: A review of the literature. *Reliab. Ing. Syst. Saf.*, *141*, 131–141. doi:10.1016/j.ress.2015.03.008

Bhamidipaty, A., Lotlikar, R., & Banavar, G. (2007). RMI: A Framework for Modeling and Assessing the Resilience Maturity of IT Service Organizations. *IEEE International Conference on Services Computing (SCC 2007)*, 300–307. 10.1109/SCC.2007.94

Bhamra, R., Dani, S., & Burnard, K. (2011). Resilience: The concept, a review of the literature, and future directions. *International Journal of Production Research*, *49*(18), 5375–5393. doi:10.1080/00207543.2011.563826

Bieńkowska, Tworek, & Zablocka-klucza. (2020). Organizational reliability: information technology and human resource management. London, UK: Routledge.

Blundel, R. (2013). *Britain's Quarterly Small Business Survey Special Topic: Resilience and Recovery 2013*. Open University.

Borges, F., & Menegon, N. (2012). Different roles in the search for system resilience. *Job*, *41*, 3238–3245. PMID:22317211

Burnard, K., & Bhamra, R. (2011). Organizational resilience: Development of a conceptual framework for organizational responses. *International Journal of Production Research*, *49*(18), 5581–5599. doi:10.1080/00207543.2011.563827

Cañizares, J., Copeland, S., & Doorn, N. (2021). Make sense of resilience. *Sustainability*, *13*(15), 8538. doi:10.3390u13158538

Carmeli, A., & Markman, G. (2011). Capture, governance, and resilience: Strategic implications of the history of Rome. *Strategic Management Journal*, *32*(3), 322–341. doi:10.1002mj.880

Chan, J. (2011). Improving Organizational Resilience: Applying the Viable System Model and MCDA in a Small Business in Hong Kong. *International Journal of Production Research*, *49*(18), 5545–5563. doi:10.1080/00207543.2011.563829

Collis, D. (1991). A Resource-Based Analysis of Global Competition: The Case of the Bearing Industry. *Strategic Management Journal*, *12*(S1), 49–68. doi:10.1002mj.4250120906

Coullahan, R., & Pastor, C. (2008). Improved business resilience in the commercial facilities sector. *Magazine of Business Continuity and Emergency Planning*, *3*(1), 5–18.

Dahles, H., & Susilowati, T. (2015). Business resilience in times of growth and crisis. *Annals of Tourism Research*, *51*, 34–50. doi:10.1016/j.annals.2015.01.002

Dalziell, E., & McManus, S. (2004). Resilience, vulnerability, and adaptability: implications for system performance. *International Forum for Engineering Decision Making*.

Daneses, S., Lee, J., Amarapurkar, S., Stafford, K., Haynes, G., & Brewton, K. (2009). Determinants of the resilience of the family business after a natural disaster by gender of the business owner. *Journal of Developmental Entrepreneurship*, *14*(4), 333–354. doi:10.1142/S1084946709001351 de Oliveira-Teixeira E. & Werther W. (2013). Resilience: continuous renewal of competitive advantages. *Horiz Bus, 56*, 333–342.

Dekker, S. (2008). *Fair culture: balance between safety and responsibility.* Ashgate Publishing Co.

Demmer, W., Vickery, S., & Calantone, R. (2011). Building Resilience in Small and Medium-sized Enterprises (SMEs): A Demmer Corporation Case Study. *International Journal of Production Research, 49*, 5395–5413. doi:10.1080/00207543.2011.563903

Denyer, D., & Pilbeam, P. (2015). *Change management in extreme contexts (Routledge studies on change and organizational development).* Routledge.

Dewald, J., & Bowen, F. (2010). Storm Clouds and Silver Lights: Responding to Disruptive Innovations through Cognitive Resilience. *Entrepreneurship Theory and Practice, 34*(1), 197–218. doi:10.1111/j.1540-6520.2009.00312.x

Di Gravio, G., Mancini, M., Patriarca, R., & Costantino, F. (2015). Overall safety performance of the air traffic management system: Forecast and monitoring. *Safety Science, 72*, 351–362. doi:10.1016/j.ssci.2014.10.003

Doern, R. (2016). Entrepreneurship and Crisis Management: The Experiences of Small Businesses During the London Riots 2011. *International Small Business Magazine., 34*(3), 276–302. doi:10.1177/0266242614553863

Earvolino-Ramirez, M. (2007). Resilience: A concept analysis. *Nursing Forum, 42*(2), 73–82. doi:10.1111/j.1744-6198.2007.00070.x PMID:17474940

ECLAC. (2020). *MSMEs and COVID-19.* Retrieved October 12, 2021, from https://www.cepal.org/es/euromipyme/mipymes-covid-19

Erol, O., Sauser, B., & Mansouri, M. (2010). A Framework for Extended Business Resilience Research. *Enterprise Information Systems, 4*(2), 111–136. doi:10.1080/17517570903474304

Fiksel, J. (2006). Sustainability and resilience: towards a systems approach. Sustainability: Science, Practice. *Policy., 2*(2), 14–21.

Fleming, J., & Ledogar, R. (2008). Resilience, an Evolving Concept: A Review of the Relevant Literature for Aboriginal Research. *Pimatziwin, 6*(2), 7–23. PMID:20963184

Fletcher, D., & Sarkar, M. (2013). Psychological resilience: Review and critique of definitions, concepts, and theory. *European Psychologist, 18*(1), 12–23. doi:10.1027/1016-9040/a000124

Folke, C. (2006). Resilience: The emergence of a perspective for the analysis of socio-ecological systems. *Global Environmental Change, 16*(3), 253–267. doi:10.1016/j.gloenvcha.2006.04.002

Folke, C. (2016). Resilience (republished). *Ecology and Society, 21*(4), 1–44. doi:10.5751/ES-09088-210444

Gao, S., Sung, M., & Zhang, J. (2013). Developing Risk Management Capacity in SMEs: A Social Capital Perspective. *International Small Business Journal, 31*(6), 677–700. doi:10.1177/0266242611431094

Gečienė, J. (2021). Management of organizational resilience to the crisis: results of a survey of social service institutions before and during a covid-19 pandemic. *Contemporary research on management and administration of organizations, 9*(1), 32-42.

Gittell, J., Cameron, K., Lim, S., & Rivas, V. (2006). Relationships, Layoffs, and Organizational Resilience: Airline Industry Responses to 9/11. *The Journal of Applied Behavioral Science, 42*(3), 300–329. doi:10.1177/0021886306286466

Grøtan, T., & Asbjørnslett, B. (2007). ICT in resilient global logistics. *Proceedings of ESREL 2007*, 2349-2356.

Hamel, G., & Välikangas, L. (2003). The search for resilience. *Harvard Business Review, 81*(9), 52–63. PMID:12964393

Handmer, J., & Dovers, S. (1996). A typology of resilience: Rethinking institutions for sustainable development. *Organization & Environment, 9*, 482–511.

Herbane, B. (2019). Rethinking organizational resilience and strategic renewal in SMEs. *Entrepreneurship and Regional Development, 31*(5-6), 476–495. doi:10.1080/08985626.2018.1541594

Hillmann, J., & Guenther, E. (2020). Organizational Resilience: A Valuable Construct for Management Research? *International Magazine of Managerial Reviews*, 1-38.

Hoffmann, G. (2016). *Organisationale Resilienz. Grundlagen und Handlungsempfehlungen für Entscheidungsträger und Führungskräfte*. Springer. doi:10.1007/978-3-658-12890-6

Hollnagel, E. (2010). How resilient is your organization? Introduction to the Resilience Analysis Grid (RAG). In Sustainable transformation: Building a resilient organization. Academic Press.

Hollnagel, E., Woods, D., & Leveson, N. (2006). *Resilience engineering: concepts and precepts*. Ashgate Publishing.

Horne, J. III, & Orr, J. (1998). Assess behaviors that create resilient organizations. *Employment Relations Today, 24*(4), 29–39.

Howard-Grenville, J., Buckle, S., Hoskins, B., & George, G. (2014). From the editors: Climate change and management. Academy of Management Journal, 57, 615-623.

Hu, Y., Li, J., & Holloway, L. (2008). Towards modeling resilience dynamics in manufacturing companies: Literature review and problem formulation. *CASE, 2008*, 279–284.

Huber, G., Gomes, J., & Carvalho, P. (2012). A program to support the construction and evaluation of resilience indicators. *Job., 41*, 2810–2816. doi:10.3233/WOR-2012-0528-2810 PMID:22317145

IBM Corporation. (2004). *Business Resilience: Proactive Measures for Forward-Looking Companies*. Available at: www-935.ibm.com/services/us/bcrs/pdf/br_business-resilience.pdf

Ismail, H., Poolton, J., & Sharifi, H. (2011). The role of agile strategic capabilities in achieving resilience in small manufacturing companies. *International Journal of Production Research, 49*(18), 5469–5487. doi:10.1080/00207543.2011.563833

Jaramillo, A., & Jaramillo, M. (2016). 2008 financial crisis: Effect on companies listed on the Mexican Stock Exchange. *Mexican Journal of Economics and Finance*, *11*(3), 161–177.

Jüttner, U., & Maklan, S. (2011). Supply chain resilience in the global financial crisis: An empirical study. *Supply Chain Management*, *16*(4), 246–259. doi:10.1108/13598541111139062

Kantur, D. & Iseri-Say, A. (2012). Organizational Resilience: An Integrative Conceptual Framework. *Management and Organization Magazine*, *18*(6), 762-773.

Kikuchi, A. & Yamaguchi, H. (2012) A clue to the synthetic understanding of resilience in organization: recomposition through the crossing of two dimensions of time series and different dimensions of objects. *Journal of Human Interface Society: Human Interface*, *14*(2), 3-108.

Kiuchi, T., & Shireman, B. (1999). Metrics for Business in the New Economy: An economic change of seasons creates demands for new business metrics. *Environmental Quality Management*, *9*, 79–90.

Lee, A., Vargo, J., & Seville, E. (2013). Developing a tool to measure and compare the resilience of organizations. *Natural Hazards Review*, *14*(1), 29–41. doi:10.1061/(ASCE)NH.1527-6996.0000075

Lengnick-Hall, C., Beck, T., & Lengnick-Hall, M. (2011). Develop organizational resilience capacity through strategic human resource management. *Human Resource Management Review*, *21*(3), 243–255. doi:10.1016/j.hrmr.2010.07.001

Linnenluecke, M., & Griffiths, A. (2012). Assessment of organizational resilience to climate and extreme weather events: Complexities and methodological pathways. *Climatic Change*, *113*(3-4), 933–947. doi:10.100710584-011-0380-6

Mafabi, S., Munene, J., & Ahiauzu, A. (2015). Creative climate and organizational resilience: The mediating role of innovation. *The International Journal of Organizational Analysis*, *23*(4), 564–587. doi:10.1108/IJOA-07-2012-0596

Mafabi, S., Munene, J., & Ntayi, J. (2012). Knowledge management and organizational resilience: Organizational innovation as a mediator in Ugandan parastatals. *J Strategy Manag.*, *5*, 57–80. doi:10.1108/17554251211200455

Mamouni-Limnios, E., Mazzarol, T., Ghadouani, A., & Schilizzi, S. (2014). The resilience architecture framework: Four organizational archetypes. *European Management Journal*, *32*(1), 104–116. doi:10.1016/j.emj.2012.11.007

Manfield, R., & Newey, L. (2015). Escape the trap of collapse: Remain capable without capabilities. Strategic change. *Briefings in Entrepreneurial Finance.*, *24*(4), 373–387.

Marcus, A., & Nichols, M. (1999). On the edge: Heeding warnings of unusual events. *Organization Science*, *10*(4), 482–499. doi:10.1287/orsc.10.4.482

Marwa, S., & Milner, C. (2013). Underwriting Corporate Resilience Through Creativity: The Flexibility Model. Total. *Qual Manag Bus.*, *24*, 835–846.

Masten, A. (2014). *Ordinary magic: resilience in development*. Guildford Press.

McManus, S., Seville, E., Vargo, J., & Brunsdon, D. (2008). Facilitated process to improve organizational resilience. *Natural Hazards Review*, 9(2), 81–90. doi:10.1061/(ASCE)1527-6988(2008)9:2(81)

Nemeth, C. (2009). The ability to adapt. In C. P. Nemeth, E. Hollnagel, & S. Dekker (Eds.), *Resilience Engineering Perspectives*. Ashgate Publishing.

O'Regan, N., & Ghobadian, A. (2007). Formal Strategic Planning: Annual Raindance or Wheel of Success? *Strategic Change*, 16(1/2), 11–22. doi:10.1002/jsc.777

Ocampo, J., Stallings, B., Belloso, H., & Frenkel, R. (2014). *The Latin American debt crises from the historical perspective. Santiago de Chile*. United Nations.

Øien, K. (2013). Remote operation in environmentally sensitive areas: Development of early warning indicators. *Journal of Risk Research*, 16(3-4), 323–336. doi:10.1080/13669877.2012.729523

Omidvar, M., Mazloumi, A., Mohammad, I., & Nirumand, F. (2017). Development of a framework for resilience measurement: Suggestion of diffuse resilience degree (RG) and diffuse resilience early warning degree (REWG). *WOR*, 56, 463–474. doi:10.3233/WOR-172512 PMID:28269808

Patterson, M., & Deutsch, E. (2015). Safety-I, Safety-II, and resilience engineering. *Health Care*, 45, 382–389. PMID:26549146

Pelling, M. (2003). *The vulnerabilities of cities: natural disasters and social resilience*. Earthscan.

Pellissier, R. (2011). The implementation of resilience engineering to enhance organizational innovation in a complex environment. *International Journal of Business and Management*, 6(1), 145–164.

Pettit, T., Croxton, K., & Fiksel, J. (2013). Ensuring the resilience of the supply chain: Development and implementation of an assessment tool. *Journal of Business Logistics*, 34(1), 46–76. doi:10.1111/jbl.12009

Pettit, T., Fiksel, J., & Croxton, K. (2010). Ensuring Supply Chain Resilience: Developing a Conceptual Framework. *Journal of Business Logistics*, 31(1), 1–21. doi:10.1002/j.2158-1592.2010.tb00125.x

Peyrefitte, J. (2012). The relationship between communication with stakeholders on mission statements and shareholder value. Journal of Leadership. *Responsibility and Ethics.*, 9(3), 28–40.

Pimm, S. (1984). The complexity and stability of ecosystems. *Nature*, 307(5949), 321–326. doi:10.1038/307321a0

Ponomarov, S., & Holcolmb, M. (2009). Understanding the concept of supply chain resilience. *International Journal of Logistics Management*, 20(1), 124–143. doi:10.1108/09574090910954873

Quiñonez, R. & Prado-Solis, M. (2017). Organizational resilience: ideas for debate in the Ecuadorian context. *Mastery of the Sciences*, 3, 488-504.

Rankin, A., Lundberg, J., & Woltjer, R. (2014). A framework for learning from adaptive performance. In Becom. Resilient. Ashgate Publishing, Ltd.

Rapoport, M. & Brenta, N. (2010). The global economic crisis: The outcome of forty years of instability? *Developmental Problems, 41*(163), 7-30.

Reinmoeller, P., & van Baardwijk, N. (2005). The link between diversity and resilience. *MIT Sloan Management Review*, *46*, 61–65.

Romero, I. (2006). SMEs in the global economy. Towards a business development strategy. Developmental problems. *Latin American Journal of Economics*, *37*(146), 31–50.

Sheffi, Y., & Rice, J. (2005). A vision of the resilient enterprise supply chain. *MIT Sloan Management Review*, *47*, 41–48.

Speight, P. (2011). Business continuity. *Journal of Applied Security Research*, *6*(4), 529–554. doi:10.1080/19361610.2011.604021

Starr, R., Newfrock, J. & Delurey, M. (2003). Business Resilience: Risk Management in the Network Economy. *Strategy and Business, 30*, 70-79.

Suire, R., & Vicente, J. (2014). Cluster Clusters for Cluster Life (s): Looking for Critical Cluster Resilience Factors. *Entrepreneurship and Regional Development*, *26*(1–2), 142–164. doi:10.1080/08985626.2013.877985

Sullivan-Taylor, B., & Branicki, L. (2011). Building Resilient SMEs: Why One Size May Not Fit All. *International Journal of Production Research*, *49*(18), 5565–5579. doi:10.1080/00207543.2011.563837

Sutcliffe, K. & Vogus, T. (2003). Organize for resilience. *Positive Organizational Scholarship*, 94-110.

Ungar, M. (2021). *Multisystemic resilience: adaptation and transformation in contexts of change*. Oxford University Press. doi:10.1093/oso/9780190095888.001.0001

Vogus, T., & Sutcliffe, K. (2007). Organizational Resilience: Towards a Theory and Research Agenda. Institute of Electrical and Electronic Engineers.

Woods, D., & Hollnagel, E. (2006). *Joint Cognitive Systems: Patterns in Cognitive Systems Engineering*. Taylor and Francis. doi:10.1201/9781420005684

Zsidisin, G., & Wagner, S. (2010). Are the perceptions coming true? The moderating role of supply chain resilience in the occurrence of disruptions. *Journal of Business Logistics*, *31*, 1–20. doi:10.1002/j.2158-1592.2010.tb00140.x

Chapter 15
Implications of the Environmental Planning and Policing Systems to Promote Organizational Green Practices, Marketing Management, and Strategic Change

José G. Vargas-Hernández
https://orcid.org/0000-0003-0938-4197
Posgraduate and Research Department, Tecnológico Mario Molina Unidad Zapopan, Mexico

ABSTRACT

This study has the objective to analyze the implications of the environmental planning and policing systems to promote organizational green practices, marketing management, and strategic change. It is assumed that organizational environmental strategic change must be planned and policed based on the transformation of green practices and marketing management. The method employed is the analytical-descriptive and reflective steaming from the theoretical and empirical research on these environmental issues. It is concluded that organizational environmental planning and policing systems are relevant to promote the strategic change in organizations towards green activities and marketing management.

INTRODUCTION

The sustainable development strategy needs to focus on environmental planning and policing systems based on green practices, marketing management and strategic change, which have an impact on organizational profitability and quality. The emergence of the green marketing requires to go green in all practices and activities to have a positive impact on environmental protection and safety. Green

DOI: 10.4018/978-1-6684-5109-0.ch015

individual and organizational factors contribute to consolidate knowledge affecting the organizational pro-environmental behaviors, practices and activities and environmental performance.

Organizations focused on strong environment orientation are more committed to embrace the green perspective. Green behaviors are defined as the behaviors, actions and practices on which employees and stakeholders engage linked with and contribute to environmental sustainability (Ones & Dilchert, 2012). Green behaviors at the workplace are of the category of transforming and have direct influence on enhancing the environmental sustainability of organizational work processes and products through the environmental planning and policing systems based on green practices and leaded by marketing management and strategic change.

Environmentally oriented organizations attain the capacity to create green products with green competitiveness. Green environmental productivity combines a set of environmental and productivity eco-friendly options of technologies, techniques, and tools to reduce the environmental impact of organizational activities while providing a healthy quality life and enhancing the competitive advantage and profitability. The implementation of the green-lean approach focuses on environmentally sustainable operations and goods, waste elimination and reduction.

Green organizations create competitive advantages by investing in environmental sustainability. The new organizational greener ways of conducting systematically the processes, operations, and practices as the critical components of a new green business model interconnected in the ecosystem aimed to align decisions in accordance with the green vision.

Managerial activities of planning and policing green practices such as sensemaking about the vision for sense giving and sense making related to the organizational identity of environmental sustainability, are needed to operationalize strategic change in green organizational models. The green vision should be recreated in the imagination considering the imperative of managerial agency in decoupling the operational logics to determine the revenue streams in the organizational ecosystem. It must be calculated in terms of sense giving acknowledging, the creation of a competitive advantage against the consequences of sustainability.

Organizations produce trustworthy and green products possessing ecological reputation and the capability of satisfying green needs and requirements of customers through green practices, marketing management and strategic change. Organizations operationalize mitigation of negative effects upon environment and ecology. Environmental customer wellbeing is the respect to the legal and moral rights of customers by disclosing complete information regarding products and services for the customer satisfaction.

Organizations identified as green by customers, they get committed to green practices in their products and services (Du et al., 2007). The measures of green competitive advantage enhance attainment of sustainable environment development (Lin and Chen 2017) are the green marketing management based on low-cost regarding green management, offering better quality products and investing in environmental development and green innovation than competitors.

ENVIRONMENTAL PLANNING AND POLICING SYSTEMS

Planning and executing eco-friendly policies create a green environment. Environmental policy has an impact on environmental sustainability projects and practices, among others in the reduction of gas emissions and environmental footprint, efficient use of natural resources and energy increasing resilience by reducing fossil fuels, waste management, etc., by installing green energy technologies. Green policy activities are aimed at urban sustainable development. The positive attitude of society to comply with green policy for sustainable development has a positive attitude of residents to buy in residential premises.

Sustainable organizational development incorporates ecological practices in managerial human resources strategies and policies to respond to the challenges posed by catastrophes and threatens brought by climate change. Some governments had not ratified the Kyoto Protocol (1997), repelled a scheme for large polluters (Crowley, 2017) and cut funding for climate science and policy. Other governments support institutional corporate greenwashing (Wright & Nyberg, 2014), and repeatedly cuts funds for climate science and policy.

The strategic green innovation integrates and promotes cooperation between management into production considering the environmental policies and regulations, green innovation practices and activities, environmental protection, and consumers awareness.

Economic considerations, reducing costs, practices and activities should be publicizing to assure quality and ensure it constantly to consumers and to gain support from non-government organizations. Organizational green workforce innovates on cost-efficient practices, processes, procedures, products, etc. Organizational green innovation practices bridge the organizational activities and the stakeholders' satisfaction (DiPietro et al., 2013). Organizational green innovation practices are influencing factors at institutional, organizational, and individual level and their implementation improve organizational legitimacy in response to institutional regulatory, normative, and imitation pressures. The complex process of green innovation practices.

Managerial agency is identified within categories in ecosystem-related change organizational practices. Organizations practicing lean activities and moving to green initiatives and practices leading to rising organizational sustainable performance. Organizational lean and green practices are paradigms applied to ensure organizational sustainable performance (Azevedo et al., 2016).

The philosophies of lean-green agile resilient practices, social management synergies and best organizational practices have an impact on organizational sustainable manufacturing on performance (Hallam and Contreras, 2016; Bergmiller and McCright, 2009; Cabral et al., 2012; D€ues et al., 2013; Galeazzo et al., 2014; Farias et al., 2019; Thanki et al., 2016; Khalili et al., 2016; Hartini and Ciptomulyono, 2015; Henao et al., 2019; Wu et al., 2015; Wiese et al., 2015; Azevedo et al., 2016). Lean practices have an influence on green practices affecting the sustainable performance measures Organizational lean–green has influence in organizational sustainable performance and practices (Kovilage, 2021).

Best practices, green and lean integrated in a benchmarking tool has been developed for improving the leanness, agility, resilience, and greenness practices of the supply chain (Weise et al. 2015; Azevedo et al. 2016) The individual impact between lean and green practices on the improvement the organizational performance. Individual practical environmental actions should be directed towards energy conservation, recycling (Lamm, Tosti-Kharas, and Williams 2013). Lean practices affect green practices, and these are moderating factors that affect sustainable performance measures.

Changes in organizational perspectives in relation to environmental initiatives can be in policy statements, capital investments, environmental job practices, product design and development, production processes, marketing strategies, etc. (Molina-Azorín, Claver-Cortés, Pereira-Moliner, & Tarí, 2009; Sharfman & Fernando, 2008). Green products are more environmentally friend products that cause less harm to humankind and offer long-term practical opportunities for a social and economic development.

There is an ongoing debate about the urban green space and population density which has led to the compensation hypothesis (Byrne and Sipe 2010) with the notion that as density increases should green space do also and more to be considered when planning and development. Green urban and sustainability spaces have different typologies in different economic, social, and political contexts to incorporate the existing urban green spaces into the needs. An assessment of the different typologies of urban green spaces and parks, urban sustainable planning and development should consider catering different demographic urban groups and cultural differences to determine the design and capacity of the green urban public spaces.

Models of urban spatial planning for green infrastructure are based on socio ecological criteria such as access to green space, landscape vulnerability, social vulnerability, urban heat island effect, air quality, stormwater management (Meerow and Newell 2017) A model developed to facilitate urban spatial planning must address the research gap in planning models aimed to investigate socio ecological tradeoffs and synergies. The realization of projects of technology programs accessible through various channels to those policy makers investors, residents, who are interested in learning about the construction and maintenance of urban green innovation areas based on green roofs

Urban sustainable planning and development must incorporate green innovation areas that respond to the demand of urban green spaces in compact cities. Urban sustainable planning initiatives of open green spaces and green roofs reinforce one another as part of the urban city open spaces network. A network of urban green open spaces is considered as a green infrastructure development that might be connected to open space with reference to climate resilience planning. An element of local policy in local governments is a tool that enable to motivate the various groups of stakeholders, local entities, and residents to construct urban green areas and green roofs.

Areas of open space need green covers and might be more suitable to be prioritized for social and environmental vulnerable communities to implement green roofs in urban planning and development. Fragmented sustainable urban planning with multiple different agendas and regulations makes difficult to realize a multifunctional green infrastructure and to adopt spatial planning. Green innovation areas and roofs can be connected into urban green space planning and created a relationship between public and private open green spaces expanding and enhancing a network in urban development.

Sustainable development open spaces planning strategies including incentives of multifunctional green roofs and policy motivations. Green roof incentives and regulations should intend to expand the multi-functionality urban green areas and to apply open spatial planning strategies for green infrastructure. Incentives from regional and local government policies rise the social awareness to construct green roofs, stimulate its development and maintain in good conditions (Chen, 2013; Olubunmi, Xia & Skitmore, 2016).

The construction of green urban innovation areas and urban green roofs requires to develop motivational policies, strategies, and instruments, including financial incentives, promotion, social dialogue, and legal provisions. The policy motivation for the implementation of the different options, initiatives and solutions of urban green roofs must held training sessions to educate the city staff to design constructions and remove all the barriers and receive all the benefits. The installation of urban green roofs and other new green spaces, including sustainable development policies to mandate requiring design standards for green roof on new residential developments, commercial and institutional buildings, and the provision of incentives.

Incentive programs for urban green areas and green roof should be integrated into green space planning and incorporated to implement private initiatives, exploring to increase green covers, and encouraging to provide options for properties considering on-the-ground green spaces. Current incentive programs for green areas and green roofs may lack initiative without fully realizing the environmental benefits to be incorporated into a climate resilience policy.

Implications of the Environmental Planning and Policing Systems

The implementation of green infrastructure including the drivers of green roof policy initiatives mostly single function. Regional and local government policies combine the types of subsidies with the obligation to construct a green roof involving the requirements such as the green roof inclination. Local government policy initiatives led to stormwater control with the development of green roofs resulting in the enhancement of climate resilience and urban heat island effect. Urban green initiatives are considered a single function detached from sustainable urban planning initiative.

Green infrastructure including the green roofs, is defined under different sustainable planning systems based on the concept of create and integrated green space in high density landscape. A comprehensive urban planning should incorporate urban green innovation areas and green roof development. The adoption of urban green innovation areas is promoted by the development of policies and other socio-economic green solutions, social awareness of the benefits. Urban green spatial planning and green roofs initiatives, regulations, and policy formulation must be part of a large comprehensive plan. Urban green areas and green roof planning should be developed according to the community resources and characteristics. Legal regulations concerning spatial planning of urban green areas and the construction of green roofs need to be implemented with a good strategy.

Land developers can use a range of planning tools and options to combine types of areas and surfaces, among others the green space factor, density of built up and green area-per-capita factor green points system (Kruuse, 2011). Diversity of planning control, green infrastructure can be hindered by funding policies framework to be translated from national to regional and local levels (Mell 2010). Green roofs are adopted for aesthetic matching the development of urban green areas with social and environmental vulnerability criteria based on policy programs, zoning and building planning to promote development

Urban green space is a compensatory element in sustainable urban planning and development and perception of meaning and use of green spaces explored under the lens of people´s cultures, differences and similarities, typologies, designs, and ownership. The Garden City model has inspired urban planning and development leading to the origin of shape-related models such as greenbelts and green fingers. Urban green space inventory should be protected and utilized in connection with the green areas and roof planning and development looking into the clustered locations for a proportional distribution in neighborhoods and to find potential social vulnerability areas to enhance climate change.

Landscape connectivity has different interpretation between urban green roofs policies and open space planning. The green areas and roofs installations mismatch the suitability in need to green covers indicating the lack of landscape connectivity and spatial planning and in open space management. Landscape connectivity is not always an issue in open green space and green building planning in relation to green infrastructure and climate initiatives. Landscape connectivity should be considered in urban green open space planning aimed to leverage the existing resources to enhance accessibility of community and neighborhoods

Green building spaces at the workplace of organizations is an alternative to traditional spaces by fulfilling a reduction of natural resources utilized in construction. Green building includes enhanced green practices in renewable and efficiency energy, storm water management, etc. Green buildings are being adopted at great upsurge by organizations. Compact green development may be able where space is scarce and putting under pressure urban green space planning and development (Coolen and Meesters 2012).

Other tools are also based on promoting green roofs and their benefits in terms of pro-environmental actions such as reduction of energy consumption, improve microclimate, aimed to improve the life quality of residents. The concept of green roofs is related to urban green space planning. Local government initiatives on green roofs development are one of the best management practices in stormwater management. Green roofs as an urban green space do not need much space compared to other urban green areas and have a relevant role and impact in urban green space planning because it has a reduction in energy consumption, reduction of greenhouse gas emission, mitigation of urban heat island effect and controlling storm water (Vijayaraghavan 2016).

Existing open spaces must be considered by applying the spatial planning elements for the development of green infrastructure and green roofs. Urban green roofs are multifunctional despite that they are being integrated into urban open space management. The first program of initiatives was introduced in Germany in the 197s for the construction of urban green roofs considering the benefits (Brudermann & Sangkakool, 2017) which have derived in investments for green policies for sustainable urban development. Expansion of the definition of urban green roofs, the ground urban green space should satisfy the property footprint as a requirement of green space planning initiatives and best practices of stormwater management for protecting biodiversity, quality life, energy consumption and urban heat island effect.

Communicating and reporting organizational green practices and activities has become required in sustainable business environment (Hartmann, P., et. al., 2005, Aaker, 1991, Keller 2003, Namkung and Jang, 2012). Organizational environmental protection standards implemented through green innovation activities and practices should be provided with incentives.

The reduction of non-value practices minimizes energy, water and natural resource consumption, and non-hazardous solid wastes considered green (Duarte & Cruz-Machado, 2019). Green nanotechnology revolutionizes drug manufacturing, delivery, diagnostics, and regenerative medicines treatment procedures and practices, monitors side effects and attitudes. Planning and controlling green nanotechnology development led to social and environmental sustainability on issues related to economic, social, environmental, health, etc. However, this situation may result in the risk of a predicted green go effect of overrun nanoengineered organisms. Production, distribution and marketing of green nanotechnology goods and services based on open science and innovation in different industries should be sustained in a rewarding policy.

GREEN PRACTICES

Organizations need to balance the economic growth and to preserve the environment by endorsing green practices (Daily and Huang 2001) with profits for the firms (Murari & Bhandari, 2011). Green practices reduce the negative environmental effects has affected the formulation of industrial strategies to reduce waste, manage and renew energy, foster more healthy environmental practices and so forth (Vandenbrande 2019).

The environmental considerations express and manifests the proclamations, commitments, and expectations to improve the wellbeing and livelihood of people through practices and activities that include sustainable manufacturing materials, eco-friendly packaging, recycling water, energies, and other waste material, etc., allowing consumers to return the packaging materials (Liu et al., 2016).

Management of green organizations engage in green practices such as energy and water conservation, recycling and reusing, use of renewal energies, waste reduction (Kim, Kim, Choi, & Phetvaroon, 2019; Pham, Tuč ková, & Jabbour, 2019). Green organizations committed to sustainable policies and sustainability include green building design principles for workspace in green buildings. Adoption of green resource management practices enhances the organizational environmental performance (Roscoe, Subramanian, Jabbour, Chong, 2019). Improvement of organizational sustainable development performance initiates with lean and green practices and activities managed through one unit and reducing the overlapping and separate implementation. The model identifies and explains the interactions among the lean, green, and sustainable performance measures.

Tasks and practices related to organizational sustainability are based on social and ecological concerns aimed to improve the branding position. Organizations must move forward in a top-down approach by designing, approving, and implementing environmental sustainability practices. Environmental sustainability is related to managerial agency and organizational identity in all the practices of the organizational ecosystem. Organizational identity is internalized and infused with the notion of environmental sustainability differentiating with practices of other organizations beyond the operational control. Competencies in management practices required in radical change of the organizational model transformation, are at the core in organizational identity (O'Connor and Ayers 2005)

Reconfiguring the organizational ecosystem for sustainable organizational practices needs new capabilities and resource-intensive processes to solve all the socio-technical challenges. Many organizations that claim to be green and they are not practicing it are doing greenwashing.

The environmental extra-roles and in-roles green organizational behaviors are discrete categories in which green employees develop and execute the environmental in-role behaviors in more proactive organizational environmental policies and practices (Ciocirlan (2016). Green psychological climate is a mediator variable that entails shared perceptions about the organizational environmental policies and procedures and enhance green values based on environmental sustainability (Ramus and Steger, 2000; Norton et al., 2014; Dumont et al., 2017; Zhou et al., 2018). The enthusiasm of the green employer to achieve environmental goals and the rating on parameters of sustainability includes the green job descriptions, eco-friendly locations, environmental green policies among other critical activities.

Focusing on green behaviors at the workplace according to determined parameters rather than by practices, references, or attitudes (To, Lam, & Lai, 2015; de Groot & Steg, 2008). The psychological green climate is related to the perceptions and interpretations of organizational policies, procedures, and practices on environmental sustainability (Norton et al., 2012, p. 212). The perception about those organizational policies and procedures contribute to environmental sustainability encourages the engagement of the involved stakeholders in the promotion of environmental behaviors and enhances organizational green performance (Seroka-Stolka and Lukomska-Szarek, 2016; Zientara and Zamojska, 2018; Tuan, 2019; Wang et al., 2019).

Compliance of organizational green strategies and policies, organizations take actions to evaluate perceptions of ecological practices to enhance ecologically friendly behavior. The major trends in the measurement of green behaviors at the working place focus on extra-role behaviors prioritizing green office in predominant quantitative studies in green practices such as double-sided printing, paper recycling, turning off lights, etc., concealing the contingency green behaviors at the workplace. Qualitative studies examine other types of green organizational behaviors other than the green office practices and not necessarily is a developmental approach.

Global economies have shared the benefits of the green tendencies and the incorporation or organizational culture practices. Organizational green culture is considered the holistic concept of internal marketing involving production, distribution, logistics, consumption, waste and disposal practices and activities. The green organizational culture concept is described by diversified terms includes environmental and eco-friendly cultures, sustainable oriented culture, based on organizational culture extended to green contexts.

Pro-environmental organizational culture meeting the perceptual and practical criteria in environment conservation and protection (Norton et al. 2015; Schein (1990). Green organizational culture is a debated concept concerned with realizing the ecological balance (Mohezara et al., 2016). Green organizational culture is defined as a set of collective shared beliefs, values, norms, perspectives, and practices, and so forth related to external environment.

Green organizational culture ensures all the organizational practices and activities with the green movement of environmental sustainability (Cordeiro and Tewari, 2015). Organizational learning and development practices focus on developing attitudes, knowledge, and skills to create awareness about environmental sustainability, to use methods and tools to save energy and resource and reduce waste, to take opportunities for environmental protection and maintenance mindset. Green organizational culture ensures all the organizational practices and activities with the green movement of environmental sustainability (Cordeiro and Tewari, 2015).

Organizational members engagement and commitment to environmental sustainability is a dimension embedded in organizational green practices (Aragon-Correa, Martin-Tapia, & Hurtado-Torres, 2013; Renwick, Redman, & Maguire, 2013). Employee engagement in an organization-wide initiative tends to develop organizational citizenship behaviors embedding environmental activities and practices within operational functions (Boiral, 2009). Social consciousness of organizational practices and activities lead to growth (Yang and Gong, 2020).

Human practices that are more harmful to the environment must be questioned. Organizations must develop employees and train them on the best green initiatives and practices. The adoption of green training is positively correlated with green supply chain, purchasing practices and cooperation with customers (Teixeira et al. 2016, p. 170). Environmental values must be induced onto employees to develop willingness towards green innovative practices. However, despite the rewards and compensation improve green initiatives not always free from malpractices.

Climate change poses global challenges for organizations considered contributors of pro-environmental initiatives in different practices of organizational environmental sustainability. Organizations are being pushed to become environmentally proactive and low carbon balancing economic and environmental performance by implementing green innovation practices. Organizational green innovation practices are critical to green development and to improve the performance of organizations. Organizational green innovation practices are related to organizational performance. Organizational green innovation practices improve resource productivity, efficiency in use of energy, water, raw materials, labor, etc. and reduce or offset the costs of environmental protection.

GREEN MARKETING MANAGEMENT

Green marketing, environmental marketing, and sustainable marketing, refer to the designing, promoting, distributing, and pricing products that do not harm the environment (Pride and Ferrell 1993). Green marketing is defined as the activities to generate and facilitate exchanges intended to meet and satisfy human needs and wants with the minimal impact on the natural environment (Polonsky, 1994). Green marketing management is the process of planning and executing to facilitate the production, distribution, promotion, packaging activities responsive to ecological concerns.

Green marketing influences multiple economic agents to benefit consumers, companies, corporate strategy, production processes, supply chain, developing economies and environment. Salzman and

Implications of the Environmental Planning and Policing Systems

Hunter, 2007; Kosnett, 2007; Ottman, Stafford, and Hartman, 2007). Green marketing to become environmentally safe incorporates activities of product modification and process, packaging, and advertising modifications.

Green marketing strategy is an environmental protection. Green strategies eliminate waste in the delivery process through the loading and route planning of the supply chain. The approaches to green purchasing are the strategy oriented, organization commitments and small-scale purchases. Strategic commitments are the green purchasing policies, green contracts, green purchasing, etc. Green purchasing may be influences by the policies and strategies of top management (Yen & Yen, 2012).

Green purchasing is referred also as environmentally preferable purchasing is the selection and acquisition of products and services that reduce the negative environmental impacts over manufacturing, logistics, transportation, distribution, consumption and recycling or disposal. Some of the benefits of green purchasing are the reduction of water and energy consumption improving the efficiency of resources, reduce the waste disposal and pollution, lower the environmental impacts, improves the environmental health impacts and the viability of recycling, and encourage the adoption of cleaner technologies

Environmental marketing, ecological marketing and green marketing are different terms referring to the growing awareness and increasing sensitiveness of marketing consumption and disposal of products and services that have environmental implications of global warming and the impacts of pollutants and non-biodegradable solid waste. The shift from traditional marketing to green marketing practices has advantages in the long-term Stafford, and Hartman, 1996; Cornelissen, et all, 2008, Brundtland, 1987).

Organizational social and consumers environmental awareness improves green innovation practices enhancing market competitiveness and opening new markets for green products. Green products have contextual extensions on green services, processes, and practices. Green products are those that are originally grown or manufactured with natural ingredients through green technology without causing environmental hazards for the conservation of natural resources, are reusable, recyclable ingredients and biodegradable, non-toxic chemical, do not harm and pollute the environment, are not tested on animals, and have eco-friendly packaging.

Green products can be certified and eco-labeled as green managerial and marketing strategies to enable sustainable economic, social, and environmental results. An analytical framework based on internal social marketing, widens the proposition of the direct and indirect influence aimed at modifying the green behaviors and extending the influence on all the organizational members (Smith and O'Sullivan 2012)

Green production and marketing reduce climate modify. The consumer is concerned with green Marketing that benefits the environment and have an influence in its variables, climate change, air, water, soil conservation, reduction of energy consumption. These benefits influence consumer decision making in the extent in which value.

Green marketing initiatives and strategies contribute to improve the environment by incorporating value propositions for consumers. Green marketing strategies need to be based on eco-design, eco-packaging, and eco-labeling to achieve a positive environmental impact.

Corporate brand may integrate green attributes, practices, and initiatives to improve the environmental commitments (Too and Bajracharya, 2013). lace marketing branding has a relevant and strategic role in promoting sustainable practices among all the tourism destinations and business they seek to attract (Frig, Sorsa, 2020; Andersson, James, 2018; Zouganeli, Trihas, Antonaki, Kladou, 2012).

Sustainability on place marketing branding in tourism management focuses more on green environmental sustainability and smart growth (Pant, 2005; Andersson, 2016, Acuti, Grazzini, Mazzoli, Aiello, 2019; Maheshwari, Vandewalle, Bamber, 2011). City marketing can be implemented in direct reference to sustainability, since green urban politics has moved in different directions such as in tourism management. In city marketing branding, strategy green spaces are a blending element that contributes to live in the open and green area in a more perfect and creative city.

Environmental and green sustainability is present in tourism marketing. Tourism visitors like more embedding organizational logic of sustainable practices as a tourist destination products and other aspects of economic, social, cultural, and environmental sustainability considerations (Hanna, Font, Scarles, Weeden, Harrison, 2018; Taecharungroj, Muthuta, Boonchaiyapruek, 2019).

STRATEGIC CHANGE

Organizational environmental sustainability must be supported and oriented by strategic change into practices in operation in the organizational ecosystems (Green et al., 2012; Robinson, 2004; Stubbs and Cocklin, 2008; Seuring and Gold,2013). The foundations for a sustainable development of a city are the spatial urban development plans must reflect the development changes and restrictions for further development of a polycentric city to avoid urban sprawl, urban green spaces protections and strengthen housing in the inner city and should be considered as competitive advantage.

Managerial agency in a sustainable organizational model change consists of sensemaking and sense giving activities that are needed to promote green innovation. Green managerial support is crucial in organizational model change in green economic solutions and benefits in real economic growth, corporate green brand, green differentiation, and customer loyalty. An analysis of organizational model change identifies the links between the organizational model and the contingencies of the organizational ecosystem. Institutionalizing green business models must overcome the barriers across the multi-actor value systems for institutional change.

Green innovation practices are categorized as green innovation strategy, eco-design, and green innovation actions as green operation (Srivastav, 2007; Xu et al., 2017; Zhang et al., 2015). To absorb new environmental knowledge from external partners is required to design and implement a green innovation strategy and policy, which may have positive impacts on the organizational performance and productivity (Aldieri et al., 2019).

The new green economy has changed the core nature of job performance and created the need of new green jobs able to display more discretionary behaviors contributing to environmental performance embedded into individual and organizational behavior to reach sustainable organizational and environmental development (Anderson and White, 2011; Aguinis and Glavas, 2013). Individual differences and psychological characteristics contribute to green behaviors that pressure change when there are benefits (Morris and Venkatesh, 2000).

Greenhouse gases emission is a contributor to global climate change. Green roofs alleviate global and local environmental impacts adaptation to climate change. Green roof development incorporated in existing buildings including changes of codes could be a window of opportunity. A grass root initiative of green roof movement may increase the vegetable gardens at the top of buildings aimed to improve stormwater quality and to mitigate the urban carbon footprint leading to the urban heat island effect. These are efforts to combat climate change and improve the urban sustainability.

Livestock production is being threatened by climate change while animal production is a higher contributor of greenhouse gases (Narayan, Barreto, Hantzopoulou, Tilbrook, 2021). Caro, Davis, Bastianoni, Caldeira, 2017).

A minimalist approach and business-as usual encouragement to implement adaptive measures (Head, 2014) towards climate change denies climate science and agreements on climate actions (Forino, von Meding, 2021; Bowden et al., 2019; Bowden, 2018), is a brake to economic growth (Hamilton, 2001). Businesses distrust about climate change and environmental issues and skepticism on adaptive attempts that have a negative impact on profits (Bowden 2018)

Ones, & Dilchert, (2012) describe the economic organizational workplaces and activities, amid unprecedented change on their relations with the natural environment. Implementation of green and lean 5S and VSM tools to the firms needs employee engagement and management commitment to eliminate the non-value-adding activities and reduce the lead time and address the changes to achieve sustainability performance of the production system. The training perspectives of green training human resources management identify the enabling of compliance and conformance to technical regulations, awareness of the organizational agenda and managing changes in organizational culture.

Building up strategic collaborations with partners to create and adapt green innovations, reinforce sustainability by favoring the identity by designing and implementing green policies, collecting green programs and products, and eco-activities, influence the organizational ecosystem.

The corporate green strategy is being incorporated into organizations, although not all of practitioners are aware of the benefits and comfortable in the human resources environment. Organizational social responsibility in strategic planning focuses on issues related to green economy for sustainable development by building up relations between organizations and local communities (Khaled Zamoum, and Serra Gorpe, 2021). Green economy is aimed to protecting and maintaining a healthy sustainable environment focusing on the establishment of green cities with the use of clean renewable energy free of pollutants.

CONCLUSION

Organizational environmental planning and policing systems are relevant to promote the strategic change in organizations towards green activities and marketing management. Organizational environmental and health issues and concerns must be aligned to interest of all the stakeholders and incorporated into the core organizational practices due to the growth of the organization. Leveraging the structural change process towards a greener and low-carbon economy, achieves sustainable development, creates green jobs, and promotes social protection

Organizational green creativity is the behavior that integrates environmental knowledge and advanced thinking related and applied to products and services, organizational processes and practices aimed to implement green innovation.

The sustainable urban planning system must create opportunities and benefits to integrate urban green infrastructure into green open space planning systems. Planning of urban green areas initiatives and developments must identify opportunities for coordination and provide recommendations to incorporate a climate resilience plan.

Organizations inducing change must be convinced of the necessity of radical alteration of routine operations into the greener mindset.

REFERENCES

Aaker, D. (1991). *Brand equity. La gestione del valore della marca*. FrancoAngeli.

Acuti, D., Grazzini, L., Mazzoli, V., & Aiello, G. (2019). Stakeholder engagement in green place branding: A focus on user-generated content. *Corporate Social Responsibility and Environmental Management, 2019*(26), 492–501. doi:10.1002/csr.1703

Aguinis, H., & Glavas, A. (2013). Embedded versus peripheral corporate social responsibility: Psychological foundations. *Ind. Organ. Psychol., 6*(4), 314–332. doi:10.1111/iops.12059

Aldieri, L., Kotsemir, M., & Vinci, C. P. (2019, July 6). Environmental innovations and productivity: Empirical evidence from Russian regions. *Resources Policy*, 1–9.

Anderson, R. C., & White, R. A. (2011). *Business Lessons from a Radical Industrialist*. St. Martin's Griffin.

Andersson, I. (2016). Green cities' going greener? Local environmental policy-making and place branding in the 'Greenest City in Europe. *European Planning Studies, 24*(6), 1197–1215. doi:10.1080/09654313.2016.1152233

Andersson, I., & James, L. (2018). Altruism or entrepreneurialism? The co-evolution of green place branding and policy tourism in Växjö, Sweden. *Urban Studies (Edinburgh, Scotland), 2018*(55), 3437–3453. doi:10.1177/0042098017749471

Aragon-Correa, J. A., Martin-Tapia, I., & Hurtado-Torres, N. E. (2013). Proactive environmental strategies and employee inclusion: The positive effects on information sharing and promoting collaboration and the influence of uncertainty. *Organization & Environment, 40*(2), 1–23. doi:10.1177/1086026613489034

Azevedo, S. G., Carvalho, H., & Cruz-Machado, V. (2016). LARG index: A benchmarking tool for improving the leanness, agility, resilience and greenness of the automotive supply chain. *Benchmark, 23*(6), 1472–1499. doi:10.1108/BIJ-07-2014-0072

Bergmiller, G. G., & McCright, P. R. (2009), *Parallel models for Lean and green operations*. Paper presented at the Industrial Engineering Research Conference, Miami, FL. https://pdfs.semanticscholar.org/0a67/c7f0f6d60ba0506e037aaf17cfe8b3a89e7d.pdf

Boiral, O. (2009). Greening the corporation through organizational citizenship behaviors. *Journal of Business Ethics, 87*(2), 221–236. doi:10.100710551-008-9881-2

Bowden, V. (2018). Life. Brought to you by'… coal? business responses to climate change in the hunter valley, NSW, Australia. *Environmental Sociology, 4*(2), 275–285. doi:10.1080/23251042.2017.1382032

Bowden, V., Nyberg, D., & Wright, C. (2019). Planning for the past: Local temporality and the construction of denial in climate change adaptation. *Global Environmental Change, 57*, 101939. doi:10.1016/j.gloenvcha.2019.101939

Brudermann, T., & Sangkakool, T. (2017). Green roofs in temperate climate cities in Europe– an analysis of key decision factors. *Urban Forestry & Urban Greening, 21*, 224–234. doi:10.1016/j.ufug.2016.12.008

Brundtland, G. (1987). *Our Common Future: The World Commission on Environment and Development.* Oxford University Press.

Byrne, J., & Sipe, N. (2010). *Green and open space planning for urban consolidation – A review of the literature and best practice.* Griffith University Urban Research Program.

Cabral, I., Grilo, A., & Cruz-Machado, V. (2012). A decision-making model for Lean, Agile, Resilient and Green supply chain management. *International Journal of Production Research, 50*(17), 4830-4845.

Caro, D., Davis, S., Bastianoni, S., & Caldeira, K. (2017). Greenhouse gas emissions due to meat production in the last fifty years. In A. Mukhtar & C. O. Stockle (Eds.), *Quantification of Climate Variability, Adaptation and Mitigation for Agricultural Sustainability* (pp. 27–37). Springer. doi:10.1007/978-3-319-32059-5_2

Chen, C. F. (2013). Performance evaluation and development strategies for green roofs in Taiwan: A review. *Ecological Engineering, 52*, 51–58. doi:10.1016/j.ecoleng.2012.12.083

Ciocirlan, C. E. (2016). Environmental workplace behaviors: Definition matters. *Organization & Environment, 30*(1), 51–70. doi:10.1177/1086026615628036

Coolen, H., & Meesters, J. (2012). Private and public green spaces: Meaningful but different settings. *Journal of Housing and the Built Environment, 27*(1), 49–67. doi:10.100710901-011-9246-5

Cordeiro, J. J., & Tewari, M. (2015). Firm Characteristics, Industry Context, and Investor Reactions to Environmental CSR: A Stakeholder Theory Approach. *Journal of Business Ethics, 130*(4), 833–849. doi:10.100710551-014-2115-x

Cornelissen, G., Pandelaere, M., Warlop, L., & Dewitte, S. (2008). Positive Cueing: Promoting Sustainable Consumer Behavior by Cueing Common Environmental Behaviors as Environmental. *International Journal of Research in Marketing, 25*(1), 46–55. doi:10.1016/j.ijresmar.2007.06.002

Crowley, K. (2017). Up and down with climate politics 2013–2016: The repeal of carbon pricing in Australia. *Wiley Interdisciplinary Reviews: Climate Change, 8*(3), e458. doi:10.1002/wcc.458

Daily, B., & Huang, S. (2001). Achieving sustainability through attention to human resource factors in environmental management. *International Journal of Operations & Production Management, 21*(12), 1539–1552. doi:10.1108/01443570110410892

de Groot, J. I. M., & Steg, L. (2008). Value orientations to explain beliefs related to environmental significant behavior. *Environment and Behavior, 40*(3), 330–354. doi:10.1177/0013916506297831

DiPietro, R. B., Cao, Y., & Partlow, C. (2013). Green practices in upscale foodservice operations: Customer perceptions and purchase intentions. *International Journal of Contemporary Hospitality Management, 25*(5), 779–796. doi:10.1108/IJCHM-May-2012-0082

Du, S., Bhattacharya, C. B., & Sen, S. (2007). Reaping relationship rewards from corporate social responsibility: The role of competitive positioning. *International Journal of Research in Marketing, 24*(3), 224–241. doi:10.1016/j.ijresmar.2007.01.001

Duarte, S., & Cruz-Machado, V. (2019). Green and lean supply-chain transformation: A roadmap. *Production Planning and Control*, *30*(14), 1170–1183. doi:10.1080/09537287.2019.1595207

D€ues, C., Tan, K., & Lim, M. (2013). Green as the new Lean: how to use Lean practices as a catalystto greening your supply chain. *Journal of Cleaner Production*, *40*, 93.

Dumont, J., Shen, J., & Deng, X. (2017). Effects of green HRM practices on employee workplace green behavior: The role of psychological green climate and employee green values. *Human Resource Management*, *56*, 613–627. doi:10.1002/ hrm.21792

Farias, L. M. S., Santos, L. S., Gohr, C. F., & Rocha, L. O. (2019). An ANP-based approach for lean andgreen performance assessment. *Resources, Conservation and Recycling*, *143*, 77–89.

Forino, G., & von Meding, J. (2021). Climate change adaptation across businesses in Australia: interpretations, implementations, and interactions. *Environ Dev Sustain*. doi:10.1007/s10668-021-01468-z

Frig, M., & Sorsa, V. P. (2020). Nation branding as sustainability governance: A comparative case analysis. *Business & Society*, *2020*(59), 1151–1180.

Galeazzo, A., Furlan, A., & Vinelli, A. (2014). Understanding environmental-operations integration: The case of pollution prevention projects. *International Journal of Production Economics*, *153*(c), 149–160.

Green Jr., K.W., Zelbst, P.J., Meacham, J., Bhadauria, V.S., (2012). Green supply chain management practices: impact on performance. *Supply C. Man. An Int. J.*, *17*(3), 290-305.

Hallam, C., & Contreras, C. (2016). Integrating lean and green management. *Management Decision*, *54*(9), 2157–2187.

Hamilton, C. (2001). *Running from the storm: the development of climate change policy in Australia*. UNSW Press.

Hanna, P., Font, X., Scarles, C., Weeden, C., & Harrison, C. (2018). Tourist destination marketing: From sustainability myopia to memorable experiences. *Journal of Destination Marketing & Management*, *2018*(9), 36–43.

Hartini, S., & Ciptomulyono, U. (2015). The relationship between lean and sustainable manufacturing on performance: Literature review. *Procedia Manufacturing*, *4*, 38–45.

Hartmann, P., & Apaolaza Ibáñez, V. (2006). Green value added. *Marketing Intelligence & Planning*, *24*(7), 673–680.

Head, B. W. (2014). Evidence, uncertainty, and wicked problems in climate change decision making in Australia. *Environment and Planning. C, Government & Policy*, *32*(4), 663–679.

Henao, R., Sarache, W., & Gomez, I. (2019). Lean manufacturing and sustainable performance: Trends and future challenges. *Journal of Cleaner Production*, *208*, 99–116.

Keller, K. (2003). Understanding brands, branding and brand equity. *Journal of Direct, Data and Digital Marketing Practice*, *5*, 7–20. https://doi.org/10.1057/palgrave.im.4340213

Khalili, A., Ismail, M. Y., Karim, A. N. M., & Daud, M. R. C. (2016). Relationships of lean, green manufacturing and sustainable performance: assessing the applicability of the proposed model. *International Conference on Industrial Engineering and Operations Management*. Available at: http://ieomsociety.org/ieom_2016/pdfs/179.pdf

Kim, Y. J., Kim, W. G., Choi, H. M., & Phetvaroon, K. (2019). The effect of green human resource management on hotel employees' eco-friendly behavior and environmental performance. *International Journal of Hospitality Management, 76*, 83–93.

Kosnett, J. R. (2007, Oct.). Green is the Next Big Thing. *Kiplinger's Personal Finance*, 32-34.

Kovilage, M. P. (2021). Influence of lean–green practices on organizational sustainable performance. *Journal of Asian Business and Economic Studies, 28*(2), 121–142. https://doi.org/10.1108/JABES-11-2019-0115

Kruuse, A. (2011). *GRaBS expert paper 6: The green space factor and the green points system*. Academic Press.

Lamm, E., Tosti-Kharas, J., & Williams, E. G. (2013). Read this article, but don't print it: Organizational citizenship behavior toward the environment. *Group & Organization Management, 38*, 163–197.

Lin, R. J., Chen, R. H., & Huang, F. H. (2014). Green innovation in the automobile industry. *Industrial Management & Data Systems, 114*(6), 886–903. https://doi.org/10.1108/IMDS-11-2013-0482

Liu, H. B., McCarthy, B., & Chen, T. (2016). Green food consumption in China: segmentation based on attitudes toward food safety. *J. Int. Food Agribus. Market., 28*, 1–17. doi: .00091.x doi:10.1111/j.1745-4565.2007

Maheshwari, V., Vandewalle, I., & Bamber, D. (2011). Place branding's role in sustainable development. *J. Place Manag. Dev, 2011*(4), 198–213.

Meerow, S., & Newell, J. P. (2017). Detroit, Spatial planning for multifunctional green infrastructure: Growing resilience in. *Landscape and Urban Planning*, 62-75.

Mell, I. C. (2010). *Green infrastructure: Concepts, perceptions, and its use in spatial planning* [Doctoral Thesis]. School of Architecture, Planning and Landscape, Newcastle University.

Mohezara, S., Nazria, M., Kaderb, M. A. R. A., Alib, R., & Yunusb, N. K. M. (2016). Corporate social responsibility in the malaysian food retailing industry: An exploratory study. *Int. Acad. Res. J. Soc. Sci, 2*, 66–72.

Molina-Azorín, J. F., Claver-Cortés, E., Pereira-Moliner, J., & Tarí, J. J. (2009). Environmental practices and firm performance: An empirical analysis in the Spanish hotel industry. *Journal of Cleaner Production, 17*, 516–524.

Morris, M. G., & Venkatesh, V. (2000). Age differences in technology adoption decisions: implications for a changing workforce. *Pers. Psychol., 53*, 375–403. doi:.2000.tb00206.x doi:10.1111/j.1744-6570

Murari, K., & Bhandari, M. (2011). Green HR: Going green with pride. *Journal of Social Welfare and Management, 3*, 107–110.

Namkung, Y., & Jang, S. (2012). Effects of restaurant green practices on brand equity formation: Do green practices really matter? *International Journal of Hospitality Management*, *41*(3), 85–95. https://doi.org/10.1016/j.ijhm.2012.06.006

Narayan, E., Barreto, M., Hantzopoulou, G.-C., & Tilbrook, A. A. (2021). Retrospective Literature Evaluation of the Integration of Stress Physiology Indices, Animal Welfare and Climate Change Assessment of Livestock. *Animals (Basel)*, *11*(5), 1287. https://doi.org/10.3390/ani11051287

Norton, T. A., Zacher, H., & Ashkanasy, N. M. (2012). On the importance of pro-environmental organizational climate for employee green behavior. *Ind. Organ. Psychol.*, *5*, 497–500. doi: .01487.x doi:10.1111/j.1754-9434.2012

Norton, T. A., Zacher, H., & Ashkanasy, N. M. (2014). Organisational sustainability policies and employee green behaviour: The mediating role of work climate perceptions. *Journal of Environmental Psychology*, *38*, 49–54. doi:10.1016/j.jenvp.2013.12.008

Norton, T. A., Zacher, H., & Ashkanasy, N. M. (2014). Organisational sustainability policies and employee green behaviour: The mediating role of work climate perceptions. *Journal of Environmental Psychology*, *38*, 49–54. doi:10.1016/j.jenvp.2013.12.008

Norton, T. A., Zacher, H., & Ashkanasy, N. M. (2015). *Pro-environmental organizational culture and climate. In the psychology of green organizations*. Oxford Univeristy Press.

O'Connor, G.C., & Ayers, A.D., (2005). Building a radical innovation competency. *Res.Technol. Manag.*, *48*(1), 23-31.

Olubunmi, O. A., Xia, P. B., & Skitmore, M. (2016). Green building incentives: A review. *Renewable & Sustainable Energy Reviews*, *59*(C), 1611–1621.

Ones, D. S., & Dilchert, S. (2012). Environmental sustainability at work: A call to action. *Industrial and Organizational Psychology: Perspectives on Science and Practice*, *5*, 444–466.

Ottman, J., Stafford, E. R., & Hartman, C. L. (2007). Avoiding Green Marketing Myopia. *Environment*, *48*(5), 22–36.

Pant, D. R. (2005). A place brand strategy for the Republic of Armenia: 'Quality of context' and 'sustainability' as competitive advantage. *Place Brand*, *1*, 273–282.

Pham, N. T., Tucˇková, Z., & Jabbour, C. J. C. (2019). Greening the hospitality industry: How do green human resource management practices influence organizational citizenship behavior in hotels? A mixed methods study. *Tourism Management*, *72*, 386–399.

Polonsky, M. J. (1991). Australia Sets Guidelines for Green Marketing. *Marketing News*, *24*(21), 6–18.

Pride, W. M., & Ferrell, O. C. (1993). *Marketing: Study Guide*. Houghton Mifflin School.

Ramus, C. A., & Steger, U. (2000). The roles of supervisory support behaviors and environmental policy in employee "eco initiatives" at leading-edge European companies. *Academy of Management Journal*, *43*(4), 605–626.

Renwick, D., Redman, T., & Maguire, S. (2013). Green human resource management: A review and research agenda. *International Journal of Management Review*, *15*(1), 1–14. doi:.00328.x doi:10.1111/j.1468-2370.2011

Robinson, J. (2004). Squaring the circle? Some thoughts on the idea of sustainable development. *Ecol. Econ.*, *48*, 369-384.

Salzman, J., & Hunter, D. (2007). *Negligence in the Air: The Duty of Care in Climate Change Litigation*. Working paper no. 95, Duke University Law School.

Schein, E. H. (1990). *Organizational Culture* (Vol. 45). American Psychological Association.

Seroka-Stolka, O., & Lukomska-Szarek, J. (2016). Barriers to the adoption of proactive environmental strategies in polish companies. *Proceedings of international academic conferences*.

Seuring, S., & Gold, S. (2013). Sustainability management beyond corporate boundaries: from stakeholders to performance. *J. Clean. Prod.*, *56*(1), 1-6.

Sharfman, M. P., & Fernando, C. S. (2008). Environmental risk management and the cost of capital. *Strategic Management Journal*, *29*, 569–592. https://dx.doi.org/10.1002/(ISSN)1097-0266

Smith, A. M., & O'Sullivan, T. (2012). Environmentally responsible behaviour in the workplace: An internal social marketing approach. *Journal of Marketing Management*, *28*, 469–493.

Srivastav, A. K. (2007). Stress in organizational roles-individual and organizational implications. *Icfaian Journal of Management Research*, *6*, 64–74.

Stafford, E. R., & Hartman, C. L. (1996). Green Alliances: Strategic Relations between Businesses and Environmental Groups. *Business Horizons*, *2*, 50–59.

Stubbs, W., & Cocklin, C. (2008). Conceptualizing a sustainability business model. *Org. Env.*, *21*(2), 103-127.

Taecharungroj, V., Muthuta, M., & Boonchaiyapruek, P. (2019). Sustainability as a place brand position: A resident-centric analysis of the ten towns in the vicinity of Bangkok. *Place Branding and Public Diplomacy*, *2019*(15), 210–228.

Teixeira, A. A., Jabbour, C. J. C., Lopes de Sousa, A. B., Hengky Latan, J., & Caldeira De Oliveira, J. H. (2016). Green training and green supply chain management: Evidence from Brazilian firms. *Journal of Cleaner Production*, *116*, 170–176.

Thanki, S. J., & Thakkar, J. J. (2016). Value-value load diagram: A graphical tool for lean-green performance assessment. *Production Planning and Control*, *27*, 1280–1297.

To, W. M., Lam, K. H., & Lai, T. M. (2015). Importance-performance ratings for environmental practices among Hong Kong professional-level employees. *Journal of Cleaner Production*, *108*, 699–706.

Too, L., & Bajracharya, B. (2015). Sustainable Campus: Engaging the community in sustainability. *International Journal of Sustainability in Higher Education*, *16*(1), 57–71.

Tuan, L. T. (2019). Catalyzing employee OCBE in tour companies: The role of environmentally specific charismatic leadership and organizational justice for pro-environmental behaviors. *Journal of Hospitality & Tourism Research (Washington, D.C.), 43*, 682–711. doi:10.1177/1096348018817582

Vandenbrande, W. W. (2019). Quality for a sustainable future. *Total Quality Management & Business Excellence,* 1–9. doi:10.1080/14783363.2019.1588724

Wiese, A., Luke, R., Heyns, G. J., & Pisa, N. M. (2015). The integration of lean, green, and best practice business principles. *Journal of Transport and Supply Chain Management, 9*(1), 192–202.

Wright, C., & Nyberg, D. (2014). Creative self-destruction: Corporate responses to climate change as political myths. *Environmental Politics, 23*(2), 205–223.

Wu, L., Subramanian, N., Abdulrahman, M. D., Liu, C., Lai, K., & Pawar, K. S. (2015). The impact of integrated practices of lean, green, and social management systems on firm sustainability performance-evidence from Chinese fashion auto-parts suppliers. *Sustainability, 7*(4), 3838–3858.

Xu, X., Maki, A., Chen, C., Dong, B., & Day, J. K. (2017). Investigating willingness to save energy and communication about energy use in the American workplace with the attitude-behavior-context model. *Energy Research & Social Science, 32*, 13–22. doi:10.1016/j.erss.2017.02.011

Yen, Y. X., & Yen, S. Y. (2012). Top-management's role in adopting green purchasing standards in high-tech industrial firms. *Journal of Business Research, 65*(7), 951–959.

Zamoum, K., & Gorpe, S. T. (2021). Corporate social responsibility in the Emirati Vision Strategy for year 2021. *Proceedings CSRCOM 2017 The 4th International CSR Communication Conference Austrian Academy of Sciences.*

Zhang, B., Wang, Z., & Lai, K. H. (2015). Mediating effect of managers' environmental concern: Bridge between external pressures and firms' practices of energy conservation in China. *Journal of Environmental Psychology, 43*, 203–215.

Zientara, P., & Zamojska, A. (2018). Green organizational climates and employee pro-environmental behaviour in the hotel industry. *Journal of Sustainable Tourism,* 26.

Zouganeli, S., Trihas, N., Antonaki, M., & Kladou, S. (2012). Aspects of sustainability in the destination branding process: A bottom-up approach. *Journal of Hospitality Marketing & Management, 2012*(21), 739–757.

Chapter 16
Strategic Analysis of Organizational Learning Approaches to Dynamic Resilient Capability

José G. Vargas-Hernández
https://orcid.org/0000-0003-0938-4197
Posgraduate and Research Department, Tecnológico Mario Molina Unidad Zapopan, Mexico

ABSTRACT

The purpose of this study is to analyze the strategic organizational learning approach to dynamic resilient capabilities. A scoping review of the theoretical and empirical literature on organizational dynamic resilience capability reveals gaps to be addressed to improve the conceptualization. Under the assumption of some attributes and properties, it is viable to study the organizational resilience learning process leading to the analysis of the organizational resilience strategies.

INTRODUCTION

Organizations are complex and dynamic systems continuously changing (Norris et al., 2008; Tyler & Moench, 2012; Young, 2010). Resilience is the organizational function of the overall awareness, management of vulnerabilities, and adaptive capacity in a complex, uncertain, dynamic, and interconnected environment. Resilience is shaped by an adaptive system based on multilevel dynamics interaction aiming to change (Masten, 2007: 926) which in turn resists increasing vulnerability and enhances resilience (Walker & Salt, 2012: 24).

Organizational resilience is related to change phenomena such as ecological unexpected and disruptive events and to environmental characteristics such as complexity, uncertainty, turbulence, dynamic, etc. Resilience organizations develop the ability to be dynamic and stable to continue operations after any major mishap (Woods & Hollnagel, 2006).

DOI: 10.4018/978-1-6684-5109-0.ch016

Organizational resilience is a function of the situation awareness, management of vulnerabilities, adaptive capacity of an organization in a complex, uncertain, dynamic, and interdependent environment. The economic, social, political, and cultural organizational environment are being considered as dynamic trait that may enhance organizational resilience.

A scoping review of the literature on organizational resilience reveals gaps to be addressed to improve the conceptualization, often presented as a normative, and the dynamic adaptation in emergent patterns of the systemic interactions. One school promotes the actions to cope with turbulences and the other fosters the dynamic ability to develop new capabilities to monitor changes and take actions to mitigate environmental challenges.

Organizational resilience frameworks align to build a system adaptation based on dynamic capabilities constructs (Limnios et al., 2014). The contribution of other disciplines to the resilience conceptualization is critical to understand the dynamics or organizational resilience capabilities related to the issues where there are gaps of information, such as in areas of the role of organizational knowledge, culture, structure, determinants of the resilience process, preparation for unexpected events, abilities to deal with threatening events at different levels of analysis.

Research on organizational resilience has been undertaken in high-reliability organizations operating in uncertain, complex, and dynamic environments where errors may lead to catastrophic consequences (Bigley & Roberts, 2001; Weick & Roberts, 1993; Weick & Sutcliffe, 2001; Weick et al., 2005). Resilience offers different thinking to contribute to the theoretical debates based on resource-based and dynamic capabilities. Theory building of organizational development is focusing on heuristic based dynamic capabilities under strategic and resource collapse conditions (McGrath, 1999; Mellahi & Wilkinson, 2004; Probst & Raisch, 2005; Sheppard & Chowdhury, 2005).

Economic theories assert that organizations aim to efficient economy balanced by turnarounds and dynamic capabilities (Barker & Duhaime, 1997; Morrow, Sirmon, Hitt, & Holcomb, 2007; Shein, 2011) and dynamic capabilities (Helfat et al., 2007; Teece, 2007; Zahra, Sapienza, & Davidsson, 2006) and the ability of organizations to endure, recover and adapt from distress.

The concept of resilience is complex and dynamic. Organizational resilience includes several attributes and elements (Gibson & Tarrant, 2010). Organizational resilience is essentially a dynamic capability used to manage unstable organizational systems to develop reliable functions (Weick & Sutcliffe, 2007). Organizational resilience is dynamic and incremental (Alexiou, 2014; Kamalahmadi & Parast, 2016; Ortiz-de-Mandojana & Bansal, 2015).

The study begins with the conceptualization of the dynamic resilient capability leading to consider the attributes and properties that are relevant in the organizational resilience learning process. Finally, it is analyzed the organizational resilience strategy.

CONCEPTUALIZATION OF THE DYNAMIC RESILIENT CAPABILITY

Resilience is a dynamic concept and evolves over time from fragile to antifragile (Taleb, 2012). The notion of organizational resilience is related to the concept of dynamic capabilities. The conceptual and empirical study of organizational resilience provide evidence of the dual change mechanism of dynamic capabilities construct used as a framework to reconfigure existent routines and resources, creating opportunities through alliances and entrepreneurial actions (Peteraf et al., 2013, Zahra, Sapienza, & Davidsson, 2006, Alvarez & Barney, 2007; Barreto, 2012).

Strategic Analysis

To build a conceptualization of organizational resilience it is necessary to clarify and use some assumptions to underlie different orientations to enable the building and development of dynamic capabilities. The assumptions of resilience can be accommodated in the dynamic capabilities framework as the platform to build the foundations for the conceptualization of organizational resilience.

Organizational resilience is the ability to strengthen firms by harnessing experience to become adaptive, robust, agile, and competitive in increasingly ever-changing, dynamic, and complex environment and embracing opportunities. Organizational resilience is the dynamic capability of exploitative adaptations or engineering resilience, explorative transformation, or ecological resilience to maintain performance and longevity (Eltantawy, 2016). Ecological resilience requires the anticipation of risks, reduction of environmental degradation, and organizational preparedness of ecosystem dynamics dependent upon natural resources (Whiteman and Cooper 2011). The engineering resilience akin to self-restoring equilibrium dynamics in mainstream economics. The conceptualization of capability performance provides insights into the complex dynamics to rebuild opportunities and development.

Organizational resilience is a strategic ability to adapt, integrate and reconfigure internal and external organizational skills, resources, and functional competences to match the requirements of a changing environment resulting from a set of dynamic capabilities (Limnios *et al.* 2014). A dynamic capabilities perspective of organizational resilience provides more understanding of adaptive conditions of adversity with the purpose.

Organizational resilience is the ability to anticipate, cope effectively, learn from these events from trends and potential threats with unexpected events to produce a dynamic capability directed towards organizational change (Duchek, 2014). Organizational resilience is the ability to continually evolve and thrive over time in the face of adverse and hostile circumstances which naturally arise in dynamic environments (Demmer *et al.* 2011).

The impact of resilience on dynamic capabilities of the organization is well known. Organizational resilience encourages recovery and growth from adversity that may involve adopting an entrepreneurial mindset and develops dynamic capabilities that turns adverse experiences into opportunities for strategic renewal. Organizations build dynamic capabilities in resilience to design strategic opportunities out of adversity.

Organizational resilience is the ability to continually evolve and thrive in adverse and hostile circumstances arising in dynamics environments (Demmer *et al.* 2011). Organizational resilience is a trait to thrive in a dynamic and volatile business environment (Chan, 2011). Organizational resilience is concerned with the adaptation process to challenge complex environmental conditions through the capability dynamic alignment aimed to avoid a path dependency approach and rebuild efficient performance (Lengnick-Hall & Beck, 2009; Sydow, Schreyögg & Koch, 2009; Eisenhardt et al., 2010). Organizational resilience is the ability and the dynamic capability of an organization to resist, absorb, cope, recover, and adapt to the altered environment following a disaster (Kahan, Allen, George, & Thompson, 2009; McManus, Seville, Vargo, & Brunsdon, 2008).

Resilience is conceptualized as a dynamic process of ongoing and reciprocal transactions between the organizations and the environment (Vanderbilt-Adriance & Shaw, 2008: 31). Organizational resilience is the intrinsic ability of a system to maintain a dynamic stable state and continue operations after a mishap in the presence of a continuous stress (Woods and Hollnagel, 2006). Organizational resilience is the ability to thrive in a dynamic environment (Cho *et al.* 2006).

Luthar et al. (2000) defines resilience as the dynamic processes encompassing positive adaptation in a context of significant adversity (p. 543) and adapting to sudden changes. The resilience process-oriented is a dynamic nature interaction between the organization and the environment (Williams et al. 2017, p. 20) responding before, during and after to adverse events (Linnenluecke et al. 2012; Alliger et al. 2015; Williams et al. 2017).

Organizational resilience is the dynamic organizational capability to facilitate organizational change through the development of abilities to anticipate, cope and learn from potential threats, unexpected events, and trends. Resilience is conceptualized as a normative construct the system of capabilities for dynamics adaptive process and outcomes. The sociological resilience of organizational system is more dynamic and determined by the adaptation process undergoing during the adaptive cycle.

Dynamic and operating capabilities and division of routines in the context of organizational resilience contributes to build adaptations through segmented actions at several levels. From this perspective, a reliable action of resilience beyond the evolution and revolution phases addressing sequences of crisis for growth and maturity functioning of the organization (Greiner, 1972). The resilience capability perspective incorporates a hierarchy of activities that yield competitive advantages while reconfiguring responses as dynamic capabilities to environmental changes (Ambrosini et al., 2009; Danneels, 2012; Hine, Parker, Pregelj, & Verreynne, 2014).

PROPERTIES AND ATTRIBUTES

Resilience is conceptualized as a generic quality linked to dynamic capabilities. Organizational resilience as an emergent system is a dynamic property that integrates the processes of adaptation and integration processes in inter-systemic in nature (Clement and Rivera 2017: 30). The dynamic nature of organizational resilience provides the inference of causality in a longitudinal evaluation that contributes to organizational renewal based on employee work-role performance (Gover & Duxbury, 2018). Organizational resilience uses the interactions of assets, attributes and routines that recognize the effects of risk over time and their emerge in unexpected ways (Vanderbilt-Adriance & Shaw, 2008: 30-31). Organizational resilience is a dynamic capacity that develops over time (Wildavsky, 1988)

As a dynamical property, organizational resilience requires new core properties of the system's capacity to be ready to respond by anticipating and synchronizing events and proactively learn (Hollnagel and Woods 2017). Resilience can be desirable and non-desirable depending on the proactive development and adaptation of dynamic capabilities (Limnios et al. 2014). The socio-ecological systems have derived in the resilience (Folke, 2006) referring to a dynamic capacity of adaptation and to the system's capacity to absorb the internal and external disruption and perturbations and return to a stable state.

Organizational resilience analysis as a dynamic property requires building inter and transdisciplinary bridges aimed to integrate processes of both organizational adaptation and transformation of the operative ecosystems and dependent networks to build and enhance resilience aligned to more holistic sustainable development goals (Folke et al., 2010).

Organizational resiliency is a relevant attribute when dealing during crisis through preparation, dynamic and flexible planning and proactive behavior built with specific training on psychological capital of personnel. Risk readiness is a concept developed in a dynamic model associated with resilience (Cook and Rasmussen 2005). The concept of resilience links to the change from a static to more dynamic paradigm of safety management. Organizational resilience in safety of complex systems copes with highly risky variability (Bergström et al., 2015), although safety is a dynamic non-event and the ability of dealing with shocks and unexpected events (Weick and Sutcliffe 2001).

It remains unclear how organizations may achieve resilience (Boin and van Eeten, 2013; Duit, 2016) and their antecedents, relationships, interactions and drivers between the different stages in an explicit conceptual framework for a comprehensive conceptual and dynamics understanding (Lynham, 2002, p. 232; Meredith, 1993; Jabareen, 2009; Burnard and Bhamra, 2011). Some principles of organizational resilience are the learning, flexibility, and adaptability.

Organizational resilience is an intrinsic attribute to the ethos of the organization and provides a shared common platform adapted to the dynamic complexity of the organizational environment, providing confidence to take measured risks, and responding appropriately. To ensure organizational resilience is important to develop a dynamic leadership, understanding the needs of all the stakeholders involved and have well-trained staff.

The different nature of organizational resilience capabilities is based on the antecedents either a heuristics-based dynamic capability, or the adoption of routine actions in the absence of survival conditions. An organizational resilience capability loop can be based on heuristic dynamic capabilities. Heuristics in organizational resilience are linked with dynamic capabilities (Bingham & Eisenhardt, 2011). Heuristics-based dynamic capabilities must be pertinent to some contextual circumstances while others may require routine-based capabilities to provide the organizational resilience. Organizations tend to use more heuristic-based resilience dynamic capabilities in scenarios of major resource loss and uncertainty.

Dynamic organizational resilience capabilities resilience focuses on the shift from the capability hierarchy perspective to heuristics-based capabilities (Barreto, 2010; Hine et al., 2014). The heuristics insight provides a decision structure to assess the organizational resilience preserving behavioral flexibility to deal with the collapse in any dynamic nature of a specific context. Organizational resilience can be assessed based on the functions of monitoring, responding, anticipating, and learning (Apneseth *et al.* 2013) and on the ability to respond, monitor, anticipate and learn (Hollnagel 2010).

According to the resilience orientations framework of Teece (2007) the reintegration, homeostasis, and loss have different dynamic capabilities for sensing, seizing, and transforming. Heuristic processes with recovery and growth from adversity can be invoked to build a dynamic resilience building with the support or sensing, seizing, and transforming processes in response to specific threats. A comprehensive heuristic dynamic capability model characterizes threats for the types of strategic, operating and resource disorganization.

Each type of disorganizations requires deployment of different heuristic resilience dynamic capability at different times and across the processes of sensing, seizing, and transforming. The result of these processes differs in resilience outcomes. The heuristics-based dynamic capabilities (Bingham et al., 2007) and the operating capabilities built on routines (Helfat et al., 2007) for organizational resilience under conditions of sustainability and competitive advantage (Peteraf, di Stefano & Verona, 2013).

An elaborate dynamic organizational resilience capability supported by a portfolio of heuristics (Gigerenzer & Brighton, 2009) the organization is challenged to deploy sensing, seizing and transformation. The heuristic-based dynamic organizational resilience capability portfolio is more critical for an unstable organization more than resources and routines. Under stable conditions of resource management and strategy, the heuristic-based dynamic capabilities can configure and re-configure the operating routing-based and entrepreneurial capabilities (Hine, Parker, Pregelj, & Verreynne, 2014; Teece, 2012; Teece et al., 1997).

Resilience is an emergent property of complex systems related to the capacity of a system to reorganize after internal or external disturbances (Folke, 2006) and adapt to organizational settings through the emergence of new behavioral patterns, learning and changes in the structure of social interactions.

THEORETICAL AND EMPIRICAL LITERATURE REVIEW

A systematic theoretical foundation of organizational research has not been formed and developed until now. The organizational dynamic resilience perspective indicates the growing of resilience to maintain a positive position to face crisis. The micro foundations of the dynamic capabilities are explored by Tabaklar, Sorkun, Yurt, and Yu, (2021) and propose a social innovation framework in highly dynamic settings to build and reconfigure capabilities that may apply in organizational resilience.

Because organizational resilience is an effective means to achieve sustainable growth in crisis situations, Chen, Liu, and Zhou, F. (2021), using the mapping and literature analysis methods, have developed an organizational resilience framework for research. Global health actors can harness the opportunities offered by pathways of change, according to Held, Kickbusch, McNally, Piselli, Told, (2019), one of which is the degree of organizational learning and active feedback loops between organizational epistemic and practice communities aimed to enhance a polycentric system of governance and the political leadership for governance innovation. An organizational dynamic resilience perspective from the capability perspective considers that resilience is a dynamic developmental and progressive process-based of organizations in improvisational response to crisis and involving identity management (Ishak, and Williams, 2018; McCarthy, Collard, and Johnson, 2017).

A theoretical organizational learning frame has been developed by Willems, Busscher, van den Brink, and Arts, (2018) to analyze the anticipation of change in agencies and the empirical research implications into the practice of waterway renewal in practice in which change is pragmatic. The dynamic capability perspective of organizational resilience research is based on evolutionary economics, the resource base view, and capabilities (Davies, and Brady, 2016).

Flexible and changing organizations only can thrive to keep aligned in a volatile environment enhancing the ability to be able to respond to crisis and supported by organizational learning, the organization can develop the dynamic resilient capacities to promote change (Duchek, 2014). Organizational learning theory is incorporated into organizational resilience by Umoh et al. (2014) and developed a measurement scale based on McManus *et al.*, (2008) to include planning capacity, organizational learning capacity, dynamic capacity, and adaptive capacity. Only flexible, changing, and agile organizations can thrive in dynamic and evolving environments (Lengnick-Hall *et al.* 2011)

One of the promised perspectives is the theory of organizational resilience based on the dynamic capability theory considered as the ability of firms to perceive threats and opportunities, make decisions, solve problems, and change their resource bases (Barreto, 2010). Internalized the dynamic capability as the organizational resilience based on the safety audit of resilience engineering by Huber *et al.* (2009), the results of their research show that the organizational dynamic capability determined the safety performance.

Organizational resilience is the function of the ability of adaptation to the dynamic environment of the organization (Wicker, Filo, and Cuskelly, 2013, Mcmanus, Seville, Vargo, and Brunsdon, 2008). Dynamic capabilities evolve with the changing environment where learning plays an important role (Zollo & Winter, 2002). The organizational dynamic capability was proposed by Teece *et al.* (1997) as the ability of the firm to establish and reconfigure its internal and external resources to gain competitive advantage in the turbulent and changing environment.

Strategic Analysis

ORGANIZATIONAL RESILIENCE LEARNING PROCESS

The resilience is the combination of anticipating, learning, responding, and monitoring sociotechnical systems comply with the variability of activities, the nature of work and the nonlinear activities (Patriarca, Di Gravio, Constantino, Falegnami, Bilotta, 2017). In the broad social sciences, resilience is the anticipated effort to predict and prevent potential dangers and the capacity to cope after the dangers manifest, learning to bounce back (Wildavsky, 1988: 61).

Organizational resilience is the ability to handle and respond threats and hazards to unexpected trouble, using pre-existing and pre-planned capabilities, by learning, changing, and developing new capabilities (Dalgaard-Nielson, 2017). Organizational resilience is the capacity and ability to respond positively, adaptively for adaptation, for learning, withstand in disruptive change and external shocks (Stewart and O'Donnel, 2007). The organization can evaluate its resilience and learn after the event in terms of the resources employed and the capacity to absorb the impact of the climate change and extreme weather event and recover. Organizational learning after these events can develop new resilience and adaptation capacities (March et al., 2003)

Organizational resilience is critical in a volatile environment and adversity where some organizations survive, others thrive, and others perish. Organizations must manage their specific resources, structures, capabilities, etc. Some building blocks affect anticipating, coping with and adapting and learning from adversity, entailing leadership, environmental scanning, initiating change processes and resilience planning in the complexity and uncertainty of the world (Vakilzadeh and Haase, 2020). Leadership enhances organizational resilience in times of change as capacity to respond adaptively to disruptive change, and implies the ability to withstand shocks and the capacity for adaptation and learning (Stewart and O'Donnell 2007)

Organizational Resilience is about learning to bounce back (Wildavsky,1988) and the ability to bounce forward (Manyena, O'Brien, O'Keefe, and Rose, 2011) to grow and prosper (Reich, 2006) through the mechanisms of performance optimization and adaptive innovation. Organizational resilience is the response to a crisis and learning over time how to face with new challenges (Sutcliffe & Vogus, 2003). Organizational resilience is linked to overcoming the crisis and emerge strengthened successful to growth (Freeman *et al.* 2004, Sutcliffe and Vogus 2003; Teo *et al.* 2017) and learning to develop new capabilities and the ability to thrive despite diversity (Dalgaard-Nielsen 2017; Stewart and O'Donnell 2007; Teo *et al.* 2017; Wildavsky, 1988; Williams *et al.* 2017; Chan 2011; Cho *et al.* 2006).

Organizational resilience comprises adaptation implying long-term learning (Madni & Jackson, 2009). Long-term adaptation of anticipatory adjustments and learning to respond to the impacts on ecological discontinuities from climate vulnerabilities and weather extremes should be considered in the design and implementation of resilience strategies. Resilience is a learning process of protective actions to build resilience against perceived vulnerabilities over time that needs to be explicit for organizations (Hale & Heijer, 2006; Masten, 2001).

The social-ecological perspective of resilience incorporates learning, adaptation and transformation beyond constancy and recovery. The concept of resilience has gradually moved from an assumption of single equilibrium to multiple equilibrium in socio-ecological systems with the increasing recognition of complexity, uncertainty, variation and learning in living systems (Folke 2006). Socioecology systems resilience can be supported by heuristics to build anticipation, recovery, learning and adaptation (Walker et al., 2006; Madni & Jackson, 2009).

Organizational resilience may result of learning from disasters (Roberts, Madsen, & Desai, 2005) and from unexpected events. Resilience must respond to what is happening by the identification, anticipation and learning from the critical problems (Hollnagel, 2009).

Organizational resilience is an iterative practice of learning the dynamic capabilities to reconfigure resources and activities for strategic opportunities by enhancing change and unintended consequences (Teece, 2007: 1343). Unlearning facilitates organizational resilience (Morais-Storz and Nguyen 2017). The transformational perspective of organizational resilience capacity is tied to a dynamic process embedded in the individuals' knowledge, skills, and abilities (King et al., 2016; Kuntz et al., 2017). Organizational resilience relates to the redundancy of humans and equipment (Azadeh et al. 2016) that promotes the robustness of the system and implies learning and adaptive changes.

Resilience capabilities can be state-like open to development through training programs or on-the-job training in dynamic capability to cope and bounce back with significant change from risk and adversities. Also, organizational resilience can be trait-like stable of the individual, team, group, and organization (Luthans 2002; Coutu 2002). In a dialectic process, resilience is influenced by different levels considered as the capability of individuals, groups, and organizations to cope in dynamic context (Cho et al. 2006).

A cultural learning process of organizational resilience enables the abilities and capabilities needed by the organizations to respond properly to deal with incidents and disturbances. Some cultural factors identified include the organizational learning and learning from past experiences. Organizational culture, learning from past experiences and professional servant leadership are some of the factors that affect organizational resilience (Erol *et al.* 2010; and Boin and McConnell 2007).

Organizational learning from incidents experience at facing external environmental, socio ecosystems, spatial, societal, sectoral, etc., crises events, has an influence on the adoption of responses and other resilience activities (Toft and Reynolds, 1997) through isomorphic learning from events of other organizations with improvements and planning (Deverell, 2009; Weick and Sutcliffe, 2003). Cross-sectional learning is implicit in organizational resilience to avoid failure and cope with crisis (Crichton et al. 2009).

Nevertheless, large organizations have organizational resilience rooted in both locations and relationships, rather than resilience formalization and isomorphic learning from other vicinities and neighborhoods characterized by their strategic resilience planning formalization activities, resources, roles, and agreements to recover from disruptive events.

The experience of mild and strong dysfunctional events and disruptions may be used for learning organizational resilience reintegration with cognitive and behavioral solutions and predominant heuristic-based responses (March 1991). Seizing from reintegration resilience is learning from threats and become open to large scale organizational change as part of the organizational growth in response to uncertainty and adversity. The resilience learning capability enable organizational survival and growth to exploit advantages (McGrat, 2013). The resilience reintegration orientation engages in a deep learning process against threats.

Organizational resilience can be increased to achieve robustness by learning from previous failures. Learning from failures facilitates organizational resilience (Crichton et al. 2009). The improvement of organizational resilience learning from multiple past failures in the network and disaster recovery, quickly identify, locate, and assess the grid resilience elements of previous errors for critical missions aimed to correct and improve processes, optimize recovery efforts, and mitigate the impacts (Chen et al., 2014). Personal networks and norms of generalized reciprocity for organizational development can be identified in the context of resilience, social learning, community recovery of disasters (Chamlee-Wright, 2010, p.21)

Strategic Analysis

Group resilience develops the capacity of learning through the imperfections and failures with the combination of accountability and psychological safety as critical ingredients (Edmonson 2007). Communities approach resilience with other associated concepts and terms seeking to improve it by learning from demonstration to achieve robust designs, high-reliability, and complex adaptive systems.

Resilience stages depend on the prior organizational knowledge former crisis, the environment, actions, etc., and influence learning and knowledge base to be used in anticipation as learning for crisis, in coping by learning as crisis and adaptation as learning from crisis (Smith and Elliott 2007). Action priority can build organizational resilience through the access to information and learning. Action learning facilitates organizational learning and change leading to organizational resilience as the ability to recover unexpected exogenous environmental change (O'Hara et al. 2007).

The organizational knowledge base is enhanced by learning for and through rare unexpected events in close relationship between the anticipation and coping phases of organizational resilience (Christianson et al. 2009) and also illustrated by the feedback loop between the anticipation and adaptation. Outcomes of organizational learning at individual level facilitate change and resilience (O'Hara et al. 2007).

Organizational resilience dynamic capabilities are not concreted things or objects and do not have any boundaries, rather is dynamic consisting in a repertoire of knowledge, skills, processes, and heuristics learnt from experiences of adversity events. The dynamic capability of organizational resilience is based on learning integration skills to reduce vulnerability. Organizational resilience as a dynamic capability is a multidisciplinary concept embracing the mechanisms of learning.

The perspective of the systems, the organizational systems is a multifaceted concept used to develop capabilities to implement adaptive responses to disruptions and create organizational learning (Francis & Bekera, 2014; Lee et al., 2013; Maitlis & Christianson, 2014; Thiel et al., 2012). Richardson (2016) applied the metatheory of resilience postulating the qualities inquiring and learning to achieve mastery as the result of change

Organizations may increase resilience by learning from errors and dynamic plans. Organizations develop different resilience capacities subject to their past experiences and leading to different threats, high risks, and disorganizations disturbances, which may require behavioral flexibility and heuristics in dynamic capabilities. Past experiences, learning and creativity are resources that influence facilitates resilience in smaller businesses (Glover 2012; Richtnér and Löfsten 2014).

Organizations develop resilience capability after coping with collapse aligned with the decision dynamic context, constraints in resources, opportunities and heuristics with a decision making. Organizational collapses are source of learning resilience capabilities to build organizational resilience an applied across the operating conditions. Heuristics is an efficient mechanism embedding learning from adversity to become more resilient (Gigerenzer, 2008).

The concept of organizational resilience informs organizational practices to bring more experiential learning and knowledge to prevent challenges of future scenarios, such as demographic, social, and economic changes (Bento and Garotti, 2019) such as in the situation of post-covid-19. The application of Bayesian network models in organizational resilience has implications with business models to open spaces for communication, learning and adaptation to prevent crisis.

Organizational adaptation is a concept in organizational resilience processes (Burnard and Bhamra 2011) that comprises the phases of detection and activation, response and organizational learning. Organizational resilience includes adaptation capabilities to critical events and the ability to make adjustments using change for organizational long term learning and advancement and increasing the knowledge for anticipation (Limnios et al. 2014; Madni and Jackson, 2009).

Adaptation is a key capability that includes reflection, learning and organizational change aimed to avoid and reduce negative effects of unexpected events (Carley, 1991; Carley and Harrald, 1997). The adaptation processes in organizational resilience have implications in operational safety practices and others, becoming relevant for the emergence of learning and knowledge creation as a respond to crisis and unexpected events.

The organizational resilience process model is a framework to build and develop dynamic capabilities as high order process to respond to tensions created by adverse unknown events and disturbances that require reconfiguration of organizational resources and activities and changing environmental negative circumstances (Burnard & Bhamra, 2011: 5595). Organizational resilience building is enabled by dynamics and impact of unexplored events (Burnard & Bhamra, 2011: 5595).

Organizational resilience building covers the management of human resources, cognitive adaptation to environmental situations, reducing vulnerabilities and propensity to disruptive events and desirability of dynamic states (Limnios et al., 2014; Lengnick-Hall, Beck, & Lengnick-Hall, 2011; Watts & Paciga, 2011; Sheffi, 2005). Organizational resilience dynamic capability building proceeds across the decline, collapse, and re-building stages to withstand failure and managing collapse.

The resilience dynamic capability development of the organization requires to learn heuristics and skills emerging from specific events and cases triggered by the different stakeholders in boundary and rebuilding transitions. An organization should learn to develop a dynamic organizational resilience-based view of capability using heuristics instead of routines, enabling strategic change and reducing the threats of collapse. Development of organizational resilience enhances organizational learning enacted through routines oriented toward specific targets (Levitt & March,1988).

The organizational resilience-based view may develop supported by dynamic capabilities and heuristics to regain stability after adversity. Resilience is a mechanism of learning and change to foster practices for stability (Bingham, Eisenhard and Davis 2007). Resilience as stability and change (Farjoun 2010) provides empirical evidence to facilitate learning and capability development for organizational change (Bingham, Eisenhard and Davis 2007).

The process model of resilience capability integrates the insights to provide resilience dynamic capability by deploying a set of skills and heuristics to bounce back from collapse.

ORGANIZATIONAL RESILIENCE STRATEGIES

Cycles of organizational learning and unlearning achieve strategic organizational resilience (Morais-Storz and Nguyen 2017)

The best organizational resilience response occurs when strategies are designed to specific disturbance although may be cognitively demanding but still manageable (Masten, 2014). Organizational resilience is a strategy aimed to face the challenges of a dynamic, complex, and uncertain and continually changing environment. Organizational resilience is a strategy based on the adoption of best practices to survive, improve, and prosper in a context of dynamic global environment by building capabilities across all the organizational areas. Design and implementation of organizational resilience strategies requires information availability and flexibility and adaptability processes through sharing of information flow and mission resilience awareness and assurance of the dynamic environment.

Organizational resilience strategies aim to mitigate errors and error recovery (Weick & Sutcliffe, 2007), to overcome barriers and incentive adaptation and learning (Howard & Irving, 2013; Li et al., 2012).

Strategic Analysis

The strategic resilience enables the organizations to reinvent dynamic models and strategies as the circumstances and situations change (Hamel and Vaelikangas 2003; Vaelikangas and Romme 2013). This conceptualization is similar to the strategic offense (Limnios et al. 2014). The dynamics of organizational resilience when facing challenges of unknow events, natural disasters, socio-economic trends, etc., requires organizations to respond, to adapt and protect continuing sustainable performance and growth (Stephenson, 2010).

The dynamics of emerging organizational behaviors may arise from environmental changes such as disasters and unknown events (Burnard and Bhamra, 2011). Organizational resilience is an approach to disaster management based on identification of resources and assets that can support adaptive response and dynamic recovery (O'Sullivan, Corneil, Kuziemsky, & Toal-Sullivan, 2015).

An approach to organizational resilience in a dynamic environment requires a balance of efficiency and reliability through flexibility and implementing measures of information availability to detect potential disruptions. Resilience are optimization and renewal as lagged indicators, and protective factors as proactive indicators are equal partners leading to the ability to evolve and thrive in the face of adversity which arise in dynamic environments (Demmer et al. 2011). Measures for organizational resilience in the context of specific goal may require moderate implementation of a feedback loop development for building dynamic emergency procedures to integrate the information required for the assessment of possible risks.

The intra and inter-groups dynamics assess the organizational resilience in which the different occupational groups distribute their activities. The notion of resilience qualifies better based on informal arrangements affected by the inter-group dynamics with negotiated and articulated tasks. The resilience of a team group increases in the face of unexpected events managed in a strong community practice. Assessing resilience requires the costs of change representing the involved working groups in their intra- and inter-group dynamics confronted with the crisis. An organizational resilience approach of containing crises regards high reliable organizations as the essence of resilience, the ability to maintain and regain a dynamic stable state in the presence of an uncertainty and vulnerability.

The dynamic capability model development has implications for the organizational resilience when resources dissipate the strategy fails to foster a long-term adversity period. The resilience dynamic capability operates the ability to manage collapse and shift towards stability and re-building. SMEs resilience is tied to strategic planning and its aspirations in terms of development of dynamic capabilities in response to a crisis, such as innovativeness, responsiveness, competition, renewal, uncertainty, etc. (Macpherson, Herbane, and Jones, 2015). The dynamic integration of logistics capabilities facilitates readiness, response, and recovery of the supply chain resilience (Ponomarov and Holcomb 2009)

CONCLUSION

Resilience is addressed through turnaround and dynamic capabilities. Organizational resilience is critical to possessing dynamic capabilities attracting new resources, design strategies and learn to overcome rigidity and regain stability. Organizational resilience is the ability to manage workflow disturbances and regain a dynamic stable state.

A conceptual organizational resilience and adaptation focuses on a dynamic interplay between organizational activities and weather variabilities. Organizational resilience involves more than a strategic imperative and the ability of the organization to survive but enables to harness its experience and flourishes embracing the opportunities in a dynamic, complex, and interconnected environment.

Some of the ex-ante decisions are planning, learning and back-up systems and some of the ex-post adjustments are changing routines, minimizing strains on infrastructure and external support. Resilience differs from continuity management in that this one is returning to business as before, while resilience enables organizations to continue but evolves and growth from a disturbance through the transformation processes by learning, flourish, and progress.

Resilience emphasizes learning from failures and success to become reliable organizations. Organizational resilience cannot be boosted on trial and error due to the high cost but by focusing on learning from failures. Resilience is related to experiential knowledge constructed by learning beyond cumulative logic from the unexpected and open communication across units and agents. Group resilience is promoted by the interactions between individuals developing organizational learning and resilience.

Resilience can integrate findings from other areas and disciplines which can be related to other resilience stages and levels such as the anticipation through high reliability organizations, coping using crisis management adaptation to unexpected events supported by organizational learning. The organizational resilience leverages learning and experience to adjust and forge new organizational development.

The development of the resilience capability occurs when learning is embedded into the conscious mind of individuals in the organization and becomes experiential knowledge to be used in future adversity events. The resilience model becomes a resilience planning and implementing tool for organizational resilience that contributes to learning from mistakes and events underestimated.

REFERENCES

Alexiou, A. (2014). Taming the waves of adversity: Exploring the multidimensional construct of organizational resilience. In D. G. Assimakopoulos, I. Oshri, & K. Pandza (Eds.), *Managing Emerging Technologies for Socio-Economic Impact*. Edward Elgar Publishing. doi:10.4337/9781782547884.00026

Alliger, G. M., Cerasoli, C. P., Tannenbaum, S. I., & Vessey, W. B. (2015). Team resilience: How teams flourish under pressure. *Organizational Dynamics*, *44*(3), 176–184. doi:10.1016/j.orgdyn.2015.05.003

Alvarez, S. A., & Barney, J. B. (2007). Discovery and Creation: Alternative Theories of Entrepreneurial Action. *Strategic Entrepreneurship Journal*, *1*(1), 11–26. doi:10.1002ej.4

Ambrosini, V., Bowman, C., & Collier, N. (2009). Dynamic Capabilities: An Exploration of How Firms Renew their Resource Base. *British Journal of Management*, *20*(S1), S9–S24. doi:10.1111/j.1467-8551.2008.00610.x

Apneseth, K., Wahl, A., & Hollnagel, E. (2013). Measuring resilience in integrated planning. In E. Albrechtsen & D. Besnard (Eds.), *Oil and Gas, Technology and Humans: Assessing the Human Factors of Technological Change*. CRC Press.

Azadeh, A., Hasannia Kolaee, M., & Salehi, V. (2016). The impact of redundancy on resilience engineering in a petrochemical plant by data envelopment analysis. *Proceedings of the Institution of Mechanical Engineers. Part O, Journal of Risk and Reliability*, *230*(3), 285–296. doi:10.1177/1748006X16629866

Barker, V. L. III, & Duhaime, I. M. (1997). Strategic Change in the Turnaround Process: Theory and Empirical Evidence. *Strategic Management Journal*, *18*(1), 13–38. doi:10.1002/(SICI)1097-0266(199701)18:1<13::AID-SMJ843>3.0.CO;2-X

Barreto, I. (2010). Dynamic Capabilities: A Review of Past Research and an Agenda for the Future. *Journal of Management*, *36*(1), 256–280. doi:10.1177/0149206309350776

Barreto, I. (2012). Solving the Entrepreneurial Puzzle: The Role of Entrepreneurial Interpretation in Opportunity Formation and Related Processes. *Journal of Management Studies*, *49*(2), 356–380. doi:10.1111/j.1467-6486.2011.01023.x

Bento, F., & Garotti, L. (2019). Resilience beyond Formal Structures: A Network Perspective towards the Challenges of an Aging Workforce in the Oil and Gas Industry. *J. Open Innovat. Technol. Market Complexity*, *5*(1), 1–15. doi:10.3390/joitmc5010015

Bergström, J., van Winsen, R., & Henriqson, E., (2015). On the rationale of resilience in the domain of safety: A literature review. *Reliab. Eng. Syst. Saf.*, *141*, 131–141. . doi:10.1016/j.ress.2015.03.008

Bigley, G. A., & Roberts, K. H. (2001). The incident command system: High reliability organizing for complex and volatile task environments. *Academy of Management Journal*, *44*(6), 1281–1299.

Bingham, C. B., & Eisenhardt, K. M. (2011). Rational Heuristics: The 'Simple Rules' that Strategists Learn from Process Experience. *Strategic Management Journal*, *32*(13), 1437–1464. doi:10.1002mj.965

Bingham, C. B., Eisenhardt, K. M., & Davis, J. P. (2007). *Opening the black box of organizational expertise: understanding what firms learn from their process experience and how that learning unfolds over time*. University of Maryland Working Paper.

Bingham, C. B., Eisenhardt, K. M., & Furr, N. R. (2007). What Makes a Process a Capability? Heuristics, Strategy and Effective Capture of Opportunities. *Strategic Entrepreneurship Journal*, *1*(1), 27–47. doi:10.1002ej.1

Boin, A., & McConnell, A. (2007). Preparing for critical infrastructure breakdowns: The limits of crisis management and the need for resilience. *Journal of Contingencies and Crisis Management*, *15*(1), 50–59. doi:10.1111/j.1468-5973.2007.00504.x

Boin, A., & van Eeten, M. J. B. (2013). The Resilient Organization—A critical appraisal. *Public Management Review*, *15*(3), 429–445. doi:10.1080/14719037.2013.769856

Burnard, K., & Bhamra, R. (2011). Organisational resilience: Development of a conceptual framework for organisational responses. *International Journal of Production Research*, *49*(18), 5581–5599. doi:10.1080/00207543.2011.563827

Carley, K. M. (1991). Designing organizational structures to cope with communication breakdowns: A simulation model. *Industrial Crisis Quarterly*, *5*(1), 19–57. doi:10.1177/108602669100500102

Carley, K. M., & Harrald, J. R. (1997). Organizational learning under fire: Theory and practice. *The American Behavioral Scientist*, *40*(3), 310–332. doi:10.1177/0002764297040003007

Chamlee-Wright, E. (2010). *The Cultural and Political Economy of Recovery: Social Learning in a Post-Disaster Environment* (Vol. 12). Routledge. doi:10.4324/9780203855928

Chan, J. K. (2011). Enhancing Organisational Resilience: Application of Viable System Model and MCDA in a Small Hong Kong Company. *International Journal of Production Research, 49*(18), 5545–5563. doi:10.1080/00207543.2011.563829

Chen, J.-C., Li, W. T., Wen, C. K., Teng, J. H., & Ting, P. (2014, July). Efficient Identification Methods for Power Line Outages in the Smart Power Grid. *IEEE Transactions on Power Systems, 29*(4), 1788–1800. doi:10.1109/TPWRS.2013.2296897

Chen, R., Liu, Y., & Zhou, F. (2021). Turning Danger into Safety: The Origin, Research Context and Theoretical Framework of Organizational Resilience. IEEE Access, 9, 48899-48913. doi:10.1109/ACCESS.2021.3069301

Cho, S., Mathiassen, L., & Robey, D. (2006). Dialectics of resilience: a multi-level analysis of a telehealth innovation. *J Inf Technol, 22*, 24–35. ave.jit.2000088 doi:10.1057/palgr

Cho, S., Mathiassen, L., & Robey, D. (2006) The Dialectics of Resilience: A Multilevel Analysis of a Telehealth Innovation. *IFIP International Working Conference on the Transfer and Diffusion of Information Technology for Organizational Resilience.* 10.1007/0-387-34410-1_22

Christianson, M. K., Farkas, M. T., Sutcliffe, K. M., & Weick, K. E. (2009). Learning through rare events: Significant interruptions at the Baltimore and Ohio Railroad Museum. *Organization Science, 20*(5), 846–860. doi:10.1287/orsc.1080.0389

Clement, V., & Rivera, J. (2017). From adaptation to transformation: An extended research agenda for organizational resilience to adversity in the natural environment. *Organization & Environment, 30*(4), 346–365. doi:10.1177/1086026616658333

Cook, R., & Rasmussen, J. (2005). Going Solid: A Model of System Dynamics and Consequences for Patient Safety. *Quality & Safety in Health Care, 14*(2), 130–134. doi:10.1136/qshc.2003.009530 PMID:15805459

Coutu, D. L. (2002). How resilience works. *Harvard Business Review, 80*(5), 46–55. PMID:12024758

Crichton, M. T., Ramsay, C. G., & Kelly, T. (2009). Enhancing organizational resilience through emergency planning: Learnings from cross-sectorial lessons. *Journal of Contingencies and Crisis Management, 17*(1), 24–37. doi:10.1111/j.1468-5973.2009.00556.x

Dalgaard-Nielsen, A. (2017). Organizational resilience in national security bureaucracies: Realistic and practicable? *Journal of Contingencies and Crisis Management, 25*(4), 341–349. doi:10.1111/1468-5973.12164

Danneels, E. (2012). Second-order competences and Schumpeterian rents. *Strategic Entrepreneurship Journal, 6*(1), 42–58. doi:10.1002ej.1127

Davies, A., & Brady, T. (2016). Explicating the dynamics of project capabilities. *Int. J. Project Manage., 34*(2), 314-327.

Demmer, W. A., Vickery, S. K., & Calantone, R. (2011). Engendering resilience in small-and medium-sized enterprises (SMEs): A case study of Demmer Corporation. *International Journal of Production Research*, *49*(18), 5395–5413. doi:10.1080/00207543.2011.563903

Deverell, E. (2009). Crises as Learning Triggers: Exploring a Conceptual Framework of Crisis-Induced Learning. *Journal of Contingencies and Crisis Management*, *17*(3), 179–188. doi:10.1111/j.1468-5973.2009.00578.x

Duchek, S. (2014). Growth in the face of crisis: The role of organizational resilience capabilities. *Academy of Management Proceedings*, *2014*(1), 13487. doi:10.5465/ambpp.2014.225

Duit, A. (2016). Resilience thinking: Lessons for Public Administration. *Public Administration*, *94*(2), 364–380. doi:10.1111/padm.12182

Edmondson, A. C. (2007). The competitive imperative of learning. *Harvard Business Review*, *86*(7-8), 60–67. PMID:18681298

Eisenhardt, K. M., Furr, N. R., & Bingham, C. B. (2010). Microfoundations of Performance: Balancing Efficiency and Flexibility in Dynamic Environments. *Organization Science*, *21*(6), 1263–1273. doi:10.1287/orsc.1100.0564

Eltantawy, R. A. (2016). The role of supply management resilience in attaining ambidexterity: A dynamic capabilities approach. *Journal of Business and Industrial Marketing*, *31*(1), 123–134. doi:10.1108/JBIM-05-2014-0091

Erol, O., Sauser, B., & Mansouri, M. (2010). A framework for investigation into extended enterprise resilience. *Enterprise Information Systems*, *4*(2), 111–136. doi:10.1080/17517570903474304

Farjoun, M. (2010). Beyond dualism: Stability and change as a duality. *Academy of Management Review*, *35*(2), 202–225.

Folke, C., (2006). Resilience: The emergence of a perspective for social–ecological systems analyses. *Global Environ. Change*, *16*(3), 253–267. .gloenvcha.2006.04.002 doi:10.1016/j

Folke, C., Carpenter, S. R., Walker, B., Scheffer, M., Chapin, T., & Rockström, J. (2010). Resilience thinking: Integrating resilience, adaptability, and transformability. *Ecology and Society*, *15*(4), art20. doi:10.5751/ES-03610-150420

Francis, R., & Bekera, B. (2014). A metric and frameworks for resilience analysis of engineered and infrastructure systems. *Reliability Engineering & System Safety*, *121*, 90–103. doi:10.1016/j.ress.2013.07.004

Freeman, S. F., Hirschhorn, L., & Maltz, M. (2004). *Organizational resilience and moral purpose: Sandler O'Neill & Partners in the aftermath of 9/11/01*. Paper presented at the Annual Meeting of the Academy of Management, New Orleans, LA.

Gibson, C., & Tarrant, M. (2010). A "Conceptual Models" approach to organisational resilience. *Australian Journal of Emergency Management*, *25*(2), 8–14.

Gigerenzer, G. (2008). Why Heuristics Work. *Perspectives on Psychological Science*, *3*(1), 20–29. doi:10.1111/j.1745-6916.2008.00058.x PMID:26158666

Gigerenzer, G., & Brighton, H. (2009). Homo Heuristicus: Why Biased Minds Makes Better inferences. *Topics in Cognitive Science*, *1*(1), 107–143. doi:10.1111/j.1756-8765.2008.01006.x PMID:25164802

Glover, J. (2012). Rural resilience through continued learning and innovation. *Local Economy*, *27*(4), 355–372. doi:10.1177/0269094212437833

Gover, L., & Duxbury, L. (2018). Making sense of organizational change: Is hindsight really 20/20. *Journal of Organizational Behavior*, *39*(1), 39–51. doi:10.1002/job.2208

Greiner, L. E. (1972). Evolution and Revolution as Organizations Grow. *Harvard Business Review*, *50*(4), 37–46. PMID:10179654

Hale, A., & Heijer, T. (2006). Defining Resilience. In E. Hollnagel, D. D. Woods, & N. Leveson (Eds.), *Resilience Engineering: Concepts and Precepts* (pp. 35–40). Ashgate.

Hamel, G., & Välikangas, L. (2003). The quest for resilience. *Harvard Business Review*, *81*(9), 52–63.

Held, D., Kickbusch, I., McNally, K., Piselli, D., & Told, M. (2019). Gridlock, Innovation and Resilience in Global Health Governance. *Global Policy*, *10*(2), 161–177. doi:10.1111/1758-5899.12654

Helfat, C. E., Finklestein, S., Mitchell, W., Peteraf, M. A., Singh, H., Teece, D. J., & Winter, S. G. (2007). *Dynamic Capabilities: Understanding strategic change in organizations*. Blackwell Publishing.

Hine, D., Parker, R., Pregelj, L., & Verreynne, M.-L. (2014). Deconstructing and Reconstructing the Capability Hierarchy. *Industrial and Corporate Change*, *23*(5), 1299–1325. doi:10.1093/icc/dtt046

Hollnagel, E. (2009). The four cornerstones of resilience engineering. In C. Nemeth & E. Hollnagel (Eds.), *Resilience Engineering Perspectives*. Ashgate Publishing Company.

Hollnagel, E. (2010). *How Resilient Is Your Organisation? An Introduction to the Resilience Analysis Grid (RAG). Sustainable Transformation*. Building a Resilient Organization.

Hollnagel, E., & Woods, D. D. (2017). Epilogue: Resilience engineering precepts. In E. Hollnagel, D. D. Woods, & N. Leveson (Eds.), *Resilience engineering: Concepts and precepts* (pp. 347–358). CRC Press. doi:10.1201/9781315605685-30

Huber, S., van Wijgerden, I. de Witt, A., & Dekker, S. W. A. (2009). Learning from organizational incidents: Resilience engineering for high-risk process environments. *Process Saf. Prog.*, *28*(1), 90-95.

Ishak, A. W., & Williams, E. A. (2018). A dynamic model of organizational resilience: Adaptive and anchored approaches,. *Editorial Advisory Board*, *23*(2), 180-196.

Jabareen, Y. (2009). Building a conceptual framework: Philosophy, definitions, and procedure. *International Journal of Qualitative Methods*, *8*(4), 49–62. doi:10.1177/160940690900800406

Kahan, J., Allen, A., George, J., & Thompson, W. (2009). *Concept development: An operational framework for resilience*. Homeland Security Studies and Analysis Institute. Available from http://www.homelandsecurity.org/

Kamalahmadi, M., & Parast, M. M. (2016). A review of the literature on the principles of enterprise and supply chain resilience: Major findings and directions for future research. *International Journal of Production Economics*, *171*, 116–133. doi:10.1016/j.ijpe.2015.10.023

King, D. D., Newman, A., & Luthans, F. (2016). Not if, but when we need resilience in the workplace. *Journal of Organizational Behavior*, *37*(5), 782–786. doi:10.1002/job.2063

Kuntz, J. R., Malinen, S., & Näswall, K. (2017). Employee resilience: Directions for resilience development. *Consulting Psychology Journal*, *69*(3), 223–242. doi:10.1037/cpb0000097

Lee, A. V., Vargo, J., & Seville, E. (2013). Developing a tool to measure and compare organizations'' resilience. *Natural Hazards Review*, *14*(1), 29–41. doi:10.1061/(ASCE)NH.1527-6996.0000075

Lengnick-Hall, C. A., & Beck, T. E. (2009). Resilience capacity and strategic agility: Prerequisites for thriving in a dynamic environment. In Resilience engineering perspectives, Volume 2. Preparation and restoration. Ashgate Publishing.

Lengnick-Hall, C. A., Beck, T. E., & Lengnick-Hall, M. L. (2011). Developing a Capacity for Organizational Resilience through Strategic Human Resource Management. *Human Resource Management Review*, *21*(3), 243–255. doi:10.1016/j.hrmr.2010.07.001

Levitt, B., & March, J. G. (1988). Organizational Learning. *Annual Review of Sociology*, *14*(1), 319–340. doi:10.1146/annurev.so.14.080188.001535

Limnios, E. A. M., Mazzarol, T., Ghadouani, A., & Schilizzi, S. G. M. (2014). The resilience architecture framework: Four organizational archetypes. *European Management Journal*, *32*(1), 104–116. doi:10.1016/j.emj.2012.11.007

Linnenluecke, M. K., & Griffiths, A. (2012). Assessing organizational resilience to climate and weather extremes: Complexities and methodological pathways. *Climatic Change*, *113*(3-4), 933–947. doi:10.100710584-011-0380-6

Luthans, F. (2002a). Positive organizational behavior: Developing and managing psychological strengths. *The Academy of Management Executive*, *16*(1), 57–72. doi:10.5465/ame.2002.6640181

Luthar, S. S., Cicchetti, D., & Becker, B. (2000). T*he construct of resilience: A critical evaluation and guidelines for future work*. Child Development, *71*(3), 543–562. doi:10.1111/1467-8624.00164 PMID:10953923

Lynham, S. A. (2002). The general method of theory-building research in applied disciplines. *Advances in Developing Human Resources*, *4*(3), 221–241. doi:10.1177/1523422302043002

Macpherson, A., Herbane, B., & Jones, B. (2015). Developing Dynamic Capabilities through Resource Accretion: Expanding the Entrepreneurial Solution Space. *Entrepreneurship and Regional Development*, *27*(5–6), 259–291. doi:10.1080/08985626.2015.1038598

Madni, A. M., & Jackson, S. (2009). Towards a conceptual framework for Resilience Engineering. *IEEE Systems Journal*, *3*(2), 181–191. doi:10.1109/JSYST.2009.2017397

Maitlis, S., & Christianson, M. (2014). Sense making in organizations: Taking stock and moving forward. *The Academy of Management Annals, 8*(1), 57–125. doi:10.5465/19416520.2014.873177

Manyena, S. B., O'Brien, G., O'Keefe, P., & Rose, J. (2011). Disaster resilience: A bounce back or bounce forward ability? *Local Environment, 16*(5), 417–424. doi:10.1080/13549839.2011.583049

March, J. G. (1991). Exploration and Exploitation in Organizational Learning. *Organization Science, 2*(1), 71–87. doi:10.1287/orsc.2.1.71

March, J. G., Sproull, L. S., & Tamuz, M. (2003). Learning from samples of one or fewer. *Organization Science, 2*(1), 1–13. doi:10.1287/orsc.2.1.1 PMID:14645764

Masten, A. S. (2001). Ordinary magic: Resilience processes in development. *The American Psychologist, 56*(3), 227–238. doi:10.1037/0003-066X.56.3.227 PMID:11315249

Masten, A. S. (2007). Resilience in Developing Systems: Progress and Promise as the Fourth Wave Rises. *Development and Psychopathology, 19*(3), 921–930. doi:10.1017/S0954579407000442 PMID:17705908

Masten, A. S. (2014). *Ordinary Magic: Resilience in Development*. Guilford Press.

McCarthy, I. P., Collard, M., & Johnson, M. (2017). Adaptive organizational resilience: An evolutionary perspective. *Current Opinion Environ. Sustainability, 28*, 33-40.

McGrath, R. G. (1999). Falling Forward: Real Options Reasoning and Entrepreneurial Failure. *Academy of Management Review, 24*(1), 13–30. doi:10.5465/amr.1999.1580438

McGrath, R. G. (2013). *The End of Competitive Advantage: How to Keep your Strategy Moving as Fast as your Business*. Harvard Business Review Press.

Mcmanus, S., Seville, E., Vargo, J., & Brunsdon, D. (2008). Facilitated process for improving organizational resilience. *Natural Hazards Rev., 9*(2), 81-90.

McManus, S., Seville, E., Vargo, J., & Brunsdon, D. (2008). Facilitated process for improving organizational resilience. *Natural Hazards Review, 9*(2), 81–90. doi:10.1061/(ASCE)1527-6988(2008)9:2(81)

Mellahi, K., & Wilkinson, A. (2004). Organizational Failure: A Critique of Recent Research and a Proposed Integrative Framework. *International Journal of Management Reviews, 5/6*(1), 21–41. doi:10.1111/j.1460-8545.2004.00095.x

Meredith, J. (1993). Theory building through conceptual methods. *International Journal of Operations & Production Management, 13*, 3–11.

Morais-Storz, M., & Nguyen, N. (2017). The role of unlearning in metamorphosis and strategic resilience. *The Learning Organization, 24*(2), 93–106. doi:10.1108/TLO-12-2016-0091

Morrow, J. L., Sirmon, D. G., Hitt, M. A., & Holcomb, T. R. (2007). Creating Value in the Face of Declining Performance: Firm Strategies and Organizational Recovery. *Strategic Management Journal, 28*(3), 271–283. doi:10.1002mj.579

Norris, F. H., Stevens, S. P., Pfefferbaum, B., Wyche, K. F., & Pfeffer-baum, R. L. (2008). Community resilience as a metaphor, theory, set of capacities, and strategy for disaster readiness. *American Journal of Community Psychology, 41*(1–2), 127–150. doi:10.100710464-007-9156-6 PMID:18157631

O'Hara, S., Murphy, L., & Reeve, S. (2007). Action learning as leverage for strategic transformation: A case study reflection. *Strategic Change*, *16*(4), 177–190. doi:10.1002/jsc.792

O'Sullivan, T. L., Corneil, W., Kuziemsky, C. E., & Toal-Sullivan, D. (2015). Use of the structured interview matrix to enhance community resilience through collaboration and inclusive engagement. *Systems Research and Behavioral Science*, *32*(6), 616–628. doi:10.1002res.2250

Ortiz-de-Mandojana, N., & Bansal, P. (2015). The long-term benefits of organizational resilience through sustainable business practices. *Strategic Management Journal*. Advance online publication. doi:10.1002mj.2410

Patriarca, R., Di Gravio, G., Constantino, F., Falegnami, A., & Bilotta, F. (2017). *An Analytic Framework to Assess Organizational Resilience*. doi:10.1016/j.shaw.2017.10.005

Peteraf, M., Di Stefano, G., & Verona, G. (2013). The Elephant in the Room of Dynamic Capabilities: Bringing Two Diverging Conversations Together. *Strategic Management Journal*, *34*(12), 1389–1410. doi:10.1002mj.2078

Ponomarov, S. Y., & Holcolmb, M. C. (2009). Understanding the Concept of Supply Chain Resilience. *International Journal of Logistics Management*, *20*(1), 124–143. doi:10.1108/09574090910954873

Probst, G., & Raisch, S. (2005). Organizational Crisis: The Logic of Failure. *The Academy of Management Executive*, *19*(1), 90–105. doi:10.5465/ame.2005.15841958

Reich, J. W. (2006). Three psychological principles of resilience in natural disasters. *Disaster Prevention and Management*, *15*(5), 793–798. doi:10.1108/09653560610712739

Richardson, G. E. (2016). The applied metatheory of resilience and resiliency. In U. Kumar (Ed.), *The Routledge International Handbook of Psychological Resilience* (pp. 124–135). Routledge.

Richtnér, A., & Löfsten, H. (2014). Managing in turbulence: How the capacity for resilience influences creativity. *R & D Management*, *44*(2), 137–151. doi:10.1111/radm.12050

Roberts, K. H., Madsen, P. M., & Desait, V. M. (2005). The space between in space transportation: A relational analysis of the failure of STS-107. In W. H. Starbuck & M. Farjoun (Eds.), *Organization at the limit—NASA and the Columbia Disaster* (pp. 81–98). Blackwell.

Sheffi, Y. (2005). Building a Resilient Supply Chain. *Harvard Business Review Supply Chain Strategy Newsletter*, *1*(8). https://sheffi.mit.edu/sites/default/files/genmedia.buildingresilientsupplychain.pdf

Sheppard, J. P., & Chowdhury, S. D. (2005). Riding the Wrong Wave: Organizational Failure as a Failed Turnaround. *Long Range Planning*, *38*(3), 239–260. doi:10.1016/j.lrp.2005.03.009

Smith, D., & Elliott, D. (2007). Exploring the barriers to learning from crisis -Organizational learning and crisis. *Management Learning*, *38*(5), 519–538. doi:10.1177/1350507607083205

Stephenson, A. (2010). *Benchmarking the Resilience of Organizations* [Unpublished PhD Thesis]. Civil and Natural Resources Engineering Department, University of Canterbury.

Stewart, J., & O'Donnell, M. (2007). Implementing change in a public agency. *International Journal of Public Sector Management*, *20*(3), 239–251. doi:10.1108/09513550710740634

Sutcliffe, K. M., & Vogus, T. J. (2003). Organizing for resilience. *Positive Organizational Scholarship*, 94-110.

Sydow, J., Schreyögg, G., & Koch, J. (2009). Organizational Path Dependence: Opening the Black Box. *Academy of Management Review, 34*(4), 689–709.

Tabaklar, T., Sorkun, M. F., Yurt, O., & Yu, W. (2021). Exploring the microfoundations of dynamic capabilities for social innovation in a humanitarian aid supply network setting. *Industrial Marketing Management, 96*, 147–162. doi:10.1016/j.indmarman.2021.04.012

Taleb, N. N. (2012). *Antifragile: Things that Gain from Disorder* (Vol. 3). Random House.

Teece, D. J. (2007). Explicating Dynamic Capabilities: The Nature and Microfoundations of (Sustainable) Enterprise Performance. *Strategic Management Journal, 28*(13), 1319–1350. doi:10.1002mj.640

Teece, D. J. (2012). Dynamic Capabilities: Routines versus Entrepreneurial Action. *Journal of Management Studies, 49*(8), 1395–1401. doi:10.1111/j.1467-6486.2012.01080.x

Teece, D. J., Pisano, G., & Shuen, A. (1997). Dynamic capabilities and strategic management. *Strategic Management Journal, 18*(7), 509–533. doi:10.1002/(SICI)1097-0266(199708)18:7<509::AID-SMJ882>3.0.CO;2-Z

Teo, W. L., Lee, M., & Lim, W.-S. (2017). The relational activation of resilience model: How leadership activates resilience in an organizational crisis. *Journal of Contingencies and Crisis Management, 25*(3), 136–147. doi:10.1111/1468-5973.12179

Thiel, C. E., Bagdasarov, Z., Harkrider, L., Johnson, J. F., & Mumford, M. D. (2012). Leader ethical decision-making in organizations: Strategies for sense making. *Journal of Business Ethics, 107*(1), 49–64. doi:10.100710551-012-1299-1

Toft, B., & Reynolds, S. (1997). *Learning from Disasters* (2nd ed.). Perpetuity Press.

Tyler, S., & Moench, M. (2012). A framework for urban climate resilience. *Climate and Development, 4*(4), 311–326. doi:10.1080/17565529.2012.745389

Umoh, G. I., Amah, E., & Wokocha, H. I. (2014). Management development and organizational resilience: A case study of some selected manufacturing firms in Rivers State, Nigeria. *IOSR J. Bus. Manage., 16*(2), 7-16.

Vaelikangas, L., & Romme, A. G. L. (2013). How to design for strategic resilience: A case study in retailing. *Journal of Organization Design, 2*(2), 44–53. doi:10.7146/jod.7360

Vakilzadeh, K., & Haase, A. (2020). *The building blocks of organizational resilience: a review of the empirical literature. Continuity & Resilience Review*. doi:10.1108/CRR-04-2020-0002

Vanderbilt-Adriance, E., & Shaw, D. S. (2008). Conceptualizing and re-evaluating resilience across levels of risk, time, and domains of competence. *Clinical Child and Family Psychology Review, 11*(1-2), 30–58. doi:10.100710567-008-0031-2 PMID:18379875

Walker, B. H., & Salt, D. A. (2006). *Resilience Thinking: Sustaining Ecosystems and People in a Changing World*. Island Press.

Watts, G., & Paciga, J. J. (2011). Conscious Adaptation: Building Resilient Organizations. In T. Carmichael (Ed.), *Complex Adaptive Systems: Energy, Information, and Intelligence*. Arlington VA: AAAI Fall Symposium Series.

Weick, K. E., & Roberts, K. H. (1993). Collective mind in organizations: Heedful interrelating on flight decks. *Administrative Science Quarterly*, *38*(3), 357–381. doi:10.2307/2393372

Weick, K. E., & Sutcliffe, K. (2003). Hospitals as Cultures of Entrapment: A Re-Analysis of the Bristol Royal Infirmary. *California Management Review*, *45*(2), 73–84. doi:10.2307/41166166

Weick, K. E., & Sutcliffe, K. M. (2001). *Managing the Unexpected: Assuring High Performance in an Age of Complexity*. Jossey-Bass.

Weick, K. E., & Sutcliffe, K. M. (2007). Managing the unexpected: Resilient performance in an age of uncertainty (2nd ed.). San Francisco, CA: Jossey-Bass.

Weick, K. E., Sutcliffe, K. M., & Obstfeld, D. (2005). Organizing and the process of sensemaking. *Organization Science*, *16*(4), 409–421. doi:10.1287/orsc.1050.0133

Whiteman, G., & Cooper, W. H. (2011). Ecological sensemaking. *Academy of Management Journal*, *43*, 1265–1282.

Wicker, P., Filo, K., & Cuskelly, G. (2013). Organizational resilience of community sport clubs impacted by natural disasters. *J. Sport Manage.*, *27*(6), 510-525.

Wildavsky, A. (1988). *Searching for Safety*. Transaction Press.

Willems, J. J., Busscher, T., van den Brink, M., & Arts, J. (2018). Anticipating water infrastructure renewal: A framing perspective on organizational learning in public agencies. *Environment and Planning C. Politics and Space*, *36*(6), 1088–1108.

Williams, T. A., Gruber, D. A., Sutcliffe, K. M., Shepherd, D. A., & Zhao, E. Y. (2017). Organizational response to adversity: Fusing crisis management and resilience research streams. *The Academy of Management Annals*, *11*(2), 733–769. doi:10.5465/annals.2015.0134

Woods, D. D., & Hollnagel, E. (2006). *Joint Cognitive Systems: Patterns in Cognitive Systems Engineering*. Taylor and Francis. doi:10.1201/9781420005684

Young, O. (2010). *Institutional dynamics: Emergent patters in international environmental governance*. MIT Press. doi:10.7551/mitpress/8457.001.0001

Zahra, S. A., Sapienza, H. J., & Davidsson, P. (2006). Entrepreneurship and Dynamic Capabilities: A review, model, and research agenda. *Journal of Management Studies*, *43*(4), 917–955. doi:10.1111/j.1467-6486.2006.00616.x

Zollo, M., & Winter, S. G. (2002). Deliberate learning and the evolution of dynamic capabilities. *Org. Sci.*, *13*(3), 339-351.

Compilation of References

Aaker, D. (1991). *Brand equity. La gestione del valore della marca*. FrancoAngeli.

Abdeen, A., Kharvari, F., O'Brien, W., & Gunay, B. (2021). The impact of the COVID-19 on households' hourly electricity consumption in Canada. *Energy and Building*, *250*, 111280. doi:10.1016/j.enbuild.2021.111280 PMID:35125633

Abdelwahab, Z. (2012). Renewable Energy, Sustainable Development and Environmental Protection in Ksours (Case of Algeria). *Energy Procedia*, *18*, 666–671. doi:10.1016/j.egypro.2012.05.081

Abedi, V., Olulana, O., Avula, V., Chaudhary, D., Khan, A., Shahjouei, S., Li, J., & Zand, R. (2021). Racial, economic, and health inequality and COVID-19 infection in the United States. *Journal of Racial and Ethnic Health Disparities*, *8*(3), 732–742. doi:10.100740615-020-00833-4 PMID:32875535

Abu-Bakar, H., Williams, L., & Hallett, S. H. (2021). Quantifying the impact of the COVID-19 lockdown on household water consumption patterns in England. *NPJ Clean Water*, *4*(1), 1–9. doi:10.103841545-021-00103-8

Abulibdeh, A. (2021). Modeling electricity consumption patterns during the COVID-19 pandemic across six socioeconomic sectors in the State of Qatar. *Energy Strategy Reviews*, *38*, 100733. doi:10.1016/j.esr.2021.100733

Acar, W., & Winfrey, F. (1994). The resilient organization: Maintaining organizational renewal and performance. *J Strateg Change.*, *3*(3), 165–173. doi:10.1002/jsc.4240030307

Accenture. (2022). *COVID-19: Retail consumer habits shift long-term*. https://www.accenture.com/usen/insights/retail/coronavirus-consumer-habits

Acquaah, M., Amoako-Gyampah, K., & Jayaram, J. (2011). Resilience in Family and Non-Family Businesses: An Examination of the Relationships Between Manufacturing Strategy, Competitive Strategy, and Business Performance. *International Journal of Production Research*, *49*(18), 5527–5544. doi:10.1080/00207543.2011.563834

Acuti, D., Grazzini, L., Mazzoli, V., & Aiello, G. (2019). Stakeholder engagement in green place branding: A focus on user-generated content. *Corporate Social Responsibility and Environmental Management*, *2019*(26), 492–501. doi:10.1002/csr.1703

Adamik, A., & Nowicki, M. (2020). Barriers of Creating Competitive Advantage in the Age of Industry 4.0: Conclusions from International Experience. In Contemporary Challenges in Cooperation and Coopetition in the Age of Industry 4.0 (pp:3-42). Springer. doi:10.1007/978-3-030-30549-9_1

Agba, A. O., Ocheni, S. I., & Agba, M. S. (2020). COVID-19 and the world of work dynamics: A critical review. *Journal of Educational and Social Research*, *10*(5), 119–119. doi:10.36941/jesr-2020-0093

Agrawal, S., De Smet, A., Lacroix, S., & Reich, A. (2020). *To Emerge Stronger from the COVID-19 Crisis, Companies Should Start Reskilling Their Workforces Now*. McKinsey & Company.

Compilation of References

Aguinis, H., & Glavas, A. (2013). Embedded versus peripheral corporate social responsibility: Psychological foundations. *Ind. Organ. Psychol.*, *6*(4), 314–332. doi:10.1111/iops.12059

Ahmad, W. N. K. W., Rezaei, J., de Brito, M. P., & Tavasszy, L. A. (2016). The influence of external factors on supply chain sustainability goals of the oil and gas industry. *Resources Policy*, *49*, 302–314. doi:10.1016/j.resourpol.2016.06.006

Ahmed, U., Abdul Majid, A. H., Mohd Zin, M. L., Phulpoto, W., & Umrani, W. A. (2016). Role and impact of reward and accountability on training transfer. *Business and Economics Journal*, *7*(1), 1–6.

Akgün, M., & Halit, K. (2014). Organizational resilience and firm product innovation and performance. *International Journal of Production Research*, *52*(23), 6918–6937. doi:10.1080/00207543.2014.910624

Akhavan, A. R., Abzari, M., Isfahani, A. N., & Fathi, S. (2017). Generational differences in job engagement: A case study of an industrial organization in Iran. *Industrial and Commercial Training*, *49*(3), 106–115. doi:10.1108/ICT-10-2016-0068

Akin, C. S. (2014). The impact of foreign trade, energy consumption and income on CO2 emissions. *International Journal of Energy Economics and Policy*, *4*(3), 465.

Alam, S., Fatima, A., & Butt, M. S. (2007). Sustainable development in Pakistan in the context of energy consumption demand and environmental degradation. *Journal of Asian Economics*, *18*(5), 825–837. doi:10.1016/j.asieco.2007.07.005

Alblas, A. & Jayaram, J. (2015). Designing resilience in the context of the fuzzy interface (FFE): an empirical examination. *International Journal of Research on Production*, *53*(22), 6820-6838.

Aldieri, L., Kotsemir, M., & Vinci, C. P. (2019, July 6). Environmental innovations and productivity: Empirical evidence from Russian regions. *Resources Policy*, 1–9.

Aldieri, L., & Vinci, C. P. (2018). Green economy and sustainable development: The economic impact of innovation on employment. *Sustainability*, *10*(10), 3541. doi:10.3390u10103541

Alesi, P. (2008). Build resilience across the company by integrating business continuity capability into day-to-day business culture and technology. *Journal of Business Continuity & Emergency Planning*, *2*, 214–220. PMID:21339108

Alexiou, A. (2014). Taming the waves of adversity: Exploring the multidimensional construct of organizational resilience. In D. G. Assimakopoulos, I. Oshri, & K. Pandza (Eds.), *Managing Emerging Technologies for Socio-Economic Impact*. Edward Elgar Publishing. doi:10.4337/9781782547884.00026

Alhajeri, H. M., Almutairi, A., Alenezi, A., & Alshammari, F. (2020). Energy demand in the state of Kuwait during the COVID-19 pandemic: Technical, economic, and environmental perspectives. *Energies*, *13*(17), 4370. doi:10.3390/en13174370

Ali, Q., Parveen, S., Yaacob, H., Zaini, Z., & Sarbini, N. A. (2021). COVID-19 and dynamics of environmental awareness, sustainable consumption and social responsibility in Malaysia. *Environmental Science and Pollution Research International*, *28*(40), 56199–56218. doi:10.100711356-021-14612-z PMID:34050516

Alliger, G. M., Cerasoli, C. P., Tannenbaum, S. I., & Vessey, W. B. (2015). Team resilience: How teams flourish under pressure. *Organizational Dynamics*, *44*(3), 176–184. doi:10.1016/j.orgdyn.2015.05.003

Almeida, F., Santos, J. D., & Monteiro, J. A. (2020). The challenges and opportunities in the digitalization of companies in a post-COVID-19 World. *IEEE Engineering Management Review*, *48*(3), 97–103. doi:10.1109/EMR.2020.3013206

Al-Mulali, U., Ozturk, I., & Solarin, S. A. (2016). Investigating the environmental Kuznets curve hypothesis in seven regions: The role of renewable energy. *Ecological Indicators*, *67*, 267–282. doi:10.1016/j.ecolind.2016.02.059

Alvarez, S. A., & Barney, J. B. (2007). Discovery and Creation: Alternative Theories of Entrepreneurial Action. *Strategic Entrepreneurship Journal*, *1*(1), 11–26. doi:10.1002ej.4

Ambrosini, V., Bowman, C., & Collier, N. (2009). Dynamic Capabilities: An Exploration of How Firms Renew their Resource Base. *British Journal of Management*, *20*(S1), S9–S24. doi:10.1111/j.1467-8551.2008.00610.x

Amin, Z. S., Hossein, I. S., & Mohammadreza, M. (2021). Introducing a new market-based system using game theory approach to promote energy efficiency: Case of Iranian energy market. *Energy Efficiency*, *14*(6), 1–16. doi:10.100712053-021-09977-6

Amparore, D., Claps, F., Cacciamani, G. E., Esperto, F., Fiori, C., Liguori, G., Serni, S., Trombetta, C., Carini, M., Porpiglia, F., Checcucci, E., & Campi, R. (2020). Impact of the COVID-19 pandemic on urology residency training in Italy. *Minerva Urologica e Nefrologica*, *72*(4), 505–509. doi:10.23736/S0393-2249.20.03868-0 PMID:32253371

Andersen, A. L., Hansen, E. T., Johannesen, N., & Sheridan, A. (2020). *Consumer responses to the COVID-19 crisis: Evidence from bank account transaction data.* https://ideas.repec.org/p/cpr/ceprdp/14809.html

Andersen, P. (2007). What is web 2.0. *Ideas, technologies and implications for education*, *1*(1), 1-64.

Andersen, M. S. (2007). An introductory note on the environmental economics of the circular economy. *Sustainability Science*, *2*(1), 133–140. doi:10.100711625-006-0013-6

Anderson, R. C., & White, R. A. (2011). *Business Lessons from a Radical Industrialist.* St. Martin's Griffin.

Andersson, I. (2016). Green cities' going greener? Local environmental policy-making and place branding in the 'Greenest City in Europe. *European Planning Studies*, *24*(6), 1197–1215. doi:10.1080/09654313.2016.1152233

Andersson, I., & James, L. (2018). Altruism or entrepreneurialism? The co-evolution of green place branding and policy tourism in Växjö, Sweden. *Urban Studies (Edinburgh, Scotland)*, *2018*(55), 3437–3453. doi:10.1177/0042098017749471

Annarelli, A., & Nonino, F. (2016). Strategic and Operational Management of Organizational Resilience: Current Status of Research and Future Directions. *Omega*, *62*, 1–18. doi:10.1016/j.omega.2015.08.004

Apergis, N., Payne, J. E., Menyah, K., & Wolde-Rufael, Y. (2010). On the causal dynamics between emissions, nuclear energy, renewable energy, and economic growth. *Ecological Economics*, *69*(11), 2255–2260. doi:10.1016/j.ecolecon.2010.06.014

Apneseth, K., Wahl, A., & Hollnagel, E. (2013). Measuring resilience in integrated planning. In E. Albrechtsen & D. Besnard (Eds.), *Oil and Gas, Technology and Humans: Assessing the Human Factors of Technological Change.* CRC Press.

Apokin, A. (2019). LNG Trade Flows In The Case Of Oversupplied Markets And Its Consequent Impact On Prices And Investment. In *Local Energy, Global Markets, 42nd IAEE International Conference.* International Association for Energy Economics.

Aragon-Correa, J. A., Martin-Tapia, I., & Hurtado-Torres, N. E. (2013). Proactive environmental strategies and employee inclusion: The positive effects on information sharing and promoting collaboration and the influence of uncertainty. *Organization & Environment*, *40*(2), 1–23. doi:10.1177/1086026613489034

Arora, N. K., & Mishra, J. (2020). COVID-19 and importance of environmental sustainability. *Environmental Sustainability*, *3*(2), 117–119. doi:10.100742398-020-00107-z

Arora, P., & Suri, D. (2020). Redefining, relooking, redesigning, and reincorporating HRD in the post Covid 19 context and thereafter. *Human Resource Development International*, *23*(4), 438–451. doi:10.1080/13678868.2020.1780077

Compilation of References

Arthur-Nyarko, E., & Kariuki, M. G. (2019). Learner Access to Resources for eLearning and Preference for Elearning Delivery Mode in Distance Education Programs in Ghana. *International Journal of Educational Technology*, *6*(2), 1–8.

Aruga, K., Islam, M., & Jannat, A. (2020). Effects of COVID-19 on Indian energy consumption. *Sustainability*, *12*(14), 5616. doi:10.3390u12145616

Ash'aari, Z. H., Aris, A. Z., Ezani, E., Ahmad Kamal, N. I., Jaafar, N., Jahaya, J. N., Manan, S. A., & Saifuddin, M. F. (2020). Spatiotemporal variations and contributing factors of air pollutant concentrations in Malaysia during movement control order due to pandemic COVID-19. *Aerosol and Air Quality Research*, *20*(10), 2047–2061. doi:10.4209/aaqr.2020.06.0334

Asiaei, K., Bontis, N., Alizadeh, R., & Yaghoubi, M. (2021). Green intellectual capital and environmental management accounting: Natural resource orchestration in favor of environmental performance. *Business Strategy and the Environment*, *31*(1), 76–93. doi:10.1002/bse.2875

Ates, A., & Bititci, U. (2011). Change Process: A Key Enabler for Building Resilient SMEs. *International Journal of Production Research*, *49*(18), 5601–5618. doi:10.1080/00207543.2011.563825

Azadeh, A., Hasannia Kolaee, M., & Salehi, V. (2016). The impact of redundancy on resilience engineering in a petrochemical plant by data envelopment analysis. *Proceedings of the Institution of Mechanical Engineers. Part O, Journal of Risk and Reliability*, *230*(3), 285–296. doi:10.1177/1748006X16629866

Azevedo, S. G., Carvalho, H., & Cruz-Machado, V. (2016). LARG index: A benchmarking tool for improving the leanness, agility, resilience and greenness of the automotive supply chain. *Benchmark*, *23*(6), 1472–1499. doi:10.1108/BIJ-07-2014-0072

Azhgaliyeva, D., Mishra, R., & Karymshakov, K. (2021). *Household energy consumption behaviors during the COVID-19 pandemic in Mongolia* (No. 1292). ADBI Working Paper.

Baars, J., Domenech, T., Bleischwitz, R., Melin, H. E., & Heidrich, O. (2021). Circular economy strategies for electric vehicle batteries reduce reliance on raw materials. *Nature Sustainability*, *4*(1), 71–79. doi:10.103841893-020-00607-0

Babbitt, C. W., Babbitt, G. A., & Oehman, J. (2021). Behavioral impacts on residential food provisioning, use, and waste during the COVID-19 pandemic. *Sustainable Production and Consumption*, *28*, 315–325. doi:10.1016/j.spc.2021.04.012 PMID:34722846

Babran, S., & Honarbakhsh, N. (2007). Water Crisis in Iran and the World. Environment and Sustainable Development Studies Research Journal. *Time*, *1*.

Bag, S., Pretorius, J. H. C., Gupta, S., & Dwivedi, Y. K. (2021). Role of institutional pressures and resources in the adoption of big data analytics powered artificial intelligence, sustainable manufacturing practices and circular economy capabilities. *Technological Forecasting and Social Change*, *163*, 120420. doi:10.1016/j.techfore.2020.120420

Bag, S., Wood, L. C., Mangla, S. K., & Luthra, S. (2020). Procurement 4.0 and its implications on business process performance in a circular economy. *Resources, Conservation and Recycling*, *152*, 104502. doi:10.1016/j.resconrec.2019.104502

Bahgat, G. (2008). Gas OPEC? Rhetoric Versus Reality. *The Journal of Social, Political, and Economic Studies*, *33*(3), 281.

Bahmani-Oskooee, M., & Chomsisengphet, S. (2002). Stability of M2 money demand function in industrial countries. *Applied Economics*, *34*(16), 2075–2083. doi:10.1080/00036840210128744

Bailey, I., & Caprotti, F. (2014). The green economy: Functional domains and theoretical directions of enquiry. *Environment & Planning A*, *46*(8), 1797–1813. doi:10.1068/a130102p

Bailey, K., & Breslin, D. (2021). The COVID-19 Pandemic: What can we learn from past research in organizations and management? *International Journal of Management Reviews*, *23*(1), 3–6. doi:10.1111/ijmr.12237

Baker, D.; Greenberg, C. & Hemingway, C. (2007). *Empresas Felices=Empresas Rentables*. Barcelona: Ediciones Gestión 2000.

Baldwin, T. T., Kevin Ford, J., & Blume, B. D. (2017). The state of transfer of training research: Moving toward more consumer-centric inquiry. *Human Resource Development Quarterly*, *28*(1), 17–28. doi:10.1002/hrdq.21278

Baltagi, B. H. (2021). *Econometric analysis of panel data*. Springer Nature. doi:10.1007/978-3-030-53953-5

Baravalle, R., Rosso, O. A., & Montani, F. (2018). Causal shannon–fisher characterization of motor/imagery movements in eeg. *Entropy (Basel, Switzerland)*, *20*(9), 660. doi:10.3390/e20090660 PMID:33265749

Barbier, E. (2011). The policy challenges for green economy and sustainable economic development. *Natural Resources Forum*, *35*(3), 233–245. doi:10.1111/j.1477-8947.2011.01397.x

Barbier, E. B. (2004). Water and economic growth. *The Economic Record*, *80*(248), 1–16. doi:10.1111/j.1475-4932.2004.00121.x

Barbier, E. B., & Burgess, J. C. (2020). Sustainability and development after COVID-19. *World Development*, *135*, 105082. doi:10.1016/j.worlddev.2020.105082 PMID:32834381

Bar, H. (2021). COVID-19 lockdown: Animal life, ecosystem and atmospheric environment. *Environment, Development and Sustainability*, *23*(6), 8161–8178. doi:10.100710668-020-01002-7 PMID:33020695

Barker, V. L. III, & Duhaime, I. M. (1997). Strategic Change in the Turnaround Process: Theory and Empirical Evidence. *Strategic Management Journal*, *18*(1), 13–38. doi:10.1002/(SICI)1097-0266(199701)18:1<13::AID-SMJ843>3.0.CO;2-X

Barnes, D. F., Krutilla, K., & Hyde, W. F. (2010). *The urban household energy transition: social and environmental impacts in the developing world*. Routledge. doi:10.4324/9781936331000

Barney, J. (2001). Resource-Based Theories of Competitive Advantage: A Ten-Year Retrospective on the Resource-Based View. *Journal of Management*, *6*(6), 643–650. doi:10.1177/014920630102700602

Barney, J. (2001a). Is the resource-based "vision" a useful perspective for strategic management research? Yes. *Academy of Management Review*, *26*(1), 41–56.

Barone, A. S., Matheus, J. R. V., De Souza, T. S. P., Moreira, R. F. A., & Fai, A. E. C. (2021). Green-based active packaging: Opportunities beyond COVID-19, food applications, and perspectives in circular economy—a brief review. *Comprehensive Reviews in Food Science and Food Safety*, *20*(5), 4881–4905. doi:10.1111/1541-4337.12812 PMID:34355490

Barreto, I. (2010). Dynamic Capabilities: A Review of Past Research and an Agenda for the Future. *Journal of Management*, *36*(1), 256–280. doi:10.1177/0149206309350776

Barreto, I. (2012). Solving the Entrepreneurial Puzzle: The Role of Entrepreneurial Interpretation in Opportunity Formation and Related Processes. *Journal of Management Studies*, *49*(2), 356–380. doi:10.1111/j.1467-6486.2011.01023.x

Barro, R. J. (1990). Government spending in a simple model of endogeneous growth. *Journal of Political Economy*, *98*(5, Part 2), S103–S125. doi:10.1086/261726

Barro, R. J., & Sala-i-Martin, X. (1992). Public finance in models of economic growth. *The Review of Economic Studies*, *59*(4), 645–661. doi:10.2307/2297991

Compilation of References

Barua, A. (2021). *A spring in consumers' steps: Americans prepare to get back to their spending ways.* https://www2.deloitte.com/us/en/insights/economy/us-consumer-spending-after-covid.html

Batjargal, B. (2007). Internet Entrepreneurship: Social Capital, Human Capital, and Performance of Internet Ventures in China. *Research Policy, 36*(5), 605–618. doi:10.1016/j.respol.2006.09.029

Bauer, W., Hämmerle, M., Schlund, S., & Vocke, C. (2015). Transforming to a hyper-connected society and economy-towards an Industry 4.0. *Procedia Manufacturing, 3,* 417–424. doi:10.1016/j.promfg.2015.07.200

Baxter, L. A., & Babbie, E. R. (2004). *The basics of communication research.* Thomson Learning.

Beier, M. E., & Kanfer, R. (2009). Motivation in training and development: A phase perspective. In Learning, Training, and Development in Organizations (pp. 90-122). Routledge.

Bell, M. (2002). *The five principles of organizational resilience.* Gartner Research.

BennettN.LemoineG. J. (2014). What VUCA really means for you. *Harvard Business Review, 92*(1/2). Available at: https://ssrn.com/abstract=2389563

Bento, F., & Garotti, L. (2019). Resilience beyond Formal Structures: A Network Perspective towards the Challenges of an Aging Workforce in the Oil and Gas Industry. *J. Open Innovat. Technol. Market Complexity, 5*(1), 1–15. doi:10.3390/joitmc5010015

Bergmiller, G. G., & McCright, P. R. (2009), *Parallel models for Lean and green operations.* Paper presented at the Industrial Engineering Research Conference, Miami, FL. https://pdfs.semanticscholar.org/0a67/c7f0f6d60ba0506e037aaf-17cfe8b3a89e7d.pdf

Bergstrom, J., van Winsen, R., & Henriqson, E. (2015). On the justification of resilience in the field of security: A review of the literature. *Reliab. Ing. Syst. Saf., 141,* 131–141. doi:10.1016/j.ress.2015.03.008

Bernstad Saraiva, A., Souza, R. G., Mahler, C. F., & Valle, R. A. B. (2018). Consequential lifecycle modelling of solid waste management systems–Reviewing choices and exploring their consequences. *Journal of Cleaner Production, 202,* 488–496. doi:10.1016/j.jclepro.2018.08.038

Bertram, C., Luderer, G., Creutzig, F., Bauer, N., Ueckerdt, F., Malik, A., & Edenhofer, O. (2021). COVID-19-induced low power demand and market forces starkly reduce CO2 emissions. *Nature Climate Change, 11*(3), 193–196. doi:10.103841558-021-00987-x

Bhamidipaty, A., Lotlikar, R., & Banavar, G. (2007). RMI: A Framework for Modeling and Assessing the Resilience Maturity of IT Service Organizations. *IEEE International Conference on Services Computing (SCC 2007),* 300–307. 10.1109/SCC.2007.94

Bhamra, R., Dani, S., & Burnard, K. (2011). Resilience: The concept, a review of the literature, and future directions. *International Journal of Production Research, 49*(18), 5375–5393. doi:10.1080/00207543.2011.563826

Bhattarai, M. (2004). *Irrigation Kuznets Curve, governance and dynamics of irrigation development: a global cross-country analysis from 1972 to 1991* (Vol. 78). IWMI.

Bhatti, M. A., Juhari, A. S., & Umrani, W. A. (2018). Addressing generational issues in training and development at Aerospace Composites Malaysia. *Global Business and Organizational Excellence, 38*(1), 47–52. doi:10.1002/joe.21900

Bielecki, S., Skoczkowski, T., Sobczak, L., Buchoski, J., Maciąg, Ł., & Dukat, P. (2021). Impact of the lockdown during the COVID-19 pandemic on electricity use by residential users. *Energies, 14*(4), 980. doi:10.3390/en14040980

Bieńkowska, Tworek, & Zablocka-klucza. (2020). *Organizational reliability: information technology and human resource management*. London, UK: Routledge.

Bigley, G. A., & Roberts, K. H. (2001). The incident command system: High reliability organizing for complex and volatile task environments. *Academy of Management Journal*, *44*(6), 1281–1299.

Bingham, C. B., Eisenhardt, K. M., & Davis, J. P. (2007). *Opening the black box of organizational expertise: understanding what firms learn from their process experience and how that learning unfolds over time*. University of Maryland Working Paper.

Bingham, C. B., & Eisenhardt, K. M. (2011). Rational Heuristics: The 'Simple Rules' that Strategists Learn from Process Experience. *Strategic Management Journal*, *32*(13), 1437–1464. doi:10.1002mj.965

Bingham, C. B., Eisenhardt, K. M., & Furr, N. R. (2007). What Makes a Process a Capability? Heuristics, Strategy and Effective Capture of Opportunities. *Strategic Entrepreneurship Journal*, *1*(1), 27–47. doi:10.1002ej.1

Blume, B. D., Ford, J. K., Baldwin, T. T., & Huang, J. L. (2010). Transfer of training: A meta-analytic review. *Journal of Management*, *36*(4), 1065–1105. doi:10.1177/0149206309352880

Blundel, R. (2013). *Britain's Quarterly Small Business Survey Special Topic: Resilience and Recovery 2013*. Open University.

Böckerman, P., Bryson, A., Kauhanen, A., & Kangasniemi, M. (2020). Does job design make workers happy? *Scottish Journal of Political Economy*, *67*(1), 31–52. doi:10.1111jpe.12211

Boin, A., & McConnell, A. (2007). Preparing for critical infrastructure breakdowns: The limits of crisis management and the need for resilience. *Journal of Contingencies and Crisis Management*, *15*(1), 50–59. doi:10.1111/j.1468-5973.2007.00504.x

Boin, A., & van Eeten, M. J. B. (2013). The Resilient Organization—A critical appraisal. *Public Management Review*, *15*(3), 429–445. doi:10.1080/14719037.2013.769856

Boiral, O. (2009). Greening the corporation through organizational citizenship behaviors. *Journal of Business Ethics*, *87*(2), 221–236. doi:10.100710551-008-9881-2

Boiral, O., Heras-Saizarbitoria, I., & Brotherton, M. (2019). Corporate sustainability and indigenous community engagement in the extractive industry. *Journal of Cleaner Production*, *235*, 701–711. doi:10.1016/j.jclepro.2019.06.311

Bolman, L. G., & Deal, T. E. (2015). Think-or sink. Leading in a VUCA world. *Leader to Leader*, *76*(76), 35–40. doi:10.1002/ltl.20176

Bonesso, S., Bruni, E., & Gerli, F. (2020). Emotional and Social Intelligence Competencies in the Digital Era. In S. Bonesso, E. Bruni, & F. Gerli (Eds.), *Behavioral Competencies of Digital Professionals* (pp. 41–62). Palgrave MacMillan. doi:10.1007/978-3-030-33578-6_3

Boons, F., Montalvo, C., Quist, J., & Wagner, M. (2013). Sustainable innovation, business models and economic performance: An overview. *Journal of Cleaner Production*, *45*, 1–8. doi:10.1016/j.jclepro.2012.08.013

Bordeianu, S. (1995). Political risk services and political risk yearbook: Edited William D. Coplin and Michael K. O'Leary. Syracuse, NY: Political Risk Services, 1994. 7 vols. $5,570.00 commercial subscribers (to the services), $750.00 (to the Yearbook). Journal of Government Information, 22(2), 186-188.

Borden, R. J., & Schettino, A. P. (1979). Determinants of Environmentally Responsible Behavior. *The Journal of Environmental Education*, *10*(4), 35–39. doi:10.1080/00958964.1979.9941906

Borges, F., & Menegon, N. (2012). Different roles in the search for system resilience. *Job*, *41*, 3238–3245. PMID:22317211

Bostancı, S. H., & Yıldırım, S. (2022). The Role of Municipalities in Achieving Water Security: The Case of Turkey. In R. Castanho (Ed.), *Handbook of Research on Sustainable Development Goals, Climate Change, and Digitalization* (pp. 268–286). IGI Global. doi:10.4018/978-1-7998-8482-8.ch017

Botke, J. A., Jansen, P. G., Khapova, S. N., & Tims, M. (2018). Work factors influencing the transfer stages of soft skills training: A literature review. *Educational Research Review*, *24*, 130–147. doi:10.1016/j.edurev.2018.04.001

Bovenberg, A. L., & van der Ploeg, F. (1994). Environmental policy, public finance and the labour market in a second-best world. *Journal of Public Economics*, *55*(3), 349–390. doi:10.1016/0047-2727(93)01398-T

Bowden, V. (2018). Life. Brought to you by'... coal? business responses to climate change in the hunter valley, NSW, Australia. *Environmental Sociology*, *4*(2), 275–285. doi:10.1080/23251042.2017.1382032

Bowden, V., Nyberg, D., & Wright, C. (2019). Planning for the past: Local temporality and the construction of denial in climate change adaptation. *Global Environmental Change*, *57*, 101939. doi:10.1016/j.gloenvcha.2019.101939

Braidot, N. (2014). *Neuromanagement. The neuroscientific revolution in organisations, from management to neuromanagement*. Granica.

Broad, M. L., & Newstrom, J. W. (1992). *Transfer of training: Action Packed Strategies to Ensure High Payoff from Training Investments*. Addison-Wesley.

Brudermann, T., & Sangkakool, T. (2017). Green roofs in temperate climate cities in Europe– an analysis of key decision factors. *Urban Forestry & Urban Greening*, *21*, 224–234. doi:10.1016/j.ufug.2016.12.008

Brundtland, G. (1987). *Our Common Future: The World Commission on Environment and Development*. Oxford University Press.

Buğday, E. B., & Tunçel, N. (2022, January). *"Do-It-Yourself" consumer activities in the Covid era and the role of demographics* [Paper presented]. *38th EBES Conference*, University of Warsaw, Warsaw, Poland.

Bull, S. R. (2001). Renewable energy today and tomorrow. *Proceedings of the IEEE*, *89*(8), 1216–1226. doi:10.1109/5.940290

Burke, L. A., & Baldwin, T. T. (1999). Workforce training transfer: A study of the effect of relapse prevention training and transfer climate. *Human Resource Management*, *38*(3), 227-241.

Burke, L. A., Hutchins, H. M., & Saks, A. M. (2013). Best practices in training transfer. In M. A. Paludi (Ed.), *Psychology for Business Success* (pp. 115–132). Praeger/ABC-CLIO.

Burke, L. A., & Hutchins, H. M. (2008). A study of best practices in training transfer and proposed model of transfer. *Human Resource Development Quarterly*, *19*(2), 107–128. doi:10.1002/hrdq.1230

Burke, L. A., & Saks, A. M. (2009). Accountability in training transfer: Adapting Schlenker's model of responsibility to a persistent but solvable problem. *Human Resource Development Review*, *8*(3), 382–402. doi:10.1177/1534484309336732

Burnard, K., & Bhamra, R. (2011). Organizational resilience: Development of a conceptual framework for organizational responses. *International Journal of Production Research*, *49*(18), 5581–5599. doi:10.1080/00207543.2011.563827

Burton, E. (2000). The compact city: Just or just compact? A preliminary analysis. *Urban Studies (Edinburgh, Scotland)*, *37*(11), 1969–2006. doi:10.1080/00420980050162184

Byrne, J., & Sipe, N. (2010). *Green and open space planning for urban consolidation – A review of the literature and best practice*. Griffith University Urban Research Program.

Cabral, I., Grilo, A., & Cruz-Machado, V. (2012). A decision-making model for Lean, Agile, Resilientand Green supply chain management. *International Journal of Production Research*, *50*(17), 4830-4845.

Caldwell, C., Dixon, R., Floyd, L., Chaudoin, J., Post, J., & Cheokas, G. (2012). Transformative Leadership: Achieving Unparalleled Excellence. *Journal of Business Ethics*, *109*(2), 175–187. Advance online publication. doi:10.100710551-011-1116-2

Cambefort, M. (2020). How the COVID-19 pandemic is challenging consumption. *Markets, Globalization &. Developmental Review*, *5*(1), 1–13.

Campbell, N. (2021). *The Covid-19 pandemic: impact on consumers' environmental consciousness and food choices in California* [Unpublished honor thesis]. Berkeley University, CA, United States.

Campos, M. A. S., Carvalho, S. L., Melo, S. K., Gonçalves, G. B. F. R., dos Santos, J. R., Barros, R. L., Morgado, U. T. M. A., da Silva Lopes, E., & Abreu Reis, R. P. (2021). Impact of the COVID-19 pandemic on water consumption behaviour. *Water Supply*, *21*(8), 4058–4067. doi:10.2166/ws.2021.160

Cañizares, J., Copeland, S., & Doorn, N. (2021). Make sense of resilience. *Sustainability*, *13*(15), 8538. doi:10.3390u13158538

Cannon, W. R., Zucker, J. D., Baxter, D. J., Kumar, N., Baker, S. E., Hurley, J. M., & Dunlap, J. C. (2018). Prediction of metabolite concentrations, rate constants and post-translational regulation using maximum entropy-based simulations with application to central metabolism of neurospora crassa. *Processes (Basel, Switzerland)*, *6*(6), 63. doi:10.3390/pr6060063 PMID:33824861

Capello, R., & Camagni, R. (2000). Beyond optimal city size: An evaluation of alternative urban growth patterns. *Urban Studies (Edinburgh, Scotland)*, *37*(9), 1479–1496. doi:10.1080/00420980020080221

Carley, K. M. (1991). Designing organizational structures to cope with communication breakdowns: A simulation model. *Industrial Crisis Quarterly*, *5*(1), 19–57. doi:10.1177/108602669100500102

Carley, K. M., & Harrald, J. R. (1997). Organizational learning under fire: Theory and practice. *The American Behavioral Scientist*, *40*(3), 310–332. doi:10.1177/0002764297040003007

Carlsson-Szlezak, P., Reeves, M., & Swartz, P. (2020). What coronavirus could mean for the global economy. *Harvard Business Review*, *3*(10).

Carmeli, A., & Markman, G. (2011). Capture, governance, and resilience: Strategic implications of the history of Rome. *Strategic Management Journal*, *32*(3), 322–341. doi:10.1002mj.880

Caro, D., Davis, S., Bastianoni, S., & Caldeira, K. (2017). Greenhouse gas emissions due to meat production in the last fifty years. In A. Mukhtar & C. O. Stockle (Eds.), *Quantification of Climate Variability, Adaptation and Mitigation for Agricultural Sustainability* (pp. 27–37). Springer. doi:10.1007/978-3-319-32059-5_2

Carvalho, V. M., Garcia, J. R., Hansen, S., Ortiz, Á., Rodrigo, T., Rodríguez Mora, J. V., & Ruiz, P. (2020). Tracking the COVID-19 crisis with high-resolution transaction data. *Royal Society Open Science*, *8*(8), 210218. doi:10.1098/rsos.210218 PMID:34401194

Chae, M.-J. (2021). Effects of the COVID-19 pandemic on sustainable consumption. *Social Behavior and Personality*, *49*(6), e10199. doi:10.2224bp.10199

Chakraborty, I., & Maity, P. (2020). Covid-19 Outbreak: Migration, effects on society, global environment and prevention. *The Science of the Total Environment*, *728*, 138882. doi:10.1016/j.scitotenv.2020.138882 PMID:32335410

Chakraborty, P., Mittal, P., Gupta, M. S., Yadav, S., & Arora, A. (2021). Opinion of students on online education during the COVID-19 pandemic. *Human Behavior and Emerging Technologies*, *3*(3), 357–365. doi:10.1002/hbe2.240

Chamlee-Wright, E. (2010). *The Cultural and Political Economy of Recovery: Social Learning in a Post-Disaster Environment* (Vol. 12). Routledge. doi:10.4324/9780203855928

Chang, C. H., & Chen, Y. (2012). The determinants of green intellectual capital. *Management Decision*, *50*(1), 74–94. doi:10.1108/00251741211194886

Chan, J. (2011). Improving Organizational Resilience: Applying the Viable System Model and MCDA in a Small Business in Hong Kong. *International Journal of Production Research*, *49*(18), 5545–5563. doi:10.1080/00207543.2011.563829

Chauhan, R., Ghosh, P., Rai, A., & Shukla, D. (2016). The impact of support at the workplace on transfer of training: A study of an Indian manufacturing unit. *International Journal of Training and Development*, *20*(3), 200–213. doi:10.1111/ijtd.12083

Chen, R., Liu, Y., & Zhou, F. (2021). Turning Danger into Safety: The Origin, Research Context and Theoretical Framework of Organizational Resilience. IEEE Access, 9, 48899-48913. doi:10.1109/ACCESS.2021.3069301

Chen, C. F. (2013). Performance evaluation and development strategies for green roofs in Taiwan: A review. *Ecological Engineering*, *52*, 51–58. doi:10.1016/j.ecoleng.2012.12.083

Chen, J.-C., Li, W. T., Wen, C. K., Teng, J. H., & Ting, P. (2014, July). Efficient Identification Methods for Power Line Outages in the Smart Power Grid. *IEEE Transactions on Power Systems*, *29*(4), 1788–1800. doi:10.1109/TPWRS.2013.2296897

Chen, S. Y., Wathen, C., & Speciale, M. (2020). Online Clinical Training in the Virtual Remote Environment: Challenges, Opportunities, and Solutions. *The Professional Counselor*, *10*(1), 78–91. doi:10.15241yc.10.1.78

Chen, X., Rahman, M. K., Rana, M. S., Gazi, M. A. I., Rahaman, M. A., & Nawi, N. C. (2022). Predicting consumer green product purchase attitudes and behavioral intention during COVID-19 pandemic. *Frontiers in Psychology*, *12*, 760051. doi:10.3389/fpsyg.2021.760051 PMID:35145450

Chen, Y. (2008). The positive effect of green intellectual capital on competitive advantages of firms. *Journal of Business Ethics*, *77*(3), 271–286. doi:10.100710551-006-9349-1

Cheshmehzangi, A. (2020). COVID-19 and household energy implications: What are the main impacts on energy use? *Heliyon*, *6*(10), e05202. doi:10.1016/j.heliyon.2020.e05202 PMID:33052318

Chetty, S. (1996). The case study method for research in small-and medium-sized firms. *International Small Business Journal*, *15*(1), 73–85. doi:10.1177/0266242696151005

Chiaburu, D. S., & Lindsay, D. R. (2008). Can do or will do? The importance of self-efficacy and instrumentality for training transfer. *Human Resource Development International*, *11*(2), 199–206. doi:10.1080/13678860801933004

Ching, J., & Kajino, M. (2020). Rethinking air quality and climate change after COVID-19. *International Journal of Environmental Research and Public Health*, *17*(14), 5167. doi:10.3390/ijerph17145167 PMID:32708953

Cho, S., Mathiassen, L., & Robey, D. (2006). Dialectics of resilience: a multi-level analysis of a telehealth innovation. *J Inf Technol, 22*, 24–35. ave.jit.2000088 doi:10.1057/palgr

Cho, S., Mathiassen, L., & Robey, D. (2006) The Dialectics of Resilience: A Multilevel Analysis of a Telehealth Innovation. *IFIP International Working Conference on the Transfer and Diffusion of Information Technology for Organizational Resilience*. 10.1007/0-387-34410-1_22

Christianson, M. K., Farkas, M. T., Sutcliffe, K. M., & Weick, K. E. (2009). Learning through rare events: Significant interruptions at the Baltimore and Ohio Railroad Museum. *Organization Science*, *20*(5), 846–860. doi:10.1287/orsc.1080.0389

Cieciuch, J. (2017a). Exploring the complicated relationship between values and behavior. In S. Roccas & L. Sagiv (Eds.), *Values and Behavior. Taking a Cross-Cultural Perspective* (pp. 237–247). Springer International Publishing.

Çınar, D. (2021). A research on the evaluation of consumers' voluntary simplicity lifestyle tendency in the Covid-19 period. *International Journal of Social Sciences and Education Research*, *7*(1), 12–23.

Ciocirlan, C. E. (2016). Environmental workplace behaviors: Definition matters. *Organization & Environment*, *30*(1), 51–70. doi:10.1177/1086026615628036

Ciulla, J. B. (2020). The importance of leadership in shaping business values. In J. B. Ciulla (Ed.), *The Search for Ethics in Leadership, Business, and Beyond* (pp. 153–163). Springer. doi:10.1007/978-3-030-38463-0_10

Claessens, S., & Yurtoglu, B. B. (2013). Corporate governance in emerging markets: A survey. *Emerging Markets Review*, *15*, 1–33. doi:10.1016/j.ememar.2012.03.002

Cleary, J. (2009). Life cycle assessments of municipal solid waste management systems: A comparative analysis of selected peer-reviewed literature. *Environment International*, *35*(8), 1256–1266. doi:10.1016/j.envint.2009.07.009 PMID:19682746

Clement, V., & Rivera, J. (2017). From adaptation to transformation: An extended research agenda for organizational resilience to adversity in the natural environment. *Organization & Environment*, *30*(4), 346–365. doi:10.1177/1086026616658333

Cobo Romaní, C. (2010). New Literacies, Old Problems: The New World of Work and the Unfinished Business of Education. *Reason and Word*, *22*(100), 577–588.

Cobo, S., Dominguez-Ramos, A., & Irabien, A. (2018). From linear to circular integrated waste management systems: A review of methodological approaches. *Resources, Conservation and Recycling*, *135*, 279–295. doi:10.1016/j.resconrec.2017.08.003

Cohen, M. J. (2020). Does the COVID-19 outbreak mark the onset of a sustainable consumption transition? *Sustainability: Science*. *Practice and Policy*, *16*(1), 1–3.

Cole, M. A. (2004). Trade, the pollution haven hypothesis and the environmental Kuznets curve: Examining the linkages. *Ecological Economics*, *48*(1), 71–81. doi:10.1016/j.ecolecon.2003.09.007

Cole, M. A., & Neumayer, E. (2004). Examining the impact of demographic factors on air pollution. *Population and Environment*, *26*(1), 5–21. doi:10.1023/B:POEN.0000039950.85422.eb

Collis, D. (1991). A Resource-Based Analysis of Global Competition: The Case of the Bearing Industry. *Strategic Management Journal*, *12*(S1), 49–68. doi:10.1002mj.4250120906

Cook, R., & Rasmussen, J. (2005). Going Solid: A Model of System Dynamics and Consequences for Patient Safety. *Quality & Safety in Health Care*, *14*(2), 130–134. doi:10.1136/qshc.2003.009530 PMID:15805459

Coolen, H., & Meesters, J. (2012). Private and public green spaces: Meaningful but different settings. *Journal of Housing and the Built Environment*, *27*(1), 49–67. doi:10.100710901-011-9246-5

Corbetta, P. (2007). *Metodología y técnicas de investigación social*. McGraw-Hill.

Cordeiro, J. J., & Tewari, M. (2015). Firm Characteristics, Industry Context, and Investor Reactions to Environmental CSR: A Stakeholder Theory Approach. *Journal of Business Ethics*, *130*(4), 833–849. doi:10.100710551-014-2115-x

Cornelissen, G., Pandelaere, M., Warlop, L., & Dewitte, S. (2008). Positive Cueing: Promoting Sustainable Consumer Behavior by Cueing Common Environmental Behaviors as Environmental. *International Journal of Research in Marketing*, *25*(1), 46–55. doi:10.1016/j.ijresmar.2007.06.002

Cornellá, A. (2009). *Infoxication: seeking order in information*. Infonomia Books.

Cosgrove, W. J., & Rijsberman, F. R. (2014). *World water vision: making water everybody's business*. Routledge. doi:10.4324/9781315071763

Costantini, V., Gracceva, F., Markandya, A., & Vicini, G. (2007). Security of energy supply: Comparing scenarios from a European perspective. *Energy Policy*, *35*(1), 210–226. doi:10.1016/j.enpol.2005.11.002

Coullahan, R., & Pastor, C. (2008). Improved business resilience in the commercial facilities sector. *Magazine of Business Continuity and Emergency Planning*, *3*(1), 5–18.

CountUsIn. (n.d.). *Making Changes That Matter*. Retrieved March 9, 2022, from https://www.count-us-in.org/en-gb/

Coutu, D. L. (2002). How resilience works. *Harvard Business Review*, *80*(5), 46–55. PMID:12024758

Cox, P. T., Grover, C. W., & Siskin, B. (1971). Effect of water resource investment on economic growth. *Water Resources Research*, *7*(1), 32–38. doi:10.1029/WR007i001p00032

Cremer, J., & Weitzman, M. L. (1976). OPEC and the monopoly price of world oil. *European Economic Review*, *8*(2), 155–164. doi:10.1016/0014-2921(76)90010-6

Crenshaw, E. M., & Jenkins, J. C. (1996). Social structure and global climate change: Sociological propositions concerning the greenhouse effect. *Sociological Focus*, *29*(4), 341–358. doi:10.1080/00380237.1996.10570650

Crichton, M. T., Ramsay, C. G., & Kelly, T. (2009). Enhancing organizational resilience through emergency planning: Learnings from cross-sectorial lessons. *Journal of Contingencies and Crisis Management*, *17*(1), 24–37. doi:10.1111/j.1468-5973.2009.00556.x

Cristea, A., Hummels, D., Puzzello, L., & Avetisyan, M. (2013). Trade and the greenhouse gas emissions from international freight transport. *Journal of Environmental Economics and Management*, *65*(1), 153–173. doi:10.1016/j.jeem.2012.06.002

Crosby, D. L., & Sharma, A. (2020). Insights on otolaryngology residency training during the COVID-19 pandemic. *Otolaryngology - Head and Neck Surgery*, *163*(1), 38–41. doi:10.1177/0194599820922502 PMID:32312158

Crowley, K. (2017). Up and down with climate politics 2013–2016: The repeal of carbon pricing in Australia. *Wiley Interdisciplinary Reviews: Climate Change*, *8*(3), e458. doi:10.1002/wcc.458

Cui, Y., Lissillour, R., Cheben, J., Lančarič, D., & Duan, C. (2022). The position of financial prudence, social influence, and environmental satisfaction in the sustainable consumption behavioural model: Cross-market intergenerational investigation during the COVID-19 pandemic. *Corporate Social Responsibility and Environmental Management*, 1–25. doi:10.1002/csr.2250

Cuomo, F., Mallin, C., & Zattoni, A. (2016). Corporate governance codes: A review and research agenda. *Corporate Governance*, *24*(3), 222–241. doi:10.1111/corg.12148

D'Auria, G., & De Smet, A. (2020). Leadership in a crisis: Responding to the coronavirus outbreak and future challenges. *Psychology (Irvine, Calif.)*, *22*(2), 273–287.

D€ues, C., Tan, K., & Lim, M. (2013). Green as the new Lean: how to use Lean practices as a catalystto greening your supply chain. *Journal of Cleaner Production*, *40*, 93.

Dahl, A. L. (2012). Achievements and gaps in indicators for sustainability. *Ecological Indicators*, *17*, 14–19. doi:10.1016/j.ecolind.2011.04.032

Dahles, H., & Susilowati, T. (2015). Business resilience in times of growth and crisis. *Annals of Tourism Research*, *51*, 34–50. doi:10.1016/j.annals.2015.01.002

Daily, B., & Huang, S. (2001). Achieving sustainability through attention to human resource factors in environmental management. *International Journal of Operations & Production Management*, *21*(12), 1539–1552. doi:10.1108/01443570110410892

Dai, Q., Ding, J., Hou, L., Li, L., Cai, Z., Liu, B., Song, C., Bi, X., Wu, J., Zhang, Y., Feng, Y., & Hopke, P. K. (2021). Haze episodes before and during the COVID-19 shutdown in Tianjin, China: Contribution of fireworks and residential burning. *Environmental Pollution*, *286*, 117252. doi:10.1016/j.envpol.2021.117252 PMID:33990050

Dal Mas, F., & Paoloni, P. (2019). A relational capital perspective on social sustainability; the case of female entrepreneurship in Italy. *Measuring Business Excellence*, *24*(1), 114–130. doi:10.1108/MBE-08-2019-0086

Dalgaard-Nielsen, A. (2017). Organizational resilience in national security bureaucracies: Realistic and practicable? *Journal of Contingencies and Crisis Management*, *25*(4), 341–349. doi:10.1111/1468-5973.12164

Dalziell, E., & McManus, S. (2004). Resilience, vulnerability, and adaptability: implications for system performance. *International Forum for Engineering Decision Making*.

Damiano, S. (2014). *Leadership is upside down.* About My Brain.

Daneses, S., Lee, J., Amarapurkar, S., Stafford, K., Haynes, G., & Brewton, K. (2009). Determinants of the resilience of the family business after a natural disaster by gender of the business owner. *Journal of Developmental Entrepreneurship*, *14*(4), 333–354. doi:10.1142/S1084946709001351

Daniel, J. (2020). Education and the COVID-19 pandemic. *Prospects*, *49*(1), 91–96. doi:10.100711125-020-09464-3 PMID:32313309

Danneels, E. (2012). Second-order competences and Schumpeterian rents. *Strategic Entrepreneurship Journal*, *6*(1), 42–58. doi:10.1002ej.1127

Dasgupta, P. (2007). The idea of sustainable development. *Sustainability Science*, *2*(1), 5–11. doi:10.100711625-007-0024-y

Das, N., Dasgupta, S., Roy, J., Langhelle, O., & Assadi, M. (2021). Emission Mitigation and Energy Security Trade-Off: Role of Natural Gas in the Indian Power Sector. *Energies*, *14*(13), 3787. doi:10.3390/en14133787

Davenport, T., & Prusak, L. (1998). *Working knowledge: How organizations manage what they know.* Harvard Business Press.

Davies, A., & Brady, T. (2016). Explicating the dynamics of project capabilities. *Int. J. Project Manage.*, *34*(2), 314-327.

Davis, I. (2009). The New Normal. *The McKinsey Quarterly*. https://www.mckinsey.com/ business-functions/strategy-and-corporate-finance/our-insights/the-new-normal

De Almeida, S. T., & Borsato, M. (2019). Assessing the efficiency of End of Life technology in waste treatment—A bibliometric literature review. *Resources, Conservation and Recycling*, *140*, 189–208. doi:10.1016/j.resconrec.2018.09.020

de Groot, J. I. M., & Steg, L. (2008). Value orientations to explain beliefs related to environmental significant behavior. *Environment and Behavior*, *40*(3), 330–354. doi:10.1177/0013916506297831 de Oliveira-Teixeira E. & Werther W. (2013). Resilience: continuous renewal of competitive advantages. *Horiz Bus, 56*, 333–342.

De Pascale, A., Arbolino, R., Szopik-Depczyńska, K., Limosani, M., & Ioppolo, G. (2021). A systematic review for measuring circular economy: The 61 indicators. *Journal of Cleaner Production, 281*, 124942. doi:10.1016/j.jclepro.2020.124942

Deb, P., Furceri, D., Ostry, J. D., & Tawk, N. (2021). The economic effects of Covid-19 containment measures. *Open Economies Review*, 1–32.

Degli Esposti, P., Mortara, A., & Roberti, G. (2021). Sharing and sustainable consumption in the era of COVID-19. *Sustainability, 13*(4), 1903. doi:10.3390u13041903

Deka, B. J., Bohra, V., Alam, W., Sanasam, S., Guo, J., Borana, L., & An, A. K. (2020). Environment impact assessment of COVID-19. In M. K. Goyal & A. K. Gupta (Eds.), *Integrated risk of pandemic: Covid-19 impacts, resilience and recommendations* (pp. 169–195). Springer. doi:10.1007/978-981-15-7679-9_8

Dekker, S. (2008). *Fair culture: balance between safety and responsibility*. Ashgate Publishing Co.

Delgado-Verde, M., Amores-Salvadó, J., Martín-de Castro, G., & Navas-López, J. (2014). Green intellectual capital and environmental product innovation: The mediating role of green social capital. *Knowledge Management Research and Practice, 12*(3), 261–275. doi:10.1057/kmrp.2014.1

Demmer, W., Vickery, S., & Calantone, R. (2011). Building Resilience in Small and Medium-sized Enterprises (SMEs): A Demmer Corporation Case Study. *International Journal of Production Research, 49*, 5395–5413. doi:10.1080/00207543.2011.563903

Denyer, D., & Pilbeam, P. (2015). *Change management in extreme contexts (Routledge studies on change and organizational development)*. Routledge.

Deverell, E. (2009). Crises as Learning Triggers: Exploring a Conceptual Framework of Crisis-Induced Learning. *Journal of Contingencies and Crisis Management, 17*(3), 179–188. doi:10.1111/j.1468-5973.2009.00578.x

Dewald, J., & Bowen, F. (2010). Storm Clouds and Silver Lights: Responding to Disruptive Innovations through Cognitive Resilience. *Entrepreneurship Theory and Practice, 34*(1), 197–218. doi:10.1111/j.1540-6520.2009.00312.x

Dhaka, B. L., Vatta, L., & Chayal, K. (2018). Workplace Factors Affecting Training Transfer–A Meta Evaluation. *Indian Research Journal of Extension Education, 18*(2), 91–92.

Di Gravio, G., Mancini, M., Patriarca, R., & Costantino, F. (2015). Overall safety performance of the air traffic management system: Forecast and monitoring. *Safety Science, 72*, 351–362. doi:10.1016/j.ssci.2014.10.003

Diab-Bahman, R., & Al-Enzi, A. (2020). The impact of COVID-19 pandemic on conventional work settings. *The International Journal of Sociology and Social Policy, 40*(9/10), 909–927. doi:10.1108/IJSSP-07-2020-0262

Dietz, T., & Rosa, E. A. (1997). Effects of population and affluence on CO2 emissions. *Proceedings of the National Academy of Sciences of the United States of America, 94*(1), 175–179. doi:10.1073/pnas.94.1.175 PMID:8990181

DiPietro, R. B., Cao, Y., & Partlow, C. (2013). Green practices in upscale foodservice operations: Customer perceptions and purchase intentions. *International Journal of Contemporary Hospitality Management, 25*(5), 779–796. doi:10.1108/IJCHM-May-2012-0082

Dixit, R. (2021). Facilitating Training Transfer of Patient Service Skills through Healthcare Learning Champion (HLC) Interventions. *Psychology and Education Journal, 58*(4), 4468–4474.

Dixit, R. R. (2019). Enhancing service experience through excellence in patient relationship (EPR) training programs. *Indian Journal of Public Health Research & Development*, *10*(5), 771–776. doi:10.5958/0976-5506.2019.01105.7

Dixit, R., & Sinha, V. (2019). Leveraging augmented reality for training transfer: A case of healthcare service providers in ophthalmology. *Development and Learning in Organizations*, *34*(6), 33–36. doi:10.1108/DLO-09-2019-0211

Dixit, R., & Sinha, V. (2020). Addressing Training and Development Bottlenecks in HRM: Facilitating a Paradigm Shift in Building Human Capital in Global Organizations. In *Contemporary Global Issues in Human Resource Management*. Emerald Publishing Limited. doi:10.1108/978-1-80043-392-220201012

Dixit, R., & Sinha, V. (2021). Is feedforward the way forward? A case of managers in a manufacturing firm. *Development and Learning in Organizations*, *35*(2), 7–10. doi:10.1108/DLO-10-2019-0254

Dixit, R., & Sinha, V. (2021). Training as a Strategic HRM Tool to Foster Employee Development in SMEs. In *Handbook of Research on Strategies and Interventions to Mitigate COVID-19 Impact on SMEs* (pp. 609–628). IGI Global. doi:10.4018/978-1-7998-7436-2.ch030

Djankov, S., McLiesh, C., & Klein, M. U. (Eds.). (2004). *Doing business in 2004: understanding regulation* (Vol. 1). World Bank Publications.

Dobrowolski, Z. (2020). The supreme audit institutions readiness to uncertainty. *Entrepreneurship and Sustainability Issues*, *8*(1), 513–525. doi:10.9770/jesi.2020.8.1(36)

Doern, R. (2016). Entrepreneurship and Crisis Management: The Experiences of Small Businesses During the London Riots 2011. *International Small Business Magazine.*, *34*(3), 276–302. doi:10.1177/0266242614553863

Doh, J. P., & Quigley, N. R. (2014). Responsible leadership and stakeholder management: Influence pathways and organizational outcomes. *The Academy of Management Perspectives*, *28*(3), 255–274. doi:10.5465/amp.2014.0013

Dosi, C., & Easter, K. W. (2002). Water scarcity: institutional change, water markets, and privatization. In *Economic Studies on Food, Agriculture, and the Environment* (pp. 91–115). Springer. doi:10.1007/978-1-4615-0609-6_6

Du, Y., Ruan, B., & Zhou, C. (2020). *In the post-epidemic era, focus on sustainable fashion consumers in China*. https://www.sohu.com/a/ 424435411_650547/

Duarte, R., Pinilla, V., & Serrano, A. (2013). Is there an environmental Kuznets curve for water use? A panel smooth transition regression approach. *Economic Modelling*, *31*, 518–527. doi:10.1016/j.econmod.2012.12.010

Duarte, S., & Cruz-Machado, V. (2019). Green and lean supply-chain transformation: A roadmap. *Production Planning and Control*, *30*(14), 1170–1183. doi:10.1080/09537287.2019.1595207

Duchek, S. (2014). Growth in the face of crisis: The role of organizational resilience capabilities. *Academy of Management Proceedings*, *2014*(1), 13487. doi:10.5465/ambpp.2014.225

Dudley, B. (2018). BP statistical review of world energy. *BP Statistical Review*, *6*(2018), 00116.

Duháček Šebestová, J. (2021). Crisis Situation and Financial Planning for Sustainability: A Case of the Czech SMEs. In C. Popescu & R. Verma (Eds.), *Sustainable and Responsible Entrepreneurship and Key Drivers of Performance* (pp. 59–82). IGI Global., doi:10.4018/978-1-7998-7951-0.ch003

Duit, A. (2016). Resilience thinking: Lessons for Public Administration. *Public Administration*, *94*(2), 364–380. doi:10.1111/padm.12182

Compilation of References

Dumont, J., Shen, J., & Deng, X. (2017). Effects of green HRM practices on employee workplace green behavior: The role of psychological green climate and employee green values. *Human Resource Management*, *56*, 613–627. doi:10.1002/hrm.21792

Du, S., Bhattacharya, C. B., & Sen, S. (2007). Reaping relationship rewards from corporate social responsibility: The role of competitive positioning. *International Journal of Research in Marketing*, *24*(3), 224–241. doi:10.1016/j.ijresmar.2007.01.001

Dzimińska, P., Drzewiecki, S., Ruman, M., Kosek, K., Mikołajewski, K., & Licznar, P. (2021). The use of cluster analysis to evaluate the impact of COVID-19 pandemic on daily water demand patterns. *Sustainability*, *13*(11), 5772. doi:10.3390u13115772

Dźwigoł, H., Dźwigoł-Barosz, M., Zhyvko, Z., Miśkiewicz, R., & Pushak, H. (2019). Evaluation of the energy security as a component of national security of the country. *Journal of Security & Sustainability Issues*, *8*(3), 307–317. doi:10.9770/jssi.2019.8.3(2)

Earvolino-Ramirez, M. (2007). Resilience: A concept analysis. *Nursing Forum*, *42*(2), 73–82. doi:10.1111/j.1744-6198.2007.00070.x PMID:17474940

ECLAC. (2020). *MSMEs and COVID-19*. Retrieved October 12, 2021, from https://www.cepal.org/es/euromipyme/mipymes-covid-19

Eden, S. E. (1993). Individual Environmental Responsibility and its Role in Public Environmentalism. *Environment and Planning A. Economy and Space*, *25*(12), 1743–1758. doi:10.1068/a251743

Edigin, E., Eseaton, P. O., Shaka, H., Ojemolon, P. E., Asemota, I. R., & Akuna, E. (2020). Impact of COVID-19 pandemic on medical postgraduate training in the United States. *Medical Education Online*, *25*(1), 1774318. doi:10.1080/10872981.2020.1774318 PMID:32493181

Edmondson, A. C. (2007). The competitive imperative of learning. *Harvard Business Review*, *86*(7-8), 60–67. PMID:18681298

Edvinsson, L. (1997). Developing intellectual capital at Skandia. *Long Range Planning*, *30*(3), 366–373. doi:10.1016/S0024-6301(97)90248-X

Edvinsson, L., & Malone, M. (1997). *Intellectual Capital: Realizing your company's true value by finding its hidden brainpower*. Oxford University Press, New York.

Edvinsson, L., & Malone, M. S. (1999). *Intellectual Capital*. Barcelona: *Gestion*.

Ehrlich, P. R., & Holdren, J. P. (1971). Impact of population growth. *Science*, *171*(3977), 1212–1217. doi:10.1126cience.171.3977.1212 PMID:5545198

Eisenhardt, K. M., Furr, N. R., & Bingham, C. B. (2010). Microfoundations of Performance: Balancing Efficiency and Flexibility in Dynamic Environments. *Organization Science*, *21*(6), 1263–1273. doi:10.1287/orsc.1100.0564

Elkington, R., Pearse, N. J., Moss, J., Van der Steege, M., & Martin, S. (2017). Global leaders' perceptions of elements required for effective leadership development in the twenty-first century. *Leadership and Organization Development Journal*, *38*(8), 1038–1056. doi:10.1108/LODJ-06-2016-0145

Elmaslar Özbaş, E., Akın, Ö., Güneysu, S., Özcan, H. K., & Öngen, A. (2021). Changes occurring in consumption habits of people during COVID-19 pandemic and the water footprint. *Environment, Development and Sustainability*, 1–17. doi:10.100710668-021-01797-z PMID:34483718

Eltantawy, R. A. (2016). The role of supply management resilience in attaining ambidexterity: A dynamic capabilities approach. *Journal of Business and Industrial Marketing*, *31*(1), 123–134. doi:10.1108/JBIM-05-2014-0091

Engle, R. F., & Granger, C. W. (1987). Co-integration and error correction: Representation, estimation, and testing. *Econometrica*, *55*(2), 251–276. doi:10.2307/1913236

Erol, O., Sauser, B., & Mansouri, M. (2010). A Framework for Extended Business Resilience Research. *Enterprise Information Systems*, *4*(2), 111–136. doi:10.1080/17517570903474304

Ertz, M. (2020). The COVID-19 pandemic crisis: Catalyst of the reconfiguration of commercial exchanges through responsible consumption? *Revue Organisations & Territoires*, *29*(3), 91–93. doi:10.1522/revueot.v29n3.1203

Estadística de Puertos del Estado. (2020). https://www.puertos.es/es-es/estadisticas/EstadisticaMensual/03%20Marzo%20 2020.pdf

Eurasian Economic Commission (EEC), United Nations Conference on Trade and Development (UNCTAD), & Interstate Bank (IB). (2019). *Inclusive growth of the Eurasian Economic Union Member States: Assessments and opportunities*. http://www.eurasiancommission.org/ru/act/integr_i_makroec/dep_makroec_pol/Documents/Inclusive_growth_in_EAEU_Member.pdf

Euromonitor. (2020). *From Sustainability to Purpose: New Values Driving Purpose-Led Innovation*. Euromonitor International.

European Commission (EC). (2020a). *Shaping Europe's Digital Future*. Luxembourg: Publications Office of the European Union. https://ec.europa.eu/info/sites/default/files/communication-shaping-europes-digital-future-feb2020_en_4.pdf doi:10.2759/48191

European Commission (EC). (2020b). *Assessment and Roadmap for the Digital Transformation of the Energy Sector Towards an Innovative Internal Energy Market*. Luxembourg: Publications Office of the European Union. https://www.euneighbours.eu/sites/default/files/publications/2020-03/MJ0220185ENN.en_.pdf doi:10.2833/36433

European Commission (EC). (2020c). *Eco-Innovation and Digitalisation Case studies, environmental and policy lessons from EU Member States for the EU Green Deal and the Circular Economy EIO Biennial report 2020*. https://ec.europa.eu/environment/ecoap/sites/default/files/eio5_eco-innovation_and_digitalisation_nov2020.pdf

European Commission (EC). (2020d). *Shaping the Digital Transformation in Europe. European Commission DG Communications Networks, Content & Technology. Final Report: A study prepared for the European Commission DG Communications Networks, Content and Technology*. https://www.ospi.es/export/sites/ospi/documents/documentos/Sstudy_Shaping_the_digital_transformation_in_Europe_Final_report_202009.pdf

European Commission (EC). (2021). *Proposal for a Decision Of The European Parliament And Of The Council establishing the 2030 Policy Programme "Path to the Digital Decade" (Text with EEA relevance) {SWD(2021) 247 final}. Brussels, 15.9.2021 COM(2021) 574 final 2021/0293 (COD)*. https://www.digitales.es/wp-content/uploads/2021/11/COM_2021_574_final_act_EN_v8_ptPK7Tb1DRDE7515KeapWlChi8_79300.pdf

European Commission (EC). (2022). *Joint European Roadmap towards lifting COVID-19 containment measures*. https://ec.europa.eu/info/sites/default/files/communication_-_a_european_roadmap_to_lifting_coronavirus_containment_measures_0.pdf

European Commission (EC). (2022). *Shaping Europe's digital future. Procurement of ICT innovation*. https://digital-strategy.ec.europa.eu/en/policies/innovation-procurement

Compilation of References

European Observatory on Health Systems and Policies & World Health Organization. (2007). *Mental Health Policy and Practice across Europe. The future direction of mental health care.* Open University Press. https://www.euro.who.int/__data/assets/pdf_file/0007/96451/E89814.pdf

European Parliament (EP). (2019). *Briefing. EU policies – Delivering for citizens EPRS*. European Parliamentary Research Service. https://www.europarl.europa.eu/RegData/etudes/BRIE/2019/633171/EPRS_BRI(2019)633171_EN.pdf

European Parliament (EP). (2021). *Briefing. Initial Appraisal of a European Commission Impact Assessment. Artificial intelligence act Impact assessment (SWD(2021) 84, SWD(2021) 85 (summary)) accompanying a Commission proposal for a regulation of the European Parliament and of the Council laying down harmonized rules on artificial intelligence (Artificial Intelligence Act) and amending certain Union legislative acts(COM(2021) 206)*. EPRS. European Parliamentary Research Service. https://www.europarl.europa.eu/RegData/etudes/BRIE/2021/694212/EPRS_BRI(2021)694212_EN.pdf

European Union (EU). (2017). *Joint Action on Mental Health and Well-being (MH-WB): Mental Health and Schools. Situation analysis and recommendations for action, published by the European Union, in the framework of the Health Program.* The Second Programme for Community Action for Health 2008-2013. https://ec.europa.eu/health/system/files/2017-07/2017_mh_schools_en_0.pdf

Fahlquist, J. N. (2009). Moral Responsibility for Environmental Problems—Individual or Institutional? *Journal of Agricultural & Environmental Ethics*, *22*(2), 109–124. doi:10.100710806-008-9134-5

Falkenmark, M., Lundqvist, J., Klohn, W., Postel, S., Wallace, J., Shuval, H., ... Rockström, J. (1998). Water scarcity as a key factor behind global food insecurity: Round table discussion. *Ambio*, •••, 148–154.

Fani, M., & Norouzi, N. (2020). Using Social and Economic Indicators for Modeling, Sensitivity Analysis and Forecasting the Gasoline Demand in the Transportation Sector: An ANN Approach in case study for Tehran metropolis. *Iranian Journal of Energy*, *23*(2), 71–91.

Fan, Y., Liu, L. C., Wu, G., & Wei, Y. M. (2006). Analyzing impact factors of CO2 emissions using the STIRPAT model. *Environmental Impact Assessment Review*, *26*(4), 377–395. doi:10.1016/j.eiar.2005.11.007

Farias, L. M. S., Santos, L. S., Gohr, C. F., & Rocha, L. O. (2019). An ANP-based approach for lean andgreen performance assessment. *Resources, Conservation and Recycling*, *143*, 77–89.

Farjoun, M. (2010). Beyond dualism: Stability and change as a duality. *Academy of Management Review*, *35*(2), 202–225.

Faurés, J. M., Vallée, D., Eliasson, Ă., & Hoogeveen, J. (2001). *Statistics on Water Resources by Country in FAO's AQUASTAT Programme*. Joint ECE/EUROSTAT Work Session on Methodological Ossues of Environmental Statistics.

Febrianti, F. D., Sugiyanto, S., & Fitria, J. R. (2020). Green Intellectual Capital Conservatism Earning Management, To Future Stock Return As Moderating Stock Return (Study Of Mining Companies In Indonesia Listed On Idx For The Period Of 2014-2019). *The Accounting Journal Of Binaniaga*, *5*(2), 141–154. doi:10.33062/ajb.v5i2.407

Felstead, A., Green, F., & Jewson, N. (2012). An analysis of the impact of the 2008–9 recession on the provision of training in the UK. *Work, Employment and Society*, *26*(6), 968–986. doi:10.1177/0950017012458016

Ferasso, M., Beliaeva, T., Kraus, S., Clauss, T., & Ribeiro-Soriano, D. (2020). Circular economy business models: The state of research and avenues ahead. *Business Strategy and the Environment*, *29*(8), 3006–3024. doi:10.1002/bse.2554

Ferrara, M., Romano, V., Steel, D. H., Gupta, R., Iovino, C., van Dijk, E. H., & Romano, M. R. (2020). Reshaping ophthalmology training after COVID-19 pandemic. *Eye (London, England)*, *34*(11), 2089–2097. doi:10.103841433-020-1061-3 PMID:32612174

FEV. (2019). *El sector del vino y el papel de la FEV en los Objetivos de Desarrollo Sostenible*. Disponible en: http://www.fev.es/fev/sostenibilidad-y-responsabilidad/objetivos-de-desarrollo-sostenible_122_1_ap.html

Fielden, K. (2005). Mindfulness: An Essential Quality of Integrated Wisdom. In J. Courtney, J. Haynes, & D. Paradice (Eds.), *Inquiring Organizations: Moving from Knowledge Management to Wisdom* (pp. 211–228). IGI Global. doi:10.4018/978-1-59140-309-8.ch011

Fiksel, J. (2006). Sustainability and resilience: towards a systems approach. Sustainability: Science, Practice. *Policy.*, *2*(2), 14–21.

Finon, D. (2007). Russia and the 'Gas-OPEC': Real or Perceived Threat?. *Russie. Nei. Visions*, 24.

Finon, D. (2011). The EU foreign gas policy of transit corridors: Autopsy of the stillborn Nabucco project. *OPEC Energy Review*, *35*(1), 47–69. doi:10.1111/j.1753-0237.2010.00185.x

Fiore, M., Silvestri, R., Contò, F., & Pellegrini, G. (2017). Understanding the relationship between green approach and marketing innovations tools in the wine sector. *Journal of Cleaner Production*, *142*, 4085–4091. doi:10.1016/j.jclepro.2016.10.026

Fleming, J., & Ledogar, R. (2008). Resilience, an Evolving Concept: A Review of the Relevant Literature for Aboriginal Research. *Pimatziwin*, *6*(2), 7–23. PMID:20963184

Fletcher, D., & Sarkar, M. (2013). Psychological resilience: Review and critique of definitions, concepts, and theory. *European Psychologist*, *18*(1), 12–23. doi:10.1027/1016-9040/a000124

Flint, R. W. (2013). *Basics of Sustainable Development BT - Practice of Sustainable Community Development: A Participatory Framework for Change*. Springer. doi:10.1007/978-1-4614-5100-6_2

Folke, C., (2006). Resilience: The emergence of a perspective for social–ecological systems analyses. *Global Environ. Change, 16*(3), 253–267. .gloenvcha.2006.04.002 doi:10.1016/j

Folke, C. (2006). Resilience: The emergence of a perspective for the analysis of socio-ecological systems. *Global Environmental Change*, *16*(3), 253–267. doi:10.1016/j.gloenvcha.2006.04.002

Folke, C. (2016). Resilience (republished). *Ecology and Society*, *21*(4), 1–44. doi:10.5751/ES-09088-210444

Folke, C., Carpenter, S. R., Walker, B., Scheffer, M., Chapin, T., & Rockström, J. (2010). Resilience thinking: Integrating resilience, adaptability, and transformability. *Ecology and Society*, *15*(4), art20. doi:10.5751/ES-03610-150420

Foncubierta-Rodríguez, M. J., & Sánchez-Montero, J. M. (2019). Towards happiness in workplace: Taking care of motivations and eliminating "digital fears", *Challenges. Revista de Ciencias de la Administración y Economía*, *9*(18), 239–257. doi:10.17163/ret.n18.2019.04

Forino, G., & von Meding, J. (2021). Climate change adaptation across businesses in Australia: interpretations, implementations, and interactions. *Environ Dev Sustain*. doi:10.1007/s10668-021-01468-z

Francis, R., & Bekera, B. (2014). A metric and frameworks for resilience analysis of engineered and infrastructure systems. *Reliability Engineering & System Safety*, *121*, 90–103. doi:10.1016/j.ress.2013.07.004

Freeman, S. F., Hirschhorn, L., & Maltz, M. (2004). *Organizational resilience and moral purpose: Sandler O'Neill & Partners in the aftermath of 9/11/01*. Paper presented at the Annual Meeting of the Academy of Management, New Orleans, LA.

Frig, M., & Sorsa, V. P. (2020). Nation branding as sustainability governance: A comparative case analysis. *Business & Society*, *2020*(59), 1151–1180.

Gabriel, S. A., Rosendahl, K. E., Egging, R., Avetisyan, H. G., & Siddiqui, S. (2012). Cartelization in gas markets: Studying the potential for a "Gas OPEC". *Energy Economics*, *34*(1), 137–152. doi:10.1016/j.eneco.2011.05.014

Galeazzo, A., Furlan, A., & Vinelli, A. (2014). Understanding environmental-operations integration: The case of pollution prevention projects. *International Journal of Production Economics*, *153*(c), 149–160.

Gallagher, T. M., & Buchmeier, M. J. (2001). Coronavirus spike proteins in viral entry and pathogenesis. *Virology*, *279*(2), 371–374. doi:10.1006/viro.2000.0757 PMID:11162792

Gao, S., Sung, M., & Zhang, J. (2013). Developing Risk Management Capacity in SMEs: A Social Capital Perspective. *International Small Business Journal*, *31*(6), 677–700. doi:10.1177/0266242611431094

García-Buades, M. E., Peiró, J. M., Montañez-Juan, M. I., Kozusznik, M. W., & Ortiz-Bonnín, S. (2020). Happy-Productive Teams and Work Units: A Systematic Review of the "Happy-Productive Worker Thesis". *International Journal of Environmental Research and Public Health*, *17*(1), 69. doi:10.3390/ijerph17010069

Gatto, E., & Lanzafame, M. (2005). *Water resource as a factor of production: water use and economic growth*. Paper presented at the 45th ERSA Conference, Amsterdam.

GECF Secretariat. (2018). *Energy and Gas Market Analysis*. www.gecf.org

Gečienė, J. (2021). Management of organizational resilience to the crisis: results of a survey of social service institutions before and during a covid-19 pandemic. *Contemporary research on management and administration of organizations*, *9*(1), 32-42.

Gegenfurtner, A. (2013). Dimensions of motivation to transfer: A longitudinal analysis of their influence on retention, transfer, and attitude change. *Vocations and Learning*, *6*(2), 187–205. doi:10.100712186-012-9084-y

Gegenfurtner, A., Festner, D., Gallenberger, W., Lehtinen, E., & Gruber, H. (2009). Predicting autonomous and controlled motivation to transfer training. *International Journal of Training and Development*, *13*(2), 124–138. doi:10.1111/j.1468-2419.2009.00322.x

Geisler, M., Berthelsen, H., & Muhonen, T. (2019). Retaining social workers: The role of quality of work and psychosocial safety climate for work engagement, job satisfaction, and organizational commitment. *Human Service Organizations, Management, Leadership & Governance*, *43*(1), 1–15. doi:10.1080/23303131.2019.1569574

Georgescu-Roegen, N. (2013). *The entropy law and the economic process*. Harvard University Press.

Gibson, C., & Tarrant, M. (2010). A "Conceptual Models" approach to organisational resilience. *Australian Journal of Emergency Management*, *25*(2), 8–14.

Gifford, R., & Sussman, R. (2012). Environmental attitudes. In *The Oxford handbook of environmental and conservation psychology* (pp. 65–88). Oxford University Press. doi:10.1093/oxfordhb/9780199733026.013.0004

Gigerenzer, G. (2008). Why Heuristics Work. *Perspectives on Psychological Science*, *3*(1), 20–29. doi:10.1111/j.1745-6916.2008.00058.x PMID:26158666

Gigerenzer, G., & Brighton, H. (2009). Homo Heuristicus: Why Biased Minds Makes Better inferences. *Topics in Cognitive Science*, *1*(1), 107–143. doi:10.1111/j.1756-8765.2008.01006.x PMID:25164802

Gilinsky, A. Jr, Newton, S., & Vega, R. (2016). Sustainability in the global wine industry: Concepts and cases. *Agriculture and Agricultural Science Procedia*, *8*, 37–49. doi:10.1016/j.aaspro.2016.02.006

Gittell, J., Cameron, K., Lim, S., & Rivas, V. (2006). Relationships, Layoffs, and Organizational Resilience: Airline Industry Responses to 9/11. *The Journal of Applied Behavioral Science*, *42*(3), 300–329. doi:10.1177/0021886306286466

Gleick, P. H. (2000). Water conflict chronology. *The World's Water 2008-2009: The Biennial Report on Freshwater Resources*, 151-196.

Gleick, P. H. (1998). *The world's water 1998-1999: the biennial report on freshwater resources*. Island Press.

Global Wellness Institute (GWI). (2019). *Move to be Well: The Global Economy of Physical Activity*. https://globalwellnessinstitute.org/wp-content/uploads/2019/10/2019-Physical-Activity-Economy-FINAL-NEW-101019.pdf

Glover, J. (2012). Rural resilience through continued learning and innovation. *Local Economy*, *27*(4), 355–372. doi:10.1177/0269094212437833

Goklany, I. M. (2002). Comparing 20th century trends in US and global agricultural water and land use. *Water International*, *27*(3), 321–329. doi:10.1080/02508060208687012

Gordon-Wilson, S. (2021). Consumption practices during the COVID-19 crisis. *International Journal of Consumer Studies*, *46*(2), 575–588. doi:10.1111/ijcs.12701 PMID:34220342

Gouldson, A., & Murphy, J. (1997). *Ecological modernisation: Economic restructuring and the environment*. Academic Press.

Gover, L., & Duxbury, L. (2018). Making sense of organizational change: Is hindsight really 20/20. *Journal of Organizational Behavior*, *39*(1), 39–51. doi:10.1002/job.2208

Green Jr., K.W., Zelbst, P.J., Meacham, J., Bhadauria, V.S., (2012). Green supply chain management practices: impact on performance. *Supply C. Man. An Int. J.*, *17*(3), 290-305.

Greiner, L. E. (1972). Evolution and Revolution as Organizations Grow. *Harvard Business Review*, *50*(4), 37–46. PMID:10179654

Grodzinska-Jurczak, M., Krawzyck, A., Jurczak, A., Strzelecka, M., Bockowski, M., & Rechcinski, M. (2020). Environmental choices vs. Covid-19 pandemic fear – plastic governance re-assessment. *Socialist Register*, *4*(2), 49–66. doi:10.14746r.2020.4.2.04

Grossman, R., & Salas, E. (2011). The transfer of training: What really matters. *International Journal of Training and Development*, *15*(2), 103–120. doi:10.1111/j.1468-2419.2011.00373.x

Grøtan, T., & Asbjørnslett, B. (2007). ICT in resilient global logistics. *Proceedings of ESREL 2007*, 2349-2356.

Grupe, D. W., Smith, C., & McGehee, C. (2021). Introducing Mindfulness Training and Research Into Policing: Strategies for Successful Implementation. In E. Arble & B. Arnetz (Eds.), *Interventions, Training, and Technologies for Improved Police Well-Being and Performance* (pp. 125–149). IGI Global. doi:10.4018/978-1-7998-6820-0.ch007

Gumilar, V. T. (2020). *Sustainable consumer behavior in times of COVID-19* [Unpublished master thesis]. National Sun Yat-Sen University, Taiwan.

Guo, M., Nowakowska-Grunt, J., Gorbanyov, V., & Egorova, M. (2020). Green technology and sustainable development: Assessment and green growth frameworks. *Sustainability*, *12*(16), 6571. doi:10.3390u12166571

Gupta, S. K. (Ed.). (2022). *Handbook of Research on Clinical Applications of Meditation and Mindfulness-Based Interventions in Mental Health*. IGI Global. doi:10.4018/978-1-7998-8682-2

Hacıoğlu, S., Känzig, D., & Surico, P. (2020). *Consumption in the time of COVID-19: Evidence from UK transaction data*. https://papers.ssrn.com/sol3/papers.cfm?abstract_id=3603964

Compilation of References

Hale, A., & Heijer, T. (2006). Defining Resilience. In E. Hollnagel, D. D. Woods, & N. Leveson (Eds.), *Resilience Engineering: Concepts and Precepts* (pp. 35–40). Ashgate.

Hall, A. K., Nousiainen, M. T., Campisi, P., Dagnone, J. D., Frank, J. R., Kroeker, K. I., Brzezina, S., Purdy, E., & Oswald, A. (2020). Training disrupted: Practical tips for supporting competency-based medical education during the COVID-19 pandemic. *Medical Teacher*, *42*(7), 756–761. doi:10.1080/0142159X.2020.1766669 PMID:32450049

Hallam, C., & Contreras, C. (2016). Integrating lean and green management. *Management Decision*, *54*(9), 2157–2187.

Hall, R. D., & Rowland, C. A. (2016). Leadership development for managers in turbulent times. *Journal of Management Development*, *35*(8), 942–955. doi:10.1108/JMD-09-2015-0121

Hamdouch, A., & Depret, M. H. (2010). Policy integration strategy and the development of the 'green economy': Foundations and implementation patterns. *Journal of Environmental Planning and Management*, *53*(4), 473–490. doi:10.1080/09640561003703889

Hamel, G., & Välikangas, L. (2003). The quest for resilience. *Harvard Business Review*, *81*(9), 52–63.

Hamel, G., & Välikangas, L. (2003). The search for resilience. *Harvard Business Review*, *81*(9), 52–63. PMID:12964393

Hamilton, C. (2001). *Running from the storm: the development of climate change policy in Australia*. UNSW Press.

Handmer, J., & Dovers, S. (1996). A typology of resilience: Rethinking institutions for sustainable development. *Organization & Environment*, *9*, 482–511.

Hanif, U., Syed, S. H., Ahmad, R., Malik, K. A., & Nasir, M. (2010). Economic Impact of Climate Change on the Agricultural Sector of Punjab. *Pakistan Development Review*, *49*(4), 771–798. doi:10.30541/v49i4IIpp.771-798

Hanna, P., Font, X., Scarles, C., Weeden, C., & Harrison, C. (2018). Tourist destination marketing: From sustainability myopia to memorable experiences. *Journal of Destination Marketing & Management*, *2018*(9), 36–43.

Hao, W., Shah, S. M. A., Nawaz, A., Asad, A., Iqbal, S., Zahoor, H., & Maqsoom, A. (2020). The impact of energy cooperation and the role of the one belt and road initiative in revolutionizing the geopolitics of energy among regional economic powers: An analysis of infrastructure development and project management. *Complexity*, *2020*, 2020. doi:10.1155/2020/8820021

Harris, S., Martin, M., & Diener, D. (2021). Circularity for circularity's sake? Scoping review of assessment methods for environmental performance in the circular economy. *Sustainable Production and Consumption*, *26*, 172–186. doi:10.1016/j.spc.2020.09.018

Hartini, S., & Ciptomulyono, U. (2015). The relationship between lean and sustainable manufacturing on performance: Literature review. *Procedia Manufacturing*, *4*, 38–45.

Hartley, K., van Santen, R., & Kirchherr, J. (2020). Policies for transitioning towards a circular economy: Expectations from the European Union (EU). *Resources, Conservation and Recycling*, *155*, 104634. doi:10.1016/j.resconrec.2019.104634

Hartmann, P., & Apaolaza Ibáñez, V. (2006). Green value added. *Marketing Intelligence & Planning*, *24*(7), 673–680.

Hayek, F. A. (1945). The use of knowledge in society. *The American Economic Review*, *35*(4), 519–530.

Head, B. W. (2014). Evidence, uncertainty, and wicked problems in climate change decision making in Australia. *Environment and Planning. C, Government & Policy*, *32*(4), 663–679.

Heilig, G. K. (2012). World urbanization prospects: The 2011 revision. United Nations, Department of Economic and Social Affairs (DESA), Population Division. *Population Estimates and Projections Section, New York*, *14*, 555.

Held, D., Kickbusch, I., McNally, K., Piselli, D., & Told, M. (2019). Gridlock, Innovation and Resilience in Global Health Governance. *Global Policy*, *10*(2), 161–177. doi:10.1111/1758-5899.12654

Helfat, C. E., Finklestein, S., Mitchell, W., Peteraf, M. A., Singh, H., Teece, D. J., & Winter, S. G. (2007). *Dynamic Capabilities: Understanding strategic change in organizations*. Blackwell Publishing.

Henao, R., Sarache, W., & Gomez, I. (2019). Lean manufacturing and sustainable performance: Trends and future challenges. *Journal of Cleaner Production*, *208*, 99–116.

Herbane, B. (2019). Rethinking organizational resilience and strategic renewal in SMEs. *Entrepreneurship and Regional Development*, *31*(5-6), 476–495. doi:10.1080/08985626.2018.1541594

Hillmann, J., & Guenther, E. (2020). Organizational Resilience: A Valuable Construct for Management Research? *International Magazine of Managerial Reviews*, 1-38.

Hine, D., Parker, R., Pregelj, L., & Verreynne, M.-L. (2014). Deconstructing and Reconstructing the Capability Hierarchy. *Industrial and Corporate Change*, *23*(5), 1299–1325. doi:10.1093/icc/dtt046

Hobbs, J. E. (2020). Food supply chains during the COVID-19 pandemic. *Canadian Journal of Agricultural Economics/Revue Canadienne D'agroeconomie*, *68*(2), 171-176.

Hoffmann, G. (2016). *Organisationale Resilienz. Grundlagen und Handlungsempfehlungen für Entscheidungsträger und Führungskräfte*. Springer. doi:10.1007/978-3-658-12890-6

Holl, K. D., & Howarth, R. B. (2000). Paying for Restoration. *Restoration Ecology*, *8*(3), 260–267. doi:10.1046/j.1526-100x.2000.80037.x

Hollnagel, E. (2010). How resilient is your organization? Introduction to the Resilience Analysis Grid (RAG). In Sustainable transformation: Building a resilient organization. Academic Press.

Hollnagel, E. (2009). The four cornerstones of resilience engineering. In C. Nemeth & E. Hollnagel (Eds.), *Resilience Engineering Perspectives*. Ashgate Publishing Company.

Hollnagel, E. (2010). *How Resilient Is Your Organisation? An Introduction to the Resilience Analysis Grid (RAG). Sustainable Transformation*. Building a Resilient Organization.

Hollnagel, E., & Woods, D. D. (2017). Epilogue: Resilience engineering precepts. In E. Hollnagel, D. D. Woods, & N. Leveson (Eds.), *Resilience engineering: Concepts and precepts* (pp. 347–358). CRC Press. doi:10.1201/9781315605685-30

Hollnagel, E., Woods, D., & Leveson, N. (2006). *Resilience engineering: concepts and precepts*. Ashgate Publishing.

Horne, J. III, & Orr, J. (1998). Assess behaviors that create resilient organizations. *Employment Relations Today*, *24*(4), 29–39.

Howard-Grenville, J., Buckle, S., Hoskins, B., & George, G. (2014). From the editors: Climate change and management. Academy of Management Journal, 57, 615-623.

Howe, C. W. (1976). The effects of water resource development on economic growth the conditions for success. *Natural Resources Journal*, *16*(4), 939–955.

Hsu, L. Y., Chia, P. Y., & Vasoo, S. (2020). A midpoint perspective on the COVID-19 pandemic. *Singapore Medical Journal*, *61*(7), 381–383. doi:10.11622medj.2020036 PMID:32211911

Huang, C., & Kung, F. (2011). Environmental consciousness and intellectual capital management: Evidence from Taiwan's manufacturing industry. *Management Decision*, *49*(9), 1405–1425. doi:10.1108/00251741111173916

Compilation of References

Huber, S., van Wijgerden, I. de Witt, A., & Dekker, S. W. A. (2009). Learning from organizational incidents: Resilience engineering for high-risk process environments. *Process Saf. Prog.*, *28*(1), 90-95.

Huber, G., Gomes, J., & Carvalho, P. (2012). A program to support the construction and evaluation of resilience indicators. *Job.*, *41*, 2810–2816. doi:10.3233/WOR-2012-0528-2810 PMID:22317145

Hughes, A. M., Zajac, S., Woods, A. L., & Salas, E. (2020). The role of work environment in training sustainment: A meta-analysis. *Human Factors*, *62*(1), 166–183. doi:10.1177/0018720819845988 PMID:31136198

Hussain, M. E., & Haque, M. (2016). Impact of economic freedom on the growth rate: A panel data analysis. *Economies*, *4*(2), 5. doi:10.3390/economies4020005

Hu, W., & Wang, D. (2020). How does environmental regulation influence China's carbon productivity? An empirical analysis based on the spatial spillover effect. *Journal of Cleaner Production*, *257*, 120484. doi:10.1016/j.jclepro.2020.120484

Hu, Y., Li, J., & Holloway, L. (2008). Towards modeling resilience dynamics in manufacturing companies: Literature review and problem formulation. *CASE*, *2008*, 279–284.

IBM Corporation. (2004). *Business Resilience: Proactive Measures for Forward-Looking Companies*. Available at: www-935.ibm.com/services/us/bcrs/pdf/br_business-resilience.pdf

Ibn-Mohammed, T., Mustapha, K. B., Godsell, J., Adamu, Z., Babatunde, K. A., Akintade, D. D., Acquaye, A., Fujii, H., Ndiaye, M. M., Yamoah, F. A., & Koh, S. C. L. (2021). A critical analysis of the impacts of COVID-19 on the global economy and ecosystems and opportunities for circular economy strategies. *Resources, Conservation and Recycling*, *164*, 105169. doi:10.1016/j.resconrec.2020.105169 PMID:32982059

Ikiz, E., Maclaren, V. W., Alfred, E., & Sivanesan, S. (2021). Impact of COVID-19 on household waste flows, diversion and reuse: The case of multi-residential buildings in Toronto, Canada. *Resources, Conservation and Recycling*, *164*, 105111. doi:10.1016/j.resconrec.2020.105111 PMID:32839638

ILO (International Labour Organization). (2020). ILO Monitor: COVID-19 and the world of work. Available at: ilo.org/global

IMF (International Monetary Fund), World Economic Outlook Database. (2020). Available at: http://www.imf.org.

Inglehart, R., Haerpfer, C., Moreno, A., Welzel, C., Kizilova, K., Diez-Medrano, J., Lagos, M., & Norris, P. E. P., & B. P. (Eds.). (2014). *World Values Survey: All Rounds - Country-Pooled Datafile Version*. https://www.worldvaluessurvey.org/WVSDocumentationWVL.jsp

International Labor Organization (ILO). (2018). *Global Commission on the future of work. New business models for inclusive growth. Issue Brief*. Prepared for the 2nd Meeting of the Global Commission on the Future of Work. https://www.ilo.org/wcmsp5/groups/public/---dgreports/---cabinet/documents/publication/wcms_618172.pdf

Ishak, A. W., & Williams, E. A. (2018). A dynamic model of organizational resilience: Adaptive and anchored approaches,. *Editorial Advisory Board*, *23*(2), 180-196.

Ishak, N. M., Bakar, A., & Yazid, A. (2014). Developing Sampling Frame for Case Study: Challenges and Conditions. *World Journal of Education*, *4*(3), 29–35.

Ismail, H., Poolton, J., & Sharifi, H. (2011). The role of agile strategic capabilities in achieving resilience in small manufacturing companies. *International Journal of Production Research*, *49*(18), 5469–5487. doi:10.1080/00207543.2011.563833

Ivanova, G., & Tranter, B. (2008). Paying for Environmental Protection in a Cross-national Perspective. *Australian Journal of Political Science*, *43*(2), 169–188. doi:10.1080/10361140802035705

Iwata, H., Okada, K., & Samreth, S. (2010). Empirical study on the environmental Kuznets curve for CO2 in France: The role of nuclear energy. *Energy Policy*, *38*(8), 4057–4063. doi:10.1016/j.enpol.2010.03.031

Jabareen, Y. (2008). A New Conceptual Framework for Sustainable Development. *Environment, Development and Sustainability*, *10*(2), 179–192. doi:10.100710668-006-9058-z

Jabareen, Y. (2009). Building a conceptual framework: Philosophy, definitions, and procedure. *International Journal of Qualitative Methods*, *8*(4), 49–62. doi:10.1177/160940690900800406

Jacobi, P., Kjellen, M., McGranahan, G., Songsore, J., & Surjadi, C. (2010). *The citizens at risk: from urban sanitation to sustainable cities*. Routledge. doi:10.4324/9781849776097

Jaffe, A. M., & Soligo, R. (1970). Market structure in the new gas economy: is cartelization possible? *Natural Gas and Geopolitics*, 439-464.

Jalilian, H., Kirkpatrick, C., & Parker, D. (2007). The impact of regulation on economic growth in developing countries: A cross-country analysis. *World Development*, *35*(1), 87–103. doi:10.1016/j.worlddev.2006.09.005

Jaramillo, A., & Jaramillo, M. (2016). 2008 financial crisis: Effect on companies listed on the Mexican Stock Exchange. *Mexican Journal of Economics and Finance*, *11*(3), 161–177.

Jenks, M., Burton, E., & Williams, K. (1996). Compact cities and sustainability: an introduction. *The compact city: A sustainable urban form*, 11-12.

Jian, Y., Yu, I. Y., Yang, M. X., & Zeng, K. J. (2020). The impacts of fear and uncertainty of covid-19 on environmental concerns, brand trust, and behavioral intentions toward green hotels. *Sustainability*, *12*(20), 8688. doi:10.3390u12208688

Jirakraisiri, J., Badir, Y., & Frank, B. (2021). Translating green strategic intent into green process innovation performance: The role of green intellectual capital. *Journal of Intellectual Capital*, *22*(7), 43–67. doi:10.1108/JIC-08-2020-0277

Johansen, S. (1988). Statistical analysis of cointegration vectors. *Journal of Economic Dynamics & Control*, *12*(2-3), 231–254. doi:10.1016/0165-1889(88)90041-3

Jribi, S., Ben Ismail, H., Doggui, D., & Debbabi, H. (2020). COVID-19 virus outbreak lockdown: What impacts on household food wastage? *Environment, Development and Sustainability*, *22*(5), 3939–3955. doi:10.100710668-020-00740-y PMID:32837271

Jüttner, U., & Maklan, S. (2011). Supply chain resilience in the global financial crisis: An empirical study. *Supply Chain Management*, *16*(4), 246–259. doi:10.1108/13598541111139062

Kadir, B. A., Broberg, O., & da Conceição, C. S. (2019). Current research and future perspectives on human factors and ergonomics in Industry 4.0. *Computers & Industrial Engineering*, *137*. doi:10.1016/j.cie.2019.106004

Kagti, S. (2020). *When You Work from a PG, It's a Fight for Internet*. Accessed 5 November 2021. https://www.livemint.com/mint-lounge/business-of-life/when-you-work-from-a-pg-it-s-a-fight-for-internet-11586186976325.html

Kahan, J., Allen, A., George, J., & Thompson, W. (2009). *Concept development: An operational framework for resilience*. Homeland Security Studies and Analysis Institute. Available from http://www.homelandsecurity.org/

Kamalahmadi, M., & Parast, M. M. (2016). A review of the literature on the principles of enterprise and supply chain resilience: Major findings and directions for future research. *International Journal of Production Economics*, *171*, 116–133. doi:10.1016/j.ijpe.2015.10.023

Compilation of References

Kang, H., An, J., Kim, H., Ji, C., Hong, T., & Lee, S. (2021). Changes in energy consumption according to building use type under COVID-19 pandemic in South Korea. *Renewable & Sustainable Energy Reviews*, *148*, 111294. doi:10.1016/j.rser.2021.111294 PMID:34234624

Kantur, D. & Iseri-Say, A. (2012). Organizational Resilience: An Integrative Conceptual Framework. *Management and Organization Magazine*, *18*(6), 762-773.

Kanwar, A., & Mishra, S. (2021). *Research in Open Learning: Lessons for a Post-COVID World*. Academic Press.

Katouzian, M. A. (1978). Oil versus agriculture a case of dual resource depletion in Iran. *The Journal of Peasant Studies*, *5*(3), 347–369. doi:10.1080/03066157808438052

Katz, D. (2015). Water use and economic growth: Reconsidering the Environmental Kuznets Curve relationship. *Journal of Cleaner Production*, *88*, 205–213. doi:10.1016/j.jclepro.2014.08.017

Kaufmann, D., Kraay, A., & Mastruzzi, M. (2005). *Governance matters IV: governance indicators for 1996-2004*. World bank policy research working paper series, (3630).

Kaufmann, D., Kraay, A., & Mastruzzi, M. (2004). Governance matters III: Governance indicators for 1996, 1998, 2000, and 2002. *The World Bank Economic Review*, *18*(2), 253–287. doi:10.1093/wber/lhh041

Keller, K. (2003). Understanding brands, branding and brand equity. *Journal of Direct, Data and Digital Marketing Practice*, *5*, 7–20. https://doi.org/10.1057/palgrave.im.4340213

Khalili, A., Ismail, M. Y., Karim, A. N. M., & Daud, M. R. C. (2016). Relationships of lean, green manufacturing and sustainable performance: assessing the applicability of the proposed model. *International Conference on Industrial Engineering and Operations Management*. Available at: http://ieomsociety.org/ieom_2016/pdfs/179.pdf

Khan, S. N. (Ed.). (2022). Leadership and Followership in an Organizational Change Context. IGI Global. https://doi.org/10.4018/978-1-7998-2807-5.

Khatri, P., & Hayasaka, T. (2021). Impacts of COVID-19 on air quality over China: Links with meteorological factors and energy consumption. *Aerosol and Air Quality Research*, *21*(10), 1–18. doi:10.4209/aaqr.200668

Khoshnava, S. M., Rostami, R., Zin, R. M., Štreimikienė, D., Yousefpour, A., Strielkowski, W., & Mardani, A. (2019). Aligning the criteria of green economy (GE) and sustainable development goals (SDGs) to implement sustainable development. *Sustainability*, *11*(17), 4615. doi:10.3390u11174615

Kikuchi, A. & Yamaguchi, H. (2012) A clue to the synthetic understanding of resilience in organization: recomposition through the crossing of two dimensions of time series and different dimensions of objects. *Journal of Human Interface Society: Human Interface, 14*(2), 3-108.

Kim, H., Shoji, Y., Tsuge, T., Aikoh, T., & Kuriyama, K. (2020). Understanding services from ecosystem and facilities provided by urban green spaces: A use of partial profile choice experiment. *Forest Policy and Economics*, *111*, 102086. doi:10.1016/j.forpol.2019.102086

Kim, N. L., & Kim, T. H. (2022). Why buy used clothing during the pandemic? Examining the impact of COVID-19 on consumers' second-hand fashion consumption motivations. *International Review of Retail, Distribution and Consumer Research*, 1–16.

Kim, Y. J., Kim, W. G., Choi, H. M., & Phetvaroon, K. (2019). The effect of green human resource management on hotel employees' eco-friendly behavior and environmental performance. *International Journal of Hospitality Management*, *76*, 83–93.

King, D. D., Newman, A., & Luthans, F. (2016). Not if, but when we need resilience in the workplace. *Journal of Organizational Behavior*, *37*(5), 782–786. doi:10.1002/job.2063

Kirk, C. P., & Rifkin, L. S. (2020). I'll trade you diamonds for toilet paper: Consumer reacting, coping and adapting behaviors in the COVID-19 pandemic. *Journal of Business Research*, *117*, 124–131. doi:10.1016/j.jbusres.2020.05.028 PMID:32834208

Kitz, R., Walker, T., Charlebois, S., & Music, S. (2021). Food packaging during the COVID-19 pandemic: Consumer perceptions. *International Journal of Consumer Studies*, *46*(2), 434–448. doi:10.1111/ijcs.12691 PMID:34230811

Kiuchi, T., & Shireman, B. (1999). Metrics for Business in the New Economy: An economic change of seasons creates demands for new business metrics. *Environmental Quality Management*, *9*, 79–90.

Kiviaho, J., Nikkinen, J., Piljak, V., & Rothovius, T. (2014). The co-movement dynamics of European frontier stock markets. *European Financial Management*, *20*(3), 574–595. doi:10.1111/j.1468-036X.2012.00646.x

Klein, T. (2018). Trends and contagion in WTI and Brent crude oil spot and futures markets-The role of OPEC in the last decade. *Energy Economics*, *75*, 636–646. doi:10.1016/j.eneco.2018.09.013

Kolmogorov, A. N., & Tikhomirov, V. M. (1959). ε-entropy and ε-capacity of sets in function spaces. *Uspekhi Matematicheskhi Nauk*, *14*(2), 3–86.

Konoplyanik, A. A. (2012). Russian gas at European energy market: Why adaptation is inevitable. *Energy Strategy Reviews*, *1*(1), 42–56. doi:10.1016/j.esr.2012.02.001

Kopnina, H. (2017). Sustainability: New strategic thinking for business. *Environment, Development and Sustainability*, *19*(1), 27–43. doi:10.100710668-015-9723-1

Kosnett, J. R. (2007, Oct.). Green is the Next Big Thing. *Kiplinger's Personal Finance*, 32-34.

Kováč, E., Vinogradov, V., & Žigić, K. (2010). Technological leadership and persistence of monopoly under endogenous entry: Static versus dynamic analysis. *Journal of Economic Dynamics & Control*, *34*(8), 1421–1441. https://doi.org/10.1016/j.jedc.2010.03.011

Kovilage, M. P. (2021). Influence of lean–green practices on organizational sustainable performance. *Journal of Asian Business and Economic Studies*, *28*(2), 121–142. https://doi.org/10.1108/JABES-11-2019-0115

Kronborg, M. T. (2014). Optimal consumption and investment with labor income and European/American capital guarantee. *Risks*, *2*(2), 171–194. doi:10.3390/risks2020171

Kruuse, A. (2011). *GRaBS expert paper 6: The green space factor and the green points system*. Academic Press.

Kuntz, J. R., Malinen, S., & Näswall, K. (2017). Employee resilience: Directions for resilience development. *Consulting Psychology Journal*, *69*(3), 223–242. doi:10.1037/cpb0000097

La Porta, R., Lopez-de-Silanes, F., Shleifer, A., & Vishny, R. (2002). Investor protection and corporate valuation. *The Journal of Finance*, *57*(3), 1147–1170. doi:10.1111/1540-6261.00457

La Porta, R., Lopez-de-Silanes, F., Shleifer, A., & Vishny, R. W. (1997). Legal determinants of external finance. *The Journal of Finance*, *52*(3), 1131–1150. doi:10.1111/j.1540-6261.1997.tb02727.x

Lagadec, P. (2009). A new cosmology of risks and crises: time for a radical shift in paradigm and practice. *Review of Policy Research*, *26*(4), 473-487. Recuperado de https://hal.archives-ouvertes.fr/hal-00338386

Lahti, T., Wincent, J., & Parida, V. (2018). A definition and theoretical review of the circular economy, value creation, and sustainable business models: Where are we now and where should research move in the future? *Sustainability*, *10*(8), 2799. doi:10.3390u10082799

Laker, D. R., & Powell, J. L. (2011). The differences between hard and soft skills and their relative impact on training transfer. *Human Resource Development Quarterly*, *22*(1), 111–122. doi:10.1002/hrdq.20063

Laksono, B. A. (2021). The Strategy of Education and Training During The Covid-19 Pandemic. *Aksara: Jurnal Ilmu Pendidikan Nonformal*, *7*(3), 855–864.

Lamm, E., Tosti-Kharas, J., & Williams, E. G. (2013). Read this article, but don't print it: Organizational citizenship behavior toward the environment. *Group & Organization Management*, *38*, 163–197.

Larson, K. (2020). Serious games and gamification in the corporate training environment: A literature review. *TechTrends*, *64*(2), 319–328. doi:10.100711528-019-00446-7

Lash, S. (2005). *Critique of Information*. Amorrortu.

Lawrence, A. (2010). Managing disputes with nonmarket stakeholders: Wage a fight, withdraw, wait, or work it out? *California Management Review*, *53*(1), 90–113. doi:10.1525/cmr.2010.53.1.90

Lee, A., Vargo, J., & Seville, E. (2013). Developing a tool to measure and compare the resilience of organizations. *Natural Hazards Review*, *14*(1), 29–41. doi:10.1061/(ASCE)NH.1527-6996.0000075

Leitch, A., Haley, B., & Hastings-Simon, S. (2019). Can the oil and gas sector enable geothermal technologies? Sociotechnical opportunities and complementarity failures in Alberta, Canada. *Energy Policy*, *125*, 384–395. doi:10.1016/j.enpol.2018.10.046

Lekakis, J. N., & Kousis, M. (2001). Demand for and supply of environmental quality in the environmental Kuznets curve hypothesis. *Applied Economics Letters*, *8*(3), 169–172. doi:10.1080/13504850150504531

Lengnick-Hall, C. A., & Beck, T. E. (2009). Resilience capacity and strategic agility: Prerequisites for thriving in a dynamic environment. In Resilience engineering perspectives, Volume 2. Preparation and restoration. Ashgate Publishing.

Lengnick-Hall, C., Beck, T., & Lengnick-Hall, M. (2011). Develop organizational resilience capacity through strategic human resource management. *Human Resource Management Review*, *21*(3), 243–255. doi:10.1016/j.hrmr.2010.07.001

Levitt, B., & March, J. G. (1988). Organizational Learning. *Annual Review of Sociology*, *14*(1), 319–340. doi:10.1146/annurev.so.14.080188.001535

Liddle, B., & Lung, S. (2010). Age-structure, urbanization, and climate change in developed countries: Revisiting STIRPAT for disaggregated population and consumption-related environmental impacts. *Population and Environment*, *31*(5), 317–343. doi:10.100711111-010-0101-5

Li, J., & Lin, B. (2016). Green economy performance and green productivity growth in China's cities: Measures and policy implication. *Sustainability*, *8*(9), 947. doi:10.3390u8090947

Li, J., & Tartarini, F. (2020). Changes in air quality during the COVID-19 lockdown in Singapore and associations with human mobility trends. *Aerosol and Air Quality Research*, *20*(8), 1748–1758. doi:10.4209/aaqr.2020.06.0303

Lim, D. H., & Nowell, B. (2014). Integration for training transfer: Learning, knowledge, organizational culture, and technology. In *Transfer of Learning in Organizations* (pp. 81–98). Springer. doi:10.1007/978-3-319-02093-8_6

Li-na, X., Tao, Z., Xiao-feng, Y., & Yan-dong, Z. (2013). Analysis the Impact of Urbanization on Carbon Emissions Using the Stirpat Model in Tianjin, China. *Journal of Applied Sciences*, *13*(21), 4608–4611. doi:10.3923/jas.2013.4608.4611

Linnenluecke, M. K. (2017). Resilience in business and management research: A review of influential publications and a research agenda. *International Journal of Management Reviews, 19*(1), 4–30. doi:10.1111/ijmr.12076

Linnenluecke, M., & Griffiths, A. (2012). Assessment of organizational resilience to climate and extreme weather events: Complexities and methodological pathways. *Climatic Change, 113*(3-4), 933–947. doi:10.100710584-011-0380-6

Lin, R. J., Chen, R. H., & Huang, F. H. (2014). Green innovation in the automobile industry. *Industrial Management & Data Systems, 114*(6), 886–903. https://doi.org/10.1108/IMDS-11-2013-0482

Liu, C. (2010). Developing green intellectual capital in companies by AHP. In *2010 8th International Conference on Supply Chain Management and Information* (pp. 1-5). IEEE.

Liu, H. B., McCarthy, B., & Chen, T. (2016). Green food consumption in China: segmentation based on attitudes toward food safety. *J. Int. Food Agribus. Market., 28*, 1–17. doi: .00091.x doi:10.1111/j.1745-4565.2007

Liu, Y. (2013). Energy production and regional economic growth in China: A more comprehensive analysis using a panel model. *Energies, 6*(3), 1409–1420. doi:10.3390/en6031409

Liu, Y., Cooper, C. L., & Tarba, S. Y. (2019). Resilience, wellbeing and HRM: A multidisciplinary perspective. *International Journal of Human Resource Management, 30*(8), 1227–1238. doi:10.1080/09585192.2019.1565370

Liu, Z., Ciais, P., Deng, Z., Lei, R., Davis, S. J., Feng, S., ... He, P. (2020). Near-real-time data captured record decline in global CO2 emissions due to COVID-19. *Nature Communications, 11*, 1–12. doi:10.103841467-020-20254-5

Ljunggren Söderman, M., Eriksson, O., Björklund, A., Östblom, G., Ekvall, T., Finnveden, G., Arushanyan, Y., & Sundqvist, J. O. (2016). Integrated economic and environmental assessment of waste policy instruments. *Sustainability, 8*(5), 411. doi:10.3390u8050411

Loiseau, E., Saikku, L., Antikainen, R., Droste, N., Hansjürgens, B., Pitkänen, K., Leskinen, P., Kuikman, P., & Thomsen, M. (2016). Green economy and related concepts: An overview. *Journal of Cleaner Production, 139*, 361–371. doi:10.1016/j.jclepro.2016.08.024

López-Regalado, M. E., Ahumada-Tello, E., & Ravina-Ripoll, R. (2020). University Social Responsibility from the perspective of Happiness Management. The case of the Faculty of Accounting and Administration of the Autonomous University of Baja California (Tijuana-Mexico). *Revista ESPACIOS, 41*(4), 26.

Lotfi, T., Golmohammadi, V., & Sarmadi, H. (2016). Political Consideration and Development of Economic Relations, Economic Cooperation Capacities of Iran and the Republic of Azerbaijan. *Mediterranean Journal of Social Sciences, 7*(3), 72.

Lucarelli, C., Mazzoli, C., & Severini, S. (2020). Applying the theory of planned behavior to examine pro-environmental behavior: The moderating effect of COVID-19 beliefs. *Sustainability, 12*(24), 10556. doi:10.3390u122410556

Lu, H., Guo, L., Azimi, M., & Huang, K. (2019). Oil and Gas 4.0 era: A systematic review and outlook. *Computers in Industry, 111*, 68–90. doi:10.1016/j.compind.2019.06.007

Lund, H. (2007). Renewable energy strategies for sustainable development. *Energy, 32*(6), 912–919. doi:10.1016/j.energy.2006.10.017

Luo, Z., Xie, F., Zhang, B., & Qiu, D. (2018). Quantifying the Nonlinear Dynamic Behavior of the DC-DC Converter via Permutation Entropy. *Energies, 11*(10), 2747. doi:10.3390/en11102747

Luque González, A., Coronado Martín, J. Á., Vaca-Tapia, A. C., & Rivas, F. (2021). How Sustainability Is Defined: An Analysis of 100 Theoretical Approximations. *Mathematics, 2021*(9), 1308. doi:10.3390/math9111308

Luque, A. (2021). Practicality, support or premeditated calculation in the digital age: The case of Ecuador. *Revista Venezolana de Gerencia*, *26*(6), 29–46. doi:10.52080/rvgluz.26.e6.3

Luque, A. (2022). Analysis of the concept of informal economy through 102 definitions: Legality or necessity. *Open Research Europe*, *2022*(1), 134. doi:10.12688/openreseurope.13990.2

Luque, A., & Herrero-García, N. (2019). How corporate social (ir)responsibility in the textile sector is defined, and its impact on ethical sustainability: An analysis of 133 concepts. *Corporate Social Responsibility and Environmental Management*, *26*(6), 1–22. doi:10.1002/csr.1747

Luthans, F. (2002a). Positive organizational behavior: Developing and managing psychological strengths. *The Academy of Management Executive*, *16*(1), 57–72. doi:10.5465/ame.2002.6640181

Luthar, S. S., Cicchetti, D., & Becker, B. (2000). The construct of resilience: A critical evaluation and guidelines for future work. *Child Development*, *71*(3), 543–562. doi:10.1111/1467-8624.00164 PMID:10953923

Lyman, P., & Varian, H. R. (2003). *How much information*. UC Berkeley.

Lynham, S. A. (2002). The general method of theory-building research in applied disciplines. *Advances in Developing Human Resources*, *4*(3), 221–241. doi:10.1177/1523422302043002

Macpherson, A., Herbane, B., & Jones, B. (2015). Developing Dynamic Capabilities through Resource Accretion: Expanding the Entrepreneurial Solution Space. *Entrepreneurship and Regional Development*, *27*(5–6), 259–291. doi:10.1080/08985626.2015.1038598

Madani, K. (2014). Water management in Iran: What is causing the looming crisis? *Journal of Environmental Studies and Sciences*, *4*(4), 315–328. doi:10.100713412-014-0182-z

Madani, K., AghaKouchak, A., & Mirchi, A. (2016). Iran's socio-economic drought: Challenges of a water-bankrupt nation. *Iranian Studies*, *49*(6), 997–1016. doi:10.1080/00210862.2016.1259286

Madni, A. M., & Jackson, S. (2009). Towards a conceptual framework for Resilience Engineering. *IEEE Systems Journal*, *3*(2), 181–191. doi:10.1109/JSYST.2009.2017397

Mafabi, S., Munene, J., & Ahiauzu, A. (2015). Creative climate and organizational resilience: The mediating role of innovation. *The International Journal of Organizational Analysis*, *23*(4), 564–587. doi:10.1108/IJOA-07-2012-0596

Mafabi, S., Munene, J., & Ntayi, J. (2012). Knowledge management and organizational resilience: Organizational innovation as a mediator in Ugandan parastatals. *J Strategy Manag.*, *5*, 57–80. doi:10.1108/17554251211200455

Magistris, T., & Gracia, A. (2016). The decision to buy organic food products in Southern Italy. *British Food Journal*, *110*(9), 929–947. doi:10.1108/00070700810900620

Maheshwari, V., Vandewalle, I., & Bamber, D. (2011). Place branding's role in sustainable development. *J. Place Manag. Dev*, *2011*(4), 198–213.

Mainieri, T., Barnett, E. G., Valdero, T. R., Unipan, J. B., & Oskamp, S. (1997). Green Buying: The Influence of Environmental Concern on Consumer Behavior. *The Journal of Social Psychology*, *137*(2), 189–204. doi:10.1080/00224549709595430

Maitlis, S., & Christianson, M. (2014). Sense making in organizations: Taking stock and moving forward. *The Academy of Management Annals*, *8*(1), 57–125. doi:10.5465/19416520.2014.873177

Majumdar, R. (2020). *Firms Need Built-In Anti-Phishing Solutions for Employees: Microsoft*. Accessed 5 November 2021. https://www.livemint.com/industry/infotech/firms-need-built-in-antiphishing-solutions-for-employees-microsoft-11589349297916.html

Malik, S., Cao, Y., Mughal, Y., Kundi, G., Mughal, M., & Ramayah, T. (2020). Pathways towards sustainability in organizations: Empirical evidence on the role of green human resource management practices and green intellectual capital. *Sustainability*, *12*(8), 3228. doi:10.3390u12083228

Maliszewska, M., Mattoo, A., & Van Der Mensbrugghe, D. (2020). *The potential impact of COVID-19 on GDP and trade: A preliminary assessment*. World Bank Policy Research Working Paper, (9211).

Mamouni-Limnios, E., Mazzarol, T., Ghadouani, A., & Schilizzi, S. (2014). The resilience architecture framework: Four organizational archetypes. *European Management Journal*, *32*(1), 104–116. doi:10.1016/j.emj.2012.11.007

Manfield, R., & Newey, L. (2015). Escape the trap of collapse: Remain capable without capabilities. Strategic change. *Briefings in Entrepreneurial Finance.*, *24*(4), 373–387.

Manovich, L. (2006). *The language of the new media*. Paidós.

Mansoor, A., Jahan, S., & Riaz, M. (2021). Does green intellectual capital spur corporate environmental performance through green workforce? *Journal of Intellectual Capital*, *22*(5), 823–839. doi:10.1108/JIC-06-2020-0181

Manyena, S. B., O'Brien, G., O'Keefe, P., & Rose, J. (2011). Disaster resilience: A bounce back or bounce forward ability? *Local Environment*, *16*(5), 417–424. doi:10.1080/13549839.2011.583049

March, J. G. (1991). Exploration and Exploitation in Organizational Learning. *Organization Science*, *2*(1), 71–87. doi:10.1287/orsc.2.1.71

March, J. G., Sproull, L. S., & Tamuz, M. (2003). Learning from samples of one or fewer. *Organization Science*, *2*(1), 1–13. doi:10.1287/orsc.2.1.1 PMID:14645764

Marco-Lajara, B., Seva-Larrosa, P., Martínez-Falcó, J., & Sánchez-García, E. (2021a). How Has COVID-19 Affected The Spanish Wine Industry? An Exploratory Analysis. *Natural Volatiles & Essential Oils Journal*, *8*(6), 2722–2731.

Marco-Lajara, B., Seva-Larrosa, P., Ruiz-Fernández, L., & Martínez-Falcó, J. (2021b). The Effect of COVID-19 on the Spanish Wine Industry. In A. Coşkun (Ed.), *Impact of Global Issues on International Trade* (pp. 211–232). IGI Global.

Marco-Lajara, B., Zaragoza-Sáez, P., Martínez-Falcó, J., & Sánchez-García, E. (2022). Green Intellectual Capital in the Spanish Wine Industry. In C. Goi (Ed.), *Innovative Economic, Social, and Environmental Practices for Progressing Future Sustainability* (pp. 102–120). IGI Global.

Marcus, A., & Nichols, M. (1999). On the edge: Heeding warnings of unusual events. *Organization Science*, *10*(4), 482–499. doi:10.1287/orsc.10.4.482

Marini, A., & Genereux, R. (1995). The challenge of teaching for transfer. In A. McKeough, J. Lupart, & A. Marini (Eds.), *Teaching for Transfer: Fostering Generalization in Learning* (pp. 1–19). Lawrence Erlbaum Associates, Inc.

Martínez-Zarzoso, I., & Maruotti, A. (2011). The impact of urbanization on CO2 emissions: Evidence from developing countries. *Ecological Economics*, *70*(7), 1344–1353. doi:10.1016/j.ecolecon.2011.02.009

Marwa, S., & Milner, C. (2013). Underwriting Corporate Resilience Through Creativity: The Flexibility Model. Total. *Qual Manag Bus.*, *24*, 835–846.

Maskin, E. (2003). Coalitional bargaining with externalities. *Keynote lecture for the European Economic Association Conference*.

Massenberg, A. C., Spurk, D., & Kauffeld, S. (2015). Social support at the workplace, motivation to transfer and training transfer: A multilevel indirect effects model. *International Journal of Training and Development*, *19*(3), 161–178. doi:10.1111/ijtd.12054

Massol, O., & Tchung-Ming, S. (2010). Cooperation among liquefied natural gas suppliers: Is rationalization the sole objective? *Energy Economics*, *32*(4), 933–947. doi:10.1016/j.eneco.2010.02.008

Masten, A. (2014). *Ordinary magic: resilience in development*. Guildford Press.

Masten, A. S. (2001). Ordinary magic: Resilience processes in development. *The American Psychologist*, *56*(3), 227–238. doi:10.1037/0003-066X.56.3.227 PMID:11315249

Masten, A. S. (2007). Resilience in Developing Systems: Progress and Promise as the Fourth Wave Rises. *Development and Psychopathology*, *19*(3), 921–930. doi:10.1017/S0954579407000442 PMID:17705908

Masten, A. S. (2014). *Ordinary Magic: Resilience in Development*. Guilford Press.

McCarthy, I. P., Collard, M., & Johnson, M. (2017). Adaptive organizational resilience: An evolutionary perspective. *Current Opinion Environ. Sustainability*, *28*, 33-40.

McGranahan, G., & Songsore, J. (1994). Wealth, health, and the urban household: Weighing environmental burdens in…. *Environment*, *36*(6), 4–45. doi:10.1080/00139157.1994.9929172

McGrath, R. G. (1999). Falling Forward: Real Options Reasoning and Entrepreneurial Failure. *Academy of Management Review*, *24*(1), 13–30. doi:10.5465/amr.1999.1580438

McGrath, R. G. (2013). *The End of Competitive Advantage: How to Keep your Strategy Moving as Fast as your Business*. Harvard Business Review Press.

McMahon, C. J., Gallagher, S., James, A., Deery, A., Rhodes, M., & van Merriënboer, J. J. (2021). Does high-variation training facilitate transfer of training in paediatric transthoracic echocardiography? *Cardiology in the Young*, *31*(4), 602–608. doi:10.1017/S1047951120004412 PMID:33300481

Mcmanus, S., Seville, E., Vargo, J., & Brunsdon, D. (2008). Facilitated process for improving organizational resilience. *Natural Hazards Rev.*, *9*(2), 81-90.

McManus, S., Seville, E., Vargo, J., & Brunsdon, D. (2008). Facilitated process to improve organizational resilience. *Natural Hazards Review*, *9*(2), 81–90. doi:10.1061/(ASCE)1527-6988(2008)9:2(81)

Meerow, S., & Newell, J. P. (2017). Detroit, Spatial planning for multifunctional green infrastructure: Growing resilience in. *Landscape and Urban Planning*, 62-75.

Mehrotra, K. (2020). *Is Your Organization Ready for Work from Home (WFH)?* Accessed 5 November 2021. https://cio.economictimes.indiatimes.com/news/corporate-news/is-yourorganization-ready-for-work-from-home-wfh/74644617

Mehta, S., Saxena, T., & Purohit, N. (2020). The new consumer behaviour paradigm amid COVID-19: Permanent or transient? *Journal of Health Management*, *22*(2), 291–301. doi:10.1177/0972063420940834

Mell, I. C. (2010). *Green infrastructure: Concepts, perceptions, and its use in spatial planning* [Doctoral Thesis]. School of Architecture, Planning and Landscape, Newcastle University.

Mellahi, K., & Wilkinson, A. (2004). Organizational Failure: A Critique of Recent Research and a Proposed Integrative Framework. *International Journal of Management Reviews*, *5/6*(1), 21–41. doi:10.1111/j.1460-8545.2004.00095.x

Mende, M., & Misra, V. (2020). Time to flatten the curves of COVID-19 and climate change. Marketing can help. *Journal of Public Policy & Marketing*, *40*(1), 94–96. doi:10.1177/0743915620930695

Meredith, J. (1993). Theory building through conceptual methods. *International Journal of Operations & Production Management*, *13*, 3–11.

Meyer, A. (2016). Is unemployment good for the environment? *Resource and Energy Economics*, *45*, 18–30. doi:10.1016/j.reseneeco.2016.04.001

Milani, B. (2000). *Designing the green economy: The postindustrial alternative to corporate globalization*. Rowman & Littlefield.

Minton, C. A. B. (2019). Counselor Education and Supervision: 2017 inaugural review. *Counselor Education and Supervision*, *58*(1), 4–17. doi:10.1002/ceas.12120

Mirzaei Khalilabadi, H., & Abrishami, H. (2004). *The role of water in the development of the agricultural sector*. University of Tehran, Faculty of Economics.

Mishra, D., Nair, A. G., Gandhi, R. A., Gogate, P. J., Mathur, S., Bhushan, P., ... Singh, M. K. (2020). The impact of COVID-19 related lockdown on ophthalmology training programs in India–Outcomes of a survey. *Indian Journal of Ophthalmology*, *68*(6), 999. doi:10.4103/ijo.IJO_1067_20 PMID:32461413

Mohabeer, R. N. (2021). COVID bread-porn: Social stratification through displays of self-management. *Cultural Studies*, *35*(2-3), 403–411. doi:10.1080/09502386.2021.1898031

Mohammadjani, E., & Yazdanian, N. (2014). Analysis of the state of the water crisis in the country and its management requirements. *Quarterly Trend*, *21*, 117–144.

Mohezara, S., Nazria, M., Kaderb, M. A. R. A., Alib, R., & Yunusb, N. K. M. (2016). Corporate social responsibility in the malaysian food retailing industry: An exploratory study. *Int. Acad. Res. J. Soc. Sci*, *2*, 66–72.

Mol, A. P., & Spaargaren, G. (2000). Ecological modernisation theory in debate: A review. *Environmental Politics*, *9*(1), 17–49. doi:10.1080/09644010008414511

Moles, A., & Costa, J. (1989). *La imagen didáctica*. CEAC.

Molina-Azorín, J. F., Claver-Cortés, E., Pereira-Moliner, J., & Tarí, J. J. (2009). Environmental practices and firm performance: An empirical analysis in the Spanish hotel industry. *Journal of Cleaner Production*, *17*, 516–524.

Molina-Sánchez, E., Leyva-Díaz, J. C., Cortés-García, F. J., & Molina-Moreno, V. (2018). Proposal of sustainability indicators for the waste management from the paper industry within the circular economy model. *Water (Basel)*, *10*(8), 1014. doi:10.3390/w10081014

Morais-Storz, M., & Nguyen, N. (2017). The role of unlearning in metamorphosis and strategic resilience. *The Learning Organization*, *24*(2), 93–106. doi:10.1108/TLO-12-2016-0091

Moriarty, P., & Honnery, D. (2012). What is the global potential for renewable energy? *Renewable & Sustainable Energy Reviews*, *16*(1), 244–252. doi:10.1016/j.rser.2011.07.151

Morris, M. G., & Venkatesh, V. (2000). Age differences in technology adoption decisions: implications for a changing workforce. *Pers. Psychol.*, *53*, 375–403. doi:.2000.tb00206.x doi:10.1111/j.1744-6570

Morrison, P. (2011). Meeting the Environmental Challenge with Technology. In SPE Digital Energy Conference and Exhibition. OnePetro. doi:10.2118/143837-MS

Morrow, J. L., Sirmon, D. G., Hitt, M. A., & Holcomb, T. R. (2007). Creating Value in the Face of Declining Performance: Firm Strategies and Organizational Recovery. *Strategic Management Journal*, *28*(3), 271–283. doi:10.1002mj.579

Morseletto, P. (2020). Targets for a circular economy. *Resources, Conservation and Recycling*, *153*, 104553. doi:10.1016/j.resconrec.2019.104553

Mozammel, S. (2019). Understanding Post-Training Factors and Job Performance Relationship: Review of Literature for Transfer of Training Enthusiasts. *Annals of Contemporary Developments in Management & HR*, *1*(3), 33–38. doi:10.33166/ACDMHR.2019.03.004

Mukherjee, A., Babu, S. S., & Ghosh, S. (2020). Thinking about water and air to attain sustainable development goals during times of COVID-19 pandemic. *Journal of Earth System Science*, *129*(1), 180. doi:10.100712040-020-01475-0

Murari, K., & Bhandari, M. (2011). Green HR: Going green with pride. *Journal of Social Welfare and Management*, *3*, 107–110.

Naeem, M. (2020). Understanding the customer psychology of impulse buying during COVID-19 pandemic: Implications for retailers. *International Journal of Retail & Distribution Management*, *49*(3), 377–393. doi:10.1108/IJRDM-08-2020-0317

Namkung, Y., & Jang, S. (2012). Effects of restaurant green practices on brand equity formation: Do green practices really matter? *International Journal of Hospitality Management*, *41*(3), 85–95. https://doi.org/10.1016/j.ijhm.2012.06.006

Nandi, S., Sarkis, J., Hervani, A. A., & Helms, M. M. (2021). Redesigning supply chains using blockchain-enabled circular economy and COVID-19 experiences. *Sustainable Production and Consumption*, *27*, 10–22. doi:10.1016/j.spc.2020.10.019 PMID:33102671

Narayan, E., Barreto, M., Hantzopoulou, G.-C., & Tilbrook, A. A. (2021). Retrospective Literature Evaluation of the Integration of Stress Physiology Indices, Animal Welfare and Climate Change Assessment of Livestock. *Animals (Basel)*, *11*(5), 1287. https://doi.org/10.3390/ani11051287

Narayan, P. K., & Narayan, S. (2010). Carbon dioxide emissions and economic growth: Panel data evidence from developing countries. *Energy Policy*, *38*(1), 661–666. doi:10.1016/j.enpol.2009.09.005

Nattagh, N. (1986). *Agriculture and regional development in Iran*. Middle East and North African Studies Press.

Nazli, N. N. N. N., & Khairudin, S. M. H. S. (2018). The factors that influence transfer of training and its effect on organizational citizenship behaviour. *Journal of Workplace Learning*, *30*(2), 121–146. doi:10.1108/JWL-09-2017-0080

Nchanji, E. B., & Lutomia, C. K. (2021). COVID-19 challenges to sustainable food production and consumption: Future lessons for food systems in eastern and southern Africa from a gender lens. *Sustainable Production and Consumption*, *27*, 2208–2220. doi:10.1016/j.spc.2021.05.016

Nemeth, C. (2009). The ability to adapt. In C. P. Nemeth, E. Hollnagel, & S. Dekker (Eds.), *Resilience Engineering Perspectives*. Ashgate Publishing.

Newman, P. G., & Kenworthy, J. R. (1989). *Cities and automobile dependence: An international sourcebook*. Academic Press.

Noe, R. A. (1986). Trainees' attributes and attitudes: Neglected influences on training effectiveness. *Academy of Management Review*, *11*(4), 736–749. doi:10.2307/258393

Norouzi, N. (2021a). The Pahlev Reliability Index: A measurement for the resilience of power generation technologies versus climate change. *Nuclear Engineering and Technology*, *53*(5), 1658–1663. doi:10.1016/j.net.2020.10.013

Norouzi, N. (2021b). Post-COVID-19 and globalization of oil and natural gas trade: Challenges, opportunities, lessons, regulations, and strategies. *International Journal of Energy Research*, *45*(10), 14338–14356. doi:10.1002/er.6762 PMID:34219899

Norouzi, N., & Ataei, E. (2021). Covid-19 Crisis and Environmental law: Opportunities and challenges. *Hasanuddin Law Review*, *7*(1), 46–60. doi:10.20956/halrev.v7i1.2772

Norouzi, N., de Rubens, G. Z., Choupanpiesheh, S., & Enevoldsen, P. (2020a). When pandemics impact economies and climate change: Exploring the impacts of COVID-19 on oil and electricity demand in China. *Energy Research & Social Science*, *68*, 101654. doi:10.1016/j.erss.2020.101654 PMID:32839693

Norouzi, N., & Fani, M. (2020a). The impacts of the novel corona virus on the oil and electricity demand in Iran and China. *Journal of Energy Management and Technology*, *4*(4), 36–48.

Norouzi, N., & Fani, M. (2020b). Black gold falls, black plague arise-An Opec crude oil price forecast using a gray prediction model. *Upstream Oil and Gas Technology*, *5*, 100015. doi:10.1016/j.upstre.2020.100015

Norouzi, N., & Fani, M. (2021a). The prioritization and feasibility study over renewable technologies using fuzzy logic: A case study for Takestan plains. *Journal of Energy Management and Technology*, *5*(2), 12–22.

Norouzi, N., & Fani, M. (2021b). Environmental Sustainability and Coal: The Role of Financial Development and Globalization in South Africa. Iranian (Iranica). *Journal of Energy & Environment*, *12*(1), 68–80. doi:10.5829/IJEE.2021.12.01.09

Norouzi, N., Fani, M., Hashemi Bahramani, E., Hemmati, M. H., & Bashash Jafarabadi, Z. (2021c). Behavioral Economics and Energy consumption: Investigating the Role of Attitudes and Beliefs on Household Electricity Consumption in Iran. *Journal of Artificial Intelligence and Big Data*, *1*(1).

Norouzi, N., Fani, M., & Ziarani, Z. K. (2020b). The fall of oil Age: A scenario planning approach over the last peak oil of human history by 2040. *Journal of Petroleum Science Engineering*, *188*, 106827. doi:10.1016/j.petrol.2019.106827

Norouzi, N., & Kalantari, G. (2020). The sun food-water-energy nexus governance model a case study for Iran. *Water-Energy Nexus*, *3*, 72–80. doi:10.1016/j.wen.2020.05.005

Norouzi, N., Khanmohammadi, H. U., & Ataei, E. (2021b). The Law in the Face of the COVID-19 Pandemic: Early Lessons from Uruguay. *Hasanuddin Law Review*, *7*(2), 75–88. doi:10.20956/halrev.v7i2.2827

Norouzi, N., Zarazua de Rubens, G. Z., Enevoldsen, P., & Behzadi Forough, A. (2021a). The impact of COVID-19 on the electricity sector in Spain: An econometric approach based on prices. *International Journal of Energy Research*, *45*(4), 6320–6332. doi:10.1002/er.6259

Norris, F. H., Stevens, S. P., Pfefferbaum, B., Wyche, K. F., & Pfeffer-baum, R. L. (2008). Community resilience as a metaphor, theory, set of capacities, and strategy for disaster readiness. *American Journal of Community Psychology*, *41*(1-2), 127–150. doi:10.100710464-007-9156-6 PMID:18157631

Norton, T. A., Zacher, H., & Ashkanasy, N. M. (2012). On the importance of pro-environmental organizational climate for employee green behavior. *Ind. Organ. Psychol.*, *5*, 497–500. doi: .01487.x doi:10.1111/j.1754-9434.2012

Norton, T. A., Zacher, H., & Ashkanasy, N. M. (2014). Organisational sustainability policies and employee green behaviour: The mediating role of work climate perceptions. *Journal of Environmental Psychology*, *38*, 49–54. doi:10.1016/j.jenvp.2013.12.008

Norton, T. A., Zacher, H., & Ashkanasy, N. M. (2015). *Pro-environmental organizational culture and climate. In the psychology of green organizations*. Oxford Univeristy Press.

Norwegian Ministry of the Environment. (1994). *Oslo roundtable on sustainable production and consumption* (Oslo Symposium). Author.

Núñez-Barriopedro, E., Cuesta-Valiño, P., Rodríguez, P. G., & Ravina-Ripoll, R. (2021). How does happiness influence the loyalty of karate athletes? A model of structural equations from the constructs: Consumer Satisfaction, Engagement, and Meaningful. *Frontiers in Psychology*, *12*. doi:10.3389/fpsyg.2021.653034

Nuñez-Cacho, P., Górecki, J., Molina-Moreno, V., & Corpas-Iglesias, F. A. (2018b). What gets measured, gets done: Development of a circular economy measurement scale for building industry. *Sustainability*, *10*(7), 2340. doi:10.3390u10072340

Núñez-Cacho, P., Molina-Moreno, V., Corpas-Iglesias, F. A., & Cortés-García, F. J. (2018a). Family businesses transitioning to a circular economy model: The case of "Mercadona". *Sustainability*, *10*(2), 538. doi:10.3390u10020538

O'Hara, S., Murphy, L., & Reeve, S. (2007). Action learning as leverage for strategic transformation: A case study reflection. *Strategic Change*, *16*(4), 177–190. doi:10.1002/jsc.792

O'Regan, N., & Ghobadian, A. (2007). Formal Strategic Planning: Annual Raindance or Wheel of Success? *Strategic Change*, *16*(1/2), 11–22. doi:10.1002/jsc.777

O'Sullivan, T. L., Corneil, W., Kuziemsky, C. E., & Toal-Sullivan, D. (2015). Use of the structured interview matrix to enhance community resilience through collaboration and inclusive engagement. *Systems Research and Behavioral Science*, *32*(6), 616–628. doi:10.1002res.2250

Ocampo, J., Stallings, B., Belloso, H., & Frenkel, R. (2014). *The Latin American debt crises from the historical perspective*. Santiago de Chile. United Nations.

O'Connor, G.C., & Ayers, A.D., (2005). Building a radical innovation competency. *Res.Technol. Manag.*, *48*(1), 23-31.

OECD. (2020). *Food supply-chains and COVID-19: Impacts and policy lessons*. https://www.oecd.org/coronavirus/policy-responses/food-supply-chains-and-covid-19-impacts-and-policy-lessons-71b57aea/

Øien, K. (2013). Remote operation in environmentally sensitive areas: Development of early warning indicators. *Journal of Risk Research*, *16*(3-4), 323–336. doi:10.1080/13669877.2012.729523

OIV. (2004). *Resolution CST 1/2004-Develpment of Sustainable Vitivinivulture*. Pareis.

OIV. (2008). *Resolution CST/2008-OIV Guidelines for Sustainable Vitiviniculture: Production, Processing and Packaging of Products*. Verone/it.

OIV. (2016). *Resolution CST 518/2016-OIV General Principles of Sustainable Vitiviniculture – Environmental - Social - Economic and Cultural Aspects*. Brento Gonçalves.

Olabi, A. G., & Abdelkareem, M. A. (2022). Renewable energy and climate change. *Renewable & Sustainable Energy Reviews*, *158*, 112111. doi:10.1016/j.rser.2022.112111

Ollo-López, A., & Aramendía-Muneta, M. E. (2012). ICT impact on competitiveness, innovation and environment. *Telematics and Informatics*, *29*(2), 204–210. doi:10.1016/j.tele.2011.08.002

Olubunmi, O. A., Xia, P. B., & Skitmore, M. (2016). Green building incentives: A review. *Renewable & Sustainable Energy Reviews*, *59*(C), 1611–1621.

Omidvar, M., Mazloumi, A., Mohammad, I., & Nirumand, F. (2017). Development of a framework for resilience measurement: Suggestion of diffuse resilience degree (RG) and diffuse resilience early warning degree (REWG). *WOR*, *56*, 463–474. doi:10.3233/WOR-172512 PMID:28269808

Ones, D. S., & Dilchert, S. (2012). Environmental sustainability at work: A call to action. *Industrial and Organizational Psychology: Perspectives on Science and Practice*, *5*, 444–466.

Organisation for Economic Co-operation and Development (OECD). (2018). *Preparing Our Youth for an Inclusive and Sustainable World: The OECD PISA global competence framework*. https://www.oecd.org/education/Global-competency-for-an-inclusive-world.pdf

Organisation for Economic Co-operation and Development (OECD). (2019). *Future of Education and Skills 2030: Curriculum Analysis. Draft - The Science of Mindfulness-Based Interventions and Learning: A Review for Educators.* 10th Informal Working Group. 23 – 25 October 2019. Ilsan and Seoul, Korea. EDU/EDPC(2019)15. Directorate For Education And Skills Education Policy Committee. https://www.oecd.org/officialdocuments/publicdisplaydocumentpdf/?cote=EDU/EDPC(2019)15&docLanguage=En

Organization for Economic Co-operation and Development (OECD). (2019). *A measurement roadmap for the future, in Measuring the Digital Transformation: A Roadmap for the Future.* OECD Publishing. www.oecd.org/going-digital/measurement-roadmap.pdf. https://www.oecd.org/digital/measurement-roadmap.pdf

Organization for Economic Co-operation and Development (OECD). (2019). *Latin American Economic Outlook 2019: Development in Transition.* OECD Publishing. doi:10.1787/g2g9ff18-

Organization for Economic Co-operation and Development (OECD). (2020). *Education Policy Outlook.* https://www.oecd.org/education/policy-outlook/country-profile-Finland-2020.pdf

Organization for Economic Co-operation and Development (OECD). (2020). *The role of international co-operation in the digital age, in Latin American Economic Outlook 2020: Digital Transformation for Building Back Better.* OECD Publishing. https://www.oecd-ilibrary.org/docserver/7d3929e1-en.pdf?expires=1648890283&id=id&accname=guest&checksum=8B23F2183B460C897B762B09B9065C3E

Organization for Economic Co-operation and Development (OECD). (2022a). *National growth through regional prosperity: OECD Regions at a Glance.* https://www.oecd.org/newsroom/nationalgrowththroughregionalprosperityoecdregionsataglance.htm

Organization for Economic Co-operation and Development (OECD). (2022b). *OECD-FAO Guidance for Responsible Agricultural Supply Chains.* http://mneguidelines.oecd.org/rbc-agriculture-supply-chains.htm

Organization for Economic Co-operation and Development (OECD). (2022c). *OECD Due Diligence Guidance for Meaningful Stakeholder Engagement in the Extractive Sector.* http://mneguidelines.oecd.org/stakeholder-engagement-extractive-industries.htm

Ortiz-de-Mandojana, N., & Bansal, P. (2015). The long-term benefits of organizational resilience through sustainable business practices. *Strategic Management Journal.* Advance online publication. doi:10.1002mj.2410

Othman Ahmed, K. (2021). Impact of COVID-19 Pandemic on Hand Washing Process and Water Consumption. *Eurasian Journal of Science & Engineering, 7*(1), 228–245.

Ottman, J., Stafford, E. R., & Hartman, C. L. (2007). Avoiding Green Marketing Myopia. *Environment, 48*(5), 22–36.

Ouabdesselam, L., & Sayad, A. (2021). Food packaging and COVID-19. *European Journal of Basic Medical Science, 11*(2), 23–26.

Ouakouak, M. L., Zaitouni, M. G., & Arya, B. (2020). Ethical leadership, emotional leadership, and quitting intentions in public organizations. *Leadership and Organization Development Journal, 41*(2), 257–279. https://doi.org/10.1108/LODJ-05-2019-0206

Özsungur, F. (2021a). Corporate Elderly Entrepreneurship in the Digital World. In K. Sandhu (Ed.), *Handbook of Research on Management and Strategies for Digital Enterprise Transformation* (pp. 149–172). IGI Global. doi:10.4018/978-1-7998-5015-1.ch008

Compilation of References

Özsungur, F. (2021b). Business Management and Strategy in Cybersecurity for Digital Transformation. In K. Sandhu (Ed.), *Handbook of Research on Advancing Cybersecurity for Digital Transformation* (pp. 144–162). IGI Global. doi:10.4018/978-1-7998-6975-7.ch008

Oztemel, E., & Gursev, S. (2020). Literature review of Industry 4.0 and related technologies. *Journal of Intelligent Manufacturing*, *31*(1), 127–182. https://doi.org/10.1007/s10845-018-1433-8

Paavola, J. (2001). Towards sustainable consumption: Economics and ethical concerns for the environment in consumer choices. *Review of Social Economy*, *59*(2), 227–248.

Pahle, M., Pachauri, S., & Steinbacher, K. (2016). Can the Green Economy deliver it all? Experiences of renewable energy policies with socio-economic objectives. *Applied Energy*, *179*, 1331–1341. doi:10.1016/j.apenergy.2016.06.073

Pant, D. R. (2005). A place brand strategy for the Republic of Armenia: 'Quality of context' and 'sustainability' as competitive advantage. *Place Brand*, *1*, 273–282.

Panwar, N. L., Kaushik, S. C., & Kothari, S. (2011). Role of renewable energy sources in environmental protection: A review. *Renewable & Sustainable Energy Reviews*, *15*(3), 1513–1524. doi:10.1016/j.rser.2010.11.037

Parikh, J., & Shukla, V. (1995). Urbanization, energy use and greenhouse effects in economic development: Results from a cross-national study of developing countries. *Global Environmental Change*, *5*(2), 87–103. doi:10.1016/0959-3780(95)00015-G

Pascuta, M. S., & Vodnar, D. C. (2022). Nanocarriers for sustainable active packaging: An overview during and post COVID-19. *Coatings*, *12*, 102.

Patriarca, R., Di Gravio, G., Constantino, F., Falegnami, A., & Bilotta, F. (2017). *An Analytic Framework to Assess Organizational Resilience*. doi:10.1016/j.shaw.2017.10.005

Patterson, M., & Deutsch, E. (2015). Safety-I, Safety-II, and resilience engineering. *Health Care*, *45*, 382–389. PMID:26549146

Pearce, D. W., & Turner, R. K. (1990). *Economics of natural resources and the environment*. JHU press.

Pelling, M. (2003). *The vulnerabilities of cities: natural disasters and social resilience*. Earthscan.

Pellissier, R. (2011). The implementation of resilience engineering to enhance organizational innovation in a complex environment. *International Journal of Business and Management*, *6*(1), 145–164.

Peluso, A. M., Pichierri, M., & Pino, G. (2021). Age-related effects on environmentally sustainable purchases at the time of COVID-19: Evidence from Italy. *Journal of Retailing and Consumer Services*, *60*, 102443.

Perkins, K. M., Munguia, N., Ellenbecker, M., Moure-Eraso, R., & Velazquez, L. (2021). COVID-19 pandemic lessons to facilitate future engagement in the global climate crisis. *Journal of Cleaner Production*, *290*, 125178.

Perlman, S. R., Lane, T. E., & Buchmeier, M. J. (1999). Coronaviruses: Hepatitis, peritonitis, and central nervous system disease. *Effects of Microbes on the Immune System*, *1*, 331-348.

Perman, R., Ma, Y., McGilvray, J., & Common, M. (2003). *Natural resource and environmental economics*. Pearson Education.

Pesaran, M. H., Shin, Y., & Smith, R. J. (2001). Bounds testing approaches to the analysis of level relationships. *Journal of Applied Econometrics*, *16*(3), 289–326. doi:10.1002/jae.616

Peteraf, M., Di Stefano, G., & Verona, G. (2013). The Elephant in the Room of Dynamic Capabilities: Bringing Two Diverging Conversations Together. *Strategic Management Journal*, *34*(12), 1389–1410. doi:10.1002mj.2078

Pettit, T., Croxton, K., & Fiksel, J. (2013). Ensuring the resilience of the supply chain: Development and implementation of an assessment tool. *Journal of Business Logistics*, *34*(1), 46–76. doi:10.1111/jbl.12009

Pettit, T., Fiksel, J., & Croxton, K. (2010). Ensuring Supply Chain Resilience: Developing a Conceptual Framework. *Journal of Business Logistics*, *31*(1), 1–21. doi:10.1002/j.2158-1592.2010.tb00125.x

Peyrefitte, J. (2012). The relationship between communication with stakeholders on mission statements and shareholder value. Journal of Leadership. *Responsibility and Ethics.*, *9*(3), 28–40.

Pham, N. T., Tuc̆ková, Z., & Jabbour, C. J. C. (2019). Greening the hospitality industry: How do green human resource management practices influence organizational citizenship behavior in hotels? A mixed methods study. *Tourism Management*, *72*, 386–399.

Pimm, S. (1984). The complexity and stability of ecosystems. *Nature*, *307*(5949), 321–326. doi:10.1038/307321a0

Pineda-Escobar, M. (2019). Moving the 2030 agenda forward: SDG implementation in Colombia. *Corporate Governance: The International Journal of Business in Society*, *19*(1), 176–188. doi:10.1108/CG-11-2017-0268

Pineda, P. (2010). Evaluation of training in organisations: A proposal for an integrated model. *Journal of European Industrial Training*, *34*(7), 673–693. doi:10.1108/03090591011070789

Polonsky, M. J. (1991). Australia Sets Guidelines for Green Marketing. *Marketing News*, *24*(21), 6–18.

Ponce de Leon Barido, D., & Marshall, J. D. (2014). Relationship between urbanization and CO2 emissions depends on income level and policy. *Environmental Science & Technology*, *48*(7), 3632–3639. doi:10.1021/es405117n PMID:24422489

Ponomarov, S., & Holcolmb, M. (2009). Understanding the concept of supply chain resilience. *International Journal of Logistics Management*, *20*(1), 124–143. doi:10.1108/09574090910954873

Popescu C. R. G. (2019a). Corporate Social Responsibility, Corporate Governance and Business Performance: Limits and Challenges Imposed by the Implementation of Directive 2013/34/EU in Romania. *Sustainability, 11*(19), 5146.

Popescu, C. R. (2022a). Mindfulness at Work, a Sound Business Investment: Focusing on the Employee Well-Being While Increasing Creativity and Innovation. In C. Popescu (Ed.), Handbook of Research on Changing Dynamics in Responsible and Sustainable Business in the Post-COVID-19 Era (pp. 1–34). IGI Global. https://doi.org/10.4018/978-1-6684-2523-7.ch001.

Popescu, C. R. (2022b). Mindfulness Business Principles: Producing Outstanding Value and Encouraging Community Connections. In C. Popescu (Ed.), COVID-19 Pandemic Impact on New Economy Development and Societal Change (pp. 196–228). IGI Global. https://doi.org/10.4018/978-1-6684-3374-4.ch010.

Popescu, C. R. (2022c). Environmental, Social, and Corporate Governance by Avoiding Management Bias and Tax Minimization: Reaching a General Consensus Regarding a Minimum Global Tax Rate. In C. Popescu (Ed.), COVID-19 Pandemic Impact on New Economy Development and Societal Change (pp. 94–132). IGI Global. https://doi.org/10.4018/978-1-6684-3374-4.ch006.

Popescu, C. R. G. & Popescu, G. N. (2019b). An Exploratory Study Based on a Questionnaire Concerning Green and Sustainable Finance, Corporate Social Responsibility, and Performance: Evidence from the Romanian Business Environment. *Journal of Risk and Financial Management, 12*(4), 162. . doi:10.3390/jrfm12040162

Popescu, C. R. G. (2017). The Role Of Total Quality Management In Developing The Concept Of Social Responsibility To Protect Public Interest In Associations Of Liberal Professions. *Amfiteatru Economic, 19,* 1091-1106.

Popescu, C. R. G. (2018). "Intellectual Capital" - Role, Importance, Components and Influences on the Performance of Organizations - A Theoretical Approach. *32nd Conference of the International-Business-Information-Management-Association (IBIMA). Vision 2020: Sustainable Economic Development And Application Of Innovation Management.*

Popescu, C. R. G. (2019a). Business Development Opportunities: Demonstrating Present And Future Performance, Auditing Intellectual Capital: A Case Study On Romanian Organizations. *33rd International-Business-Information-Management-Association (IBIMA) Conference. Vision 2025: Education Excellence and Management of Innovations through Sustainable Economic Competitive Advantage.*

Popescu, C. R. G. (2019b). Business Development Opportunities: Demonstrating Present And Future Performance, Auditing Intellectual Capital: A Case Study On Romanian Organizations. *33rd International-Business-Information-Management-Association (IBIMA) Conference. Vision 2025: Education Excellence and Management of Innovations through Sustainable Economic Competitive Advantage.*

Popescu, C. R. G. (2019b). Intellectual Capital, Integrated Strategy and Performance: Focusing on Companies' Unique Value Creation Mechanism and Promoting Better Organizational Reporting In Romania: A Framework Dominated By the Impact of Green Marketing and Green Marketing Strategies. *33rd International-Business-Information-Management-Association (IBIMA) Conference. Vision 2025: Education Excellence and Management of Innovations through Sustainable Economic Competitive Advantage.*

Popescu, C. R. G. (2019c). Demonstrating How Universities Extend Value Creation And Performance: Convergence Between Intellectual Capital Contributions And Research Quality - A Romanian Collective Intelligence Framework. *11th International Conference on Education and New Learning Technologies (EDULEARN). EDULEARN19: 11th International Conference On Education And New Learning Technologies.*

Popescu, C. R. G. (2019c). Intellectual Capital, Integrated Strategy and Performance: Focusing on Companies' Unique Value Creation Mechanism and Promoting Better Organizational Reporting In Romania: A Framework Dominated By the Impact of Green Marketing and Green Marketing Strategies. *33rd International-Business-Information-Management-Association (IBIMA) Conference. Vision 2025: Education Excellence and Management of Innovations through Sustainable Economic Competitive Advantage.*

Popescu, C. R. G. (2019d). Demonstrating How Universities Extend Value Creation And Performance: Convergence Between Intellectual Capital Contributions And Research Quality - A Romanian Collective Intelligence Framework. *11th International Conference on Education and New Learning Technologies (EDULEARN). EDULEARN19: 11th International Conference On Education And New Learning Technologies.*

Popescu, C. R. G. (2019d). Using Intellectual Capital Measurements In Universities To Assess Performance - Evidence From The Romanian Education System. *11th International Conference on Education and New Learning Technologies (EDULEARN). EDULEARN19: 11th International Conference On Education And New Learning Technologies.*

Popescu, C. R. G. (2019e). Intellectual Capital Evaluation And Measuring Effectiveness - A Case Study On Romania's Experience In Terms Of Performance And Excellence. *13th International Technology, Education And Development Conference (INTED2019). 13th International Technology, Education and Development Conference (INTED).*

Popescu, C. R. G. (2019e). Using Intellectual Capital Measurements In Universities To Assess Performance - Evidence From The Romanian Education System. *11th International Conference on Education and New Learning Technologies (EDULEARN). EDULEARN19: 11th International Conference On Education And New Learning Technologies.*

Popescu, C. R. G. (2019f). Intellectual Capital Evaluation And Measuring Effectiveness - A Case Study On Romania's Experience In Terms Of Performance And Excellence. *13th International Technology, Education And Development Conference (INTED2019). 13th International Technology, Education and Development Conference (INTED).*

Popescu, C. R. G. (2019g). Evaluating Intellectual Capital And Its Influence On Companies' Performance - A Case Study On Romania's Experience. *13th International Technology, Education And Development Conference (INTED2019). 13th International Technology, Education and Development Conference (INTED).*

Popescu, C. R. G. (2020d). Sustainability Assessment: Does the OECD/G20 Inclusive Framework for BEPS (Base Erosion and Profit Shifting Project) Put an End to Disputes Over The Recognition and Measurement of Intellectual Capital? *Sustainability, 12*(23), 10004. . doi:10.3390/su122310004

Popescu, C. R. G., & Dumitrescu, M. (2019). About Decisions: International Environment For Business And Perspectives Before And After The Financial Crisis - Roles Played By Corporate Governance, Knowledge Asymmetry And Intellectual Capital In The Romanian Business Environment. *34th International-Business-Information-Management-Association (IBIMA) Conference. Vision 2025: Education Excellence and Management of Innovations through Sustainable Economic Competitive Advantage.*

Popescu, C. R. G., & Popescu, G. N. (2014). Theoretical contributions concerning performance - the way to achieve excellence. *24th International-Business-Information-Management-Association Conference (IBIMA) Conference. Crafting Global Competitive Economies: 2020 Vision Strategic Planning & Smart Implementation.*

Popescu, C. R. G., & Popescu, G. N. (2015). What is Total Quality Management and how Can It Be Used in the Development of an Economy - A Case Study on Romania's Experience. *6th LUMEN International Conference on Rethinking Social Action Core Values. Rethinking Social Action. Core Values.*

Popescu, C. R. G., & Popescu, G. N. (2018). Methods of Evaluating "Intellectual capital" of an Organization and Ways of Enhancing Performance in the Knowledge-based Economy - A Synthetically Approach. *32nd Conference of the International-Business-Information-Management-Association (IBIMA). Vision 2020: Sustainable Economic Development And Application Of Innovation Management.*

Popescu, C. R. G., & Popescu, G. N. (2018). Risks of cyber attacks on financial audit activity. *The Audit Financiar Journal, 16*(149), 140-140. https://ideas.repec.org/a/aud/audfin/v16y2018i149p140.html

Popescu, C. R. G., & Popescu, G. N. (2019a). The Social, Economic, and Environmental Impact of Ecological Beekeeping in Romania. In G. Popescu (Ed.), Agrifood Economics and Sustainable Development in Contemporary Society (pp. 75-96). IGI Global. doi:10.4018/978-1-5225-5739-5.ch004

Popescu, C. R. G., & Popescu, G. N. (2019c). International Environment For Business: Economic Growth, Sustainable Development, Competitiveness And The Power Of Intellectual Capital - Focus On Romanian Business Environment. *34th International-Business-Information-Management-Association (IBIMA) Conference. Vision 2025: Education Excellence and Management of Innovations through Sustainable Economic Competitive Advantage.*

Popescu, C. R. G., & Popescu, V. A. (2014). The concept of excellence in business organizations - Case of Romania. *24th International-Business-Information-Management-Association Conference (IBIMA) Conference. Crafting Global Competitive Economies: 2020 Vision Strategic Planning & Smart Implementation.*

Popescu, C. R. G., & Popescu, V. A. (2015). Enhancing Learning by Improving Organizational Performance in the Quality Field - A Case Study on Romania's Experience on Business Process Management. *6th LUMEN International Conference on Rethinking Social Action Core Values. Rethinking Social Action.*

Compilation of References

Popescu, C. R. G., Popescu, G. N., & Popescu, V. A. (2015). Corporate Governance in Romania: Theories and Practices. In Corporate Governance And Corporate Social Responsibility: Emerging Markets Focus (pp. 375-401). World Scientific Publ Co Pte Ltd.

Popescu, C. R. G., Popescu, G. N., & Popescu, V. A. (2015). Corporate Governance in Romania: Theories and Practices. In *Corporate Governance And Corporate Social Responsibility: Emerging Markets Focus* (pp. 375-401). World Scientific Publ Co Pte Ltd. https://www.worldscientific.com/doi/abs/10.1142/9789814520386_0014 doi:10.1142/9789814520386_0014

Popescu, C. R. G., Popescu, G. N., & Popescu, V. A. (2017a). Assessment Of The State Of Implementation Of Excellence Model Common Assessment Framework (CAF) 2013 By The National Institutes Of Research - Development - Innovation In Romania. *Amfiteatru Economic, 19*(44), 41-60.

Popescu, C. R. G., Popescu, G. N., & Popescu, V. A. (2017b). Sustainability Leadership, the Key to a Better World - A Case Study on Romania's Situation. *29th International-Business-Information-Management-Association Conference (IBIMA). Sustainable Economic Growth, Education Excellence, And Innovation Management Through Vision 2020.*

Popescu, C. R. G., Popescu, G. N., & Popescu, V. A. (2017c). International Migration, Attempting To Create a Better World - A Case Study on Romania's Situation. *29th International-Business-Information-Management-Association Conference (IBIMA). Sustainable Economic Growth, Education Excellence, And Innovation Management Through Vision 2020.*

Popescu, C. R. G., Popescu, G. N., & Popescu, V. A. (2017d). Illusion of Diversity and Certitude of ChangeIn Buyers Tastes - Soft Drinks Industry Global Overview: Nowadays Key Trends. *30th International Business-Information-Management-Association Conference (IBIMA). Vision 2020: Sustainable Economic Development, Innovation Management, And Global Growth.*

Popescu, C. R. G., Popescu, G. N., & Popescu, V. A. (2017e). The What, Why and How of Performance-Driven Funding In Sports Industry - Economics and Management of Sports Industry's Competitive Strategy. *30th International Business-Information-Management-Association Conference (IBIMA). Vision 2020: Sustainable Economic Development, Innovation Management, And Global Growth.*

Popescu, C. R. G., Popescu, V. A., & Popescu, G. N. (2009). New Economy From Supremacy - To The Sudden Crisis. *Metalurgia International, 14*, 109-112.

Popescu, C. R. G., Popescu, V. A., & Popescu, G. N. (2011). Alternative Fuels - New Perspectives For A Bright Future. In *Crises After The Crisis: Inquiries From A National, European And Global Perspective, Vol. IV. 18th International Economic Conference on Crisis After the Crisis - Inquiries from a National European and Global Perspective.*

Popescu, C. R. G., Popescu, V. A., & Popescu, G. N. (2014). Excellence models for performance management: Case study: The evolution of "quality concept" in Japan - the Japanese model of excellence. Academic Press.

Popescu, C. R. G., Popescu, V. A., & Popescu, G. N. (2015). The Entrepreneur's Role In The Performance Growth Of The Financial Audit Activity In Romania. *Amfiteatru Economic, 17*(38), 228-246.

Popescu, C. R. G., Popescu, V. A., & Popescu, G. N. (2017). Forecasting Of Labour Market And Skill Needs In Nowadays Society - A Case Study On Romania's Situation Facing The Challenges Of The New Economy. *11th International Conference on Technology, Education and Development (INTED). INTED2017: 11th International Technology, Education And Development Conference.*

Popescu, C. R. G., Roman, C., & Popescu, V. A. (2009). Study On The Costs Of Implementing The European Union's Environmental Policy And The Results Of Applying The European Environmental Standards On Competitiveness In Romania. *Metalurgia International, 14*(4), 149-153.

Popescu, G. N., Popescu, C. R. G., & Popescu, V. A. (2016a). The Challenges Of Nowadays Companies, As Economic Organizations - A Case Study On Romania's Situation. *10th International Management Conference (IMC) - Challenges of Modern Management. Proceedings Of The 10th International Management Conference: Challenges Of Modern Management (IMC 2016).*

Popescu, G. N., Popescu, C. R. G., & Popescu, V. A. (2017). The Role And The Importance Of The University- Industry Collaboration - A Case Study On Romania's Situation Concerning Today's Educational Trends. *11th International Conference on Technology, Education and Development (INTED). INTED2017: 11th International Technology, Education And Development Conference.*

Popescu, G. N., Popescu, V. A., & Popescu, C. R. G. (2009). Research For Defining The Standards And Identifying The Opportunities For Increasing The Role Of The Green It In The Context Of Improving The Global Economy Management And Monitoring. *Metalurgia International, 14*(8), 48-53.

Popescu, G. N., Popescu, V. A., & Popescu, C. R. G. (2013). What Is Business Intelligence And How Can It Be Used In The Development Of An Economy - A Case Study On Romania's Experience. *7th International Technology, Education And Development Conference (INTED2013).*

Popescu, V. A., Popescu, G. N., & Popescu, C. R. G. (2009a). The Effects Of Informatics Revolution On Organizing The Modern Management, Accounting, Control And Financial Audit. *Metalurgia International, 14*(9), 156-164.

Popescu, V. A., Popescu, G. N., & Popescu, C. R. G. (2010). Global Trends - How Countries Can Learn From History. *Metalurgia International, 14*(5), 186-193.

Popescu, V. A., Popescu, G. N., & Popescu, C. R. G. (2011). "Liquid Assets" Or Turning Fine Wines In A Very Profitable Investment. In Crises After The Crisis: Inquiries From A National, European And Global Perspective, Vol. IV. *18th International Economic Conference on Crisis After the Crisis - Inquiries from a National European and Global Perspective.*

Popescu, V. A., Popescu, G. N., & Popescu, C. R. G. (2012a). Building a culture for innovation through competitive intelligence and accountability: case of Romania. *Innovation And Sustainable Competitive Advantage: From Regional Development To World Economies, Vols. 1-5. 18th International-Business-Information-Management-Association Conference (IBIMA).*

Popescu, V. A., Popescu, G. N., & Popescu, C. R. G. (2012b). Knowledge And Knowledge Management - New Challenges And Future Perspectives. *EDULEARN12: 4th International Conference On Education And New Learning Technologies. Book Series: EDULEARN Proceedings. 4th International Conference on Education and New Learning Technologies (EDULEARN).*

Popescu, V. A., Popescu, G. N., & Popescu, C. R. G. (2013). The Impact Of Higher Education On The Development Of Nowadays Society - A Case Study On Romania's Experience. *7th International Technology, Education And Development Conference (INTED2013). Book Series: INTED Proceedings. 7th International Technology, Education and Development Conference (INTED).*

Popescu, V. A., Popescu, G. N., & Popescu, C. R. G. (2014). The Economic And Social Dimensions Of Romania's Metallurgical Industry. *Metalurgija, 53*(1), 113-115.

Popescu, V. A., Popescu, G. N., & Popescu, C. R. G. (2015a). The Relation Productivity - Environment In The Context Of Sustainable Development - Case Study On The Romanian Industry. *Metalurgija, 54*(1), 286-288.

Popescu, V. A., Popescu, G. N., & Popescu, C. R. G. (2015b). Competitiveness And Sustainability - A Modern Economic Approach To The Industrial Policy. *Metalurgija, 54*(2), 426-428.

Popescu, V. A., Popescu, G. N., & Popescu, C. R. G. (2015c). The Impact Of Global Crisis On The Dominant Sectors Of The Economy At The Romanian Industry. *Metalurgija, 54*(2), 289-291.

Popescu, V. A., Popescu, G. N., Roman, C., & Popescu, C. R. G. (2009b). From Creative Accounting To The Moral And Financial Crisis. *Metalurgia International, 14*(9), 141-149.

Popescu, C. R. (2021a). Sustainable and Responsible Entrepreneurship for Value-Based Cultures, Economies, and Societies: Increasing Performance Through Intellectual Capital in Challenging Times. In C. Popescu & R. Verma (Eds.), *Sustainable and Responsible Entrepreneurship and Key Drivers of Performance* (pp. 33–58). IGI Global. doi:10.4018/978-1-7998-7951-0.ch002

Popescu, C. R. (2021b). Measuring Progress Towards the Sustainable Development Goals: Creativity, Intellectual Capital, and Innovation. In C. Popescu (Ed.), *Handbook of Research on Novel Practices and Current Successes in Achieving the Sustainable Development Goals* (pp. 125–136). IGI Global. doi:10.4018/978-1-7998-8426-2.ch006

Popescu, C. R. (2022a). Mindfulness at Work, a Sound Business Investment: Focusing on the Employee Well-Being While Increasing Creativity and Innovation. In C. Popescu (Ed.), *Handbook of Research on Changing Dynamics in Responsible and Sustainable Business in the Post-COVID-19 Era* (pp. 1–34). IGI Global. doi:10.4018/978-1-6684-2523-7.ch001

Popescu, C. R. (2022b). Impact of Innovative Capital on the Global Performance of the European Union: Implications on Sustainability Assessment. In C. Popescu (Ed.), *Handbook of Research on Novel Practices and Current Successes in Achieving the Sustainable Development Goals* (pp. 90–124). IGI Global. doi:10.4018/978-1-7998-8426-2.ch005

Popescu, C. R. (2022c). Mindfulness Business Principles: Producing Outstanding Value and Encouraging Community Connections. In C. Popescu (Ed.), *COVID-19 Pandemic Impact on New Economy Development and Societal Change* (pp. 196–228). IGI Global. doi:10.4018/978-1-6684-3374-4.ch010

Popescu, C. R. (2022d). Environmental, Social, and Corporate Governance by Avoiding Management Bias and Tax Minimization: Reaching a General Consensus Regarding a Minimum Global Tax Rate. In C. Popescu (Ed.), *COVID-19 Pandemic Impact on New Economy Development and Societal Change* (pp. 94–132). IGI Global. doi:10.4018/978-1-6684-3374-4.ch006

Popescu, C. R. G. (2020a). Developing a Model for Entrepreneurship Competencies: Innovation, Knowledge Management, and Intellectual Capital – Success Competences for Building Inclusive Entrepreneurship and Organizational Performance. In J. Šebestová (Ed.), *Developing Entrepreneurial Competencies for Start-Ups and Small Business* (pp. 1–22). IGI Global. doi:10.4018/978-1-7998-2714-6.ch001

Popescu, C. R. G. (2020b). Analyzing the Impact of Green Marketing Strategies on the Financial and Non-Financial Performance of Organizations: The Intellectual Capital Factor. In V. Naidoo & R. Verma (Eds.), *Green Marketing as a Positive Driver Toward Business Sustainability* (pp. 186–218). IGI Global. doi:10.4018/978-1-5225-9558-8.ch008

Popescu, C. R. G. (2020c). Approaches to Sustainable and Responsible Entrepreneurship: Creativity, Innovation, and Intellectual Capital as Drivers for Organization Performance. In B. Hernández-Sánchez, J. Sánchez-García, & A. Moreira (Eds.), *Building an Entrepreneurial and Sustainable Society* (pp. 75–95). IGI Global. doi:10.4018/978-1-7998-2704-7.ch004

Popescu, C. R. G. (2022e). Fostering Creativity in Business: Empowering Strong Transformational Leaders. In C. Popescu (Ed.), *Handbook of Research on Changing Dynamics in Responsible and Sustainable Business in the Post-COVID-19 Era* (pp. 349–381). IGI Global. doi:10.4018/978-1-6684-2523-7.ch017

Popescu, C. R. G. (Ed.). (2021d). *Handbook of Research on Novel Practices and Current Successes in Achieving the Sustainable Development Goals*. IGI Global. doi:10.4018/978-1-7998-8426-2

Popescu, C. R. G. (Ed.). (2022f). *COVID-19 Pandemic Impact on New Economy Development and Societal Change*. IGI Global. doi:10.4018/978-1-6684-3374-4

Popescu, C. R. G. (Ed.). (2022g). *Handbook of Research on Changing Dynamics in Responsible and Sustainable Business in the Post-COVID-19 Era*. IGI Global. doi:10.4018/978-1-6684-2523-7

Popescu, G. N., Popescu, C. R. G., & Popescu, V. A. (2016b). The Textile Industry in the Context of Economic Growth, Economic Development and Sustainable Development - A Nowadays Economic and Managerial Approach. *28th International Business-Information-Management-Association Conference (IBIMA)*.

Porter, M. E., & Van der Linde, C. (1995). Toward a new conception of the environment-competitiveness relationship. *The Journal of Economic Perspectives*, *9*(4), 97–118. doi:10.1257/jep.9.4.97

Poumanyvong, P., & Kaneko, S. (2010). Does urbanization lead to less energy use and lower CO2 emissions? A cross-country analysis. *Ecological Economics*, *70*(2), 434–444. doi:10.1016/j.ecolecon.2010.09.029

Pradhan, P., Subedi, D. R., Khatiwada, D., Joshi, K. K., Kafle, S., Chhetri, R. P., ... Bhuju, D. R. (2021). The COVID-19 Pandemic Not Only Poses Challenges, but Also Opens Opportunities for Sustainable Transformation. *Earth's Future*, *9*(7).

Prata, J. C., Silva, A. L., Walker, T. R., Duarte, A. C., & Rocha-Santos, T. (2020). COVID-19 pandemic repercussions on the use and management of plastics. *Environmental Science & Technology*, *54*(13), 7760–7765.

Pride, W. M., & Ferrell, O. C. (1993). *Marketing: Study Guide*. Houghton Mifflin School.

Probst, G., & Raisch, S. (2005). Organizational Crisis: The Logic of Failure. *The Academy of Management Executive*, *19*(1), 90–105. doi:10.5465/ame.2005.15841958

Qarnain, S. S., Sattanathan, M., Sankaranarayanan, B., & Ali, S. M. (2020). Analyzing energy consumption factors during coronavirus (COVID-19) pandemic outbreak: A case study of residential society. *Energy Sources. Part A, Recovery, Utilization, and Environmental Effects*, 1–20.

Quiñonez, R. & Prado-Solis, M. (2017). Organizational resilience: ideas for debate in the Ecuadorian context. *Mastery of the Sciences, 3*, 488-504.

Rada, E. C., Ragazzi, M., Torretta, V., Castagna, G., Adami, L., & Cioca, L. I. (2018). Circular economy and waste to energy. In AIP Conference Proceedings (Vol. 1968, No. 1, p. 030050). AIP Publishing LLC. doi:10.1063/1.5039237

Ragazzi, M., Fedrizzi, S., Rada, E. C., Ionescu, G., Ciudin, R., & Cioca, L. I. (2017). Experiencing urban mining in an Italian municipality towards a circular economy vision. *Energy Procedia*, *119*, 192–200. doi:10.1016/j.egypro.2017.07.068

Rago, A., Ribeiro, N., Cunha, M. P., & Jesuino, J. C. (2011). How happiness mediates the organizational virtuousness and affective commitment relationship. *Journal of Business Research*, *64*(5), 524–532. https://doi.org/10.1016/j.jbusres.2010.04.009

Rahyuda, A. G., Soltani, E., & Syed, J. (2018). Preventing a relapse or setting goals? Elucidating the impact of post-training transfer interventions on training transfer performance. *International Journal of Training Research*, *16*(1), 61–82. doi:10.1080/14480220.2017.1411287

Ramus, C. A., & Steger, U. (2000). The roles of supervisory support behaviors and environmental policy in employee "eco initiatives" at leading-edge European companies. *Academy of Management Journal*, *43*(4), 605–626.

Rani, N., & Samuel, A. (2016). A study on generational differences in work values and person-organization fit and its effect on turnover intention of Generation Y in India. *Management Research Review*, *39*(12), 1695–1719. https://doi.org/10.1108/MRR-10-2015-0249

Compilation of References

Rankin, A., Lundberg, J., & Woltjer, R. (2014). A framework for learning from adaptive performance. In *Becom. Resilient*. Ashgate Publishing, Ltd.

Rao, M. S. (2009). Is cutting development and training in a recession a good idea? Looking at the IT and ITeS sector in India. *Development and Learning in Organizations, 23*(5), 7–9. doi:10.1108/14777280910982915

Rapoport, M. & Brenta, N. (2010). The global economic crisis: The outcome of forty years of instability? *Developmental Problems, 41*(163), 7-30.

Rasheed, R. A., Kamsin, A., & Abdullah, N. A. (2020). Challenges in the online component of blended learning: A systematic review. *Computers & Education, 144*, 103701. doi:10.1016/j.compedu.2019.103701

Ravina-Ripoll, R., Nunez-Barriopedro, E., Almorza-Gomar, D., & Tobar-Pesantez, L. B. (2021). Happiness Management: A Culture to Explore from Brand Orientation as a Sign of Responsible and Sustainable Production. *Frontiers in Psychology, 12*. doi:10.3389/fpsyg.2021.727845

Raynor, M. E. (2007). Solving the strategy paradox: How to reach for the fruit without going out on a limb. *Strategy and Leadership, 35*(4), 4–10. doi:10.1108/10878570710761327

Rebelo, S. (1991). Long-run policy analysis and long-run growth. *Journal of Political Economy, 99*(3), 500–521. doi:10.1086/261764

Reed, S. E. (1984). The behaviour of recent isolates of human respiratory coronavirus in vitro and in volunteers: Evidence of heterogeneity among 229E-related strains. *Journal of Medical Virology, 13*(2), 179–192. doi:10.1002/jmv.1890130208 PMID:6319590

Reich, J. W. (2006). Three psychological principles of resilience in natural disasters. *Disaster Prevention and Management, 15*(5), 793–798. doi:10.1108/09653560610712739

Reinmoeller, P., & van Baardwijk, N. (2005). The link between diversity and resilience. *MIT Sloan Management Review, 46*, 61–65.

Renwick, D., Redman, T., & Maguire, S. (2013). Green human resource management: A review and research agenda. *International Journal of Management Review, 15*(1), 1–14. doi:.00328.x doi:10.1111/j.1468-2370.2011

Rényi, A. (1961). On measures of entropy and information. In *Proceedings of the Fourth Berkeley Symposium on Mathematical Statistics and Probability*, Volume 1*: Contributions to the Theory of Statistics* (pp. 547-561). University of California Press.

Restorick, T. (2020). *How has covid-19 changed our eating habits?* https://www.hubbub.org.uk/ blog/how-has-covid-19-changed-our-eating-habits

Richardson, G. E. (2016). The applied metatheory of resilience and resiliency. In U. Kumar (Ed.), *The Routledge International Handbook of Psychological Resilience* (pp. 124–135). Routledge.

Richtnér, A., & Löfsten, H. (2014). Managing in turbulence: How the capacity for resilience influences creativity. *R & D Management, 44*(2), 137–151. doi:10.1111/radm.12050

Rizvi, S., Rustum, R., Deepak, M., Wright, G. B., & Arthur, S. (2021). Identifying and analyzing residential water demand profile; including the impact of COVID-19 and month of Ramadan, for selected developments in Dubai, United Arab Emirates. *Water Supply, 21*(3), 1144–1156.

Roberts, K. H., Madsen, P. M., & Desait, V. M. (2005). The space between in space transportation: A relational analysis of the failure of STS-107. In W. H. Starbuck & M. Farjoun (Eds.), *Organization at the limit—NASA and the Columbia Disaster* (pp. 81–98). Blackwell.

Robinson, J. (2004). Squaring the circle? Some thoughts on the idea of sustainable development. *Ecol. Econ., 48*, 369-384.

Roca, J. (2003). Do individual preferences explain the Environmental Kuznets curve? *Ecological Economics, 45*(1), 3–10. doi:10.1016/S0921-8009(02)00263-X

Roccas, S., & Sagiv, L. (2010). Personal values and behavior: Taking the cultural context into account. *Social and Personality Psychology Compass, 4*(1), 30–41. https://www.doi.org/10.1111/j.1751-9004.2009.00234.x

Rock, M. T. (1998). Freshwater use, freshwater scarcity, and socioeconomic development. *Journal of Environment & Development, 7*(3), 278–301. doi:10.1177/107049659800700304

Rodriguez, A., & Rodriguez, Y. (2015). Metaphors for today's leadership: VUCA world, millennial and Cloud Leaders. *Journal of Management Development, 34*(7), 854–866. https://doi.org/10.1108/JMD-09-2013-0110

Rodríguez-P'erez, C., Molina-Montes, E., Verardo, V., Artacho, R., García-Villanova, B., Guerra-Hernandez, E. J., & Ruíz-Lopez, '. M. D. (2020). Changes in dietary behaviours during the COVID-19 outbreak confinement in the Spanish COVIDiet study. *Nutrients, 12*(6), 1–19.

Romer, D. (2018). *Macroeconomic theory*. University of California.

Romero-Hernández, O., & Romero, S. (2018). Maximizing the value of waste: From waste management to the circular economy. *Thunderbird International Business Review, 60*(5), 757–764. doi:10.1002/tie.21968

Romero, I. (2006). SMEs in the global economy. Towards a business development strategy. Developmental problems. *Latin American Journal of Economics, 37*(146), 31–50.

Rosati, F., & Faria, L. (2019). Addressing the SDGs in sustainability reports: The relationship with institutional factors. *Journal of Cleaner Production, 215*, 1312–1326. doi:10.1016/j.jclepro.2018.12.107

Roson, R., & Hubert, F. (2015). Bargaining power and value sharing in distribution networks: A cooperative game theory approach. *Networks and Spatial Economics, 15*(1), 71–87. doi:10.100711067-014-9270-6

Rouleau, J., & Gosselin, L. (2021). Impacts of the COVID-19 lockdown on energy consumption in a Canadian social housing building. *Applied Energy, 287*, 116565.

Ruiz, A. (2015). *Reliability and Validity: Conceptualization and calculation procedures with Spss*. University of Barcelona. Retrieved from http://diposit.ub.edu/dspace/bitstream/2445/65322/1/Fiabilidad_Validez.pdf

Rume, T., & Islam, S. D. U. (2020). Environmental effects of COVID-19 pandemic and potential strategies of sustainability. *Heliyon, 6*(9), e04965.

Russell, J. E. (2008). Promoting subjective well-being at work. *Journal of Career Assessment, 16*(1), 117–131. https://doi.org/10.1177/1069072707308142

Rutigliano, N. K., Samson, R. M., & Frye, A. S. (2017). Mindfulness: Spiriting Effective Strategic Leadership and Management. In V. Wang (Ed.), *Encyclopedia of Strategic Leadership and Management* (pp. 460–469). IGI Global. doi:10.4018/978-1-5225-1049-9.ch033

Saboori, B., Sulaiman, J., & Mohd, S. (2012). Economic growth and CO2 emissions in Malaysia: A cointegration analysis of the Environmental Kuznets Curve. *Energy Policy, 51*, 184–191. doi:10.1016/j.enpol.2012.08.065

Sachs, J. D., Schmidt-Traub, G., Mazzucato, M., Messner, D., Nakicenovic, N., & Rockström, J. (2019). Six Transformations to achieve the Sustainable Development Goals. *Nature Sustainability*, *2*(9), 805–814. doi:10.103841893-019-0352-9

Sadorsky, P. (2014). The effect of urbanization on CO2 emissions in emerging economies. *Energy Economics*, *41*, 147–153. doi:10.1016/j.eneco.2013.11.007

Saks, A. M. (2002). So what is a good transfer of training estimate? A reply to Fitzpatrick. *The Industrial-Organizational Psychologist*, *39*(3), 29–30.

Saks, A. M., & Belcourt, M. (2006). An investigation of training activities and transfer of training in organizations. *Human Resource Management*, *45*(4), 629–648. doi:10.1002/hrm.20135

Salas, E., Tannenbaum, S. I., Kraiger, K., & Smith-Jentsch, K. A. (2012). The science of training and development in organizations: What matters in practice. *Psychological Science in the Public Interest*, *13*(2), 74–101. doi:10.1177/1529100612436661 PMID:26173283

Salas-Vallina, A., Alegre, J., & Fernández Guerrero, R. (2018). Happiness at work in knowledge-intensive contexts: Opening the research agenda. *European Research on Management and Business Economics*, *24*(3), 149–159. https://doi.org/10.1016/j.iedeen.2018.05.003

Salazar Estrada, J. G., Guerrero Pupo, J. C., Machado Rodríguez, Y. B., & Cañedo Andalia, R. (2009). Clima y cultura organizacional: Dos componentes esenciales en la productividad laboral. *Acimed*, *20*(4), 67–75.

Salzano, G., Passanisi, S., Pira, F., Sorrenti, L., La Monica, G., Pajno, G. B., ... Lombardo, F. (2021). Quarantine due to the COVID-19 pandemic from the perspective of adolescents: The crucial role of technology. *Italian Journal of Pediatrics*, *47*(1), 1–5.

Salzman, J., & Hunter, D. (2007). *Negligence in the Air: The Duty of Care in Climate Change Litigation*. Working paper no. 95, Duke University Law School.

Sánchez-Vázquez, J. F. (2018). El significado vital en las organizaciones: aportaciones de la economía de la felicidad. *Cauriensia*, *13*, 143-156. doi:10.17398/2340-4256.13.143

Sánchez-Vázquez, J. F., & Sánchez-Ordóñez, R. (2019). Happiness Management: Review of scientific literature in the framework of happiness at work. *Retos. Revista de Ciencias de la Administración y Economía*, *9*(18), 259-271. doi:10.17163/ret.n18.2019.05

Sangkala, M., Ahmed, U., & Pahi, H. M. (2016). Empirical investigating on the role of supervisor support, job clarity, employee training and performance appraisal in addressing job satisfaction of nurses. *International Business Management*, *10*(23), 5481–5486.

Santiago, I., Moreno-Munoz, A., Quintero-Jiménez, P., Garcia-Torres, F., & Gonzalez-Redondo, M. J. (2021). Electricity demand during pandemic times: The case of the COVID-19 in Spain. *Energy Policy*, *148*, 111964.

Santos, A., & Stuart, M. (2003). Employee perceptions and their influence on training effectiveness. *Human Resource Management Journal*, *13*(1), 27–45. doi:10.1111/j.1748-8583.2003.tb00082.x

Sarigöllü, E. (2008). A Cross-Country Exploration of Environmental Attitudes. *Environment and Behavior*, *41*(3), 365–386. doi:10.1177/0013916507313920

Sarkar, A. (2016). We live in a VUCA World: The importance of responsible leadership. *Development and Learning in Organizations*, *30*(3), 9–12. https://dx.doi.org/10.1108/DLO-07-2015-0062

Sarmento, P., Motta, M., Scott, I. J., Pinheiro, F. L., & de Castro Neto, M. (2022). Impact of COVID-19 lockdown measures on waste production behavior in Lisbon. *Waste Management (New York, N.Y.)*, *138*, 189–198.

Schaffer, M. B. (2008). The great gas pipeline game: Monopolistic expansion of Russia's Gazprom into European markets. *Foresight*, *10*(5), 11–23. doi:10.1108/14636680810918478

Schäufele, I., & Hamm, U. (2017). Consumers' perceptions, preferences and willingness-to-pay for wine with sustainability characteristics: A review. *Journal of Cleaner Production*, *147*, 379–394. doi:10.1016/j.jclepro.2017.01.118

Schein, E. H. (1990). *Organizational Culture* (Vol. 45). American Psychological Association.

Schmitt, V. G. H., Cequea, M. M., Vásquez Neyra, J. M., & Ferasso, M. (2021). Consumption behavior and residential food waste during the COVID-19 pandemic outbreak in Brazil. *Sustainability*, *13*(7), 3702.

Schwartz, S. H. (2011). Values: Individual and cultural. In F. J. R. Van de Vijver, A. Chasiotis, & S. M. Breugelmans (Eds.), *Fundamental Questions in Cross-Cultural Psychology* (pp. 463–493). Cambridge University Press.

Scott, D., & Willits, F. K. (1994). Environmental Attitudes and Behavior: A Pennsylvania Survey. *Environment and Behavior*, *26*(2), 239–260. doi:10.1177/0013916594026002006

Seibel, S., Santos, I., & Silveira, I. (2021). Covid-19's Impact on Society, Fashion Trends and Consumption. *Strategic Design Research Journal*, *14*(1), 92–101.

Seiberling, C., & Kauffeld, S. (2017). Volition to transfer: Mastering obstacles in training transfer. *Personnel Review*, *46*(4), 809–823. doi:10.1108/PR-08-2015-0202

Seligman, M. E. P. (1990). *Learned Optimism*. Knopf. Free Press.

Seroka-Stolka, O., & Lukomska-Szarek, J. (2016). Barriers to the adoption of proactive environmental strategies in polish companies. *Proceedings of international academic conferences*.

Seuring, S., & Gold, S. (2013). Sustainability management beyond corporate boundaries: from stakeholders to performance. *J. Clean. Prod.*, *56*(1), 1-6.

Severo, E. A., De Guimarães, J. C. F., & Dellarmelin, M. L. (2021). Impact of the COVID-19 pandemic on environmental awareness, sustainable consumption and social responsibility: Evidence from generations in Brazil and Portugal. *Journal of Cleaner Production*, *286*, 124947.

Seyf, A. (2009). Population and agricultural development in Iran, 1800–1906. *Middle Eastern Studies*, *45*(3), 447–460. doi:10.1080/00263200902853439

Shaharuddin, B., Sany, S., & Hasan, N. N. N. (2021). Challenges and Solutions to Shortage of Personal Protective Equipment during Covid-19 Pandemic: A Case Study on Corporate and Community Response. *Journal of Sustainability Science and Management*, *16*(8), 248–255.

Shaheen, S. A., Mallery, M. A., & Kingsley, K. J. (2012). Personal vehicle sharing services in North America. *Research in Transportation Business & Management*, *3*, 71–81. doi:10.1016/j.rtbm.2012.04.005

Shakoury, K. (2018). *Critical discourse analysis of Iranian Presidents' Addresses to the United Nations General Assembly (2007-2016)* (Doctoral dissertation). University of Saskatchewan.

Shannon, C. E. (1948). A mathematical theory of communication. *The Bell System Technical Journal*, *27*(3), 379–423. doi:10.1002/j.1538-7305.1948.tb01338.x

Compilation of References

Sharfman, M. P., & Fernando, C. S. (2008). Environmental risk management and the cost of capital. *Strategic Management Journal*, 29, 569–592. https://dx.doi.org/10.1002/(ISSN)1097-0266

Sharma, H. B., Vanapalli, K. R., Cheela, V. S., Ranjan, V. P., Jaglan, A. K., Dubey, B., ... Bhattacharya, J. (2020). Challenges, opportunities, and innovations for effective solid waste management during and post COVID-19 pandemic. *Resources, Conservation and Recycling*, 162, 105052.

Sharma, S. S. (2011). Determinants of carbon dioxide emissions: Empirical evidence from 69 countries. *Applied Energy*, 88(1), 376–382. doi:10.1016/j.apenergy.2010.07.022

Sheffi, Y. (2005). Building a Resilient Supply Chain. *Harvard Business Review Supply Chain Strategy Newsletter*, 1(8). https://sheffi.mit.edu/sites/default/files/genmedia.buildingresilientsupplychain.pdf

Sheffi, Y., & Rice, J. (2005). A vision of the resilient enterprise supply chain. *MIT Sloan Management Review*, 47, 41–48.

Shen, J., & Tang, C. (2018). How does training improve customer service quality? The roles of transfer of training and job satisfaction. *European Management Journal*, 36(6), 708–716. doi:10.1016/j.emj.2018.02.002

Sheppard, J. P., & Chowdhury, S. D. (2005). Riding the Wrong Wave: Organizational Failure as a Failed Turnaround. *Long Range Planning*, 38(3), 239–260. doi:10.1016/j.lrp.2005.03.009

Sherman, A., & Barokas, G. (2019). Are happy people more employable? Evidence from field experiments. *Applied Economics Letters*, 26(17), 1384–1387. https://doi.org/10.1080/13504851.2018.1558345

Sherwin, W. B. (2018). Entropy, or information, unifies ecology and evolution and beyond. *Entropy (Basel, Switzerland)*, 20(10), 727. doi:10.3390/e20100727 PMID:33265816

Shore, L. M., Coyle-Shapiro, J. A.-M., Chen, X.-P., & Tetrick, L. E. (2009). Social exchange in work settings: Content, process, and mixed models. *Management and Organization Review*, 5, 289–302. https://doi.org/10.1111/j.1740-8784.2009.00158.x

Silva, L. E. N., Neto, M. B. G., da Rocha Grangeiro, R., & de Nadae, J. (2020). Covid-19 pandemic: why does it matter for consumer research? [Paper presentation]. CLAV 2020, Sao Paulo, Brasil.

Silva, A. L. P., Prata, J. C., Walker, T. R., Duarte, A. C., Ouyang, W., Barceló, D., & Rocha-Santos, T. (2021). Increased plastic pollution due to COVID-19 pandemic: Challenges and recommendations. *Chemical Engineering Journal*, 405, 126683.

Smith, A. M., & O'Sullivan, T. (2012). Environmentally responsible behaviour in the workplace: An internal social marketing approach. *Journal of Marketing Management*, 28, 469–493.

Smith, D., & Elliott, D. (2007). Exploring the barriers to learning from crisis -Organizational learning and crisis. *Management Learning*, 38(5), 519–538. doi:10.1177/1350507607083205

Sneader, K., & Singhal, S. (2020). *From Thinking about the Next Normal to Making it Work: What to Stop, Start, and Accelerate*. McKinsey & Company.

Sneader, K., & Sternfels, R. A. (2020). *From surviving to thriving: Reimagining the Post-COVID-19 Return*. McKinsey & Company.

Sneyd, J. R., Mathoulin, S. E., O'Sullivan, E. P., So, V. C., Roberts, F. R., Paul, A. A., ... & Balkisson, M. A. (2020). The impact of the COVID-19 pandemic on anaesthesia trainees and their training. *British Journal of Anesthesia*. doi:10.1016/j.bja.2020.07.011

Snow, W. H., Lamar, M. R., Hinkle, J. S., & Speciale, M. (2018). Current Practices in Online Counselor Education. *The Professional Counselor*, *8*(2), 131–145. doi:10.15241/whs.8.2.131

Soerensen, P., Stegeager, N., & Bates, R. (2017). Applying a Danish version of the Learning Transfer System Inventory and testing it for different types of education. *International Journal of Training and Development*, *21*(3), 177–194. doi:10.1111/ijtd.12102

Sookhai, F., & Budworth, M. H. (2010). The trainee in context: Examining the relationship between self-efficacy and transfer climate for transfer of training. *Human Resource Development Quarterly*, *21*(3), 257–272. doi:10.1002/hrdq.20044

Sovacool, B. K. (2009). Energy policy and cooperation in Southeast Asia: The history, challenges, and implications of the trans-ASEAN gas pipeline (TAGP) network. *Energy Policy*, *37*(6), 2356–2367. doi:10.1016/j.enpol.2009.02.014

Spangenberg, J. H. (2002). Environmental space and the prism of sustainability: Frameworks for indicators measuring sustainable development. *Ecological Indicators*, *2*(3), 295–309. doi:10.1016/S1470-160X(02)00065-1

Speight, P. (2011). Business continuity. *Journal of Applied Security Research*, *6*(4), 529–554. doi:10.1080/19361610.2011.604021

Srivastav, A. K. (2007). Stress in organizational roles-individual and organizational implications. *Icfaian Journal of Management Research*, *6*, 64–74.

Stafford, E. R., & Hartman, C. L. (1996). Green Alliances: Strategic Relations between Businesses and Environmental Groups. *Business Horizons*, *2*, 50–59.

Stahel, W. R. (2017). Analysis of the structure and values of the European Commission's Circular Economy Package. In *Proceedings of the Institution of Civil Engineers-Waste and Resource Management* (Vol. 170, No. 1, pp. 41-44). Thomas Telford Ltd. 10.1680/jwarm.17.00009

Starr, R., Newfrock, J. & Delurey, M. (2003). Business Resilience: Risk Management in the Network Economy. *Strategy and Business, 30*, 70-79.

Statista. (2020, June 24). *How COVID-19 has impacted US spending levels*. https://www.statista.com/chart/22091/change-in-consumer-spending-due-to-coronavirus/

Stenling, A., & Tafvelin, S. (2016). Transfer of training after an organizational intervention in Swedish sports clubs: A self-determination theory perspective. *Journal of Sport & Exercise Psychology*, *38*(5), 493–504. doi:10.1123/jsep.2016-0084 PMID:27736273

Stephenson, A. (2010). *Benchmarking the Resilience of Organizations* [Unpublished PhD Thesis]. Civil and Natural Resources Engineering Department, University of Canterbury.

Stewart, J., & O'Donnell, M. (2007). Implementing change in a public agency. *International Journal of Public Sector Management*, *20*(3), 239–251. doi:10.1108/09513550710740634

Stiglitz, J. (1998). The private uses of public interests: Incentives and institutions. *The Journal of Economic Perspectives*, *12*(2), 3–22. doi:10.1257/jep.12.2.3

Strand, V., & Bosco-Ruggiero, S. (2011). Implementing transfer of learning in training and professional development in a US public child welfare agency: What works? *Professional Development in Education*, *37*(3), 373–387. doi:10.1080/19415257.2010.509675

Stratoulias, D., & Nuthammachot, N. (2020). Air quality development during the COVID-19 pandemic over a medium-sized urban area in Thailand. *The Science of the Total Environment*, *746*, 141320.

Stubbs, W., & Cocklin, C. (2008). Conceptualizing a sustainability business model. *Org. Env., 21*(2), 103-127.

Sturges, J., Conway, N., & Liefooghe, A. (2010). Organizational support, individual attributes, and the practice of career self-management behavior. *Group & Organization Management, 35*(1), 108–141. doi:10.1177/1059601109354837

Suazo, M. M., Martínez, P. G., & Sandoval, R. (2009). Creating psychological and legal contracts through human resource practices: A signaling theory perspective. *Human Resource Management Review, 19*(2), 154–166. doi:10.1016/j.hrmr.2008.11.002

Suire, R., & Vicente, J. (2014). Cluster Clusters for Cluster Life (s): Looking for Critical Cluster Resilience Factors. *Entrepreneurship and Regional Development, 26*(1–2), 142–164. doi:10.1080/08985626.2013.877985

Sullivan, C. (2002). Calculating a water poverty index. *World Development, 30*(7), 1195–1210. doi:10.1016/S0305-750X(02)00035-9

Sullivan-Taylor, B., & Branicki, L. (2011). Building Resilient SMEs: Why One Size May Not Fit All. *International Journal of Production Research, 49*(18), 5565–5579. doi:10.1080/00207543.2011.563837

Sun, C. (2001). Paying for the Environment in China: The Growing Role of the Market. *China Environment Series, 4*, 32–42. http://citeseerx.ist.psu.edu/viewdoc/download?doi=10.1.1.201.7949&rep=rep1&type=pdf

Sun, X., Su, W., Guo, X., & Tian, Z. (2021). The impact of awe induced by COVID-19 pandemic on green consumption behavior in China. *International Journal of Environmental Research and Public Health, 18*(2), 543.

Sutcliffe, K. & Vogus, T. (2003). Organize for resilience. *Positive Organizational Scholarship*, 94-110.

Sutcliffe, K. M., & Vogus, T. J. (2003). Organizing for resilience. *Positive Organizational Scholarship*, 94-110.

Sydow, J., Schreyögg, G., & Koch, J. (2009). Organizational Path Dependence: Opening the Black Box. *Academy of Management Review, 34*(4), 689–709.

Szolnoki, G. (2013). A cross-national comparison of sustainability in the wine industry. *Journal of Cleaner Production, 53*, 243–251. doi:10.1016/j.jclepro.2013.03.045

Szyja, P. (2016). The role of the state in creating green economy. *Oeconomia Copernicana, 7*(2), 207–222. doi:10.12775/OeC.2016.013

Tabaklar, T., Sorkun, M. F., Yurt, O., & Yu, W. (2021). Exploring the microfoundations of dynamic capabilities for social innovation in a humanitarian aid supply network setting. *Industrial Marketing Management, 96*, 147–162. doi:10.1016/j.indmarman.2021.04.012

Taecharungroj, V., Muthuta, M., & Boonchaiyapruek, P. (2019). Sustainability as a place brand position: A resident-centric analysis of the ten towns in the vicinity of Bangkok. *Place Branding and Public Diplomacy, 2019*(15), 210–228.

Taleb, N. N. (2012). *Antifragile: Things that Gain from Disorder* (Vol. 3). Random House.

Taylor, P. J., Russ-Eft, D. F., & Chan, D. W. (2005). A meta-analytic review of behavior modeling training. *The Journal of Applied Psychology, 90*(4), 692–709. doi:10.1037/0021-9010.90.4.692 PMID:16060787

Tchetchik, A., Kaplan, S., & Blass, V. (2021). Recycling and consumption reduction following the COVID-19 lockdown: The effect of threat and coping appraisal, past behavior and information. *Resources, Conservation and Recycling, 167*, 105370.

Teece, D. J. (2007). Explicating Dynamic Capabilities: The Nature and Microfoundations of (Sustainable) Enterprise Performance. *Strategic Management Journal, 28*(13), 1319–1350. doi:10.1002mj.640

Teece, D. J. (2012). Dynamic Capabilities: Routines versus Entrepreneurial Action. *Journal of Management Studies*, *49*(8), 1395–1401. doi:10.1111/j.1467-6486.2012.01080.x

Teece, D. J., Pisano, G., & Shuen, A. (1997). Dynamic capabilities and strategic management. *Strategic Management Journal*, *18*(7), 509–533. doi:10.1002/(SICI)1097-0266(199708)18:7<509::AID-SMJ882>3.0.CO;2-Z

Teixeira, A. A., Jabbour, C. J. C., Lopes de Sousa, A. B., Hengky Latan, J., & Caldeira De Oliveira, J. H. (2016). Green training and green supply chain management: Evidence from Brazilian firms. *Journal of Cleaner Production*, *116*, 170–176.

Teo, W. L., Lee, M., & Lim, W.-S. (2017). The relational activation of resilience model: How leadership activates resilience in an organizational crisis. *Journal of Contingencies and Crisis Management*, *25*(3), 136–147. doi:10.1111/1468-5973.12179

Thanki, S. J., & Thakkar, J. J. (2016). Value-value load diagram: A graphical tool for lean-green performance assessment. *Production Planning and Control*, *27*, 1280–1297.

Thiagarajan, A., & Sekkizhar, J. (2017). The Impact of Green Intellectual Capital on Integrated Sustainability Performance in the Indian Auto-component Industry. *Journal of Contemporary Research in Management*, *12*(4), 21–78.

Thiel, C. E., Bagdasarov, Z., Harkrider, L., Johnson, J. F., & Mumford, M. D. (2012). Leader ethical decision-making in organizations: Strategies for sense making. *Journal of Business Ethics*, *107*(1), 49–64. doi:10.100710551-012-1299-1

Thilagaraj, A. (2021). Training and Development in a Post-Covid-19 Workplace. *Utkal Historical Research Journal*, *34*(19), 77-80.

Thomas, H., & Hedrick-Wong, Y. (2019). Enabling models of inclusive growth: Addressing the need for financial and social inclusion. *Global Focus Magazine. The EFMD Business Magazine.* https://www.globalfocusmagazine.com/enabling-models-of-inclusive-growth-addressing-the-need-for-financial-and-social-inclusion/

Tir, N. A., Momeni, F., & Boboevich, G. T. (2014). Exploring the effects of water sector investment in economic development in Iran. *Procedia: Social and Behavioral Sciences*, *131*, 396–405. doi:10.1016/j.sbspro.2014.04.137

Toft, B., & Reynolds, S. (1997). *Learning from Disasters* (2nd ed.). Perpetuity Press.

Tomprou, M., Xanthopoulou, D., & Vakola, M. (2020). Socio-emotional and monetary employee-organization resource exchanges: Measurement and effects on daily employee functioning. *Work and Stress*, *34*(2), 189–214. https://doi.org/10.1080/02678373.2019.1616333

Too, L., & Bajracharya, B. (2015). Sustainable Campus: Engaging the community in sustainability. *International Journal of Sustainability in Higher Education*, *16*(1), 57–71.

To, W. M., Lam, K. H., & Lai, T. M. (2015). Importance-performance ratings for environmental practices among Hong Kong professional-level employees. *Journal of Cleaner Production*, *108*, 699–706.

Tsallis, C. (1988). Possible generalization of Boltzmann-Gibbs statistics. *Journal of Statistical Physics*, *52*(1), 479–487. doi:10.1007/BF01016429

Tseng, M. L., Wong, W. P., & Soh, K. L. (2018). An overview of the substance of resource, conservation and recycling. *Resources, Conservation and Recycling*, *136*, 367–375. doi:10.1016/j.resconrec.2018.05.010

Tsuda, K., & Sakuragi, M. (2020). Co-design of do-it-yourself face shield in Japan under COVID-19 Pandemic. *Strategic Design Research Journal*, *13*(3), 502–510.

Tuan, L. T. (2019). Catalyzing employee OCBE in tour companies: The role of environmentally specific charismatic leadership and organizational justice for pro-environmental behaviors. *Journal of Hospitality & Tourism Research (Washington, D.C.)*, *43*, 682–711. doi:10.1177/1096348018817582

Tukker, A., Cohen, M., De Zoysa, U., Hertwich, E., Hofstetter, P., Inaba, A., ... Sto, E. (2008). The Oslo declaration on sustainable consumption. *Journal of Industrial Ecology*, *10*(1-2), 9–14.

Tuncer, F. F. (2020). The spread of fear in the globalizing world: The case of COVID-19. *Journal of Public Affairs*, *20*(4), e2162.

Tyagi, B., Choudhury, G., Vissa, N. K., Singh, J., & Tesche, M. (2021). Changing air pollution scenario during COVID-19: Redefining the hotspot regions over India. *Environmental Pollution*, *271*, 116354.

Tyler, S., & Moench, M. (2012). A framework for urban climate resilience. *Climate and Development*, *4*(4), 311–326. doi:10.1080/17565529.2012.745389

Ullah, H., Wang, Z., Bashir, S., Khan, A., Riaz, M., & Syed, N. (2021). Nexus between IT capability and green intellectual capital on sustainable businesses: Evidence from emerging economies. *Environmental Science and Pollution Research International*, *28*(22), 27825–27843. doi:10.100711356-020-12245-2 PMID:33515153

Umoh, G. I., Amah, E., & Wokocha, H. I. (2014). Management development and organizational resilience: A case study of some selected manufacturing firms in Rivers State, Nigeria. *IOSR J. Bus. Manage.*, *16*(2), 7-16.

Underdown, K. O., McCabe, C. L., & McCabe, M. F. (2022). Creating and Maintaining Balance: Work-Life Balance, Self-Care, and Mindfulness. In S. Ramlall, T. Cross, & M. Love (Eds.), *Handbook of Research on Future of Work and Education: Implications for Curriculum Delivery and Work Design* (pp. 533–545). IGI Global. doi:10.4018/978-1-7998-8275-6.ch031

UNEP. (2021). *Ecosystem restoration for people, nature and climate*. https://wedocs.unep.org/bitstream/handle/20.500.11822/36251/ERPNC.pdf

UNEP. (2022). *Noise, Blazes and Mismatches-Emerging Issues of Environmental Concern*. https://www.unep.org/frontiers

UNEP. (n.d.). *About UN Environment Programme*. Retrieved March 8, 2022, from https://www.unep.org/about-un-environment

Ungar, M. (2021). *Multisystemic resilience: adaptation and transformation in contexts of change*. Oxford University Press. doi:10.1093/oso/9780190095888.001.0001

United Nations (UN). (2015). *Transforming Our World: The 2030 Agenda for Sustainable Development A/RES/70/1*. sustainabledevelopment.un.org. https://sustainabledevelopment.un.org/content/documents/21252030%20Agenda%20for%20Sustainable%20Development%20web.pdf

United Nations (UN). (2020a). *Secretary General's Roadmap for Digital Cooperation*. https://www.un.org/en/content/digital-cooperation-roadmap/assets/pdf/Roadmap_for_Digital_Cooperation_EN.pdf

United Nations (UN). (2020b). *United Nations E-Government Survey 2020. Digital Government in the Decade of Action for Sustainable Development*. The Department of Economic and Social Affairs of the United Nations Secretariat. United Nations. https://publicadministration.un.org/egovkb/Portals/egovkb/Documents/un/2020-Survey/2020%20UN%20E-Government%20Survey%20(Full%20Report).pdf

United Nations (UN). (2021). *The Sustainable Development Goals Report 2021*. https://unstats.un.org/sdgs/report/2021/The-Sustainable-Development-Goals-Report-2021.pdf

United Nations Development Program (UNDP). (2020). *Sustainable Development Goals (SDGs)*. Booklet. United Nations Development Program.

United Nations Economic Commission for Europe (UNECE). (2021). *SPECA Workshop on digitalization of transport services (eTIR and eCMR)*. https://unece.org/transport/events/speca-workshop-digitalization-transport-services-etir-and-ecmr-nur-sultan

Vaelikangas, L., & Romme, A. G. L. (2013). How to design for strategic resilience: A case study in retailing. *Journal of Organization Design*, 2(2), 44–53. doi:10.7146/jod.7360

Vakilzadeh, K., & Haase, A. (2020). *The building blocks of organizational resilience: a review of the empirical literature*. Continuity & Resilience Review. doi:10.1108/CRR-04-2020-0002

Van der Waal, J., & Thijssens, T. (2020). Corporate involvement in sustainable development goals: Exploring the territory. *Journal of Cleaner Production*, 252, 119625. doi:10.1016/j.jclepro.2019.119625

Van der Wielen, W., & Barrios, S. (2021). Economic sentiment during the COVID pandemic: Evidence from search behaviour in the EU. *Journal of Economics and Business*, 115, 105970.

Vandekerkhof, P., Steijvers, T., Hendriks, W., & Voordeckers, W. (2018). Socio-emotional wealth separation and decision-making quality in family firm TMTs: The moderating role of psychological safety. *Journal of Management Studies*, 55(4), 648–676. https://doi.org/10.1111/joms.12277

Vandenbrande, W. W. (2019). Quality for a sustainable future. *Total Quality Management & Business Excellence*, 1–9. doi:10.1080/14783363.2019.1588724

Vanderbilt-Adriance, E., & Shaw, D. S. (2008). Conceptualizing and re-evaluating resilience across levels of risk, time, and domains of competence. *Clinical Child and Family Psychology Review*, 11(1-2), 30–58. doi:10.100710567-008-0031-2 PMID:18379875

Vargas-Hernández, J. G. (2021). Socio-Intercultural Entrepreneurship Capability Building and Development. In C. Popescu (Ed.), Handbook of Research on Novel Practices and Current Successes in Achieving the Sustainable Development Goals (pp. 259–276). IGI Global. https://doi.org/10.4018/978-1-7998-8426-2.ch013.

Vigersky, R. A., Velado, K., Zhong, A., Agrawal, P., & Cordero, T. L. (2021). The effectiveness of virtual training on the MiniMed™ 670G system in people with type 1 diabetes during the COVID-19 pandemic. *Diabetes Technology & Therapeutics*, 23(2), 104–109. doi:10.1089/dia.2020.0234 PMID:32678672

Visenescu, R. S. (2018). Russian-ASEAN cooperation in the natural gas sector. Lessons from the Russian-Vietnamese relation. *Energy Policy*, 119, 515–517. doi:10.1016/j.enpol.2018.05.006

Vogus, T., & Sutcliffe, K. (2007). Organizational Resilience: Towards a Theory and Research Agenda. Institute of Electrical and Electronic Engineers.

Von Neumann, J., & Morgenstern, O. (2007). *Theory of games and economic behavior*. Princeton university press.

Vörösmarty, C. J., Green, P., Salisbury, J., & Lammers, R. B. (2000). Global water resources: vulnerability from climate change and population growth. *Science, 289*(5477), 284-288.

Vukovic, N., Pobedinsky, V., Mityagin, S., Drozhzhin, A., & Mingaleva, Z. (2019). A study on green economy indicators and modeling: Russian context. *Sustainability*, 11(17), 4629. doi:10.3390u11174629

Vuola, M., Korkeakoski, M., Vähäkari, N., Dwyer, M. B., Hogarth, N. J., Kaivo-oja, J., Luukkanen, J., Chea, E., Thuon, T., & Phonhalath, K. (2020). What is a green economy? Review of national-level green economy policies in Cambodia and Lao PDR. *Sustainability*, *12*(16), 6664. doi:10.3390u12166664

Wachyuni, S. S., & Wiweka, K. (2020). The changes in food consumption behavior: A rapid observational study of COVID-19 pandemic. *International Journal of Management Innovation & Entrepreneurial Research*, *6*(2), 77–87.

Wagbara, O. N. (2007). How would the gas exporting countries forum influence gas trade? *Energy Policy*, *35*(2), 1224–1237. doi:10.1016/j.enpol.2006.03.017

Walker, B. H., & Salt, D. A. (2006). *Resilience Thinking: Sustaining Ecosystems and People in a Changing World*. Island Press.

Wang, X., Lei, S. M., Le, S., Yang, Y., Zhang, B., Yao, W., ... Cheng, S. (2020). Bidirectional influence of the COVID-19 pandemic lockdowns on health behaviors and quality of life among Chinese adults. *International Journal of Environmental Research and Public Health*, *17*(15), 5575.

Watanabe, T. (2020). *The responses of consumption and prices in Japan to the COVID-19 crisis and the Tohoku Earthquake*. https://academiccommons.columbia.edu/doi/10.7916/d8-qs4v-q792

Watts, G., & Paciga, J. J. (2011). Conscious Adaptation: Building Resilient Organizations. In T. Carmichael (Ed.), *Complex Adaptive Systems: Energy, Information, and Intelligence*. Arlington VA: AAAI Fall Symposium Series.

Web, M. D. (2020). *Covid-19 is giving us a lesson-and a warning-about our environment*. https://blogs.webmd.com/webmd-doctors/20200422/covid19-is-giving-us-a-lession-and-a-warning-about-our-environment

Weick, K. E., & Sutcliffe, K. M. (2007). Managing the unexpected: Resilient performance in an age of uncertainty (2nd ed.). San Francisco, CA: Jossey-Bass.

Weick, K. E., & Roberts, K. H. (1993). Collective mind in organizations: Heedful interrelating on flight decks. *Administrative Science Quarterly*, *38*(3), 357–381. doi:10.2307/2393372

Weick, K. E., & Sutcliffe, K. (2003). Hospitals as Cultures of Entrapment: A Re-Analysis of the Bristol Royal Infirmary. *California Management Review*, *45*(2), 73–84. doi:10.2307/41166166

Weick, K. E., & Sutcliffe, K. M. (2001). *Managing the Unexpected: Assuring High Performance in an Age of Complexity*. Jossey-Bass.

Weick, K. E., Sutcliffe, K. M., & Obstfeld, D. (2005). Organizing and the process of sensemaking. *Organization Science*, *16*(4), 409–421. doi:10.1287/orsc.1050.0133

Wendtlandt, M., & Wicker, P. (2021). The effects of sport activities and environmentally sustainable behaviors on subjective well-being: A comparison before and during COVID-19. *Frontiers in Sports and Active Living*, *3*, 659837.

Whiteman, G., & Cooper, W. H. (2011). Ecological sensemaking. *Academy of Management Journal*, *43*, 1265–1282.

Whiteman, W. E. (1998). *Training and educating army officers for the 21st Century: Implications for the United States Military Academy*. Defense Technical Information Center.

Wicker, P., Filo, K., & Cuskelly, G. (2013). Organizational resilience of community sport clubs impacted by natural disasters. *J. Sport Manage.*, *27*(6), 510-525.

Wiese, A., Luke, R., Heyns, G. J., & Pisa, N. M. (2015). The integration of lean, green, and best practice business principles. *Journal of Transport and Supply Chain Management*, *9*(1), 192–202.

Wildavsky, A. (1988). *Searching for Safety*. Transaction Press.

Willems, J. J., Busscher, T., van den Brink, M., & Arts, J. (2018). Anticipating water infrastructure renewal: A framing perspective on organizational learning in public agencies. *Environment and Planning C. Politics and Space*, *36*(6), 1088–1108.

Willerton, J. P., Goertz, G., & Slobodchikoff, M. O. (2015). Mistrust and hegemony: Regional institutional design, the FSU-CIS, and Russia. *International Area Studies Review*, *18*(1), 26–52. doi:10.1177/2233865914562256

Williams, T. A., Gruber, D. A., Sutcliffe, K. M., Shepherd, D. A., & Zhao, E. Y. (2017). Organizational response to adversity: Fusing crisis management and resilience research streams. *The Academy of Management Annals*, *11*(2), 733–769. doi:10.5465/annals.2015.0134

Wood, A. D., Mason, C. F., & Finnoff, D. (2016). OPEC, the Seven Sisters, and oil market dominance: An evolutionary game theory and agent-based modeling approach. *Journal of Economic Behavior & Organization*, *132*, 66–78. doi:10.1016/j.jebo.2016.06.011

Woods, D., & Hollnagel, E. (2006). *Joint Cognitive Systems: Patterns in Cognitive Systems Engineering*. Taylor and Francis. doi:10.1201/9781420005684

World Bank. (2012). *Inclusive green growth: The pathway to sustainable development*. The World Bank.

World Health Organization (WHO). (2005). *Promoting Mental Health. Concepts. Emerging Evidence. Practice*. A Report of the World Health Organization, Department of Mental Health and Substance Abuse in collaboration with the Victorian Health Promotion Foundation and The University of Melbourne. https://www.who.int/mental_health/evidence/MH_Promotion_Book.pdf

Wormer, B. A., Augenstein, V. A., Carpenter, C. L., Burton, P. V., Yokeley, W. T., Prabhu, A. S., Harris, B., Norton, S., Klima, D. A., Lincourt, A. E., & Heniford, B. T. (2013). The green operating room: Simple changes to reduce cost and our carbon footprint. *The American Surgeon*, *79*(7), 666–671. doi:10.1177/000313481307900708 PMID:23815997

Wosik, J., Fudim, M., Cameron, B., Gellad, Z. F., Cho, A., Phinney, D., Curtis, S., Roman, M., Poon, E. G., Ferranti, J., Katz, J. N., & Tcheng, J. (2020). Telehealth transformation: COVID-19 and the rise of virtual care. *Journal of the American Medical Informatics Association: JAMIA*, *27*(6), 957–962. doi:10.1093/jamia/ocaa067 PMID:32311034

Wright, C., & Nyberg, D. (2014). Creative self-destruction: Corporate responses to climate change as political myths. *Environmental Politics*, *23*(2), 205–223.

Wu, L., Subramanian, N., Abdulrahman, M. D., Liu, C., Lai, K., & Pawar, K. S. (2015). The impact of integrated practices of lean, green, and social management systems on firm sustainability performance-evidence from Chinese fashion auto-parts suppliers. *Sustainability*, *7*(4), 3838–3858.

Xiao, S., Dong, H., Geng, Y., & Brander, M. (2018). An overview of China's recyclable waste recycling and recommendations for integrated solutions. *Resources, Conservation and Recycling*, *134*, 112–120. doi:10.1016/j.resconrec.2018.02.032

Xiao, Y., & Torok, M. E. (2020). Taking the right measures to control COVID-19. *The Lancet. Infectious Diseases*, *20*(5), 523–524. doi:10.1016/S1473-3099(20)30152-3 PMID:32145766

Xie, J., & Saltzman, S. (2000). Environmental policy analysis: An environmental computable general-equilibrium approach for developing countries. *Journal of Policy Modeling*, *22*(4), 453–489. doi:10.1016/S0161-8938(97)00076-8

Xu, X., Maki, A., Chen, C., Dong, B., & Day, J. K. (2017). Investigating willingness to save energy and communication about energy use in the American workplace with the attitude-behavior-context model. *Energy Research & Social Science*, *32*, 13–22. doi:10.1016/j.erss.2017.02.011

Yadav, G., Luthra, S., Jakhar, S. K., Mangla, S. K., & Rai, D. P. (2020). A framework to overcome sustainable supply chain challenges through solution measures of industry 4.0 and circular economy: An automotive case. *Journal of Cleaner Production*, *254*, 120112. doi:10.1016/j.jclepro.2020.120112

Yadiati, W., Nissa, N., Paulus, S., Suharman, H., & Meiryani, M. (2019). The role of green intellectual capital and organizational reputation in influencing environmental performance. *International Journal of Energy Economics and Policy*, *9*(3), 261–267. doi:10.32479/ijeep.7752

Yang, C., Peijun, L., Lupi, C., Yangzhao, S., Diandou, X., Qian, F., & Shasha, F. (2009). Sustainable management measures for healthcare waste in China. *Waste Management (New York, N.Y.)*, *29*(6), 1996–2004. doi:10.1016/j.wasman.2008.11.031 PMID:19157834

Yaw, D. C. (2008). Tools for transfer. *Industrial and Commercial Training*, *40*(3), 152–155. doi:10.1108/00197850810868658

Yawson, R. (2020). Strategic flexibility analysis of HRD research and practice post COVID-19 pandemic. *Human Resource Development International*, *23*(4), 406–417. doi:10.1080/13678868.2020.1779169

Yawson, R. M., & Greiman, B. C. (2016). A systems approach to identify skill needs for agrifood nanotechnology: A multiphase mixed methods study. *Human Resource Development Quarterly*, *27*(4), 517–545. doi:10.1002/hrdq.21266

Yawson, R. M., & Greiman, B. C. (2017). Strategic flexibility analysis of agrifood nanotechnology skill needs identification. *Technological Forecasting and Social Change*, *118*, 184–194. doi:10.1016/j.techfore.2017.02.019

Yelp. (2020). *Yelp: Coronavirus economic impact report*. https://blog.yelp.com/news/yelp-coronavirus-economic-impact-report/

Yen, Y. X., & Yen, S. Y. (2012). Top-management's role in adopting green purchasing standards in high-tech industrial firms. *Journal of Business Research*, *65*(7), 951–959.

Yong, J., Yusliza, M., Ramayah, T., & Fawehinmi, O. (2019). Nexus between green intellectual capital and green human resource management. *Journal of Cleaner Production*, *215*, 364–374. doi:10.1016/j.jclepro.2018.12.306

York, R., Rosa, E. A., & Dietz, T. (2003). STIRPAT, IPAT and ImPACT: Analytic tools for unpacking the driving forces of environmental impacts. *Ecological Economics*, *46*(3), 351–365. doi:10.1016/S0921-8009(03)00188-5

Young, O. (2010). *Institutional dynamics: Emergent patters in international environmental governance*. MIT Press. doi:10.7551/mitpress/8457.001.0001

Yusliza, M., Yong, J., Tanveer, M., Ramayah, T., Faezah, J., & Muhammad, Z. (2020). A structural model of the impact of green intellectual capital on sustainable performance. *Journal of Cleaner Production*, *249*, 119334. doi:10.1016/j.jclepro.2019.119334

Yusoff, Y., Omar, M., Zaman, M., & Samad, S. (2019). Do all elements of green intellectual capital contribute toward business sustainability? Evidence from the Malaysian context using the Partial Least Squares method. *Journal of Cleaner Production*, *234*, 626–637. doi:10.1016/j.jclepro.2019.06.153

Zahra, S. A., Sapienza, H. J., & Davidsson, P. (2006). Entrepreneurship and Dynamic Capabilities: A review, model, and research agenda. *Journal of Management Studies*, *43*(4), 917–955. doi:10.1111/j.1467-6486.2006.00616.x

Zainudin, N., Lau, J. L., & Munusami, C. (2020). Micro-Macro Measurements of Sustainability BT - Affordable and Clean Energy. Springer International Publishing. doi:10.1007/978-3-319-71057-0_91-1

Zambrano-Monserrate, M. A., Ruano, M. A., & Sanchez-Alcalde, L. (2020). Indirect effects of COVID-19 on the environment. *The Science of the Total Environment*, *728*, 138813.

Zambrano-Monserrate, M. A., Silva-Zambrano, C. A., & Ruano, M. A. (2018). The economic value of natural protected areas in Ecuador: A case of Villamil Beach National Recreation Area. *Ocean and Coastal Management*, *157*, 193–202. doi:10.1016/j.ocecoaman.2018.02.020

Zamoum, K., & Gorpe, S. T. (2021). Corporate social responsibility in the Emirati Vision Strategy for year 2021. *Proceedings CSRCOM 2017 The 4th International CSR Communication Conference Austrian Academy of Sciences*.

Zelezny, L. C., Chua, P. P., & Aldrich, C. (2000). Elaborating on gender differences in environmentalism. *The Journal of Social Issues*, *56*(3), 443–457. doi:10.1111/0022-4537.00177

Zeus, J. H., & Reif, K. (1990). Evolution of Environmental Attitudes in the European Community. *Scandinavian Political Studies*, *13*(2), 119–146. doi:10.1111/j.1467-9477.1990.tb00433.x

Zhang, B., Wang, B., & Wang, Z. (2017). Role of renewable energy and non-renewable energy consumption on EKC: Evidence from Pakistan. *Journal of Cleaner Production*, *156*, 855–864. doi:10.1016/j.jclepro.2017.03.203

Zhang, B., Wang, Z., & Lai, K. H. (2015). Mediating effect of managers' environmental concern: Bridge between external pressures and firms' practices of energy conservation in China. *Journal of Environmental Psychology*, *43*, 203–215.

Zhang, X., Shao, X., Jeong, E., & Olson, E. (2021). I am worth more than you think I am: Investigating the effects of upcycling on event attendees' recycling intention. *International Journal of Hospitality Management*, *94*, 102888.

Zhang, Y., Sun, J., Yang, Z., & Wang, Y. (2020). Critical success factors of green innovation: Technology, organization and environment readiness. *Journal of Cleaner Production*, *264*, 121701. doi:10.1016/j.jclepro.2020.121701

Zhao, H., Guo, S., & Zhao, H. (2018). Impacts of GDP, fossil fuel energy consumption, energy consumption intensity, and economic structure on SO2 emissions: A multi-variate panel data model analysis on selected Chinese provinces. *Sustainability*, *10*(3), 657. doi:10.3390u10030657

Zhao, M., Liu, F., Song, Y., & Geng, J. (2020). Impact of air pollution regulation and technological investment on sustainable development of green economy in Eastern China: Empirical analysis with panel data approach. *Sustainability*, *12*(8), 3073. doi:10.3390u12083073

Zientara, P., & Zamojska, A. (2018). Green organizational climates and employee pro-environmental behaviour in the hotel industry. *Journal of Sustainable Tourism*, 26.

Zollo, M., & Winter, S. G. (2002). Deliberate learning and the evolution of dynamic capabilities. *Org. Sci.*, *13*(3), 339-351.

Zouganeli, S., Trihas, N., Antonaki, M., & Kladou, S. (2012). Aspects of sustainability in the destination branding process: A bottom-up approach. *Journal of Hospitality Marketing & Management*, *2012*(21), 739–757.

Zsidisin, G., & Wagner, S. (2010). Are the perceptions coming true? The moderating role of supply chain resilience in the occurrence of disruptions. *Journal of Business Logistics*, *31*, 1–20. doi:10.1002/j.2158-1592.2010.tb00140.x

About the Contributors

Cristina Raluca Gh. Popescu is Full-Professor Habil. at the University of Bucharest, Bucharest, Romania and PhD. Supervisor and Doctoral School Member at The Bucharest University of Economic Studies, Bucharest, Romania. Having more than 21 years of experience, focuses on helping students learn and apply the subjects more effectively, and centers on improving scientific research excellence. Values a special environment where her in-depth knowledge of creative thinking and academic writing can help deliver accurate research results. She is skilled in Business Administration, Economics, Management, Accounting, and Audit. Collaborations: The National Institute for Research and Development in Environmental Protection (I.N.C.D.P.M.), Romania; National Research and Development Institute for Gas Turbines COMOTI, Romania; University of Craiova, Romania; Ministry of Research and Innovation, Romania. She is Member of Chamber of Financial Auditors of Romania (CAFR), Romania as Financial Auditor, and Member of Authority for the Public Oversight of the Statutory Audit Activity (ASPAAS), Ministry of Public Finance, Romania as Financial auditor. Single author and coauthor of more than 287 scientific works, with national and international publishers, having national and international coauthors: books, book chapters, articles, conference papers. She has more than 860 citations in national and international publications. Member of Scientific Committee (SC): International Congress of Management, Economy and Policy (ICOMEP), Turkey; Symposium on Migration and Asylum in Turkey, Tekirdağ Namık Kemal Üniversitesi (Tekirdag Namık Kemal University), Turkey; International Congress "Multidimensional Sustainability: Transitions and Convergences", Instituto Superior Politécnico Gaya (ISPGAYA), Portugal. Editor and Editorial Advisory Board (EAB) member: IGI Global – Publishing House (Pennsylvania, USA). Guest Editor and Academic Editor for Multidisciplinary Digital Publishing Institute (MDPI, Basel, Switzerland): Mathematics, Journal of Risk and Financial Management (JRFM), Businesses. Topic Editor for Multidisciplinary Digital Publishing Institute (MDPI, Basel, Switzerland): Mathematics, Businesses. Associate Editor for The International Academy of Organizational Behavior Management (IAOBM): International Journal of the Academy of Organizational Behavior Management (IJAOBM); The International Journal of Management Science and Information Technology (IJMSIT). Editorial Advisory Board (EAB) Member for North American Institute of Science and Information Technology (NAISIT) (The International Journal of Management Science and Information Technology (IJMSIT)); Journal of Emerging Economies and Policy (JOEEP). Review Board member: IBIMA Conferences and IBIMA Publishing, USA (Journal of E-Government Studies and Best Practices, The MENA Journal of Business Case Studies); International Conference on Decision Making for Small and Medium-Sized Enterprises (DEMSME 2021); IGI Global – Publishing House (Pennsylvania, USA); University of Bucharest (International Journal of Health Economics (IJHE)); Multidisciplinary Digital Publishing Institute (MDPI, Basel, Switzerland) (Sustainability, Symmetry, Journal of Risk and Financial Management (JRFM), Mathematics, Economies, Risks, Journal of Open Innovation: Technology, Market, and Complexity (JOItmC), Journal of Administrative Sciences, World, Informatics, Water, Agriculture, Businesses, Microorganisms, Energies, Agronomy, Urban Science). Invited reviewer: Management Decision (MD), Sustainable Development (SD), Corporate Social Responsibility & Environmental Management (CSREM), Journal of Business Economics and Management (JBEM), Engineering Economics (Inzinerine Ekonomika), International Journal of Sustainable Development and Planning (IJSDP), Transformations in Business & Economics (TIBE), Open Research Europe (ORE), Coffee Science (CS).

* * *

Esna Betül Buğday is an Assistant Professor at Hacettepe University, Department of Family and Consumer Sciences. She completed her master's study at Gazi University and received her Ph.D. at Hacettepe University, Department of Family and Consumer Sciences. After receiving her Ph.D., she has been to the University of Autonoma as a visiting scholar. She has attended several international conferences and published numerous papers in national and international scientific journals. Her research interests include Consumer Behavior, Conscious Consumption, Sustainable Consumption, and Consumer Education. Also, since 2016, she has been serving as a deputy manager of the Center of Consumer and Market Research, Consulting, Test, and Education.

Ramnath Dixit is a Behavioral Training Facilitator and Proprietor at Squirrel Interventions, a training and development entity. He has been conducting behavioral training workshops for global organizations on areas of leadership, communication, customer service, team building and various other topics of business relevance. In a career spanning over 15 years he has delivered trainings at over 125 organizations spanning 25 industry verticals and covering more than 7000 participants. Ramnath has to his credit a research paper related to Training & Development, published in a Scopus Indexed Journal. Some of his noteworthy credentials include the following: Life-member and Diploma in Training & Development (Dip. T & D from ISTD, New Delhi, India), Certified Behavioral Trainer (Dale Carnegie Training, India), Neuro-linguistic Practitioner (School of Excellence, India) and Belbin Team Role Assessor (CERT, India). He is currently pursuing his research from Symbiosis International (Deemed University) (SIU), Pune, India.

Arturo Luque is full professor at the Technical University of Manabí, Ecuador, and member of Euro-Mediterranean Observatory on Public Policies and Democratic Quality at the University King Juan Carlos (Spain) and visiting Professor at the University of Rosario, Colombia. He holds a Ph.D. in Social Sciences and Law and a Master of two years about Labor Relations. He supervises several doctoral theses (Ph.D.) in Córdoba (Spain) and in the Basque Country (GEZKI Institute) like a director and co-director. It has 69 indexed articles and his latest publications includes topics about digitalization (Practicality, support or premeditated calculation in the digital age: the case of Ecuador), Globalization (Analysis of the concept of informal economy through 102 definitions: legality or necessity), corporate social (Ir)responsibility (How corporate social (ir)responsibility in the textile sector is defined, and its impact on ethical sustainability: An analysis of 133 concepts), transnational companies (The transnational textile companies relationship with environment: a Delphi analysis approach) and their relations with ethics (Corruption in the transnational textile industry: an exception or the rule?), social economy and cooperative system like economic alternative (Socially responsible public management: case spinning

About the Contributors

development in Ecuador), media analysis and social conflicts (Analysis of the indigenous uprising of Ecuador, 2019: between a measured legal response and lawfare, 2019) and sustainability (Public Strategy and Eco-Social Engagement in Latin American States: An Analysis of Complex Networks Arising from Their Constitutions). Arturo Luque, Technical University of Manabí, Portoviejo, (Ecuador) and Euro-Mediterranean Observatory on Public Policies and Democratic Quality, Rey Juan Carlos University (Spain). https://orcid.org/0000-0002-7447-7560.

María José Foncubierta-Rodríguez has been developing research, teaching and management functions since its incorporation to the university. Regarding research activity, she has published articles in specialized journals in her area of knowledge, all of them integrated into the main databases (SSCI, SCOPUS, LATINDEX, Scielo, etc.). In addition, she has published several book chapters in different prestigious publishers. Her research activity is complemented with the actively participates in various scientific congress (national and international), as well as their participation in research projects financed by public funding. These projects are about human resources competences as a general line: the importance of on-the-job training, professional skills, gender perspective of competences to work, and, currently, on intellectual capital in academic groups. She develops two novel lines of research, focused on the Principal Investigator of the research teams, and on the competences for Happiness Management at work.

Esra Karapınar Kocağ received her PhD in Economics from University of Reading in the UK in 2019. After finishing her PhD, she worked as a lecturer in Economics Department at Gümüşhane University/Turkey between 2019-2021. Since then, she has been working as an Assistant Professor in Social Service and Counselling Department at Gümüşhane University/Turkey. Her research area covers microeconomics, migration economics, labour economics, and welfare economics.

Bartolomé Marco-Lajara (PhD) is Professor at the University of Alicante. His research interests are strategic management and tourism management. He is the author of several books, book chapters and international articles related to the areas above mentioned. He is a member of the Tourism Research Institute at the University of Alicante since its foundation and the main researcher of the European project 'Next Tourism Generation Alliance' at his University, as well as of the public competitive project for the creation of the Tourist Observatory of the Valencian Community (Spain). He has taken part in others public and private projects, such as the development of the strategic plan of the Alicante province for the period 2010-2020. He is the Head of the Department of Management at the University of Alicante, and previously was the Assistant Dean of the Economics Faculty for the Business Degree.

Javier Martínez Falcó is Assistant Professor in the Department of Management at the University of Alicante. In the field of research, he focuses his interest on issues related to the Strategic Management of the Company, specifically in the areas of Knowledge Management and Corporate Sustainability of wine companies, on which he has written several publications in the form of articles, book chapters and contributions to conferences. He has also participated in several national research projects and teaches Strategic Management on the ADE, TADE and DADE degree courses.

Luis A. Millan-Tudela is assistant professor at University of Alicante. Awarded as one of the top graduates in mechanical engineering in Spain (2020), he redirected his career taking a Master of Business Administration. He is currently developing his doctorate dissertation while giving management classes.

He focuses his research on business failure and survival, all within the Department of Management at University of Alicante.

Nima Norouzi graduated his primary, high school, and college education from the Iranian special NODET (National organization for Intellectual people) primary Education system. he took the national university entrance exam and, with rank 365 (among 164000), entered the Amirkabir University of Technology and started his education in system management and engineering in the B.Sc. degree. After his graduation with his B.Sc. degree, and because of his various educational and research field successes, he has been appreciated many times by the university. After that, he took a master's in energy system engineering in one year, and he got a green economics degree at Bournemouth University, UK. Then got his Ph.D. in Energy and Economics from Amirkabir university. Nima currently does research in techno-economic, techno-environmental, techno-social, and legal aspects of Energy and natural resources economics.

Sajedeh Rabipour is one of the youngest researchers in the field of healthcare policy. Her research mainly covers fields of political healthcare economy and public healthcare system.

Rafael Ravina-Ripoll holds a PhD in History since 2015. He has been a Professor of Business Organisation at the University of Cadiz (Spain) since 2008-1996. His priority lines of research are happiness, happiness management, well-being and business. He is the author of more than 100 research papers published in several indexed academic journals (Corporate Governance, Quality & Quantity, Entrepreneurship and Sustainability Issues, Polish Journal of Management Studies, International Journal of Entrepreneurship, International Journal. Environmental Research Public Health, Journal of Risk and Financial Management, Energies, International Journal of Business Environment, Academy of Entrepreneurship Journal, Journal of Legal, Ethical and Regulatory Issues, Frontiers in Psychology, Sustainability, Retos, etc.) and in numerous chapters published in the most relevant international publishing houses in economics (Springer, Peter Lang, Tirant lo Blanch, Aranzadi, Akal, Narcea, Comares, Dykinson, etc.). According to the Google Scholar database, his research has more than 300 citations, and his h-index is equal to 11. He is a founding member of the International University Network of Happiness and the Research Institute for Sustainable Social Development of the University of Cadiz (INDESS), guest editor of Energies and Journal Corporate Governance. He is on the editorial board of Decision Analytics Journal and Healthcare Analytics, Retos, Cuadernos de Administración and Revista Jurídicas CUC. He is also the Director of the University Research Group Happiness Management, Creativity and Well-being in Industry 4.0 from social sciences and humanities.

Vinita Sinha is a Professor (OB & HR) at Symbiosis Center of Management & Human Resource Development, a constituent of Symbiosis International University, Pune, India. She is doctorate in Psychology and Masters in Psychology with specialization in Organizational Behavior. She also holds Post Graduate Diploma in Human Resource Management, Post Graduate Diploma in Health Psychology & Behavior Modification and Masters Diploma in Higher Education and Andragogy. She has 14 years of work experience in core teaching and research. She is also a recognized research supervisor at Symbiosis International University. Her areas of interest in teaching and research stretch out from Psychology to OB & HR viz. evolving trends in management and education, social media, accreditation, psychological issues at work, quality aspects of work, psychological well-being, work stress, role stress, attrition trends,

About the Contributors

etc. She has presented many papers in international conferences and published more than 30 research papers in refereed international and national journals of repute.

Niray Tunçel is working as an Assistant Professor at Hacettepe University, Department of Business Administration. She earned a master's degree in Marketing at Bahçeşehir University. Then, she received her Ph.D. in Business Administration from Hacettepe University. In her doctoral period, she spent a semester at the University of Primorska conducting a cross-cultural study. She also researched at the University of Mannheim as a visiting fellow after her Ph.D. Besides, she has participated in various international conferences, been involved in different research projects, and published several papers in international scientific journals. Her research interests include Consumer Behavior, Consumer Ethics, Digital Marketing, Sharing Economy, and Sustainable Consumption.

José G. Vargas-Hernández, M.B.A., Ph.D., Member of the National System of Researchers of Mexico and a research professor at Tecnológico Mario Molina Unidad Zapopan formerly at University Center for Economic and Managerial Sciences, University of Guadalajara. Professor Vargas-Hernández has a Ph. D. in Public Administration and a Ph.D. in Organizational Economics. He has undertaken studies in Organisational Behaviour and has a Master of Business Administration, published four books and more than 200 papers in international journals and reviews (some translated to English, French, German, Portuguese, Farsi, Chinese, etc.) and more than 300 essays in national journals and reviews. He has obtained several international Awards and recognition.

Patrocinio Zaragoza-Sáez (PhD, University of Alicante, Spain) is a Professor at the Department of Management at the University of Alicante, Spain. She is the Coordinator of the University Master's Degree in Tourism Management and Planning. Her primary research interests are strategic management, knowledge management and intellectual capital, tourist districts, ambidexterity and tourism industry. She has published research papers in international journals including Journal of Business Research, Journal of Knowledge Management, Journal of Intellectual Capital, Journal of Sustainable Tourism, Current Issues in Tourism, Tourism Management, International Journal of Contemporary Hospitality Management, Knowledge Management Research and Practice and Business Strategy & Environment, among others.

Index

A

Assembly of Gas Exporting Countries 225

B

business 1-5, 8-9, 11, 22-23, 26-27, 29-32, 54, 58, 60-68, 71-76, 79, 81, 84-95, 103, 109, 112, 117, 121, 123, 125-126, 141, 145, 156, 159-160, 162, 166-172, 174, 176-179, 182-184, 186, 188-190, 193-196, 199-200, 220, 223, 239, 242, 275, 278-279, 281-282, 288-289, 292-298, 300, 304, 307-308, 310-313, 315-316, 319, 325, 328, 330-332, 334-336

C

case study 26, 56-57, 88-93, 111-112, 115, 122-124, 143, 161-162, 182, 275, 277, 294, 331, 335-336
Circular Economics 143
circular economy 52, 117, 121, 129, 141, 144-149, 154-156, 158-164, 172, 179-181, 223, 242, 278
circularity 141, 160, 164, 223, 242, 278
climate change 27, 43, 46-47, 50, 52-53, 55, 67-68, 75, 77, 85, 94-96, 112, 120-121, 126, 131, 139-143, 161, 164-165, 222-224, 242-245, 249, 255-258, 263-264, 266, 270, 272-273, 276, 278-279, 295, 301, 303, 306-312, 314-316, 323
Continuously Changing Environment 31
COVID-19 2, 9, 25, 29, 31, 36-58, 60-61, 64-65, 67-69, 72, 76-78, 86, 88-89, 94-98, 102-110, 124, 128, 156, 160-162, 166-167, 169-174, 176-180, 183-187, 190, 192, 194-199, 201-202, 276-277, 280-283, 289-290, 294-295
creativity 1-2, 22-23, 25, 29, 31, 65, 71, 75, 85, 87-89, 113, 284-285, 288, 296, 309, 325, 335
Creativity in Business 31, 89

D

decision-making 6, 30, 33, 86, 144, 177, 244, 270, 311, 336
degradation 98, 100, 138, 142, 144, 165, 224, 243-246, 254-256, 260, 264, 269, 274, 279, 319
development theory 204
Digital Business Process Management (DBPM) 170, 183
Digital Business Processes (DBP) 170, 183
Digital Organization (DO) in the Post-COVID-19 Era 170, 183
Digital Skills Transformation (DST) in the Post-COVID-19 Era 169, 184
digitalization 27, 166-174, 177-180, 183-184, 195
digitalization to restart the economy 166-167, 169, 171-172, 174, 177-180, 184
Do It Yourself 42, 58
Do It Yourself Activities 58
DYNAMIC RESILIENT CAPABILITY 317-318

E

Eco commerce 141, 223, 242, 278
Ecological Economics 140, 142, 224, 243, 258, 274-275, 279
economic growth 37, 65, 68, 71, 77, 85, 90-92, 95-96, 99-103, 105-106, 109-110, 127, 131-132, 143-144, 149-150, 155, 160, 168, 171, 175, 184, 204-205, 207-209, 213-215, 218, 220-223, 247, 258, 265-267, 269-270, 274-275, 281, 304, 308-309
Eco-Tariffs 141, 223, 242, 278
Effects of Association of Socio-Demographic Variables on the Leader's Competencies 1-3, 26, 31
emissions trading 141, 223, 242, 278
employee training 185, 187, 189, 200
energy consumption 36, 39-41, 48-51, 54, 56, 101-102, 110, 130, 132-135, 138, 157, 162-163, 264, 266-267, 269-271, 273-274, 277, 303-304, 307

Index

Energy Economics 125, 130, 140, 143, 235, 240-241, 258, 274
energy intensity 110, 130, 135, 137-138
environment 1-2, 4-5, 9, 18, 22-23, 25-26, 31, 35, 37, 39, 43-50, 52-58, 60-61, 63-68, 71-76, 79, 84-85, 90, 93-95, 98, 100-101, 110, 112-113, 115, 117, 120, 123, 126-127, 129, 131-132, 138-144, 148-149, 159-162, 166-174, 177-179, 181, 184, 186, 188-189, 191-193, 197-199, 220-224, 226, 242-250, 252-260, 264-266, 269-275, 277-280, 282-284, 286-287, 289, 295, 297, 300, 304, 306-307, 309-314, 317-323, 325-328, 330, 333-334, 337
environmental degradation 98, 100, 138, 142, 144, 165, 224, 243-246, 254-256, 260, 269, 274, 279, 319
environmental enterprise 141, 223, 242, 279
environmental planning 275, 299-300, 309
Environmental-friendly Behaviour 244
environmentally friendly consumption 36, 43, 49

G

gas trade 161, 225-226, 232, 238, 241, 276
global economic environment 166-169, 171-174, 177-179, 184
Global Economic Environment (GEE) for Sustainable Development (SD) 171, 184
global knowledge societies (GKS) for sustainable development (SD) 65-66, 71, 75-76, 84, 94-95
Green Economics 130, 140-141, 143, 163-164, 263, 271-273, 278
green economy 142, 204, 224, 243, 263-277, 279, 308-309
Green Human Capital 111, 113, 126, 128
green intellectual capital 111-112, 116, 118, 123-126, 128
Green politics 142, 224, 243, 279
green practices 299-301, 303-306, 311, 313-314
Green Relational Capital 111, 113, 126, 129
Green Structural Capital 111, 113, 126, 128
green, resilient, and inclusive development (GRID) 66-68, 75-76, 84, 94-95
greenhouse gases 142, 157, 224, 243, 263, 270, 279, 308

H

Health Financing 97
Healthcare economics 97
Healthcare management 97
Healthcare policy 97
Human Resource 1, 60, 65, 71, 73, 75, 85, 114, 124-125, 185, 187, 196-202, 288, 293, 296, 311-315, 333
Human Resource Development (HRD) 202
human resources 2-3, 6, 8, 10, 22-25, 64-65, 75, 85, 155, 166-169, 171-172, 174, 184, 186, 194, 269, 288, 301, 309, 326, 333

I

Information and Communications Technology (ICT) 5, 202
innovation 1-2, 22-23, 25, 29, 31, 34, 54, 58, 60, 65, 71, 73, 75, 85, 87-92, 112-114, 123-124, 126, 131, 149, 166-167, 172, 175-176, 181-182, 274, 277, 282, 284-286, 290-292, 296-297, 300-304, 306-309, 313-314, 322-323, 330, 332, 336
intangible assets 22, 64, 75, 85, 113, 126, 166-167, 172
Intellectual Capital 1, 22, 25, 27, 60, 64-65, 71, 73, 75, 85, 87-90, 111-113, 116, 118, 123-126, 128, 166-167, 172, 182
ISO 14000 116-117, 126

K

knowledge 1-5, 9, 22-23, 31, 33, 36-37, 40-41, 48-50, 60-63, 65-66, 68, 71, 73, 75-76, 78, 80-81, 83-86, 89-90, 92, 94-95, 111-114, 116-117, 121, 123, 126, 128, 166-167, 170-172, 174, 178-180, 183-187, 189-195, 199, 203, 254-255, 275, 284-285, 287-288, 290, 296, 300, 306, 308-309, 318, 324-326, 328

L

leadership 1-6, 8-9, 18, 22-35, 60-61, 65, 71, 73, 75, 85, 91, 93, 175, 177-178, 195, 197, 200, 284, 287-288, 297, 316, 321-324, 336
Leadership in the Post-COVID-19 Era 31
learning and development 185-193, 203, 306
learning transfer 185-187, 191-192, 195, 201-203
low-carbon economy 142, 224, 243, 279, 309

M

marketing management 299-300, 306, 309, 315, 336
Middle East 103, 135, 143, 145, 222, 267, 270
mindfulness 22-23, 29, 31, 60-69, 71-76, 78-88, 93-95
mindfulness into the business environment 60, 64-65, 67-68, 72, 74-76, 84, 95
mindfulness movement in organizations 60-65, 68, 71-73, 75-76, 78, 80-83, 85, 95

N

natural gas 41, 49, 106, 161, 225-228, 231-242, 276
natural resource economics 142, 164, 224, 243, 279
natural resources 36-37, 59, 84, 100, 120, 142, 145-146, 148. 157-158, 162, 164-165, 204, 208, 221-222, 224, 243, 263-265, 269-270, 275, 279, 300, 303, 307, 319, 335
natural sources 36, 38, 40-41, 48-50, 249
New Leadership for a New Era 1-3, 8-9, 22-23, 26, 31

O

ordered probit model 247, 252, 256, 260
organizational culture 2, 22, 65, 71, 73, 75, 85, 117, 121, 199, 287-288, 305-306, 309, 314-315, 324
organizational learning 192, 306, 317, 322-326, 328-329, 333-334, 337
organizational resilience 190, 280-293, 295-298, 317-328, 330-337

P

pandemic 2, 9, 26, 29, 31, 36-58, 60-61, 64-65, 67-69, 72, 76-78, 88-89, 94-97, 110, 162, 166-167, 169-170, 172-173, 177-178, 180, 183-190, 193-198, 201-202, 277, 280-281, 283, 289, 295
Pandemic costs 97
policing 68, 87, 299-300, 309
Powerful Leaders 31
preferences 44, 125, 170, 183, 211, 244-247, 249, 252, 254-256, 258
pro-environmental behaviour 256, 260, 316
Promoting Mental Health 75-76, 79, 94-95

R

Ranking of Assembly Members 225
recycling 41-43, 47-49, 54, 57-58, 128, 141, 144-150, 155, 157-161, 163-165, 223, 235-236, 242, 271-272, 278, 301, 304-305, 307, 312
renewable energies 263-264, 273
renewable energy market 263, 273
resilience and inclusive growth 68, 75, 77, 84, 95
restart the economy 166-169, 171-172, 174, 177-180, 184
reuse 38, 42, 49, 54, 117, 141, 144-145, 148, 155, 157, 164-165, 223, 242, 278
reusing 41-43, 49, 59, 149, 304

S

SMEs 4, 27, 186, 197, 280-283, 289-290, 292, 294-295, 298, 327, 331
STIRPAT model 130, 133-135, 139
Strategic Analysis 317
strategic change 288, 296-297, 299-300, 308-309, 326, 329, 332, 335
strategies 25, 29, 56, 67-68, 76-77, 79, 85, 87-89, 95-96, 121, 157, 159-161, 163, 170, 172-173, 182, 186, 190, 193, 196-197, 233, 239, 258, 263, 270, 276, 280, 282, 285-290, 292, 301-302, 304-305, 307, 310-311, 315, 317, 323, 326-327, 334, 336
sustainability 27, 37-38, 45-47, 51-57, 67, 76, 84, 88-89, 91, 93-94, 112, 116-117, 121, 123-129, 131-132, 139, 142-143, 159-163, 165, 171, 179, 181, 184, 194-195, 198, 224, 239-240, 243, 245-246, 255, 257-259, 265-266, 274-277, 279, 293-294, 300-301, 304-309, 311-312, 314-316, 321, 334
Sustainable city 130
sustainable consumption 36-38, 42, 44, 47-53, 56-59
Sustainable Development 2, 22-23, 27, 30-31, 37-38, 47, 55, 60-69, 71-73, 75-81, 83-85, 87-90, 92-96, 99, 111-114, 116, 120, 125, 129, 131, 138, 140, 142, 144, 157, 165-169, 171-174, 177-180, 183-184, 204, 220, 224, 226, 243-244, 246, 257-259, 265-266, 270-272, 274-277, 279, 295, 299, 301-302, 304, 308-309, 313, 315, 320
Sustainable Development Goals (SDGs) 2, 22-23, 37, 60-66, 68-69, 71, 75-79, 81, 84-85, 93-96, 111-112, 167-169, 171-172, 180, 184, 276
Sustainable Development Goals (SDGs) for Building Inclusive Global Knowledge Societies 171, 180, 184
Sustainable Economics 130, 143
sustainable economy 204
sustainable food consumption 45, 50
sustainable packaging 36, 44, 50

T

Training Barriers 185
training intervention 185, 189, 191, 194, 203
Training investment 195, 203
training investments 185, 187, 195-196
training transfer 185-187, 189-200, 203
Transformational Leaders 31, 89

V

Voluntary Simplicity 53, 59

Index

VUCA environment 1, 4-5, 9, 22

W

waste valorization 141, 164-165, 223, 242, 278
water economy 204
well-being 1, 3, 6, 9, 22-23, 25, 29-31, 37, 58, 61, 63, 65-69, 71-73, 75-88, 94-96, 99, 102, 127, 145, 175, 188, 285
wine industry 111-112, 117, 120-122, 124-126
Wineries for Climate Protection 115, 117, 127
Work from Home (WFH) 194, 199, 203
World Values Survey 245, 247, 255, 257

Recommended Reference Books

IGI Global's reference books are available in three unique pricing formats:
Print Only, E-Book Only, or Print + E-Book.

Shipping fees may apply.

www.igi-global.com

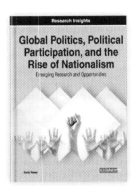

ISBN: 9781799873433
EISBN: 9781799873457
© 2021; 213 pp.
List Price: US$ 175

ISBN: 9781799841562
EISBN: 9781799841579
© 2021; 374 pp.
List Price: US$ 195

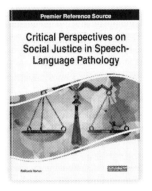

ISBN: 9781799871347
EISBN: 9781799871361
© 2021; 355 pp.
List Price: US$ 195

ISBN: 9781799837299
EISBN: 9781799837312
© 2021; 301 pp.
List Price: US$ 185

ISBN: 9781799870043
EISBN: 9781799870067
© 2021; 290 pp.
List Price: US$ 195

ISBN: 9781799836650
EISBN: 9781799836674
© 2021; 301 pp.
List Price: US$ 195

Do you want to stay current on the latest research trends, product announcements, news, and special offers?
Join IGI Global's mailing list to receive customized recommendations, exclusive discounts, and more.
Sign up at: **www.igi-global.com/newsletters**.

Publisher of Timely, Peer-Reviewed Inclusive Research Since 1988

Ensure Quality Research is Introduced to the Academic Community

Become an Evaluator for IGI Global Authored Book Projects

 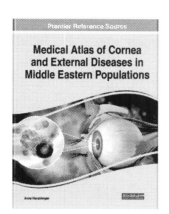  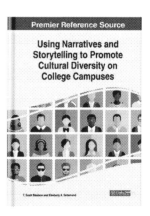

The overall success of an authored book project is dependent on quality and timely manuscript evaluations.

Applications and Inquiries may be sent to:
development@igi-global.com

Applicants must have a doctorate (or equivalent degree) as well as publishing, research, and reviewing experience. Authored Book Evaluators are appointed for one-year terms and are expected to complete at least three evaluations per term. Upon successful completion of this term, evaluators can be considered for an additional term.

If you have a colleague that may be interested in this opportunity, we encourage you to share this information with them.

Increase Your Manuscript's Chance of Acceptance
IGI Global Author Services

Copy Editing & Proofreading

Professional, native English language copy editors improve your manuscript's grammar, spelling, punctuation, terminology, semantics, consistency, flow, formatting, and more.

Scientific & Scholarly Editing

A Ph.D. level review for qualities such as originality and significance, interest to researchers, level of methodology and analysis, coverage of literature, organization, quality of writing, and strengths and weaknesses.

Figure, Table, Chart & Equation Conversions

Work with IGI Global's graphic designers before submission to enhance and design all figures and charts to IGI Global's specific standards for clarity.

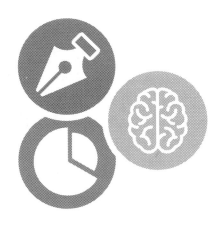

- Professional Service
- Quality Guarantee & Certificate
- Timeliness
- Affordable Pricing

What Makes IGI Global Author Services Stand Apart?

Services/Offerings	IGI Global Author Services	Editage	Enago
Turnaround Time of Projects	3-5 Business Days	6-7 Busines Days	6-7 Busines Days
Pricing	Fraction of our Competitors' Cost	Up to 2x Higher	Up to 3x Higher

Learn More or Get Started Here:

For Questions, Contact IGI Global's Customer Service Team at cust@igi-global.com or 717-533-8845

6,600+ E-BOOKS.
ADVANCED RESEARCH.
INCLUSIVE & ACCESSIBLE.

IGI Global e-Book Collection

- **Flexible Purchasing Options** (Perpetual, Subscription, EBA, etc.)
- Multi-Year Agreements with **No Price Increases** Guaranteed
- **No Additional Charge** for Multi-User Licensing
- No Maintenance, Hosting, or Archiving Fees
- Transformative **Open Access Options** Available

Request More Information, or Recommend the IGI Global e-Book Collection to Your Institution's Librarian

Among Titles Included in the IGI Global e-Book Collection

Research Anthology on Racial Equity, Identity, and Privilege (3 Vols.)
EISBN: 9781668445082
Price: US$ 895

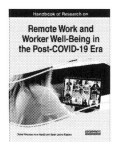

Handbook of Research on Remote Work and Worker Well-Being in the Post-COVID-19 Era
EISBN: 9781799867562
Price: US$ 265

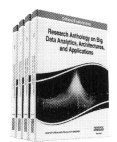

Research Anthology on Big Data Analytics, Architectures, and Applications (4 Vols.)
EISBN: 9781668436639
Price: US$ 1,950

Handbook of Research on Challenging Deficit Thinking for Exceptional Education Improvement
EISBN: 9781799888628
Price: US$ 265

Acquire & Open

When your library acquires an IGI Global e-Book and/or e-Journal Collection, your faculty's published work will be considered for immediate conversion to Open Access *(CC BY License)*, at no additional cost to the library or its faculty *(cost only applies to the e-Collection content being acquired)*, through our popular **Transformative Open Access (Read & Publish) Initiative**.

For More Information or to Request a Free Trial, Contact IGI Global's e-Collections Team: eresources@igi-global.com | 1-866-342-6657 ext. 100 | 717-533-8845 ext. 100